W9-BMN-854
http://www.hbschool.com
SPLIT/RESET
SELECT
MODE
START/STOP
SET
MODEL 221
SUN MON TUE WED THU FRI SAT
MIN
SEC
1/100
SPORTLINE
WATERTIGHT

http://www.hbschool.com

Harcourt Brace & Company

Orlando • Atlanta • Austin • Boston • San Francisco • Chicago • Dallas • New York • Toronto • London

http://www.hbschool.com

Grateful acknowledgment is made to Little, Brown and Company for permission to reprint the cover illustration by Louis Darling from *The Enormous Egg* by Oliver Butterworth. Copyright © 1956 by Oliver Butterworth.

Printed in the United States of America

ISBN 0-15-305672-X

8 9 10 048 2000

Senior Authors

Grace M. Burton
Chair, Department of Curricular Studies
Professor, School of Education
University of North Carolina at Wilmington
Wilmington, North Carolina

Evan M. Maletsky
Professor of Mathematics
Montclair State University
Upper Montclair, New Jersey

Authors

George W. Bright
Professor of Mathematics Education
The University of North Carolina at Greensboro
Greensboro, North Carolina

Sonia M. Helton
Professor of Childhood Education
Coordinator, College of Education
University of South Florida
St. Petersburg, Florida

Loye Y. (Mickey) Hollis
Professor of Mathematics Education
Director of Teacher Education and Undergraduate Programs
University of Houston
Houston, Texas

Howard C. Johnson
Dean of the Graduate School
Associate Vice Chancellor for Academic Affairs
Professor, Mathematics and Mathematics Education
Syracuse University
Syracuse, New York

Joyce C. McLeod
Visiting Professor
Rollins College
Winter Park, Florida

Evelyn M. Neufeld
Professor, College of Education
San Jose State University
San Jose, California

Vicki Newman
Classroom Teacher
McGaugh Elementary School
Los Alamitos Unified School District
Seal Beach, California

Terence H. Perciante
Professor of Mathematics
Wheaton College
Wheaton, Illinois

Karen A. Schultz
Associate Dean and Director of Graduate Studies and Research
Research Professor, Mathematics Education
College of Education
Georgia State University
Atlanta, Georgia

Muriel Burger Thatcher
Independent Mathematics Consultant
Mathematical Encounters
Pine Knoll Shores, North Carolina

Advisors

Anne R. Biggins
Speech-Language Pathologist
Fairfax County Public Schools
Fairfax, Virginia

Carolyn Gambrel
Learning Disabilities Teacher
Fairfax County Public Schools
Fairfax, Virginia

Asa G. Hilliard, III
Fuller E. Callaway Professor of Urban Education
Georgia State University
Atlanta, Georgia

Marsha W. Lilly
Secondary Mathematics Coordinator
Alief Independent School District
Alief, Texas

Clementine Sherman
Director, Division of USI Mathematics and Science
Dade County Public Schools
Miami, Florida

Judith Mayne Wallis
Elementary Language Arts/Social Studies/Gifted Coordinator
Alief Independent School District
Houston, Texas

CONTENTS

WHOLE NUMBER OPERATIONS — CHAPTERS 1–4

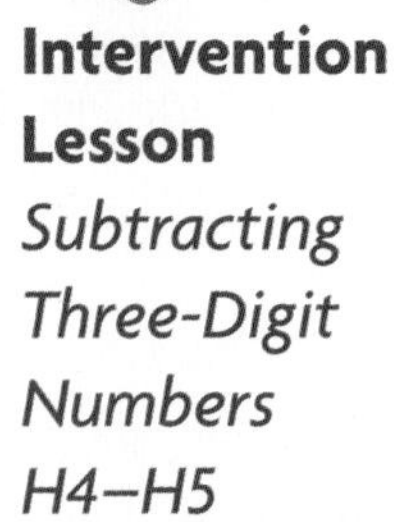

* **Algebra Readiness**

* **Algebra Readiness**

Intervention Lesson
Value of a Digit
H10–H11

CHAPTER 6 Place Value of Whole Numbers 86

Intervention Lesson
Relating Ones, Tens, and Hundreds
H12–H13

CHAPTER 7 Comparing and Ordering Numbers .. 102

Intervention Lesson
Modeling to Compare
H14–H15

CHAPTER 8 Understanding Time 118

Intervention Lesson
Measuring Time
H16–H17

* **Algebra Readiness**

Assessment Checkpoint ✓ Chapters 5–8

STATISTICS, GRAPHING, AND PROBABILITY CHAPTERS 9–11

*** Algebra Readiness**

GEOMETRY — CHAPTERS 12–15

* **Algebra Readiness**

Intervention Lesson
Characteristics of Plane Figures
H24–H25

CHAPTER 14 Perimeter and Area of Polygons 226

Extension Lesson
Making Equal Areas
H38–H39

CHAPTER 15 Geometry and Motion 242

Extension Lesson
Transformations in Designs
H40–H41

Assessment Checkpoint ✓ Chapters 12–15

* **Algebra Readiness**

CHAPTER 16 Multiplying by One-Digit Numbers . . 264

Intervention Lesson
Multiplication Facts
H26–H27

CHAPTER 17 Multiplying by Two-Digit Numbers . . 280

Extension Lesson
Lattice Multiplication
H42–H43

CHAPTER 18 Dividing by One-Digit Numbers 296

Intervention Lesson
Division Facts
H28–H29

* **Algebra Readiness**

CHAPTER 19 More About Dividing by One-Digit Numbers 314

Assessment Checkpoint ✓ Chapters 16–19

FRACTIONS AND DECIMALS — CHAPTERS 20–23

CHAPTER 20 Understanding Fractions 336

* **Algebra Readiness**

* **Algebra Readiness**

MEASUREMENT — CHAPTERS 24–26

* **Algebra Readiness**

* **Algebra Readiness**

CHAPTER 28

Fractions and Decimals in Circle Graphs 470

Extension Lesson
Making a Circle Graph from a Bar Graph

Assessment Checkpoint ✓ Chapters 27–28

STUDENT HANDBOOK

* **Algebra Readiness**

As you work on math this year, use your book as a tool that makes learning easier—and more fun! Look for these things:

- **Team-Up Time** You'll work with a group of your classmates on activities that will help you become a good problem solver.
- **Why Learn This?** One way is answered for you at the beginning of every lesson. You can find other answers in all the ways you use math every day—at school, at home, and everywhere you go!
- **Word Power** Knowing the meanings of math words will help you solve problems and understand directions in your book and on your tests.
- **Remember** These boxes will remind you of math skills you've already learned that will help you in the new lesson.
- **Mixed Review** It's easy to forget how to do something when you haven't done it for a while. These sets of problems will help you keep your math skills sharp.
- **Math Fun** Games and activities you can do with classmates or family members will make learning math *fun*.
- **Technology Link** Computer and calculator activities will give you new ways to learn math and practice your math skills.
- **Links to Science, Social Studies, History, Language Arts, Health, and Physical Education** You'll learn how math is used in your other subjects.
- **Cultural Link** You'll find out how math is used in other cultures.

Math Advantage gives you "power tools" that will help you become a real mathematician!

The Authors

BE A GOOD PROBLEM SOLVER

Good problem solvers need to be good thinkers. They also need to know these strategies.

- Draw a Diagram
- Work Backward
- Use or Make a Table or Graph
- Act It Out
- Find a Pattern
- Account for All Possibilities
- Make a Model
- Guess and Check
- Write a Number Sentence
- Use a Formula
- Solve a Simpler Problem
- Make an Organized List

This plan can help you think through a problem.

Understand the problem.

Ask yourself...	Then try this.
What is the problem about?	Retell the problem in your own words.
What is the question?	Say the question as a fill-in-the-blank sentence.
What information is given?	List the information given in the problem.

Plan how to solve it.

Ask yourself...	Then try this.
What strategies might I use?	List some strategies you can use.
About what will the answer be?	Predict what your answer will be. Make an estimate if it will help.

Solve it.

Ask yourself...	Then try this.
How can I solve the problem?	Follow your plan and show your solution.
How can I write my answer?	Write your answer in a complete sentence.

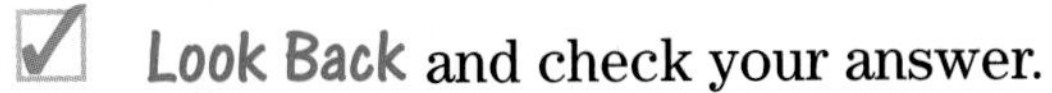

Look Back and check your answer.

Ask yourself...	Then try this.
How can I tell if my answer is reasonable?	Compare your answer to your estimate. Check your answer by redoing your work. Match your answer to the question.
How else might I have solved the problem?	Try using another strategy to solve the problem.

You can be a good problem solver! Remember these important words—**Understand**, **Plan**, **Solve**, **Look Back**. Ask yourself questions as you think through the problem. Then be proud of your success!

CHAPTER 1

USING ADDITION AND SUBTRACTION

DID YOU KNOW . . .

Children in Mexico, Puerto Rico, and Cuba often have a piñata at their birthday celebrations.

If you know the number of toys and the number of candies, you can add to find the total number of objects in a piñata.

Who Needs to Add and Subtract?

You use numbers and operations every day. Work with a group to make a list of things you might do today in which you might use addition or subtraction. Try to be the group with the longest list.

Work with a group. Your job is to

- brainstorm ideas about when you use addition and subtraction.
- make a list of your ideas.
- for each idea, write a problem that can be solved using addition and a problem that can be solved using subtraction.
- solve some of the problems you have written.
- share your ideas with the class.

DID YOU

- ✓ brainstorm ideas and make a list?
- ✓ write and solve problems using addition and subtraction?
- ✓ share your ideas with the class?

When Do You Use Addition...

1. When finding the total number of friends coming to a party
2. When figuring out how many prizes to buy
3. When figuring out how many invitations to send
4. To find the total number of points in a birthday game
5. To find out how old you will be in five years

When Do You Use Subtraction...

1. To find how many pieces of cake will be left over
2. To find how many more party hats are needed
3. To find how many more invitations are needed
4. To find how many years ago your last big party was
5. To figure out how old you were when you received skates
6. To find how many more years it will be until you are 15

Modeling Addition or Subtraction Situations

You will investigate when to add and when to subtract by modeling problems.

Why learn this? You will know when to use addition or subtraction.

Explore

Act out each problem. Then use counters to model it. Decide whether to add or subtract.

MATERIALS: 12 counters

1. Lisa had 8 tapes. Tyler gave her 4 more. How many tapes does Lisa have in all?

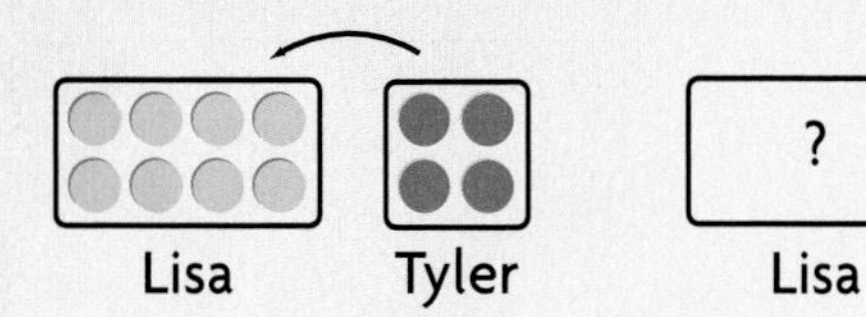

2. Lisa had some tapes. Tyler gave her 4 more. Now Lisa has 12 tapes. How many tapes did she have to begin with?

3. Lisa had 8 tapes. Tyler gave her some more. Now she has 12 tapes. How many did Tyler give her?

4. Melinda had 12 pens. She gave 4 pens to Tim. How many pens does Melinda have now?

5. Melinda had 12 pens. She gave some to Tim. Now she has 8 pens. How many did she give to Tim?

6. Melinda had some pens. She gave 4 to Tim. Now she has 8 pens left. How many pens did Melinda have to begin with?

Record

Draw a model for each problem. Then write a number sentence to show addition or subtraction.

Talk About It

- For which problems did you use addition? subtraction?
- Compare Problems 1, 2, and 3. How are they different?
- Compare Problems 4, 5, and 6. How did they change?

Technology Link

E-Lab • Activity 1 Available on CD-ROM and the Internet at http://www.hbschool.com/elab

Now, investigate five other types of problems.

Try This

Act out and then model each problem. Write a number sentence for each. Record your models.

7. Kathy has 12 pens. James has 8 pens. How many more does Kathy have than James?

8. James has 4 more pens than Kathy. Kathy has 8 pens. How many does James have?

9. Kathy has 12 pens. She has 4 more than James. How many does James have?

- How did comparing numbers help you solve each problem?

10. Lynn has 4 red candles and 8 blue candles. How many candles does she have?

11. Lynn has 12 candles. Eight are red and the rest are blue. How many blue candles does she have?

- How did the colors of the items help you solve each problem?

Talk About It

- For which problems did you use addition? subtraction?
- How are these two sets of problems different from each other? different from the problems on page 2?

HANDS-ON PRACTICE

Decide if you should add or subtract. Write the answer and the number of the problem (1–11) that is the most similar to each one below.

12. Todd had some folders. He gave 2 to Tracy. Now he has 8. How many folders did Todd have to begin with?

13. Erin had 6 pens. Justin gave her some more. Now she has 9 pens. How many did Justin give her?

14. Jan has 5 more puzzles than Rob. Rob has 3. How many puzzles does Jan have?

15. Shane has 17 pencils. Eight are red and the rest are blue. How many blue pencils does he have?

MORE PRACTICE Student Handbook page H68

Using Mental Math

You will learn how addition and subtraction and mental math can help you make equal amounts.	**Why learn this?** You can use mental math to solve many problems in your head.	**WORD POWER** equation

An **equation** is a kind of number sentence. It uses an equals sign to show that two amounts are equal.

$4 + 9 = 13 \qquad 5 + 3 = 1 + 7 \qquad 10 - 7 = 12 - 9$

4 + 9 = 13
5 + 3 = 1 + 7

Suppose you want to solve this equation.

$9 + 2 = \underline{\ ?\ } + 3$

Here is one way to do it.

$9 + 2 = \underline{\ ?\ } + 3$

$11 = \underline{\ ?\ } + 3$ **Think:** 11 − 3 = 8.

So, $9 + 2 = \underline{\mathbf{8}} + 3$.

Here is another way to solve.

$9 + 2 = \underline{\ ?\ } + 3$

$9 + 2 = (\underline{9 - 1}) + 3$ **Think:** Since 3 is 1 more than 2, subtract 1 from 9.

So, $9 + 2 = \underline{\mathbf{8}} + 3$.

You can use mental math to make both sides of an equation equal even though the signs are different.

$8 + 4 = \underline{\ ?\ } - 6$

Since $8 + 4 = 12$, $12 = \underline{\ ?\ } - 6$ **Think:** 12 + 6 = 18, and 18 − 6 = 12.

So, $8 + 4 = \underline{18} - 6$.

Check Your Understanding

CRITICAL THINKING

Use mental math to complete each equation.

1. $6 + \underline{\ ?\ } = 14 - 3$
2. $18 - 6 = \underline{\ ?\ } + 2$
3. $5 + 9 = \underline{\ ?\ } - 0$
4. $12 - 7 = 3 + \underline{\ ?\ }$
5. How did you solve Exercise 2?
6. What do you know about zero that helps you complete the equation in Exercise 3?

Social Studies Link

Mathematicians once used these symbols:

for addition — for subtraction

The symbols + and − came into use before the late 1400's. How are those symbols like our plus and minus signs?

PRACTICE

Copy and complete each equation. Show how you solved it.

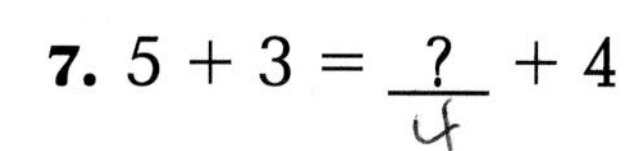

7. $5 + 3 = \underline{\ ?\ } + 4$ **8.** $7 + 2 = 6 + \underline{\ ?\ }$ **9.** $4 + \underline{\ ?\ } = 5 + 5$

Use mental math to complete each equation.

10. $6 + 2 = 4 + \underline{\ ?\ }$ **11.** $8 - 3 = \underline{\ ?\ } - 2$ **12.** $4 + \underline{\ ?\ } = 6 + 3$

13. $10 - 3 = 3 + \underline{\ ?\ }$ **14.** $5 + 4 = \underline{\ ?\ } - 1$ **15.** $\underline{\ ?\ } - 4 = 5 + 3$

16. $14 - \underline{\ ?\ } = 1 + 8$ **17.** $\underline{\ ?\ } + 0 = 10 - 2$ **18.** $16 - 5 = 2 + \underline{\ ?\ }$

Mixed Applications

Use the price tags to solve.

19. Leslie has three $5 bills. Write an equation to show how she could spend her money.

20. Juan has two $5 bills and six $1 bills. What other item could he buy if he buys a cap?

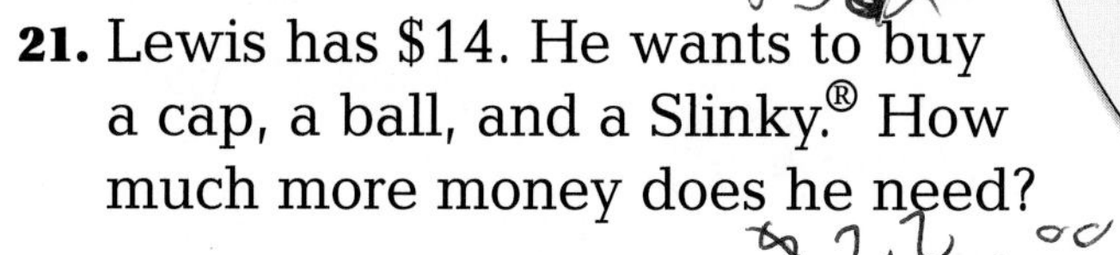

21. Lewis has $14. He wants to buy a cap, a ball, and a Slinky.® How much more money does he need?

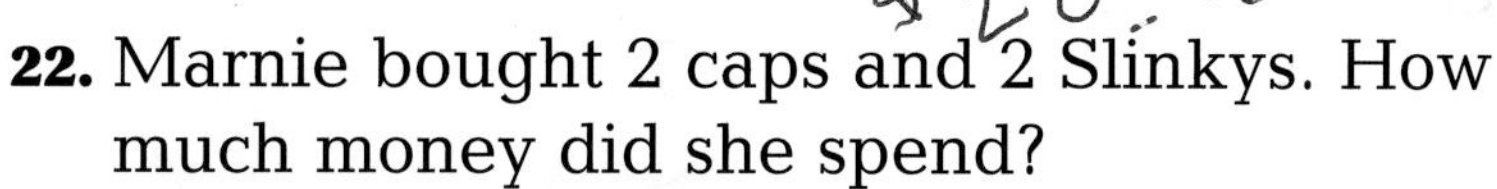

22. Marnie bought 2 caps and 2 Slinkys. How much money did she spend?

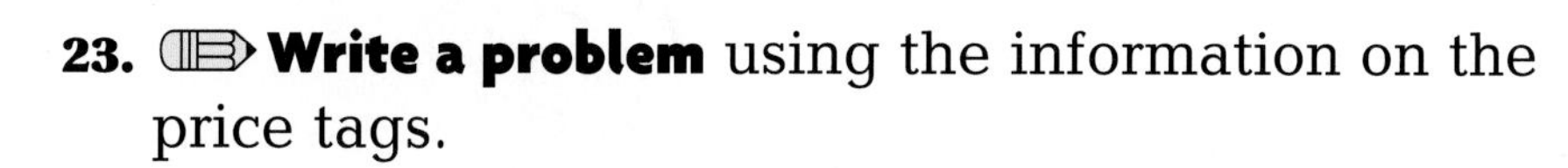

23. **Write a problem** using the information on the price tags.

Mixed Review

Write $<$, $>$, or $=$ for the ● to complete each equation. (taught in Grade 3)

24. $15 - 8$ ● $7 + 4$ **25.** $9 - 3$ ● $12 - 6$ **26.** $14 + 6$ ● $8 + 7$

27. $11 - 7$ ● $14 - 9$ **28.** $16 - 9$ ● $6 + 1$ **29.** $4 + 5$ ● $13 - 4$

30. $6 + 7$ ● $15 - 2$ **31.** $12 - 4$ ● $5 + 4$ **32.** $5 + 6$ ● $14 - 3$

Find the sum or difference. (taught in Grade 3)

33. $6 + 3 + 4 = \underline{\ ?\ }$ **34.** $2 + 7 + 9 = \underline{\ ?\ }$ **35.** $4 + 5 + 8 = \underline{\ ?\ }$

36. $3 + 6 + 3 = \underline{\ ?\ }$ **37.** $17 - 8 = \underline{\ ?\ }$ **38.** $15 - 7 = \underline{\ ?\ }$

39. $13 - 5 = \underline{\ ?\ }$ **40.** $16 - 7 = \underline{\ ?\ }$ **41.** $7 + 4 + 8 = \underline{\ ?\ }$

MORE PRACTICE Student Handbook page H68

PART

1 Adding Three or More Addends

You will learn to use three or more addends to find perimeter.

Why learn this? You can find the distance around something, such as a fenced yard for a pet.

WORD POWER

Grouping Property of Addition

What is the perimeter of this rectangle?

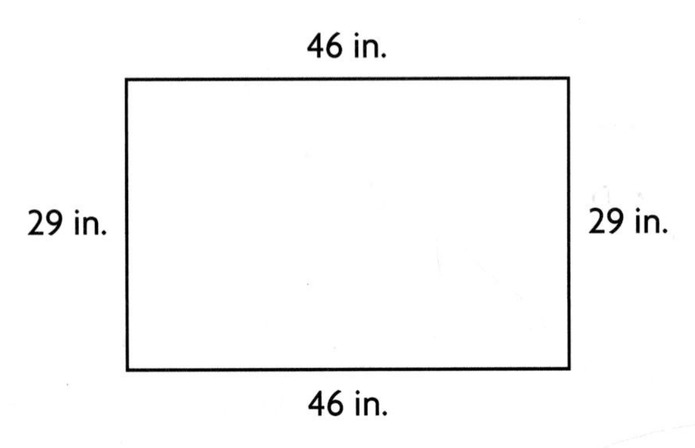

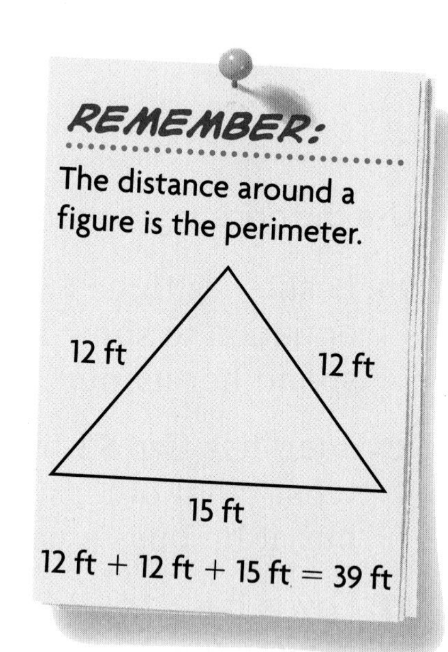

Add to find the perimeter.

```
   3                 3
  29 ⟩              29 ⟩
  46 ⟩ 15           29 ⟩ 18
  29 ⟩              46 ⟩
 +46 ⟩ 15          +46 ⟩ 12
 ----              ----
150 in.            150 in.
```

The **Grouping Property of Addition** states that addends can be grouped differently but the sum does not change.

So, the perimeter of the rectangle is 150 in.

Talk About It

- Do you have to regroup to find the sum? Why?
- Will the sum change if you group the addends as (29 + 29) + (46 + 46)? Explain.

Check Your Understanding

Find the perimeter of this figure.

1. How did you find the perimeter?
2. What will happen to the sum if you change the grouping of the addends? Why?

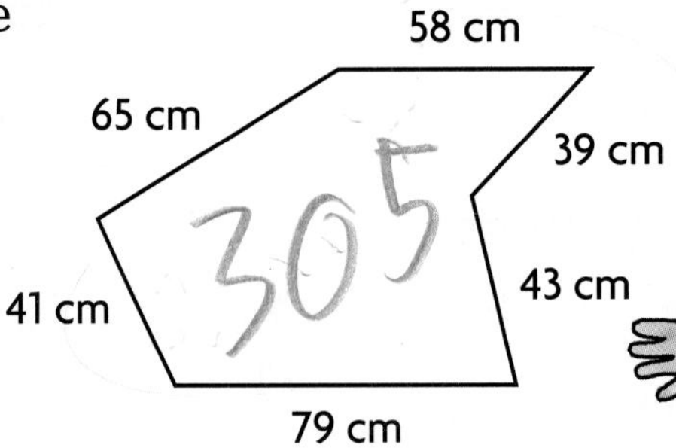

Calculator Activities page H62

PRACTICE

Find the perimeter of each figure.

3.

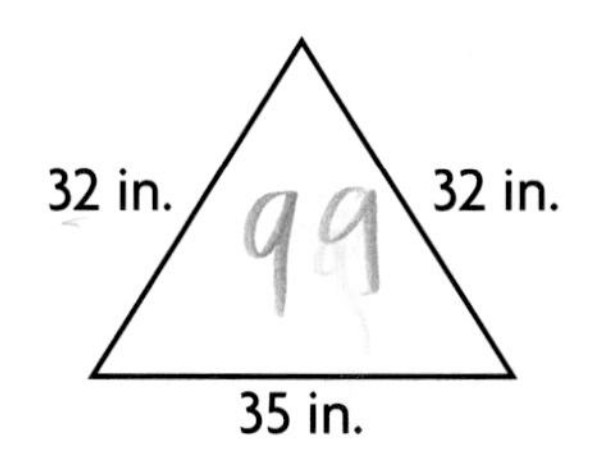

4.

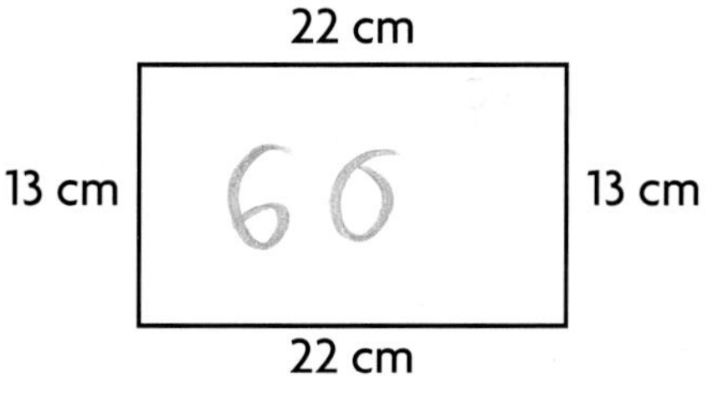

5.

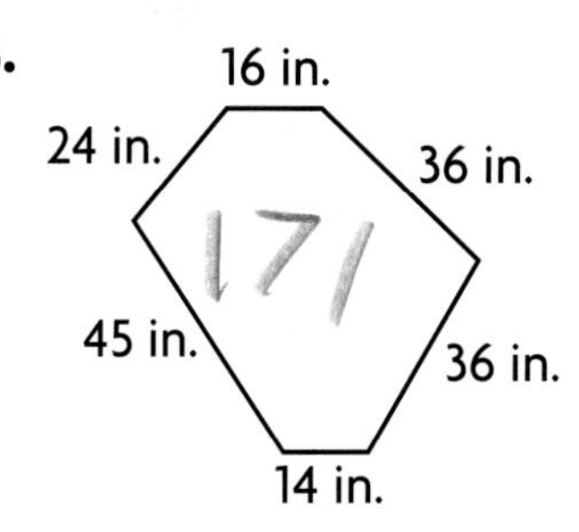

6.

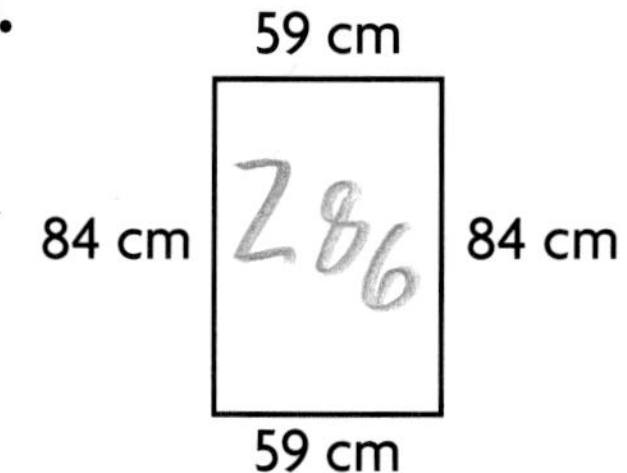

7.

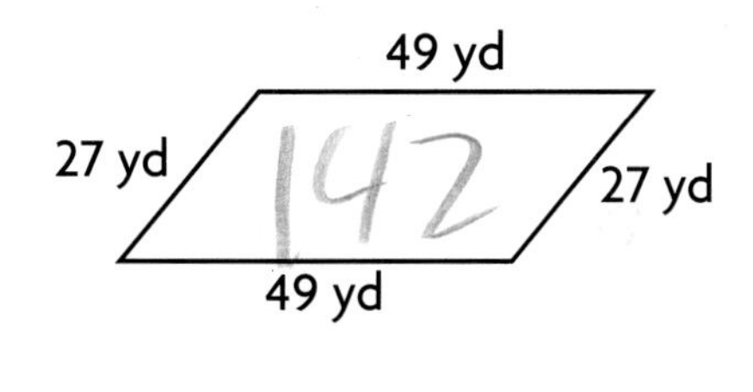

8.

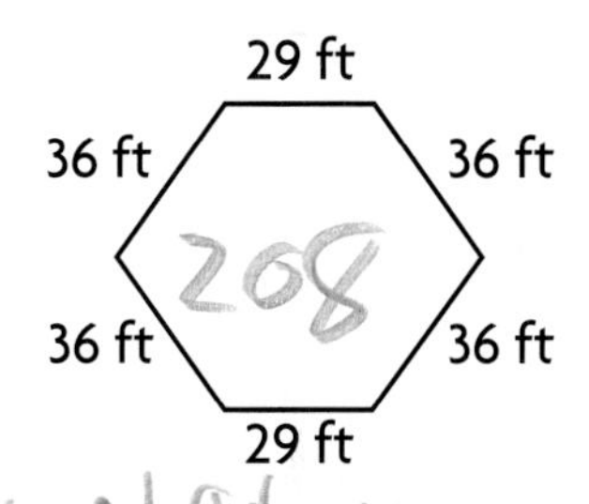

Find the sum.

9. $14 + 26 + 14$

10. $52 + 13 + 35$

11. $32 + 18 + 32 + 18$

12. $89 + 42 + 67 + 51$

13. $26 + 49 + 34$

14. $97 + 24 + 41$

15. $19 + 22 + 69$

16. $29 + 58 + 82$

17. $34 + 27 + 89$

Social Studies Link

The Parthenon is near Athens, Greece. It was built about 2,500 years ago as a temple. Its perimeter is formed by 46 columns. Each of the two ends has 8 columns. How many columns are on each of the two sides? (Hint: Draw a picture. This is tricky!)

Mixed Applications

18. Tony had 4 tiles that were each 12 inches square. He used them to make one large square. What is the perimeter of the larger square?

19. **WRITE ABOUT IT** Find 31 + 49 + 18 in two different ways to show the Grouping Property.

LESSON CONTINUES

PART 2 **PROBLEM-SOLVING STRATEGY**

Make a Model

THE PROBLEM Molly and her brother made a cage for her pet hamster. The cage floor is in the shape of a rectangle. Molly knows that the cage has a perimeter of 76 inches and that it is 22 inches long. How can she find how wide it is?

REMEMBER:
- ✓ Understand
- ✓ Plan
- ✓ Solve
- ✓ Look Back

✓ Understand

- What are you asked to find?
- What information will you use?
- Is there any information that you will not use? If so, what?

✓ Plan

- What strategy can you use to solve the problem?

  You can *make a model* with paper clips. Let one paper clip equal one inch.

✓ Solve

- What model can you make?

The cage floor is a rectangle. One side is 22 paper clips long. So, the side across from it must be 22 paper clips long.

$$\begin{array}{rl} 76 = & \text{perimeter} \\ -44 = & \text{paper clips for two sides} \\ \hline 32 = & \text{paper clips remaining} \end{array}$$

The 32 paper clips remaining make up the other two sides. Arrange your paper clips to make the whole rectangle.

Opposite sides of a rectangle are equal. So, the width must be 16 inches.

$16 + 16 + 22 + 22 = 76$ inches

✓ Look Back

- How can you decide if your answer is reasonable?
- What other strategy could you use?

PRACTICE

CHOOSE Paper/Pencil Calculator Hands-on Mental Math

Make a model to solve.

1. Ashley wants to put a border around the perimeter of her bird's cage. The cage is 22 inches long and has a perimeter of 72 inches. How wide is the cage?

2. Ken has 62 fence sections to build a rectangular pen for his dog. Suppose he uses 18 sections each for the north and south sides of the pen. How many sections will he use for the east side of the pen? the west side?

3. The snake's cage is 6 feet wide and 3 feet long. What is the perimeter of the cage?

4. The yard for the tortoise is 32 feet long and 28 feet wide. What is the perimeter of the yard?

Mixed Applications

Solve.

CHOOSE A STRATEGY

- Work Backward
- Draw a Picture
- Make a Model
- Write a Number Sentence

5. The average adult male giraffe weighs 2,420 pounds. The average adult female giraffe weighs 1,540 pounds. How much more does the male weigh?

6. Aaron spent $2 on food for the animals and $4 for his own lunch. He had $4 left when he got home. How much money did Aaron take to the zoo?

7. The teacher handed the cashier at the zoo $40 for her students' tickets. She was given back $2. Tickets are $2 each. How many students are in the class?

8. On Monday 126 fourth graders visited the zoo. On Tuesday 117 third graders visited the zoo. How many students visited in all?

9. Maria is going to the zoo in 30 minutes. At what time is she leaving for the zoo?

10. A kangaroo can travel 30 feet in 1 jump. How far can a kangaroo travel in 4 jumps?

11. Mr. Lee wants to put a fence around the petting zoo. One side of the rectangular area is 54 feet long, and the perimeter is 168 feet. How wide is the area for the petting zoo?

12. At the zoo the elephant was directly in front of the lion. The polar bear was behind the monkey and in front of the elephant. In what order were the animals?

Estimating Sums and Differences

You will learn to use rounding to estimate sums and differences.

Why learn this? You can estimate when you don't need exact answers.

You can estimate by rounding numbers to different place values. Number lines can help you. Ross flew his paper airplane 75 feet. To the nearest ten feet, how far did the airplane fly?

Round 75 to the nearest ten.

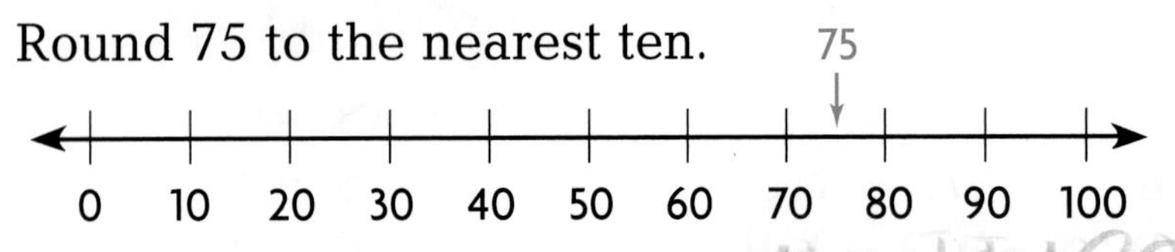

- Is 75 closer to 70 or to 80?
- To what number should you round 75?

So, the paper airplane flew about 80 feet.

Round 227 to the nearest hundred.

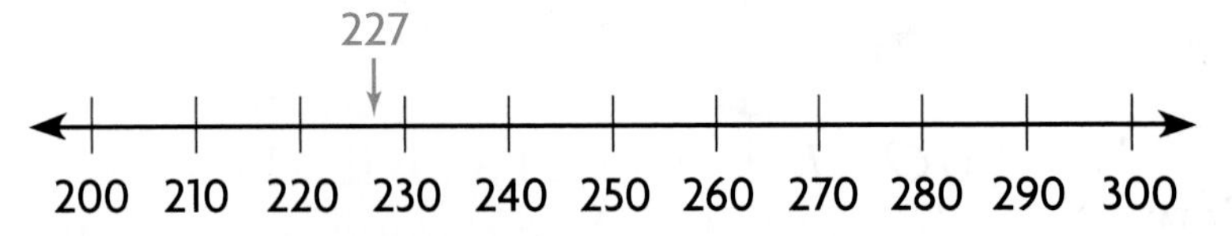

- Is 227 closer to 200 or to 300? How can you tell?

You can round numbers without a number line.

REMEMBER:

When a number is halfway between two numbers, round to the greater number.

10 11 12 13 14 15 16 17 18 19 20

15 is halfway between 10 and 20.
15 rounds to 20.

EXAMPLES

Round to the nearest ten, hundred, and thousand.

A.

86 →	90
68 →	70
+52 →	+50
	210

B.

548 →	500
−397 →	−400
	100

C.

4,119 →	4,000
−2,863 →	−3,000
	1,000

Talk About It

- To what place-value positions were the numbers rounded in Examples A–C?
- Suppose you want an estimate that is as close as possible to the exact answer. Should you round to the nearest ten, hundred, or thousand? Explain.
- When might you use an estimate instead of an exact answer?

PRACTICE

Round to the nearest *ten*.

1. 7 **2.** 21 **3.** 42 **4.** 65 **5.** 99

Round to the nearest *hundred*.

6. 75 **7.** 143 **8.** 298 **9.** 444 **10.** 950

Round $45.83 to each given amount.

11. ten cents **12.** dollar **13.** ten dollars

Estimate the sum or difference.

14. 17 + 52 + 34

15. 63 − 48

16. 374 + 548

17. $65.49 − $47.25

18. 897 − 249

19. $185.13 + $547.89

20. $746.99 − $537.28

21. 444 + 209 + 351

Consumer Link

When estimating to buy amounts of ingredients for a recipe, should you round to the greater or lesser number? Why?

Mixed Applications

Use estimation to solve.

22. Mel has $10 to buy fruit. How many bags of apples can she buy?

23. What if Mel buys a watermelon and a cantaloupe? About how much change will she receive from $10?

24. **WRITE ABOUT IT** Mel estimates that she can buy 3 cantaloupes for $3. Is she correct? Explain.

Mixed Review

Compare. Write $<$, $>$, or $=$ for ●. **(taught in Grade 3)**

25. 74 ● 74 **26.** 81 ● 87 **27.** 99 ● 89 **28.** 119 ● 111

Write the missing numbers in the pattern. **(taught in Grade 3)**

29. 35, 37, 39, _?_, _?_, _?_, 47 **30.** 276, 270, 264, _?_, _?_, _?_, 240

Adding and Subtracting with Money

You will learn to add and subtract money amounts.

Why learn this? You can add and subtract money when you go shopping.

THE PROBLEM Jonathan ate lunch in the food court at the mall. He decided to have pizza, a garden salad, and a large lemonade. How much did he spend for lunch?

Fashion Mall Food Court

		Beverages	Small	Medium	Large
Hamburger	$2.35	Lemonade	$0.89	$0.99	$1.19
Pizza Slice	$1.69	Soda	$0.99	$1.19	$1.29
Grilled Chicken	$2.49	Bottled Water	$1.95		
Taco Salad	$3.19	Cookies	2 for $0.99		
Garden Salad	$3.25	Frozen Yogurt	$2.19		

Pizza Slice	$1.69 →	Think:	169
Garden Salad	3.25 →		325
Lemonade	+ 1.19 →		+119
			613, or $6.13

(Regrouping shown above the Think column: 1 2)

REMEMBER:
When you add or subtract money amounts, separate the dollars and cents with a decimal point. Place a dollar sign in front of the sum or difference.

decimal point ↓
dollar sign → $4.78

Talk About It

- Jonathan needed to know *about* how much his lunch would cost. How could he estimate?
- When you are rounding costs of things to buy, why should you always round to the greater number?
- How is adding money amounts the same as adding whole numbers? How is it different?
- If Jonathan had $10.00, how much change would he receive?

Check Your Understanding

Suppose Jonathan's sister had $5.00 to spend for lunch.

1. What two different lunches could she have bought?

2. With each choice, how much money would she have left?

PRACTICE

Find the sum or difference.

3. $7.52 − 1.97	**4.** $9.48 − 5.73	**5.** $1.29 + 2.35 + 3.14	**6.** $14.49 − 12.75
7. $12.98 + 3.75	**8.** $1.18 + 4.32 + 2.97	**9.** $12.46 − 8.32	**10.** $15.03 − 11.93
11. $26.48 − 7.39	**12.** $18.65 + 22.05	**13.** $25.34 − 18.35	**14.** $16.72 + 14.28

Mixed Applications

Use the menu on page 12 for Problems 15–18.

15. Carroll buys a garden salad, bottled water, and frozen yogurt. How much does she spend at the food court?

16. Neil gives the clerk $6.00 for a taco salad, large soda, and two cookies. How much change will he receive?

17. Sean estimates that $5.00 will be enough money for a hamburger, small soda, and frozen yogurt. Is he correct? Explain.

18. **WRITE ABOUT IT** Suppose Samantha buys grilled chicken and a small lemonade with $5.75. Will she have enough money left to buy a frozen yogurt? Explain.

Health Link

When you're thirsty, drink the best health drink there is—WATER! Soft drinks do not make you less thirsty. That's because many contain salt, sugar, and caffeine, which make your body need more water, not less. How much water do you drink each day?

Mixed Review

Write each in expanded form. (taught in Grade 3)

19. 97 **20.** 608 **21.** 830 **22.** [illegible]1

Find the sum or difference. (taught in Grade 3)

23. 73 + 51	**24.** 39 + 28	**25.** 96 − 60	**26.** 58 − 47

MORE PRACTICE Student Handbook page H69

MATH FUN!

PRICE LIST

Item	Price
Shirt	$16
Belt	$8
Sweater	$34
Jacket	$46
Socks	$4
Jeans	$22
Cap	$9

It All Adds Up!

PURPOSE To practice adding three or more addends

Make a shopping list of three or more things you can buy for each amount.

1. \$21 **2.** \$60 **3.** \$96 **4.** \$74 **5.** \$81

ALMOST 100!

PURPOSE To practice adding two-digit numbers

YOU WILL NEED number cards (0–9)

Play with a partner or small group. One player at a time draws four number cards. He or she arranges them into two 2-digit addends whose sum is as close as possible to 100. The player whose sum is closest to 100 scores 1 point. After each round, shuffle the cards. The player with the most points wins.

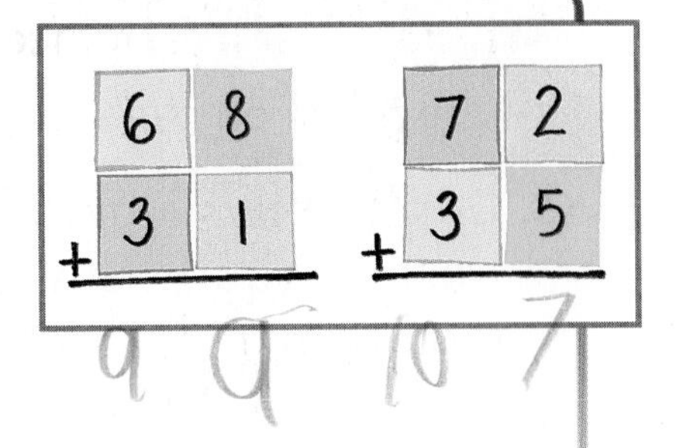

What's Your Number?

PURPOSE To get the greatest sum and the least difference

YOU WILL NEED number cube, paper and pencil

Play with a partner or small group. Each player copies the grid, rolls the number cube eight times, and fills in the eight spaces on his or her grid in any order. Then players find the sum and the difference. The player with the greatest sum and the player with the least difference get 1 point each. After five rounds the player with the highest score wins.

Make a grid with two rows of three squares. Then challenge members of your family to get the greatest sum and the least difference, using three-digit numbers.

REVIEW

✓ CHECK UNDERSTANDING

VOCABULARY

1. A number sentence that uses an equals sign to show that two amounts are equal is an __?__. (page 4)

2. The __?__ states that addends can be grouped differently but the sum does not change. (page 6)

Use mental math to complete each equation. (pages 4–5)

3. $8 + 7 = 9 + \underline{?}$

4. $6 + 7 = \underline{?} + 5$

5. $\underline{?} - 4 = 6 + 9$

✓ CHECK SKILLS

Find the sum or difference. (pages 6–7; 12–13)

6. $\begin{array}{r} 36 \\ 74 \\ +49 \\ \hline \end{array}$

7. $\begin{array}{r} 626 \\ 174 \\ +588 \\ \hline \end{array}$

8. $\begin{array}{r} \$1.96 \\ +\ 7.39 \\ \hline \end{array}$

9. $\begin{array}{r} \$6.78 \\ -\ 2.89 \\ \hline \end{array}$

10. $\begin{array}{r} 704 \\ +469 \\ \hline \end{array}$

11. $\begin{array}{r} 652 \\ -578 \\ \hline \end{array}$

12. $\begin{array}{r} 196 \\ +799 \\ \hline \end{array}$

13. $\begin{array}{r} 670 \\ -439 \\ \hline \end{array}$

Round to the nearest hundred. (pages 10–11)

14. 59 **15.** 137 **16.** 279 **17.** 973

Round $78.46 to each given amount. (pages 10–11)

18. ten cents **19.** dollar **20.** ten dollars

✓ CHECK PROBLEM SOLVING

Solve. (pages 2–3, 8–9)

CHOOSE A STRATEGY

- Work Backward
- Act It Out
- Make a Model
- Draw a Picture
- Write a Number Sentence

21. Mr. Williams is putting a fence around his garden. The garden is 36 feet long. Its perimeter is 120 feet. How wide is the garden?

22. Katie had some lunch money. She gave $0.45 to Alan. Now she has $0.95. How much lunch money did Katie have to begin with?

23. Robert has 73 basketball cards. He has 14 more cards than John. How many cards does John have?

24. Julie's bulletin board is 48 inches long and 36 inches wide. She wants to make a border for it. How much paper will she need?

CHAPTER 2

ADDING AND SUBTRACTING LARGER NUMBERS

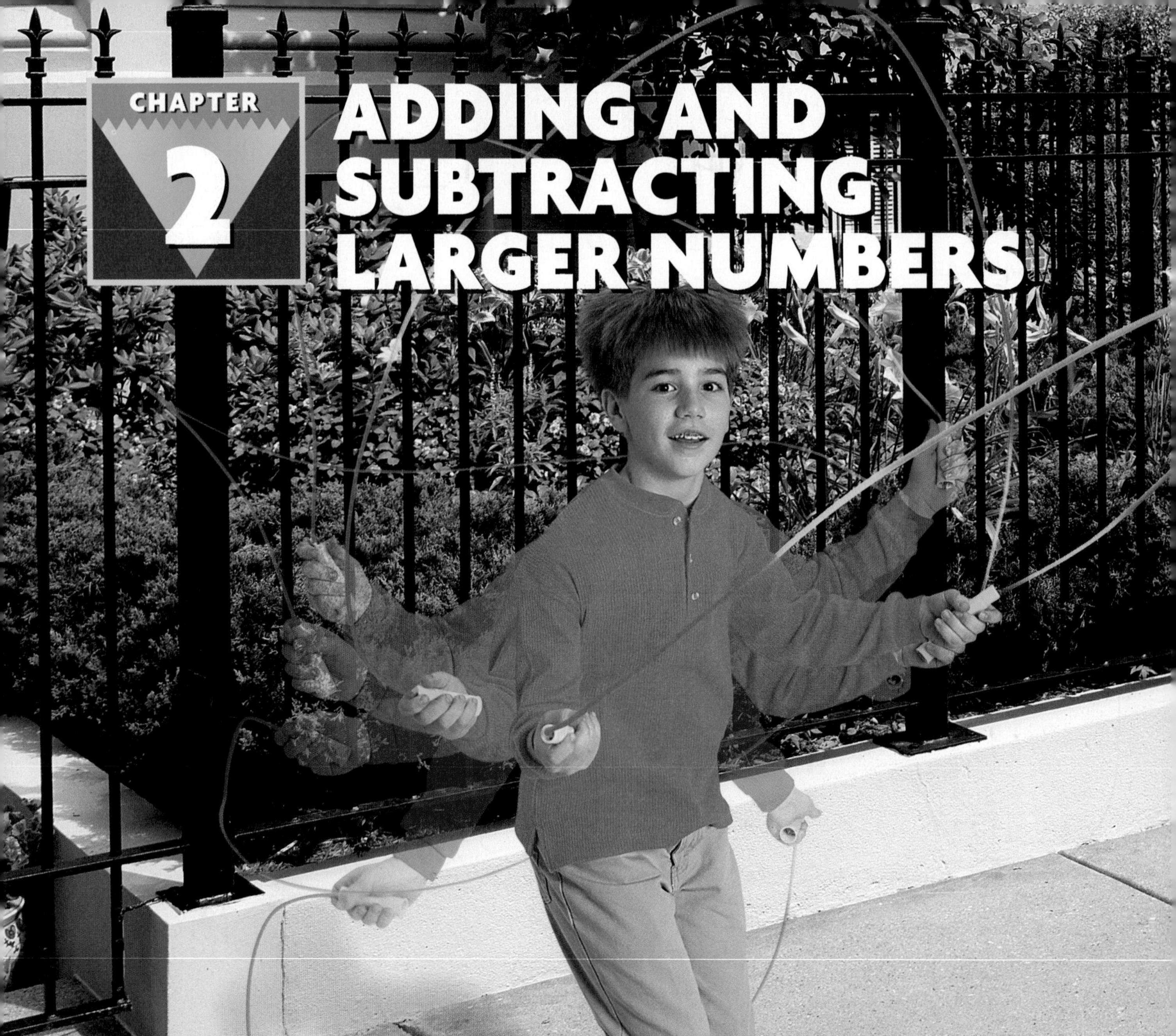

DID YOU KNOW . . .

Robert Commers of Woodbridge, New Jersey, holds the United States record for jumping rope with 13,783 turns in one hour.

Park Bong Tae of South Korea holds the world record with 14,628 turns.

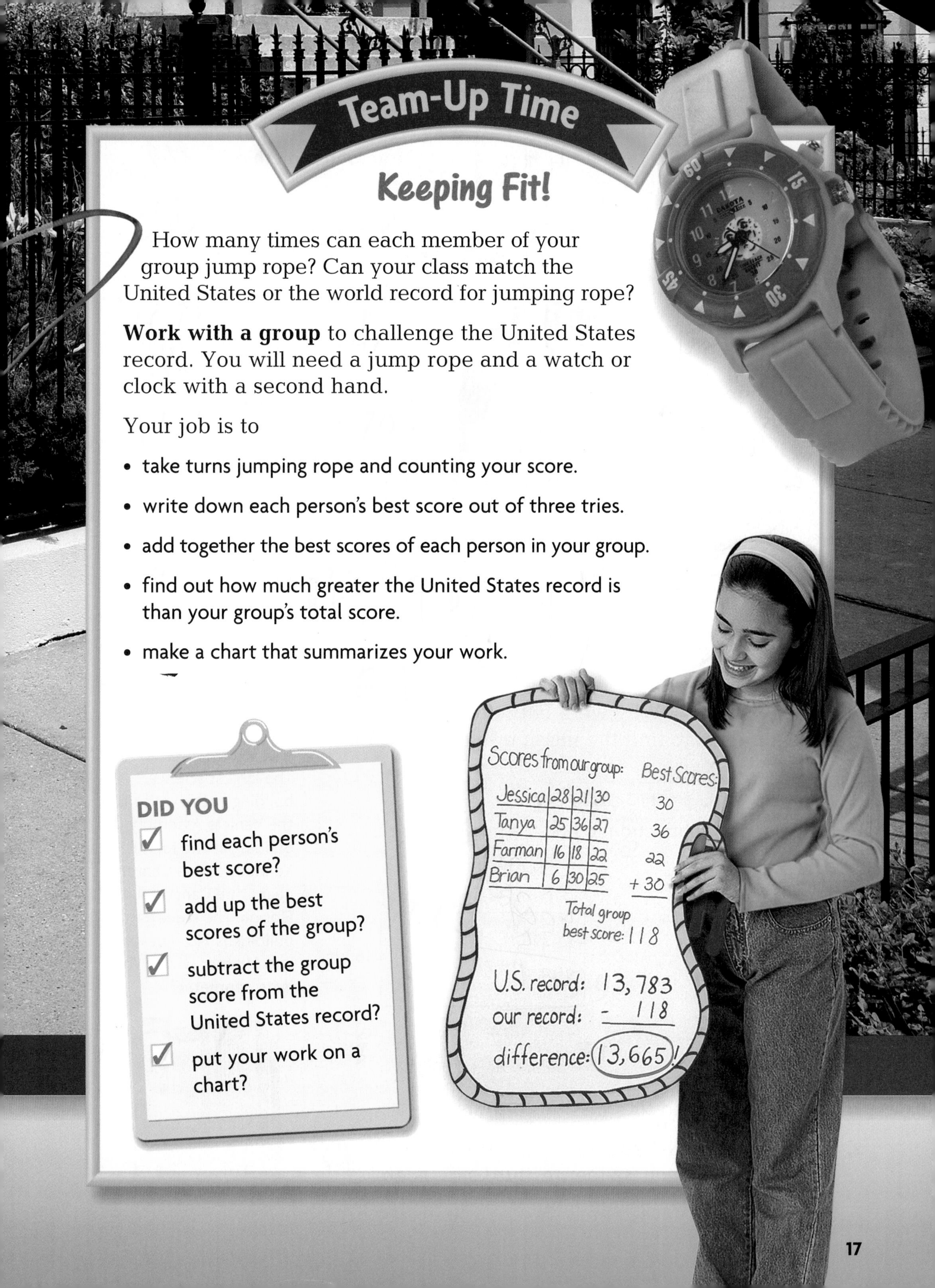

Team-Up Time

Keeping Fit!

How many times can each member of your group jump rope? Can your class match the United States or the world record for jumping rope?

Work with a group to challenge the United States record. You will need a jump rope and a watch or clock with a second hand.

Your job is to

- take turns jumping rope and counting your score.
- write down each person's best score out of three tries.
- add together the best scores of each person in your group.
- find out how much greater the United States record is than your group's total score.
- make a chart that summarizes your work.

DID YOU

- ✓ find each person's best score?
- ✓ add up the best scores of the group?
- ✓ subtract the group score from the United States record?
- ✓ put your work on a chart?

Adding and Subtracting Larger Numbers

You will learn that addition and subtraction are used to find the missing length of a side of a figure.

Why learn this? You can find the distance around something, such as a playing field.

Louis knows that the perimeter of the baseball diamond is 360 feet. He knows the lengths of three of the sides.

REMEMBER:

The distance around a figure is called the perimeter.

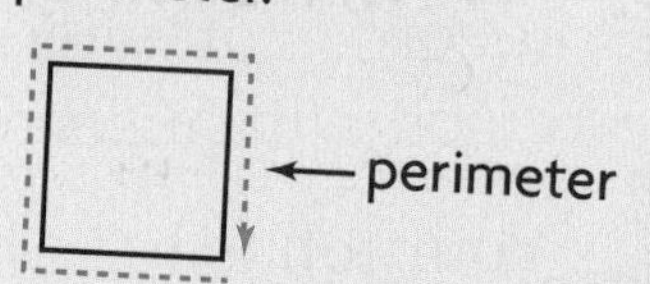

How can he use addition *and* subtraction to find the length of the fourth side?

Step 1

Make a drawing.

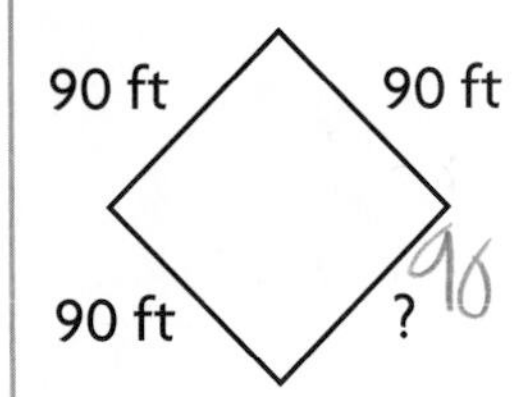

Step 2

Add the lengths of the three known sides.

$$\begin{array}{r} 90 \text{ ft} \\ 90 \text{ ft} \\ +90 \text{ ft} \\ \hline 270 \text{ ft} \end{array}$$

Step 3

Subtract that amount from the perimeter.

$$\begin{array}{r} 360 \text{ ft} \\ -270 \text{ ft} \\ \hline 90 \text{ ft} \end{array}$$

So, the length of the fourth side is 90 feet.

CRITICAL THINKING Why were both addition and subtraction used to find the missing length?

Check Your Understanding

Use addition *and* subtraction to find the missing lengths.

Basketball Court

94 ft

50 ft 50 ft

?

perimeter = 288 ft

Football Field

?

160 ft 160 ft

360 ft

perimeter = 1,040 ft

1. How did you find the missing lengths?
2. The perimeter of a swimming pool is 134 feet. Two sides are each 32 feet. A third side is 46 feet. What is the missing length?

Science Link

The largest science building in the world is the Vehicle Assembly Building at the John F. Kennedy Space Center, near Cape Canaveral, Florida. The steel-framed building is 716 feet long and 518 feet wide. What is its perimeter?

PRACTICE

Use addition *and* subtraction to find the missing length.

3. **4.** **5.**

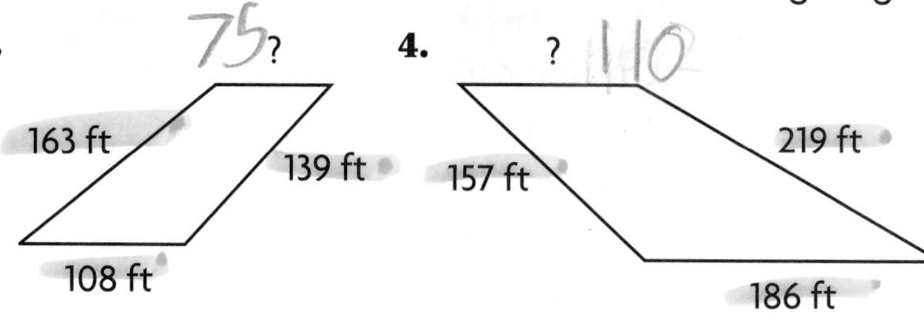

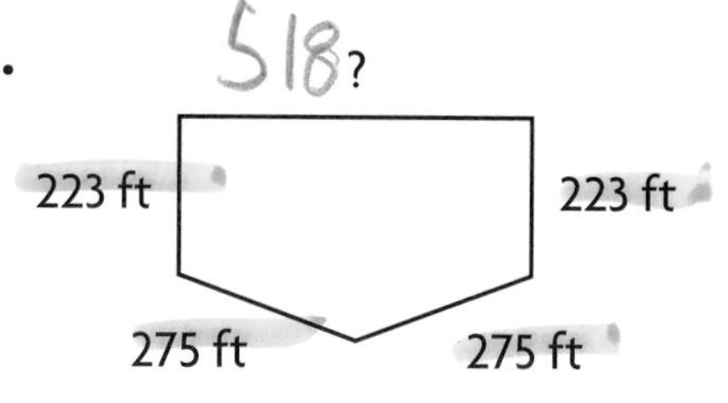

6. **WRITE ABOUT IT** When the perimeter is known, how can you use addition and subtraction to find the missing length?

Mixed Applications

7. The swim team begins practice by running around a field. Two sides of the field are 112 yards each. The other two sides are 43 yards each. What is the perimeter of the field?

8. Before her first miss, Laura jumped 36 turns of the rope. Then she jumped 33, then 44. How many turns did she jump altogether?

9. There are 425 plants on the four sides of the school building. There are 81 plants on one side, 105 on another side, and 117 on the third side. How many plants are on the fourth side of the building?

10. Part of the stadium is roped off for the band. The rope is 84 feet long. The rope stretches 16 feet across the front. It stretches 22 feet along each of the two sides. How many feet does the rope stretch across the back?

11. Sammy bought a poster and a school T-shirt. He gave the clerk $20.00. He got $3.77 change. How much money did Sammy spend?

Mixed Review

Find the sum or difference. (taught in Grade 3)

12. $90 - 17$

13. $40 - 28$

14. $70 + 55$

15. $60 - 43$

16. $80 + 64$

Write the number that is 1,000 more. (taught in Grade 3)

17. 2,679 **18.** 8,934 **19.** 1,982 **20.** 9,920 **21.** 4,804

MORE PRACTICE Student Handbook page H69

Subtracting Across Zeros

You will investigate how to subtract from numbers that have zeros.

Why learn this? When you subtract to find out how much change you should receive, you often need to subtract across zeros.

Explore

Make a model to show how to subtract 300 − 246.

MATERIALS: base-ten blocks

MODEL

Step 1

Choose the base-ten blocks that you will need.

Use 3 hundreds to show 300. Since 6 > 0, regroup the blocks to solve the problem.

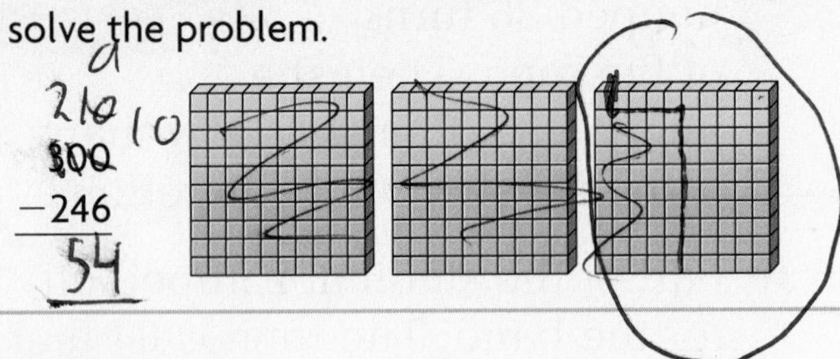

Record

Explain how you used the base-ten blocks to find the difference.

TALK ABOUT IT In which place values did you have to regroup? Why?

Try This

Use base-ten blocks to find 404 − 135.

WRITE ABOUT IT How did you regroup and subtract to find the difference?

E-Lab • Activity 2 Available on CD-ROM and the Internet at http://www.hbschool.com/elab

HANDS-ON PRACTICE

Use base-ten blocks to model the subtraction. Solve.

1. $\begin{array}{r} 200 \\ -123 \\ \hline \end{array}$ 77

2. $\begin{array}{r} 400 \\ -285 \\ \hline \end{array}$ 115

3. $\begin{array}{r} 300 \\ -192 \\ \hline \end{array}$ 108

4. $\begin{array}{r} 500 \\ -473 \\ \hline \end{array}$ 27

Applying What You Learned

Find the difference.

5. $\begin{array}{r} 600 \\ -347 \\ \hline \end{array}$ 253

6. $\begin{array}{r} 500 \\ -392 \\ \hline \end{array}$ 108

7. $\begin{array}{r} 600 \\ -583 \\ \hline \end{array}$ 17

8. $\begin{array}{r} 700 \\ -426 \\ \hline \end{array}$ 274

9. $\begin{array}{r} 400 \\ -273 \\ \hline \end{array}$ 127

10. $\begin{array}{r} 700 \\ -569 \\ \hline \end{array}$ 131

11. $\begin{array}{r} 800 \\ -658 \\ \hline \end{array}$ 142

12. $\begin{array}{r} 900 \\ -834 \\ \hline \end{array}$ 66

Mixed Applications

13. Ricky had $300 in the bank. He bought a video game for $49. How much money does Ricky have in the bank now? 251

14. In one section of an arena, there are 500 seats. There are 437 people sitting in the seats. How many of the seats are empty? 63

15. The Science Club wanted to raise money for a field trip. The club ordered 600 T-shirts to sell. The club members sold 252 shirts on Thursday and 221 shirts on Friday. How many T-shirts were left to sell? 327

16. The Science Club advertised their T-shirt sale. They gave out 509 fliers on Monday and 607 fliers on Tuesday. How many fliers did they give out in the two days? 1,116

17. This year there are 200 trophies in the school trophy case. Last year there were 178 trophies in the case. How many trophies did the school earn this year? 22

Sports Link

Football was first played in Australia around 1850. There were 40 players on the field at a time. Today Australian football is played with 18 players on the field at a time. How many more players played on an Australian football field in 1850 than today? 7 more

PART

1 More Subtracting Across Zeros

You will learn to subtract across zeros with larger numbers.	**Why learn this?** You can find out how much farther one distance is than another.

Humpback whales migrate about 8,000 miles each year.

Green turtles migrate about 2,800 miles each year.

How much farther do the whales travel than the turtles?

MODEL

Find 8,000 − 2,800.

Step 1	Step 2	Step 3	Step 4
Subtract the ones.	Subtract the tens.	Since 8 > 0, regroup 8 thousands as 7 thousands 10 hundreds. Subtract the hundreds.	Subtract the thousands.
$\begin{array}{r} 8,000 \\ -2,800 \\ \hline 0 \end{array}$	$\begin{array}{r} 8,000 \\ -2,800 \\ \hline 00 \end{array}$	$\begin{array}{r} {\scriptstyle 7\ 10} \quad \\ \not{8},\not{0}00 \\ -2,800 \\ \hline 200 \end{array}$	$\begin{array}{r} {\scriptstyle 7\ 10} \quad \\ \not{8},\not{0}00 \\ -2,800 \\ \hline 5,200 \end{array}$

So, humpback whales travel about 5,200 miles farther than green turtles.

EXAMPLES

A. $\begin{array}{r} {\scriptstyle 5\ 9\ \ 9\ 10} \ \\ \not{6}\not{0},\not{0}\not{0}5 \\ -\ \ 9,745 \\ \hline 50,260 \end{array}$ **B.** $\begin{array}{r} {\scriptstyle 2\ \ 9\ 9\ 10} \\ 1\not{3},\not{0}\not{0}\not{0} \\ -\ \ 1,573 \\ \hline 11,427 \end{array}$ **C.** $\begin{array}{r} {\scriptstyle 3\ 9\ \ 10\ 6\ 11} \\ \not{4}\not{0},\not{0}\not{7}\not{1} \\ -27,163 \\ \hline 12,908 \end{array}$

Talk About It

- How is the regrouping in Example A like the regrouping in Example B? How is it different?
- Look at Example C. Explain why there is a 10 over the hundreds column.

Science Link

Animals *migrate* to find food, to give birth, or to find a better place to live. Arctic terns travel about 25,000 miles round trip from the North Pole to the South Pole. About how much farther do the arctic terns travel than the humpback whales?

MIGRATION ROUTES
Arctic Tern
Humpback Whale
Green Turtle

PRACTICE

Find the difference.

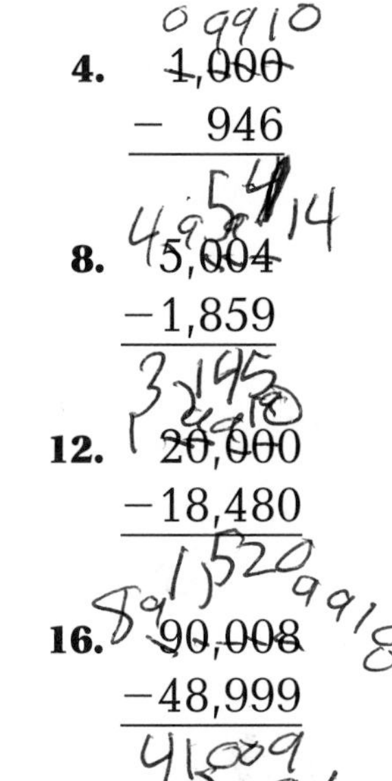

1. $\begin{array}{r}400\\-287\\\hline\end{array}$	2. $\begin{array}{r}700\\-692\\\hline\end{array}$	3. $\begin{array}{r}300\\-163\\\hline\end{array}$	4. $\begin{array}{r}1{,}000\\-\ \ 946\\\hline\end{array}$
5. $\begin{array}{r}4{,}001\\-3{,}090\\\hline\end{array}$	6. $\begin{array}{r}8{,}003\\-6{,}564\\\hline\end{array}$	7. $\begin{array}{r}2{,}005\\-1{,}978\\\hline\end{array}$	8. $\begin{array}{r}5{,}004\\-1{,}859\\\hline\end{array}$
9. $\begin{array}{r}6{,}000\\-4{,}278\\\hline\end{array}$	10. $\begin{array}{r}9{,}003\\-7{,}973\\\hline\end{array}$	11. $\begin{array}{r}10{,}000\\-\ \ 9{,}195\\\hline\end{array}$	12. $\begin{array}{r}20{,}000\\-18{,}480\\\hline\end{array}$
13. $\begin{array}{r}60{,}005\\-47{,}938\\\hline\end{array}$	14. $\begin{array}{r}30{,}000\\-28{,}743\\\hline\end{array}$	15. $\begin{array}{r}80{,}000\\-23{,}196\\\hline\end{array}$	16. $\begin{array}{r}90{,}008\\-48{,}999\\\hline\end{array}$
17. $\begin{array}{r}40{,}021\\-17{,}604\\\hline\end{array}$	18. $\begin{array}{r}70{,}000\\-52{,}347\\\hline\end{array}$	19. $\begin{array}{r}60{,}000\\-32{,}691\\\hline\end{array}$	20. $\begin{array}{r}80{,}006\\-73{,}019\\\hline\end{array}$

Mixed Applications

21. Some birds migrate 2,000 miles across the Pacific Ocean to Hawaii without rest or food. Some sea turtles migrate 1,400 miles across the Atlantic Ocean to South America. How much farther do the birds migrate than the sea turtles?

22. The box for David's turtle is 36 inches long and 28 inches wide. What is the perimeter of the box?

23. Kendra saw a male walrus that weighed 3,000 pounds. Later, she saw a female walrus. It weighed 2,380 pounds. How much more did the male walrus weigh?

24. The first seal weighs 286 pounds more than the second seal. If the second seal weighs 394 pounds, how much does the first seal weigh?

25. **Write a problem** about these animals. The leatherback sea turtle may weigh up to 1,500 pounds. The Galápagos tortoise may weigh about 600 pounds.

In ***Mighty Math Number Heroes***, the game *Quizzo* challenges you to add and subtract larger numbers.

MORE PRACTICE Student Handbook page H70

PART 2 PROBLEM-SOLVING STRATEGY
Work Backward

THE PROBLEM Quincy and his family went to Sea-Life Park. Quincy bought a book for $7.00, a T-shirt for $18.00, and sunglasses for $9.00. He had $14.75 left. How much money did Quincy have to begin with?

✓ Understand

- What are you asked to find?
- What information will you use?
- Is there any information you will not use? If so, what?

✓ Plan

- What strategy can you use to solve the problem?

  You can use the strategy *work backward*. Work from the amount Quincy has left to find the amount he started with.

✓ Solve

- How can you work backward to solve the problem?

  You can work backward from what you know by using the opposite operation, addition, to solve the problem.

  Quincy had $14.75 left. Add to that all the amounts he spent.

	$14.75	(amount left)
	9.00	(sunglasses)
	18.00	(T-shirt)
+	7.00	(book)
	$48.75	

So, Quincy had $48.75 to begin with.

✓ Look Back

- How can you decide if your answer is reasonable?
- What other strategy could you use?

Calculator Activities page H61

CHOOSE Paper/Pencil Calculator Hands-on Mental Math

PRACTICE

Work backward to solve.

1. At Sea-Life Park, Holly took 8 pictures of dolphins and 6 pictures of sea lions. She took 6 pictures at the whale show. She still had 4 pictures left. How many pictures were on the roll of film when she came to the park? 24

2. The science club members earned $58 at their car wash. The 20 new members paid dues of $2 each. The club now has $125. How much money did the science club have to begin with? $27.00

3. Rick and Mason played a number game. Rick picked a number and added 9. Then, he subtracted 4. Last, he added 10. The answer was 23. What number did Rick choose? 8

4. Peter's mother planted 24 daisies in one flower bed and 38 in another. She had 26 plants left. How many daisies did she have when she started? 88

Mixed Applications

Solve.

CHOOSE A STRATEGY

- Work Backward
- Make a Model
- Draw a Picture
- Write a Number Sentence

5. At the Snack Shack, Luisa bought a hamburger for $2.85, a salad for $1.59, and a drink for $1.25. The clerk gave her $4.31 in change. How much did Luisa give the clerk to pay for her order? 10

6. Linda, Bill, Emily, and Glenn are lined up to practice free throws. Bill's turn is before Linda's and after Glenn's. Emily's turn is before Glenn's. In what order are they lined up? E G B L

7. There were 870 people at the first baseball game and 1,003 people at the second game. How many more people were at the second baseball game? 133

8. Paul was able to jump rope 35 more times than Daniella. If Paul jumped 123 times, how many times did Daniella jump rope? 88

9. Marcus ran 50 yards down the football field in three plays. On the third play he ran 18 yards. He had run one-half that far on the second play. How far did Marcus run on the first play? 23

10. The tennis team often plays on this tennis court. What is its perimeter? 228

78 ft

36 ft

Estimating Sums and Differences

You will learn that rounding can help you estimate sums and differences.

Why learn this? Sometimes an estimate is just as useful as an exact answer.

You can estimate by rounding numbers to different place values. Follow these rules:

a. Decide on the digit to be rounded.

b. Look at the digit to its right.

c. If the digit to the right is *less than* 5, the digit being rounded stays the same.

d. If the digit to the right is 5 *or more*, the digit being rounded is increased by 1.

Suppose a stadium has 7,365 seats. How many seats are there to the nearest

thousand? **7**,3̲65 → 7,000 seats

hundred? 7,**3**6̲5 → 7,400 seats

ten? 7,3**6**5̲ → 7,370 seats

CRITICAL THINKING To round 7,365 to the nearest *thousand*, what digit did you look at? to the nearest *hundred*? to the nearest *ten*?

You can estimate sums and differences by rounding to given place values such as ten, hundred, or thousand.

You can estimate a number to any of its place values.

Sports Link

The Orlando Arena seats about 17,000 fans. The Charlotte Coliseum seats about 23,700 fans. About how many more fans can watch games at the Charlotte Coliseum than at the Orlando Arena?

EXAMPLES

A. Round to the nearest **ten**.

48	→	50
31	→	30
+**1**9	→	+20
		100

B. Round to the nearest **hundred**.

978	→	1,000
−**5**84	→	− 600
		400

C. Round to the nearest **thousand**.

4,443	→	4,000
6,925	→	7,000
+**2**,516	→	+3,000
		14,000

Find the exact answers for Examples A–C.

- How can you use the estimates to help you decide if your answers make sense?

PRACTICE

Round to the nearest *hundred*.

1. 219 **2.** 781 **3.** 147 **4.** 950

Round to the nearest *thousand*.

5. 2,690 **6.** 1,472 **7.** 8,099 **8.** 9,541

Round to the nearest *ten*, *hundred*, and *thousand*.

9. 4,261 **10.** 5,682 **11.** 7,915 **12.** 9,489

Round to the nearest *ten*, *hundred*, or *thousand*. Estimate the sum or difference.

13. 25 + 42 + 18

14. 443 − 236

15. 509 + 350 + 136

16. 6,401 − 2,658

17. 4,509 + 8,025 + 3,900

18. 194 + 657

19. 529 − 146

20. 845 + 379

21. 3,178 + 3,045

22. 2,024 − 1,896

Mixed Applications

SPORTS STORE SALE

- In-line Skates............... $44.92
- NFL Football............... $69.24
- Jogging Trampoline... $25.95
- Bicycle....................... $84.87

23. Adam wants to buy a bicycle and a pair of skates. Estimate the total cost of these things.

24. Estimate the difference in the cost of a football and the cost of a bicycle.

25. Marion wants to buy skates, a football, and a bicycle. Estimate the total cost of these things.

26. **Write a problem** that uses the data on the sign and requires an estimate.

Mixed Review

Write the next three numbers in the pattern. (taught in Grade 3)

27. 8, 12, 16, ___?___, ___?___, ___?___

28. 7, 14, 21, ___?___, ___?___, ___?___

29. 9, 18, 27, ___?___, ___?___, ___?___

30. 15, 20, 25, ___?___, ___?___, ___?___

Use mental math to complete each equation. (taught in Grade 3)

31. 4 + ___?___ = 9 + 3

32. 12 − 4 = ___?___ + 5

33. 8 + 7 = 18 − ___?___

34. 14 − 7 = 6 + ___?___

Technology Link

Data can be displayed in tables and graphs. You can use ***Graph Links*** computer software to make a graph.

Choosing the Operation

You will learn whether to add or subtract to solve a problem.

Why learn this? You can use word clues to help you decide how to solve problems.

Decide whether you would add or subtract the missing numbers to solve these problems.

A. Abraham Lincoln was born in __?__. He was elected President at the age of __?__. In what year was he elected President?

B. George Washington, the first President, died in __?__ at the age of __?__. In what year was he born?

C. John F. Kennedy was born in __?__. He was elected President in __?__. What was his age when he was elected President?

D. Thomas Jefferson, the third President, was born in __?__ and died in __?__. How old was he when he died?

Talk About It

For information use the Social Studies Link.

- In which of Problems A–D would you *add* to find the answer?
- In which of Problems A–D would you *subtract* to find the answer?
- What clues in each of the problems help you find the answer?

Check Your Understanding

CRITICAL THINKING

1. Work with a partner. Choose one of Problems A–D. Use the Social Studies Link to help you find the answer.
2. Explain how the clues in Problems A–D are different.

Social Studies Link

Abraham Lincoln was born in 1809 and was elected President at 51.

George Washington died in 1799 at the age of 67.

John F. Kennedy was born in 1917 and was elected President in 1960.

Thomas Jefferson was born in 1743 and died in 1826.

PRACTICE

Write whether you should *add* or *subtract* the missing numbers to solve. Use the table below to find the missing numbers and solve the problems.

Distance Between United States Cities	
Seattle to Omaha	1,608 miles
Omaha to Washington, D.C.	1,116 miles
Washington, D.C. to Philadelphia	140 miles

Social Studies Link

Washington, D.C., became the capital of the United States in 1800. How many years ago did Washington, D.C., become the capital?

3. The Larsens drove __?__ miles from Seattle to Omaha. Then they drove __?__ miles from Omaha to Washington, D.C. What is the distance they drove from Seattle to Washington, D.C.?

4. The Larsens drove __?__ miles from Seattle to Omaha. Then they drove __?__ miles from Omaha to Philadelphia. How many more miles did they drive from Seattle to Omaha than from Omaha to Philadelphia?

Mixed Applications

For Problems 5–7, use the table.

Capital City	Population
Montpelier, Vermont	8,247
Augusta, Maine	21,325
Helena, Montana	24,559
Juneau, Alaska	26,751

5. The number of people in Montpelier is __?__. The number of people in Augusta is __?__. How many more people are in Augusta?

6. The number of people in Helena is __?__. The number of people in Juneau is __?__. What is the total number of people in these two cities?

7. The difference in the number of people in Juneau and in Helena is __?__. The difference in the number of people in Juneau and in Augusta is __?__. Which pair of cities has the greatest difference?

Mixed Review

Write the value of the blue digit. (taught in Grade 3)

8. 3,568 **9.** 43,297 **10.** 436,271 **11.** 2,729 **12.** 39,471

Write the number that is 100 less. (taught in Grade 3)

13. 879 **14.** 1,430 **15.** 169 **16.** 1,055 **17.** 43,001

MORE PRACTICE Student Handbook pages H70–H71

CULTURAL CONNECTION

COOPERATIVE LEARNING

CINCO DE MAYO FESTIVAL

Miguel's school in Santa Fe, New Mexico, set up a booth for the city's Cinco de Mayo festival. The students sold tacos, burritos, fruit juices, and ice cream bars. Miguel kept track of the number of each item sold.

By 2:00 P.M. they had sold 165 burritos. Between 2:00 and 6:00 P.M., they sold 205 more. How many more burritos did they sell after 2:00 than before 2:00?

To solve this problem, restate the question and the facts in your own words. Replace the words in the problem with the numbers. Then find the sum or difference.

The number of burritos sold after 2:00 is 205.
The number sold before 2:00 is 165.
$205 - 165 = \underline{?}$, or $165 + \underline{?} = 205$

So, they sold 40 more burritos after 2:00 than before 2:00.

CULTURAL LINK

Cinco de Mayo (Fifth of May) is celebrated in Mexico and in the United States. The holiday celebrates the defeat of French troops in Puebla, Mexico, in 1862. In parades with horses, riders dress in charro costumes decorated with silver. During the festival, people enjoy Mexican folk dances, special foods, and the music of mariachi bands.

Work Together

1. The booth closed at 6:00 P.M. How many burritos did the students sell at the festival?
2. The students sold 401 tacos. How many more tacos than burritos did they sell?
3. In the morning, the students sold 184 ice cream bars. In the afternoon, they sold 236 ice cream bars. How many ice cream bars did they sell in all?
4. **Write a problem** about boxes of fruit juice the students sold in the morning and how many they sold in the afternoon. Exchange with a classmate. Solve.

CHAPTER 2

REVIEW

✓ CHECK UNDERSTANDING

Use addition and subtraction to find the missing length. (pages 18–19)

1.

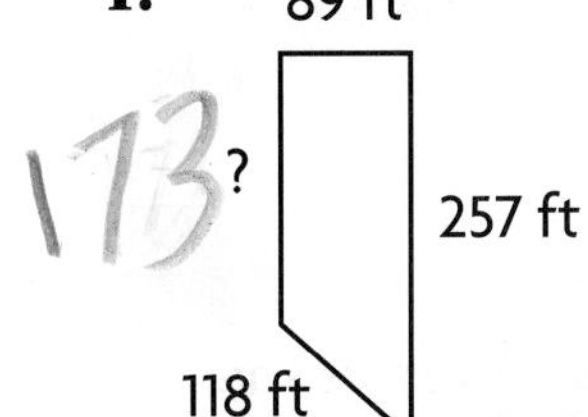

perimeter = 637 ft

2.

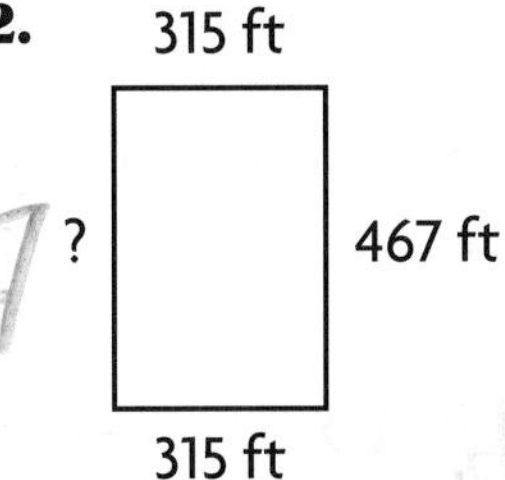

perimeter = 1,564 ft

3.

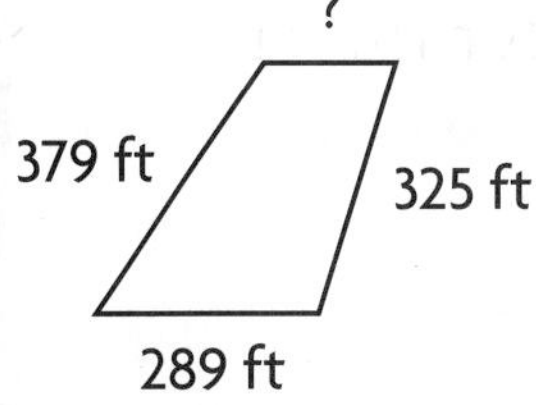

perimeter = 1,161 ft

✓ CHECK SKILLS

Find the difference. (pages 20–23)

4. 903 − 745

5. 300 − 136

6. 700 − 459

7. 801 − 177

8. 6,400 − 2,515

9. 3,000 − 1,564

10. 5,000 − 3,401

11. 7,003 − 4,900

Round to the nearest *ten, hundred,* and *thousand.* (pages 26–27)

12. 5,432

13. 1,983

14. 6,410

15. 3,755

Round to the nearest *hundred* or *thousand.* Estimate the sum or difference. (pages 26–27)

16. 639 − 215

17. 909 + 425

18. 589 − 119

19. 2,008 + 1,900

✓ CHECK PROBLEM SOLVING

Solve. (pages 24–25, 28–29)

CHOOSE A STRATEGY

- Work Backward
- Draw a Picture
- Make a Model
- Write a Number Sentence

20. Shelly bought a cassette for $14.98 and a cassette case for $6.97. She had $3.75 left. How much money did she have to begin with?

21. Susan bought a shirt that cost $2.10 less than a pair of pants. The pants cost $8.79 more than a purse. The purse cost $19.98. How much did the pants cost? the shirt?

MULTIPLICATION FACTS

DID YOU KNOW...

As a hobby, collecting rocks dates back to the 19th century. Some people collect different kinds of rocks from around the world.

Team-Up Time

Displaying Collections

Is your hobby collecting rocks, baseball cards, dolls, or stamps? Suppose you collect stamps. Multiplication can help you organize your collection. Design a stamp album. Work with your group to decide on the best way to arrange any number of stamps onto an album page with the same number of stamps in each row.

Work with a group. Your job is to

- decide how many ways you can put stamps in the rows in the album.
- show the ways.
- explain for each way how many stamps would fit on a page.
- share your ideas with the class.

DID YOU

- ✓ decide how many ways you can arrange stamps?
- ✓ show the ways?
- ✓ explain the total number of stamps on each page?
- ✓ share your ideas with the class?

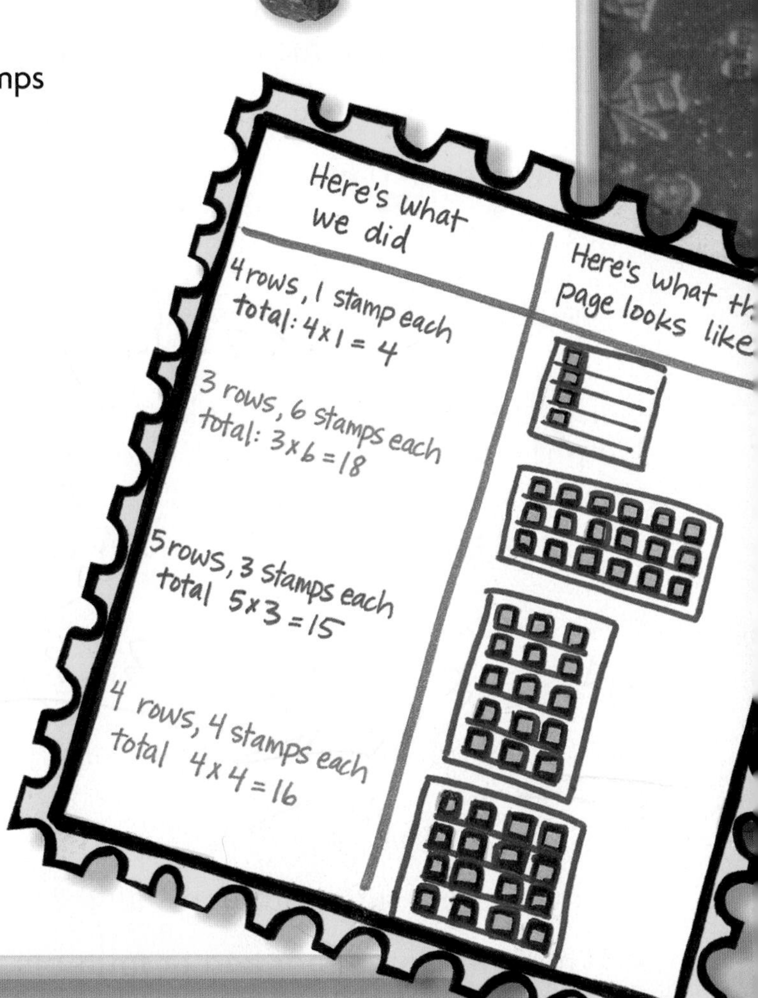

What Questions Can Multiplication Answer?

You will learn how to model different problems.	**Why learn this?** You'll know when to choose multiplication to solve a problem.

Nancy bought 3 packages of gum. There were 5 pieces of gum in each package. How many pieces of gum did Nancy buy?

- 3 packages
- 5 in each package
- $3 \times 5 = 15$

So, Nancy bought 15 pieces of gum.

Use craft sticks to model the problem.

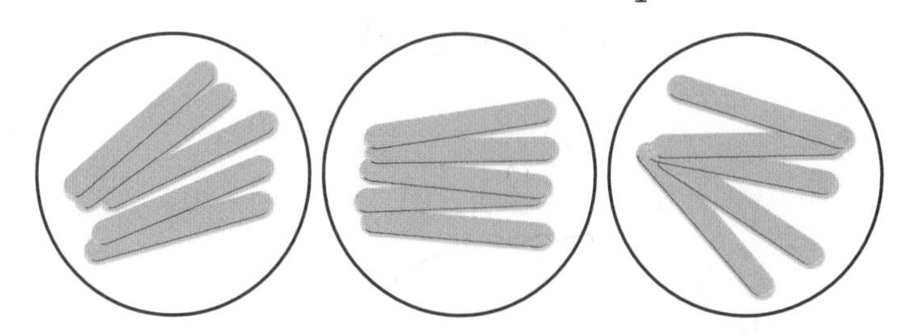

Corey walks his dog 2 times each day. How many times does he walk his dog in one week?

- 7 days in one week
- 2 walks each day
- $7 \times 2 = 14$

So, Corey walks his dog 14 times in one week.

Use a number line to model the problem.

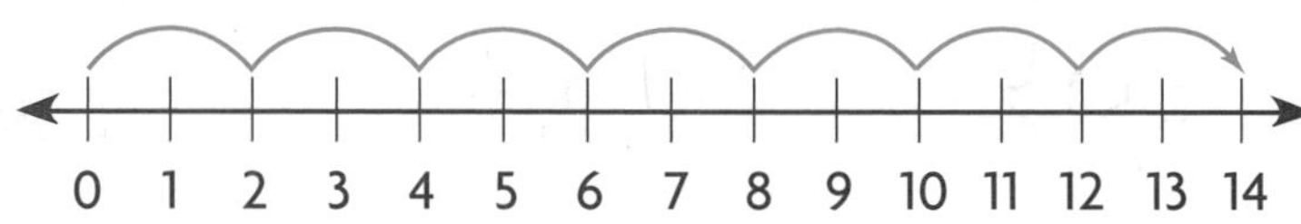

Carlos arranged his rock collection on 3 shelves. He put 6 rocks on each shelf. How many rocks did Carlos put on the shelves?

- 3 shelves
- 6 rocks on each shelf
- $3 \times 6 = 18$

So, Carlos put 18 rocks on the shelves.

Make an array to model the problem.

Talk About It

- How are the three problems alike?
- When can you either add or multiply to solve a problem?

PRACTICE

Model each problem. Solve.

1. Haley rides the school bus 2 times each day. How many times does she ride the bus in 5 days?
2. Albert put 4 ice cubes into each of 5 glasses. How many ice cubes did Albert use in all?
3. Amber has 6 bags with 4 cookies in each bag. How many cookies does Amber have?
4. Chet has 4 rows of 3 cars. How many cars does Chet have in all?
5. There are 9 boxes of envelopes on each of 3 shelves. How many boxes are there in all?
6. Sue has 5 green beads. She has 6 times as many red beads. How many red beads does Sue have?

Mixed Applications

7. Nick has 275 baseball cards. Seth has 367 baseball cards. How many more cards does Seth have than Nick?
8. Tiffany has 3 birds, 6 fish, and 1 cat. She has twice as many dogs as cats. How many pets does Tiffany have?

9. **WRITE ABOUT IT** Explain how each model in this lesson shows equal groups.

Mixed Review

Find the sum. (pages 6–7)

10.	11.	12.	13.	14.
15	12	14	23	45
15	12	14	23	45
+15	+12	+ 8	+17	+45

Find the difference. (taught in Grade 3)

15.	16.	17.	18.	19.
675	393	781	850	908
−328	−184	−462	−765	−639

20.	21.	22.	23.	24.
462	718	484	634	361
−144	−609	−329	−216	− 37

Multiplication Properties

You will learn how multiplication properties can help you remember the facts.

Why learn this? When you know the properties, you don't have to memorize so many facts.

WORD POWER
- Property of One
- Zero Property
- Order Property

Charlie saw 1 bird's nest in an oak tree. There are 5 eggs in the nest. How many eggs are there in all?

PROPERTY OF ONE
When one of the factors is 1, the product is the other factor.

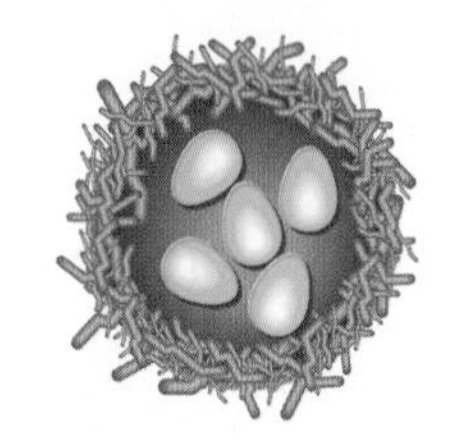

1 nest with 5 eggs in it

$1 \times 5 = 5$

So, there are 5 eggs in all.

A female robin lays three to six blue eggs that hatch in about 2 weeks.

Amanda saw 3 bird's nests in the apple tree. There are no eggs in any of the nests. How many eggs are there in all?

ZERO PROPERTY
When one of the factors is zero, the product is zero.

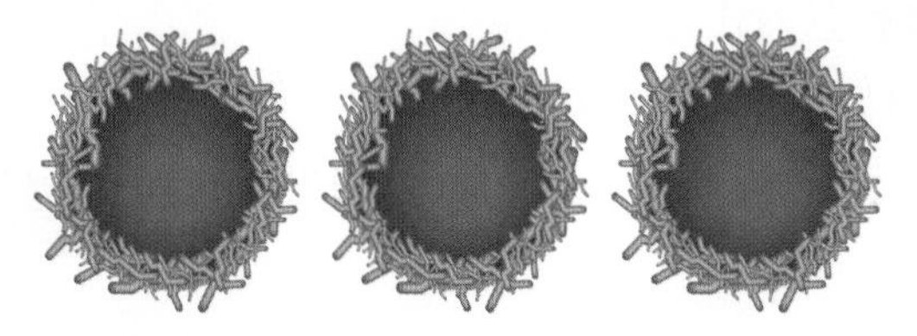

3 nests with 0 eggs in each

$3 \times 0 = 0$

So, there are 0 eggs in all.

At the pond, Justin saw 2 nests with 4 eggs in each. Matt saw 4 nests with 2 eggs in each. Who saw more eggs?

ORDER PROPERTY
Two numbers can be multiplied in any order. The product is the same.

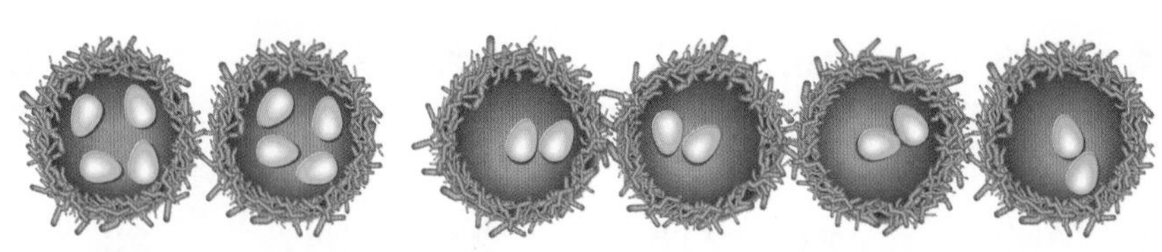

$2 \times 4 = 8$

2 nests with 4 eggs in each

$4 \times 2 = 8$

4 nests with 2 eggs in each

So, Justin and Matt each saw 8 eggs.

CRITICAL THINKING How do you think knowing these properties can help you remember the facts?

WRITE ABOUT IT Make a list of the facts you know. How can you use the Order Property to double the number of facts that you know?

PRACTICE

Write *a*, *b*, or *c* to tell which property is shown.

a. Property of One	**1.** $43 \times 1 = 43$	**2.** $6 \times 2 = 2 \times 6$
b. Zero Property	**3.** $279 \times 0 = 0$	**4.** $3 \times 5 = 5 \times 3$
c. Order Property	**5.** $1 \times 75 = 75$	**6.** $0 \times 27 = 0$

Use the multiplication properties to solve.

7. $\begin{array}{r} 6 \\ \times 0 \\ \hline \end{array}$ **8.** $\begin{array}{r} 8 \\ \times 1 \\ \hline \end{array}$ **9.** $\begin{array}{r} 0 \\ \times 5 \\ \hline \end{array}$ **10.** $\begin{array}{r} 7 \\ \times 1 \\ \hline \end{array}$ **11.** $\begin{array}{r} 1 \\ \times 4 \\ \hline \end{array}$ **12.** $\begin{array}{r} 9 \\ \times 0 \\ \hline \end{array}$

13. $8 \times 3 =$?
$3 \times 8 =$?

14. $2 \times 9 =$?
$9 \times 2 =$?

15. $6 \times 4 =$?
$4 \times 6 =$?

16. $5 \times 7 =$?
$7 \times 5 =$?

Mixed Applications

17. A canoe course down the river is 1 mile long. Felisha paddles down the river and back 2 times. How many miles does she travel?

18. On 1 canoe trip, Diana saw 3 alligators. How many alligators did she see in all?

19. Royce can see that there are not any frogs on the 4 water lilies in the pond. How many frogs are on the water lilies?

20. **Write a problem** using the Order Property to show how the number of birds in 3 trees can be the same as the number of birds in 2 trees.

Mixed Review

Find the difference. (pages 20–23)

21. $\begin{array}{r} 200 \\ -107 \\ \hline \end{array}$ **22.** $\begin{array}{r} 400 \\ -235 \\ \hline \end{array}$ **23.** $\begin{array}{r} 700 \\ -368 \\ \hline \end{array}$ **24.** $\begin{array}{r} 600 \\ -409 \\ \hline \end{array}$ **25.** $\begin{array}{r} 300 \\ -287 \\ \hline \end{array}$

Write the number that is 100 more. (taught in Grade 3)

26. 85 **27.** 169 **28.** 209 **29.** 810 **30.** 988

HANDS ON
COOPERATIVE LEARNING

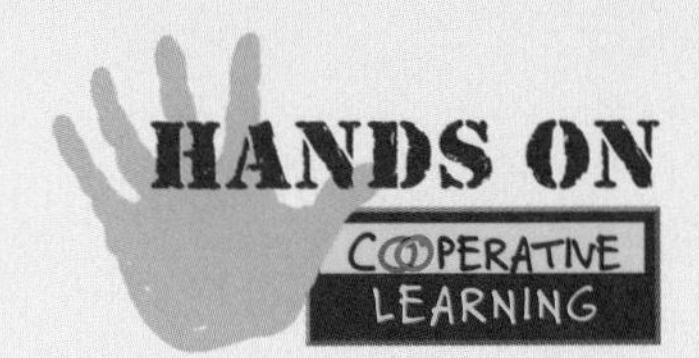

More About Multiplication Models

You will investigate a way to model multiplication of larger numbers.

Why learn this? You can find products of larger factors more easily.

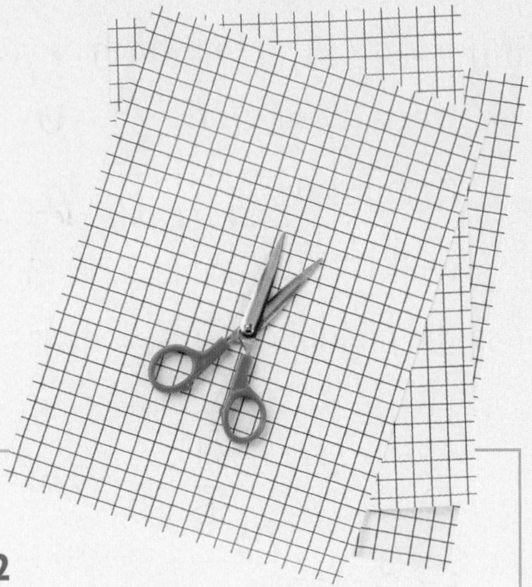

Explore

You can break apart numbers to make them easier to multiply. Model a way to find the product of 6 and 8.

MATERIALS: centimeter grid paper

MODEL

What is 6×8?

Step 1

Outline a rectangle that is 6 units high and 8 units wide.

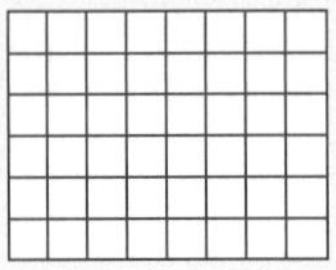

Step 2

Cut apart the rectangle to make two arrays whose products you know.

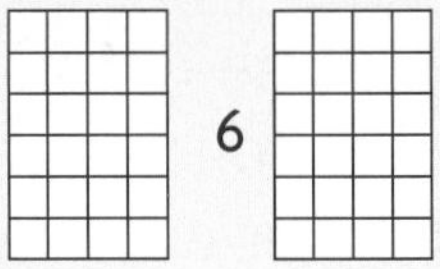

Record

Write a number sentence for each rectangle. Find the sum of the products for the two smaller rectangles.

Talk About It

- What multiplication sentence did you write for each of the two smaller rectangles?
- What is the sum of their products?
- Why is the sum the same as the product of the large rectangle?

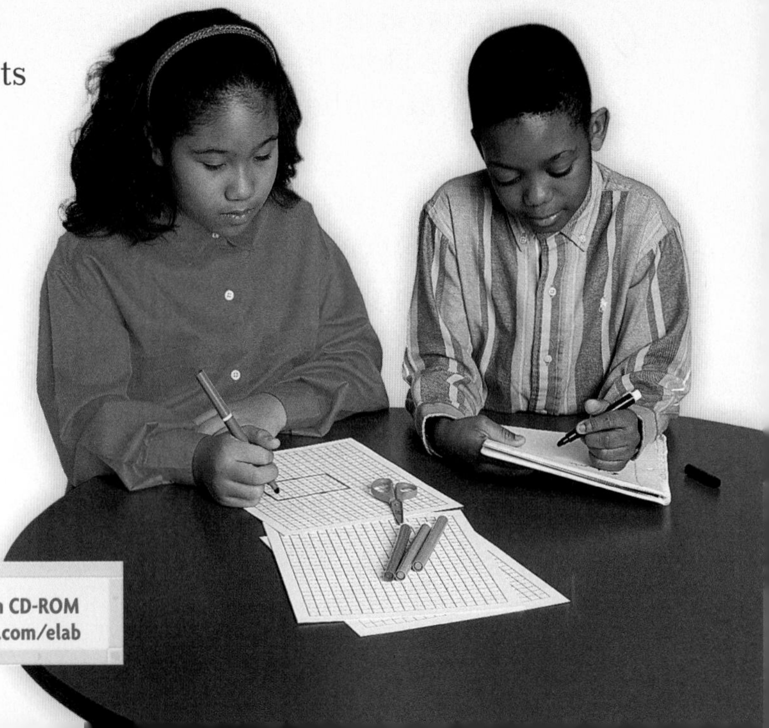

Technology Link
E-Lab • Activity 3 Available on CD-ROM and the Internet at http://www.hbschool.com/elab

Try This

Use grid paper. Break apart rectangles to find $8 \times 9 = \underline{?}$.

TALK ABOUT IT Look at your grid-paper model. How did you break apart the model to find the total product?

WRITE ABOUT IT How does breaking apart numbers help you find the product of larger factors?

HANDS-ON PRACTICE

Use the arrays. Find the products.

1. What is 5×7?

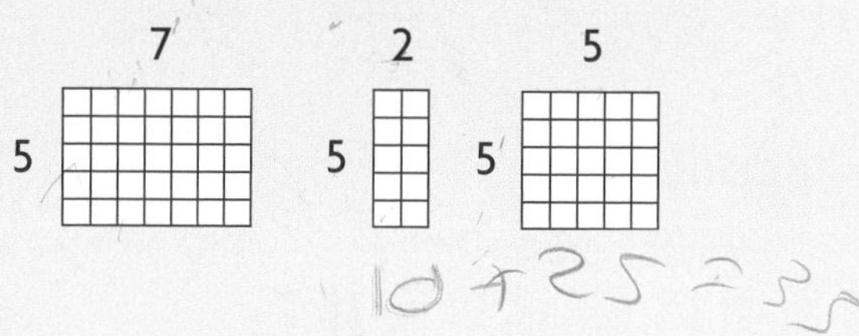

$5 \times 2 = \underline{?}$
$5 \times 5 = \underline{?}$
So, $5 \times 7 = \underline{?}$.

2. What is 8×9?

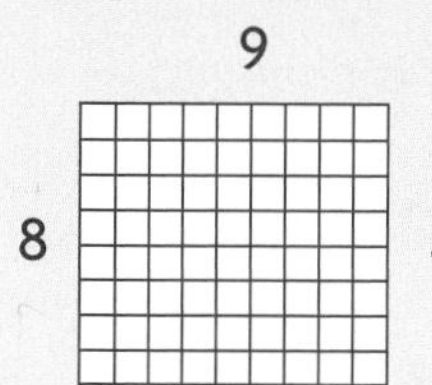

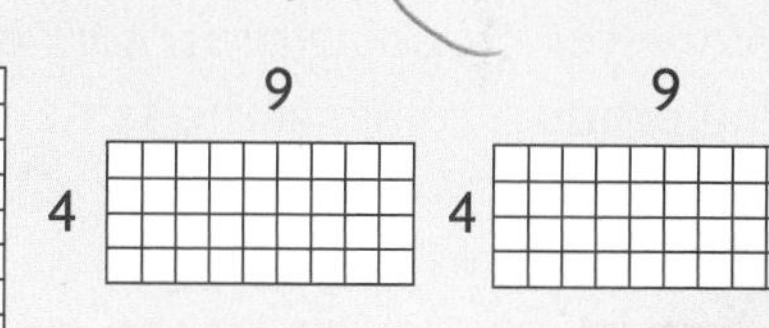

$4 \times 9 = \underline{?}$
$4 \times 9 = \underline{?}$
So, $8 \times 9 = \underline{?}$.

Use grid paper. Break apart the numbers to find the product.

3. $6 \times 7 = \underline{?}$
4. $7 \times 9 = \underline{?}$
5. $6 \times 6 = \underline{?}$
6. $8 \times 8 = \underline{?}$
7. $7 \times 7 = \underline{?}$
8. $8 \times 7 = \underline{?}$
9. $9 \times 6 = \underline{?}$
10. $7 \times 8 = \underline{?}$
11. $9 \times 9 = \underline{?}$
12. $6 \times 9 = \underline{?}$
13. $9 \times 7 = \underline{?}$
14. $7 \times 6 = \underline{?}$

Mixed Applications

15. The bus driver drives 3 miles from the school to the Nature Center and 3 miles back to the school each day for 5 days. How many miles does the bus driver travel in five days?

16. Joshua collected 14 different leaves on the field trip. Tara collected 12 leaves, and Carey collected 15 leaves. How many leaves did the three students collect in all?

17. For the field trip, the class is separated into 6 groups. There are 6 students in each group. How many students are in the class?

18. **Write a problem** about a field trip you have taken or would like to take. Use multiplication in your problem.

MORE PRACTICE Student Handbook page H71

PART 1 Multiplying Three Factors

You will learn how to multiply three factors.	**Why learn this?** You can understand the ways that three factors can be grouped to find a product.	**WORD POWER** Grouping Property

Jamal chose 4 songs from each of 2 music books. He sang each song for 5 minutes. For how many minutes did Jamal sing?

You can use tiles to help you multiply three factors in any order.

GROUPING PROPERTY

When the grouping of factors is changed, the product remains the same.

A.

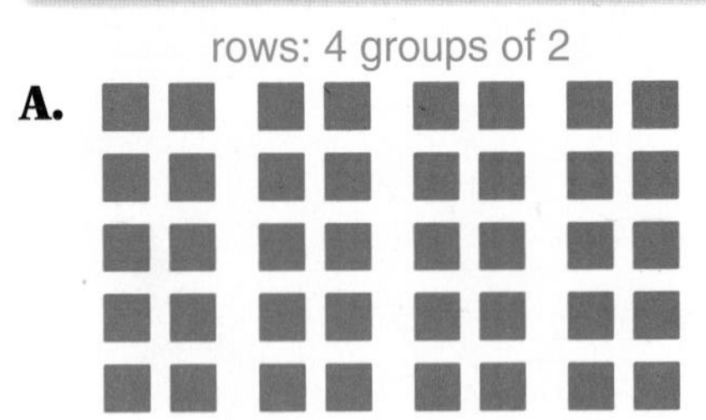

$(4 \times 2) \times 5 = \underline{?}$

$8 \times 5 = 40$

B.

rows: 2 groups of 5

4 groups of 10

$4 \times (2 \times 5) = \underline{?}$

$4 \times 10 = 40$

So, Jamal sang for 40 minutes.

REMEMBER:

Multiply the numbers in parentheses ( ) first.

Talk About It

- What two ways can you group $2 \times 3 \times 4 = \underline{?}$ to find the product?
- Are the products the same? Why or why not?

Check Your Understanding

Show two ways to group Exercises 1–6 by using parentheses ( ). Find the products.

1. $1 \times 6 \times 9 = \underline{?}$ **2.** $3 \times 2 \times 1 = \underline{?}$ **3.** $4 \times 2 \times 1 = \underline{?}$

4. $2 \times 5 \times 2 = \underline{?}$ **5.** $3 \times 2 \times 2 = \underline{?}$ **6.** $4 \times 2 \times 2 = \underline{?}$

Calculator Activities page H59

PRACTICE

Find the product.

7. $(6 \times 1) \times 5 =$? **8.** $4 \times (3 \times 3) =$? **9.** $2 \times (2 \times 4) =$?

Use the Grouping Property to solve each problem.

10. $4 \times (5 \times 1) =$? **11.** $(2 \times 2) \times 2 =$? **12.** $1 \times (5 \times 3) =$? **13.** $(7 \times 5) \times 1 =$?

14. $(3 \times 2) \times 4 =$? **15.** $4 \times (1 \times 6) =$? **16.** $(8 \times 1) \times 9 =$? **17.** $9 \times (1 \times 5) =$?

Show two ways to group Exercises 18–25 using parentheses. Find the products.

18. $4 \times 1 \times 2 =$? **19.** $2 \times 3 \times 2 =$? **20.** $2 \times 4 \times 2 =$? **21.** $7 \times 4 \times 1 =$?

22. $2 \times 3 \times 3 =$? **23.** $5 \times 8 \times 1 =$? **24.** $2 \times 1 \times 9 =$? **25.** $4 \times 4 \times 1 =$?

Mixed Applications

26. Emanuel practices the banjo 3 hours each week. Lois practices the piano 5 hours each week. How much longer does Lois practice in 4 weeks than Emanuel does?

27. In the band contest, there were 6 bands. There were 5 students in each of 3 bands. There were 6 in each of the other 3 bands. How many students were in the contest?

28. Charity's mother bought a music stand for \$14, a music book for \$12, and a new case for \$36. She gave the clerk four \$20 bills. How much money did she get back?

29. **WRITE ABOUT IT** Why is it helpful to group the factors in another way when you multiply three numbers? Give an example.

In ***Mighty Math Calculating Crew***, the game *Intergalactic Trader* challenges you to remember your multiplication facts.

PART 2 PROBLEM-SOLVING STRATEGY
Make a Model

THE PROBLEM At the pet store, the parakeets are in 2 rows of 4 large cages. There are 8 parakeets in each cage. They are given water 2 times a day. How many parakeets are there in all?

✓ Understand

- What are you asked to find?
- What information will you use?
- Is there any information that you will not use? If so, what?

✓ Plan

- What strategy can you use to solve the problem?

You can *make a model* to find the number of parakeets in all.

✓ Solve

- What model can you make to solve the problem?

Use tiles to make a model.

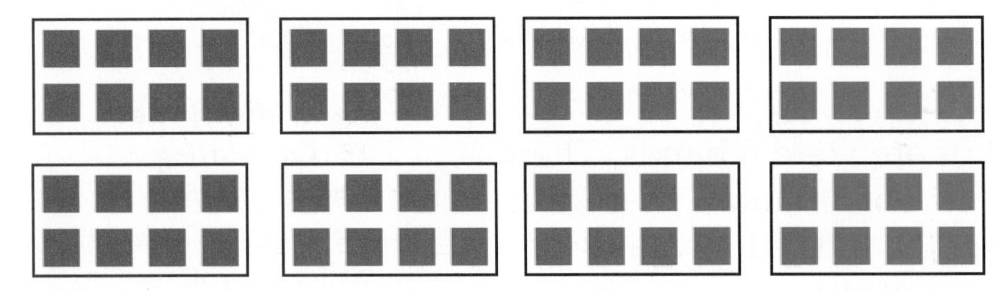

$(2 \times 4) \times 8 = 64$

(2	× 4)	× 8	= 64
number of rows	**number of cages**	**number of parakeets in each cage**	**number of parakeets in all**

So, there are 64 parakeets in all.

✓ Look Back

- How can you decide if your answer is reasonable?
- What other strategy could you use?

PRACTICE

CHOOSE Paper/Pencil Calculator Hands-on Mental Math

Make a model to solve.

1. At the pet store, the guinea pigs are in 2 rows of 3 cages. There are 4 guinea pigs in each cage. How many guinea pigs are there in all?

2. Sherry put 3 rows of 3 boxes of dog biscuits on each of 2 shelves. How many boxes of dog biscuits did she put on the shelves?

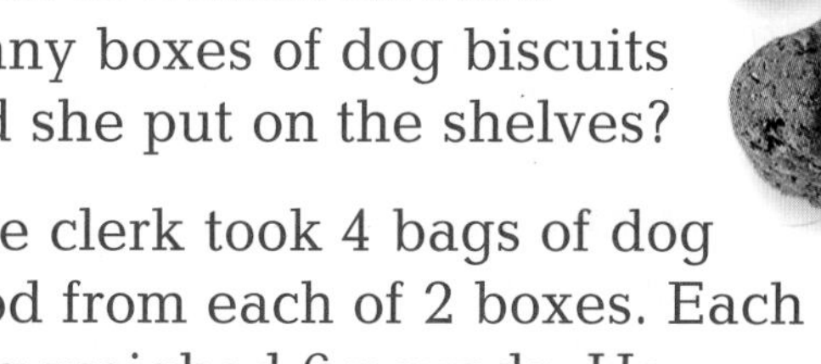

3. Dennis put 2 bowls of gerbil food in each cage of gerbils. The cages are in 3 rows of 2. How many bowls of gerbil food did he use?

4. The clerk took 4 bags of dog food from each of 2 boxes. Each bag weighed 6 pounds. How many pounds of dog food did the clerk take from the boxes?

Mixed Applications

Solve.

CHOOSE A STRATEGY

- Find a Pattern
- Work Backward
- Draw a Picture
- Make a Table
- Make a Model
- Write a Number Sentence

5. Jamie spent $10 on pet food, $3 for a pet brush, and $4 for a cat toy. She used a $2 coupon to help pay for the things. Jamie had $5 when she left the store. How much money did she take to the store?

6. Russell and Sarah have decided to take turns walking their dog. Russell will walk it on Monday, Sarah on Tuesday, and so on. What is the sixth day that Russell will walk their dog?

7. Angel feeds his dogs 3 cups of food 2 times each day. How many cups of food does he feed his dogs in 7 days?

8. Shelley has 8 gerbils, 3 cats, 2 dogs, and 1 rabbit. She has twice as many birds as cats. How many pets does Shelley have?

9. Mark and his brother counted 4 quarters, 8 dimes, 6 nickels, and 70 pennies. If they divide the coins evenly, how much money will each receive?

10. There are puppies and birds in the pet store. In all, there are 10 animals with 28 legs. How many puppies and how many birds are there?

11. Nate is building a doghouse. What is its perimeter?

36 in.

24 in.

Choosing the Operation

You will learn that addition, subtraction, and multiplication are used to answer different kinds of questions.	**Why learn this?** You will know which operation to use to find answers, such as which thing costs more.

Before you decide which operation to use, look carefully at the question.

Mr. Hall's class ordered 9 pizzas. Ms. Field's class ordered 8 pizzas. How many pizzas did the two classes order in all?

a. $9 - 8 = \underline{\ ?\ }$ **b.** $9 \times 8 = \underline{\ ?\ }$

c. $9 - \underline{\ ?\ } = 8$ **d.** $9 + 8 = \underline{\ ?\ }$

- What are you asked to find?
- Should you add, subtract, or multiply? Why?
- Which number sentence will help you solve the problem?

Check Your Understanding

Read the following exercises.

A. The cook baked 8 pizzas. Then he baked 4 more. How many pizzas did he bake?

B. Drew served 8 pizzas. The guests ate 4 of the pizzas. How many pizzas were left?

C. David, Carol, Lucy, and Frank each bought 8 pizzas for the party. How many pizzas did they buy in all?

1. Which operations would you use to solve A–C?

2. **WRITE ABOUT IT** What clues can you use to help you know when to add, subtract, or multiply to solve a problem?

Pizza is the Italian word for *pie*. How many slices of pizza would it take for each member of your family to have 2 slices?

PRACTICE

Choose the number sentences you would use to solve Problems 3–6. Then solve.

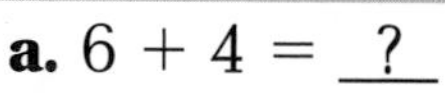

a. $6 + 4 = \underline{\ ?\ }$	**b.** $6 \times 4 = \underline{\ ?\ }$
c. $6 - 4 = \underline{\ ?\ }$	**d.** $6 - \underline{\ ?\ } = 4$

3. The chorus gave 6 concerts during the day. They sang 4 songs at each concert. How many songs did they sing during the day?

4. In the first row, there were 6 girls and 4 boys. How many students were in the first row?

5. At first, 6 chorus members were selling tickets. Then 4 of them had to leave. How many chorus members were left selling tickets?

6. The chorus will sing 6 songs in all. They have 4 songs left to sing. How many songs have they sung?

Mixed Applications

7. Vanessa made 8 signs for open house at her school. Brandon made 5 signs. How many more signs did Vanessa make than Brandon?

8. Chris is looking at 7 cakes on the table at the bake sale. Each cake has 6 slices. How many slices of cake are there?

9. Chris received 6 shirts and 4 pairs of shorts for his birthday. How many different outfits can he have?

10. **Write a problem** using the numbers 4 and 6. Use addition, subtraction, and multiplication in your problem.

Mixed Review

Find the sum or difference. (pages 12–13)

11. $12.95 − 1.83

12. $4.76 + 5.24

13. $9.06 − 4.52

14. $10.17 + 6.94

15. $14.67 − 9.58

Find the perimeter of these figures. (pages 6–7)

16.

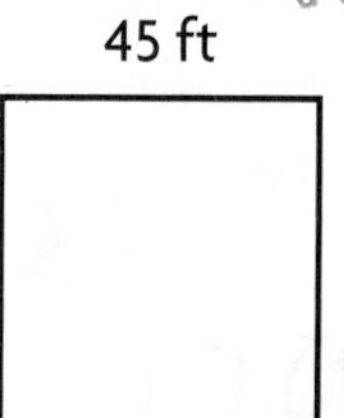

17.

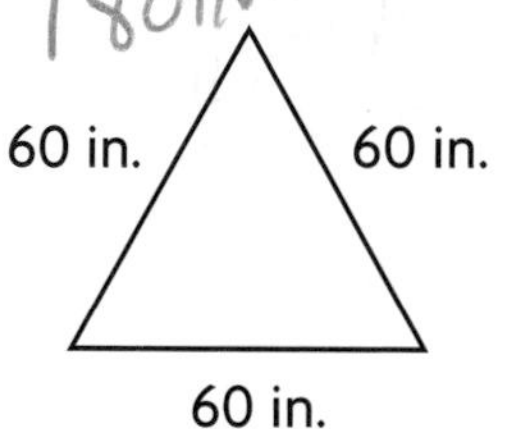

18.

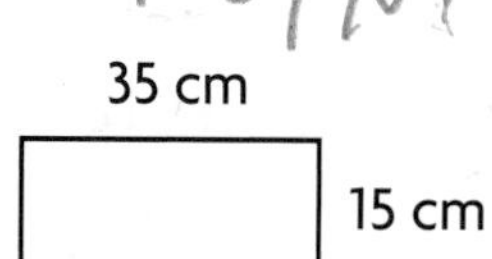

19.

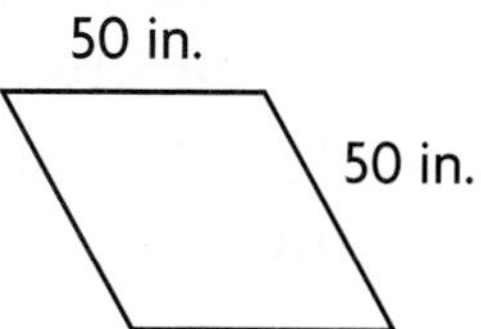

MORE PRACTICE Student Handbook page H72

MATH FUN!

NUMBER CUBE ROLL

PURPOSE To practice multiplication facts

YOU WILL NEED 2 cubes numbered 1–6

Play with a partner. Take turns rolling the number cubes. At each roll, find the product of the numbers and record it. After five turns, add your scores. The player with the higher score wins.

Multiplication Facts Bingo

PURPOSE To play a game and practice multiplication facts

YOU WILL NEED 5-by-5 grids, 2 sets of number cards (1-9), counters

Write a multiplication product between 1 and 81 in each square of your grid. Take turns choosing one number card from each set and naming the product of the two numbers. Each player covers the product if it appears on the grid.

Keep a list of the numbers drawn and their products. The player who first covers five spaces across, down, or diagonally calls, "BINGO!" Players check their answers against the list. If all the products are correct, the player wins.

Challenge family members to make grids and play Multiplication Facts Bingo with you.

WEEKLY SLEEP PATTERNS

PURPOSE To use multiplication and to show information in a pictograph

YOU WILL NEED grid paper

Make a list of the family members in your home. Find out about how many hours each person sleeps in one day. Multiply that number by 7 to find the number of hours each person sleeps in one week.

Mom	☾☾☾☾☾☾☾☾
Dad	☾☾☾☾☾☾☾
Joe	☾☾☾☾☾☾☾☾☾

Choose a symbol to show seven hours of sleep. Decide how many symbols are needed to show the number of hours each family member sleeps in one week. Show the information in a pictograph. Share your pictograph with the rest of the class.

CHAPTER 3 REVIEW

✓ CHECK UNDERSTANDING

VOCABULARY

1. $6 \times 3 = 18$ and $3 \times 6 = 18$ is an example of the _?_. (page 36)

2. $4 \times 0 = 0$ is an example of the _?_. (page 36)

3. The _?_ states that when one of the factors is 1, the product is the other number. (page 36)

4. The _?_ states that when the grouping of factors is changed, the product remains the same. (page 40)

Use the arrays. Find each product. (pages 38–41)

5. What is 7×9?

9 5 4

7 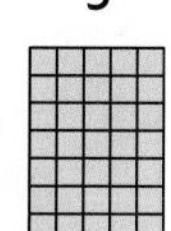 7 7

$7 \times 5 =$ _?_
$7 \times 4 =$ _?_
So, $7 \times 9 =$ _?_.

6. $3 \times (3 \times 2) =$ _?_

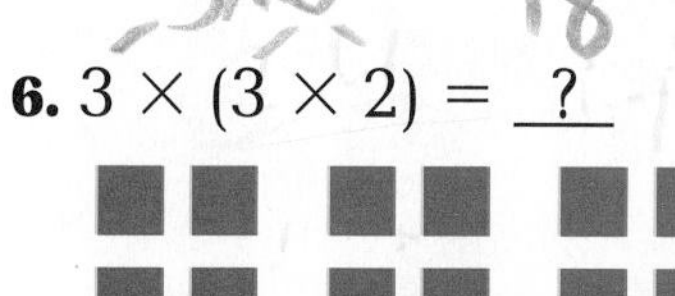

✓ CHECK SKILLS

Find the product. (pages 38–39)

7. $6 \times 8 =$ _?_ **8.** $5 \times 9 =$ _?_ **9.** $7 \times 8 =$ _?_ **10.** $9 \times 9 =$ _?_

Use the Grouping Property to solve each problem. (pages 40–41)

11. $(3 \times 3) \times 2 =$ _?_

12. $3 \times (2 \times 2) =$ _?_

13. $4 \times (2 \times 3) =$ _?_

14. $(5 \times 1) \times 7 =$ _?_

✓ CHECK PROBLEM SOLVING

Solve. (pages 42–45)

CHOOSE A STRATEGY

- Work Backward
- Draw a Picture
- Make a Model
- Write a Number Sentence

15. Tania put 4 packages of shirts in each of 2 boxes. There were 4 shirts in each package. How many shirts did Tania put in the boxes?

16. Jack spent \$2.95 for dog treats, \$1.99 for a dog toy, and \$4.98 for a leash. He had \$0.08 left. How much money did he have to begin with?

17. Birdseed is on sale in 6-pound bags. Wendy buys 8 bags. How many pounds of birdseed does she have?

DIVISION FACTS

DID YOU KNOW . . .

The largest crowd recorded for a soccer match in the United States was 101,799.

The event was France's 2–0 Olympics final win over Brazil at the Rose Bowl, Pasadena, California, on August 11, 1984.

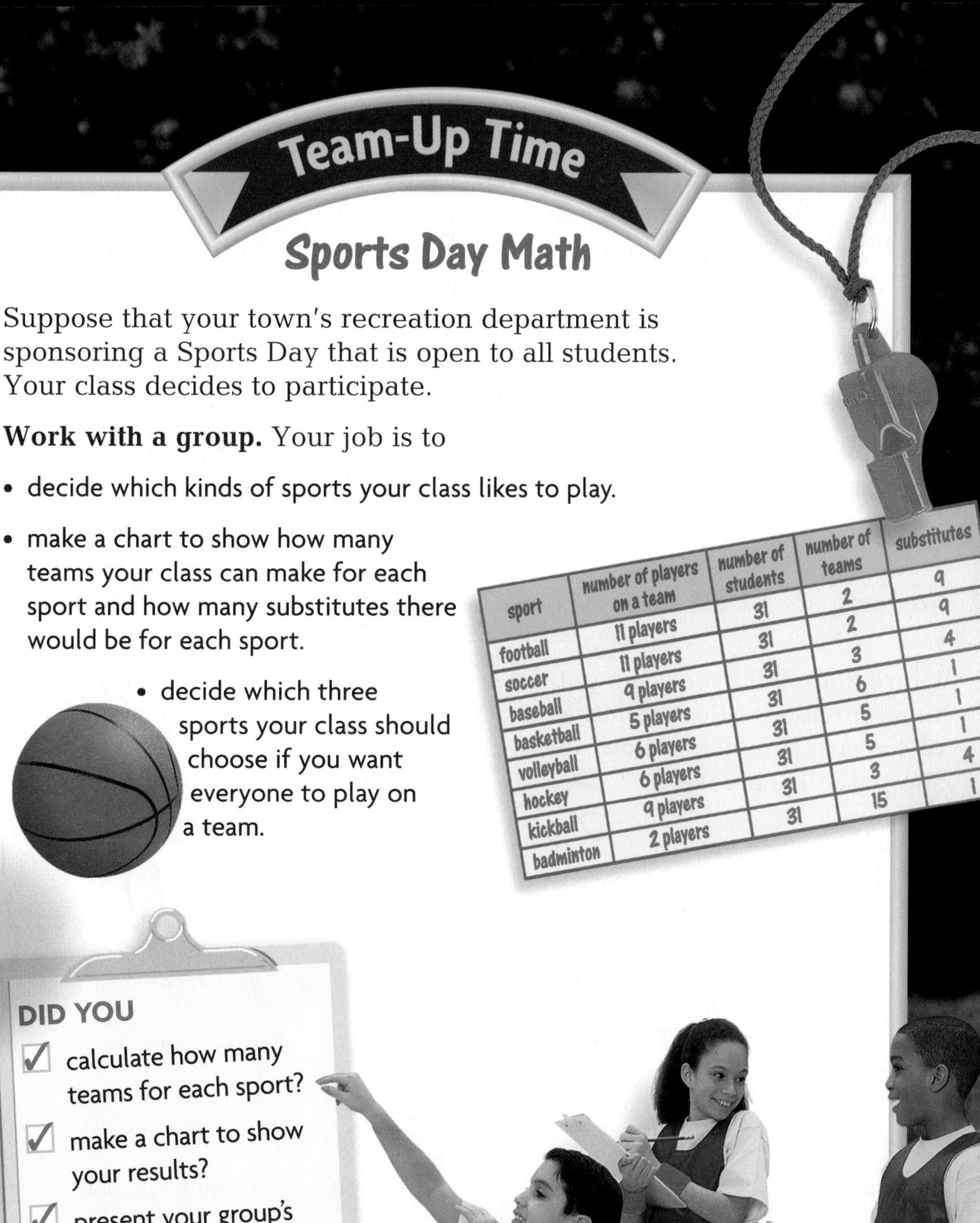

Team-Up Time

Sports Day Math

Suppose that your town's recreation department is sponsoring a Sports Day that is open to all students. Your class decides to participate.

Work with a group. Your job is to

- decide which kinds of sports your class likes to play.
- make a chart to show how many teams your class can make for each sport and how many substitutes there would be for each sport.
- decide which three sports your class should choose if you want everyone to play on a team.

sport	number of players on a team	number of students	number of teams	substitutes
football	11 players	31	2	9
soccer	11 players	31	2	9
baseball	9 players	31	3	4
basketball	5 players	31	6	1
volleyball	6 players	31	5	1
hockey	6 players	31	5	1
kickball	9 players	31	3	4
badminton	2 players	31	15	1

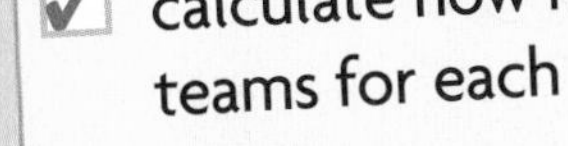

DID YOU

- ✓ calculate how many teams for each sport?
- ✓ make a chart to show your results?
- ✓ present your group's decision to the class and explain your plan?

What Questions Can Division Answer?

You will learn how to decide when you can use division to answer a question.

Why learn this? You can understand how to find equal amounts when you share something.

There are 12 tennis balls in cans. There are 3 balls in each can. How many cans of tennis balls are there?

- 12 tennis balls
- 3 balls in each can
- $12 \div 3 = 4$

So, there are 4 cans of tennis balls.

Laura had 20 flowers. She put the same number of flowers into each of 4 vases. How many flowers did she put in each vase?

- 20 flowers
- 4 vases
- $20 \div 4 = 5$

So, Laura put 5 flowers in each vase.

Rusty put several groups of 3 cookies on a plate. He put 15 cookies on the plate. How many groups of cookies did he put on the plate?

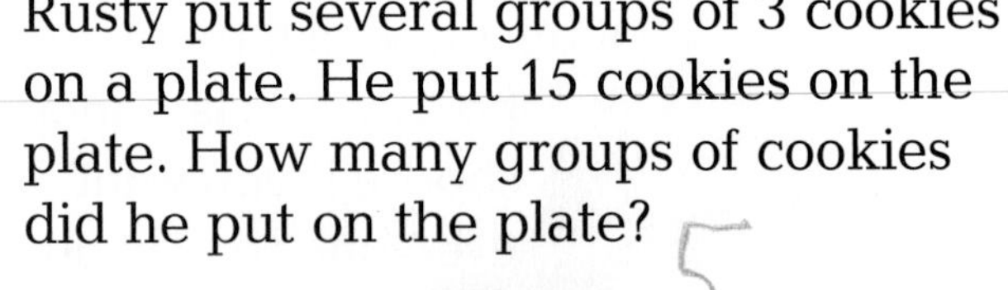

- 15 cookies in all
- 3 cookies in each group
- $15 \div 3 = 5$

So, Rusty put 5 groups of cookies on the plate.

Talk About It

- How are these three problems alike? How are they different?
- How does division help you find equal groups?
- When can you use division to solve a problem?

PRACTICE

Decide when using division will answer the question. Write *yes* or *no*. If you write *yes*, then solve.

1. There are 16 friends bowling. The same number of friends is bowling in each of 4 lanes. How many friends are bowling in each lane?

2. Mr. Diaz brought 24 books to class. He put the same number of books on each of 6 tables. How many books did Mr. Diaz put on each table?

3. The fourth graders worked on 12 art projects. They worked on 2 projects each week. For how many weeks did the fourth graders work on art projects?

4. Christy bought 6 cans of tennis balls. There are 3 tennis balls in each can. How many tennis balls did Christy buy?

Mixed Applications

5. Matthew has 20 lines to learn for the class play. He plans to learn the same number of lines each day for 5 days. How many lines should he learn each day?

6. The costume for each animal in the play will take 3 yards of cloth. There are 6 animals in the play. At $2 for each yard, how much will the cloth for all the costumes cost?

7. Melissa sold tickets to the class play. On Monday she sold 126 tickets. On Tuesday, she sold 119 tickets. How many tickets did Melissa sell on those two days?

8. **Write a problem** about the number of groups using division.

Mixed Review

Find the difference. (pages 22–23)

9. $600 - 249$ **10.** $3{,}005 - 1{,}698$ **11.** $8{,}000 - 4{,}876$ **12.** $20{,}004 - 13{,}469$ **13.** $40{,}000 - 28{,}194$

Use the multiplication properties to solve. (pages 36–37)

14. 4×1 **15.** 6×0 **16.** 1×8 **17.** 0×7

18. $3 \times 6 = \underline{\ ?\ }$; $6 \times 3 = \underline{\ ?\ }$

19. $7 \times 4 = \underline{\ ?\ }$; $4 \times 7 = \underline{\ ?\ }$

MORE PRACTICE Student Handbook page H72

Connecting Multiplication and Division

You will learn that multiplication and division are opposite operations.	**Why learn this?** You can use multiplication facts to help you solve division problems.	**WORD POWER** inverse fact family

You can use multiplication facts to find quotients because division is the **inverse** of multiplication. One operation undoes the other.

Dennis scored 18 points in the first quarter of the basketball game. Each basket was worth 2 points. How many baskets did he make?

$18 \div 2 = \underline{?}$

Think: $\underline{?} \times 2 = 18$, or $9 \times 2 = 18$

$18 \div 2 = 9$

So, Dennis made 9 baskets.

Dennis also scored 18 points in the second quarter of the game. He made 9 baskets. How many points did he score for each basket?

$18 \div 9 = \underline{?}$

Think: $9 \times \underline{?} = 18$, or $9 \times 2 = 18$

$18 \div 9 = 2$

So, Dennis scored 2 points for each basket.

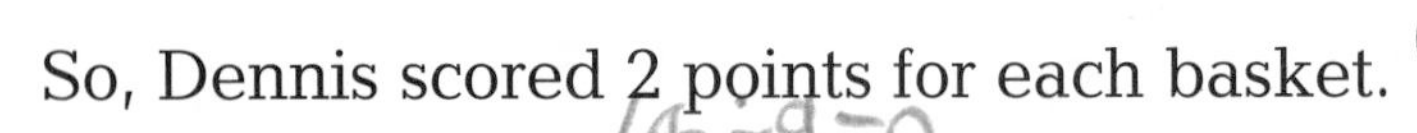

You can see the relationship between multiplication and division in a **fact family**, a set of related multiplication and division sentences using the same numbers.

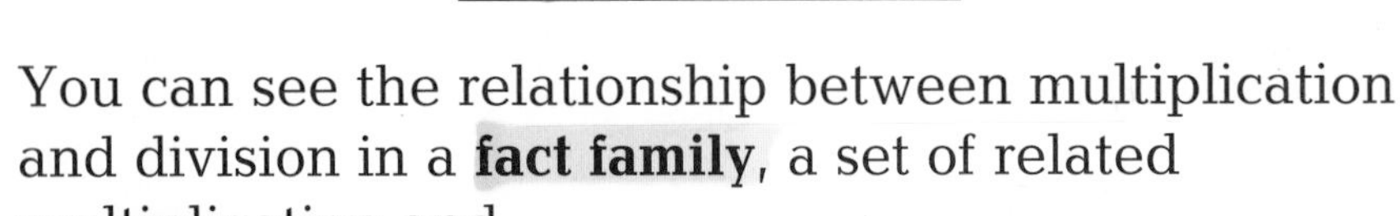

$2 \times 9 = 18$	$9 \times 2 = 18$
$18 \div 9 = 2$	$18 \div 2 = 9$

Physical Education Link

The game of basketball was invented in 1891 by James Naismith of Springfield, Massachusetts. He fastened two peach baskets to a railing 10 feet above the gym floor. His P.E. classes played the game, using a soccer ball. For about how many years has basketball been played?

Talk About It

- How do fact families show inverse operations?
- How can you use multiplication to solve a division problem?

CRITICAL THINKING Some fact families have only two number sentences. Give an example.

PRACTICE

Write a related multiplication fact.

1. $10 \div 2 = 5$
2. $12 \div 3 = 4$
3. $15 \div 5 = 3$
4. $28 \div 4 = 7$

Complete the number sentence. Write the related multiplication fact used to find the quotient.

5. $16 \div 2 =$?
6. $12 \div 4 =$?
7. $20 \div 4 =$?
8. $9 \div 3 =$?
9. $27 \div 3 =$?
10. $30 \div 5 =$?
11. $36 \div 9 =$?
12. $42 \div 6 =$?

Write the fact family for each set of numbers.

13. 2, 4, 8
14. 4, 6, 24
15. 5, 7, 35

Mixed Applications

For Problems 16–20, use the table.

MICHAEL'S CARD COLLECTION

Month	Number Collected
January	64
February	28
March	110
April	35

16. How many more cards did Michael collect in March than in January?
17. What is the total number of cards Michael collected in the four months?
18. Michael collected the same number of cards in each of the 4 weeks in February. How many cards did he collect each week?
19. In March Michael collected 20 cards the first week, 35 cards the second week, and 42 cards the third week. How many cards did Michael collect the fourth week?
20. **Write a problem** using the table.

Mixed Review

Estimate the sum or difference by rounding. (pages 26–27)

21. $35 + 18 + 52$
22. $860 - 423$
23. $438 + 691 + 715$
24. $3{,}198 - 1{,}814$
25. $2{,}509 + 1{,}487 + 4{,}375$

Make a model to solve. (pages 8–9)

26. The rabbit's cage is 5 feet long and 4 feet wide. What is the perimeter of the cage?
27. Zenia's poster is 24 inches long and 18 inches wide. How many inches of border trim does she need?

MORE PRACTICE Student Handbook page H73

Dividing with Remainders

PART 1

You will investigate what happens when you can't make all the groups equal.

Why learn this? You can find and record the amount left over when you divide.

remainder

The amount left over when you find a quotient is called the **remainder**.

REMEMBER:

20 ÷ 6 = 3 r2

The letter *r* stands for *remainder.*

Explore

Make a model to show 29 divided by 3.

MATERIALS: 29 counters

MODEL

Step 1

Use 29 counters.

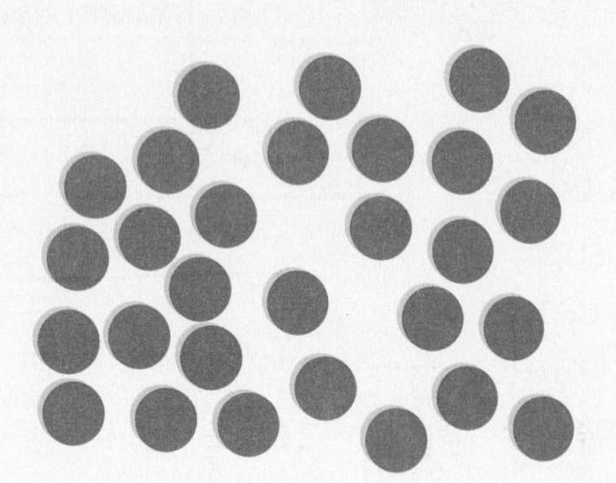

Step 2

Draw 3 circles. Divide the 29 counters into 3 equal groups by putting them in the circles.

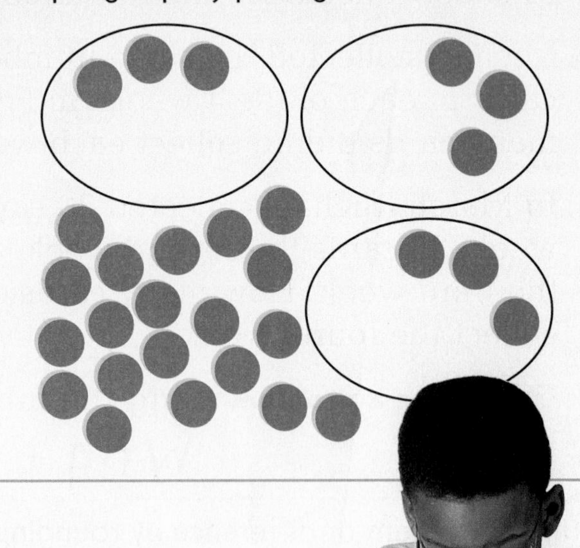

Record

Explain how you used the counters to find 29 ÷ 3.

TALK ABOUT IT How many counters are in each of the 3 groups? What is the remainder?

CRITICAL THINKING Could the remainder ever be greater than the number of circles? Why?

Technology Link

E-Lab • Activity 4 Available on CD-ROM and the Internet at http://www.hbschool.com/elab

Try This

Use counters to show 34 ÷ 6 = ?.

WRITE ABOUT IT How did you use the counters to help you find the quotient and the remainder?

HANDS-ON PRACTICE

Use counters to find the quotient and remainder.

1. 17 ÷ 3 = ? **2.** 25 ÷ 4 = ? **3.** 8 ÷ 3 = ?

4. 11 ÷ 4 = ? **5.** 15 ÷ 2 = ? **6.** 16 ÷ 5 = ?

Use the model to find the quotient.

7.

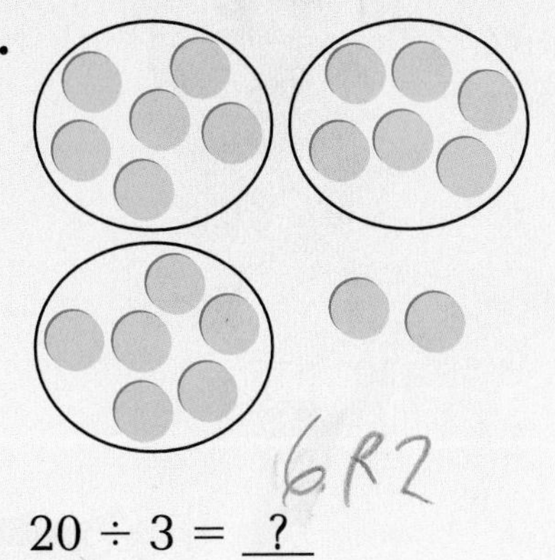

20 ÷ 3 = ?

8.

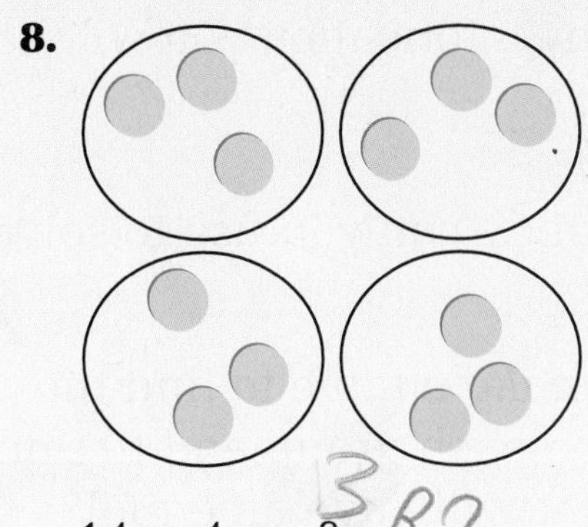

14 ÷ 4 = ?

Applying What You Learned

Find the quotient. You may wish to use a model to help you.

9. 12 ÷ 5 = ? **10.** 11 ÷ 3 = ? **11.** 14 ÷ 5 = ? **12.** 19 ÷ 7 = ?

13. 17 ÷ 2 = ? **14.** 23 ÷ 4 = ? **15.** 25 ÷ 6 = ? **16.** 27 ÷ 4 = ?

Mixed Applications

17. The band members need to learn 20 new songs. They will learn 2 songs each week for 8 weeks. How many more songs will they still need to learn?

18. The quotient is 4, and the divisor is 3. The dividend is 14. I am the remainder. What number am I?

19. The 24 students in the band are in 3 equal groups for the first song. They are in 4 equal groups for the second song. How many students are in each group for each song?

20. **WRITE ABOUT IT** What is the largest remainder you can have when you divide counters into 5 equal groups? Explain.

LESSON CONTINUES

MORE PRACTICE Student Handbook page H73

PART 2 PROBLEM-SOLVING STRATEGY
Make a Table

THE PROBLEM **Ms. Arthur's class of 30 students is going to draw a mural. She is going to divide the class into 4 to 8 groups. How many students will be in each group? In which groups will there be an equal number of students?**

5 AND 6 GROUPS

✓ Understand

- What are you asked to find?
- What information will you use?
- Is there any information you will not use? If so, what?

✓ Plan

- What strategy can you use to solve the problem?

  You can *make a table* to find the number of students in each group and to find the groups that will have an equal number of students.

✓ Solve

- How can you solve this problem?

  Make a table that shows all the groups of students.

Total Number of Students	Number of Groups	Number of Students in Each Group
30	4	30÷4=7 r2
30	5	30÷5=6
30	6	30÷6=5
30	7	30÷7=4 r2
30	8	30÷8=3 r6

So, if the students work in either 5 or 6 groups, there will be an equal number of students in each group.

✓ Look Back

- How can you decide if your answer is reasonable?
- What other strategy could you use?

PRACTICE

CHOOSE Paper/Pencil Calculator Hands-on Mental Math

Make a table to solve.

1. Mr. Mark's class of 27 students want to work on their art projects in 3 or 4 groups. How many students will be in each group? In which group will there be an equal number of students?

2. Bob needs 10 jars for a science project. He can buy the jars either one by one or in packages of 2. In how many different ways can he buy 10 jars?

3. Make a table that lists your favorite TV shows. Include the title, day, time, and your favorite thing about each show.

4. The students use 8 lemons for every 2 quarts of lemonade. How many lemons will they use for 8 quarts of lemonade?

Mixed Applications

Solve.

CHOOSE A STRATEGY

- Find a Pattern
- Work Backward
- Make a Table
- Make a Model
- Write a Number Sentence

5. The 24 oil paintings are going to be hung on 5 or 6 separate walls. How many paintings will be on each wall? Which way will there be an equal number of paintings on each wall?

6. On Saturday the snack bar sold 117 drinks in the morning and 224 drinks in the afternoon. On Sunday it sold 185 drinks in the morning and 163 drinks in the afternoon. How many more drinks did it sell on Sunday than on Saturday?

7. At the art fair, Amy bought 2 rings for $3.50 each. She also bought a small picture for $7.50 and a drink for $1.25. She had $1.25 when she got home. How much money did Amy take to the art fair?

8. Molly wants to see the Youth Chorus and the Southern Dance Company. How many minutes should she allow for these two events?

9. The art fair is 3 blocks long. There are 8 booths on each side of the street on each block. How many booths in all are there at the art fair?

Schedule of Festival Events	
Youth Chorus	1:45–2:45
Mime Theater	3:00–3:30
Southern Dance Company	3:30–4:00
Bach Choir	4:15–5:00

MORE PRACTICE Student Handbook page H73

Division on a Multiplication Table

You will learn that you can use a multiplication table to find quotients.

Why learn this? It can help you solve division problems.

Cindy's dad is planting 36 tomato plants in 4 rows of his garden. How many plants is he putting in each row?

Use a multiplication table to find the quotient.

$36 \div 4 = \underline{?}$

Think of the missing factor.

$4 \times \underline{?} = 36$

You know one factor, 4.

Find it in the top row.

Look down the column to find the product, 36. Look left across the row to find the quotient, or missing factor, 9.

$36 \div 4 = 9$

So, Cindy's dad is putting 9 tomato plants in each row.

×	0	1	2	3	4	5	6	7	8	9
0	0	0	0	0	0	0	0	0	0	0
1	0	1	2	3	4	5	6	7	8	9
2	0	2	4	6	8	10	12	14	16	18
3	0	3	6	9	12	15	18	21	24	27
4	0	4	8	12	16	20	24	28	32	36
5	0	5	10	15	20	25	30	35	40	45
6	0	6	12	18	24	30	36	42	48	54
7	0	7	14	21	28	35	42	49	56	63
8	0	8	16	24	32	40	48	56	64	72
9	0	9	18	27	36	45	54	63	72	81

CRITICAL THINKING How does the multiplication table help you find the quotient in a division problem? Give an example.

Check Your Understanding

Use the multiplication table to find the quotient.

1. $35 \div 5 = \underline{?}$

2. $49 \div 7 = \underline{?}$

3. $54 \div 6 = \underline{?}$

4. $72 \div 8 = \underline{?}$

5. $56 \div 7 = \underline{?}$

6. $36 \div 6 = \underline{?}$

7. $42 \div 7 = \underline{?}$

8. $81 \div 9 = \underline{?}$

Health Link

Students the ages of 9–12 should eat at least 3 servings daily of foods from the vegetable food group. How many servings is this in 1 week?

PRACTICE

Find the quotient. You may wish to use the multiplication table to help you.

9. $15 \div 3 = \underline{?}$ **10.** $30 \div 6 = \underline{?}$ **11.** $18 \div 3 = \underline{?}$ **12.** $32 \div 4 = \underline{?}$

13. $21 \div 7 = \underline{?}$ **14.** $35 \div 5 = \underline{?}$ **15.** $20 \div 4 = \underline{?}$ **16.** $27 \div 3 = \underline{?}$

17. $24 \div 3 = \underline{?}$ **18.** $18 \div 6 = \underline{?}$ **19.** $36 \div 9 = \underline{?}$ **20.** $45 \div 5 = \underline{?}$

21. $54 \div 9 = \underline{?}$ **22.** $63 \div 9 = \underline{?}$ **23.** $5 \div 5 = \underline{?}$ **24.** $5 \div 1 = \underline{?}$

25. $56 \div 8 = \underline{?}$ **26.** $64 \div 8 = \underline{?}$ **27.** $63 \div 7 = \underline{?}$ **28.** $72 \div 9 = \underline{?}$

Mixed Applications

29. Brandon put 2 ounces of cheese on each of 6 small pizzas. If he bought 16 ounces of cheese, how many ounces of cheese were left over?

30. Carly takes 4 dance classes a week. Her sister takes only 1 dance class a week. In 8 weeks, how many more dance classes does Carly take than her sister?

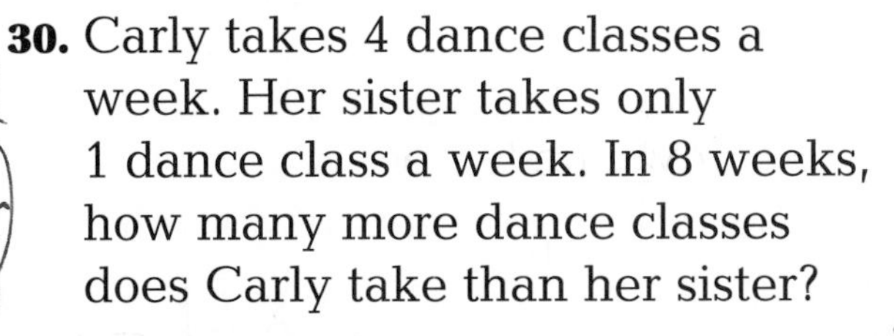

31. At the store, Martha bought corn for \$1.19, an onion for \$0.35, and lettuce for \$0.89. How much change did she receive from \$5.00?

32. **Write a problem** that uses numbers from the multiplication table and that asks for the cost of 1 notepad.

Round each number to the nearest *ten, hundred,* and *thousand.* **(pages 26–27)**

33. 3,725 **34.** 5,494 **35.** 8,916

36. 9,573 **37.** 7,089 **38.** 6,327

Find the product. **(pages 38–39)**

39. $4 \times 6 = \underline{?}$ **40.** $7 \times 7 = \underline{?}$

41. $8 \times 9 = \underline{?}$ **42.** $7 \times 5 = \underline{?}$

43. $6 \times 8 = \underline{?}$ **44.** $4 \times 9 = \underline{?}$

45. $8 \times 8 = \underline{?}$ **46.** $6 \times 9 = \underline{?}$

47. $7 \times 8 = \underline{?}$ **48.** $9 \times 9 = \underline{?}$

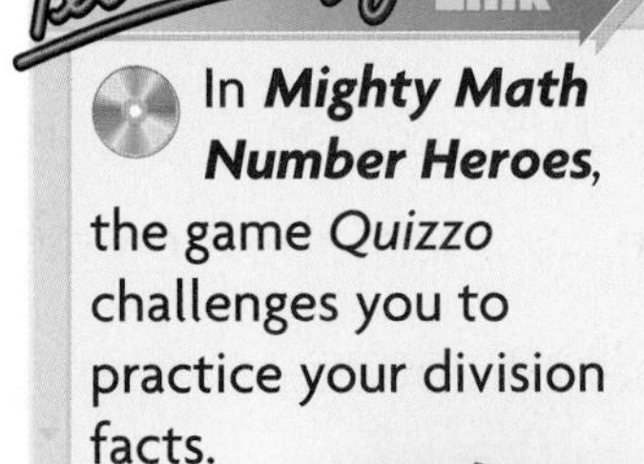

In ***Mighty Math Number Heroes***, the game *Quizzo* challenges you to practice your division facts.

MORE PRACTICE Student Handbook page H73

Recording and Practicing Division

You will learn about dividing with one and zero and about two ways to record division problems.

Why learn this? When you need to find how many equal groups there are, you will know how to record the problem.

Ms. Wood's class of 28 students is planting flowers around the school for Earth Day. The students are working in groups of 4. How many groups are there?

There are 2 ways to record division problems.

$28 \div 4 = 7$ or $4\overline{)28}$ with quotient 7

(quotient: 7; divisor: 4; dividend: 28)

Read both this way:
28 divided by 4 equals 7.

So, there are 7 groups of 4 students planting the flowers.

Division with One and Zero

Mr. Stevens has 4 trees. He gave the same number of trees to each of 4 students. How many trees did Mr. Stevens give to each student?

$4 \div 4 = 1$

So, Mr. Stevens gave each student 1 tree.

When a number is divided by itself, the quotient is always 1.

$6 \div 6 = 1$

When a number is divided by 1, the quotient is always that number.

$7 \div 1 = 7$

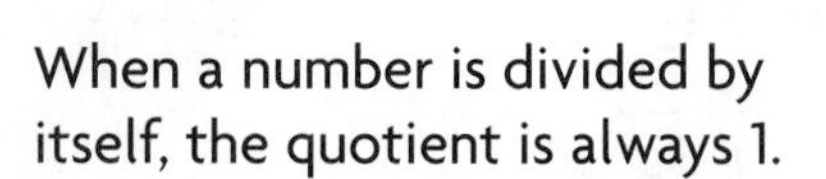

Use 12 counters. Can you put them into 0 groups?
$12 \div 0 = \underline{?}$

$12 \div 0$ does not equal 12 because 12×0 does not equal 12.

You cannot divide by zero. There is no number that when multiplied by zero will equal that number.

So, you cannot put the counters into 0 groups.

Science Link

Students at Dorseyville School in Pittsburgh, Pennsylvania, decorated 150 grocery bags with messages about Earth Day. If 25 students decorated the same number of bags, how many bags did each student decorate? 6

Talk About It

- If the dividend and divisor are the same, what is the quotient?
- Why can't you find $5 \div 0$?
- How can you use what you know about division with 0 and 1 to help you divide mentally?

PRACTICE

Find the quotient.

1. $18 \div 2 = \underline{?}$ **2.** $7 \div 7 = \underline{?}$ **3.** $27 \div 3 = \underline{?}$ **4.** $8 \div 1 = \underline{?}$

5. $24 \div 8 = \underline{?}$ **6.** $48 \div 6 = \underline{?}$ **7.** $56 \div 7 = \underline{?}$ **8.** $32 \div 8 = \underline{?}$

9. $27 \div 9 = \underline{?}$ **10.** $72 \div 8 = \underline{?}$ **11.** $36 \div 4 = \underline{?}$ **12.** $45 \div 9 = \underline{?}$

13. $6\overline{)54}$ **14.** $9\overline{)9}$ **15.** $5\overline{)45}$ **16.** $9\overline{)81}$ **17.** $4\overline{)16}$

18. $7\overline{)42}$ **19.** $3\overline{)27}$ **20.** $8\overline{)56}$ **21.** $5\overline{)40}$ **22.** $7\overline{)49}$

Mixed Applications

For Problems 23–25, use the table.

CONTAINERS COLLECTED ON ECOLOGY DAY	
Type	**Number**
Plastic	81
Glass	77
Paper	104

23. If 9 students each brought in the same number of plastic containers, how many plastic containers did they each bring in?

24. The school had a goal of collecting 250 containers. Did they meet their goal? Explain.

25. **Write a problem** using the information in the table.

Mixed Review

Choose the correct number sentence. Solve. (pages 44–45)

a. $5 \times 3 = \underline{?}$ **b.** $5 + 3 = \underline{?}$

26. The team made 5 runs. Then it made 3 more. How many runs did the team make?

27. Tracy scored 5 points in each of 3 games. How many points did Tracy score?

Show two ways to group Exercises 28–30 using parentheses. Find the products. (pages 40–41)

28. $7 \times 8 \times 1 = \underline{?}$ **29.** $8 \times 4 \times 1 = \underline{?}$ **30.** $2 \times 3 \times 3 = \underline{?}$

Choosing the Operation

You will learn that addition, subtraction, multiplication, and division are used to solve different kinds of problems.

Why learn this? You can choose the correct operation to solve a problem.

Before you can solve a problem, you must decide what the problem asks you to find. Study the problems. Decide which operation you would use to solve each.

A. John earns $5 an hour mowing lawns. If he works for 6 hours, how much money will he earn?

B. The 32 students in Mr. Miller's class want to work in groups of 4. How many groups will there be?

C. There were about 23 thousand people at the baseball game. Of that number, about 9 thousand were women. About how many men and children attended the game?

D. Mike is training for a 26-mile race. This week he ran 8 miles on Monday, 7 miles on Tuesday, 11 miles on Wednesday, and 14 miles on Friday. How many miles has he run so far this week?

Talk About It

- In your own words, tell what is being asked for in each of the problems.
- When do you use addition to solve a problem? subtraction?
- When do you use multiplication to solve a problem? division?

Check Your Understanding

1. Work with a partner. Solve Problems A–D.
2. What two operations could you have used to solve Problem A? to solve Problem B?
3. Write an addition, subtraction, multiplication, or division problem for your partner to solve.

CULTURAL LINK

The modern Olympic games began in Athens, Greece, in 1896. Only 13 countries sent athletes. In the 1996 Olympics, 197 countries sent athletes. How many more countries sent athletes in 1996 than in 1896?

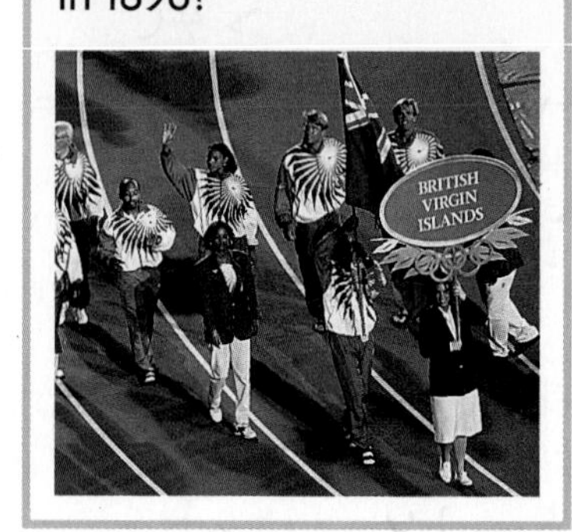

PRACTICE

Choose an operation to use. Then solve.

4. Grant earned \$3 for each day that he took care of his aunt's cat. He took care of the cat for 6 days. How much did he earn?

5. Kaitlyn read 35 pages on Saturday and 26 pages on Sunday. How many pages did she read in all?

6. Kayla earned \$12 one month for raking leaves. If she earned \$2 each time she raked, how many times did she rake leaves that month?

7. In one week David rode his bicycle for 4 more hours than Danny. David rode his bicycle for 12 hours. For how many hours did Danny ride his bicycle?

Mixed Applications

For Problems 8–12, use the table.

GARAGE SALE	
Item	**Price**
Board Games	\$0.50
Books	\$0.25
Tapes	\$0.75

8. Cara bought 2 tapes, a book, and a board game. Chad bought 4 tapes. How much more did Chad spend than Cara?

9. If Ben buys 2 board games and 6 books, how much change will he get from \$3.00?

10. Blake has \$2.00 to spend at the garage sale. What are two different groups of items he could buy?

11. Tyler bought 3 tapes and 2 books. How much did he spend?

12. **Write a problem** about how much Jessie spent at the garage sale.

Mixed Review

Find the sum or difference. (pages 12–13)

13. $\$8.45 - 6.26$

14. $\$7.19 + 6.82$

15. $\$14.39 - 9.64$

16. $\$23.01 + 12.59$

17. $\$34.70 - 24.80$

Round \$34.59 to each given amount. (pages 10–11)

18. ten cents

19. dollar

20. ten dollars

CULTURAL CONNECTION

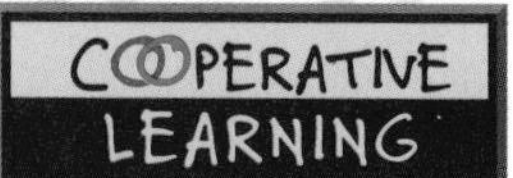

Kite Flying

Michael worked at his uncle's kite stand in Atlantic City, New Jersey, last summer. During the first week in July, Michael put together 63 delta kites. He put together the same number of kites each day of the week. How many delta kites did he put together on Monday?

$63 \div 7 = \underline{\ ?\ }$

So, Michael put together 9 delta kites on Monday.

CULTURAL LINK

Kite fighting is a popular sport in Korea and other Asian countries. Often the kite lines are coated with fine ground glass. Kite fliers try to cut the kite lines of the other fighting kites with the glass. The last kite in the air is the winner.

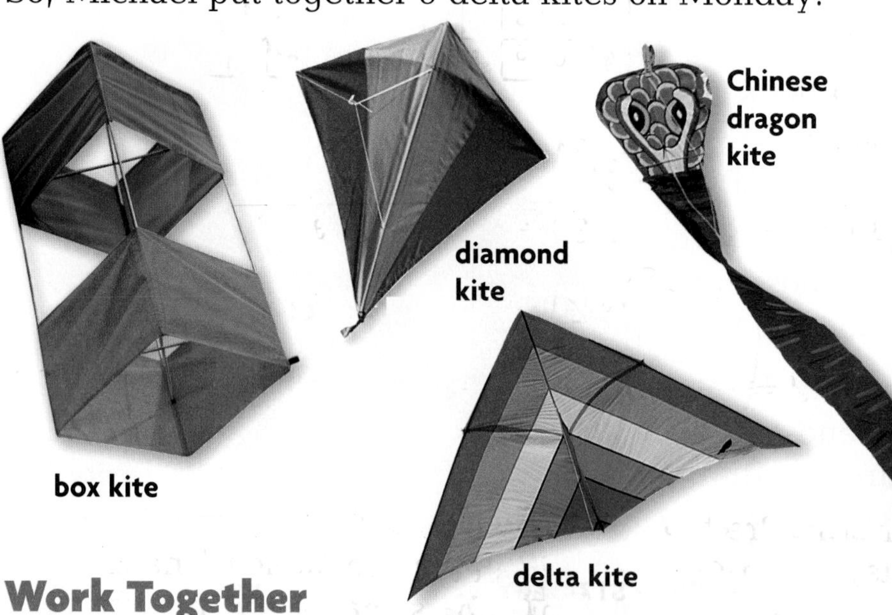

Work Together

Choose an operation. Write a number sentence to solve.

1. Michael assembled 56 diamond kites in one week. If he put together the same number each day, how many diamond kites did he assemble on Tuesday?

2. Michael put together 9 Chinese dragon kites on Wednesday. Each kite uses 3 bamboo sticks. How many bamboo sticks did Michael use in these kites?

3. Michael's uncle sold 18 delta kites the second week in July. He sold half of the kites on Saturday. How many did he sell on that day?

4. **Write a problem** about an upcoming kite-fighting competition with 81 kites competing and 9 kites being flown in each contest.

REVIEW

✓ CHECK UNDERSTANDING

VOCABULARY

1. A multiplication fact can help you find a quotient because multiplication is the __?__ of division. (page 52)

2. A __?__ is a set of related multiplication and division sentences using the same numbers. (page 52)

3. The amount left over when you find a quotient is called the __?__. (page 54)

Write the fact family for each set of numbers. (pages 52–53)

4. 4, 8, 32 **5.** 9, 7, 63 **6.** 3, 9, 27 **7.** 6, 7, 42

✓ CHECK SKILLS

Find the quotient. (pages 54–55, 58–61)

8. $24 \div 8 =$ __?__ **9.** $15 \div 7 =$ __?__ **10.** $18 \div 6 =$ __?__ **11.** $36 \div 9 =$ __?__

12. $36 \div 7 =$ __?__ **13.** $25 \div 5 =$ __?__ **14.** $48 \div 8 =$ __?__ **15.** $26 \div 4 =$ __?__

16. $6\overline{)54}$ **17.** $7\overline{)49}$ **18.** $9\overline{)72}$ **19.** $8\overline{)64}$

✓ CHECK PROBLEM SOLVING

Solve. (pages 56–57)

CHOOSE A STRATEGY

- Work Backward
- Find a Pattern
- Make a Table
- Write a Number Sentence

20. There are 9 players on the All-Star team. They will share equally 81 tickets to the game. How many tickets can each player have?

21. Sharon takes 6 diving lessons in 6 days. She takes the same number of lessons each day. How many lessons does she take each day?

22. Becky ran 10 laps the first day of practice. The second day she ran 12 laps. The third day she ran 14, and so on. How many laps did she run on the seventh day?

23. On Tuesday Tim earned some money for mowing a lawn. On Saturday he spent \$4.50. On Sunday he spent \$6.65. He still has \$3.85. How much money did he earn?

CHAPTERS 1–4

STUDY GUIDE & REVIEW

VOCABULARY CHECK

WORD BANK

- equation
- Grouping Property
- inverse
- Order Property
- Property of One
- Zero Property

Choose a term from the box to complete each sentence.

1. A number sentence that uses an equals sign to show that two amounts are equal is an ___?___. (page 4)

2. The ___?___ states that when the grouping of addends or factors is changed, the sum or product remains the same. (pages 6, 40)

3. 5 × 1 is an example of the ___?___. (page 36)

4. The ___?___ states that when one of the factors is zero, the product is zero. (page 36)

5. 4 × 5 = 20 and 5 × 4 = 20 is an example of the ___?___. (page 36)

6. A multiplication fact can help you find a quotient because multiplication is the ___?___ of division. (page 52)

STUDY AND SOLVE

CHAPTER 1

EXAMPLE

```
   21
  435
  697
 +183
 1,315
```

1. Regroup when the sum is 10 or more.
2. Add the ones.
3. Add the tens.
4. Add the hundreds.

Find the sum or difference. (pages 6–7, 10–13)

7. 542 + 686 + 451

8. $4.96 + 3.45

9. $7.54 − 2.68

10. 580 − 147

Round to the nearest hundred. (pages 10–11)

11. 151

12. 348

Solve. (pages 2–3, 8–9)

13. William is putting a fence around a dog run. The dog run will be 30 yards long and 15 yards wide. How much fence will William need?

14. Ali has saved $5.47. She buys a book that costs $2.69. How much money does Ali have left?

CHAPTER 2

EXAMPLE

```
    9  9
 3 10 10 10
  4,0 0 0
 −2,4 5 6
  1,5 4 4
```

1. Regroup when needed.
2. Subtract the ones.
3. Subtract the tens.
4. Subtract the hundreds.
5. Subtract the thousands.

Find the difference. (pages 20–23)

15. $\begin{array}{r} 805 \\ -656 \\ \hline \end{array}$

16. $\begin{array}{r} 600 \\ -166 \\ \hline \end{array}$

17. $\begin{array}{r} 9{,}004 \\ -6{,}905 \\ \hline \end{array}$

18. $\begin{array}{r} 7{,}000 \\ -3{,}468 \\ \hline \end{array}$

Round to the nearest thousand. Estimate the sum or difference. (pages 26–27)

19. $\begin{array}{r} 6{,}008 \\ -1{,}845 \\ \hline \end{array}$

20. $\begin{array}{r} 3{,}900 \\ +2{,}111 \\ \hline \end{array}$

Solve. (pages 18–19, 24–25, 28–29)

21. The Gonzales family's yard has a perimeter of 585 feet. The measurements of three of the sides are 163 feet, 158 feet, and 139 feet. What is the measurement of the other side?

CHAPTER 3

EXAMPLE

$\begin{array}{r} 8 \\ \times 6 \\ \hline 48 \end{array}$ Add. 8 + 8 + 8 + 8 + 8 + 8

Count the squares. Multiply.

Find the product. (pages 38–41)

22. $8 \times 5 =$ ___?___ **23.** $9 \times 1 =$ ___?___

24. $4 \times 6 =$ ___?___ **25.** $5 \times 0 =$ ___?___

26. $\begin{array}{r} 7 \\ \times 6 \\ \hline \end{array}$

27. $\begin{array}{r} 9 \\ \times 5 \\ \hline \end{array}$

28. $(4 \times 2) \times 8 =$ ___?___

Solve. (pages 42–45)

29. A small bag of puppy food weighs 5 pounds. Bob buys 3 bags. How many pounds of puppy food does he buy?

CHAPTER 4

EXAMPLE

13 ÷ 2 = ?

$\begin{array}{r} 6 \text{ r}1 \\ 2\overline{)13} \\ -12 \\ \hline 1 \end{array}$

1. Divide.
2. Multiply.
3. Subtract.
4. Write what is left as a remainder.

Write the fact family for each set of numbers. (pages 52–53)

30. 5, 4, 20 **31.** 4, 9, 36

Find the quotient. (pages 54–55, 58-61)

32. $72 \div 9 =$ ___?___ **33.** $49 \div 7 =$ ___?___

34. $56 \div 8 =$ ___?___ **35.** $15 \div 3 =$ ___?___

36. $4\overline{)18}$ **37.** $6\overline{)55}$

Solve. (pages 56–57)

38. Ms. Taylor has 25 students in her class. She asks them to form 5 equal groups. How many students are in each group?

CHAPTERS 1–4

WHAT DID I LEARN?

WRITE ABOUT IT

1. Explain how you could use mental math to solve each equation. Name the missing number. (pages 4–5)

   $4 + 7 = \underline{\ ?\ } + 9$ $\qquad$ $5 + 9 = \underline{\ ?\ } - 5$

2. Show each step as you find the difference for 8,000 − 5,325. Explain your method. (pages 22–23)

3. Explain how to use the properties of multiplication to solve each problem, and then solve. (pages 36–37)

   $6 \times 3 = \underline{\ ?\ }$ $\qquad$ $3 \times 6 = \underline{\ ?\ }$

   $5 \times 0 = \underline{\ ?\ }$ $\qquad$ $1 \times 9 = \underline{\ ?\ }$

4. Draw a picture to show $25 \div 6 = \underline{\ ?\ }$. Explain your method. (pages 54–55)

PERFORMANCE ASSESSMENT

Solve. Explain your method.

CHOOSE A STRATEGY

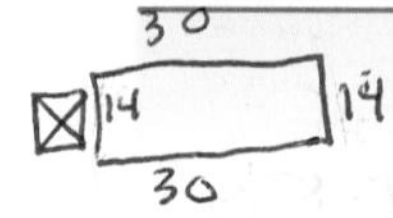

- Find a Pattern
- Act It Out
- Make a Model
- Make a Table
- Work Backward

5. Ray needs to replace the fence around three sides of his rectangular yard. He knows that the perimeter of the yard is 88 feet and the width is 14 feet. How many feet of fence will Ray need to replace one of the lengths? (pages 8–9)

6. Ella bought a tennis racket for $35.50 and 3 cans of tennis balls for $2.00 each. She had $6.50 left. How much money did she have when she walked into the store? (pages 24–25)

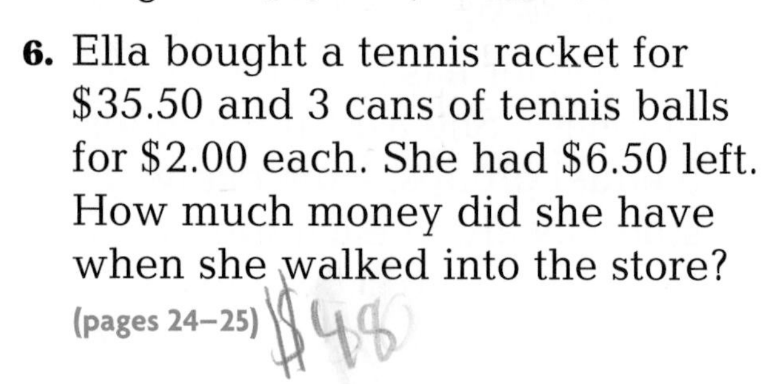

7. Bo moved books from a cart to 5 shelves. For each shelf, he made 2 trips and carried 4 books each time. How many books did Bo put on the shelves in all? (pages 42–43)

8. Mrs. Diaz wants to put 35 children on teams to play games. Game A has 5 teams. Game B has 6 teams. How many players will be on each team in each game? Which game will have extra players on some teams? (pages 56–57)

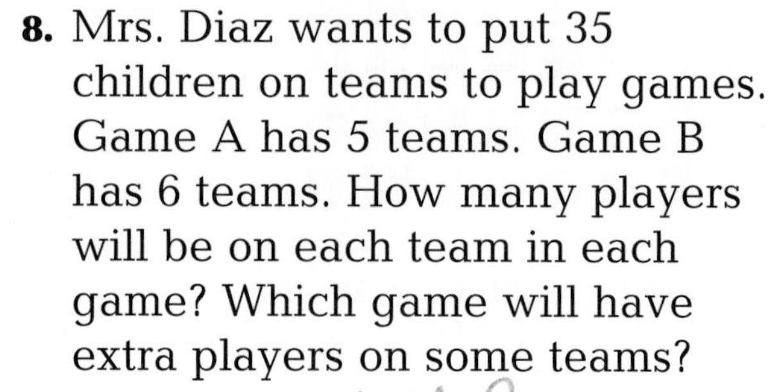

CUMULATIVE REVIEW

Solve the problem. Then write the letter of the correct answer.

1. $\begin{array}{r} 464 \\ 826 \\ +238 \\ \hline \end{array}$

A. 1,418
B. 1,428
C. 1,528
D. 1,529

(pages 6–7)

2. $\begin{array}{r} \$6.98 \\ +\ 1.99 \\ \hline \end{array}$

A. \$4.99
B. \$7.87
C. \$7.97
D. \$8.97

(pages 12–13)

3. $\begin{array}{r} 502 \\ -177 \\ \hline \end{array}$

A. 679
B. 475
C. 335
D. 325

(pages 20–21)

4. $\begin{array}{r} 4,000 \\ -2,469 \\ \hline \end{array}$

A. 1,531
B. 1,641
C. 2,641
D. 6,469

(pages 22–23)

5. $\begin{array}{r} 8 \\ \times 0 \\ \hline \end{array}$

A. 0
B. 1
C. 8
D. 16

(pages 36–37)

6. $8 \times 7 = \underline{\ ?\ }$

A. 15
B. 49
C. 56
D. 64

(pages 38–39)

7. $42 \div 6 = \underline{\ ?\ }$

A. 6
B. 7
C. 36
D. 48

(pages 52–53)

8. $5\overline{)27}$

A. 5
B. 5 r2
C. 6 r3
D. 22

(pages 54–55)

9. Peter has 454 baseball cards. Maria has 266 cards. How many cards do they have in all?

A. 188 cards
B. 610 cards
C. 20 cards
D. 720 cards

(pages 18–19)

10. Michelle took \$20.00 to the store. She bought a CD for \$10.99. How much did she have left?

A. \$9.01
B. \$9.11
C. \$10.11
D. \$30.99

(pages 22–23, 28–29)

11. A.J. has 4 cages with 3 hamsters in each cage. How many hamsters does A.J. have?

A. 2 hamsters
B. 12 hamsters
C. 35 hamsters
D. 40 hamsters

(pages 44–45)

12. The baker has a recipe for bread that calls for 24 cups of flour to make 8 loaves of bread. How many cups of flour does it take for each loaf of bread?

A. 2 cups
B. 3 cups
C. 16 cups
D. 32 cups

(pages 44–45)

CHAPTER 5 NUMBER CONCEPTS

DID YOU KNOW...

Watches, pocket watches, and grandfather clocks often have Roman numerals on their faces to show the time.

Team-Up Time

Math and History

Have you ever noticed a string of symbols on a movie video box or at the end of a film? If you have, you may have been looking at Roman numerals. Look at the Roman numerals.

ROMAN NUMERAL CLUES

I	II	III	IV	V	VI	VII	VIII	IX	X	C	M
1	2	3	4	5	6	7	8	9	10	100	1,000

Work with a group. Your job is to

- study the Roman numerals.
- figure out how the Roman numeral system works.
- write the Roman numerals for 11–20.
- present your work to the class.

DID YOU

- ✓ study the Roman numeral system and figure out how it works?
- ✓ write the Roman numerals for 11–20?
- ✓ present your work to the class?

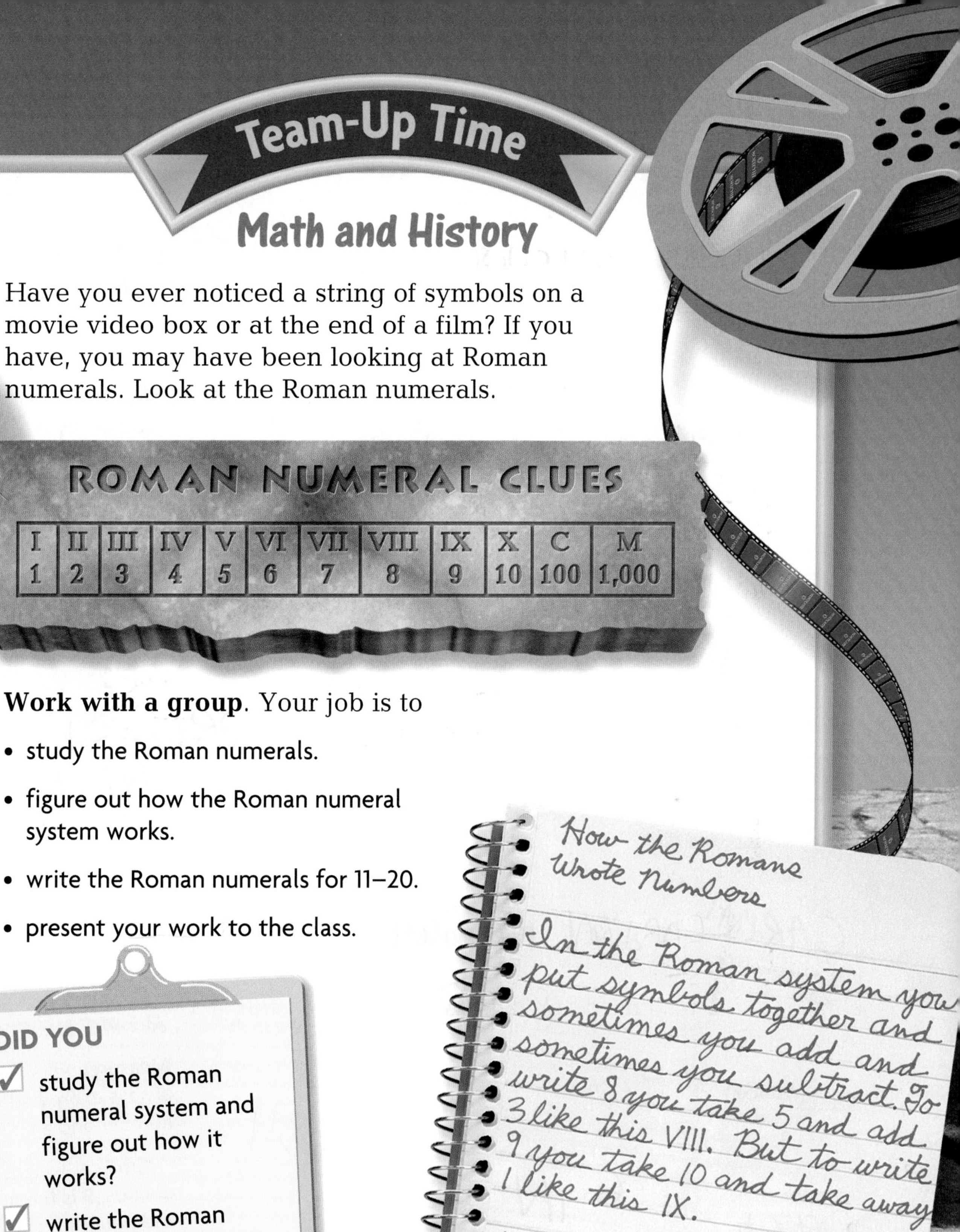

PART

1 How Numbers Are Used

You will learn that numbers have different meanings.	**Why learn this?** You can make sense of the numbers you see and use every day.

WORD POWER
cardinal
ordinal
nominal

You use numbers in different ways every day.

Cardinal numbers tell how many.		Ordinal numbers tell position or order.		Nominal numbers name things.
1	one	1st	first	telephone number
2	two	2nd	second	car license plate
25	twenty-five	25th	twenty-fifth	Interstate 4

Social Studies Link

Roman numerals can be found on clock faces, pages of books, and cornerstones. Are the Roman numerals on the clock cardinal, ordinal, or nominal?

Talk About It

- What number tells a line leader's position in line?
- What number tells how many students are in your class?

Look at the ways numbers are used in the pictures below.

- Which numbers are cardinal? ordinal? nominal?

Numbers are also used as measurements. They tell how many units.

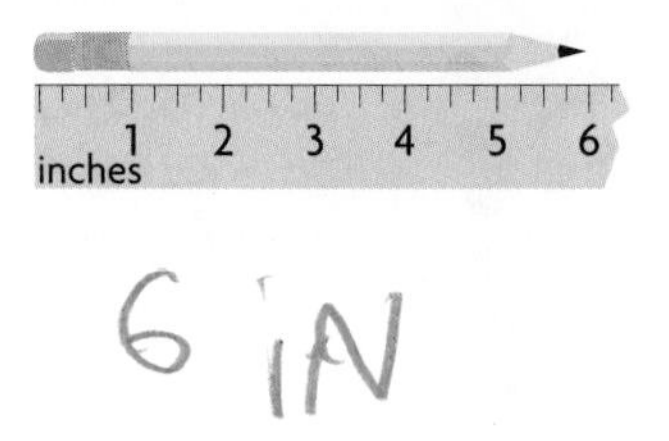

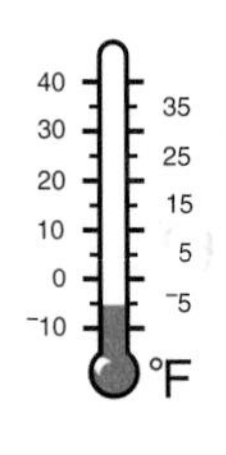

REMEMBER:

Measurements are always expressed with a number and a unit.

If Kim's cat weighs 9 pounds, *9* is the number and *pounds* is the unit.

Talk About It

- What weight is shown on the scale?
- How many inches long is the pencil?
- What temperature is shown on the thermometer?
- Why are measurements expressed with a number?

PRACTICE

Tell whether each number is *cardinal, ordinal,* or *nominal.*

1. 63rd ORdiNAl
2. (615) 555-9872 NOM,NAl
3. forty-six CARdiNAl
4. 2:00 P.M. NOMiNAl

Write each number. Tell what kind of number it is.

5. your telephone number NOMiNAl
6. your house or apartment number NOMiNAl
7. your age CARdiNAl
8. the number of students in your class ORdiNAl
9. your favorite television channel NOMINAl
10. the position in the alphabet of the first letter of your first name ORdiNAl

CULTURAL LINK

The Incas kept numerical records by using knotted and colored strings called *quipus* (KEE•pooz). How could you use a quipu to show how many? NO

Write the weight, length, or temperature shown.

11. 

110 lb.

12. 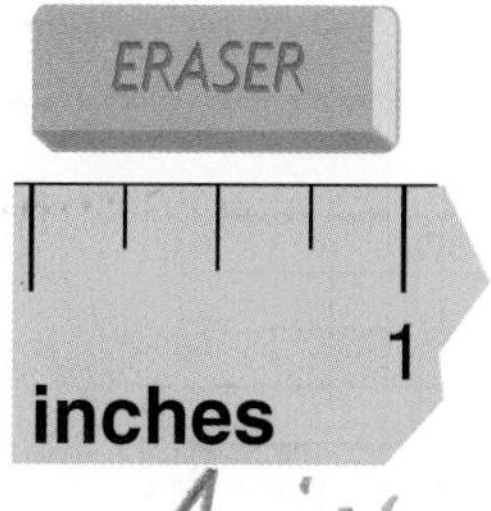

1 iN

13. 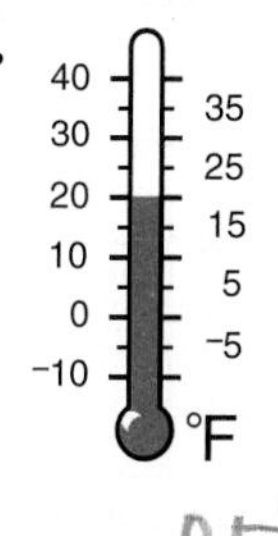

20°F

Mixed Applications

Answer the following questions by using the table Ms. Dasher made.

Favorite Day of the Week to Eat School Lunch

Mon	Tue	Weds	Thurs	Fri
0	2	9	6	13

14. How many of Ms. Dasher's students like to eat the school lunch on the first two days of the week? on the last two days of the week? 2 19

15. What is the third day of the school week? How many students like to eat the school lunch on that day? 9

16. Which day of the school week did most of Ms. Dasher's students pick as their favorite day to eat the school lunch? FRidAY

17. How many of Ms. Dasher's students like to eat the school lunch on Tuesday? on Friday? 15

18. **Write a problem** that can be answered by using the table above.

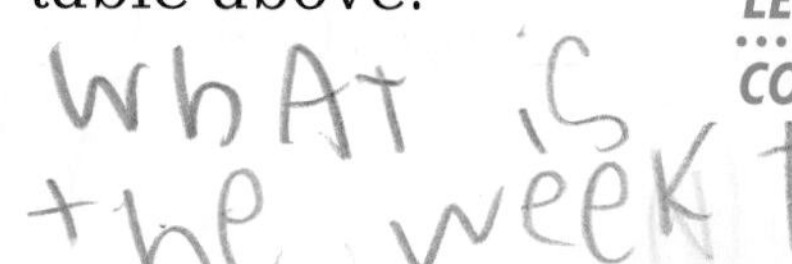
WhAT iS the week To eAT Wed. 9

LESSON CONTINUES

MORE PRACTICE Student Handbook page H74

PART 2

More About How Numbers Are Used

WORD POWER
ordered pair

You can use two numbers to locate points on a grid. The two numbers are called an **ordered pair**. The first number tells how far to move horizontally, or straight across. The second number tells how far to move vertically, or straight up.

MODEL

What ordered pair tells where the school is?

Step 1

Start at 0. Count the number of units horizontally from 0.

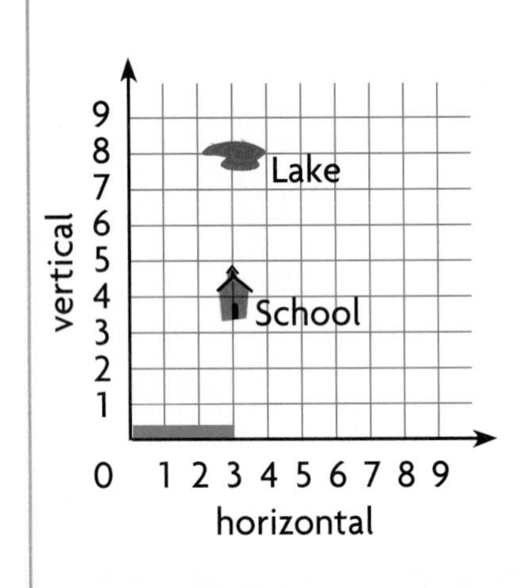

Step 2

Then count the number of units vertically.

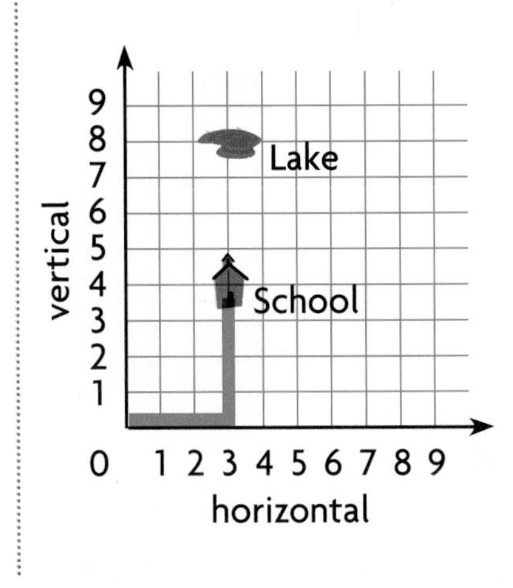

Step 3

Write the ordered pair. The number of units horizontally from 0 is always shown first.

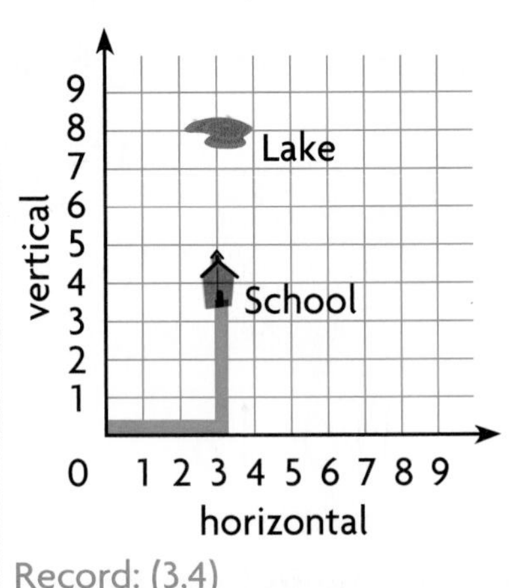

Record: (3,4)

So, the ordered pair (3,4) tells where the school is.

Talk About It

- What ordered pair tells where the lake is?
- Why is the first number in the ordered pair for the lake the same as the first number in the ordered pair for the school?
- Explain how finding (4,3) and (3,4) is different.

CRITICAL THINKING Why is the order of the numbers in an ordered pair important?

PRACTICE

Use the map to write the ordered pair for each place.

1. Historical Museum
2. Planetarium
3. Museum of American Art

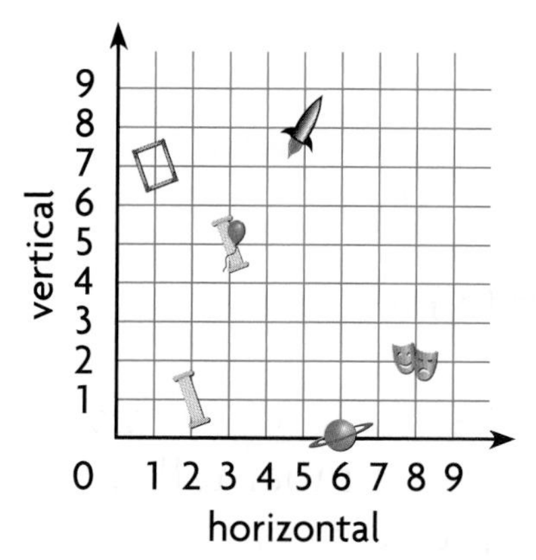

- Museum of American Art
- Air and Space Museum
- Historical Museum
- Children's Museum
- Planetarium
- Performing Arts Theater

Write the name of the place for the ordered pair.

4. (3,5) 5. (8,2) 6. (5,8)

Copy and complete the table. Use the ordered pairs to find the landmarks on the grid below.

	Ordered Pair	Landmark
7.	(1,3)	
8.	(2,6)	
9.	(3,9)	

- Art Museum
- Science Center
- Library

Social Studies Link

The first map made in America was a map of Virginia. It was drawn by John Smith. It was published in England in 1612. How would a grid help you find cities in Virginia today?

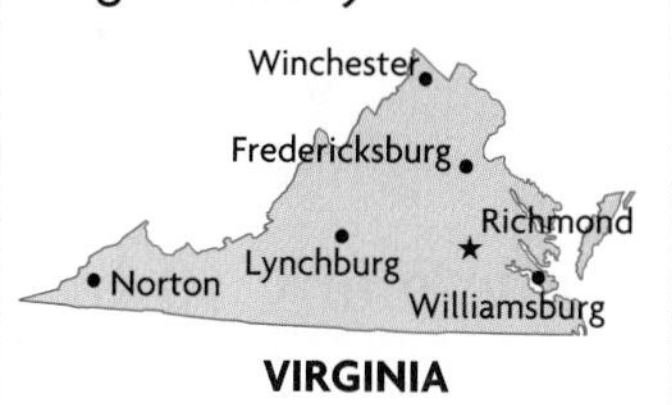

Mixed Applications

10. Rachel has 25 pieces of candy. She will divide the candy evenly among 5 friends. How many pieces will each friend get?

11. **WRITE ABOUT IT** Describe how you know where the Art Museum is on the grid above. Use an ordered pair of numbers.

Mixed Review

Break apart the numbers to find the product. (pages 38–39)

12. 8×4
13. 9×3
14. 6×5
15. 8×7
16. 5×2
17. 7×6

Find the quotient. (pages 60–61)

18. $8\overline{)64}$
19. $4\overline{)24}$
20. $3\overline{)15}$
21. $5\overline{)35}$
22. $4\overline{)16}$
23. $7\overline{)63}$

Understanding 1,000

You will investigate ways to count to 1,000.

Why learn this? You can understand the meaning of numbers in the thousands, which you see in newspapers, magazines, and books.

Explore

Make a "1,000 Squares" book. Use one 10-by-10 grid for each page of the book.

MATERIALS: 10-by-10 grids

- Decide how many pages, or 10-by-10 grids, you will need.
- Staple the pages together. Number the squares from 1 to 1,000 any way you like, as long as you can find the place of any number in the book.

REMEMBER:

A 10-by-10 grid is covered with 100 squares.

Record

Explain the plan you used for numbering your squares.

Talk About It

- How many 10-by-10 grids did you need to make the book with 1,000 squares?
- If you numbered every square, what would the first and last numbers have been on the first page of the book? on the second page?
- On what page is the number 329? the number 850?
- Why do you need more than three grids to show 329? How many more squares do you need?
- How many grids do you need to show 850?

Technology Link

E-Lab • Activity 5 Available on CD-ROM and the Internet at http://www.hbschool.com/elab

Now, investigate ways to count to 10,000.

Try This

Put your "1,000 Squares" book with some of your classmates' books to make a book of "10,000 Squares."

- How many books did you use?
- How many books would you need to make a "100,000 Squares" book?

Applying What You Learned

Look in your "1,000 Squares" book. Write the page number on which each number is found.

1. 429 **2.** 687 **3.** 920 **4.** 225

5. 136 **6.** 804 **7.** 85 **8.** 394

Mixed Applications

For Problems 9–13, use your "1,000 Squares" book.

9. Brenda's family is going on a trip. They will drive 921 miles from Nashville, Tennessee, to Miami, Florida. On what page of your book is 921?

10. Louise is entering her dog in a pet show. There are 492 pets entered so far. On what page of your book is 492? What are the first and last numbers on that page?

11. Greg collects baseball cards. He has 558 cards. On what page of your book is 558?

12. If Greg buys 175 more baseball cards, how many will he have? On what page of your book is the number of cards Greg will have?

13. Maya's family uses 75 gallons of water to take showers each day. How many gallons of water will they use in 7 days? On what page of your book is the number of gallons they will use?

14. **WRITE ABOUT IT** How could you make a "1,000,000 Squares" book?

Environmental Link

The average person uses 25 gallons of water to take a shower. That is 100 gallons of water for a family of four. If each family member showers every day, how many days will it take the family of four to use 1,000 gallons of water?

MORE PRACTICE Student Handbook page H75

PART

1 More About 1,000

You will learn to read and write numbers to thousands.	**Why learn this?** You can use what you know about 1,000 to understand the values of large numbers, such as the number of people who live in your neighborhood.

Suppose that 1,427 students attend East Elementary. How can you show 1,427 with base-ten blocks?

Thousands	Hundreds	Tens	Ones
1	4	2	7
$1 \times 1{,}000 = 1{,}000$	$4 \times 100 = 400$	$2 \times 10 = 20$	$7 \times 1 = 7$

You can show 1,427 with a calculator.

Press:

CRITICAL THINKING How many of each base-ten block do you need to show 2,336? ______

A comma is sometimes used to separate the thousands place from the hundreds place.

EXAMPLES

A. 4,000

Say: four thousand

B. 2,095

Say: two thousand, ninety-five

C. 7,683

Say: seven thousand, six hundred eighty-three

Talk About It

- How does a comma make it easier to read and understand a number in the thousands?
- What examples of 1,000 things can you name?

PRACTICE

Write the number shown by the base-ten blocks.

1.

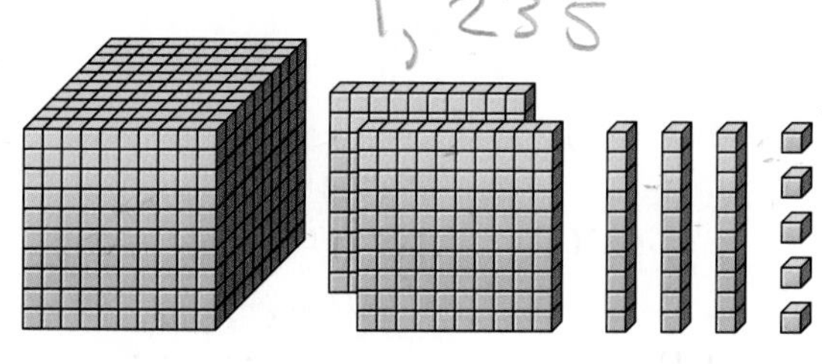

2.

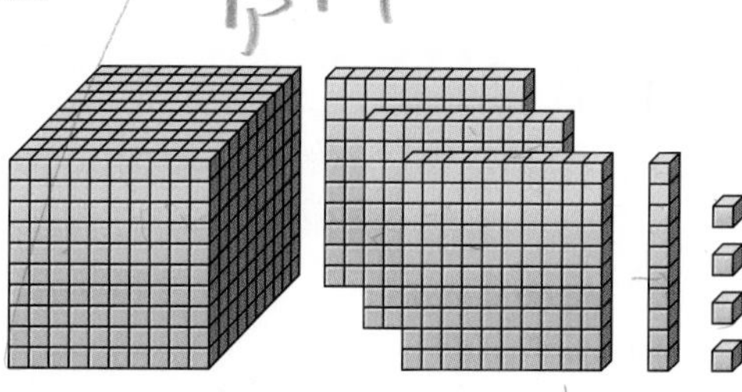

Record the number of thousands, hundreds, tens, and ones.

3. 5,901	**4.** 2,485	**5.** 7,378	**6.** 1,492	**7.** 3,566
8. 4,735	**9.** 9,124	**10.** 6,817	**11.** 8,253	**12.** 1,908

Put in the comma, and write each number in words.

13. 2000	**14.** 3045	**15.** 6723	**16.** 7846	**17.** 4001
18. 4875	**19.** 2839	**20.** 1600	**21.** 5241	**22.** 9367

Mixed Applications

23. Kerry's school collected one thousand, six hundred ninety-nine cans during the canned-food drive. Write the number, and draw a picture of how to model it with base-ten blocks.

24. Write the number that is 1,000 more than three thousand, one hundred sixteen. How many of each base-ten block do you need to show the number?

25. Brad collected seashells for three days. On Monday he collected 235. On Tuesday he collected 144. On Wednesday he collected 262. How many seashells did Brad collect? How many more does he need to make 1,000?

26. A 500-meter speed-skating race is a little more than a quarter mile, or 1,320 feet. How many feet more than 1,000 is that?

27. **WRITE ABOUT IT** How could you describe 1,000 to someone who has no idea of the size of the number?

Science Link

A 1,000-meter speed-skating race is a little more than a half mile, or 2,640 feet. How can you show 2,640 with base-ten blocks?

LESSON CONTINUES

MORE PRACTICE Student Handbook page H75

PART 2 PROBLEM-SOLVING STRATEGY
Act It Out

THE PROBLEM Ian wanted to compare the distances three Matchbox® cars would travel. He drew lines on the ground that were 1 meter apart. He rolled each car from just behind the first line. Car A stopped 21 millimeters past the 2-meter mark. Car B stopped 33 millimeters before the 2-meter mark. Car C stopped exactly on the 3-meter mark. How many millimeters did each car travel?

REMEMBER:

- ✓ Understand
- ✓ Plan
- ✓ Solve
- ✓ Look Back

✓ Understand

- What are you asked to find?
- What information will you use?
- Is there any information that you will not use? If so, what?

✓ Plan

- What strategy can you use to solve the problem?

You can *act it out* with toy cars.

✓ Solve

- How can you act it out to solve the problem?

A meter equals 1,000 mm. You can draw four lines, 1 meter apart. Place Car A 21 mm past the 2-meter line, Car B 33 mm before the 2-meter line, and Car C on the 3-meter line. Then measure the distance of each car from the starting line.

So, Car A rolled 2,021 millimeters. Car B rolled 1,967 millimeters. Car C rolled 3,000 millimeters.

✓ Look Back

- How did changing the units to millimeters help you find the distance each car traveled?
- Was the distance that each car traveled long or short? Explain.
- What other strategy could you use?

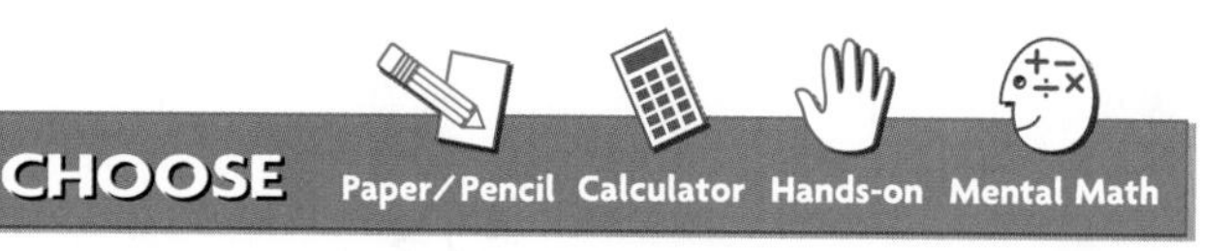

PRACTICE

Act it out to solve.

1. Ian compared the distances that three different cars traveled. Car A stopped 10 millimeters past the 2-meter mark. Car B stopped 15 millimeters before the 2-meter mark. Car C stopped exactly on the 1-meter mark. How many millimeters did each car travel?

2. Joelle and Nicole are playing a board game. In the first three turns, Joelle moves 6 spaces forward, 3 back, and 4 forward. Nicole moves 5 spaces forward, 2 back, and 5 forward. Who is ahead in the game? How far ahead is she?

3. Four students are waiting in line. Corey is standing 2 meters behind Brooke and 1 meter in front of Yasmine. Yasmine is standing an equal distance between Corey and Mike. How far away is the first student standing from the last?

4. Three friends have bought some cards. They are dividing the change evenly. The cashier hands them the amount shown. How much money does each friend receive?

Mixed Applications

Solve.

CHOOSE A STRATEGY

- **Make a Model**
- **Act It Out**
- **Make a Table**
- **Write a Number Sentence**
- **Look for a Pattern**

5. Taylor had 127 baseball cards. He gave 18 cards to Tony. Tony gave him 5 cards. How many cards did Taylor have after trading with Tony?

6. Two friends started a book club. There were 4 people at the second meeting and 6 people at the third meeting. If this pattern continues, how many people will be at the fifth meeting?

7. Hector sold school newspapers. He sold 15 newspapers on Wednesday, 23 on Thursday, and 56 on Friday. How many newspapers did Hector sell?

8. Katelin is making a design with 12 squares made up of 8 sections each, like the one shown. How many sections will make up the design?

MORE PRACTICE Student Handbook page H76

Benchmark Numbers

You will learn that a benchmark number can be used to show relationships among numbers.	Why learn this? You can estimate the number of objects by comparing them with a benchmark number.	WORD POWER benchmark

A **benchmark** is a point of reference. Benchmark numbers are often used to show number relationships.

Think about your class, your grade, and your school. Which has about 25 students? about 100 students? about 1,000 students?

Benchmark Numbers →	about **25** students in your class	about **100** students in your grade	about **1,000** students in your school

- There are 25 students in Debbie's class. There are 5 fourth-grade classes. About how many students are in the fourth grade?

Check Your Understanding

Use a benchmark number to estimate the numbers of marbles in the second and third jars.

5 marbles   **? marbles**   **? marbles**

1. In which jar are there about 20 marbles?
2. Which benchmark number would you use to estimate the number of marbles in Jar C?
3. About how many marbles are in Jar C?

A roll of quarters has 40 quarters, which equals $10.00. About how much money do you think is in the jar?

PRACTICE

Write a benchmark number for each problem. Use the benchmark to estimate.

4. In which jar are there about 50 jelly beans?

5. About how many jelly beans are in Jar C? How can you tell?

Write *more than* or *less than* for each.

6. Are there more than or less than 30 grapes in Bowl B?

7. Are there more than or less than 50 candies in Bowl D?

A B C D

Mixed Applications

8. There are 50 pennies in a roll. Angela has ten rolls. How many pennies does she have? How much money is that?

9. **Write a problem,** like Exercise 5, in which a benchmark is used to estimate the total number.

Mixed Review

Round to the nearest *ten*. (pages 10–11)

10. 5 **11.** 14 **12.** 33 **13.** 65 **14.** 79

Estimate the sum or difference. (pages 10–11)

15. $132 + 278$

16. $495 - 307$

17. $641 - 196$

18. $316 + 966$

19. $759 + 363$

20. $5,003 + 1,728$

21. $7,542 - 3,109$

22. $1,942 - 1,097$

23. $2,904 + 6,515$

24. $8,823 - 3,210$

MATH FUN!

Numbers Everywhere!

PURPOSE To practice finding and classifying numbers

YOU WILL NEED magazines, newspapers, poster board, scissors, glue

Look through magazines and newspapers for numbers. Cut out and display the numbers in these categories: *cardinal*, *ordinal*, and *nominal*.

FOUR IN A LINE

PURPOSE To practice locating points on a grid

YOU WILL NEED grid paper, 2 number cubes (1–6), marking pens

Draw a 12-by-12 grid on grid paper. Label the lines to make a coordinate grid like the one shown. Players take turns rolling two number cubes to make ordered pairs. The sum of the numbers on the first roll is the first number of the ordered pair. The sum of the numbers on the second roll is the second number.

Players locate their ordered pairs on the grid. Then, they write their initials next to the pairs.

The winner is the first player to get 4 points in a line (horizontally, vertically, or diagonally).

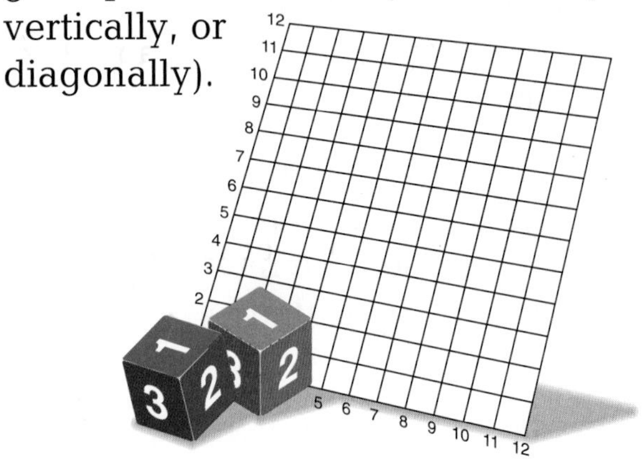

Write a Number Story

PURPOSE To practice using numbers in different ways

YOU WILL NEED paper and pencil

Write a short story about a trip you might take. Include at least ten different numbers at ten points in the story. Include numbers up to the thousands.

I will be too excited to sleep when I go white-water rafting! I am going to wake up at 7:00 in the morning to get ready. We have to drive 1,750 miles to North Carolina. The drive will take about 3 days.

Have your family help you write a number story about a trip you took together.

REVIEW

✓ CHECK UNDERSTANDING

VOCABULARY

1. An _?_ helps you locate points on a grid. (page 74)
2. A _?_ is a point of reference. (page 82)

Tell whether each number is *cardinal, ordinal,* or *nominal.* (pages 72–73)

3. 3:53 P.M.
4. 25 cars
5. 555-3167
6. fourth

Estimate the number of pumpkin seeds. Use the first pumpkin as a benchmark. (pages 82–83)

7.

8.

✓ CHECK SKILLS

Draw a coordinate grid on grid paper. Locate and label each point with the exercise number. (pages 74–75)

9. (3,4)
10. (8,1)
11. (6,5)
12. (2,9)
13. (7,0)
14. (1,6)

Record the number of thousands, hundreds, tens, and ones. (pages 78–79)

15. 3,000
16. 2,093
17. 4,719
18. 5,860

✓ CHECK PROBLEM SOLVING

Solve. (pages 80–81)

CHOOSE A STRATEGY

- Make a Model
- Act It Out
- Work Backward
- Make a Table

19. Charlotte threw her baseball 5 millimeters farther than 2 meters. Edgar threw his baseball 8 millimeters less than 2 meters. How many millimeters did each ball travel?
20. Last year the Lee family used 850 gallons of water each day. Now they use 725 gallons each day. How many fewer gallons of water do they use each day now?

PLACE VALUE OF WHOLE NUMBERS

DID YOU KNOW . . .

The *Seismosaurus* weighed about 200,000 pounds. A young elephant weighs about 2,000 pounds.

Team-Up Time

Weighing Dinosaurs

Scientists are discovering more remains of dinosaurs every year. In 1985, scientists in New Mexico discovered the largest dinosaur yet. They call it *Seismosaurus*. *Seismosaurus* may have weighed up to 100 tons. That is 200,000 pounds. A fourth grader can weigh about 100 pounds.

Work with a group. Your job is to

- figure out how many 100-pound fourth graders weigh as much as one *Seismosaurus*. Explain how you figured it out.
- plan a chart to show your findings.
- choose a symbol. Decide how many 100-pound fourth graders each symbol will represent.

DID YOU

- ✓ figure out how many 100-pound fourth graders weigh as much as one *Seismosaurus*?
- ✓ choose a symbol and decide how many fourth graders each represents?
- ✓ make a chart and share it with the class?

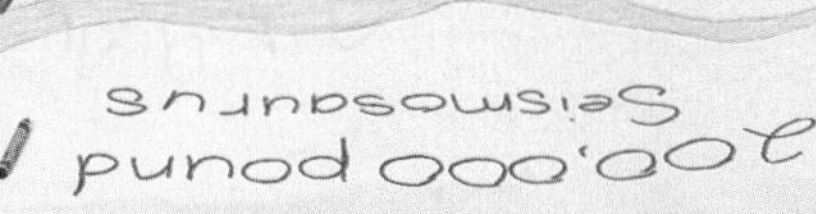

Numeration Systems

You will learn to compare place-value systems with numeration systems that do not use place value.

Why learn this? You can decide which system is easier to use.

WORD POWER
numeration system

A **numeration system** is a way of counting and naming numbers. The early Egyptians used picture symbols to name numbers. To find the value of Egyptian symbols, you add.

	Lotus Flower	Scroll	Heel Bone	Stick
Egyptian				
Standard	1,000	100	10	1

The distance around the base of the Pyramid of Khufu is 3,024 feet. The symbols the early Egyptians would have written are shown below.

Say: 1,000 + 1,000 + 1,000 + 10 + 10 + 1 + 1 + 1 + 1

There are more than two million large blocks in the Pyramid of Khufu (KOO•foo). Why is it sometimes hard to read and write large numbers using the Egyptian numeration system?

Talk About It

- Which Egyptian symbol has the same value as ten sticks? as ten heel bones? as ten scrolls?
- Is it easier to write the Egyptian symbols for 999 or the standard numeral 999? Explain.

The numeration system we use most often uses place value. The position of each digit shows its value.

EXAMPLE

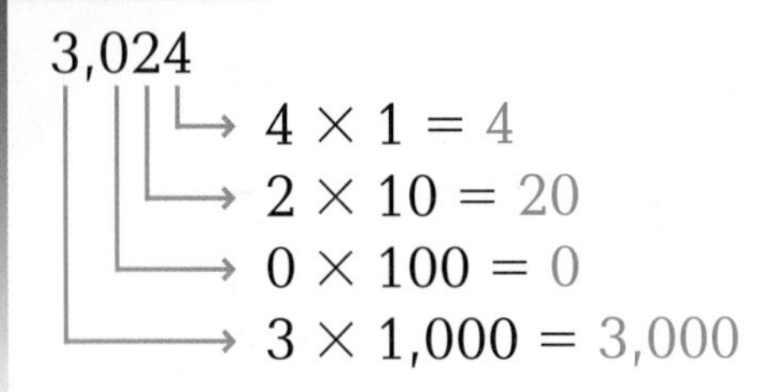

- How is this system different from the Egyptian numeration system?
- Why is a place-value system easier to use?

PRACTICE

Write the value of each group of Egyptian symbols.

1. 𓏺𓏺𓏺𓏺𓏺𓏺𓏺
2. 𓎆𓎆𓎆𓏺𓏺
3. 𓍢𓏺
4. 𓍢𓍢𓍢𓎆𓎆𓏺𓏺
5. 𓆼𓆼𓆼𓆼𓍢𓍢𓍢𓏺𓏺𓏺
6. 𓆼𓍢
7. 𓆼𓆼𓆼𓎆𓎆
8. 𓆼𓆼𓍢𓍢𓎆𓏺𓏺𓏺𓏺𓏺
9. 𓍢𓎆

Show the value of each digit in a place-value system.

10. 5 **11.** 13 **12.** 47 **13.** 90 **14.** 110

15. 123 **16.** 475 **17.** 600 **18.** 1,234 **19.** 6,030

Mixed Applications

20. The Pyramid of Khufu is 450 feet high. The Sphinx is 65 feet high. Write 450 and 65 using Egyptian symbols.

21. *Triceratops* lived 65 to 70 million years ago. It was up to 30 feet long and more than 13 feet high. Write 30 and 13 using Egyptian symbols.

22. Nicole's pet bird lives in a square cage. The length of one side of the cage is 21 inches. What is the total distance around the cage?

23. **WRITE ABOUT IT** How is the Egyptian numeration system like the place-value numeration system we use? How is it different?

Mixed Review

Estimate the sum or difference. (pages 10–11)

24. $296 + 368$

25. $708 - 471$

26. $554 - 370$

27. $138 + 190$

Find the sum. (pages 6–7)

28. $16 + 28 + 32$

29. $47 + 90 + 51$

30. $82 + 96 + 74 + 63$

31. $19 + 75 + 80 + 26$

32. $79 + 96 + 88 + 14$

Reading and Writing Numbers

You will learn that numbers can be written in different forms.

Why learn this? You can show numbers on a check in standard form and written form.

WORD POWER
expanded form

You can use a place-value chart to understand the value of each digit.

Thousands	Hundreds	Tens	Ones
1 $1 \times 1{,}000 = 1{,}000$	6 $6 \times 100 = 600$	9 $9 \times 10 = 90$	2 $2 \times 1 = 2$

Expanded form is a way to write numbers by showing the sum of the value of each digit.

The expanded form number is 1,000 + 600 + 90 + 2.

The number, in written form, is one thousand, six hundred ninety-two.

The number, in standard form, is 1,692.

Standard Form	Expanded Form	Written Form
16	10 + 6	sixteen
426	400 + 20 + 6	four hundred twenty-six
2,905	2,000 + 900 + 5	two thousand, nine hundred five

REMEMBER:
To find the value of each digit, multiply the digit by its place-value position. In 4,652 the value of the 6 is 6×100, or 600.

Use a calculator. Enter the expanded form of each number above, and read the answer on the display.

Press:

Display:

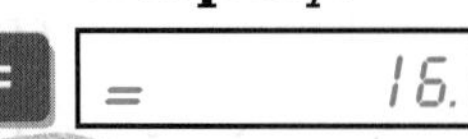

Talk About It

- How would you write *three thousand, one hundred sixty-seven* in standard form? in expanded form?
- How does expanded form show the value of each digit?
- When might you need to use the written form of a number?

Consumer Link
You use the standard and written forms of a number when you write a check. Why do you think that both standard and written forms of the amount are on a check?

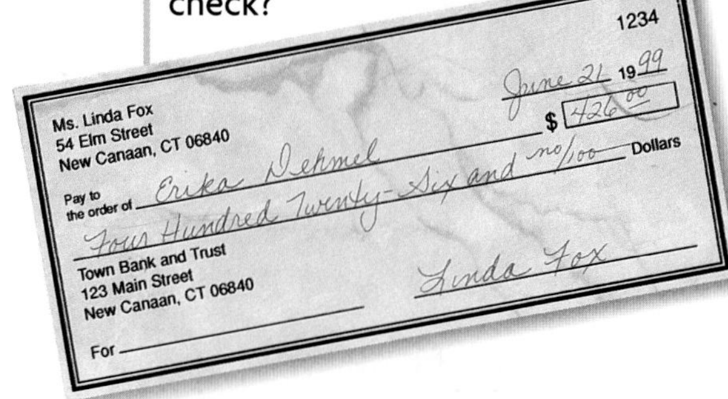

Calculator Activities, page H61

PRACTICE

Write each number in standard form.

1. thirty-seven
2. seventy-six
3. four hundred eighty-six
4. one hundred two
5. three thousand, nine hundred six
6. six thousand, six hundred ten
7. five thousand, seventeen
8. three thousand, forty-eight
9. nine thousand, eight hundred ninety-five
10. five thousand, nine hundred eighty-nine

Write each number in expanded form and written form.

11. 48
12. 165
13. 2,809
14. 6,158
15. 9,045

Write each number in two other ways.

16. 7,809
17. nine thousand, fifty-six
18. four hundred thirty-five
19. 3,962
20. 8,000 + 100 + 60 + 3
21. 7,259
22. 3,000 + 70 + 5
23. 1,000 + 200 + 30 + 4
24. six thousand, eight
25. 4,000 + 200 + 6

Mixed Applications

26. Linda paid $869 for a computer and $108 for software at Computer Corner. Write the amount she spent in standard and written form.

27. WRITE ABOUT IT Rafael bought a $20 gift certificate for Myriam. A gift certificate is written like a check. Write the amount on the gift certificate in standard form and written form.

Mixed Review

Use mental math to complete each equation. (pages 4–5)

28. 10 + 5 = 20 − _?_
29. 60 − _?_ = 20 + 30
30. _?_ − 5 = 30 + 5

Estimate the sum or difference. (pages 26–27)

31. 719 + 184
32. 190 − 117
33. 528 − 352
34. 367 + 584
35. 609 − 175

MORE PRACTICE Student Handbook pages H76–H77

Mental Math and Place Value

You will learn to use place value to name numbers in more than one way.	**Why learn this?** You can compute mentally using what you know about place-value positions.

Numbers can be named in more than one way.

A. 160	**B.** 3,100
Other names: 1 hundred 6 tens 16 tens 160 ones	Other names: 31 hundreds 310 tens 3,100 ones

CULTURAL LINK

The Persians were among the first people to use an abacus. They placed some stones on lines to show numbers. What number is shown on the abacus below?

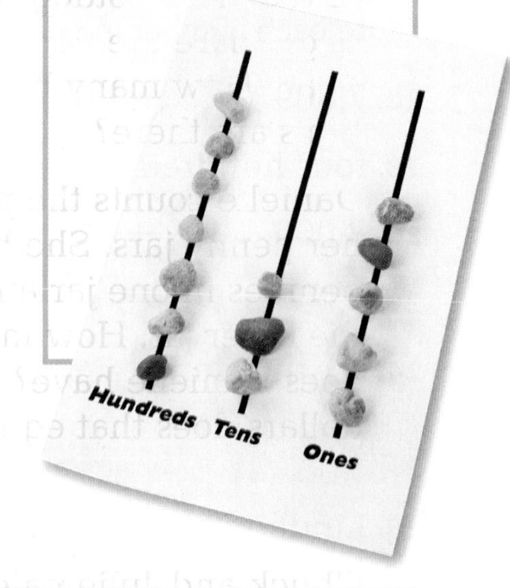

Talk About It

- In Examples A and B, how does place value help you name each number in more than one way?
- In what different ways can you name the number 430? the number 8,500?

You can use other names for numbers to compute mentally.

Sheila has 700 stickers. Tony has 500 stickers. How many stickers do they have in all?

MODEL

Add 700 and 500.

Step 1

Give the other names for each number.

700 = 7 hundreds, 70 tens, or 700 ones

500 = 5 hundreds, 50 tens, or 500 ones

Step 2

Add the one-digit numbers with the same place-value label.

$$\begin{array}{r} 7 \text{ hundreds} \\ +5 \text{ hundreds} \\ \hline 12 \text{ hundreds} \end{array}$$

Step 3

Change the sum back to standard form.

12 hundreds = 1,200

So, Sheila and Tony have 1,200 stickers in all.

CRITICAL THINKING How does using place value help you compute mentally?

PRACTICE

Use place value to name each number in two different ways.

1. 140 **2.** 380 **3.** 1,100 **4.** 2,600 **5.** 8,400

Use another name for each number and solve by using mental math.

6. $\begin{array}{r} 200 \\ +900 \\ \hline \end{array}$ **7.** $\begin{array}{r} 800 \\ +400 \\ \hline \end{array}$ **8.** $\begin{array}{r} 100 \\ +900 \\ \hline \end{array}$ **9.** $\begin{array}{r} 500 \\ +600 \\ \hline \end{array}$ **10.** $\begin{array}{r} 700 \\ +700 \\ \hline \end{array}$

11. $\begin{array}{r} 2,000 \\ +7,000 \\ \hline \end{array}$ **12.** $\begin{array}{r} 6,000 \\ +1,000 \\ \hline \end{array}$ **13.** $\begin{array}{r} 8,000 \\ +9,000 \\ \hline \end{array}$ **14.** $\begin{array}{r} 1,500 \\ +3,100 \\ \hline \end{array}$ **15.** $\begin{array}{r} 4,300 \\ +5,200 \\ \hline \end{array}$

Mixed Applications

16. There are 8 hotdog buns in each bag. There are 64 hotdog buns in all. How many bags of hotdog buns are there?

17. Nancy has 359 stamps in her stamp collection. Her brother Brian also has 359 stamps. How many stamps do they have in all?

18. Danielle counts the pennies in her penny jars. She has 1,200 pennies in one jar and 2,500 in the other jar. How many pennies does Danielle have? How many dollars does that equal?

19. On Friday 675 shakes were sold at the mall ice-cream shop. On Saturday 957 shakes were sold. How many more shakes were sold on Saturday than on Friday?

20. Chuck and Julie paid $350 for a golden retriever and $500 for a Yorkshire terrier. How much money did they spend? If they started with $1,000, how much money do they have now?

21. **WRITE ABOUT IT** The Golden Gate Bridge is 4,200 feet long. Sam read the number as 42 hundred feet. Was he correct? How else could he have read it?

Mixed Review

Use the multiplication properties to solve. (pages 36–37)

22. $\begin{array}{r} 7 \\ \times 0 \\ \hline \end{array}$ **23.** $\begin{array}{r} 1 \\ \times 5 \\ \hline \end{array}$ **24.** $\begin{array}{r} 0 \\ \times 6 \\ \hline \end{array}$ **25.** $\begin{array}{r} 8 \\ \times 1 \\ \hline \end{array}$ **26.** $\begin{array}{r} 1 \\ \times 9 \\ \hline \end{array}$ **27.** $\begin{array}{r} 3 \\ \times 0 \\ \hline \end{array}$

Find the quotient. (pages 60–61)

28. $9\overline{)20}$ **29.** $4\overline{)31}$ **30.** $7\overline{)36}$ **31.** $8\overline{)47}$ **32.** $3\overline{)28}$ **33.** $5\overline{)24}$

Place Value to 100,000

You will investigate how to show 100,000 by using models that stand for 1,000.

Why learn this? You can understand the values of larger numbers.

There are 10 tens in 1,000. If you stack 10 tens blocks, they make the shape of a cube.

Explore

Make a model that looks like a cube to show 1,000.

MATERIALS: 10-by-10 grids, scissors, tape, string

MODEL

How can you make a model of 1,000 with 10-by-10 grids?

Step 1

Cut out the faces needed to form a thousands block.

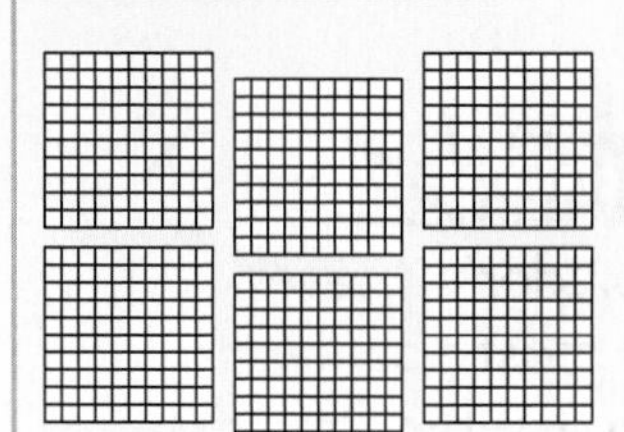

Step 2

Tape the faces together to form the shape of a cube.

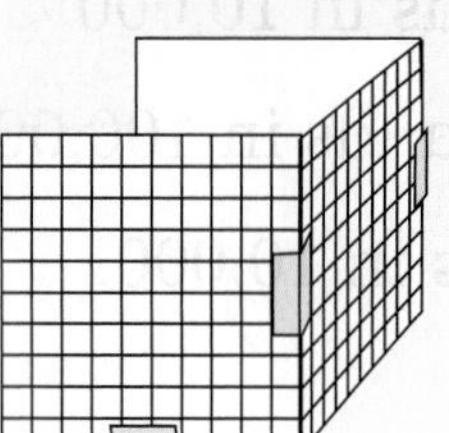

Marty's model of 1,000

Record

Explain how you know the model stands for 1,000.

- How many thousands cubes would it take to show 10,000? Explain.

100 thousands

Try This

With other members of your group, make enough models of 1,000 to show 10,000.

TALK ABOUT IT The shape of the model that shows 1,000 is a cube. What is the shape of the model that shows 10,000?

WRITE ABOUT IT Explain how you know the new model shows 10,000.

NOX WAY

Technology Link

E-Lab • Activity 6 Available on CD-ROM and the Internet at http://www.hbschool.com/elab

Now, investigate using string to outline the size of a model that shows 100,000. Cut string four times the length of your 10,000 model. Use the string and your 10,000 model to outline the size and shape of a 100,000 model.

TALK ABOUT IT What is the shape of the string outline that shows the model for 100,000?

WRITE ABOUT IT How do the shapes of the models that show 100,000; 10,000; and 1,000 compare with the shapes of the models that show 100, 10, and 1?

Applying What You Learned

Write *true* or *false* for each statement. Rewrite false statements to make them true.

1. There are exactly 10 thousands in 100,000.
2. There are exactly 100 thousands in 10,000.
3. There are exactly 10 ten thousands in 100,000.
4. There are exactly 10 thousands in 10,000.

Mixed Applications

5. Crystal has a Labrador retriever that can fetch a stick in 6 seconds. How long will it take Crystal's dog to fetch a stick 10 times? How many minutes is that?
6. Fashion Mall has a parking garage that holds 1,000 cars. Exactly 100 cars can park on each level of the garage. How many levels are there in all?
7. Carrie has 8 cubes. Each cube models 1,000. How many more cubes does she need to show 10,000?
8. **WRITE ABOUT IT** What would the model for 1,000,000 look like? Explain how you could make one.

Social Studies Link

Labrador retrievers are the most popular dog breed in the United States. In 1 year there were 126,393 Labrador retriever puppies registered with the American Kennel Club. How many more than 100,000 is that?

PART 1 Using Large Numbers

You will learn to read and write numbers to millions.	**Why learn this?** You can understand very large numbers, such as those used to measure distances and to describe populations.	**WORD POWER** period

Each group of three numbers in a large number is called a **period**. Commas separate the periods. Say the number before each comma, and then name each period. You do not name the ones period when you name a number.

Use the table to help you read the number 48,700,000.

Periods →

MILLIONS		THOUSANDS			ONES		
Tens	**Ones**	**Hundreds**	**Tens**	**Ones**	**Hundreds**	**Tens**	**Ones**
4	8 ,	7	0	0 ,	0	0	0

Say: 48 million, 700 thousand

Talk About It

- How would you read the number 3,167,541? 42,413,792? 983,032,816?
- How does naming the periods help you read the number?
- Why is it important to remember the name of each period in a large number?

One million is a very large number.

one million = one hundred thousand × ten
1,000,000 = 100,000 × 10

- Would you use *hundred thousands* or *millions* to describe the population of your state? the population of this country?

CRITICAL THINKING Give some other examples of things that can be counted in the hundred thousands or millions.

REMEMBER:

A *benchmark* is a point of reference. Suppose you know there are about 5,000 staples in 1 box. You can estimate the number of staples in a case of 10 boxes.

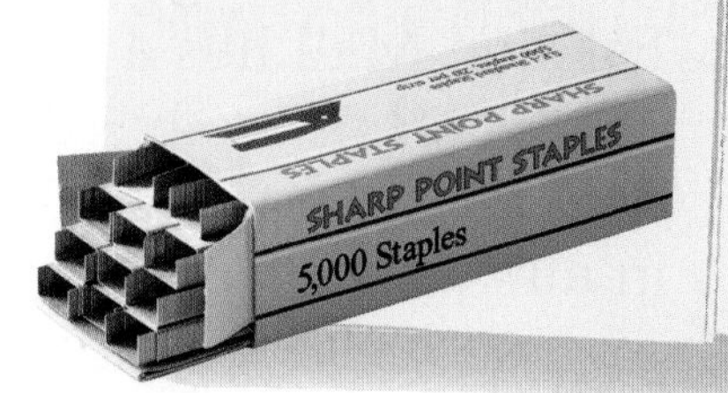

PRACTICE

Write the number as you would say it with period names.

1. 4,153,862 4 ___, 153 ___, 862
2. 10,075,463 10 ___, 75 ___, 463
3. 32,185,049 32 ___, 185 ___, 49
4. 790,008,400 790 ___, 8 ___, 400
5. 612,982 612 ___, 982

Write each number in standard form.

6. eighteen million, eight hundred eleven thousand, nine hundred sixty
7. four hundred seven million, one hundred thousand, three hundred six
8. two million, eight hundred thirty thousand, seven hundred fifty-two
9. ninety-five million, one hundred one thousand, nine hundred forty-six
10. one million, eight hundred ninety-one thousand, six hundred fifteen

Would the number of cars in the United States be about 150 or 150,000,000?

Write *yes* or *no* to tell whether each number is large enough to be counted in the hundred thousands or more.

11. the number of students in your class
12. the number of cars in the United States
13. the number of grains of sand on a beach
14. **Write a problem** about something that is counted in the hundred thousands or millions.

Mixed Applications

15. The total amount of money spent in 1 year for airline travel in the United States was $64,849,849. Write the number by naming each period.
16. The sum of two numbers is 15. Their difference is 1. Their product is 56. What are the two numbers?
17. Mr. Craig is ordering a box of staples for each person in his office. There are 20 people in his office and 10 boxes of staples in a case. How many cases should Mr. Craig order?

LESSON CONTINUES

PART 2

PROBLEM-SOLVING STRATEGY
Use a Table

THE PROBLEM The Davenport Recycling Center collects cans. The table below lists the number of cans collected from 1995 through 1998. If the center does not collect more cans in 1999 than in 1998, it will be shut down. What do you predict will happen?

REMEMBER:
- ✓ Understand
- ✓ Plan
- ✓ Solve
- ✓ Look Back

✓ Understand

- What are you asked to do?
- What information will you use?
- Is there any information you will not use? If so, what?

✓ Plan

- What strategy can you use to solve the problem?

You can *use a table* to make a prediction.

✓ Solve

- How can you use the table to solve the problem?

Find out if there were more cans or fewer cans collected from year to year. Then make your prediction.

CANS COLLECTED BY DAVENPORT RECYCLING CENTER	
Year	**Number of Cans**
1995	210,426
1996	209,873
1997	543,167
1998	621,411

Since more cans were collected every year since 1996, there will probably be more cans collected in 1999. So, the recycling center probably will not be shut down.

✓ Look Back

- Why is it helpful to make a table to organize numbers?
- What other strategy could you use to solve the problem?

Environmental Link

Every minute, an average of 113,204 aluminum beverage cans are recycled. What period do you name to say 113,204?

PRACTICE

CHOOSE Paper/Pencil Calculator Hands-on Mental Math

Use a table to solve.

LEE COUNTY EARTH DAY CELEBRATION ATTENDANCE		
Year	**Number of People**	**Increase from Previous Year**
1994	11,560	—
1995	19,780	8,220
1996	22,140	2,360
1997	31,690	9,550
1998	44,538	12,848

ROCKY BROOK LACROSSE JUNE SCHEDULE	
June 14	Parrots vs. Macaws
June 16	Hawks vs. Pelicans
June 21	Cardinals vs. Robins
June 23	Blue Jays vs. Orioles
June 28	Penguins vs. Eagles

1. Between which two years did attendance at the Earth Day Celebration increase the most?

2. How many more people attended the Earth Day Celebration in 1996 than in 1994?

3. Which teams play one week after the Cardinals and the Robins? Which ones play one week before?

4. How many days are there from the first game in June to the last game in June? How many weeks is that?

Mixed Applications

Solve.

CHOOSE A STRATEGY

- Use a Table
- Act It Out
- Make a Model
- Work Backward

5. Ian is building a rectangular recycling bin. The perimeter of the bin is 16 feet, and the length is 5 feet. How wide is the recycling bin?

6. Maurice spent $4 for a movie ticket and $4 for snacks. Then, his mother gave him $5. Maurice had $15 left. How much money did he take to the movie?

7. Sabrina, Jared, and Dave have collected 480 newspapers for a paper drive. They collected 218 newspapers on Friday and 168 on Saturday. How many papers did they collect before Friday?

8. Four friends are in line to buy tickets. Cameron is in front of Katie. Ann is between Katie and Don. In what order are the friends in line?

9. Between which two years did attendance at the fall picnic decrease? by how many people?

FALL PICNIC ATTENDANCE				
Year	1995	1996	1997	1998
People	2,051	2,104	2,007	2,595

MORE PRACTICE Student Handbook page H78

CULTURAL CONNECTION

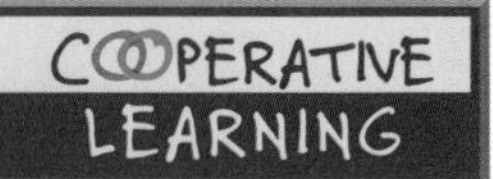

Flying to the Philippines

Maria Villanueva and her family are planning a trip to the Philippines in the summer. The airplane will stop in Hawaii on the way. The Villanuevas will spend four days there before going on to Manila. Maria estimates that the distance to Hawaii from San Francisco is about 2,400 miles. How would you write this number in expanded form? in written form?

Expanded Form
2,000 + 400

Written Form
two thousand, four hundred

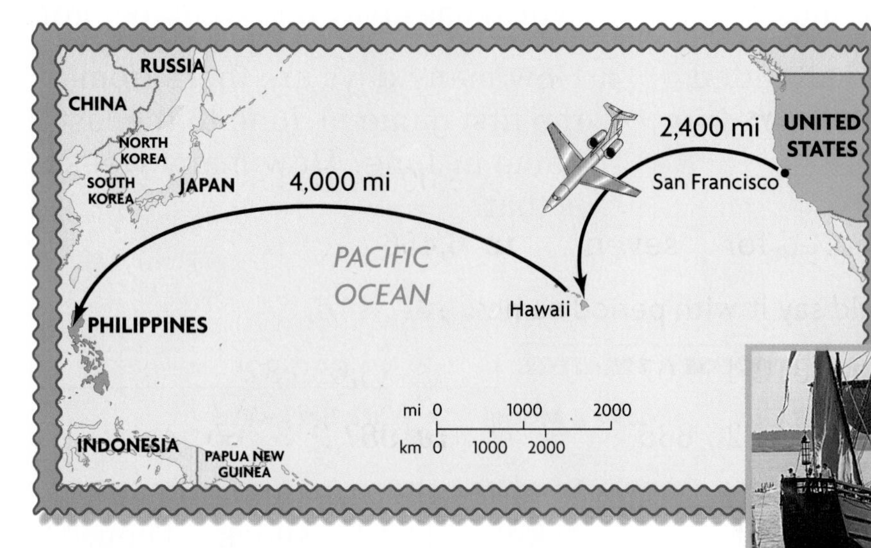

CULTURAL LINK

In the 1500's the Philippine Islands were named by the Spanish in honor of King Philip II of Spain. Spanish galleons sailed from the Philippines to Mexico. They carried spices, cloth, jewels, and other expensive items from Asia. When they returned to Manila, they carried Mexican silver. Spain controlled the Philippines until 1898, when it was taken over by the United States. Because Spain occupied the Philippines for many years, many Filipinos today have Spanish names.

Work Together

1. From San Francisco to Manila, the entire trip is about 6,400 miles. Write the distance in written form. six Thousand four hundred

2. Of the people living in the Philippines, 26,831,200 are farmers. Write the number of farmers in expanded form.
   20,000,000 6,000,000

3. The estimated population of the Philippines in 1995 was sixty-seven million, seventy-eight thousand people. Write the estimated population in standard form. 67,078,000

4. **WRITE ABOUT IT** All the islands in the Philippines cover one hundred fifteen thousand, seven hundred forty square miles. Explain how to write the number in standard form and in expanded form.
   150,740
   100,000 + 50,000 + 700 + 40

REVIEW

✓ CHECK UNDERSTANDING

VOCABULARY

1. A __?__ is a way of counting and naming numbers. (page 88)
2. __?__ is a way to write numbers by showing the sum of the value of each digit. (page 90)
3. Each group of three numbers in a large number is called a __?__. (page 96)

Use place value to name each number in two different ways. (pages 92–93)

4. 500
5. 230
6. 8,000
7. 4,900
8. 6,100

✓ CHECK SKILLS

Write each number in two other ways. (pages 90–91)

9. 3,813
10. 5,000 + 900 + 20 + 3
11. one thousand, two hundred forty-seven
12. 6,456

Write the number as you would say it with period names. (pages 96–97)

13. 378,946,388
14. 812,459,673
15. 48,650,327
16. 89,573,449
17. 14,726,835
18. 987,213,465

✓ CHECK PROBLEM SOLVING

Solve. (pages 98–99)

CHOOSE A STRATEGY

- **Make a Model**
- **Act It Out**
- **Work Backward**
- **Use a Table**

19. Brandon gave 11 grapes to Kyle, 14 to Betsy, and 12 to Stephanie. He has 20 grapes left. How many grapes did Brandon start with?

20. Felicia wants to watch all the events that will be held on Saturday. If she stays for every event, how many hours will she spend at the fair?

COMPARING AND ORDERING NUMBERS

BIG DIPPER

Star	Distance	Brightness
Alkaid	210 light-years	fairly bright
Alioth	68 light-years	fairly bright
Dubhe	105 light-years	fairly bright
Merak	78 light-years	medium
Phecda	90 light-years	medium
Mizar	88 light-years	fairly bright
Megrez	65 light-years	medium

DID YOU KNOW . . .

The constellation The Great Bear includes the seven stars of the Big Dipper. The stars form an imaginary outline.

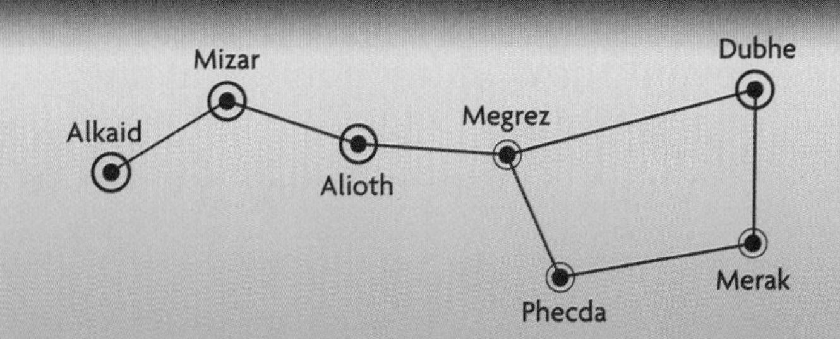

Team-Up Time

Measuring the Stars

Constellations are patterns of stars. Scientists have identified 88 star clusters as constellations. One of the easiest to see is the Big Dipper.

The stars in a constellation are different distances from the Earth. These stars can be sorted from very bright to very faint.

Find out if the brightness of a star is related to the star's distance from the Earth.

Work with a group. Your job is to

- choose a constellation to find out about.
- make a poster about your constellation.
- order the stars in your constellation by brightness and distance from the Earth.
- draw a picture of your constellation.

DID YOU

- ✓ make a poster about your constellation?
- ✓ order the stars by brightness and distance from the Earth?

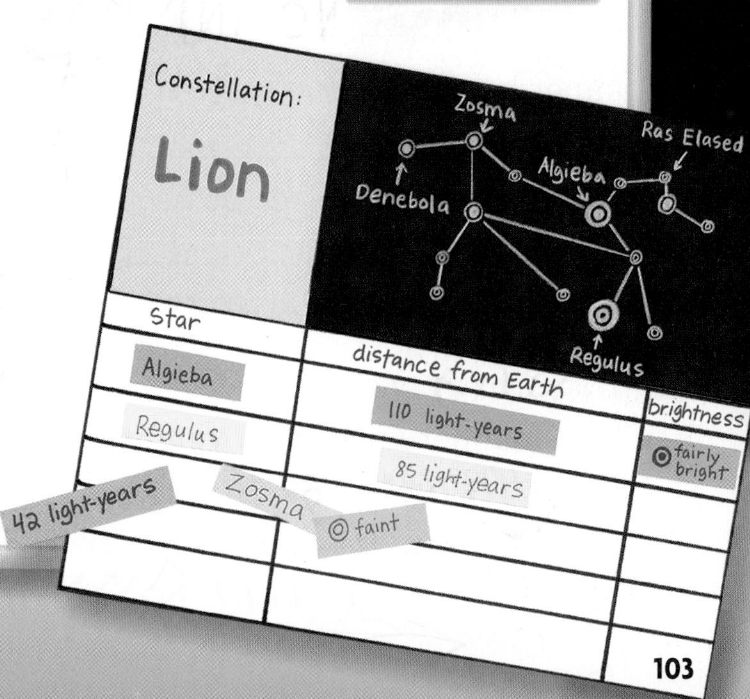

Comparing on a Number Line

You will learn how to compare numbers on a number line.

Why learn this? You can compare scores when you and your friends play a game.

Marla and Felipe are playing a game. So far Marla has 30 points, and Felipe has 40 points. Who has more points?

Locate 30 and 40 on a number line. Use words and symbols to compare them.

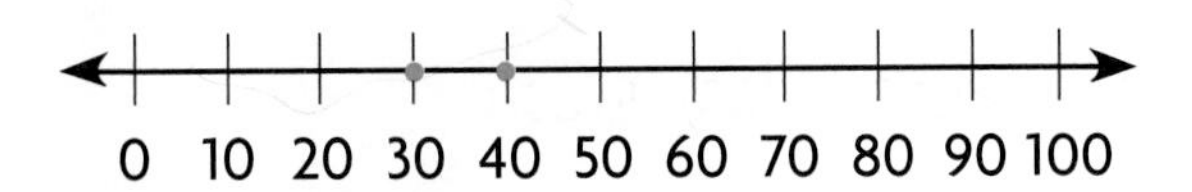

Notice that

- 40 is to the right of 30. So, 40 is greater than 30.

  $40 > 30$

- 30 is to the left of 40. So, 30 is less than 40.

  $30 < 40$

So, Felipe has more points.

Talk About It

- Is 20 greater than or less than 40? How can you tell?
- Can you use this number line to compare 195 and 165? Why or why not?

A number line does not always start at 0.

a.

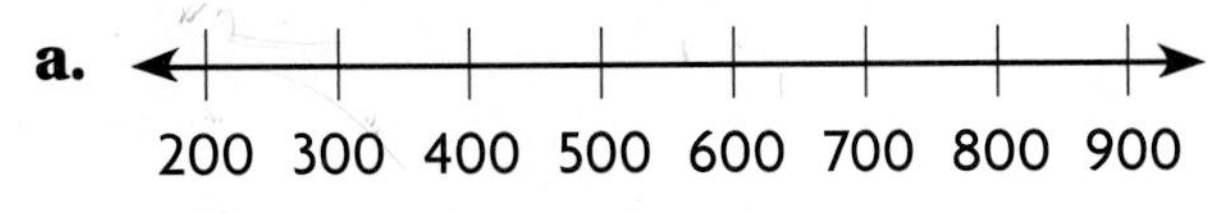

b.

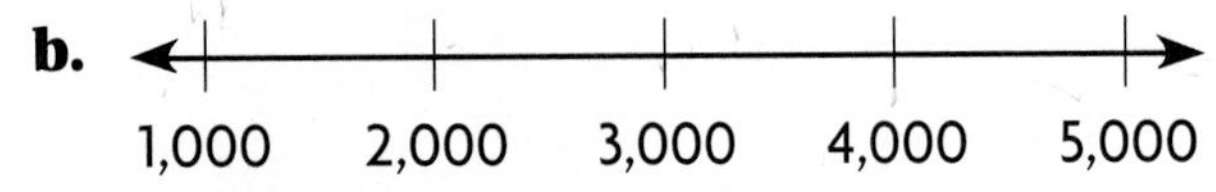

Talk About It

- Which number line would you use to compare 700 and 900? 3,000 and 2,000?
- How would you draw a number line to compare 17 and 25?

REMEMBER:

As you move from left to right on a number line, the numbers get larger. As you move from right to left, the numbers get smaller.

In ***Mighty Math Calculating Crew***, the game *Nautical Number Line* challenges you to locate numbers on a number line.

PRACTICE

Use the number line to compare. Write < or >.

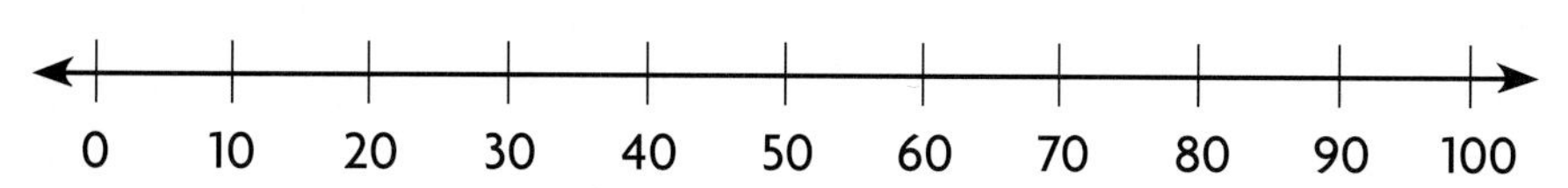

1. 10 ● 40 **2.** 50 ● 30 **3.** 70 ● 60 **4.** 90 ● 100

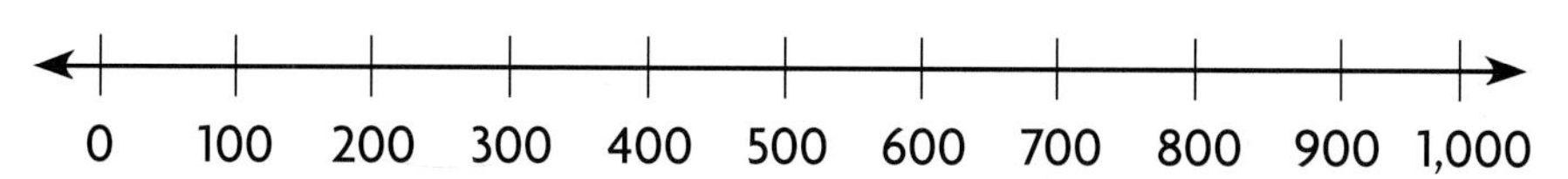

5. 200 ● 300 **6.** 800 ● 900 **7.** 600 ● 500 **8.** 900 ● 300

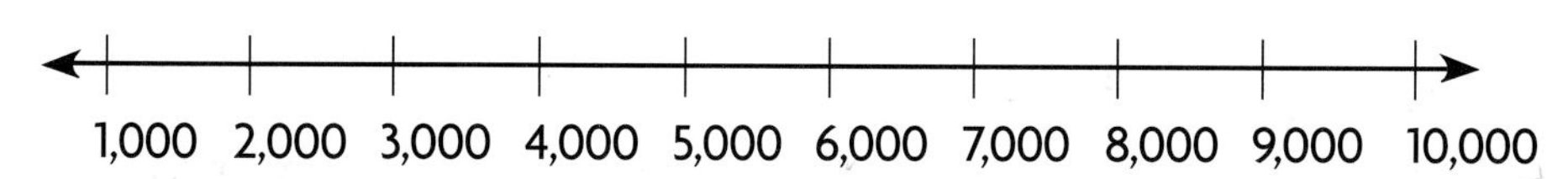

9. 1,000 ● 3,000 **10.** 9,000 ● 6,000 **11.** 7,000 ● 8,000

Compare the numbers and write < or > for the ●.

12. 300 ● 400 **13.** 28 ● 18 **14.** 550 ● 490 **15.** 8,000 ● 9,000

Mixed Applications

16. Craig counted 124 stars. Naomi counted 142 stars. Who counted more stars? How many more stars did he or she count?

17. There were 247 tickets sold for the game at school on Friday. That night, 175 more tickets were sold. How many tickets were sold in all?

18. WRITE ABOUT IT Explain why you wouldn't use a number line marked with tens to compare the numbers 1,200 and 3,100.

Mixed Review

Find the difference. (pages 20–21)

19. 600 − 79

20. 400 − 265

21. 900 − 698

22. 300 − 176

23. 900 − 897

Show two ways to group using parentheses. Find the products. (pages 40–41)

24. $4 \times 2 \times 3 =$?

25. $5 \times 6 \times 1 =$?

26. $3 \times 3 \times 2 =$?

27. $1 \times 9 \times 7 =$?

MORE PRACTICE Student Handbook pages H78–H79

PART

1 Comparing Numbers

You will learn how to use place value to compare numbers.

Why learn this? When shopping, you can compare the cost of what you want to buy with the amount of money you have.

Michael has 95¢ and Portia has 99¢. Who has more lunch money? PoRtiA

To compare 95 and 99, compare each place-value position. Start with the greatest position, and compare until the digits are different.

Step 1

Begin at the left.
Compare the tens.

95
↓
99

same number of tens

Step 2

Compare the ones.

95
↓
99

Since $5 < 9$, $95 < 99$.

Since 95¢ is less than 99¢, Michael has less lunch money. So, Portia has more lunch money.

EXAMPLES

A. Compare 342 and 342.

342 ↓ 342 — same number of hundreds	342 ↓ 342 — same number of tens	342 ↓ 342 — same number of ones $342 = 342$

B. Compare 8,629 and 8,659.

8,629 ↓ 8,659 — same number of thousands	8,629 ↓ 8,659 — same number of hundreds	8,629 ↓ 8,659 — Since 2 tens $<$ 5 tens, $8{,}629 < 8{,}659$.

- In Example B, what is the greatest place-value position in which the digits are different?

CRITICAL THINKING Why do you start at the left when you compare numbers?

PRACTICE

Write the greatest place-value position in which the digits are different. Write the greater number.

1. 85; 87 **2.** 46; 38 **3.** 95; 46 **4.** 162; 167

5. 437; 369 **6.** 756; 758 **7.** 1,498; 1,479 **8.** 3,652; 3,567

Compare the numbers. Write the comparison using <, >, or = .

9. 75
57

10. 82
82

11. 35
45

12. 165
256

13. 609
619

14. 475
475

15. 1,056
1,156

16. 2,136
2,116

Mixed Applications

17. In three plays in a football game, Kurt ran 24 yards, 14 yards, and 12 yards. What is the number of yards he ran in the three plays?

18. The Seminole track team traveled 191 miles to the state meet. The Brevard track team traveled 181 miles. Which team traveled farther? How many more miles did it travel?

19. At the end of the year, there were 18 students on the school bowling team. During the year, 6 students had joined the team and 3 students had moved away. How many students were on the team at the beginning of the year?

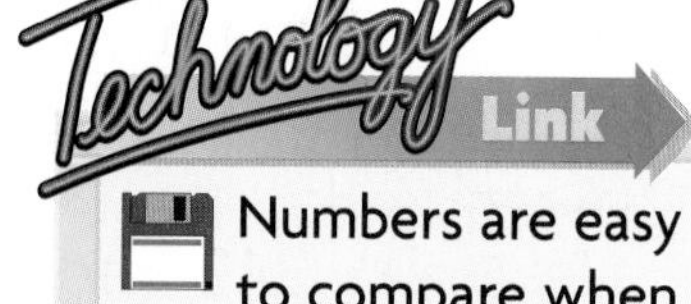

Numbers are easy to compare when they are displayed in a bar graph. You can use ***Graph Links*** computer software to make a bar graph.

For Problems 20–24, use the table.

BOWLING SCORES	
Player	**Score**
Lana	125
Jesse	124
Karlene	116

20. Does Lana or Jesse have the greater score? by how many points?

21. Who has a lower score than Jesse? How do you know?

22. How much higher is Lana's score than Karlene's?

23. Lana bowls another game and scores 118 points. What is the difference in her two scores?

24. **Write a problem** that compares two scores from the table.

LESSON CONTINUES

PART 2 PROBLEM-SOLVING STRATEGY
Guess and Check

THE PROBLEM Colleen took part in a three-day archery tournament. Each day she scored twice as many points as the day before. Her total score at the end of three days was 420 points. How many points did Colleen score each day?

REMEMBER:
✓ Understand
✓ Plan
✓ Solve
✓ Look Back

✓ Understand

- What are you asked to find?
- What information will you use?
- Is there any information you will not use? If so, what?

✓ Plan

- What strategy can you use to solve the problem?

  You can *guess and check* to find the number of points scored each day.

✓ Solve

- How can you use the strategy to solve the problem?

  Guess the number of points Colleen scored on the first day. Multiply by two to find the number of points she scored on the second day. Multiply by two again to find the number of points she scored on the third day. Check by adding the scores for the three days.

Guess	Day 1	100	50	60
	Day 2	200	100	120
	Day 3	400	200	240
Check		700	350	420
Notes		too high	too low	just right

So, Colleen scored 60 points on Day 1, 120 points on Day 2, and 240 points on Day 3.

✓ Look Back

- What facts must be true about Colleen's three scores?
- What other strategy could you use to solve the problem?

PRACTICE

CHOOSE Paper/Pencil Calculator Hands-on Mental Math

Guess and check to solve.

1. What if Colleen's total score at the end of three days had been 525 points? How many points would she have scored each day?

2. Neil has 10 coins that total $1.26. If he has at least 1 penny, 1 nickel, 1 dime, and 1 quarter, how many of each coin does he have?

3. There are 17 fourth graders on the soccer team. There are 3 more boys than girls on the team. How many boys are on the team? How many girls?

4. The sum of two numbers is 25. Their difference is 3. What are the two numbers?

Mixed Applications

Solve.

CHOOSE A STRATEGY

- **Make a Model**
- **Guess and Check**
- **Act It Out**
- **Use a Table**
- **Work Backward**

5. There are 9 teams taking part in a swim meet. Each team has 6 swimmers. How many swimmers are taking part in the swim meet?

6. Floor exercises in gymnastics are performed on a square floor mat. Each side of the mat is 40 feet long. What is the perimeter of the floor mat?

7. There are 14 teams in the youth basketball league. Last year, 5 new teams joined the league and 2 teams left. How many teams were in the basketball league at the beginning of last year?

8. Manny wants to buy new fishing gear. It costs $115. He has already saved $70. If he can save $5 a week, for how many more weeks does he need to save in order to buy the gear?

9. There are 6 boats at the dock. Each boat can hold 8 people. 4 boats are full and 2 boats can hold one more person each. How many people are in boats?

For Problems 10–11, use the table.

10. On which day will the swim team have its longest practice? its shortest practice?

11. For how many hours will the team practice in all?

Swim Team Practice Schedule	
Mon, Sep 13	3:00–4:00
Thu, Sep 16	3:00–5:00
Mon, Sep 20	3:30–5:30
Wed, Sep 22	2:30–5:30
Fri, Sep 24	3:30–5:30

MORE PRACTICE Student Handbook page H79

Ordering Numbers

You will investigate using yarn to compare distances.

Why learn this? You can compare and order measures of very large distances.

Explore

Cut lengths of yarn to model the distance of each planet from the sun.

MATERIALS: yarn, meterstick, scissors

- Cut pieces of yarn to stand for the distance of each planet from the sun. Have 1 centimeter stand for 10,000,000 miles and 1 meter stand for 1,000,000,000 miles.

PLANETS' DISTANCES FROM THE SUN		
Planet	**Distance from the Sun (rounded to the nearest 10,000,000 miles)**	**Length of Yarn to Cut**
Earth	90,000,000 miles	9 centimeters
Jupiter	480,000,000 miles	48 centimeters
Mars	140,000,000 miles	14 centimeters
Mercury	40,000,000 miles	4 centimeters
Neptune	2,800,000,000 miles	2 meters, 80 centimeters
Pluto	3,670,000,000 miles	3 meters, 67 centimeters
Saturn	890,000,000 miles	89 centimeters
Uranus	1,780,000,000 miles	1 meter, 78 centimeters
Venus	70,000,000 miles	7 centimeters

- Label each piece of yarn with the name of the planet it stands for. Order the pieces of yarn from shortest to longest.

Record

List the planets and their distances from the sun in order from the least to the greatest.

E-Lab • Activity 7 Available on CD-ROM and the Internet at http://www.hbschool.com/elab

Now, investigate how to order a different set of numbers from the least to the greatest.

Try This

Choose five items. Use yarn to measure the length of each item. Label each piece of yarn with the name of the item it stands for and its length in centimeters. Compare and order the pieces of yarn and their measures from the least to the greatest length.

TALK ABOUT IT How would you order the pieces of yarn and their measures from the *greatest* to the *least* length?

WRITE ABOUT IT How does this method help you order measures of different lengths?

Sports Link

In football the linesmen "bring out the chains" to measure a distance of 10 yards. A first down is made when the team has moved the football forward at least 10 yards. How is this like using yarn to compare distances?

Applying What You Learned

Order from the least to the greatest length.

1. a. 56 in. **b.** 22 in. **c.** 30 in.

2. a. 190 mm **b.** 120 mm **c.** 90 mm

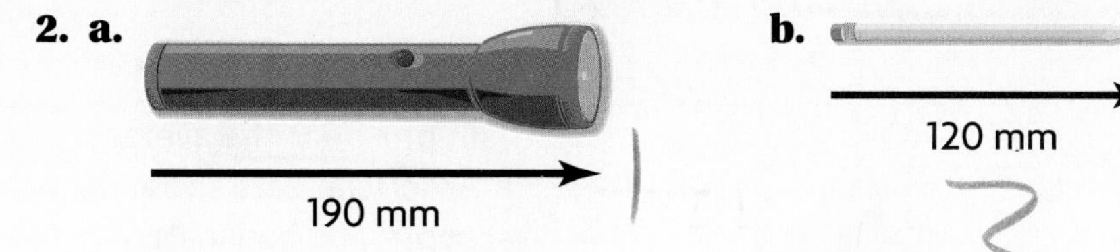

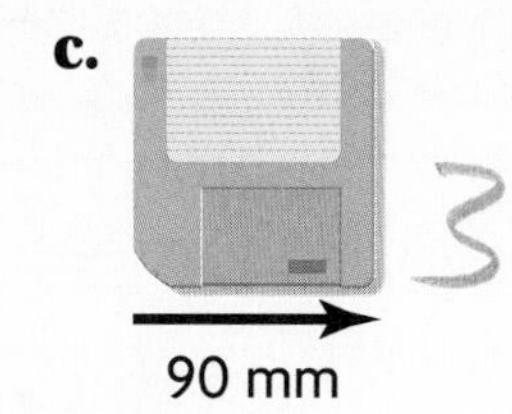

Mixed Applications

For Problems 3–6, use the map.

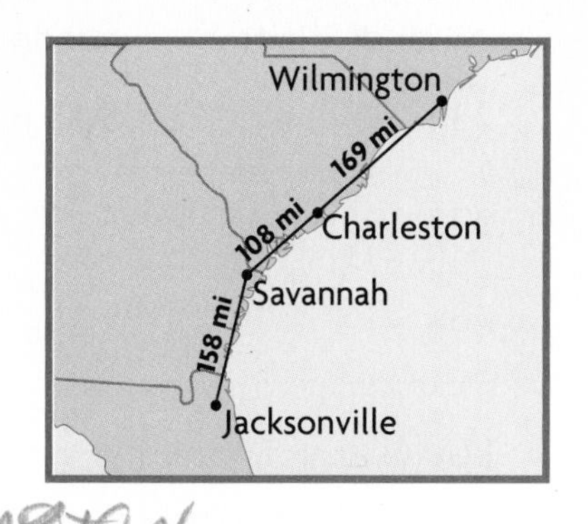

3. What is the total number of miles one must drive to go from Jacksonville to Wilmington?

4. Between which two cities is the distance greater than the distance between Jacksonville and Savannah?

5. Between which two cities is the distance the shortest to drive?

6. **Write a problem** about two distances on the map.

MORE PRACTICE Student Handbook page H79

More About Ordering Numbers

You will learn how to order numbers by using a number line and place value.	**Why learn this?** You can quickly compare large numbers, like video game scores.

Mariah, Kimberly, and Jabaar are having a contest to see who can get the highest score on a video game. Mariah scored 9,380 points, Kimberly scored 9,760 points, and Jabaar scored 9,150 points. Place their scores in order from least to greatest.

When you play video games, you compare scores to see who is the winner.

You can use a number line to compare and order.

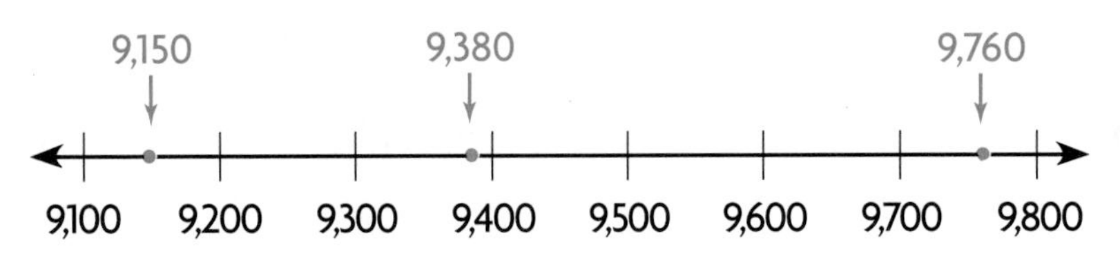

9,150 < 9,380 < 9,760

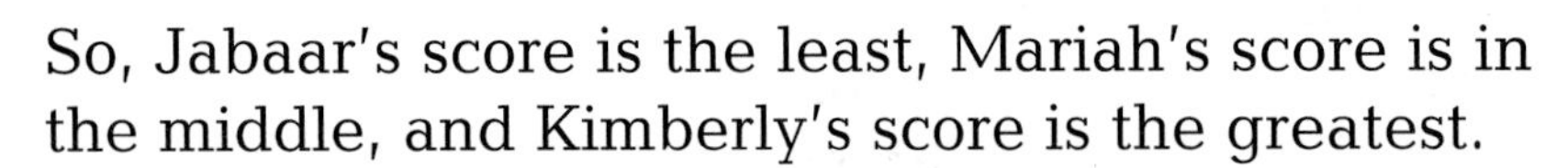

So, Jabaar's score is the least, Mariah's score is in the middle, and Kimberly's score is the greatest.

You can order numbers by comparing the digits in the same place-value position.

MODEL

How can you place 5,231, 5,922, and 5,496 in order from greatest to least?

Step 1

Compare the thousands digits.

5,231
↓
5,922 — same number of thousands
↓
5,496

Step 2

Compare the hundreds digits.

5,231
↓
5,922 — 9 > 4 > 2
↓
5,496

Step 3

Order the numbers using the hundreds digits.

Since 9 > 4 > 2, 5,922 > 5,496 > 5,231.

- How would you order these numbers from least to greatest?

CRITICAL THINKING Which method of comparing numbers is easier? Explain.

Health Link

In one year the average American eats about 60 apples, 56 bananas, 6 grapefruit, 29 bunches of grapes, and 26 oranges. Place these numbers in order from the greatest to the least.

PRACTICE

Write the numbers in order from the least to the greatest.

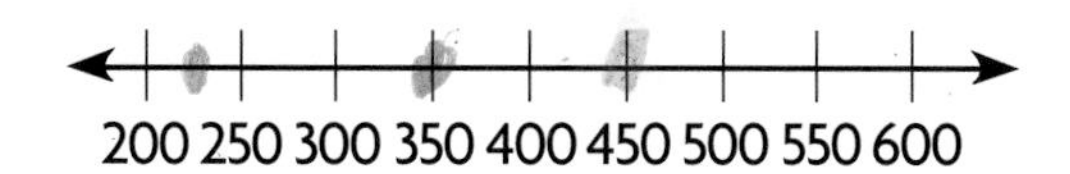

1. 350; 225; 450

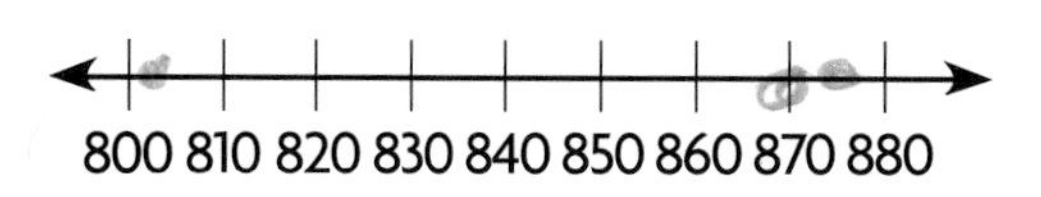

2. 870; 877; 807

3. 3,954; 3,959; 3,965

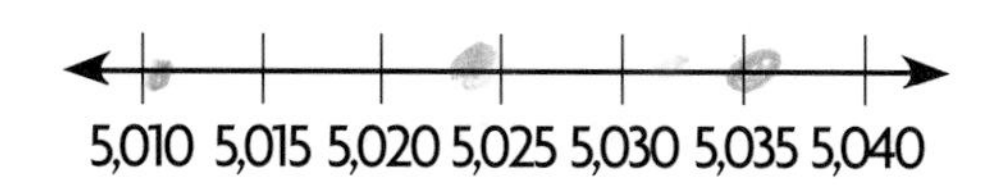

4. 5,011; 5,035; 5,023

Write the numbers in order from the greatest to the least.

5. 785; 875; 758 **6.** 695; 513; 603 **7.** 496; 946; 416

8. 1,870; 1,865; 1,869 **9.** 6,432; 8,105; 7,936 **10.** 9,107; 9,170; 9,017

Mixed Applications

11. Write in order the day the least number of tickets was sold to the day the greatest number of tickets was sold.

Ticket Sales	
Friday	2,781 tickets
Saturday	2,136 tickets
Sunday	2,948 tickets

12. Which building is the tallest? the shortest? What is the difference in height between the tallest and shortest buildings?

HEIGHTS OF BUILDINGS	
Building	**Height**
Empire State Building	1,250 ft
World Trade Center	1,368 ft
John Hancock Center	1,127 ft

13. Rita has 5 goldfish. She has 3 times as many guppies as goldfish. She has 12 fewer angelfish than guppies. How many of each kind of fish does Rita have?

14. **WRITE ABOUT IT** Explain how to place 1,234, 1,244, and 1,254 in order from least to greatest.

Mixed Review

Write the fact family for each set of numbers. (pages 52–53)

15. 3, 4, 12 **16.** 9, 7, 63 **17.** 5, 8, 40 **18.** 4, 6, 24

Record the number of thousands, hundreds, tens, and ones. (pages 78–79)

19. 5,287 **20.** 3,369 **21.** 9,407 **22.** 1,198 **23.** 2,645

Sorting and Comparing

You will learn how to sort and compare sets of numbers, using a Venn diagram.	**Why learn this?** You can compare one group of numbers with another group of numbers, such as basketball scores.	**WORD POWER** Venn diagram

A **Venn diagram** uses circles to show relationships among different sets of things. Think about how numbers are compared in each Venn diagram.

A.

DECEMBER BASKETBALL SCORES

89, 90, 91, 94, 95, 96, 99, 101, 105, 108, 109, 110, 114, 130

DECEMBER BASKETBALL SCORES

Scores Less Than 100: 94, 89, 90, 95, 99, 96, 91

Scores Greater Than 100: 109, 105, 114, 108, 110, 101, 130

B.

JANUARY BASKETBALL SCORES

82, 89, 92, 93, 94, 101, 105, 106, 107, 109, 111, 112, 114, 122

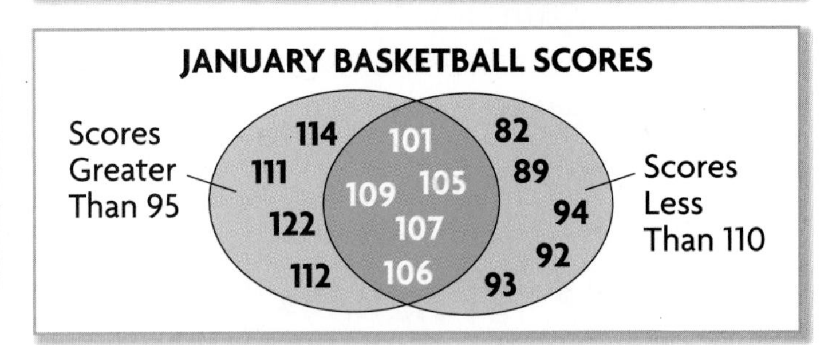

C.

FEBRUARY BASKETBALL SCORES

79, 84, 92, 93, 94, 97, 99, 104, 105, 109, 113, 115, 121

Talk About It

- Why don't the two circles in Example A overlap?
- In Example B, how are the numbers in the middle part of the diagram alike?
- In Example C, why is *Scores Less Than 100* inside *Scores Less Than 125*?
- Where would you place the number 103 in each example above?

PRACTICE

Copy the Venn diagrams. Place the numbers where they belong.

1.

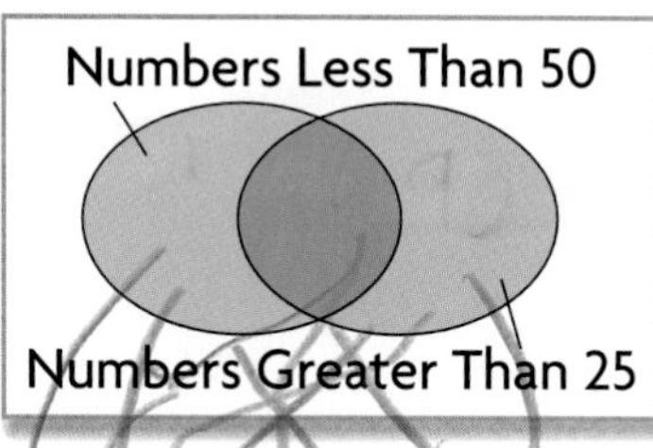

16, 5, 90, 21, 38, 26, 67, 49, 54

2.

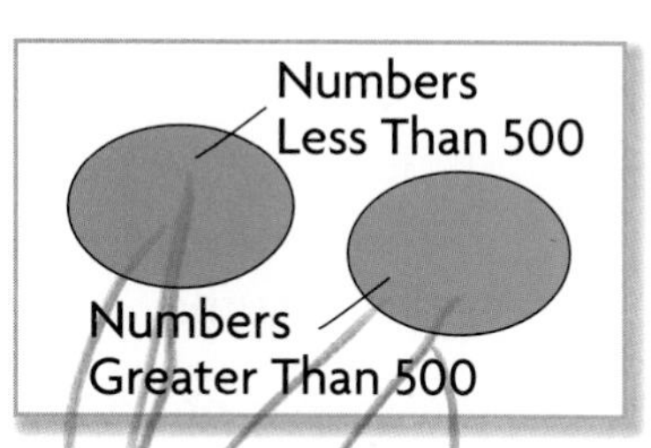

149, 501, 999, 67, 499, 750

3.

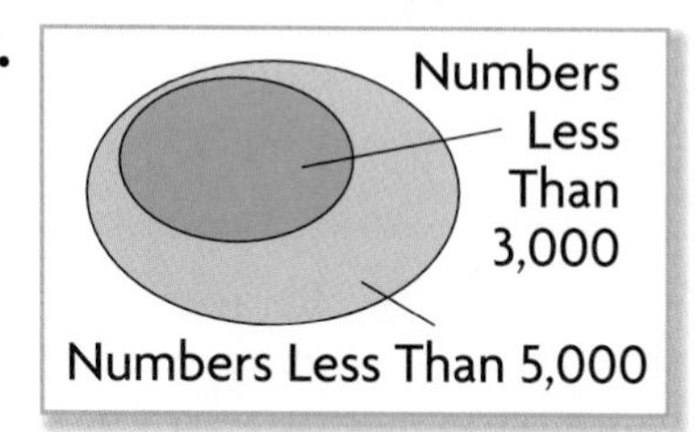

4,975; 2,816; 1,750; 3,146; 2,165

4. Draw a Venn diagram for *Numbers Greater Than 1,000* and *Numbers Less Than 2,000.* Include 1,500; 975; 3,000; 2,050; 525; and 1,950.

5. Make and label a Venn diagram comparing these numbers: 150, 600, 475, 505, 370, and 765.

Mixed Applications

For Problems 6–8, use the Venn diagram.

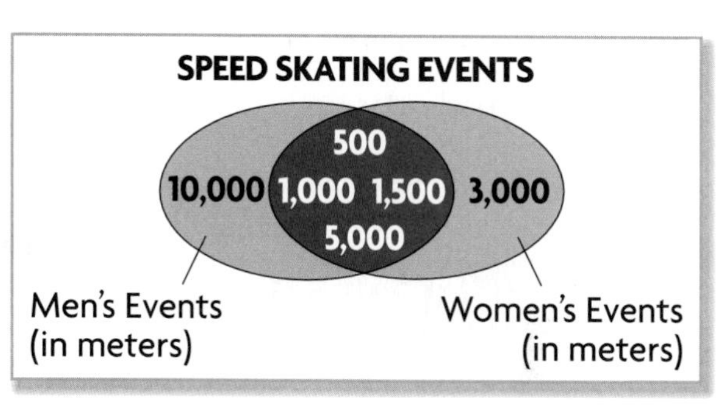

6. Do men, women, or both skate in the 5,000-meter race? Do men, women, or both skate in the 3,000-meter race?

7. Which races are the same for both men and women speed skaters?

8. In which race do only men skate?

9. Charlotte practices ice skating 3 days a week for 3 hours each day. She practices 2 days a week for 2 hours each day. How many hours does she practice in 4 weeks?

10. **WRITE ABOUT IT** Explain how using a Venn diagram to sort and compare numbers is different from using a number line to compare numbers.

Mixed Review

Find the sum or difference. (pages 12–13)

11. $7.56 + 2.14

12. $9.53 − 6.47

13. $14.08 + 15.92

14. $24.67 − 8.59

15. $32.06 + 67.95

Tell whether each number is *cardinal*, *ordinal*, or *nominal*. (pages 72–73)

16. third

17. 8:30 A.M.

18. 1,250

19. (904) 555-1050

MATH FUN!

STICK TOSS

PURPOSE To add numbers and compare sums

YOU WILL NEED 4 flat sticks, markers, paper and pencil

Make a set of sticks by copying the designs. Play with a group of four. Each player in turn "tosses" the sticks by holding them loosely, hitting the bottoms with the flat of the hand, and dropping the sticks. Here is how you earn points:

- all patterned sides down = 10 points
- all patterned sides up = 50 points
- three patterned sides up = 30 points
- two patterned sides up = 20 points
- one patterned side up = 15 points

Take turns. The first to reach 100 points wins.

THE NUMBER GAME

PURPOSE To compare numbers

YOU WILL NEED index cards numbered 1,001–1,020

Play this game with a partner. Deal ten cards face down to your partner and ten to yourself. Each of you turns over your top card at the same time. The person whose card shows the greater number wins both cards. Continue playing until you have played all ten cards. The person with more cards wins the game.

Make your own set of cards and play this game at home.

Spin a Number

PURPOSE To compare numbers

YOU WILL NEED 0–9 spinner, place-value chart

Work with a small group. Decide whether you will try for the least or greatest number. Each player spins a digit and all players place that digit in any box on their place-value charts. Then the next player spins. When four digits are placed, compare numbers to find who wins the point. The first player to earn 5 points is the winner.

CHAPTER 7 REVIEW

✓ CHECK UNDERSTANDING

1. **VOCABULARY** A __?__ uses circles to show relationships among different sets of things. (page 114)

Use the number line to compare. Write < or >. (pages 104–105)

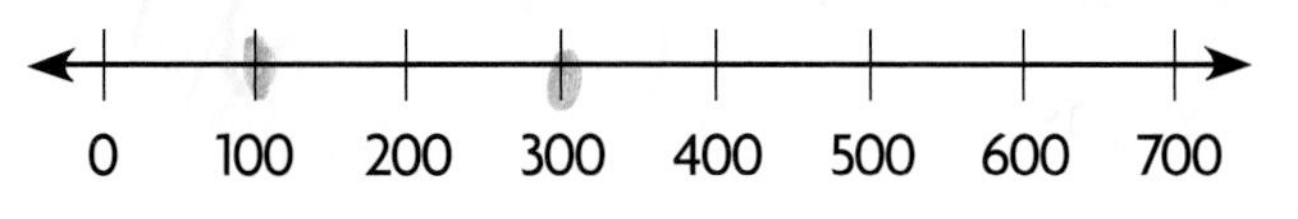

1,000 2,000 3,000 4,000 5,000 6,000 7,000

2. 300 ● 100

3. 4,000 ● 5,000

✓ CHECK SKILLS

Compare the numbers. Write the greatest place-value position in which the numbers are different. (pages 104–107)

4. 19, 12
5. 60, 90
6. 400, 700
7. 8,002; 7,992

Write the numbers in order from the least to the greatest. (pages 110–113)

8. 4,783; 3,783; 5,783
9. 6,291; 6,251; 6,215
10. 9,024; 9,022; 9,029

✓ CHECK PROBLEM SOLVING

Solve. (pages 108–109)

CHOOSE A STRATEGY

- Make a Model
- Guess and Check
- Act It Out
- Use a Table
- Work Backward

11. Jorge has 25 quarters in 2 banks. One bank has 5 more quarters than the other bank. How many quarters are in each bank?

12. A picture postcard costs 25¢. A plain postcard costs 15¢. Abby spent 95¢ on postcards. How many of each kind did she buy?

13. Complete the Venn diagram. Show that in Lisa's class 5 students have brown hair and blue eyes. Show that 13 students have brown hair but not blue eyes. Show that 7 students have blue eyes but not brown hair.

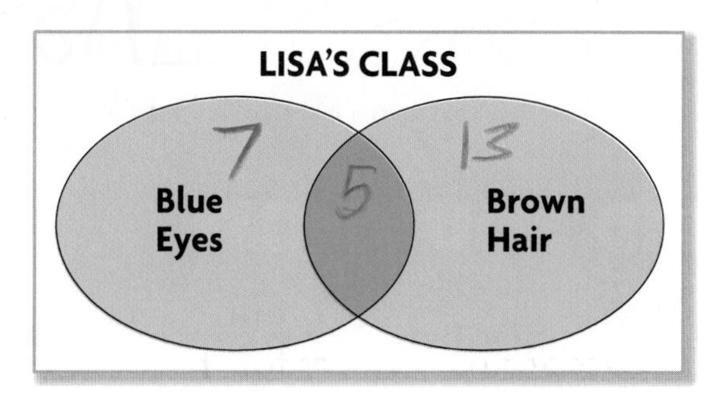

UNDERSTANDING TIME

DID YOU KNOW . . .

Sharks are fish. They are cold-blooded, have fins, live in the water, and breathe with gills. Sharks feed on a variety of fish.

Our Day at the Aquarium

Your class is visiting the aquarium. You will be there from 10:00 A.M. to 1:45 P.M. Using the schedule, plan your day at the aquarium. Allow at least 15 minutes for each exhibit. Be sure to include lunch!

Work with a group. Your job is to

- determine how many activities you will do at the aquarium.
- determine how much time you will spend on each activity.
- choose your order of events so that you will not have to retrace your steps.

Make a poster that shows when you will visit each area of the aquarium, including the special feedings and the movie. Decorate it with pictures of sea life.

AQUARIUM SCHEDULE

Today:

Sea otter feedings
(15-minute activity):
10:30 A.M.
1:30 P.M.

Kelp forest demonstration
(15-minute activity):
11:30 A.M.

Movie about MUBARI, a remote-controlled submarine
(20-minute activity):
10:30 A.M.
11:00 A.M.
11:30 A.M.
12:00 noon
12:30 P.M.
1:00 P.M.
1:30 P.M.

Every day:

The Touch Pools
Poisonous Tropical Sea Life
Jelly Fish
Kelp Lab
Habitat Exhibits: Outer Bay, Shoreline, and Reef

DID YOU

- ✓ plan your time at the aquarium and show your plan on a poster?
- ✓ decorate your work with sea-life pictures?

Telling Time

You will learn to tell time to the minute and second and give the most reasonable units of time for activities.	**Why learn this?** You can tell time so you can plan on being at a certain place at a specific time.

Aaron is going to take a bus to the aquarium. The bus leaves at 2:00. The time right now is shown on the clock at the right. Has Aaron missed the bus?

The time on the clock is 1:53, or 7 minutes before 2:00. So, Aaron has not missed the bus to the aquarium.

Digital clocks show hours and minutes. Some digital clocks also show seconds. Analog clocks show hours, minutes, and seconds.

A.

digital clock

This display shows 30 minutes past five.

B.

analog clock

The minute hand moves 1 tick when the second hand has moved once around the clock.

The hour hand moves from one number to the next while the minute hand moves once around the clock.

This display shows 30 minutes and 40 seconds past five, or 5:30 and 40 seconds.

You can use what you know about units of time to estimate how long a given activity will last.

Units of Time		
60 seconds (sec)	=	1 minute (min)
60 minutes	=	1 hour (hr)
24 hours	=	1 day

Talk About It

- How can you measure a second? a minute?
- How many seconds are in a minute? minutes are in an hour?
- What can you do in about 1 second? in about 1 minute? in about 1 hour?

Science Link

The Great Barrier Reef is a coral reef that stretches around Australia's coast for 1,240 miles. Part of this coral reef lives at The Great Barrier Reef Aquarium. If you arrived at 12:00 and left 5 hours later, what time would it be?

About how long does it take to run 1 mile?

PRACTICE

Write the letter of the unit used to measure the time. Use each answer only once.

a. days
b. hours
c. minutes
d. seconds

1. to blink your eyes

2. from sunrise to sunset

3. to run one mile

4. to complete a project for the math fair

Write the time shown on the clock. Include seconds.

5. 

6. 

7. 

8. 

Write the time as shown on a digital clock.

9. 6 minutes past one **10.** 40 minutes past eleven **11.** 28 minutes past seven

Mixed Applications

12. Bart spends about 7 hours each day at school. He goes to school 5 days each week. About how many hours does Bart spend at school in 1 week?

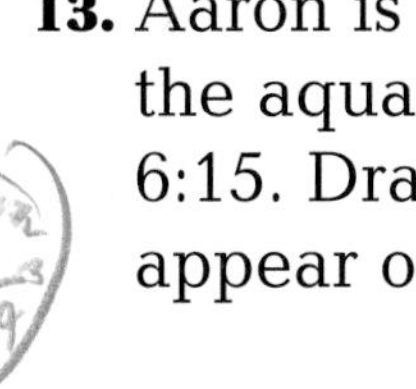

13. Aaron is taking a bus home from the aquarium. The bus leaves at 6:15. Draw the time as it would appear on an analog clock.

14. Cheryl spends 2 hours doing chores and eating meals. She wants to visit friends for 5 hours, shop for 7 hours, and sleep for 10 hours. Will Cheryl be able to do everything in one day? Explain.

15. **Write a problem** in which you need to estimate how long an activity will last.

Mixed Review

Compare the numbers and write < or > for the ●. (pages 104–105)

16. 300 ● 30 **17.** 5,000 ● 6,000 **18.** 890 ● 900 **19.** 1,200 ● 1,020

Find the quotient. (pages 58–59)

20. $81 \div 9 = \underline{?}$ **21.** $42 \div 7 = \underline{?}$ **22.** $56 \div 8 = \underline{?}$ **23.** $48 \div 8 = \underline{?}$

A.M. and P.M.

You will learn the difference between A.M. hours and P.M. hours.	**Why learn this?** You can tell from the written time whether an event is in the morning or evening.	**WORD POWER** A.M. P.M. 24-hour clock

Renee has a dance recital at 7:00 P.M. How do you know if her recital is in the morning or evening?

The hour hand on a clock goes around twice each day to measure 24 hours. **A.M.** means "before noon." The hours from midnight to noon are A.M. hours. **P.M.** means "after noon." The hours from noon to midnight are P.M. hours.

Dance Recital
7:00
Tonight

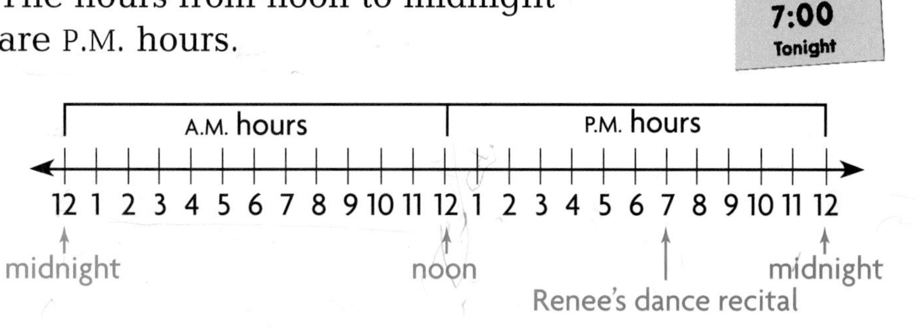

So, Renee's dance recital is at 7:00 in the evening.

Talk About It

- What are some things you do during the A.M. hours? the P.M. hours?
- Which is easier to understand when you mean 12:00 in the daytime: 12:00 P.M. or noon? Why?

Another way you can record time is to use a 24-hour clock. On a **24-hour clock**, the A.M. hours are from 2400 to 1200, and the P.M. hours are from 1200 to 2400.

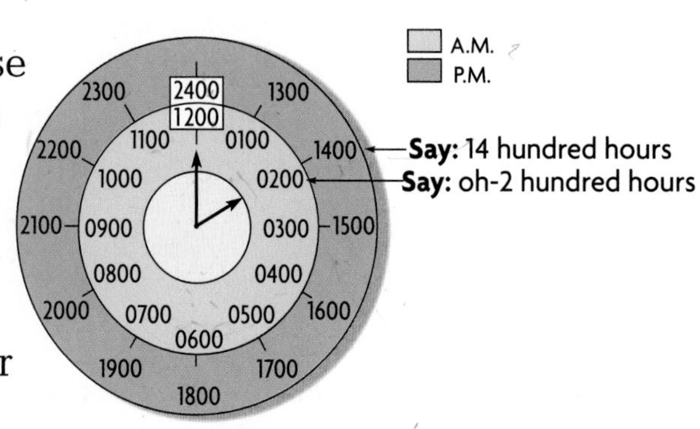

Notice that

➪ A.M. or P.M. is not used with a 24-hour clock.

CRITICAL THINKING What time is the same as 6:00 P.M. on a 24-hour clock? How do you say the time?

PRACTICE

Write the time, using A.M. or P.M.

1. when you eat dinner
2. when school starts
3. when the sun rises
4. when you go to bed
5. when the mall opens
6. when the school day ends

Write the time as shown on a 24-hour clock.

7. 7:00 A.M.
8. 3:00 P.M.
9. 11:00 A.M.
10. midnight
11. 10:00 P.M.
12. 3:00 A.M.
13. 4:00 P.M.
14. 9:00 A.M.
15. 7:00 P.M.
16. 2:00 P.M.

Write the time as shown on a 12-hour clock. Use A.M. or P.M.

17. 0100
18. 0600
19. 1700
20. 1300
21. 2300
22. 0400
23. 2100
24. 1800
25. 1000
26. 2000

Mixed Applications

27. Jason's hockey game starts at 1:00 P.M. Bradley's hockey game starts at 1400 hours. Whose game starts earlier? Write the starting time of Bradley's hockey game using A.M. or P.M.

28. Lauren jogged for 24 minutes. Then, she walked for 38 minutes. Did her jogging and walking take more than or less than 1 hour?

29. On Saturday, Ashley went to the library at 3:00 P.M. She went to the store at 10:00 A.M. and to her friend's house at noon. List the activities in the order in which Ashley did them.

30. **Write a problem** about a given amount of time you spend doing different activities during the week.

Mixed Review

Write the numbers in order from the greatest to the least. (pages 112–113)

31. 465; 456; 564
32. 897; 987; 789
33. 1,280; 1,285; 1,295

Write a related multiplication fact. (pages 52–53)

34. $24 \div 6 = 4$
35. $18 \div 3 = 6$
36. $36 \div 4 = 9$
37. $40 \div 5 = 8$

Elapsed Time on a Clock

You will investigate using an analog clock to measure elapsed time.

Why learn this? You can calculate how long an activity has lasted or when it will end.

WORD POWER
elapsed time

Elapsed time is the time that passes from the start of an activity to the end of that activity. Use a model of a clock to find elapsed time.

Find the elapsed time from 1:00 P.M. to 1:30 P.M.

Show the starting time on an analog clock.

As you move the minute hand around the clock to the ending time, count the minutes.

Notice that

- the hands move clockwise, or around the clock to the right.

So, the elapsed time from 1:00 P.M. to 1:30 P.M. is 30 minutes.

Explore

MATERIALS: analog clock

Hank is taking guitar lessons. His lesson begins at 4:15 P.M. and ends at 5:00 P.M. What is the elapsed time from the beginning to the end of Hank's guitar lesson?

Record

Draw pictures of analog clocks that show when Hank's guitar lesson begins and ends. Write the elapsed time.

E-Lab • Activity 8 Available on CD-ROM and the Internet at http://www.hbschool.com/elab

TALK ABOUT IT What if Hank's guitar lesson lasted 75 minutes? At what time would the lesson end?

Now, investigate finding the elapsed time of an activity that starts before noon and ends after noon.

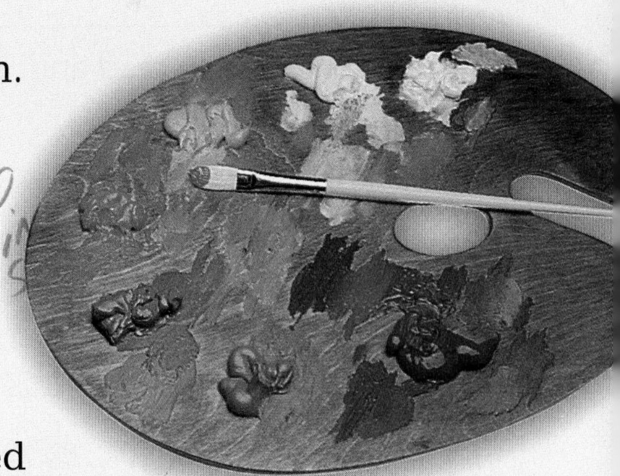

Try This

Veronica is taking art lessons. Each lesson begins at 11:45 A.M. and ends at 1:15 P.M. What is the elapsed time from the beginning to the end of her lesson?

WRITE ABOUT IT What if Veronica's lesson lasted 2 hours and 30 minutes? At what time would it end? Explain how you found your answer.

HANDS-ON PRACTICE

Use an analog clock to find the elapsed time.

1. **start:** 9:30 A.M.
   end: 4:50 P.M.
2. **start:** 11:10 A.M.
   end: 2:45 P.M.
3. **start:** 5:20 A.M.
   end: 9:05 A.M.
4. **start:** 3:15 P.M.
   end: 8:25 P.M.
5. **start:** 10:50 P.M
   end: 1:55 A.M.
6. **start:** 7:45 P.M.
   end: 1:10 A.M.

Applying What You Learned

Write the ending time.

7. **starting time:** 7:45 A.M.
   elapsed time: 4 hr 10 min
8. **starting time:** 10:45 A.M.
   elapsed time: 3 hr 25 min
9. **starting time:** 12:30 P.M.
   elapsed time: 2 hr 35 min
10. **starting time:** 6:20 P.M.
    elapsed time: 6 hr 45 min

Copy and complete the table.

	Start Time	End Time	Elapsed Time
11.	3:15 A.M.	?	50 min
12.	7:35 A.M.	5:20 P.M.	?

Mixed Applications

13. Kayla earns $6 per hour at her job. If she works 4 hours each day, how much does she earn in 2 days?

14. Mark's family drove 55 miles in 1 hour. If they continue at the same speed, how far can they travel in 3 hours?

MORE PRACTICE Student Handbook pages H80–H81

PART

1 Using a Schedule

You will learn to read and understand a schedule.

Why learn this? You can make plans based on a schedule of events, such as a listing of movie times.

The Children's Center is having Arts and Crafts Day. Each class lasts 1 hour and 45 minutes. At what time does each class end?

ARTS AND CRAFTS DAY	
Class	Starting Time
Bead Making	9:00 A.M.
Friendship Bracelets	11:10 A.M.
Tie-Dye	1:20 P.M.
Leather Crafts	3:30 P.M.

To find the time that each class ends, add 1 hour and 45 minutes to each starting time.

So, the classes end at 10:45 A.M., 12:55 P.M., 3:05 P.M., and 5:15 P.M.

It takes about 50 minutes to travel by train from Baltimore, MD, to Philadelphia, PA, and 50 minutes to travel from Philadelphia to Newark, NJ. If a train leaves Baltimore at 11:36 A.M., when will it arrive in Newark?

Talk About It

- If Rosa and Billy can stay from 10:00 A.M. to 4:30 P.M., which classes can they take?
- Why are there some classes Rosa and Billy can't take?

Check Your Understanding

Read the schedule and answer the questions. Each movie lasts about 90 minutes.

1. At about what time does each movie end?
2. Can you see all the movies in one day? Why or why not?
3. What is the elapsed time from the beginning of *Black Beauty* to the end of *Old Yeller*?

MOVIE SCHEDULE	
Title	Time
Black Beauty	1:05 P.M.
Charlotte's Web	2:55 P.M.
Bambi	4:30 P.M.
Old Yeller	5:25 P.M.

PRACTICE

For Problems 4–9, use the schedules.

CULTURAL DAY	
Activity	**Starting Time**
Costume Parade	10:00 A.M.
Food Tasting	11:15 A.M.
Drama Production	12:30 P.M.
Music and Dancing	1:30 P.M.

4. If each activity lasts 45 minutes, at what time will each one end?

5. If Alexis can stay for only 3 hours and she wants to be there for three complete activities, at what time should she arrive?

6. What is the elapsed time from the beginning of the costume parade to the end of music and dancing? ________

FLIGHTS FROM MIAMI TO NEW YORK CITY	
Each flight lasts about 2 hours and 45 minutes.	
Airline	**Departure Time**
Airline A	9:10 A.M.
Airline B	10:15 A.M.
Airline C	12:50 P.M.
Airline D	1:20 P.M.

7. At about what time does each flight arrive in New York City?

8. Will Airline B arrive in New York City before or after Airline C leaves Miami?

9. If Ms. Lane needs to be in New York City for a 3:30 P.M. meeting, on which airlines can she fly?

Mixed Applications

10. If the sun rises at 6:45 A.M. and sets the same day at 8:20 P.M., how long is there daylight on that day?

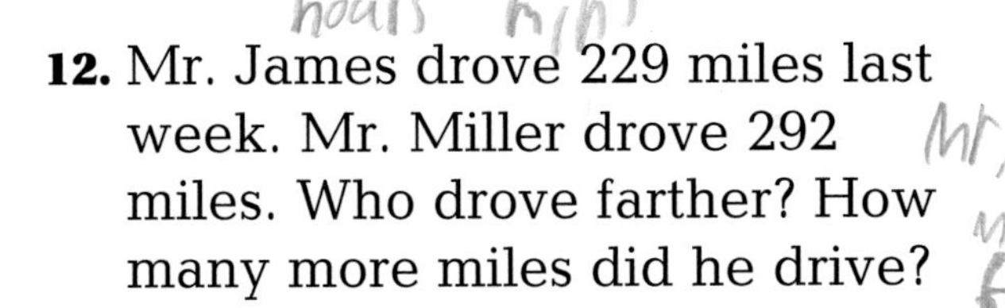

11. The cost for one ticket on a flight that leaves in the morning is $149. The cost for a ticket on a flight that leaves in the afternoon is $175. How much money can you save by leaving in the morning?

12. Mr. James drove 229 miles last week. Mr. Miller drove 292 miles. Who drove farther? How many more miles did he drive?

13. Enid has 1,000 stickers. She has 100 stickers in each book. How many books does she have?

14. Horace and his family left on Sunday for a trip to visit some friends. They returned 12 days later. On what day of the week did they return?

15. **WRITE ABOUT IT** Make a schedule of your daily routine. List the time you start and end each activity.

LESSON CONTINUES

PART 2 PROBLEM-SOLVING STRATEGY Make a Table

THE PROBLEM Kirk's school is having Team Sports Day. Each game will last about 1 hour and 30 minutes. Kirk's bus leaves for home at 3:00 P.M. It takes 15 minutes to clean up and get on the bus. Which game does Kirk have time to play?

TEAM SPORTS DAY	
Game	**Time**
Basketball	1:15 P.M.
Soccer	1:30 P.M.
Street Hockey	1:45 P.M.

✓ Understand

- What are you asked to find?
- What information will you use?
- Is there any information you will not use? If so, what?

✓ Plan

- What strategy can you use to solve the problem?

  You can *make a table* to show the time each game will end, and the time Kirk can get on the bus.

✓ Solve

- How can you use the strategy to solve the problem?

  Make a table. Add 1 hour and 30 minutes to each start time to find the end time. Add 15 minutes to each end time to find when Kirk can get on the bus.

So, Kirk has time to play basketball and be on the bus by 3:00 P.M.

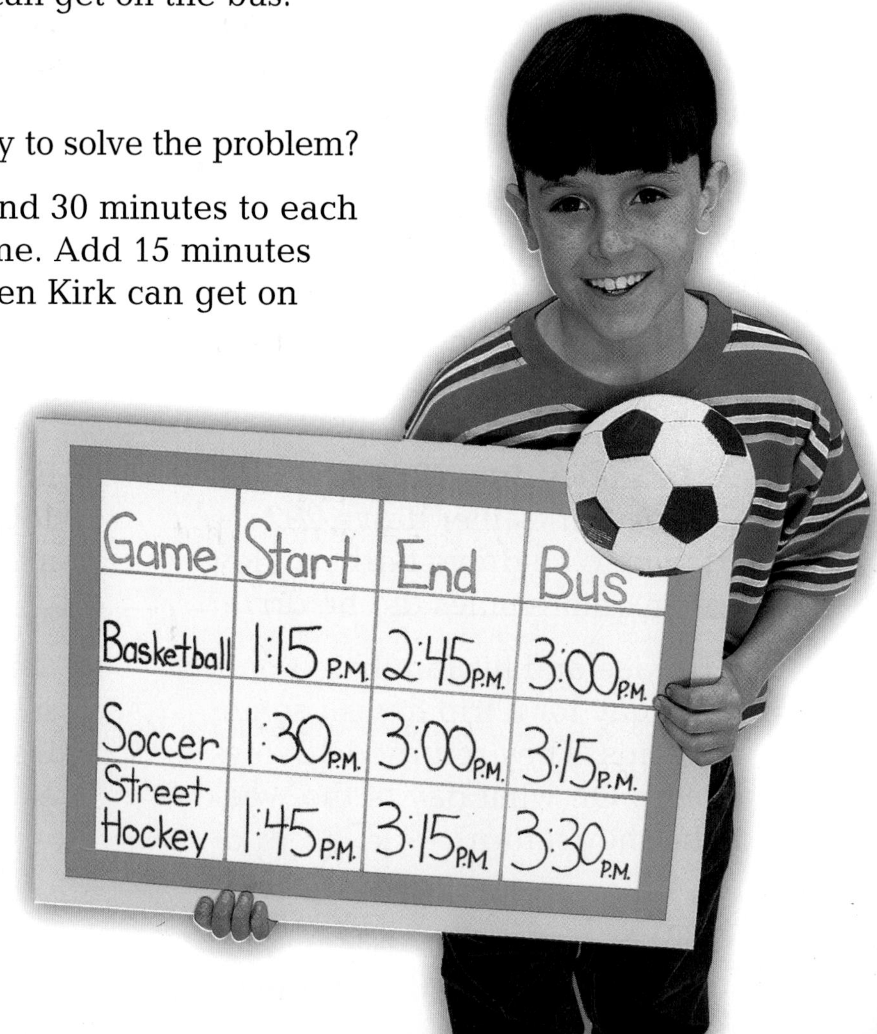

✓ Look Back

- How can you determine if your answer is reasonable?
- What other strategy could you use?

PRACTICE

CHOOSE Paper/Pencil Calculator Hands-on Mental Math

Make a table to solve.

1. Suppose Kirk's Team Sports Day schedule is wrong. Basketball starts at 1:30 P.M., soccer at 1:45 P.M., and street hockey at 2:00 P.M. Which games does Kirk have time to play? Explain.

2. Glenn takes dance lessons on Mondays at 5:15, on Wednesdays at 5:45, and on Fridays at 4:30. Each lesson lasts 1 hour 15 minutes. At what time does each lesson end?

3. Use the soccer schedule. Practice lasts 2 hours and 30 minutes on Mondays and Wednesdays, and 2 hours on Fridays. At what time does practice end each day?

STARS SOCCER PRACTICE SCHEDULE

Day	Start Time
Monday	3:15 P.M.
Wednesday	2:30 P.M.
Friday	3:15 P.M.

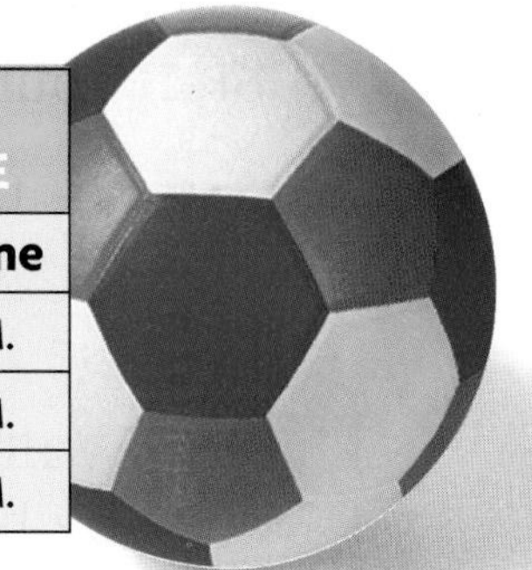

Mixed Applications

Solve.

CHOOSE A STRATEGY

- Work Backward
- Guess and Check
- Act It Out
- Use a Table
- Make a Table

4. Three friends went out for lunch. Each friend paid $4.15 for the food bill and tip. If the tip was $2.00, how much was the bill?

5. The first act in a play was twice as long as the second act. If the play was 2 hours long, how long was each act?

6. Gwen arrived home at 10:15 P.M. She had been at a play for 2 hours and 45 minutes. Before the play, she spent 45 minutes getting ready to go out. At what time did Gwen start getting ready to go out?

7. Dante has karate class Tuesday at 7:30, Thursday at 6:45, and Saturday at 9:15. His Tuesday and Thursday classes last 45 minutes. His Saturday class lasts 1 hour 15 minutes. At what time does each class end?

8. The stage in the theater is 25 feet long and 16 feet wide. What is the perimeter of the stage?

9. Ms. Ortiz has 24 students in her class. They sit in 4 equal rows. How many sit in each row?

10. How many more centimeters did Kerry's plant grow between Weeks 3 and 4 than between Weeks 1 and 2?

PLANT GROWTH

Week	Height
1	3 cm
2	6 cm
3	13 cm
4	22 cm

MORE PRACTICE Student Handbook page H81

Elapsed Time on a Calendar

You will learn to use a calendar to find elapsed time in days and months.

Why learn this? You can tell elapsed times of activities that are longer than minutes or hours.

The Walls are taking a trip. They will leave on August 4 and return on August 12. How many days will they be gone?

To find the elapsed time, count the number of days. Start counting with August 5.

So, the Walls' trip will last for 8 days.

AUGUST

Sun	Mon	Tue	Wed	Thu	Fri	Sat
			1	2	3	4
5	6	7	8	9	10	11
12	13	14	15	16	17	18
19	20	21	22	23	24	25
26	27	28	29	30	31	

Units of Time		
7 days	=	1 week (wk)
12 months (mo)	=	1 year (yr)
about 52 weeks	=	1 year
365 days	=	1 year
366 days	=	1 leap year

Talk About It

- Will the Walls' trip be more than or less than 1 week? by how many days?
- If the Walls went on a trip for 15 days, on what date would they return?

Check Your Understanding

CRITICAL THINKING

For Problems 1–4, use the calendars.

FEBRUARY

Sun	Mon	Tue	Wed	Thu	Fri	Sat
	1	2	3	4	5	6
7	8	9	10	11	12	13
14	15	16	17	18	19	20
21	22	23	24	25	26	27
28						

MARCH

Sun	Mon	Tue	Wed	Thu	Fri	Sat
	1	2	3	4	5	6
7	8	9	10	11	12	13
14	15	16	17	18	19	20
21	22	23	24	25	26	27
28	29	30	31			

APRIL

Sun	Mon	Tue	Wed	Thu	Fri	Sat
				1	2	3
4	5	6	7	8	9	10
11	12	13	14	15	16	17
18	19	20	21	22	23	24
25	26	27	28	29	30	

MAY

Sun	Mon	Tue	Wed	Thu	Fri	Sat
						1
2	3	4	5	6	7	8
9	10	11	12	13	14	15
16	17	18	19	20	21	22
23/30	24/31	25	26	27	28	29

JUNE

Sun	Mon	Tue	Wed	Thu	Fri	Sat
		1	2	3	4	5
6	7	8	9	10	11	12
13	14	15	16	17	18	19
20	21	22	23	24	25	26
27	28	29	30			

JULY

Sun	Mon	Tue	Wed	Thu	Fri	Sat
				1	2	3
4	5	6	7	8	9	10
11	12	13	14	15	16	17
18	19	20	21	22	23	24
25	26	27	28	29	30	31

1. Report cards were sent home on March 12. They will be sent home again in 9 weeks. On what date will report cards be sent home again?

2. In a leap year, February has 29 days instead of 28. How long is it from February 24 to March 4 in a regular year? in a leap year?

3. How many days are there from the last day of March to the last day of April? from the last day of June to the last day of July?

4. Rob went to the dentist on April 9. He will make his next visit 3 months after April 9. What will be the date of Rob's next visit?

Dr. Henry S. Moore, D.D.S.
An appointment for Rob
has been scheduled on April 9
at 4:00 A.M. P.M.
Please call 24 hours in advance for cancellations

PRACTICE

For Problems 5–10, use the calendars.

AUGUST

Sun	Mon	Tue	Wed	Thu	Fri	Sat
	1	2	3	4	5	6
7	8	9	10	11	12	13
14	15	16	17	18	19	20
21	22	23	24	25	26	27
28	29	30	31			

SEPTEMBER

Sun	Mon	Tue	Wed	Thu	Fri	Sat
				1	2	3
4	5	6	7	8	9	10
11	12	13	14	15	16	17
18	19	20	21	22	23	24
25	26	27	28	29	30	

OCTOBER

Sun	Mon	Tue	Wed	Thu	Fri	Sat
						1
2	3	4	5	6	7	8
9	10	11	12	13	14	15
16	17	18	19	20	21	22
23/30	24/31	25	26	27	28	29

5. About how many weeks will the exhibit last?

6. How many days is it from September 30 to the last day of the exhibit?

7. Pam bought a ticket 3 weeks before the first day of the exhibit. On what date did Pam buy her ticket?

8. Hunter bought a ticket 5 weeks before the last day of the exhibit. On what date did Hunter buy his ticket?

9. The exhibit began advertising 3 months before it came to town. In what month did it begin advertising?

10. It will take 5 days to clean up after the exhibit leaves town. What is the last date the cleanup crew will work?

Mixed Applications

11. What number can you add to 45,627 to get the sum of 47,627?

12. There are 26 seats on one bus. How many seats are on 2 buses?

13. Samantha's birthday is 4 months from June 21. Ricky's birthday is 6 days before Samantha's. When are their birthdays?

14. **WRITE ABOUT IT** Explain how to find the date that is 10 days after October 6 and the date 2 weeks after that. What are the two dates?

Mixed Review

Write the greatest place-value position in which the digits differ. Write the greater number. (pages 106–107)

15. 843; 893 **16.** 347; 345 **17.** 1,260; 1,160 **18.** 7,391; 5,739

Round $28.46 to each given amount. (pages 10–11)

19. ten cents **20.** dollar **21.** ten dollars

MORE PRACTICE Student Handbook page H81

CULTURAL CONNECTION

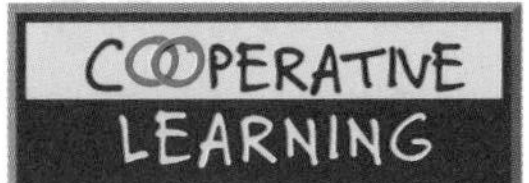

An Early Timepiece

Tony's class is learning about Washington, D.C. They learned that Benjamin Banneker, an African American, helped survey the site on the Potomac River that became our nation's capital. Benjamin Banneker also made significant achievements as an astronomer, mathematician, surveyor, and inventor. Tony read that Banneker lived from 1731 to 1806. How many years did Banneker live?

Subtract his birth year from the year of his death.

So, he lived to be 75 years old.

CULTURAL LINK

In early America an almanac provided a yearly calendar. Since most people did not own clocks, almanacs were their only way to predict important seasonal changes. Almanacs provided farmers with weather forecasts, a calendar of the moon's phases, and tables indicating planting and harvesting dates.

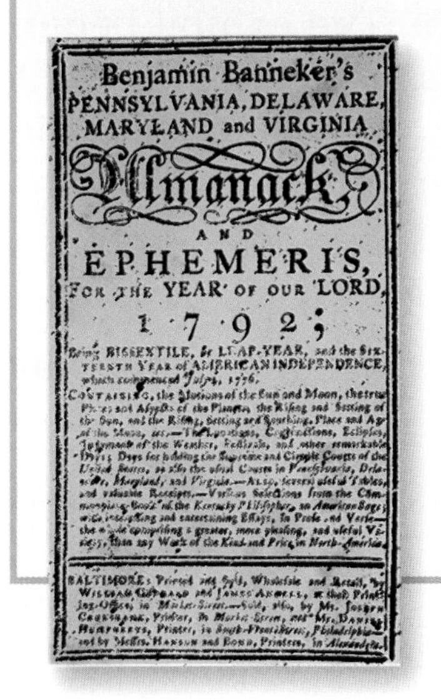
Benjamin Banneker's
PENNSYLVANIA, DELAWARE,
MARYLAND and VIRGINIA
Almanack,
AND
EPHEMERIS,
FOR THE YEAR OF OUR LORD,
1792;

Work Together

1. About 1761, Banneker invented a clock to chime every hour. The clock kept time for 50 years. What year did it stop running? If it chimed once an hour, how many times did it chime in one day?

2. If Benjamin Banneker worked on his farm duties for 11 hours a day, read astronomy books for 2 hours, and watched the night skies for 5 hours, how many hours could he sleep? If he started at 6 A.M. show his schedule for the day. Draw analog clocks to show when each task began and ended.

3. Banneker's first almanac was published in 1791. It predicted sunrise at 4:38 A.M. and sunset at 7:22 P.M. on June 21, 1792. How do these times differ from sunrise and sunset on June 1, predicted for 4:43 A.M. and 7:17 P.M.?

4. **Write a problem** using the information from the table showing the times for sunrise and sunset for the first week of June 1792.

Date	Sunrise	Sunset
June 1	4:43 A.M.	7:17 P.M.
June 2	4:42 A.M.	7:18 P.M.
June 3	4:42 A.M.	7:18 P.M.
June 4	4:41 A.M.	7:19 P.M.
June 5	4:41 A.M.	7:19 P.M.
June 6	4:41 A.M.	7:19 P.M.
June 7	4:40 A.M.	7:20 P.M.

CHAPTER 8 REVIEW

✓ CHECK UNDERSTANDING

VOCABULARY

1. _?_ means the hours from noon to midnight, and _?_ means the hours from midnight to noon. (page 122)
2. On a _?_, the P.M. hours are from 1200 to 2400. (page 122)
3. _?_ is the time that passes from the start to the end of an activity. (page 124)

Write the time, using A.M. or P.M. (pages 122–123)

4. when you eat lunch
5. when you wake up
6. when you take a shower

✓ CHECK SKILLS

Write the time shown on the clock. Include seconds. (pages 120–121)

7. 

8. 

Copy and complete the table. (pages 124–125)

	Start	End	Elapsed Time
9.	?	6:25 P.M.	2 hr 15 min
10.	11:40 A.M.	?	5 hr 40 min
11.	3:05 P.M.	6:25 P.M.	?

✓ CHECK PROBLEM SOLVING

Solve. (pages 128–129)

CHOOSE A STRATEGY

- **Work Backward**
- **Guess and Check**
- **Use a Table**
- **Make a Table**

12. Bo and his class go to the computer lab on Monday at 9:00, Wednesday at 10:15, and Thursday at 11:45. They stay for 45 minutes. When do they leave?

13. If each Family Fun Day activity ends 10 minutes before the next one, what are the elapsed times of the first five activities?

Family Fun Day Schedule	
10:00 A.M.	Parade
11:30 P.M.	Lunch
1:00 P.M.	Concert
3:15 P.M.	Games
6:30 P.M.	Dinner
9:00 P.M.	Fireworks

14. Kira came back from the school store with 91¢. She bought 2 pencils for 15¢ each and a notebook for 79¢. How much money did Kira take to the store?

CHAPTERS 5–8

STUDY GUIDE & REVIEW

VOCABULARY CHECK

Choose a term from the box to complete each sentence.

WORD BANK
A.M.
benchmark
numeration system
ordered pair
P.M.

1. An _?_ helps you locate points on a grid. (page 74)
2. A _?_ is a point of reference. (page 82)
3. A _?_ is a way of counting and naming numbers. (page 88)
4. _?_ means the hours from noon to midnight. (page 122)
5. _?_ means the hours from midnight to noon. (page 122)

STUDY AND SOLVE

CHAPTER 5

EXAMPLE

4,705 How many?

Thousands	Hundreds	Tens	Ones
4 ,	7	0	5
4,000	700	0	5
4,000 + 700 + 0 + 5 = 4,705			

Record the number of thousands, hundreds, tens, and ones. (pages 78–79)

6. 6,000
   _?_ thousands
   _?_ hundreds
   _?_ tens
   _?_ ones

7. 5,841
   _?_ thousands
   _?_ hundreds
   _?_ tens
   _?_ ones

Write the ordered pair for each point on the grid. (pages 74–75)

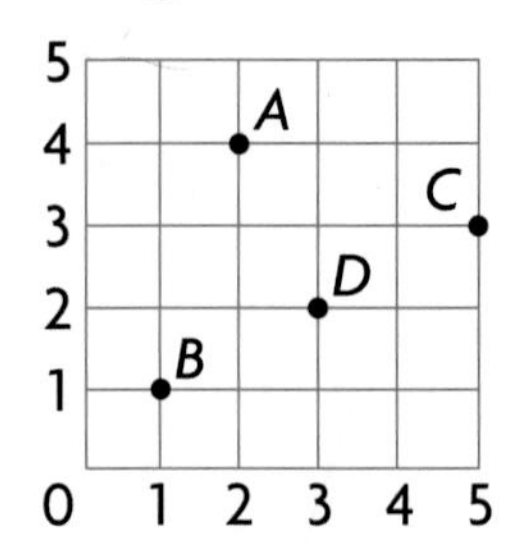

8. Point *A*
9. Point *B*
10. Point *C*
11. Point *D*

Solve. (pages 80–81)

12. In all, Jasmine has 28 baseball, basketball, and football cards. She has twice as many baseball cards as basketball cards. She has 6 basketball cards. How many football cards does she have?

CHAPTER 6

EXAMPLE

Write the number, using period names.
640,200,090

Millions			Thousands			Ones		
6	4	0 ,	2	0	0 ,	0	9	0

six hundred forty million, two hundred thousand, ninety

Write each number in expanded form. (pages 90–91)

13. 7,864
14. 1,152

Write each number in standard form. (pages 90–91)

15. two thousand, thirty

16. 4,000 + 500 + 60 + 4

Write the number as you would say it using period names. (pages 96–97)

17. 42,415,899 **18.** 500,605,000

For Problems 19–20, use the table. (pages 98–99)

MOVIE THEATER PRICES			
Year	Price	Year	Price
1950	$0.50	1980	$4.00
1960	$1.50	1990	$6.00
1970	$2.50	2000	?

19. Between which years did ticket prices increase the most?

20. How much did movie ticket prices increase between 1950 and 1990?

CHAPTER 7

EXAMPLE

To compare numbers, start with the greatest place-value position.

Compare 4,905 and 4,897.

4,905 ↓ **4,897** Compare the thousands.

4,905 ↓ **4,897** Compare the hundreds.

9 > 8. So, 4,905 > 4,897.

Compare the numbers. (pages 104–107)

21. 5,419 ● 5,421 **22.** 412 ● 408

Order the numbers from the least to the greatest. (pages 112–113)

23. 8,033; 8,031; 8,129

Solve. (pages 108–109)

24. The difference of two numbers is 400. Their sum is 1,200. What are the two numbers?

CHAPTER 8

EXAMPLE

Find the elapsed time.

start: 8:30 A.M. Count hours.
end: 3:50 P.M. Count minutes.
7 hr 20 min

Find the elapsed time. (pages 124–125)

25. start: 11:15 A.M.
end: 1:25 P.M.

Find the ending time. (pages 124–125)

26. starting time: 4:15 P.M.
elapsed time: 50 minutes

Solve. (pages 130–131)

27. Joan's birthday is 3 months before September 3. John's birthday is 3 days after Joan's. On what date is John's birthday?

CHAPTERS 5–8

WHAT DID I LEARN?

WRITE ABOUT IT

1. Put 10 counters in a group. Now take a handful of counters. Explain how you can use the group of 10 counters as a benchmark to estimate the number of counters in your handful. Estimate the number of counters in the handful. **(pages 82–83)**

Explain your method.

2. Write an 8-digit number in a place-value chart. Explain how the chart can help you
   - name the place of each digit in the number.
   - read the number with period names. **(pages 96–97)**

3. Explain how to use a number line to compare 70 and 50. Write 70 and 50 with $<$ or $>$ to compare the numbers. **(pages 104–105)**

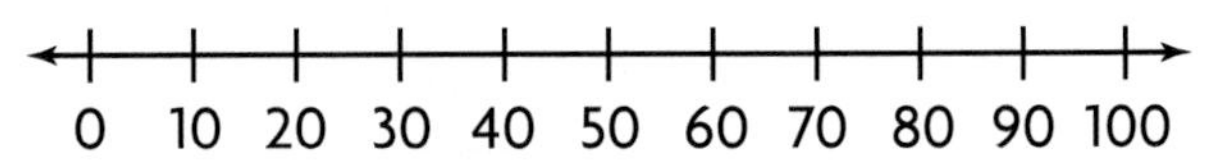

4. Look at the classroom clock. Explain how the hands on the clock are used to tell time. Give the correct time. **(pages 120–121)**

PERFORMANCE ASSESSMENT

Solve. Explain your method.

CHOOSE A STRATEGY

- **Find a Pattern** • **Guess and Check** • **Act It Out** • **Draw a Picture** • **Use a Table**
- **Make a Model** • **Write a Number Sentence**

5. Josh has 18 coins. He has 3 more nickels than dimes. Josh has 5 nickels. How many pennies, nickels, and dimes does Josh have? **(pages 80–81)**

6. Which team had the most people in all at their 2 games? **(pages 98–99)**

Game	Attendance
Lions and Hawks	15,356
Hawks and Bears	22,498
Bears and Sharks	18,107
Sharks and Lions	9,215

7. In 4 days the Boys Club cleaned 600 feet of beach front. They cleaned half as many feet each day as they had the day before. How many feet did they clean the first day? **(pages 108–109)**

8. Ann baby-sits at 6:00 P.M. She takes a computer class that begins at 3:45 P.M. and lasts 2 hours. It takes her 10 minutes to bike from class to her job. At what time will she arrive for baby-sitting? **(pages 124–125)**

CUMULATIVE REVIEW

Solve the problem. Then write the letter of the correct answer.

1. $\begin{array}{r} \$6.89 \\ +\ 2.46 \\ \hline \end{array}$

   A. \$9.36
   B. \$9.35
   C. \$8.25
   D. \$4.43

   (pages 12–13)

2. $\begin{array}{r} 5{,}000 \\ -2{,}375 \\ \hline \end{array}$

   A. 2,625
   B. 2,735
   C. 3,375
   D. 7,375

   (pages 20–21)

3. $\begin{array}{r} 7 \\ \times 1 \\ \hline \end{array}$

   A. 1 **B.** 6
   C. 7 **D.** 8

   (pages 36–37)

4. $25 \div 5 =$ __?__

   A. 5 **B.** 20
   C. 30 **D.** 125

   (pages 52–53)

5. Michael bought a shirt for \$18.95. He bought a belt for \$16.89. How much did he spend?

   A. \$2.06 **B.** \$2.14
   C. \$24.74 **D.** \$35.84

   (pages 12–13)

6. Mr. Lin wants his 27 students to form 3 equal groups. How many will be in each group?

   A. 9 students **B.** 24 students
   C. 30 students **D.** 81 students

   (pages 44–45)

7. How many tens are in 4,102?

   A. 0 tens **B.** 1 ten
   C. 2 tens **D.** 4 tens

   (pages 78–79)

8. What is five thousand, fifty-two in standard form?

   A. 552 **B.** 5,052
   C. 5,520 **D.** 500,052

   (pages 90–91)

9. Compare. 5,999 ● 6,001.

   A. $-$ **B.** $=$
   C. $<$ **D.** $>$

   (pages 106–107)

10. What is the elapsed time?
    start: 8:30 A.M.
    end: 5:00 P.M.

    A. 3 hr 15 min **B.** 7 hr 30 min
    C. 8 hr 30 min **D.** 9 hr 15 min

    (pages 124–125)

11. Elizabeth competed in a three-day board-game tournament. Each day she scored twice as many points as the day before. Her total score was 700 points. How many points did she score on the third day?

    A. 400 points **B.** 350 points
    C. 200 points **D.** 100 points

    (pages 108–109)

12. Deion went to the dentist on May 17. Around what date should he schedule his next 6-month checkup?

    A. Sep 17 **B.** Oct 17
    C. Nov 17 **D.** Dec 17

    (pages 130–131)

CHAPTER 9

UNDERSTANDING DATA

DID YOU KNOW . . .

Vitamin C is found in fruits and vegetables such as oranges, tomatoes, green peppers, and lettuce. Vitamin C helps heal cuts. It also helps our bones, mouth, and teeth.

Team-Up Time

Mixing Salads

Suppose that your school is thinking about offering a salad bar at lunchtime. Students would be able to choose any two ingredients to make their own salads. Make an attractive poster showing salad combinations.

Work with a group to make a poster for a salad bar at your school. Your job is to

- choose five salad ingredients that people in your group like.
- find out how many different salads students could make if they could choose two ingredients each day.
- make a poster to show different possible salads.

Tomatoes

Carrots

Lettuce

DID YOU

- ✓ choose five ingredients for the salad bar?
- ✓ make an attractive poster of the salad-bar choices?
- ✓ find the number of possible salads that could be made?

Day	Ingredients
Monday	lettuce, cucumbers
Tuesday	tomatoes, Carrots
Wednesday	
Thursday	
Friday	

Organizing Data in Tables

You will learn to organize and record data in tally tables and frequency tables.	**Why learn this?** You can collect and organize data about things that you want to know.	**WORD POWER** cumulative frequency

How can you find the number of students who bought orange juice in one week?

- In a tally table, tally marks (|) are used to record data.
- In a frequency table, numbers are used instead of tally marks.

TALLY TABLE	
Day	**Number of Students**
Monday	𝍸 𝍸 𝍸
Tuesday	𝍸 𝍸 III
Wednesday	𝍸
Thursday	𝍸 IIII
Friday	𝍸 𝍸 𝍸 II

FREQUENCY TABLE			
Day	**Number of Students (Frequency)**	**Total Number of Students (Cumulative Frequency)**	
Monday	15	15	
Tuesday	13	28	←15 + 13 = 28
Wednesday	5	33	←28 + 5 = 33
Thursday	9	42	←33 + 9 = 42
Friday	17	59	←42 + 17 = 59

Notice that

➪ in this frequency table, there are two columns of numbers.

➪ the numbers in the **cumulative frequency** column show the sum as each new line of data is entered.

A *frequency table* uses numbers to show how often something happens.

Example

Class	Students
Jones	25
Lee	27
Phillips	22

Talk About It

- Which table would you use to find the number who bought orange juice on Thursday? Explain your choice.
- Why are the numbers different in the frequency and cumulative frequency columns?
- Is it easier to find the number who bought orange juice in one week by using the frequency column or the cumulative frequency column? Explain.

PRACTICE

For Problems 1–8, use the frequency table.

ALUMINUM CANS COLLECTED		
Week	Number of Cans	Cumulative Frequency
1	16	16
2	20	36
3	12	48
4	9	57

1. How many cans were collected in Week 1?

2. How many cans were collected in Week 3?

3. By the end of Week 2, how many cans had been collected?

4. How many more cans were collected in Week 2 than in Week 1?

5. By the end of Week 3, how many cans had been collected?

6. How many cans in all were collected in Weeks 2 and 3?

7. How many cans in all were collected in Weeks 3 and 4?

8. How many cans were collected in all four weeks?

Mixed Applications

For Problems 9–11, use the frequency table.

Student Involvement in Community Project	
Class	Number of Students
Mr. Williams	6
Ms. Jones	5
Mr. Newton	8
Mr. Warren	4

9. How many students in Mr. Newton's class are involved in the project?

10. How many students in all are involved in the project?

11. **Write a problem** that can be answered by using the data in the frequency table.

Mixed Review

Record the number of thousands, hundreds, tens, and ones. (pages 78–79)

12. 4,261 **13.** 5,185 **14.** 7,490

15. 3,672 **16.** 1,804 **17.** 8,005

Show two ways to group Exercises 18–23 using parentheses. Find the products. (pages 40–41)

18. $4 \times 1 \times 2 = \underline{?}$ **19.** $2 \times 1 \times 7 = \underline{?}$

20. $4 \times 2 \times 2 = \underline{?}$ **21.** $8 \times 1 \times 5 = \underline{?}$

22. $7 \times 1 \times 3 = \underline{?}$ **23.** $9 \times 3 \times 1 = \underline{?}$

Health Link

You need Vitamin C to stay healthy. Here is a list of how much Vitamin C children need each day:

Age	Amount
1–3 years	40 mg
4–10 years	45 mg
11–14 years	50 mg

How can you organize this information in a tally table?

MORE PRACTICE Student Handbook page H82

PART 1 Organizing Data

You will investigate how to use a table to organize data from an experiment.

Why learn this? Organizing data in a table makes the data easier to understand.

WORD POWER
outcomes

Explore

Find a way to use a table to organize the results of an experiment in which you toss a two-color counter and spin the pointer on a spinner 20 times.

MATERIALS: two-color counters; 4-part spinner, labeled 1–4; 6-part spinner, labeled 1–6

REMEMBER:
A table can help you organize data.

column headings
Title
row headings
cell
rows
columns

MODEL

Step 1

Make a table. Use the possible results, or **outcomes**, of the experiment to name the parts of the table.

Possible outcomes:

- The counter lands with the red side up, and the pointer stops on 1, 2, 3, or 4.
- The counter lands with the yellow side up, and the pointer stops on 1, 2, 3, or 4.

Step 2

Toss the two-color counter and spin the pointer 20 times on the spinner with four parts. After each toss and spin, record the outcome in the table.

	Number			
Color	1	2	3	4
Red	|		|	
Yellow		|		|

Record

Explain how you can describe the outcomes of your experiment by using the data in your table.

Now, investigate how to organize the outcomes of an experiment in which you toss a two-color counter and spin the pointer on a spinner with six parts, labeled 1–6.

Try This

Make a new table. Toss a counter and spin the pointer 20 times. After each toss and spin, record the outcome in the table.

Technology Link
E-Lab • Activity 9 Available on CD-ROM and the Internet at http://www.hbschool.com/elab

TALK ABOUT IT How did you decide to label the parts of the tables? How did you decide to record the outcomes of the experiments in the tables?

WRITE ABOUT IT How did organizing the data in tables make the data easier to understand?

Applying What You Learned

For Problems 1–3, use the table.

Thomas and Adam made this table to organize the outcomes of an experiment in which they tossed a coin and spun the pointer on a four-color spinner.

1. What are all the possible outcomes for this experiment?
2. Why are there 8 cells where tally marks can be recorded?

EXPERIMENT RESULTS

	Red	Blue	Yellow	Green
Heads	II	II	I	I
Tails	I	I		II

3. How would the table change if you used a six-color spinner?
4. What are all the possible outcomes if you toss a coin and spin a pointer with 6 colors: red, blue, yellow, green, orange, and purple?

Mixed Applications

5. Ms. Sweeney's students began an experiment at 9:30 A.M. It took them 5 minutes to prepare materials. It took 20 minutes to do the experiment and 15 minutes to record their outcomes. At what time did they finish their work?
6. Ms. Sweeney and her class used straws to do experiments. They used 56 straws in one experiment and 47 different straws in another. How many straws did they use in all?
7. There are 28 students in Mr. Troy's fourth-grade class. There are 4 more girls than boys. How many girls are in Mr. Troy's class?
8. **Write a problem** about an experiment using a two-color counter and a number cube with the numbers 1–6.

LESSON CONTINUES

MORE PRACTICE Student Handbook page H82

PART 2 PROBLEM-SOLVING STRATEGY
Make an Organized List

THE PROBLEM Celia is choosing an after-school activity. She must choose an activity and a way of getting there. How many different combinations of choices does she have?

CELIA'S CHOICES	
Activity	**Transportation**
Music lesson	Walk
Team sports	Bicycle
Girls' Club	Parent drives

REMEMBER:
- ✓ Understand
- ✓ Plan
- ✓ Solve
- ✓ Look Back

✓ Understand
- What are you asked to find?
- What information will you use?
- Is there information you will not use? If so, what?

✓ Plan
- What strategy can you use to solve the problem?

You can *make an organized list* to show all the combinations of choices.

✓ Solve
- How can you use the strategy to solve the problem?

  You can use the table to make an organized list of all the possible choices. Start with the music lesson. List all the ways Celia could get there. There are three activities and three ways Celia could get to each activity.

So, Celia has nine different combinations of choices.

✓ Look Back
- How can you decide if your answer is reasonable?
- What other strategy could you use?

PRACTICE

CHOOSE Paper/Pencil Calculator Hands-on Mental Math

Make an organized list to solve.

1. Brandon is choosing a computer project. He can make a card, a calendar, a postcard, or a banner. He can print the project in black or red ink. In how many possible ways can he do the project?

2. Four friends want to start a club. They can have a reading club, a computer club, or a skating club. They can meet on Saturday or Sunday. In how many possible ways can the friends have a club?

3. A restaurant offers a choice of peas, carrots, or corn with any meal. The meals are chicken, pork, beef, and fish. In how many possible ways can dinner be ordered?

4. A furniture store sells chairs made of vinyl, leather, or cloth. Each kind of chair comes in black, brown, or gray. How many chair choices are there?

Mixed Applications

Solve.

CHOOSE A STRATEGY

- **Make an Organized List**
- **Act It Out**
- **Make a Model**
- **Guess and Check**
- **Write a Number Sentence**

5. There were 5 students playing a basketball game. The first three players scored 8 points each. The fourth player scored half as many points as the fifth. The total number of points scored was 54. How many points were scored by each player?

6. Helen is deciding what she will wear to school. She can choose from blue, tan, or black pants. She can choose from a white, black, brown, or pink blouse. How many possible outfits can Helen wear?

7. Mr. Howard collected and counted lunch money. He had 14 quarters, 6 dimes, 8 nickels, and 10 pennies. What was the total amount for each kind of coin? How much did he count in all?

8. Amanda is sewing together an equal number of blue and white squares to make a quilt for her bed. The quilt will be 6 squares wide and 9 squares long. How many squares of each color will Amanda need?

9. Mark has $10. He wants to buy two items. Which two items can he buy? Which two items cost too much?

MORE PRACTICE Student Handbook page H83

Understanding Surveys

You will learn how to evaluate a survey.	**Why learn this?** You can write a survey and collect data about things you care about.	**WORD POWER** survey

You are taking a **survey** when you ask several people the same questions and record their answers. You have to think carefully about the way you ask the questions. The way you ask may affect the answers you get.

Jason and Susie are in the same class of 29 students. Each wrote a survey to help them select food for their class party. Compare the surveys. Decide which survey results name the food most students want at their class party.

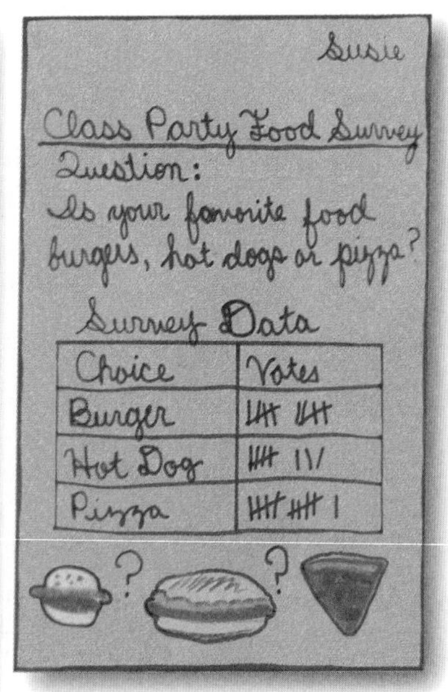

Talk About It

- How are the survey questions alike? How are they different?
- Which way of asking the question would allow ice cream as a favorite food choice?
- Why are there more food choices in Jason's survey?
- Tell whether each statement below is true or false. Explain how you know.
    - Susie's data show that pizza is the students' favorite food.
    - Jason's data show that burgers are the students' favorite food.
    - Susie's results name the food most students would want at a class party.

PRACTICE

Cicely took a survey to help her decide what kind of party to have. She asked her friends, "What is your favorite kind of party?" The table shows the results of her survey.

FAVORITE KIND OF PARTY	
Party	Votes
Skating	5
Bowling	7
Movie	4
Pool	5
Costume	8

For Problems 1–4, use the table.

1. What kind of party did the greatest number of Cicely's friends choose as the favorite?

2. Tell whether this statement is true or false: Cicely's data show that a bowling party is the least favorite choice.

3. How do you think the survey results would have been different if Cicely had asked, "Is your favorite kind of party a skating, a costume, or a bowling party?"

4. Does the survey question Cicely wrote make it easy for her to decide what kind of party to have? Explain.

Mixed Applications

5. When Bryan got home from bowling, he had $4.00. He had paid $4.50 to bowl. He had bought a drink for $0.75. How much money did Bryan start with?

6. Brandi can have a granola bar, pretzels, or raisins. She can drink apple juice or orange juice. What are all the possible combinations she could have?

7. Katrina invited a friend to go bowling with her. They paid $5.00 each to bowl. They spent $1.50 each on drinks. How much money did they spend in all?

8. **Write a problem** to help you find out the favorite fruit of the students in your class. Conduct the survey, and show the results in a table.

Mixed Review

Write the elapsed time. (pages 124–125)

9. **start:** 9:30 A.M. **end:** 10:30 P.M.

10. **start:** 11:15 A.M. **end:** 8:30 P.M.

11. **start:** 11:30 A.M. **end:** 10:30 A.M.

Find the sum. (pages 6–7)

12. $16 + 12 + 12$

13. $17 + 15 + 15$

14. $43 + 12 + 12$

15. $15 + 14 + 8$

16. $21 + 12 + 8$

MORE PRACTICE Student Handbook page H83

Comparing Graphs

You will learn to interpret data in bar graphs that look different but have the same data.

Why learn this? You can interpret bar graphs in any form.

WORD POWER
interval

It is important to compare information in graphs. Even though graphs may look different, they can show the same data. Graphs A and B show two different views of the data shown in the frequency table.

Frequency Table

FOURTH-GRADE FUND-RAISER	
Class	**Dollars Earned**
Mrs. Clark	50
Mr. Green	43
Mr. Baum	35
Mrs. Call	30

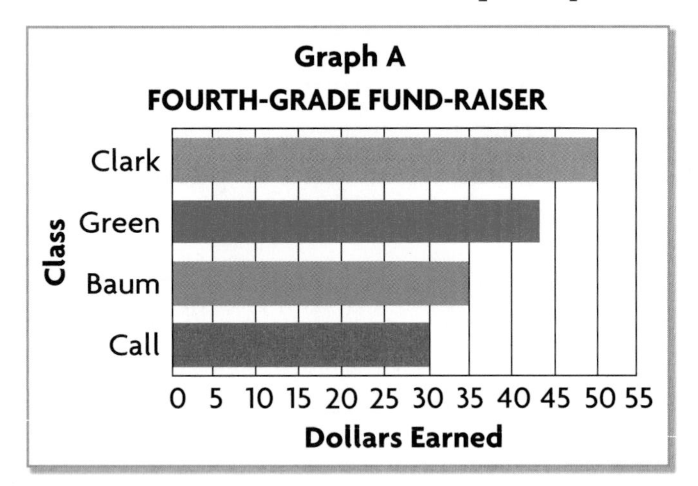

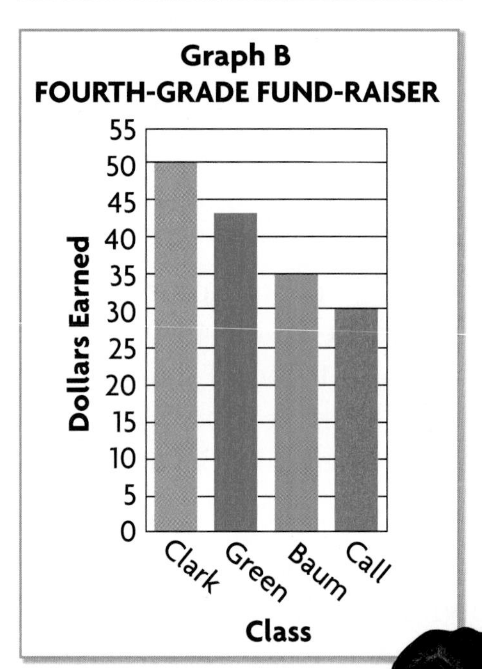

Notice that

- the bars in Graph A are horizontal. They are drawn from the left to the right. The bars in Graph B are vertical. They are drawn from the bottom to the top.
- the numbers on both graphs are the same. The **interval**, or distance between the numbers, is 5. So, the bars in both graphs are the same length.

Talk About It

- Why do you think an interval of 5 was chosen for these data?
- What other interval would be a good choice for these data?
- Which graph do you think is easier to read? Explain your choice.

PRACTICE

For Exercises 1–4, use Graphs A and B.

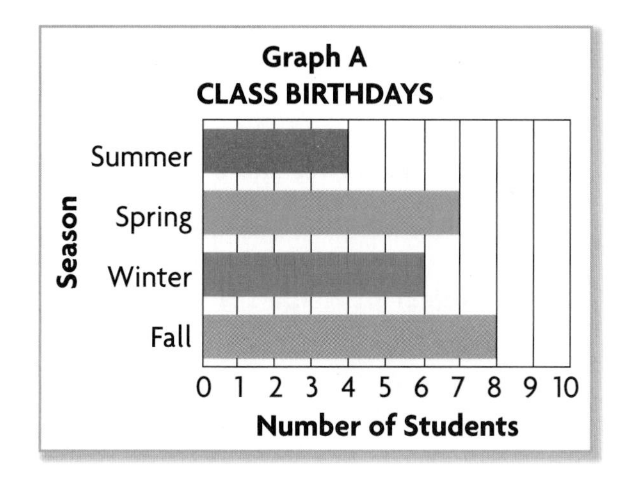

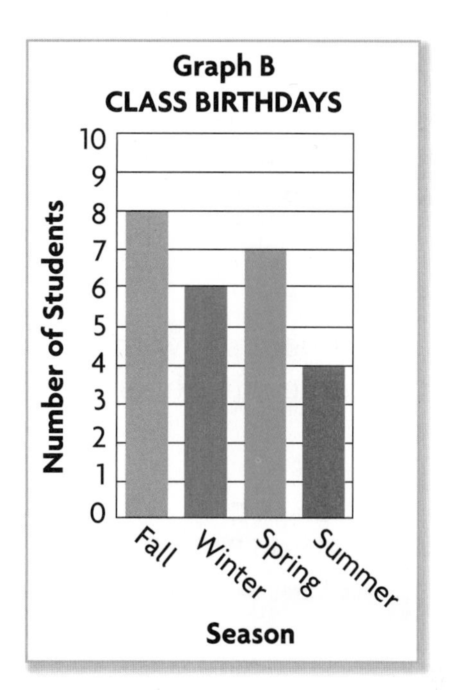

1. How are Graphs A and B different? How are they alike?

2. How many students have birthdays in the spring?

3. What interval is used in the scales of the graphs? What other interval could be used that would make the data easy to read?

4. **WRITE ABOUT IT** Make frequency tables for Graphs A and B. How do the two tables compare?

Mixed Applications

5. Ms. Resnick's class earned $68.95 from book sales. Mr. Pachay's class earned $75.49. How much money did the two classes earn?

6. **Write a problem** that can be solved by using the table.

FOURTH-GRADE BAKE SALE

Class	Dollars Earned
Mr. Davis	15
Ms. East	23
Mrs. Ride	16
Mr. Patel	25

Mixed Review

Find the difference. (pages 20–21)

7. $900 - 115$
8. $800 - 634$
9. $400 - 247$
10. $700 - 175$
11. $500 - 422$
12. $400 - 396$

Write each number in standard form. (pages 90–91)

13. two thousand, one hundred six

14. four hundred five thousand, nine hundred thirty-seven

More About Comparing Graphs

You will learn more about how to interpret data in bar graphs.	**Why learn this?** You can interpret graphs that have the same data but use different intervals in their scales.	**WORD POWER** scale

Graphs C and D both show the data from the frequency table. However, the graphs look different.

Frequency Table

FUND-RAISING PROJECTS	
Project	Number of Helpers Needed
Craft Fair	45
Bake Sale	40
Raffle	40
Carnival	35
Car Wash	23

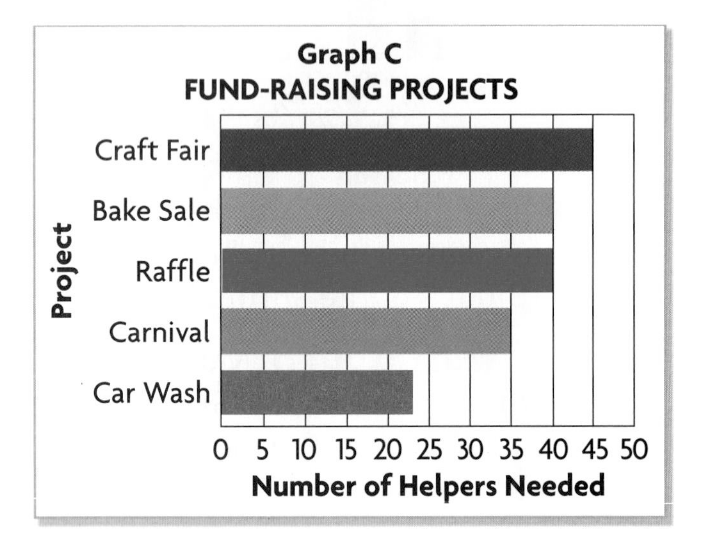

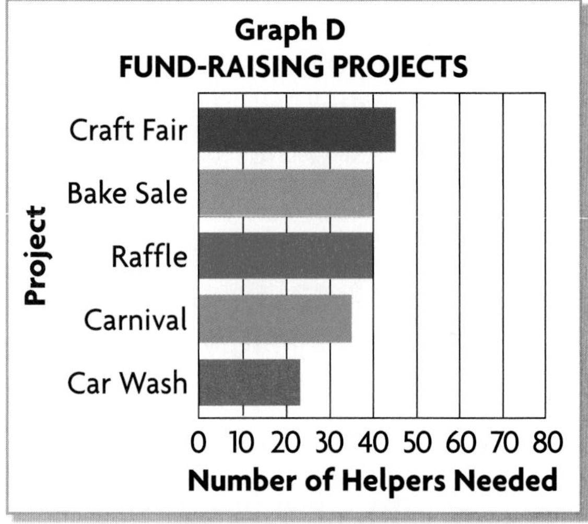

Notice that

- in Graph C, the **scale**, or series of numbers placed at fixed distances, is different from the scale in Graph D.
- the lengths of the bars in each graph are related to the numbers in the scale.

Talk About It

- What happens to the lengths of the bars when the scale numbers are less? are greater?
- In which graph do you think the intervals in the scale make the bars easier to read? Explain.
- How would the bars change if the graph had a scale with intervals of 2?

In ***Graph Links*** computer software, you can change the interval between the numbers of a graph's scale.

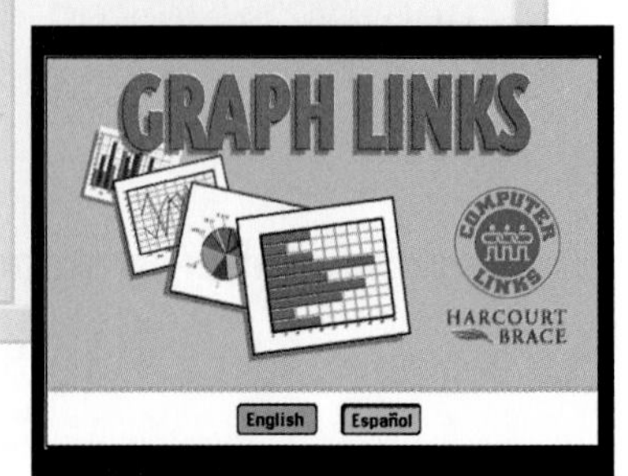

PRACTICE

Tell how the bars would change in the graph below.

1. if the interval were 1
2. if the interval were 2
3. if the interval were 20
4. if the interval were 50
5. if the interval were 3
6. if the interval were 40

Mixed Applications

For Problems 11–12, use the graph.

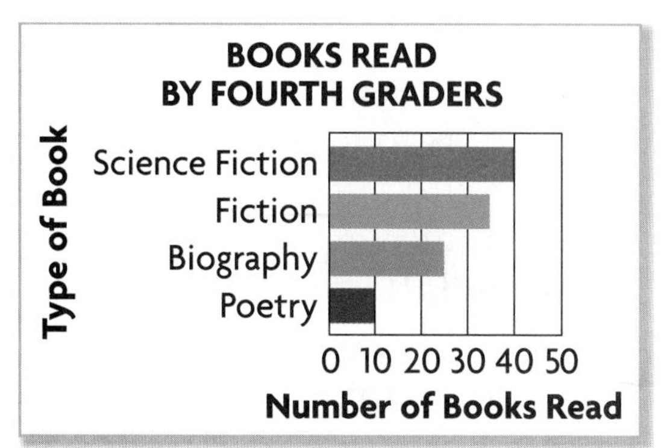

7. Each picnic table seats 8 people. There are 9 picnic tables in the park. How many people can be seated at the tables?

8. Mr. Merrick had 24 T-shirts. He gave the students in his class 3 T-shirts each. How many students are in Mr. Merrick's class?

9. Before lunch 107 students checked out books from the library. After lunch 89 students checked out books. How many more students checked out books before lunch than after lunch?

10. Dylan collected 146 cans in the first week. He collected 195 cans in the second week. How many more cans did he collect in the second week than in the first?

11. Draw a new graph with intervals of 5. Explain how it looks different from the graph shown.

12. **Write a problem** that can be solved by using the data in the graph.

Mixed Review

Find the difference. (pages 22–23)

13.	14.	15.	16.	17.
600	7,000	8,000	10,000	40,000
−451	−5,902	−6,789	−3,083	−29,995

Write *true* or *false* for each statement. Rewrite false statements to make them true. (pages 94–95)

18. There are exactly 10 thousands in 10,000.

19. There are exactly 100 hundreds in 100,000.

MATH FUN!

TEAM TAKROW

PURPOSE To record data in a table

YOU WILL NEED 2 soft rubber balls, timer or stopwatch

Players form two teams. Each team stands in a circle. The point of the game is to move the ball around the circle from player to player without players touching it with their hands and without letting it fall. Take turns passing the ball and keeping time.

Each team's time is the number of seconds the team can keep the ball in play without dropping it. Record the scores in a table. Play three rounds. Add up each team's time. The team with the lowest time wins the game.

Challenge family members to a game of Team Takrow.

Graph Whiz

PURPOSE To interpret data in a graph

YOU WILL NEED paper and pencil

Write 10 questions that can be answered using the data from the graph. Trade with a partner.

Videos Rented in the Last Five Months	
July	🎥🎥🎥🎥🎥🎥🎥🎥
August	🎥🎥🎥🎥🎥🎥🎥🎥🎥
September	🎥🎥🎥🎥🎥
October	🎥🎥🎥🎥
November	🎥🎥🎥🎥🎥🎥🎥🎥
Key: Each 🎥 stands for 50 videos.	

Decisions, Decisions

PURPOSE To practice making an organized list

YOU WILL NEED television guide or television listings

Suppose you are allowed to watch only one TV show a week on a night before a school day. You can watch a comedy, a cartoon, or a movie. You can watch on Sunday, Monday, Tuesday, Wednesday, or Thursday. Make an organized list of all the possible combinations. Use your list to choose the show and the night on which to view it.

CHAPTER 9 REVIEW

✓ CHECK UNDERSTANDING

VOCABULARY

1. On the frequency table, the numbers in the __?__ column show the sum as each new line of data is entered. (page 140)

2. Possible results are also called __?__. (page 142)

3. You are taking a __?__ when you ask several people the same questions and record their answers. (page 146)

4. On a graph, the __?__ is a series of numbers placed at fixed distances. The distance between the numbers is the __?__. (pages 148, 150)

For Problems 5–7, use the frequency table. (pages 140–141)

5. How many videos were sold in Week 2?

6. How many videos had been sold by the end of Week 3?

7. How many videos in all were sold in five weeks?

VIDEOS SOLD

Week	Number of Videos	Cumulative Frequency
Week 1	15	15
Week 2	25	40
Week 3	10	50
Week 4	30	80
Week 5	10	90

✓ CHECK SKILLS

For Problems 8–10, use the graph. (pages 148–149)

8. What interval is used in the scale of this graph?

9. What other interval could be used?

10. How many comedies were released?

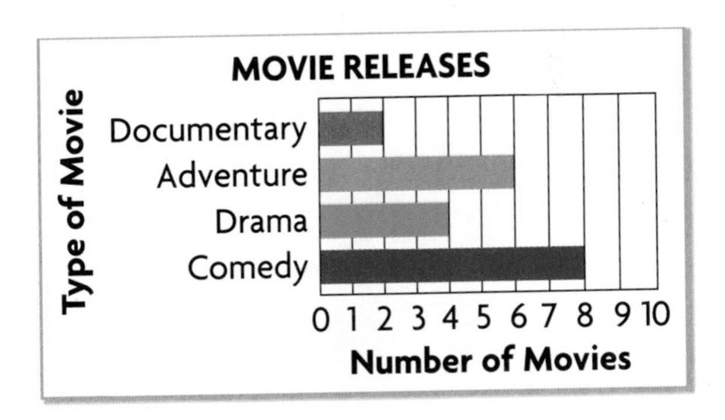

✓ CHECK PROBLEM SOLVING

Solve. (pages 144-145)

CHOOSE A STRATEGY

- Write a Number Sentence
- Make an Organized List
- Act It Out
- Guess and Check

11. A factory makes bicycles with 3, 5, 10, and 12 speeds. Each kind of bicycle comes in black, red, or green. In how many possible ways can you order a bicycle?

12. Cindy placed 3 pots of flowers on each of 2 sides of her porch. She placed 6 pots on each of the other 2 sides. How many pots did she put on her porch in all?

CHAPTER 10

REPRESENTING DATA

DID YOU KNOW . . .

Our bodies need water every day. Water helps vitamins and nutrients travel to places in the body where they are needed.

It helps to keep our temperature the same all day. Water also helps us digest food.

The Water Drop Experiment

Graphs are useful for showing the results of science experiments. You can do an experiment showing how drops of plain and soapy water stick together.

YOU WILL NEED pie pan, coin, dropper, paper towel, small containers of both plain and soapy water

Work with a partner. Your job is to

- fill the dropper with plain water, and slowly put one drop at a time on top of the coin
- make a tally mark for each drop that stays on the coin.
- dry off the coin when a drop spills over the edge.
- do the same experiment with the soapy water.
- graph the results of the experiments.

DID YOU

- ✓ find the number of drops of plain and soapy water that will stay on top of a coin?
- ✓ tally the results of the experiment?
- ✓ graph the results of the experiment?

Exploring Double-Bar Graphs

You will investigate how to show more than one set of data on a graph.

Why learn this? You can compare data from two groups.

WORD POWER
double-bar graph

Explore

Double-bar graphs are used to compare similar kinds of data. Make a double-bar graph that shows the data from the frequency table.

WATER-DROP EXPERIMENT		
	Number of Plain Water Drops	Number of Soapy Water Drops
Quarter	48	26
Dime	26	13
Penny	32	16

MATERIALS: 1-cm grid paper, red and blue crayons

MODEL

Step 1

Decide on a title, labels, and a scale for the graph.

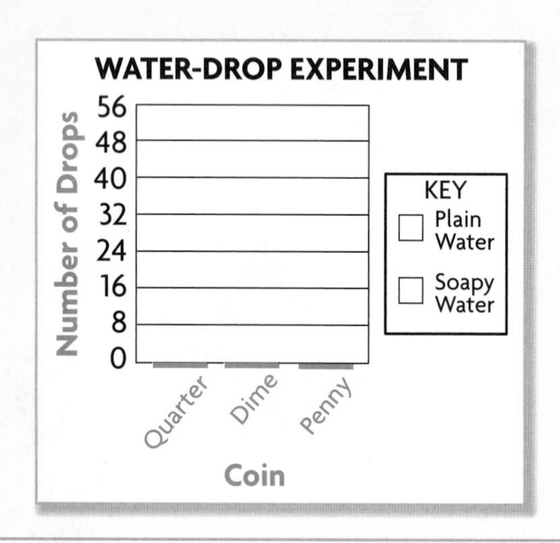

Step 2

Make the graph, using data from the frequency table. Use one color for plain water and a different color for soapy water. Make a key to show which color stands for plain water and which stands for soapy water.

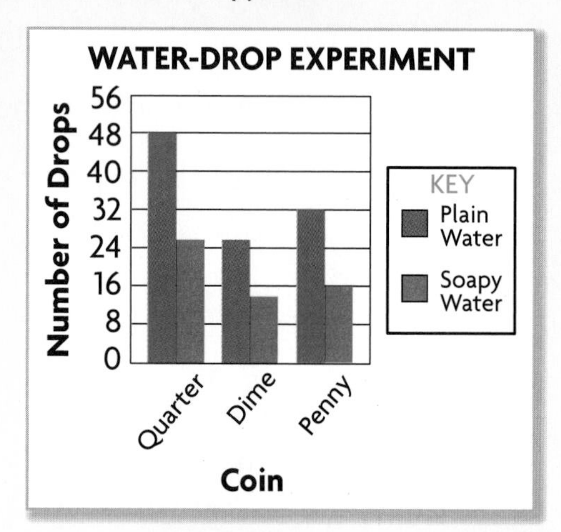

Record

Explain how the colors and the key in a double-bar graph help you compare data from two groups.

Technology Link
E-Lab • Activity 10 Available on CD-ROM and the Internet at http://www.hbschool.com/elab

Talk About It

- What does the graph show about the number of plain and soapy water drops?
- Do you think it is easier to compare the data on the graph or in the table? Explain.
- How is a double-bar graph different from a single-bar graph? How are they the same?

REMEMBER:
To decide on a scale to use, look at all the numbers in the set of data. Choose intervals that allow most of the data to fall on a line.

Now, investigate how to compare the number of books read by two fourth-grade classes.

Try This

Make a double-bar graph to compare the data of Mrs. Brown's and Mr. Fried's classes. What scale will you use? Explain.

BOOKS READ BY FOURTH GRADERS		
Type of Book	Mrs. Brown's Class	Mr. Fried's Class
Mystery	18	16
Biography	12	14
Sports	10	6
Science	8	5
Fiction	17	19

TALK ABOUT IT Why is a key needed in a double-bar graph?

WRITE ABOUT IT Explain how you could show the data in a double-bar graph in two separate bar graphs.

Applying What You Learned

Take a survey in your class or school. Collect data that you can show in a double-bar graph. After you make the graph, answer Problems 1–3.

1. What scale did you use on your graph? Why did you use that scale?
2. What does the key on your graph show?
3. Could you have made a single-bar graph of your data? Explain why or why not.

Mixed Applications

4. Kenny made a graph about students' favorite colors. He compared favorite colors of students in the first grade and fourth grade. What kind of graph could he use to show these data? Explain.
5. In our class, 16 students like red best. In another class 4 more like red best. How many students in the other class like red best?

MORE PRACTICE Student Handbook page H84

Reading a Line Graph

You will learn how to read line graphs.

Why learn this? You can read a graph that shows how data change over time.

WORD POWER
line graph

A **line graph** uses a line to show how something changes over a period of time. The line graph below shows the number of absences in a fourth-grade class over 9 months' time.

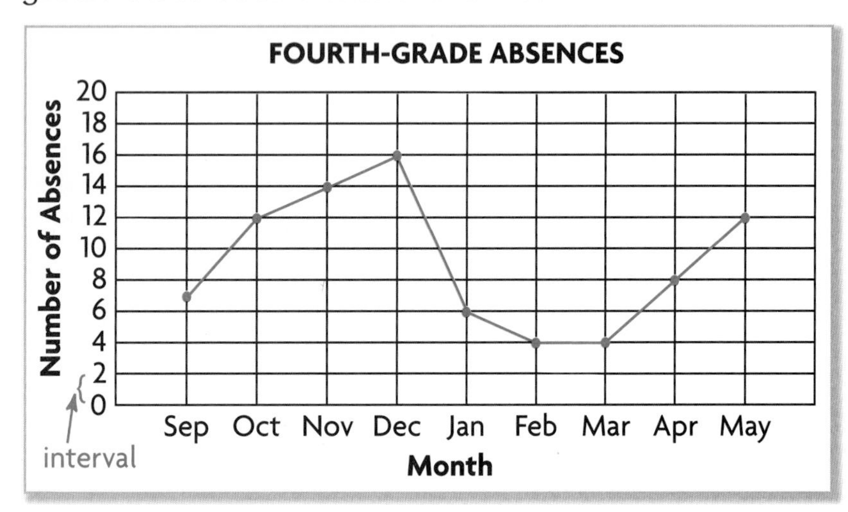

REMEMBER:

Just as in a pictograph or bar graph, the point in the middle of an interval represents the number between numbers on the scale.

Absences
4
2
0
3 absences

Notice that

- the point on the line for September is between 6 and 8 to show 7 absences.
- the labels (months) are shown on the lines, not between them as in a bar graph.
- the line connecting the points shows the increases and decreases in the number of absences over the 9 months.

Mr. Smart's class in October

Talk About It

- Between which months was there an increase in the number of absences? a decrease? no change?
- Would a line graph be the best way to show outside temperature for a week? Explain.
- How is a line graph different from a bar graph?

PRACTICE

For Problems 1–5, use the line graph.

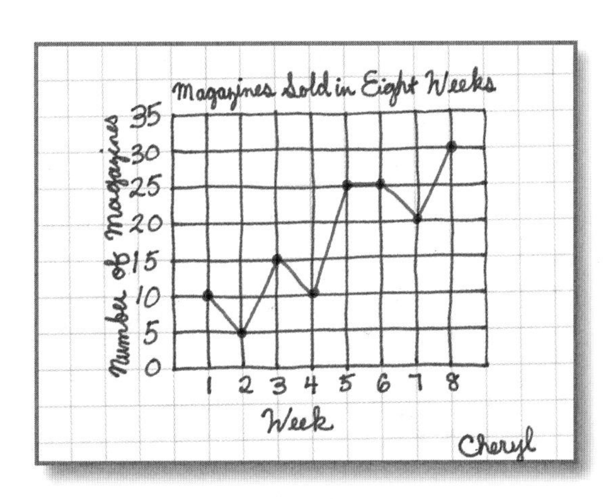

1. During which week did Cheryl sell the most magazines? the fewest?
2. How many magazines did she sell during the third week?
3. During which weeks did she sell fewer than 15 magazines?
4. For two weeks in a row, Cheryl sold the same number of magazines. How many magazines did she sell each week?
5. Between which two weeks was there the greatest increase in the number of magazines sold?

For Problems 6–7, use the table and blank graph.

6. Fill in the graph, using the data in the table.
7. **Write a problem** using the data in the graph.

Month	Jan	Feb	Mar	Apr	May	Jun
Days of Rain	6	5	6	7	10	13

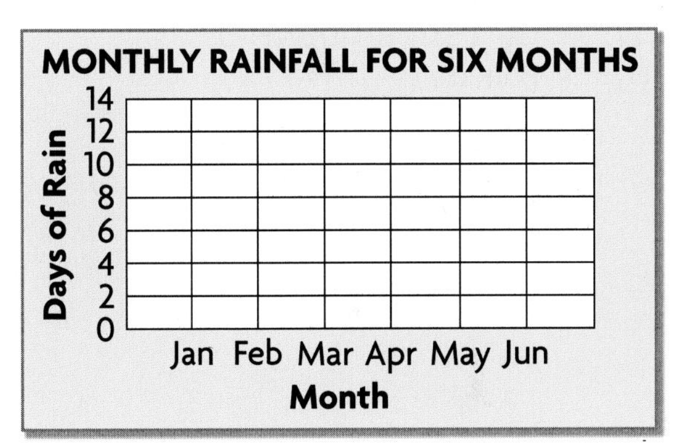

Mixed Applications

8. Paul's line graph has intervals of 3 on the scale. His data include the numbers 17, 12, 6, 22, 18, and 10. Which numbers in his data must be graphed between the numbers on the scale?
9. Maria has 4 pages to read for science class. She has twice as many pages to read for reading class, and half as many to read for social studies. How many pages in all does Maria have to read?

Mixed Review

Round to the nearest *ten, hundred,* and *thousand.* (pages 26–27)

10. 5,316 **11.** 6,537 **12.** 8,985 **13.** 9,906

Write the numbers in order from the greatest to the least. (pages 112–113)

14. 678; 665; 687 **15.** 492; 402; 429 **16.** 1,507; 1,570; 1,563

Line Plot

You will learn how to interpret and record data in a line plot.

Why learn this? You can keep track of data so you can use them to make predictions, such as how many cookies are needed for a party.

WORD POWER
line plot
range

A **line plot** is a diagram that shows the frequency of data. It can be used to keep a count of data as they are gathered. The line plot below shows the data from the table at the right.

COOKIES EATEN AT A PARTY	
Number of Cookies Eaten	**Number of Students**
0	|
1	||
2	~~||||~~ |
3	~~||||~~ ||
4	||
5	|||
6	|

The difference between the greatest and the least numbers in a set of data is called the **range**. $6 - 0 = 6$, so the line plot must be at least from 0 to 6.

REMEMBER:
This is how the data in the line plot looks on a bar graph. Compare the number of the X's to the top of each bar.

One X above the 6 means one student ate 6 cookies.

Numbers show the number of cookies.

Talk About It

- What were the greatest and the least numbers of cookies eaten by any student?
- How many students ate 3 cookies? How many cookies is that in all?
- How many cookies were eaten at the party? What operations do you use to find this number?

PRACTICE

For Problems 1–4, use the line plot at the right.

1. The X's on this line plot stand for the number of players. What do the numbers on the line plot stand for?
2. How many players made 10 baskets during free-throw practice?
3. What number of baskets did the players make most often?
4. What is the range used in this line plot?
5. Use the data in the table at the right to make a line plot.

1 2 3 4 5 6 7 8 9 10

Baskets Made During Free-Throw Practice

CARTONS OF MILK AT ONE LUNCH	
Number of Glasses	**Number of Students**
0	||
1	卌
2	||||
3	卌

Mixed Applications

6. Use the data in the table for Problem 5 to find how many cartons of milk students drank at one lunch.

7. Jessica made a line plot of the number of pennies her classmates had. The least number of pennies was 0, and the greatest number was 12. What line plot would you draw to show her data?
8. Brian's father planted 52 plants in the yard. He planted 12 bushes along each side of the house and 8 trees in the back. How many plants did he put in the front?
9. **Write a problem** using the data in the line plot you made for Problem 5.

Mixed Review

Decide when division will answer the question. Write *yes* or *no*. If you write *yes*, then solve. (pages 50–51)

10. The class can use a list of 45 ideas for making reports. Each group may choose 9 ideas. How many groups are there?
11. Ginny sold 5 boxes of candy to the people who live on her street. There were 8 bars in each box. How many bars did she sell?

Write the number as you would say it with period names. (pages 96–97)

12. 872,106
13. 5,203,112
14. 120,044,360

MORE PRACTICE Student Handbook page H85

Stem-and-Leaf Plot

You will learn how data are shown on a stem-and-leaf plot.

Why learn this? You can list data in a way that makes them easy to read.

WORD POWER
stem-and-leaf plot
mode
median

A **stem-and-leaf plot** shows groups of data arranged by place value. Data are arranged in order from the least to the greatest number.

Mrs. Zephyr's Class
Sit-Ups Completed in 1 Minute

S.E. - 47	A.L. - 39
D.C. - 43	B.J. - 38
J.N. - 50	M.R. - 43
S.K. - 37	B.F. - 50
C.D. - 34	R.K. - 50
M.H. - 51	L.E. - 47
M.M. - 40	J.M. - 46
J.L. - 38	B.S. - 51
M.D. - 52	M.E. - 36
T.J. - 40	

Mrs. Zephyr wrote the number of sit-ups her students did in 1 minute next to their initials.

Mrs. Zephyr listed the data in this way.

Stem	Leaves
3	4 6 7 8 8 9
4	0 0 3 3 6 7 7
5	0 0 0 1 1 2

Number of Sit-Ups

Each tens digit is called the *stem*.

The ones digits are called the *leaves*.

Notice that

- the right side, or the leaves, of the stem-and-leaf plot shows the ones digits for each tens digit in order from the least to the greatest.

The **mode** is the number that is listed most often in a set of data. What is the mode in this set of data? What number of sit-ups happened most often?

The **median** is the middle number in an ordered series of numbers. To find it, cross off the least leaf at the beginning of the plot and the greatest leaf at the end. Keep doing this, moving toward the middle, until one number is left. What is the median?

Talk About It

- What kind of data can be arranged in a stem-and-leaf plot?
- What were the least and the greatest numbers of sit-ups? How did you find these data?
- Would a line plot be a good way to show these data? Explain.

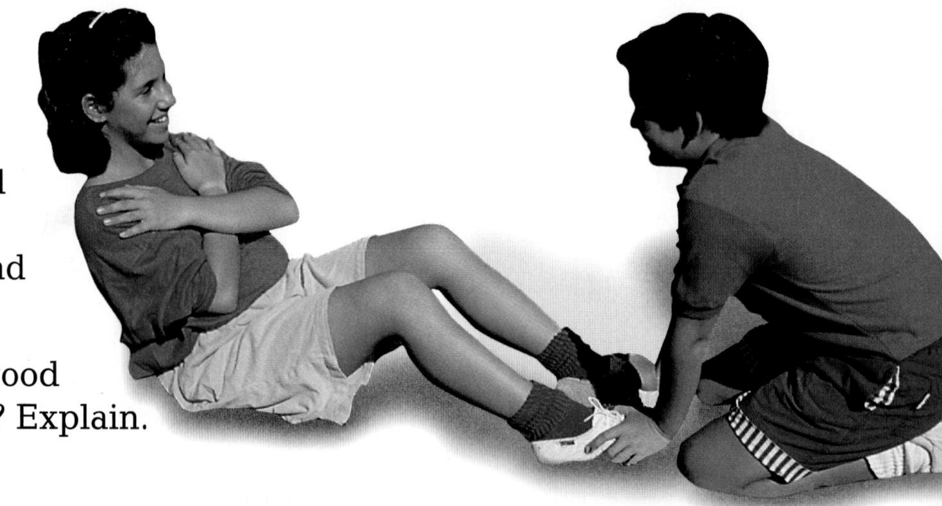

PRACTICE

The stem-and-leaf plot shows Dell's scores for 17 rounds of golf. Use it to answer Problems 1–3.

1. What were Dell's least and greatest golf scores?
2. What is the mode of Dell's scores?
3. What is the median of Dell's scores?

Stem	Leaves
7	6 7 9 9 9
8	0 2 3 5 6 8 9
9	0 0 1 2 3

Dell's Golf Scores

In Ms. Hale's class, the following scores were made on a math test: 68, 70, 75, 75, 77, 79, 82, 82, 82, 84, 84, 86, 88, 90, 90, 92, 93, 93, 93, 93, 94, 95, 97, 98, 98. Show these scores on a stem-and-leaf plot.

4. Which digits are stems? Which are leaves?
5. What is the mode in these test scores? the median?
6. What are the lowest and highest test scores?

Mixed Applications

7. Mr. Baker owns a small company. The following is a list of the ages of his workers: 23, 23, 24, 25, 25, 29, 32, 32, 32, 34, 36, 38, 42. Make a stem-and-leaf plot showing these data.
8. Angela scored 139 the first time she played her new video game. She scored 188 in her second game. How many more points did she score the second time she played?
9. Lana has 3 dimes. Bob has 2 times as many nickels as Lana has dimes. Who has more money?
10. **Write a problem** using the data in the stem-and-leaf plot you made for Problem 7.

Mixed Review

Compare the numbers and write $<$ or $>$ for the ●. (pages 104–105)

11. 200 ● 300 **12.** 48 ● 42 **13.** 98 ● 102 **14.** 6,000 ● 4,000

Write the ending time. (pages 124–125)

15. starting time: 6:15 A.M.
elapsed time: 3 hr 30 min
16. starting time: 11:05 A.M.
elapsed time: 2 hr 20 min
17. starting time: 10:30 P.M.
elapsed time: 2 hr 45 min
18. starting time: 9:35 P.M.
elapsed time: 4 hr 35 min

PART

1 Choosing a Graph

You will learn how to choose the best kind of graph to show a set of data.

Why learn this? You can choose the best graph to use when solving problems or when giving a report.

Suppose you are giving a report to your class on the speeds animals can run. Look at how Heather, Mark, and Jane showed the data. How can you decide which graph or plot works best for the data?

ANIMAL SPEEDS	
Animal	**Miles Per Hour (mph)**
Cheetah	70
Lion	50
Rabbit	35
Elephant	25
Squirrel	12

Choosing the best graph for the data is as important as making an accurate graph.

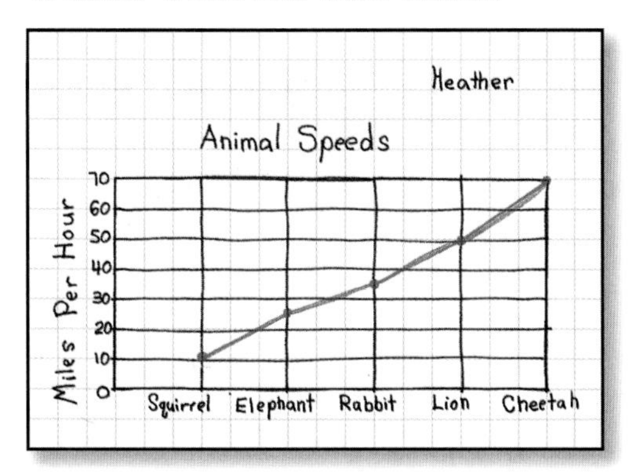

A *line graph* is used to show changes over time. So, this is not an appropriate graph to use.

Mark

Animal Speeds

Cheetah, Lion, Rabbit, Elephant, Squirrel

0 10 20 30 40 50 60 70

Miles Per Hour

A *bar graph* is used to compare facts about groups. So, this is an appropriate graph to use.

Jane

Animal Speeds

Stem	Leaves
1	2
2	5
3	5
5	0
7	0

A *stem-and-leaf plot* arranges data by place value. So, this is not the best way to display these data.

So, Mark's graph is best for displaying these data.

Talk About It

- Would a line plot be appropriate for displaying these data? Explain.
- What other type of graph or plot could you use?

Technology Link

With *Graph Links* computer software, you can make bar and line graphs to display data.

PRACTICE

Write the graph or plot you would choose to show data for each of the following.

1. to show the kinds of books read by a fourth-grade class
2. to show the favorite fast foods of your classmates
3. to show the number of family members of your classmates
4. to show the week's spelling grades of your classmates
5. to compare the favorite subjects of two classes
6. to find the median of jumping jacks for your class
7. to keep a record of how tall a plant grows
8. to show average monthly temperatures

Explain why each graph is not the best choice for the data it shows. Tell which kind of graph you think would be a better choice.

9. 10.

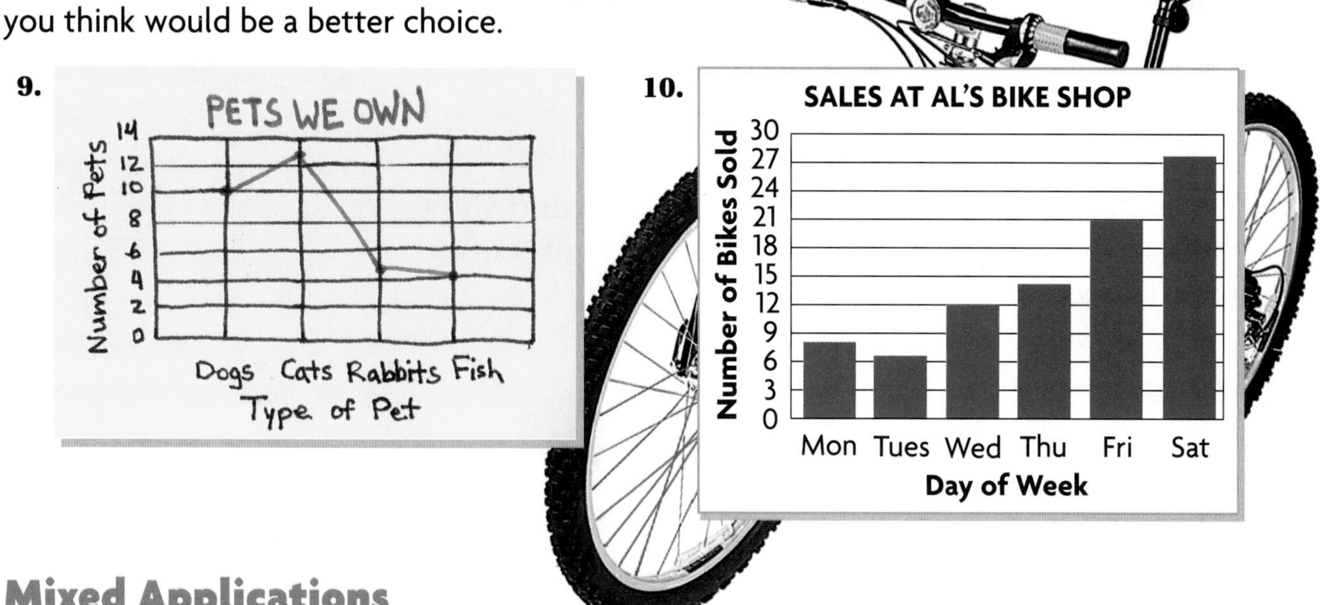

Mixed Applications

11. Carl found a graph in the newspaper showing increases in the cost of postage stamps over the past 30 years. Which kind of graph do you think it was? Explain why.
12. Ellen wants to make a graph showing the types of shoes that her classmates are wearing. She plans to make a stem-and-leaf plot. Do you agree with her choice? Explain why or why not.
13. Jake ran 5 minutes on Monday, 7 minutes on Tuesday, and 9 minutes on Wednesday. If he follows this pattern, how many minutes will he run on Sunday?
14. **WRITE ABOUT IT** Choose one kind of graph you have studied in this chapter. Describe data it shows best, and data for which it is not appropriate.

LESSON CONTINUES

PART 2 PROBLEM-SOLVING STRATEGY Make a Graph

THE PROBLEM Suppose you are planning a speech to get your classmates to agree to serve only cheese pizza at a school party. What graph or plot would you use to get your classmates to agree?

Understand

- What are you asked to find?
- What information will you use?
- Is there information you will not use? If so, what?

FOOD CHOICES FOR SCHOOL PARTY		
Type of Food	Girls	Boys
Hamburgers	5	4
Spaghetti	3	7
Cheese Pizza	14	10
Tacos	4	3

Plan

- What strategy can you use to solve the problem?

You can *make a graph or plot* to arrange and show data so that they can clearly be seen as you make your speech.

Solve

- Which graph or plot can you make to help you get your classmates to agree?

You can use a double-bar graph to show data for girls and boys. You can show that more girls prefer cheese pizza and more boys prefer cheese pizza over the other choices.

Look Back

- How can you decide if you have made the best choice of graph or plot?
- What other strategy could you use?

PRACTICE

CHOOSE Paper/Pencil Calculator Hands-on Mental Math

Make a graph or plot for each table or set of data.

1.

FAVORITE MUSIC GROUPS		
Name of Band	Girls	Boys
Blue Night	8	10
Oasis	12	18
Lenny B.	7	5
The Enforcers	15	21

2. Ages of the 12 children in Mr. Balmer's art program: 10, 11, 10, 14, 11, 10, 12, 13, 12, 12, 12, 14

3.

FAVORITE SNACK FOODS	
Snack	Number of Votes
Chips	7
Cookies or Cake	9
Candy	5
Soda	8
Fruit	4

4.

PINECONES COLLECTED ON NATURE WALK	
Number of Pinecones	Number of Children
5	III
6	~~IIII~~
7	~~IIII~~ IIII

Mixed Applications

Solve.

CHOOSE A STRATEGY

- **Make an Organized List** • **Make a Graph** • **Guess and Check** • **Write a Number Sentence**

5. Cindy has $5 more than Todd. Together they have $19. How much money does each have?

6. Denise arranged some cards in 2 rows with 13 cards in each row. How many cards did Denise arrange?

7. Andy's father said he would take out Andy and a friend. He said they could go fishing, roller skating, or bowling. They could go on Saturday or Sunday. How many choices does Andy have?

8. What is the perimeter of this figure?

86 cm

41 cm

9. A new movie theater opened on Friday. There were 986 people who went there Friday, 1,453 people who went Saturday, and 1,622 who went Sunday. How many people went to the movie theater during those three days?

10. Ronnie surveyed 30 boys and girls. Of the boys, 15 like soccer, 10 like basketball, and 5 like hockey. Of the girls, 13 like soccer, 7 like basketball, and 10 like hockey. Which activity do both girls and boys like best? How can you show this?

MORE PRACTICE Student Handbook page H86

CULTURAL CONNECTION

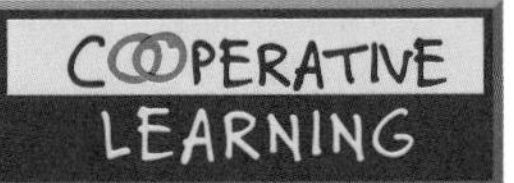

Spices from Many Lands

Hector's class held an Around-the-World lunch so students could taste foods from other countries. The students prepared reports on some of the spices they used. They found that spices come from many lands and can be used in many ways. Study the bar graph at the right listing the spices that were used.

stick cinnamon

cloves

nutmeg

ginger root

SPICES USED IN OUR FOOD

Number of Dishes: 0, 2, 4, 6, 8, 10, 12, 14, 16

Spice: Pepper, Cinnamon, Chili, Nutmeg, Ginger, Cloves

Work Together

1. Use the information in the bar graph. List the spices in order from the one used in the most foods to the one used in the fewest foods.

2. Countries that are major spice growers are Brazil, Malaysia, Sri Lanka, India, West Indies, Indonesia, and China. Make a pictograph that shows how many spices some of these countries grow.

Countries	Spices
Brazil	Cinnamon, Pepper
Malaysia	Cloves, Nutmeg, Pepper
India	Cinnamon, Chili, Pepper, Ginger
West Indies	Cinnamon, Nutmeg, Ginger
Indonesia	Cinnamon, Chili, Cloves, Pepper

3. For holiday gifts, the fourth-grade students made cloth bags, containing spices and herbs, called potpourri, cinnamon-stick wall hangers, and egg-carton herb gardens. Make a bar graph that shows the number of items the students made each week. Use intervals of 10 on the graph.

Week	Number of Items Made
1	50
2	75
3	80
4	20
5	32
6	58

REVIEW

✓ CHECK UNDERSTANDING

VOCABULARY

1. A _?_ is used to compare similar kinds of data. (page 156)
2. A _?_ is a diagram that shows the frequency of data. (page 160)
3. A _?_ uses a line to show how something changes over a period of time. (page 158)
4. The difference between the greatest and the least numbers in a set of data is called the _?_. (page 160)
5. A _?_ shows groups of data arranged by place value. Data are arranged in order from the least to the greatest number. (page 162)
6. The number that is listed most often in a set of data is the _?_. The middle number is called the _?_. (page 162)

Name each type of graph. (pages 156–163)

7. 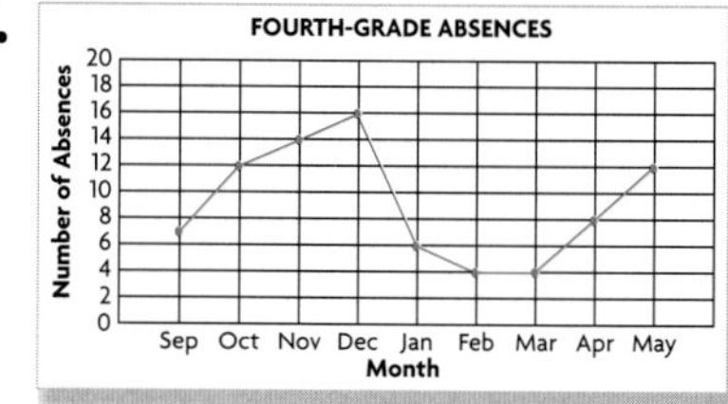

8. 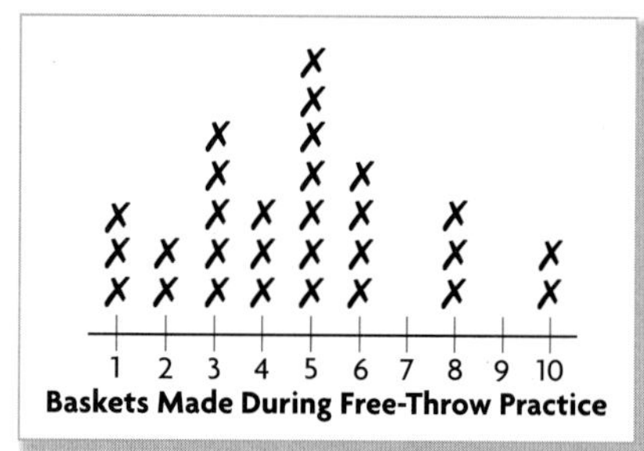

9. 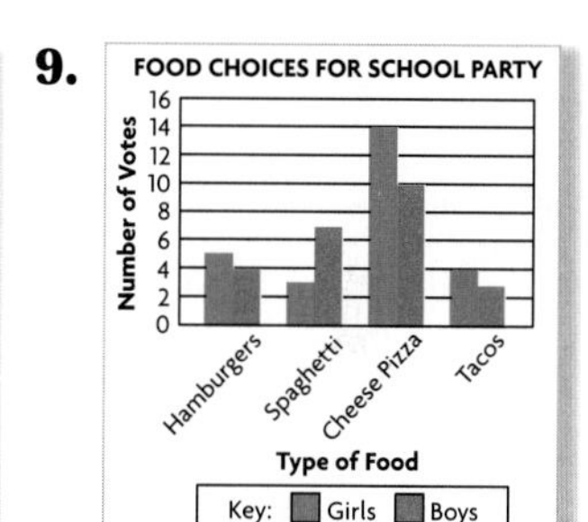

✓ CHECK SKILLS

For Problems 10–11, use the stem-and-leaf plot. (pages 162-163)

Stem	Leaves
1	7 8 9 9
2	0 2 5 5 5 5 7
3	0 1 2 2

Class Sizes at Oakview School

10. What is the smallest class size? the largest?
11. What is the mode in this data? the median?

✓ CHECK PROBLEM SOLVING

Solve. (pages 166–167)

CHOOSE A STRATEGY

- **Make a Graph**
- **Make a Model**
- **Act It Out**
- **Write a Number Sentence**

12. Kirby made a doghouse that is 58 inches long and 32 inches wide. What is its perimeter?
13. A cat was 4 in. tall in May, 6 in. tall in June, and 10 in. tall in July. When did the cat grow the most?

CHAPTER 11 PROBABILITY

DID YOU KNOW . . .

Patolli is an ancient Aztec game about probability. The Aztecs lived in what is now Mexico.

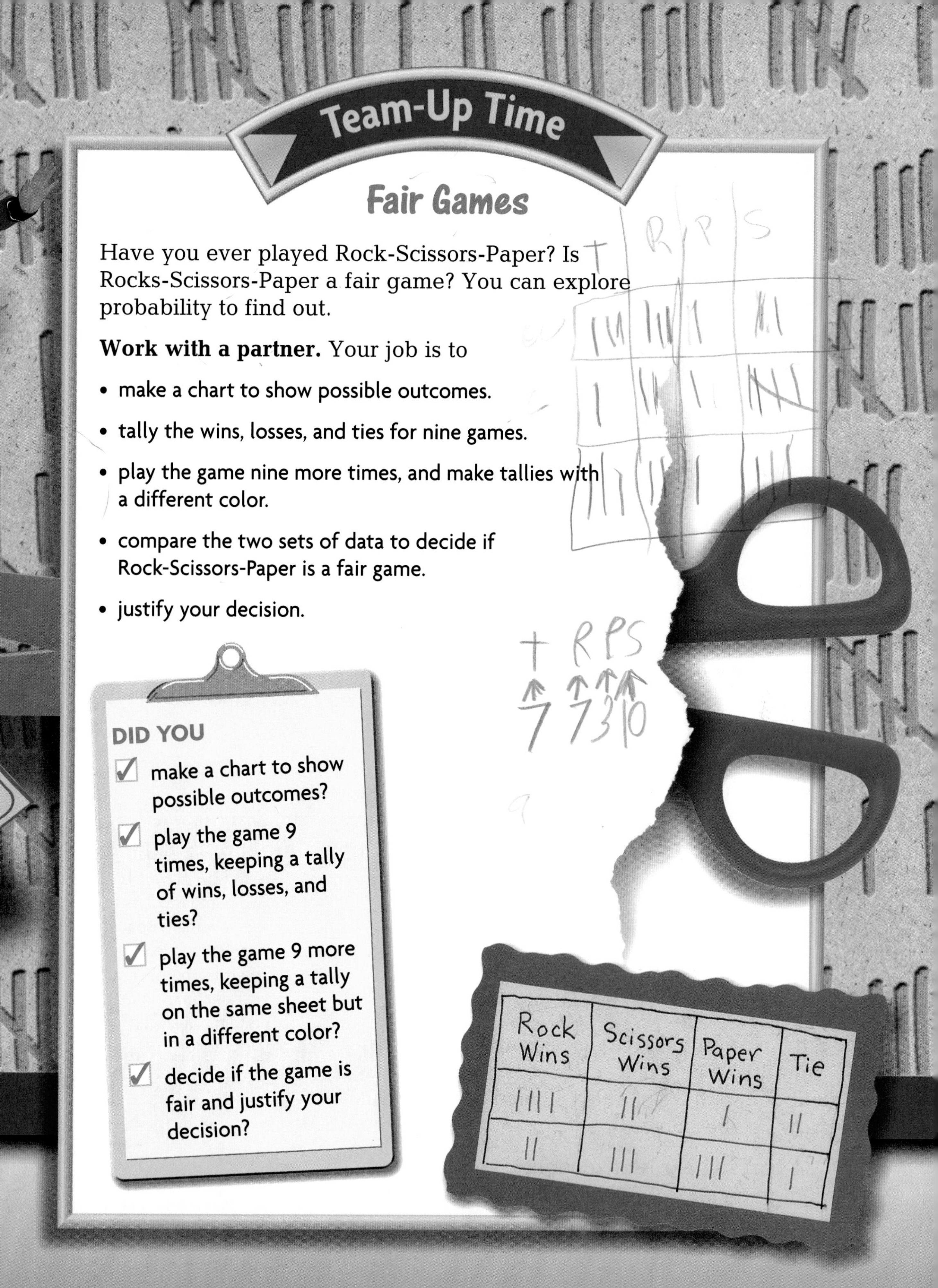

Team-Up Time

Fair Games

Have you ever played Rock-Scissors-Paper? Is Rocks-Scissors-Paper a fair game? You can explore probability to find out.

Work with a partner. Your job is to

- make a chart to show possible outcomes.
- tally the wins, losses, and ties for nine games.
- play the game nine more times, and make tallies with a different color.
- compare the two sets of data to decide if Rock-Scissors-Paper is a fair game.
- justify your decision.

DID YOU

- make a chart to show possible outcomes?
- play the game 9 times, keeping a tally of wins, losses, and ties?
- play the game 9 more times, keeping a tally on the same sheet but in a different color?
- decide if the game is fair and justify your decision?

Rock Wins	Scissors Wins	Paper Wins	Tie
IIII	II	I	II
II	III	III	I

Certain and Impossible

You will learn how to predict if events are certain or are impossible.

Why learn this? You can decide what can and cannot happen when you do an experiment.

WORD POWER
certain
impossible
predict

An event is **certain** if it will always happen.

- The Earth will rotate around the sun.
- If you throw a ball up into the air, it will come down.
- Multiplying 3 and 5 gives 15.

An event is **impossible** if it will never happen.

- A brontosaurus will walk into your classroom today.
- It will rain cats and dogs.
- Money grows on trees.

You can **predict**, or tell what will happen, when you do experiments.

Kelly made this spinner for a game she created.

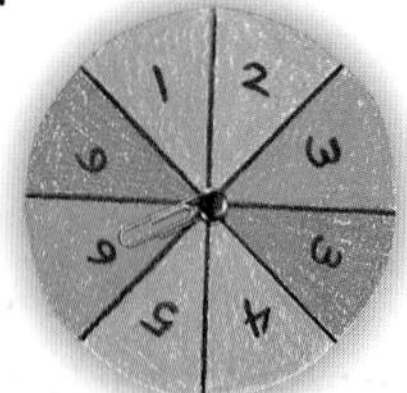

Brad put marbles into a bag for an experiment.

Talk About It

- Using Kelly's spinner, would you predict that it is certain or impossible that you will spin a number less than 10?
- Would you predict that it is certain or impossible that you will spin the number 8? Why?
- Is pulling a yellow marble from Brad's bag certain or impossible? Why?

Consumer Link

The game Monopoly® is published in 43 countries and 26 languages. Before each turn players toss two number cubes to see how many spaces they will move. When you roll 2 number cubes, what is something certain to happen? impossible?

Check Your Understanding

1. Suppose you pull five marbles at the same time from Brad's bag. Is it certain or impossible that you will pull marbles of at least two different colors? How do you know?
2. A 4-part spinner is divided into red, blue, yellow, and green parts. Predict something that is certain and something that is impossible when you spin the pointer.

PRACTICE

Tell if each event is certain or impossible.
Write *certain* or *impossible*.

3. going to Mars for lunch tomorrow

4. feeling pain if you touch a hot stove with your hand

5. pulling a blue crayon from a box with all blue crayons

6. pulling a dime from a bag that has only pennies

7. pulling a quarter from a cup that has a penny and a nickel

8. spinning a number less than 5 on a spinner with parts numbered 1, 2, 3, and 4

For Problems 9–10, use the spinner.

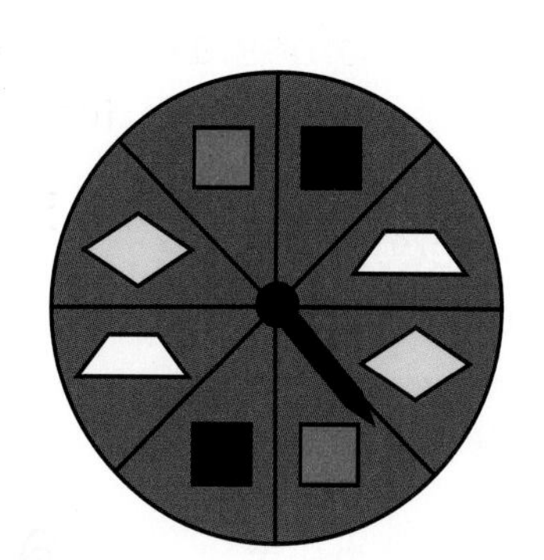

9. Is it certain or impossible that you will spin a four-sided shape?

10. Is spinning a blue shape certain or impossible?

For Problems 11–12, suppose you put five counters in a bag. Describe the counters that could be in the bag.

11. It is impossible to pick a green counter.

12. It is certain that when you pull two counters at the same time, you will pull at least two different colors.

Mixed Applications

13. Blair has 1 nickel, 2 dimes, and 3 quarters in his pocket. Is it certain or impossible that he will pull less than $0.20 if he pulls out 3 coins at the same time?

14. **WRITE ABOUT IT** How do you know if something is certain or impossible?

Mixed Review

Write the time as shown on a digital clock. (pages 120–121)

15. 15 minutes past two

16. 35 minutes past five

17. 4 minutes past eleven

Write *yes* or *no* to tell whether each number is large enough to be counted in the hundred thousands or more. (pages 96–97)

18. the number of students in your school

19. the number of raisins in a snack-size box

20. the number of stars in the sky

MORE PRACTICE Student Handbook page H86

Likely and Unlikely

You will learn how to collect, arrange, record, and use data to predict if something is likely or unlikely to happen.	**Why learn this?** You can decide what is likely and unlikely to happen when you do an experiment.	**WORD POWER** event

An **event** is something that happens in an experiment that brings about an outcome.

Jackie and Cody pulled blocks from a bag of ten blocks 25 times. After each time, they put the block back in the bag. They recorded the outcomes in a tally table.

Blocks Pulled	
Red	𝍸 𝍸 ||
Yellow	𝍸 |
Blue	𝍸 ||

Spencer and Cassie pulled blocks from the same bag 25 times. After each time, they put the block back in the bag. They recorded these outcomes.

Blocks Pulled	
Red	𝍸 𝍸 |||
Yellow	||||
Blue	𝍸 |||

Talk About It

- Did each pair of students get similar outcomes in the experiment? Explain.
- Which color block was pulled most often? Why was it likely to be pulled?
- Which color block was pulled least often? Why was it unlikely to be pulled?
- Suppose there were five red, two yellow, and three blue blocks in the bag. Do the outcomes of the experiment make sense? Explain.
- What makes an event in an experiment likely? unlikely?

Check Your Understanding

1. On the spinner at the right, which shape are you likely to spin? unlikely? How do you know?

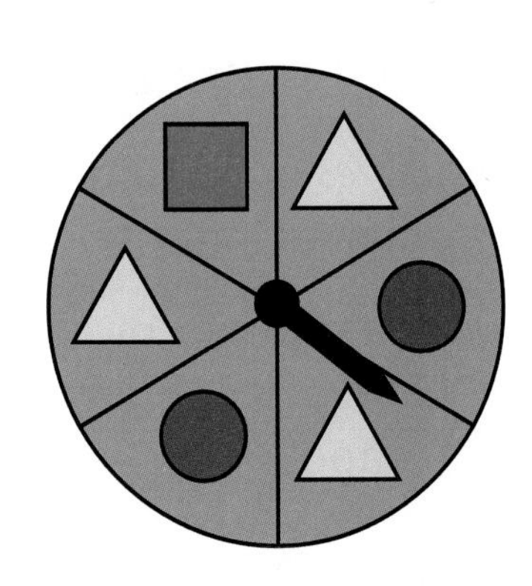

PRACTICE

For Problems 2–5, tell whether each event is *likely* or *unlikely*.

2. feeling tired after running around the track three times

3. seeing a tiger at the beach

4. spinning an even number on a spinner that is numbered 1, 2, 4, 8, 11, 12, 16, and 20

5. pulling a green marble from a bag that has five yellow, four red, and two green marbles

6. Choose one of the problems above in which you answered *unlikely*. Explain why the event is not *impossible*.

Look at the spinner and bag of marbles.

7. Which number on the spinner are you likely to spin the most in ten spins? Explain.

8. If you pull a marble from the bag ten times, which color are you unlikely to pull? Why?

Mixed Applications

9. Hilary wants to give 30 marbles to 5 of her friends. If she divides the marbles evenly, how many marbles will each friend get?

10. **WRITE ABOUT IT** Amy pulled a red counter from a bag four times, a yellow counter five times, and a blue counter five times. She said she thought it was likely that there were more yellow counters in the bag than red or blue counters. Do you agree? Explain.

Mixed Review

Write each number in standard form. (pages 90–91)

11. one hundred fourteen

12. two thousand, thirty-four

13. four thousand, one hundred six

Write the numbers in order from the least to the greatest. (pages 112–113)

14. 156, 147, 174

15. 602, 620, 612

16. 1,717; 1,707; 1,770

MORE PRACTICE Student Handbook page H86

Predicting Outcomes

You will investigate how to compare likely outcomes with all the possible outcomes of an event.

Why learn this? You can predict likely outcomes in experiments, such as rolling number cubes.

WORD POWER
equally likely
possible ways

When you roll one number cube numbered 1–6, you are **equally likely** to roll 1, 2, 3, 4, 5, or 6. Each number has the same chance of happening. When you roll two number cubes, there are many ways to roll the sums of 2 through 12.

Explore

Find all **possible ways**, or outcomes, that can happen when finding sums by using two number cubes. Predict which sums are likely to happen most often.

MATERIALS: 2 number cubes numbered 1–6; blank spinner patterns; yellow, blue, and red crayons; paper clips; brads

MODEL

Step 1

Make a table showing all the ways to roll sums with two number cubes. Then list what you think the likely outcomes will be.

Sum	Ways to Roll	Number of Ways
2	1+1	1
3	1+2, 2+1	2
4	1+3, 3+1, 2+2	3
5		

Step 2

Roll the number cubes 25 times and record each sum in a tally table.

Sum	Tallies
2	I
3	
4	II

Record

Compare your list of likely outcomes with the outcomes of rolling the number cubes. Explain why you think the outcomes were similar or different.

- Would more rolls of the number cubes change the outcomes?

Now, investigate likely outcomes on a spinner.

Try This

Make a spinner with six parts. Color three parts yellow, one part blue, and two parts red. Predict likely outcomes. Then spin the pointer 40 times and record in a tally table the color of each spin.

Talk About It

- What did you predict would be the likely outcomes in the spinner experiment? Did the outcomes support your prediction? Explain.
- How were the spinner experiment and the number cube experiment the same? different?

WRITE ABOUT IT Explain the difference between a likely outcome and a possible outcome. Give an example of each, using marbles in a bag.

HANDS-ON PRACTICE

Make a spinner for a spinner experiment. You may use colors, numbers, or shapes. Your spinner may have any number of parts between 3 and 8. Make your spinner so that it has likely outcomes as well as other outcomes.

First, spin 20 times and record the outcomes in a tally table. Spin 40 more times and record the outcomes in a different tally table. Then answer Problems 1–3.

1. Were there likely outcomes on your spinner? What makes them likely outcomes?
2. Did the likely outcomes happen more often than any of the possible outcomes in the 20-spin experiment? in the 40-spin experiment?
3. Compare your outcomes with those of your classmates. Explain why you think the outcomes were similar or why they were different.

Mixed Applications

4. Mike tossed a cube numbered 1, 1, 1, 2, 3, and 4. He tossed the cube 25 times. Which number do you think he rolled most often? Explain.
5. Kelly started making her spinner at 1:35. She finished making it 25 minutes later. At what time did Kelly finish making her spinner?

MORE PRACTICE Student Handbook page H86

Probability

You will learn to find the probability of an event.	**Why learn this?** You can give the chances of something happening, such as spinning a certain color.	**WORD POWER** probability

This spinner has three equally likely outcomes: red, blue, yellow.

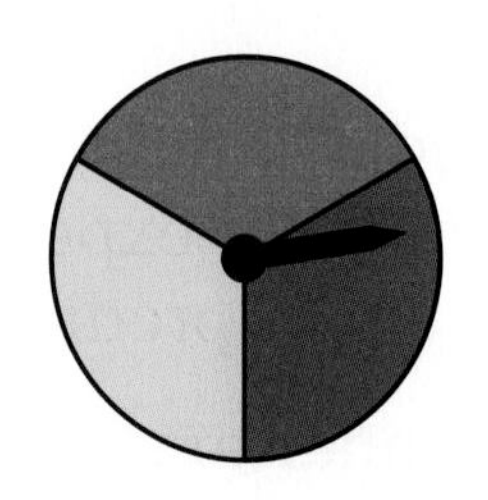

Probability is the chance that an event will happen. A number written as a fraction can be used to describe probability.

$$\text{Probability} = \frac{\text{number of ways the event happens}}{\text{number of ways all events can happen}}$$

Probability of red $= \frac{1}{3}$ ⟵ **Read:** 1 out of 3

- What is the way an event can happen for a probability of red?
- What are the ways all events can happen?
- What is the probability of spinning blue? yellow?

The number of ways an event can happen can describe more than one outcome.

Using the spinner above, find the probability.

A. What is the probability of spinning red or yellow?

$$\text{Probability red or yellow} = \frac{\text{red or yellow}}{\text{red, blue, yellow}} = \frac{2}{3}$$

B. What is the probability of spinning red, blue, or yellow?

$$\text{Probability red, blue, or yellow} = \frac{\text{red, blue, or yellow}}{\text{red, blue, yellow}} = \frac{3}{3}$$

Since the number of ways the event can happen is equal to the number of ways all events can happen, the probability is 1. It is certain to happen.

C. What is the probability of spinning green?

$$\text{Probability green} = \frac{\text{green}}{\text{red, blue, yellow}} = \frac{0}{3}$$

Since the number of ways the event can happen is zero, the probability is 0. It is impossible for green to happen.

- What is the probability of rolling a 6 on a number cube labeled 1–6?

PRACTICE

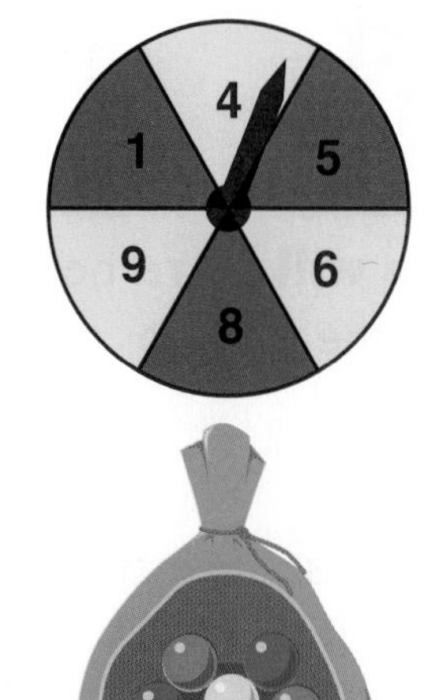

Look at the spinner at the right. Find the probability of spinning each.

1. the number 4 **2.** the number 9

3. a number less than 5 **4.** an even number

Look at the bag of marbles at the right. Find the probability of pulling each.

5. a red marble **6.** a blue marble

7. a yellow marble **8.** a white marble

For Problems 9 and 10, use the spinner at the right.

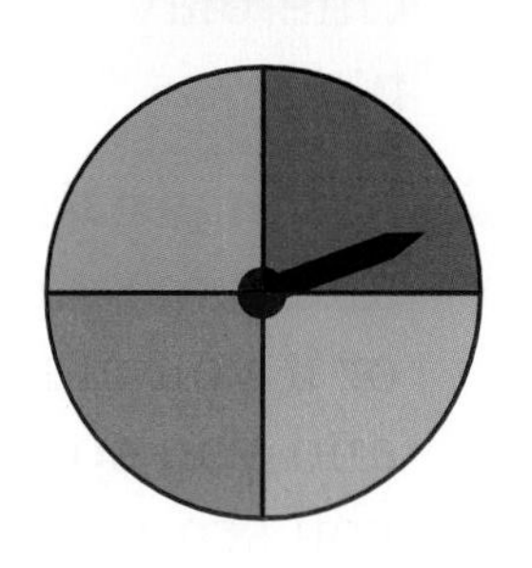

9. What is the probability of spinning red or purple?

10. What is the probability of spinning red, green, or purple?

Mixed Applications

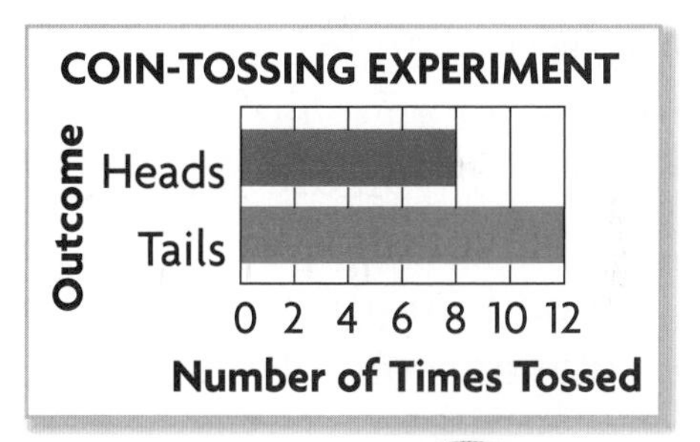

11. In this coin-tossing experiment, how many more times did tails come up than heads?

12. A spinner has 6 equal parts. In 2 parts there is a triangle. In 3 parts there is a square, and in 1 part there is a circle. What is the probability of spinning a shape with only 3 sides?

13. **Write a problem** in which you have to find the probability of an event. Write the probability as a fraction.

Mixed Review

Write the time as shown on a 12-hour clock. Use A.M. or P.M. (pages 122–123)

14. 0500 **15.** 1800 **16.** 2200 **17.** 0100 **18.** 1400

Put in the comma, and write each number in words. (pages 78–79)

19. 5010 **20.** 1001 **21.** 1300 **22.** 8500 **23.** 6012

MORE PRACTICE Student Handbook page H87

PART

1 Testing for Fairness

You will learn how to decide if a game is fair or unfair.	Why learn this? You can decide which game you want to play when you know if it is fair.	WORD POWER fairness

Fairness in a game means that one player is not more likely to win than another.

Rules for Spin-It!

1. One player is "odd" and one player is "even."
2. Decide who goes first. Take turns spinning the pointer.
3. If you are the "odd" player and you spin an odd number, or if you are the "even" player and you spin an even number, you score 5 points.

   If you are the "odd" player and you spin an even number, or if you are the "even" player and you spin an odd number, the other player scores 1 point.
4. The winner is the first player to score 25 points.

Look at each of these spinners.

Spinner A: 2, 6, 3, 5

Spinner B: 1, 8, 2, 7, 4, 6

Spinner C: 13, 56, 25, 43

Talk About It

- What is the probability of spinning an odd number on each spinner?
- Which spinner gives both players an equal chance to win at Spin-It!? Explain how you know.
- If you are the "odd" player, which spinner would you want to use? Why?
- If you are the "even" player, which spinner would you want to use? Why?

PRACTICE

Tell if each spinner is fair. Write *yes* or *no*. If your answer is *no*, explain why the spinner isn't fair.

1. 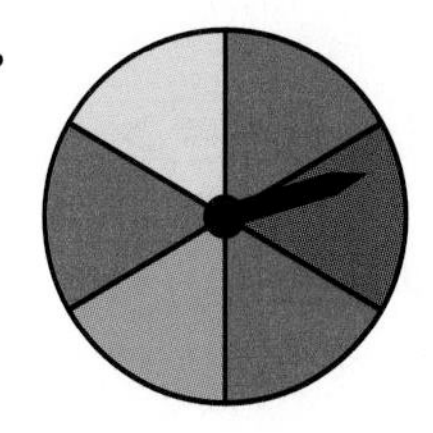

2. 

3. 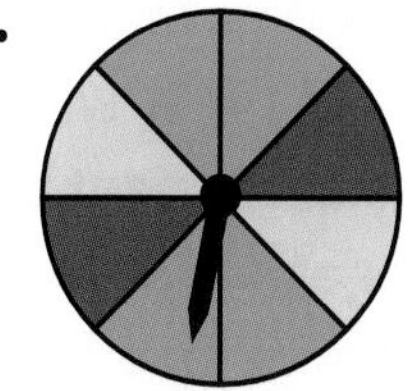

In Katie's game, players choose a shape and take turns spinning. Each time players spin their shape, they color that shape on their game card. The first player to color all of his or her shapes wins.

4. What is the probability of spinning each shape?

5. What is the probability of not spinning a square?

6. Why isn't the game fair?

7. How would you change the game to make it fair?

Mixed Applications

8. Mrs. Kaiser can type 5 pages each hour. How many pages can she type in 7 hours?

9. Lynn and Paul arranged 40 chairs in rows. They put 8 chairs in each row. How many rows were there?

10. Julie bought 2 tapes. Each tape cost $8. Then she spent $5 for a book. She had $2 left. How much money did Julie start with?

11. Melanie had 12 crackers. She gave 3 crackers to each of her friends, and kept 3 crackers for herself. With how many friends did she share her crackers?

12. In Matt's game, players take turns tossing 2 pennies. If 2 heads or 2 tails come up, Player 1 gets a point. If a head and a tail come up, Player 2 gets a point. Is this game fair? Why or why not?

13. **WRITE ABOUT IT** Suppose you are playing a game similar to Spin-It! but using two number cubes. The "odd" player scores a point if the sum of the cubes rolled is odd and the "even" player scores a point if the sum is even. Is the game fair? Explain why or why not.

LESSON CONTINUES

MORE PRACTICE Student Handbook page H87

PART 2 PROBLEM-SOLVING STRATEGY
Make a Model

THE PROBLEM Shannon looked at Kyle's spinner to decide if it was fair. It was divided into 6 unequal parts. The 2 yellow parts together were $\frac{1}{4}$ of the spinner. The 2 red parts together were also $\frac{1}{4}$ of the spinner. The blue part was the same size as the 2 yellow parts together. The green part was the same size as the blue part. Is Kyle's spinner fair?

REMEMBER:
- ✓ Understand
- ✓ Plan
- ✓ Solve
- ✓ Look Back

✓ Understand
- What are you asked to find?
- What information will you use?
- Is there information you will not use? If so, what?

✓ Plan
- What strategy can you use to solve the problem?

  You can *make a model* to decide if Kyle's spinner is fair.

✓ Solve
- What model can you make?

  You know that the spinner has 6 parts. Using one fact about the spinner at a time, color in each of the parts. Then decide if the spinner is fair.

Since there is an equal chance of spinning each color on the spinner, it is fair.

✓ Look Back
- How can you check your answer?
- What other strategy could you use?

PRACTICE

CHOOSE Paper/Pencil Calculator Hands-on Mental Math

Make a model to solve.

1. Perry's spinner is divided into 5 unequal parts. The red and green parts are the same size. Together they are $\frac{1}{2}$ of the spinner. The blue and orange parts are the same size and together are $\frac{1}{4}$ of the spinner. The yellow part is the same size as the red part. Is Perry's spinner fair? Explain.

2. A rectangle-shaped gameboard is divided into 6 unequal parts. A blue part is $\frac{1}{4}$ of the rectangle. The part beside blue is divided into yellow and green parts of equal size. A red part is $\frac{1}{4}$ of the rectangle, with equal-sized yellow and green parts beside it. Is the gameboard fair? Explain.

Mixed Applications

Solve.

CHOOSE A STRATEGY

- Use a Table
- Make a Model
- Act It Out
- Guess and Check
- Write a Number Sentence
- Work Backward

3. There are four students standing at the chalkboard. Marie is standing left of Antonio. Elise is to Antonio's right, and Marie is between John and Antonio. From left to right, in what order are the students?

4. A spinner has 12 equal parts. There are 2 red parts, 4 yellow parts, 4 blue parts, and 2 green parts. What two colors together cover more than $\frac{1}{2}$ of the spinner?

5. Bruce worked on his model airplane for 8 hours. He worked 2 more hours on Saturday than on Sunday. How long did he work on Saturday? on Sunday?

6. Tyrell got home at 5:00. After school, he went to the library for 50 minutes. Then it took him 20 minutes to ride his bicycle home. When did he leave school?

7. Myra has 5 full CD cases, with 9 CDs in each case. Ellen has 6 full CD cases, with 7 CDs in each case. Who has more CDs? How many more does she have?

8. Ian and Erika are brother and sister. The sum of their ages is 25 years. Ian is 7 years older than Erika. How old is Ian? How old is Erika?

9. Which river is longest: Colorado, Mississippi, Ohio, or Tennessee? Which is shortest? How many miles longer than the shortest river is the longest river?

UNITED STATES RIVERS

River	Length in Miles
Colorado River	1,450
Mississippi River	2,340
Ohio River	981
Tennessee River	652

MORE PRACTICE Student Handbook page H87

MATH FUN!

Multiplication Probability

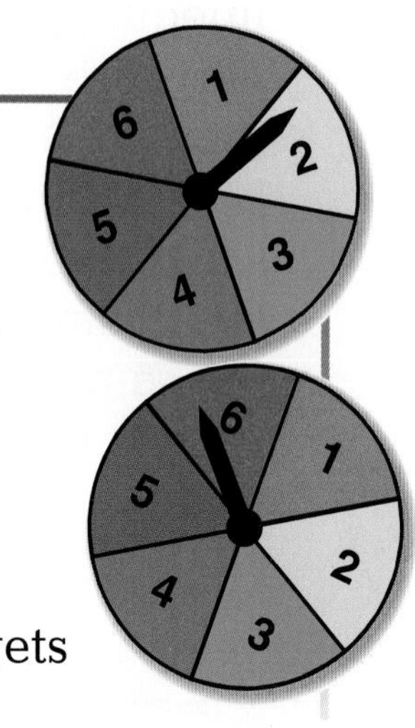

PURPOSE To test for likely and unlikely outcomes

YOU WILL NEED paper and pencil, 2 spinners marked 1–6

Test the game by playing 10 rounds. Spin the pointer on each spinner. Multiply the numbers to get a product. Record the products. Analyze your data. Is an even product more likely than an odd product? Test your prediction by spinning 30 more rounds. The player who spins an even product gets 1 point. The player who spins an odd product gets 2 points.

LICENSE PLATE PUZZLE

TEXAS
AMET
Lone Star State

PURPOSE To practice finding possible outcomes and probabilities

YOU WILL NEED paper and pencil

You are given the letters *E*, *T*, and *A* to make three-letter license plates. Make all the different combinations of three letters you can. Find the probability of making a license plate with a real English word. Then try the four letters *A*, *M*, *E*, and *T*. What is the probability of getting an English word this time?

Select three or four other letters, and challenge members of your family to make English words using these letters. Teach them how to show probability.

Tack Toss

PURPOSE To practice testing for fairness

YOU WILL NEED 10 tacks, cup or other container

Play a tack-tossing game in which Player 1 gets points for each tack that lands on its head and Player 2 gets points for each tack that lands on its side.

Shake the tacks in the cup, and toss the tacks 10 times. Record the results. After 10 tosses, tell the probability of tossing a head or a side. Decide if the game is fair, and explain. Predict how many heads and sides will be tossed if you toss the tacks 20 times in all. Try it, and record your results.

CHAPTER 11 REVIEW

✓ CHECK UNDERSTANDING

VOCABULARY

1. An event is _?_ if it will always happen and _?_ if it will never happen. (page 172)
2. You can _?_, or tell what will happen, when you do probability experiments. (page 172)
3. You can list all the _?_, or outcomes, that can happen. (page 176)
4. Outcomes that have the same chance of happening are _?_. (page 176)
5. An _?_ is something that happens in an experiment that brings about an outcome, such as tossing a coin. (page 174)
6. The chance that an event will happen is called _?_, and is often written as a fraction. (page 178)
7. _?_ is having an equal chance at winning. (page 180)

✓ CHECK SKILLS

For Problems 8–10, use the spinner. (pages 172–175, 178–179)

8. Is it certain or impossible that you will spin an even number?
9. Is it likely or unlikely that you will spin a number greater than 5?
10. What is the probability of spinning a 10?

✓ CHECK PROBLEM SOLVING

Solve. (pages 182–183)

CHOOSE A STRATEGY

- **Make a Table**
- **Make a Model**
- **Work Backward**
- **Make an Organized List**

11. Jo and Lee finished their game at 7:10 P.M. They had started it at 6:05 P.M. For how long did they play?
12. In a bag, there are 3 red marbles, 2 blue marbles, and 1 black marble. What is the probability of picking a blue marble?
13. What are all the possible outcomes if you toss a coin and roll a number cube that is numbered from 1 to 6?
14. Benjamin made a spinner with 6 equal parts. He shaded 3 parts purple, 1 part green, and 2 parts blue. Is this spinner fair? Explain.

CHAPTERS 9–11

STUDY GUIDE & REVIEW

VOCABULARY CHECK

Choose a term from the box to complete each sentence.

WORD BANK

- equally likely
- interval
- median
- mode
- predict
- probability
- range
- scale
- survey

1. When you ask people questions about something in order to collect data, you are conducting a _?_ . (page 146)
2. On a graph, the _?_ is a series of numbers placed at fixed distances. The distance between the numbers is the _?_ . (pages 148, 150)
3. The difference between the greatest and the least numbers in a set of data is called the _?_. (page 160)
4. The number that occurs most often in a set of data is the _?_. The middle number in an ordered series of numbers is called the _?_. (page 162)
5. You can _?_, or tell what will happen, when you do probability experiments. (page 172)
6. Outcomes that have the same chance of happening are _?_. (page 176)
7. The chance that an event will happen is called _?_. (page 178)

STUDY AND SOLVE

CHAPTER 9

EXAMPLE

Use the table below to answer.

How many cans were collected in Week 2? 14 cans

ALUMINUM CANS COLLECTED		
Week	Number of Cans (frequency)	Cumulative Frequency
1	20	20
2	14	34
3	16	?

For Problems 8–9, use the table. (pages 140–141)

8. What is the total number of cans collected by the end of Week 2?
9. What is the total number of cans collected at the end of 3 weeks?

Solve. (pages 144–145)

10. Some friends want to play golf, play tennis, or go fishing on Saturday or Sunday. How many possible ways can they spend the weekend?

For questions 11–12, use the graph.
(pages 148–149)

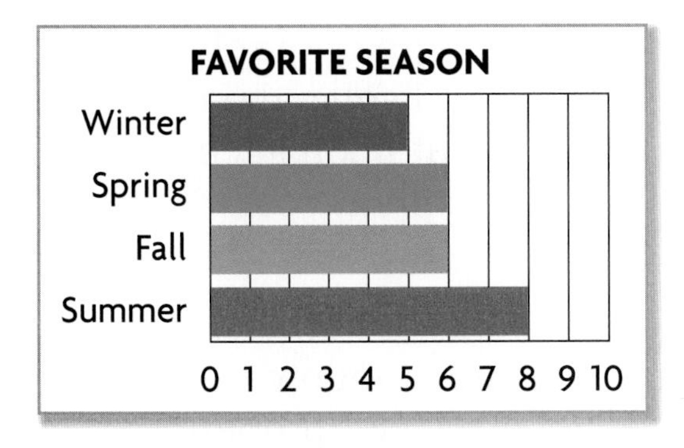

11. What interval is used on this graph?

12. Would an interval of 2, 4, or 5 be easiest to use on this graph?

CHAPTER 10

EXAMPLE

Use the plot below to answer.

How many scores are given for students in the class? 15 scores

Stem	Leaves
7	7 8 9 9
8	0 2 4 5 6 6 6
9	0 1 2 2

Science Test Scores

For questions 13–16, use the stem-and-leaf plot. (pages 160, 162–163)

13. What is the mode?

14. What is the median?

15. What is the range?

16. What is the highest score?

CHAPTER 11

EXAMPLE

A bag of marbles contains 4 blue marbles, 3 green marbles, 2 red marbles, and 1 yellow marble. What is the probability of picking a blue marble? $\frac{4 \text{ blue marbles}}{10 \text{ marbles total}}$, or $\frac{2}{5}$

For questions 17–21, use the spinner.
(pages 172–179)

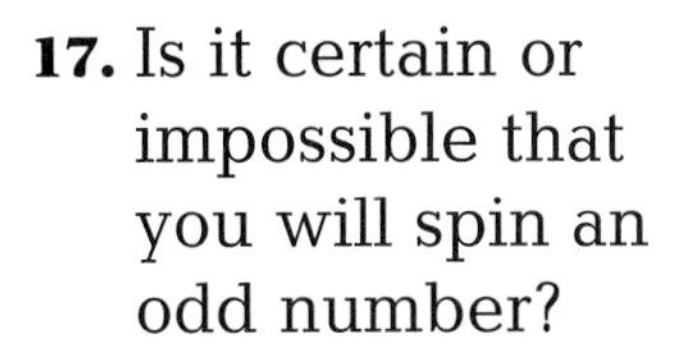

17. Is it certain or impossible that you will spin an odd number?

18. Is it likely or unlikely that you will spin a number less than 6?

19. What is the probability of spinning 3?

20. What is the probability of spinning 13?

21. Are all outcomes equally likely? Why?

Solve. (pages 182–183)

22. A square gameboard is divided into 4 sections. The blue and red sections are the same size. Together they are $\frac{1}{2}$ of the gameboard. The green and yellow sections are the same size and are each $\frac{1}{4}$ of the gameboard. Is the gameboard fair? Why?

CHAPTERS 9–11

WHAT DID I LEARN?

WRITE ABOUT IT

Choose a method to solve. Explain your method.

1. Suppose you wanted to know which sport your classmates like to watch most on TV. Which of these would be the best survey question to ask them?

- What sport do you like watching most on TV?
- Would you rather watch football, baseball, or soccer on TV?

Explain your choice. (pages 140–141)

2. Identify the type of graph you would use to display the outside temperature at noon each day for one week. Explain your choice. (pages 164–165)

3. There are 3 red marbles, 2 blue marbles, and 1 yellow marble in a bag. What is the probability of pulling: (pages 178–179)

a. a red marble?
b. a blue marble?
c. a yellow marble?

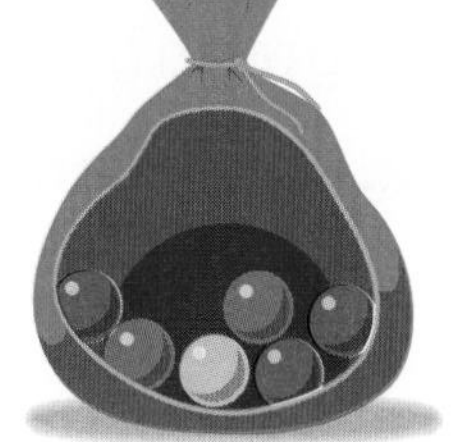

PERFORMANCE ASSESSMENT

Solve. Explain your choice.

CHOOSE A STRATEGY

- Make a Model
- Draw a Picture
- Make a Graph
- Write a Number Sentence
- Make an Organized List

4. Mel sells records, audiotapes, and CDs. He has popular music, country music, and jazz. Make a list of all the possible combinations of items that Mel can sell. (pages 144–145)

6. Jen and Sam use a spinner that has a red, a blue, and a green section. In 100 spins, the spinner lands on red 50 times, on blue 25 times, and on green 25 times. What does the spinner look like? Explain. (pages 182–183)

For Problem 5, use the table.

5. Mr. Ho's students voted to go on a class trip. Which place received the most votes? (pages 166–167)

CLASS TRIP VOTES

Place	Boys	Girls
Zoo	4	2
Museum	4	1
Theater	6	8
Nature Center	2	3

CUMULATIVE REVIEW

Solve the problem. Then write the letter of the correct answer.

1. 578
+267

A. 311
B. 735
C. 845
D. 846 (pages 6–7)

2. $20.00
− 8.72

A. $11.28
B. $12.72
C. $14.27
D. $18.38 (pages 12–13)

3. $6\overline{)38}$

A. 6 r1
B. 6 r2
C. 32
D. 46 (pages 54–55)

4. Sandy bought a blouse for $28.79. She gave the clerk $30.00. How much change did she receive?

A. $1.21 **B.** $2.21
C. $2.31 **D.** $58.79

(pages 12–13, 22–23, 28–29)

5. There are 5 rows of desks in the classroom. There are 5 desks in each row. How many desks are there in all? (pages 44–45)

A. 0 desks **B.** 1 desk
C. 10 desks **D.** 25 desks

6. What is the location of Point *Y* on the grid? (pages 74–75)

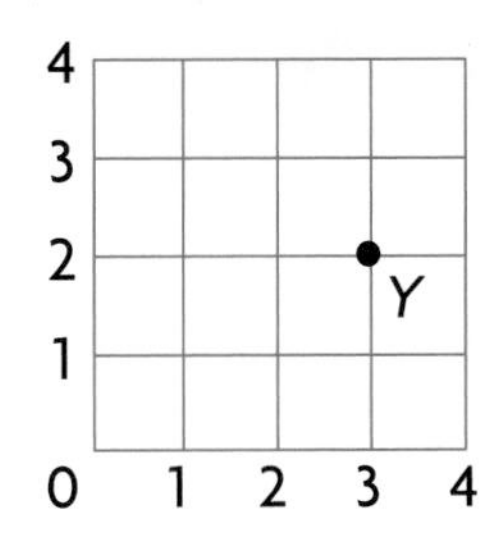

A. (1,4)
B. (3,2)
C. (2,3)
D. (4,1)

7. What is fifty million, four hundred in standard form?

A. 50,400 **B.** 50,000,004
C. 50,000,400 **D.** 50,400,000

(pages 90–91)

8. What is the cumulative frequency for October?

LIBRARY BOOKS BORROWED

	Number of Books (frequency)	Cumulative Frequency
Sep	1,067	1,067
Oct	1,134	?
Nov	1,189	?

A. 2,023 books **B.** 2,201 books
C. 2,438 books **D.** 2,500 books

(pages 140-141)

9. What is the median for this set of data? (pages 162–163)

Stem	Leaves
7	7 7 8 9
8	0 2 3 4 7 8 8
9	0 3 5 6

Math Test Scores

A. 82
B. 84
C. 87
D. 88

10. What is the probability of pulling a yellow marble from the bag?
(pages 178–179)

A. $\frac{1}{10}$
B. $\frac{2}{10}$
C. $\frac{3}{10}$
D. $\frac{4}{10}$

CHAPTER 12 ANALYZING GEOMETRIC FIGURES

DID YOU KNOW...

Triangles can be shaped in many different ways, but they always have 3 angles and 3 sides. *Tri* means "three".

Some other words with *tri* are: a *tri*cycle has 3 wheels, a *tri*ceratops has 3 horns, and *tri*ple means "times 3."

Team-Up Time

Designing Spaceships

You have probably read a story or seen a movie about spaceships. You can design a spaceship yourself using what you know about solid figures.

Work with a partner or in a small group. Your job is to

- make a triangular pyramid using straws and balls of clay to begin the ship.
- imagine how the spaceship might look and start building on to the pyramid!
- when you are finished, make a display card for your spaceship, explaining which figures were used in its construction.

DID YOU

- ✓ make a triangular pyramid?
- ✓ design and build a spaceship?
- ✓ make a display card for the spaceship, explaining which figures you used to make it?

Exploring Geometric Figures

You will learn to name, describe, and compare one-dimensional, two-dimensional, and three-dimensional figures.

Why learn this? You can make geometric figures from things you use every day. You can learn ways to measure them.

WORD POWER
dimension

Dimension is a measure in *one* direction. Geometric figures can have one, two, or three dimensions.

These figures are *one-dimensional.* They can be measured in only one direction, such as length.	These figures are *two-dimensional.* They can be measured in two directions, such as length and width.	These figures are *three-dimensional.* They can be measured in three directions, such as length, width, and height.
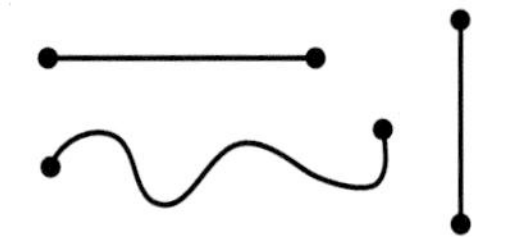	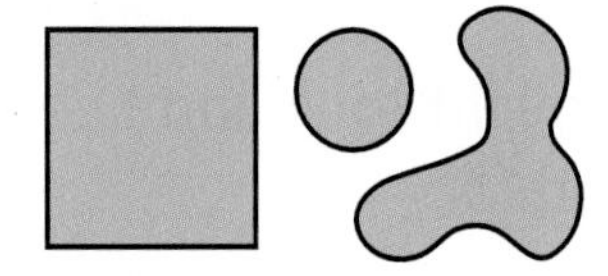	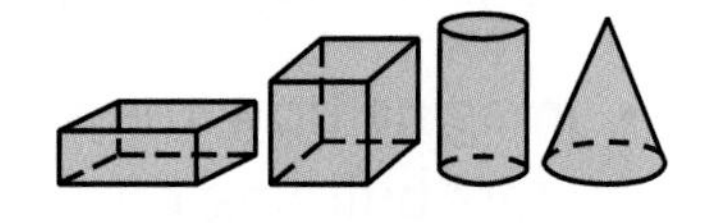
Open Plane Figures You use a linear unit, ⊢⊣, to measure a one-dimensional figure.	**Closed Plane Figures** You use a square unit, ◻, to measure the *area* of a two-dimensional figure.	**Solid Figures** You use a cubic unit, ◻, to measure the *volume* of a three-dimensional figure.

Talk About It

- Would each of the following be measured in inches, square inches, or cubic inches: a piece of string, a place mat, a shoe box?
- What in the classroom reminds you of a one-dimensional figure? a two-dimensional figure? a three-dimensional figure?

Check Your Understanding

Choose *feet, square feet,* or *cubic feet* to measure each.

1. 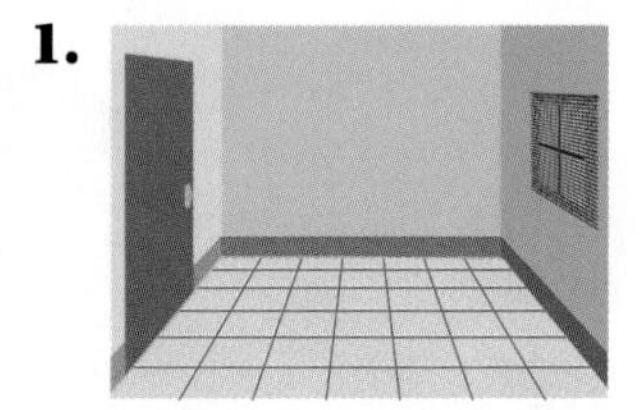

area of a floor

2. 

length of a rope

3. 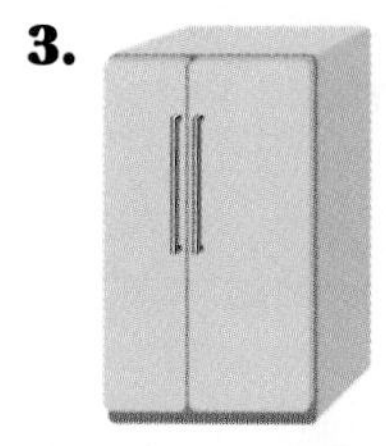

volume of a refrigerator

PRACTICE

Write *one-dimensional, two-dimensional,* or *three-dimensional* to describe each figure.

4. 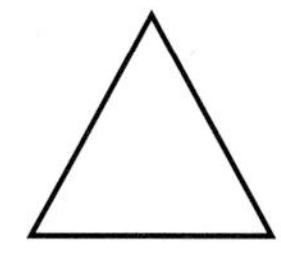

5.

6. 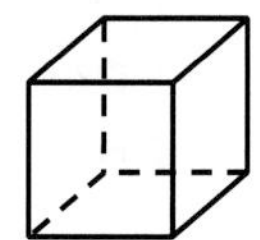

7. 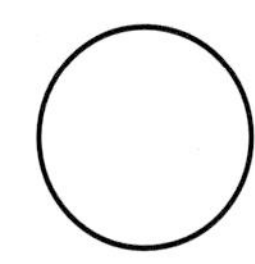

8. 

9. 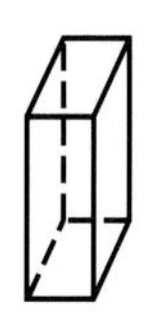

10. 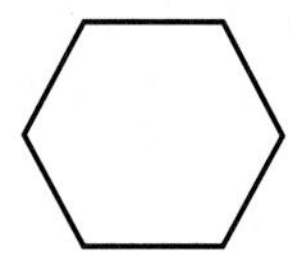

11. 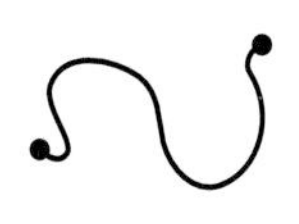

12. 

13. 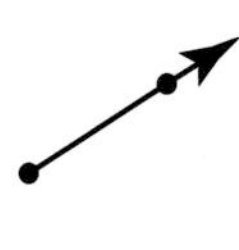

14. 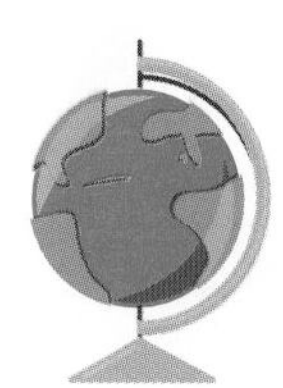

15. 

16. 

17. 

18. 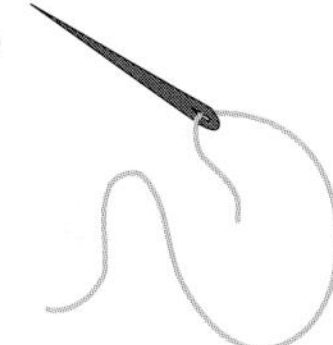

Choose the unit that can be used to measure each. Write *feet, square feet,* or *cubic feet.*

19. 

20. 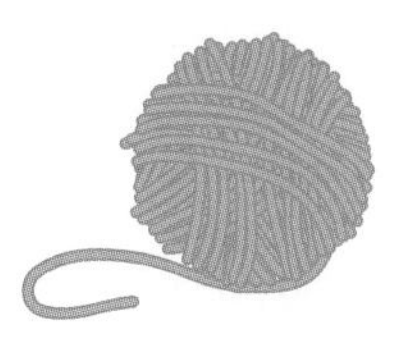

21. 

Mixed Applications

22. Shannon wants to buy a rug to cover her bedroom floor. What unit could she use to measure the area of the floor?

23. **WRITE ABOUT IT** What can you name that is one-dimensional? two-dimensional? three-dimensional? Tell the unit you would use to measure each.

Mixed Review

Find the difference. (pages 20–21)

24. $200 - 179$

25. $400 - 218$

26. $500 - 364$

27. $900 - 607$

Find the sum. (pages 6–7)

28. $8 + 7 + 11$

29. $32 + 74 + 68$

30. $73 + 89 + 26$

31. $98 + 87 + 43$

Patterns for Solid Figures

You will investigate the two-dimensional faces of three-dimensional figures.

Why learn this? You will understand how a package or box can be made from a pattern.

WORD POWER
net

Explore

Cut apart a three-dimensional box to make a two-dimensional pattern.

MATERIALS: empty container, such as a small cereal box; scissors and tape

MODEL

Step 1
Cut along some of the edges until the box is flat. Be sure each face is connected by at least one edge.

Step 2
Trace the flat shape. This is a net. A **net** is a two-dimensional pattern of a three-dimensional figure.

Step 3
Rebuild the net into a three-dimensional box. Use tape to hold it together.

Record

Draw your net. Write sentences to compare your net with your classmates' nets. How are they alike? How are they different?

Try This

Use the pattern to make a cube.

MATERIALS: the pattern of a cube; scissors and tape

- Cut out and fold the pattern. Make a cube. Put tape on each edge.
- Now, cut the cube along different edges to make a different net.
- Draw at least two different nets for a cube. Remember to put tape on all edges of the cube each time you rebuild it.

TALK ABOUT IT How many dimensions does a cube have? a net for a cube? an edge for a cube?

Technology Link
E-Lab • Activity 12 Available on CD-ROM and the Internet at http://www.hbschool.com/elab

HANDS-ON PRACTICE

Use tape, scissors, and patterns for nets to make a model of another figure.

1. Choose a different pattern, and make the figure. Cut it apart, and draw at least two different nets for that figure.

2. **WRITE ABOUT IT** What pattern did you choose? Explain how the net for the cube is different from this figure.

Technology Link

In ***Mighty Math Number Heroes***, the game *Dr. Gee's 3-D Lab* challenges you to match solid figures to their nets.

Applying What You Learned

Write the letter of the figure that is made with each net.

3. 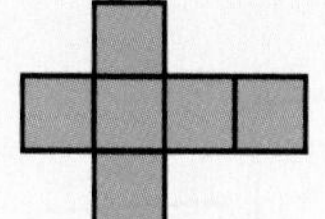

4. 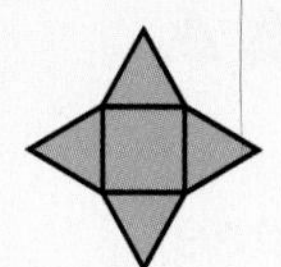

5. 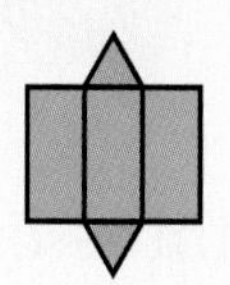

6. 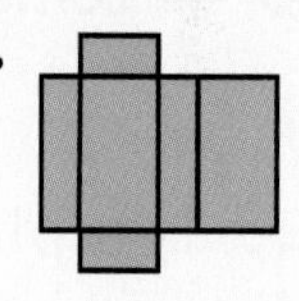

a. 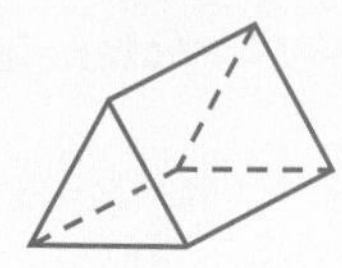

b. 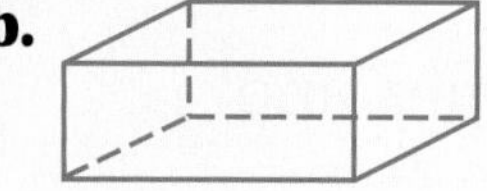

c. 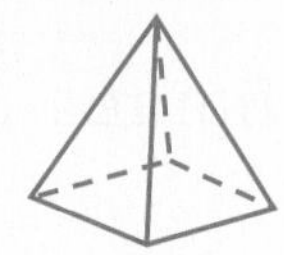

d. 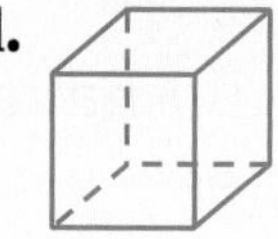

7. Which of the following nets would make a cube?

a. 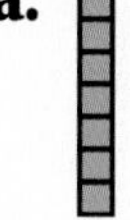

b. 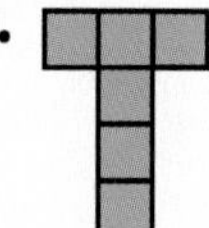

c. 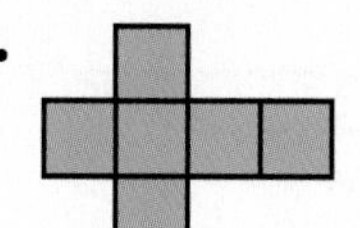

d. 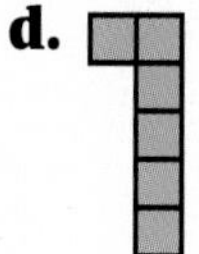

8. Which of the following nets could be folded to form the figure at the left?

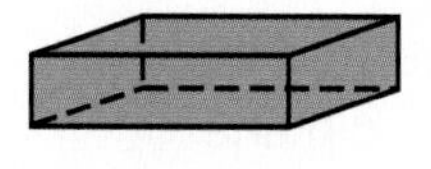

a. 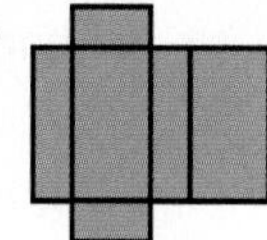

b. 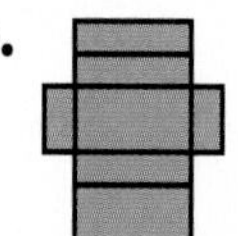

c. 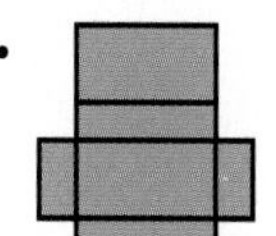

d. 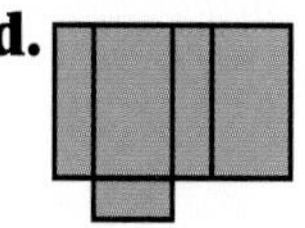

Mixed Applications

9. When Rosa finished her cereal, she opened the bottom of the box. Then she cut along one vertical edge to make a net. Draw the net that Rosa made.

10. **WRITE ABOUT IT** Write how you could make a cube into a net. Tell what net you would make, and draw a picture of the net.

MORE PRACTICE Student Handbook page H88

PART
1 Faces of Solid Figures

You will learn that faces of solid figures are made up of plane figures.	**Why learn this?** You can picture the two-dimensional shapes used to make a three-dimensional figure.	**WORD POWER** vertex

If the net for a triangular prism were cut apart, what plane figures would you have?

Look at the triangular prism.

These are the faces of the triangular prism.

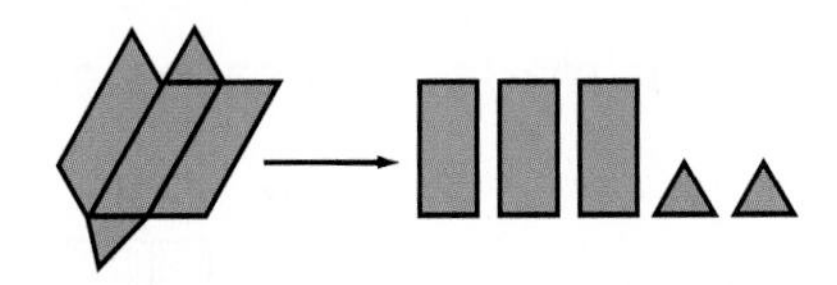

A **vertex** is a place where three or more sides meet in a solid figure. Vertices are more than one vertex.

You would have 5 plane figures: 3 rectangles and 2 triangles.

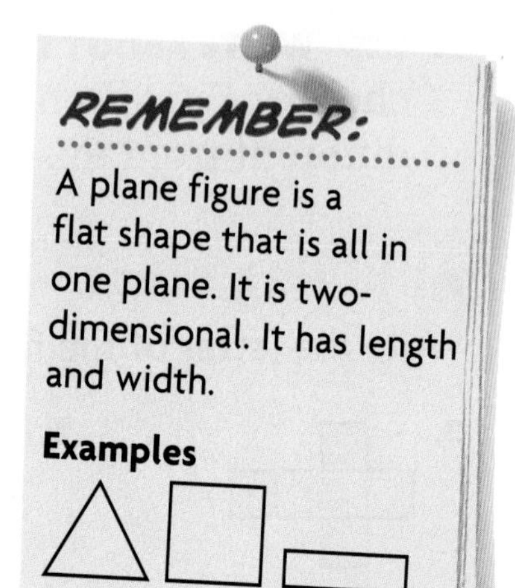

Study the faces of these solid figures.

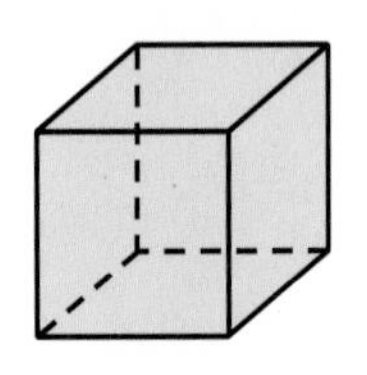

cube

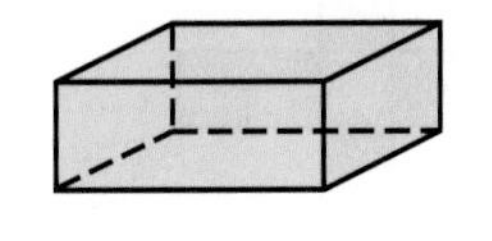

rectangular prism

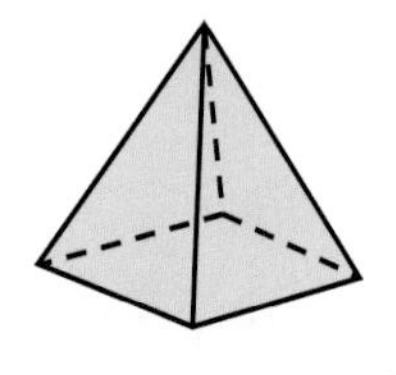

square pyramid

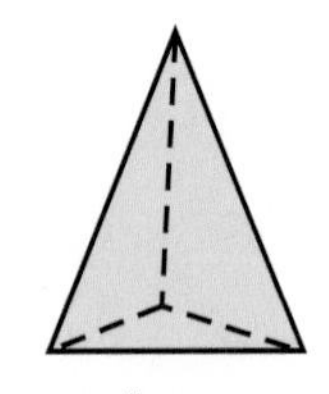

triangular pyramid

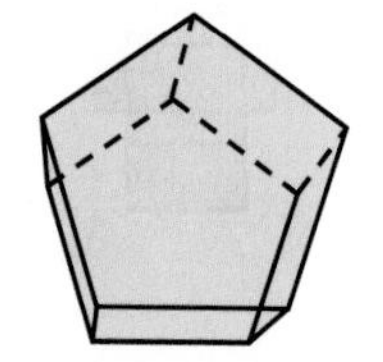

pentagonal prism

Social Studies Link

The Pentagon in Washington, D.C., is shaped like a pentagonal prism. Which plane figures do you see in the picture of the Pentagon?

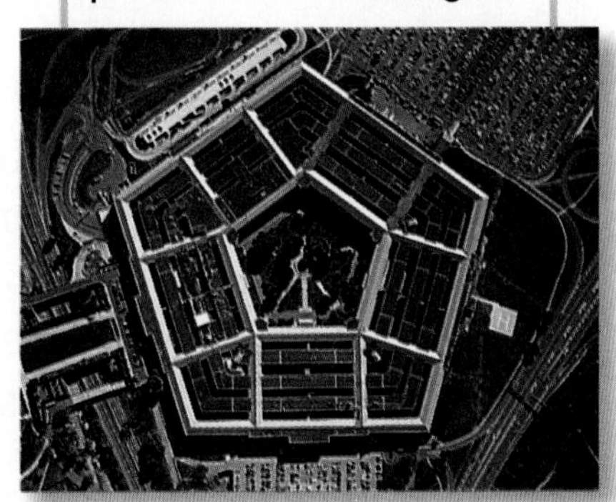

Talk About It

- What plane figures are faces of each solid figure?
- Which figure has seven faces ?
- Which solid figures have two kinds of faces?

PRACTICE

Write the names of the plane figures that are the faces of each three-dimensional figure.

1. 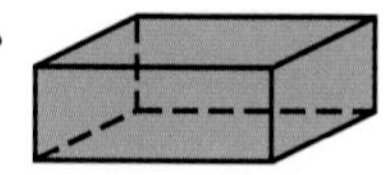

2. 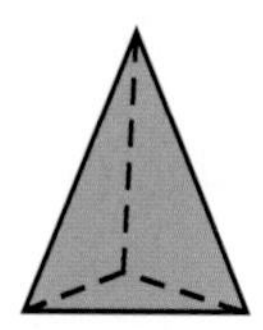

3. 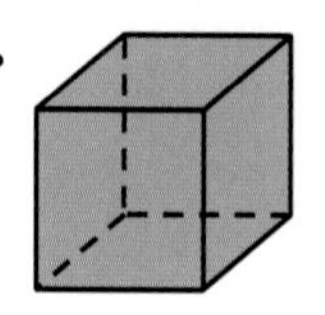

4. 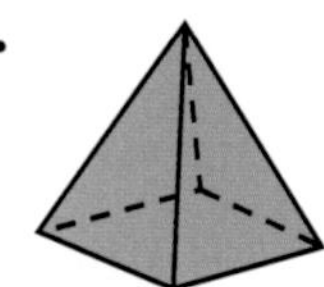

Write the number of square faces on each.

5. 

6. 

7. 

Write the names of the faces and the number of each face on the three-dimensional figure.

8. rectangular prism

9. triangular prism

10. triangular pyramid

11. cube

12. square pyramid

13. pentagonal prism

The Great Pyramid in Giza, Egypt, stands taller than a 40-story building. Its base is large enough to cover ten football fields. What plane figures make up the Great Pyramid?

Mixed Applications

14. Larry is using a number cube in his game. What plane figures make up the faces of a number cube?

15. Julio drew a picture that shows one face of a birdhouse. What three-dimensional shape does a birdhouse suggest?

16. **WRITE ABOUT IT** Susan is wrapping a gift. The gift box has 6 rectangular faces. What solid shape is the box? Draw a picture of each face. Are all of the faces of the box the same size?

PART

2 More About Solid Figures

Faces, vertices, and edges are given in the table.

Complete the table by finding the faces, vertices, and edges of the other figures.

Figure	Name of Figure	Number of Faces	Number of Vertices	Number of Edges
	Cube	6	8	12
	Rectangular prism	?	?	?
	Triangular prism	?	?	?
	Triangular pyramid	?	?	?
	Square pyramid	?	?	?

Talk About It

- How are a cube and a rectangular prism alike? How are they different?
- What plane figure forms three congruent faces of a triangular prism?
- How are a triangular pyramid and a square pyramid alike? How are they different?

Check Your Understanding

For Exercises 1–9, use the table above.

Which figures have

1. 8 vertices?

2. 6 edges?

3. the fewest edges?

4. more than 6 vertices?

Which figures have

5. all congruent faces?

6. some triangular faces?

7. some rectangular faces?

8. the fewest faces?

9. the most faces?

Social Studies Link

The World Trade Center is in New York City. What figures do you see in the faces of the buildings?

PRACTICE

Copy the drawings. Circle each vertex, outline each edge in blue, and shade one face in yellow.

10. 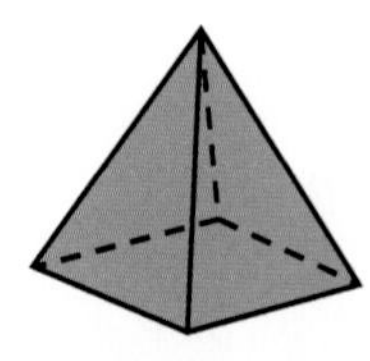

11. 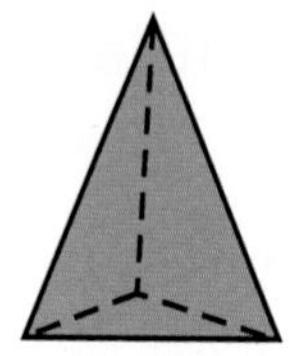

12. 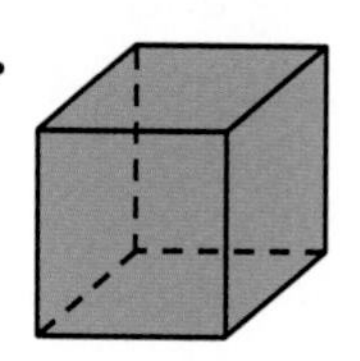

Write the letter of the figure that answers each question.

13. Which figure has more edges?
  a. a cube
  b. a triangular prism

14. Which figure has more vertices?
  a. a rectangular prism
  b. a square pyramid

15. Which figure has fewer faces?
  a. a triangular pyramid
  b. a triangular prism

16. Which figures have all congruent faces?
  a. a rectangular prism and a cube
  b. a cube and some triangular pyramids

Mixed Applications

17. I am a three-dimensional figure with 5 faces, 2 of which are triangles. What am I?

18. I am a three-dimensional figure with 5 faces, 8 edges, and 5 vertices. What am I?

19. What plane figure is always found in a pyramid?

20. **Write a problem** about a figure that has 6 faces and 12 edges.

Mixed Review

Write the time on the clock. (pages 120–121)

21. 

22. 

23. 

24. 

Find the sum or difference. (pages 12–13)

25. $5.62 + 7.92

26. $21.35 − 19.77

27. $24.52 + 48.52

28. $140.00 − 73.46

29. $60.03 + 5.99

Plane Figures on a Coordinate Grid

You will learn that plane figures can be shown by finding and connecting sets of points on a coordinate grid.

Why learn this? You can locate places on a map or play games such as Battleship.®

You can locate points on a grid using two numbers called an *ordered pair*. The first number in each pair tells how many spaces to move horizontally, or straight across. The second number tells how many spaces to move vertically, or straight up.

MATERIALS: grid paper and a straightedge

Use the ordered pairs (1,2), (8,2), and (4,5) to draw a plane figure. What plane figure did you draw?

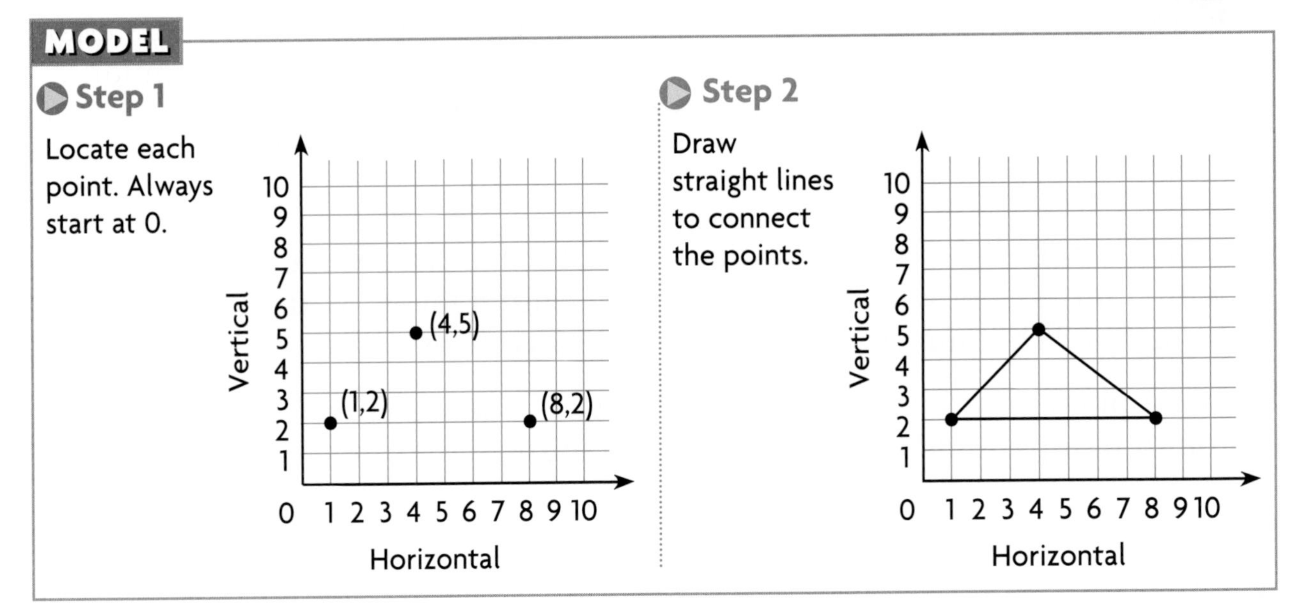

So, the plane figure you drew is a triangle.

Check Your Understanding

CRITICAL THINKING

Use grid paper to draw plane figures on a coordinate grid.

1. Locate points on the grid that are vertices of a different plane figure. Write the ordered pairs.

2. Name a set of ordered pairs. Have a partner locate the points, draw the figure, and name the figure.

Talk About It

- How does the order of the numbers in an ordered pair help you locate a point on a grid or map?
- Are the figures that you drew one-dimensional, two-dimensional, or three-dimensional? How do you know?

Social Studies Link

This sign at the mall is like a map. The ordered pairs tell where the stores are. If the Music Store is at (3,5), how can you find it on the map?

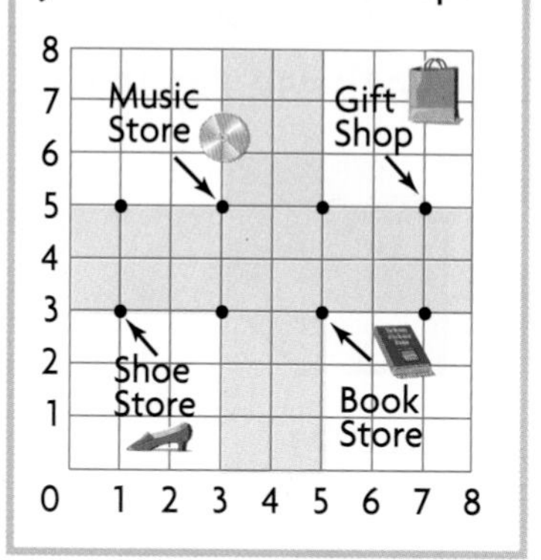

PRACTICE

Write the ordered pairs used to draw each plane figure.

3.

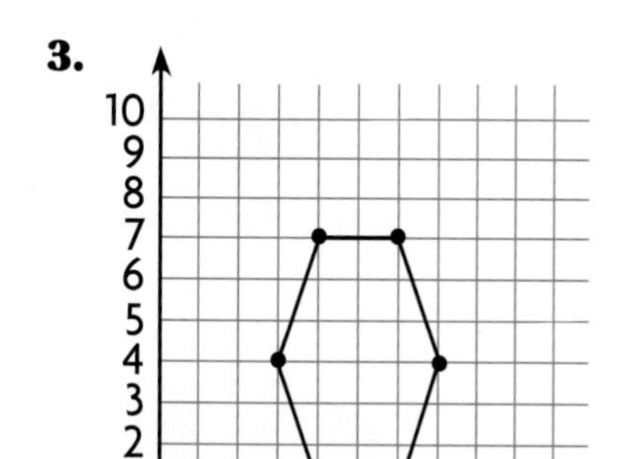

4.

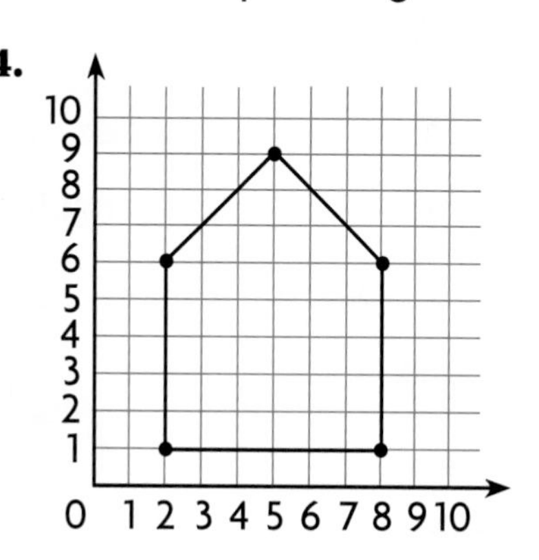

Mark the ordered pairs on grid paper. Draw a figure with vertices at the named points. Write the name of the figure.

5. (1,1), (1,2), (2,1), (2,2)

6. (1,2), (4,2), (1,4), (4,4)

7. (3,2), (3,4), (4,6), (5,4), (5,2)

8. (2,6), (3,5), (3,7), (5,5), (5,7), (6,6)

Mixed Applications

9. Claire's new classes are located on a grid map at (3,1), (3,5), and (5,5). She returns to her first class at the end of her third class. Connect the points. What plane figure is represented by Claire's path?

10. **WRITE ABOUT IT** Drake is using a grid map to plan his garden. He will plant tomatoes between the points (1,1), (1,2), (2,1), and (2,2). Draw a picture of Drake's garden. Describe the figure made by the tomato section.

Mixed Review

Write the numbers in order from the least to the greatest. (pages 110–113)

11. 2,581; 3,581; 2,518

12. 8,063; 8,636; 8,603

13. 4,161; 6,416; 4,116

Write the time as show on a digital clock. (pages 120–121)

14. 11 minutes past six

15. 27 minutes past three

16. 15 minutes before two

MORE PRACTICE Student Handbook page H89

PART 1 Classifying and Sorting Solid Figures

You will learn to sort and classify solid figures by their faces, vertices, and edges.

Why learn this? You can name characteristics of solid figures and picture them as things you use every day, such as balls, cans, or boxes.

Study these figures.

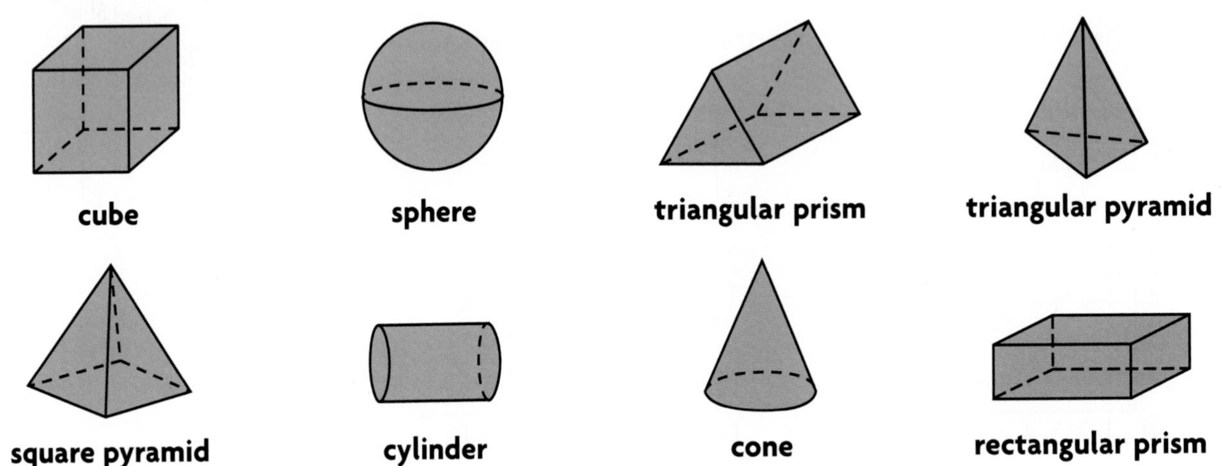

Notice that

- the solid figures can have flat faces, curved surfaces, or both flat faces and curved surfaces.

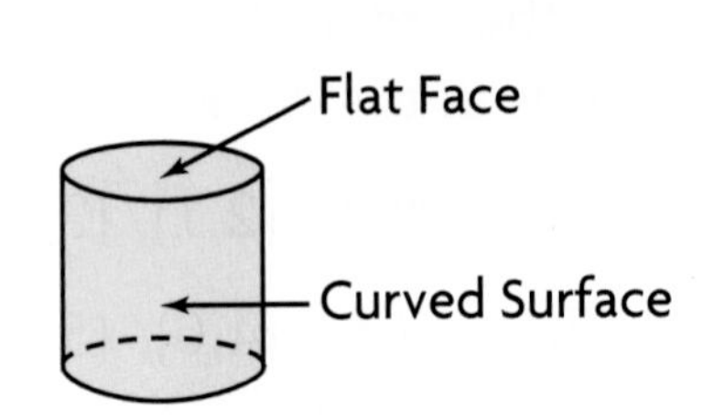

Talk About It

- How many flat faces does the square pyramid have?
- Which figures have both flat faces and curved surfaces?
- Which figure has no faces or edges?

Use a Venn diagram to show relationships among geometric figures.

Sort the figures above into a Venn diagram.

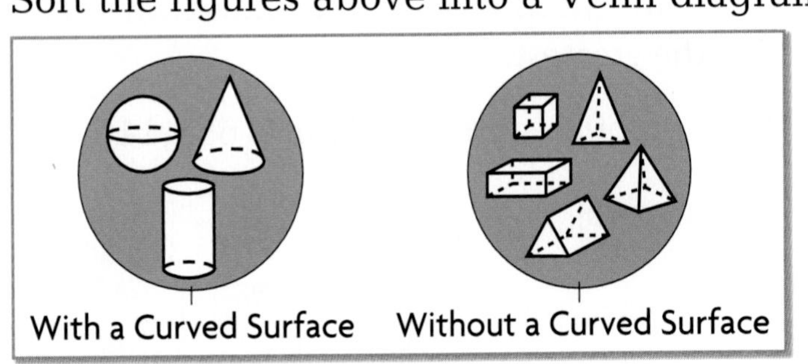

Check Your Understanding 

Use a Venn diagram to sort the figures shown at the top of page 202.

1. Write a label for each part of the Venn diagram.

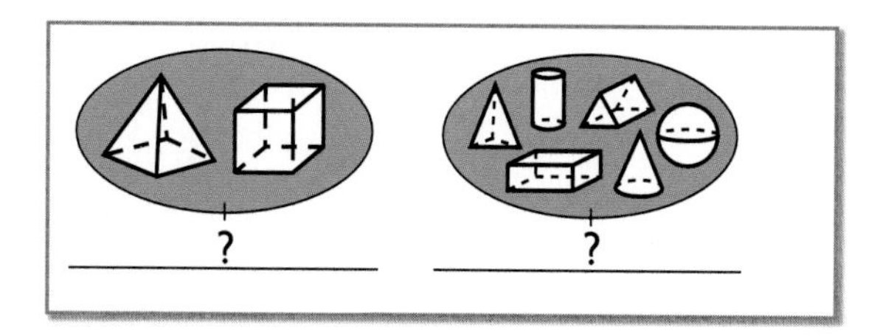

2. Sort the figures into the Venn diagram.

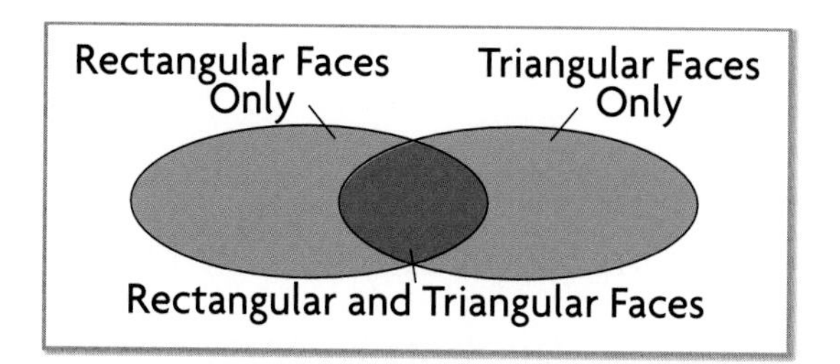

3. How can you decide if the circles in a Venn diagram should overlap?

4. Draw the Venn diagram to sort the figures in the models with and without triangular faces.

PRACTICE

Which solid figure do you see in each?

5. 

6. 

7. 

Write a label for each part of the Venn Diagram.

8. 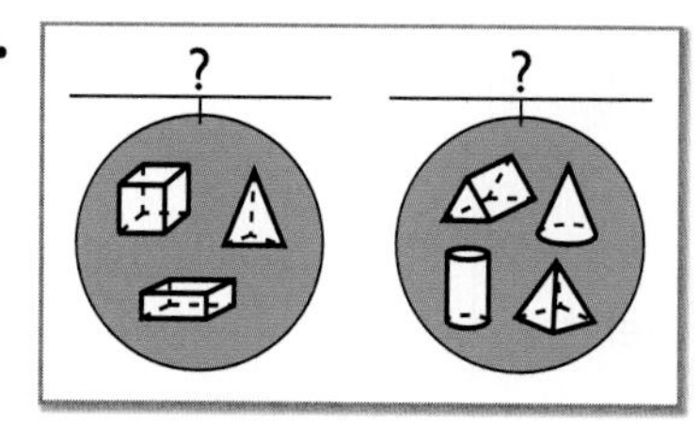

9. 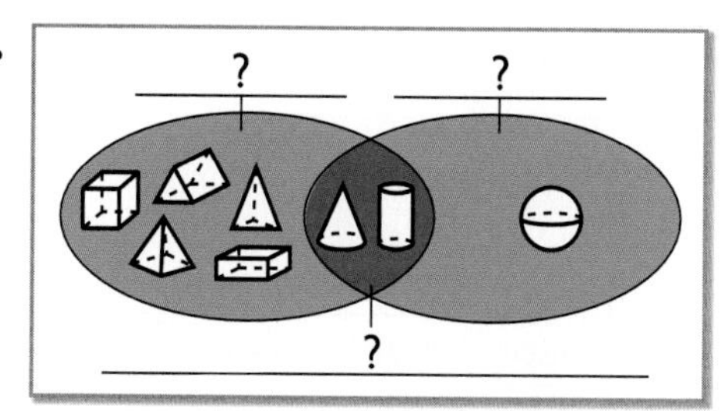

Mixed Applications

10. How many more edges does a cube have than a square pyramid?

11. Which figures on page 202 have at least one triangular face?

12. **WRITE ABOUT IT** Are there faces in a square pyramid and a triangular prism that are the same figure? Explain.

MORE PRACTICE Student Handbook page H89

PART 2 PROBLEM-SOLVING STRATEGY
Make an Organized List

THE PROBLEM Jason's job is to sort and classify the items in a gift shop. He must put all the items on the shelves and tables by their shapes. How can Jason organize the items in the gift shop?

✓ Understand

- What are you asked to find?
- What information will you use?
- Is there information you will not use? If so, what?

✓ Plan

- What strategy can you use to solve the problem?

You can *make an organized list* to solve the problem.

✓ Solve

- How can you organize your list to solve the problem?

You can make a list for each group of items with the same shape.

Box Shaped	Sphere Shaped	Cone Shaped	Cylinder Shaped	Pyramid Shaped
gift box	snow globes	party hats	cologne	paperweights
candy box	paperweights	feathered hats	lipsticks	sculptures
books	balloons	drink cups	bubble beads	gift boxes
puzzles	globes	noisemakers	straws	

So, you can list the items by their geometric shape.

✓ Look Back

- How can you decide if your answer is correct?
- What other strategy could you use?

PRACTICE

CHOOSE Paper/Pencil Calculator Hands-on Mental Math

Make an organized list to solve.

1. June found a book, a pen, a stack of writing paper, a tape recorder, chalk, a supply box, crayons, and a crayon box in her desk. Sort the objects by the three-dimensional figures they suggest.

2. The fourth-grade science room has a telescope; models of the earth, moon and sun; a small space shuttle and space capsule; and a space helmet. Sort these items into lists of the three-dimensional shapes they suggest.

3. With lunch the astronauts may choose lemonade, apple drink, or tea. For dessert, they may have cookies, fruit, or peanuts. How many combinations of drinks and desserts could they have with their meal?

4. Use the digits 4, 6, and 8. List all the three-digit numbers you can make without repeating any digits in the same number.

Mixed Applications

Solve.

CHOOSE A STRATEGY

- Look for a Pattern
- Work Backward
- Act It Out
- Make an Organized List

5. Nicholas, Holly, Ryan, and Alicia are going to do an experiment. Nicholas will have a turn after Alicia but before Holly. Ryan's turn is before Alicia's. In what order will they do the experiment?

6. On Monday, Tom drew 3 more pictures for his report and on Tuesday he added 2 more. In the report were 11 pictures. How many pictures were in the report before Monday?

7. Ms. Lopez received extra work from 2 students the first week of class. In the next three weeks, 3, 5, and 8 students turned in extra work. If the pattern goes on, how many will do extra work the fifth week of class?

8. Alfredo spent half his money for a ticket to the basketball game. Then he spent half of what was left on a snack. The picture shows how much he had left. How much money did Alfredo have at the start?

9. Nan is putting the groceries away. She has soup, cereal, straws, paper towels, and a cookbook. Sort the groceries by the three-dimensional figures they suggest.

MORE PRACTICE Student Handbook page H90

CULTURAL CONNECTION

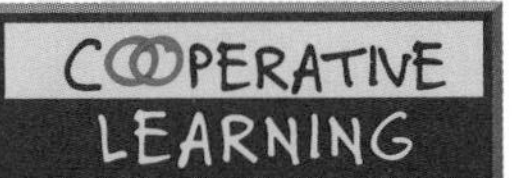

TLINGIT WOOD CARVER

On Saturdays in the summer, Alice helps her uncle and aunt in their wood shop in Ketchikan, Alaska. Tourists buy her uncle's wood carvings. He is a Tlingit (TLING•kuht) artist.

What plane and solid figures do you see in Tlingit art and architecture?

CULTURAL LINK

Many Tlingit people live in southeastern Alaska. Their ancestors carved totem poles. The brightly colored figures on the poles were birds and animals. The poles were Tlingit history books. A family story could be told about each figure. The poles were placed near the decorated Tlingit homes.

1. During the winter, Alice's uncle makes about 100 keychain totem poles. What solid figure could he use for the keychains?
2. Alice's uncle will make and paint models of Tlingit houses. What solid figures can he use to make the houses?
3. Study the photograph and the floor plan of a traditional Tlingit house. Then make a model of a Tlingit house. Copy the patterns on grid paper, cut them out, and fold them.

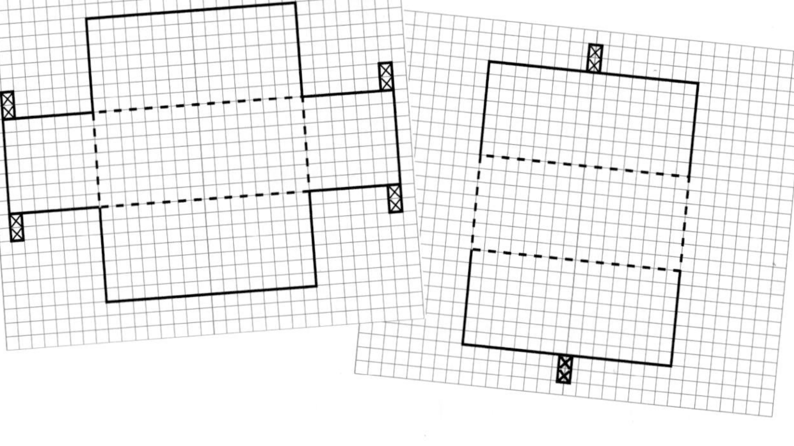

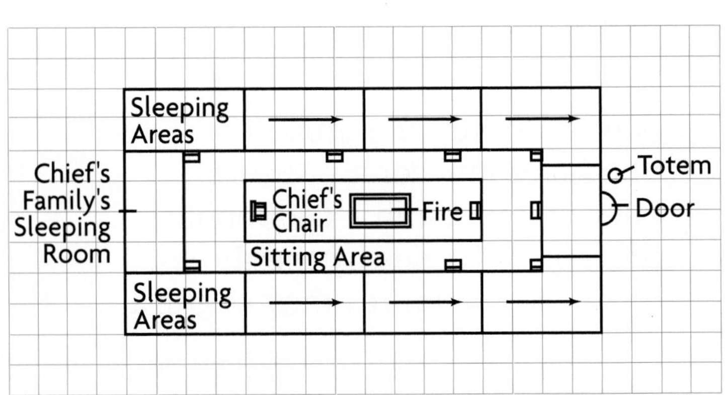

CHAPTER 12

REVIEW

✓ CHECK UNDERSTANDING

VOCABULARY

1. A measure in one direction is a _?_. (page 192)

2. A _?_ is a place where three sides meet in a solid figure. (page 196)

3. A two-dimensional pattern of a three-dimensional figure is a _?_. (page 194)

Write one-dimensional, two-dimensional, or three-dimensional. (pages 192–193)

4. 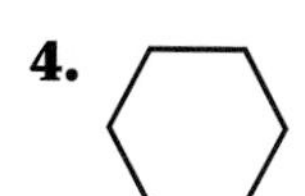

5. 

6. 

7. 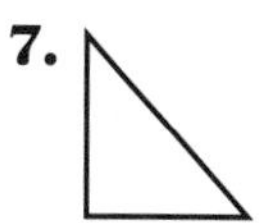

8. 

9. Which of the following nets would make a rectangular prism? (pages 194–195)

a. 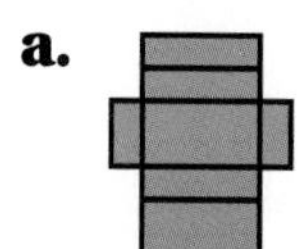

b. 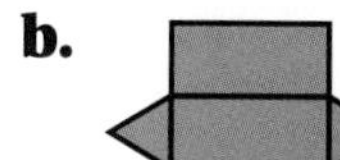

c. 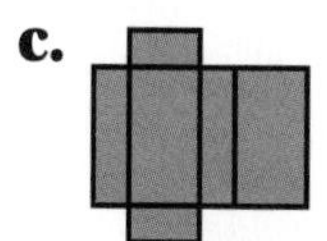

d. 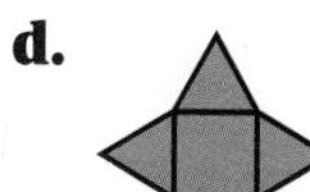

e. 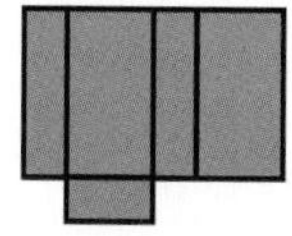

Locate the ordered pairs on grid paper. Connect the points and name the figure. (pages 200–201)

10. (1,5), (1,1), (4,1)

11. (1,3), (2,1),(3,1), (4,3), (3,5), (2,5)

✓ CHECK SKILLS

Name the solid figure. Write the plane figures that are its faces and write the number of faces, edges, and vertices. (pages 196–199)

12. 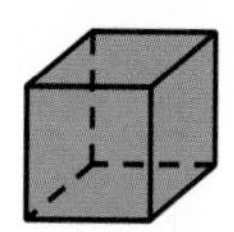

13. 

14. 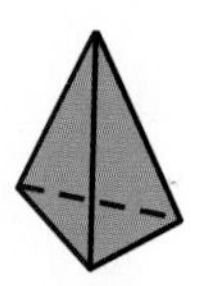

15. 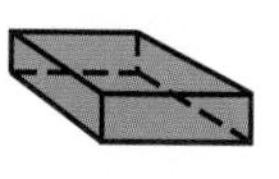

16. 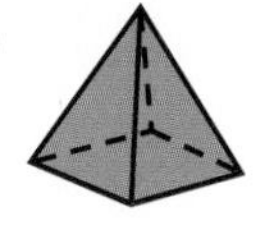

✓ CHECK PROBLEM SOLVING

Solve. (pages 204–205)

CHOOSE A STRATEGY

- Act It Out
- Make a Model
- Work Backward
- Make an Organized List

17. Use the digits 3, 5, and 7. List all the three-digit numbers you can without repeating any digit in the same number.

18. Melissa wants to take a picture of her classmates Phylisa, Ashley, and Juan. In how many different ways can Melissa line them up?

EXPLORING ONE- AND TWO-DIMENSIONAL FIGURES

DID YOU KNOW . . .

Origami is the name of the ancient art of paper folding. The word *origami* comes from two Japanese words: *Ori* means "folding" and *kami* means "paper."

Origami Geometry

The art of paper folding, *origami*, is a fun way to use geometry. By carefully following folding instructions, you can make hats or animals.

YOU WILL NEED: a square sheet of wrapping paper or newsprint and chart paper to record your findings.

Work with a partner. Your job is to

- make an origami object, and predict which figures you will see when you unfold your object: intersecting, parallel, or perpendicular line segments; acute, obtuse, or right angles; rectangles; squares; triangles; pentagons.
- unfold your origami and check your predictions.
- make a chart that shows all the different figures you found.

MAKE A HAT

1.

2.

3.

4.

5. Fold up the upper sheet. Repeat to the other side.

6. Open and wear.

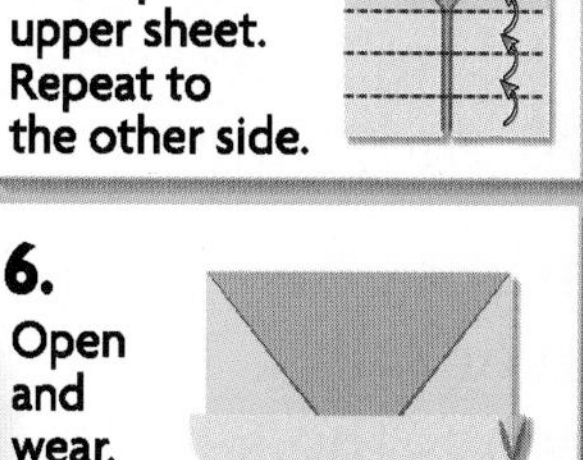

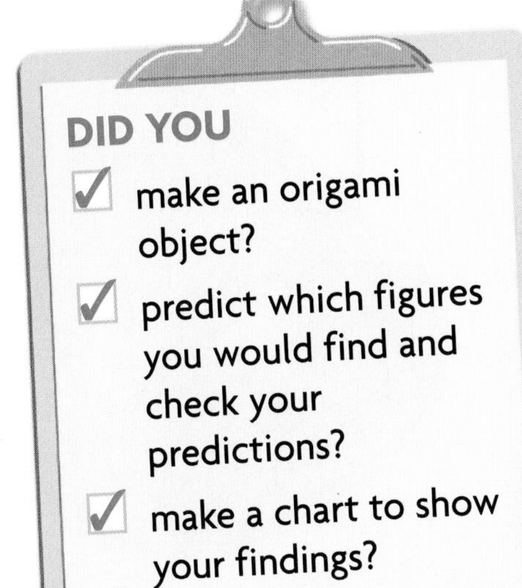

Line Segments

You will learn about geometric ideas and line segments.

Why learn this? You can find line segments all around you.

WORD POWER
- point
- plane
- line
- line segment
- parallel

These ideas will help you understand terms used in geometry.

Points name locations on objects and in space. They are named by letters.

A

point *A*

A **plane** is a flat surface with no end. Planes are named by three points in the plane.

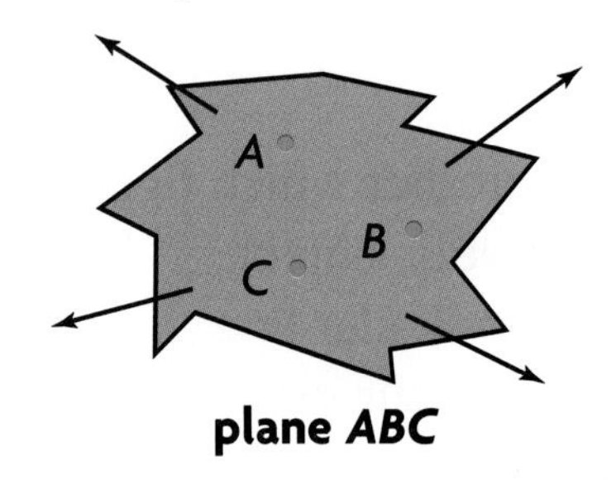

plane *ABC*

A **line** is a straight path in a plane. It has no end. It can be named by any two points on the line.

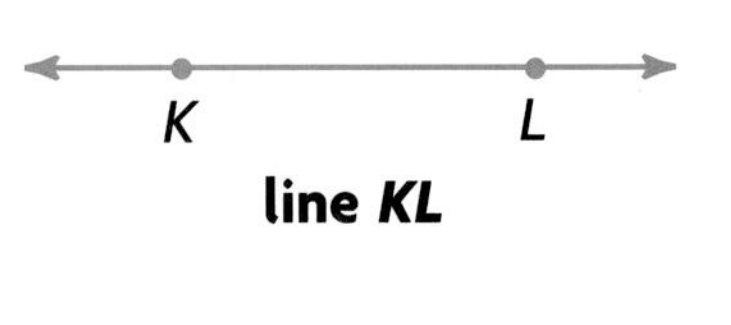

line *KL*

Use your imagination to connect these ideas to things around you. Look at the football field.

- What is *like* a point? *like* a plane? *like* a line?

A **line segment** is a part of a line between two endpoints.

Parallel line segments never cross. They are always the same distance apart.

Sports Link

What do the yard lines on a football field stand for?

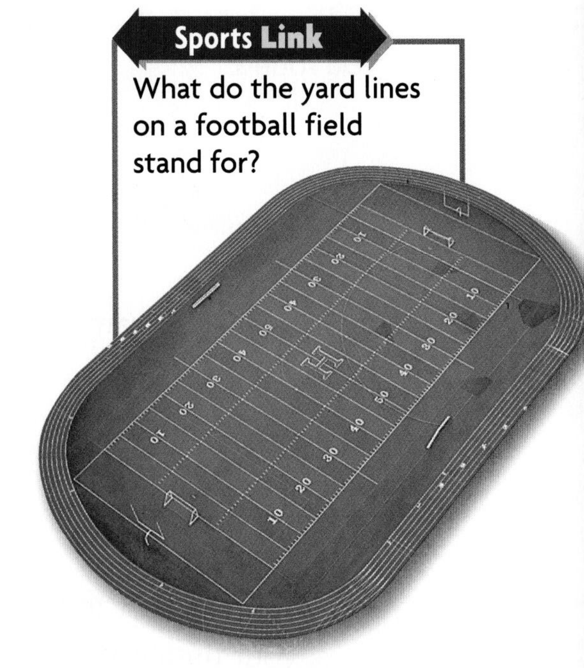

Talk About It

- How do you know that the yard lines on the football field are parallel?
- Is a football field like a plane? Explain.
- Is a goal line like a line segment? Explain.
- What examples of line segments do you see in your classroom?

PRACTICE

Write *points, line, line segment,* or *plane* to name each figure.

1. 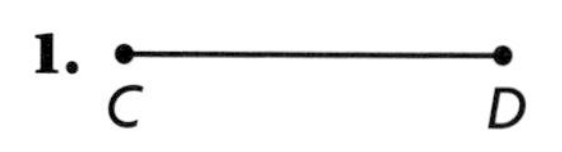

2. 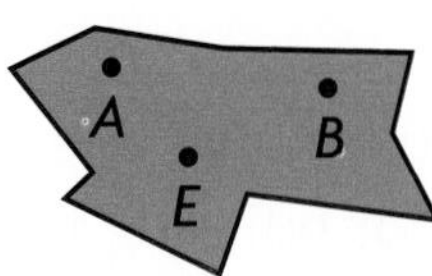

3. F G

4. J K

5. 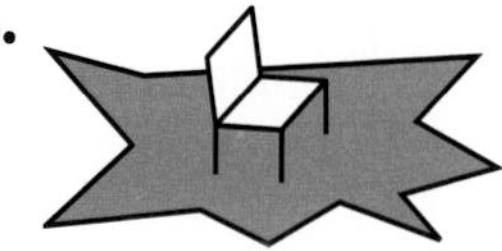

6. 

7. 

8. 

Decide if the figure is a line segment. Write *yes* or *no*.

9. 

10.

11.

12. 

Write *yes* or *no* to tell if the pair of line segments is parallel.

13. 

14. 

15. 

Mixed Applications

16. What parallel line segments do you notice on the flag in your classroom?

17. **WRITE ABOUT IT** Draw four endpoints as shown. What is the greatest number of line segments you can draw using these endpoints?

CULTURAL LINK

The ancient Chinese people discovered how to make paper. The Japanese invented, *Origami,* the art of paper folding. What figure does this origami look like?

Mixed Review

Write *one-dimensional, two-dimensional,* or *three-dimensional* to describe each figure. (pages 192–193)

18. 

19. 

20. 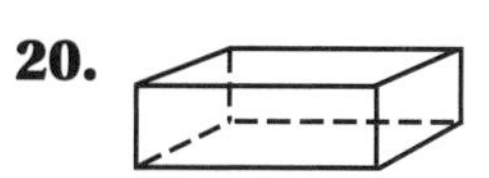

21. 

22. 

Write the names of the plane figures that are the faces of each three-dimensional figure. (pages 196–197)

23. 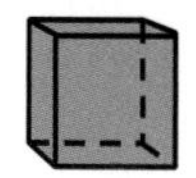

24. 

25. 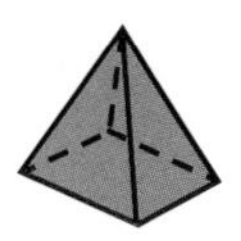

26. 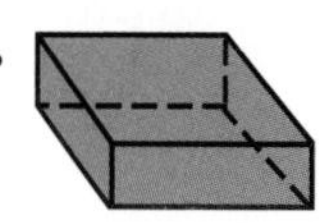

27. 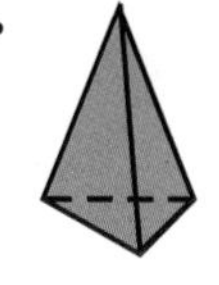

PART 1
Exploring Angles and Line Relationships

You will learn to name kinds of angles and line relationships.

Why learn this? You can use lines and angles when drawing or building two-dimensional and three-dimensional figures.

WORD POWER
ray
angle
right angle
acute angle
obtuse angle

A **ray** is part of a line and has one endpoint. It is straight and goes on and on in one direction. A ray is named by the endpoint and one other point on the ray.

How is a beam of light like a ray?

When two rays have the same endpoint, they form an **angle**. An angle is named by points on the rays and the endpoint.

A **right angle** forms a square corner.

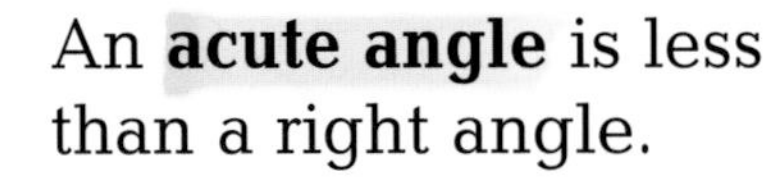

An **acute angle** is less than a right angle.

An **obtuse angle** is greater than a right angle.

Shows right angle measure.

right angle

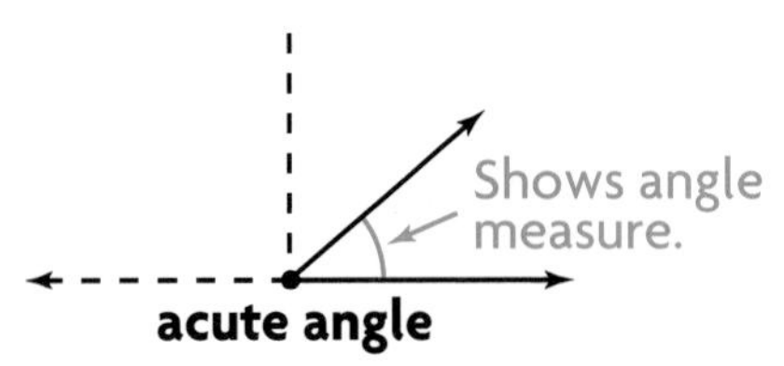

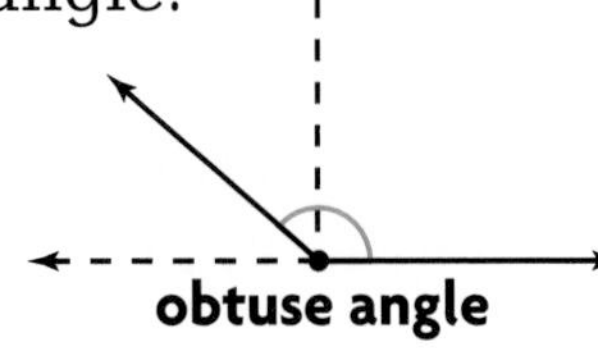

Talk About It

- How can you check to find out if an angle is a right angle?
- What are some examples of angles in your classroom?
- What kind of angle is formed by the hands on this clock?
- What angle is formed by the hands on each clock below?

a. 9:00

b. 4:45

c. 4:30

d. 3:35

PRACTICE

Write the name of each figure.

1. 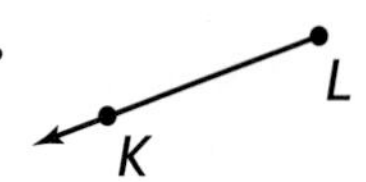
2. R S
3. S
4. O P
5. 
6. E F
7. P Q
8. A B

What kind of angle is each? Write *right*, *acute*, or *obtuse*.

9. 

10. 
11. 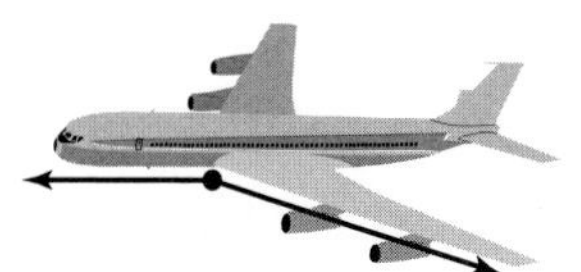
12. 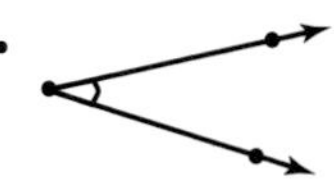
13. 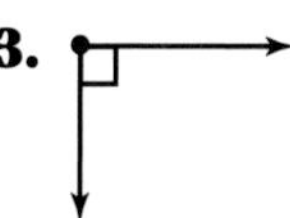
14. 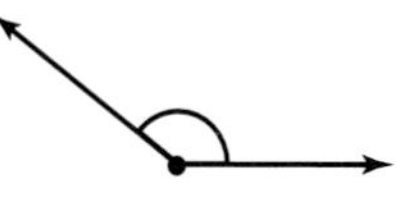
15. 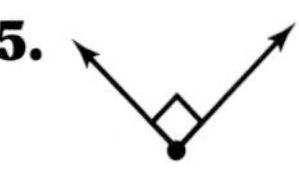
16. 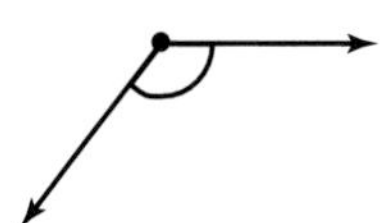
17. 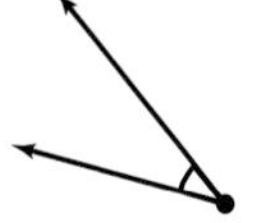

Write the number of right angles in each letter.

18. T
19. 
20. 
21. E
22. 
23. 

Mixed Applications

24. Amir is drawing a building and sees that the doors, windows, and corners of the rooms all form the same kind of angle. What kind of angle do they form?

25. When Jenny took her dog for a walk, the traffic lights were red at every other corner. The first light was red. Was the light at the fifth corner red or green?

26. Kelly arrived at her dance class at 7:30 P.M. The class was over on the hour. Kelly noticed that the clock's hands were at a right angle. How long was her dance class?

27. **WRITE ABOUT IT** As Melissa prints her name, she notices that there are three angles in the letter *M*. What kind of angles are they? Print your first name and count the angles.

MORE PRACTICE Student Handbook pages H90-H91

PART 2

More About Angles and Line Relationships

WORD POWER

intersecting lines
perpendicular lines

Look at the line relationships shown below. What angles are formed by each set of lines?

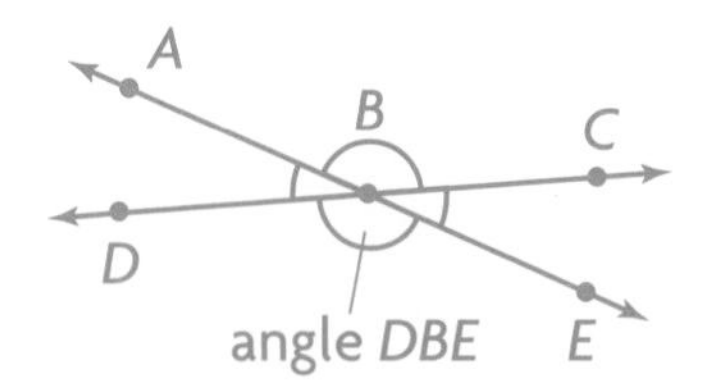

angle LMN
L
K
N
M
O

All lines that cross each other are **intersecting lines**. The lines above form two acute angles and two obtuse angles.

Lines that intersect to form four right angles are **perpendicular lines**.

On maps, lines show roads. On a map of these roads, what line relationships will you see?

Talk About It

- Can lines be *both* intersecting and perpendicular? Explain.
- Name some objects around you that suggest intersecting or perpendicular lines. Explain.

Check Your Understanding

Use the map below to answer the questions.

1. What roads intersect with Interstate 24 on the map?
2. Which streets intersect and are perpendicular to each other?
3. Which street is perpendicular to Second Street?
4. How many streets are parallel to First Street?
5. Which street is perpendicular to the railroad tracks?

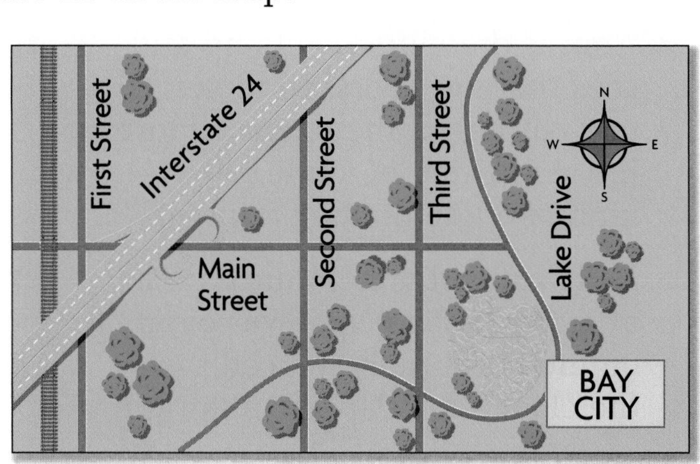

6. Write three more questions about angles and line relationships on this map. Have a classmate answer your questions.

PRACTICE

What kind of line relationship is each? Write *intersecting, parallel,* or *perpendicular.*

7. 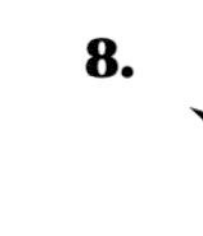

8. 

9. 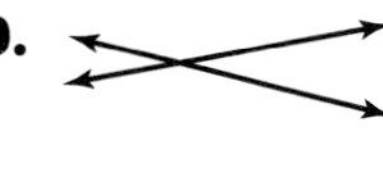

10. 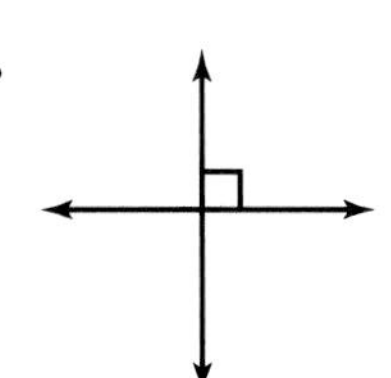

11.

12.

History Link

The oldest known map was made in about 2250 B.C. It is a clay tablet of Babylonia, which is now Iraq. What do you think the lines on the map show?

Mixed Applications

Use the map of College Park to answer Problems 13–16.

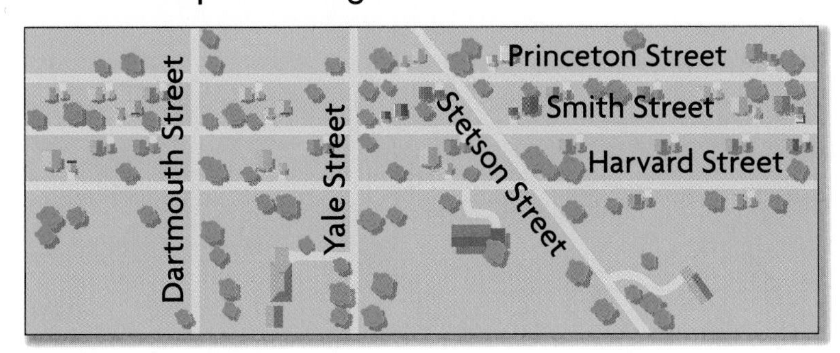

13. Name the streets that are parallel to Smith Street.

14. Name the streets that are perpendicular to Harvard Street.

15. Name the street that intersects Princeton Street but is not perpendicular to Princeton Street.

16. Name the streets that intersect with Stetson Street.

17. Conner bought a CD for $13.99, a book for $7.95 and 2 packages of paper for $0.89 each. The tax was $1.43. How much change did he receive from $30.00?

18. **WRITE A PROBLEM** Draw a map of the streets near your school or home. Write two problems about your map.

Mixed Review

Insert the comma and write the number in words. (pages 78–79)

19. 5000 **20.** 2089 **21.** 31774 **22.** 19999 **23.** 6004 **24.** 208008

Find the quotient. (pages 60–61)

25. $36 \div 9 =$? **26.** $16 \div 4 =$? **27.** $72 \div 9 =$? **28.** $56 \div 7 =$?

MORE PRACTICE Student Handbook page H91

Exploring Circles

You will investigate how to draw a circle and how the parts of a circle are used to measure it.

Why learn this? You draw circles in art, on game boards, and in sports.

WORD POWER
radius
diameter

Explore

Use a paper clip and two pencils to draw a circle.

MATERIALS: large and small paper clips, centimeter ruler, two pencils

MODEL

Step 1

Draw a point to be the center of the circle. Label it with the letter *P*.

P •

Step 2

Draw the circle by placing pencils in the ends of a paper clip. The pencil at point *P* does not move.

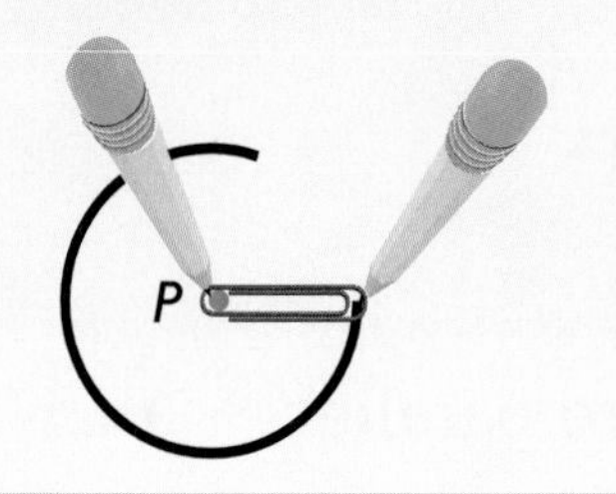

Art Link

Make patterns with circles. What can you use to make circles?

Talk About It

- How does the curved line of the circle relate to the point in the center?
- How is a circle different from other curved plane figures?

Record

Write a definition for a circle. Draw a picture of a circle as a part of your definition.

Now, investigate the parts of a circle that are used to measure it.

E-Lab • Activity 13 Available on CD-ROM and the Internet at http://www.hbschool.com/elab

A. A **radius** of a circle is a line segment. It goes from the center to any point on the circle.

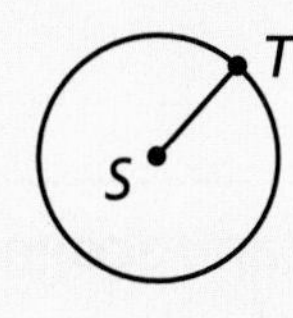

radius *ST*

B. A **diameter** of a circle is a line segment. It passes through the center and has its endpoints on the circle.

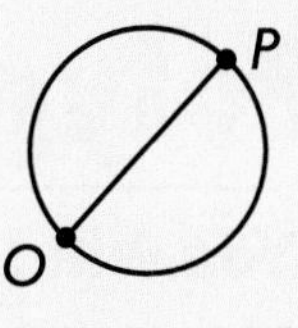

diameter *OP*

Try This

Draw a circle with each size paper clip. Use letters to name a radius and a diameter on each circle.

TALK ABOUT IT How many centimeters long are the radius and diameter of each circle you drew?

WRITE ABOUT IT In the same circle, what is the relationship of the radius to the diameter?

HANDS-ON PRACTICE

For Problems 1–4, use the drawing and a centimeter ruler.

1. The center of this circle is _?_.
2. Line segment *AB* is a _?_ of the circle. It measures _?_ cm.
3. Line segment *CD* is a _?_ of the circle. It measures _?_ cm.
4. Three points on the circle are _?_, _?_, and _?_.
5. Draw a circle. Label the center point E. Draw a radius EF. Draw a diameter GH.

Applying What You Learned

For Problem 6, use the drawings.

6. Name each radius and diameter. Name their lengths in centimeters.

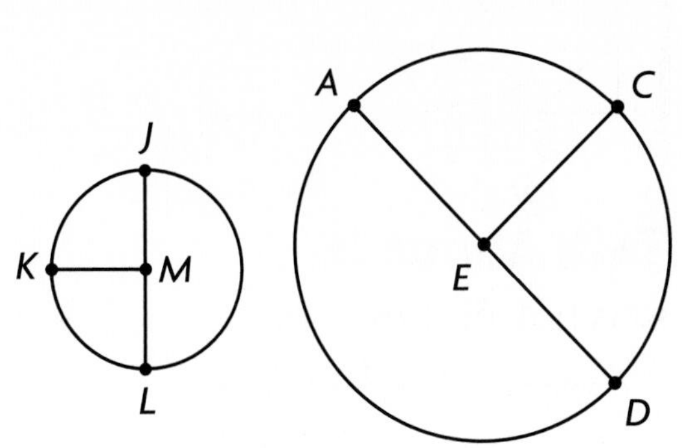

Mixed Applications

7. Angela is slicing a pie. If she makes 3 cuts from one end of the pie to another and passes through the center, how many pieces does she have?

8. Kyle and his mother left to go to the mall at 12:45 P.M. They arrived home 2 hours before dinner, which they ate at 6:00 P.M. How long were they gone?

Polygons

You will learn to name and sort polygons by their number of sides and angles.	Why learn this? You can recognize the shapes of polygons on the flat surfaces of many objects such as CDs, computer screens, and pictures.	WORD POWER polygon

A **polygon** is a closed plane figure with straight sides.

The straight sides of a polygon are line segments. Which figures are polygons? How do you know?

a. **b.** **c.** **d.**

e. **f.** **g.** **h.**

i. **j.** **k.** **l.**

So, **a, c, d, h, k,** and **l** are polygons because they are closed plane figures with straight sides.

Technology Link

In ***Mighty Math Number Heroes***, the game *GeoComputer* challenges you to identify various polygons.

Polygons are named by their number of sides or angles.

EXAMPLES

triangles

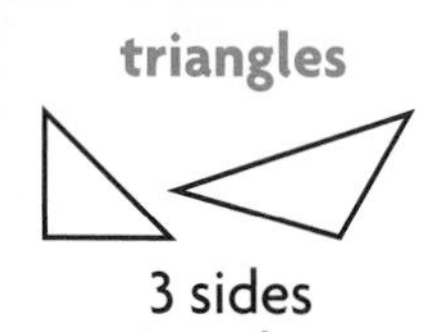

3 sides
3 angles

quadrilaterals

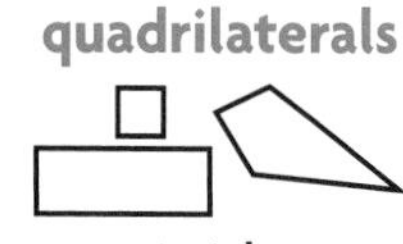

4 sides
4 angles

pentagons

5 sides
5 angles

hexagons

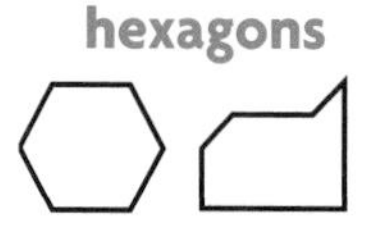

6 sides
6 angles

octagons

8 sides
8 angles

Talk About It

- What makes a polygon different from other plane figures?
- How are the two hexagons alike? How are they different?
- What polygons do you see on the faces of objects and buildings?

PRACTICE

Is the figure a polygon? Write *yes* or *no*. Give a reason for your answer.

1.  **2.** 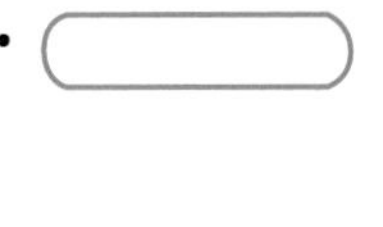 **3.**  **4.**  **5.** 

6. 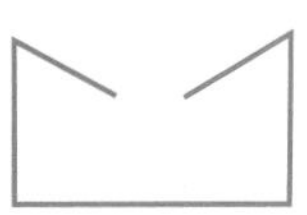 **7.** 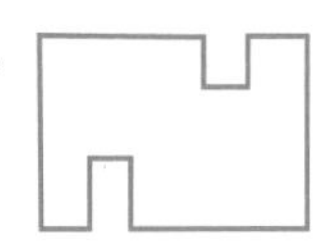 **8.** 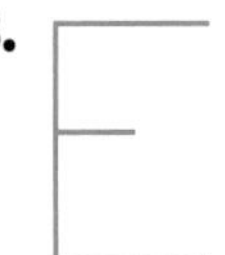 **9.**  **10.** 

Name each polygon. Tell how many sides and angles.

11.  **12.** 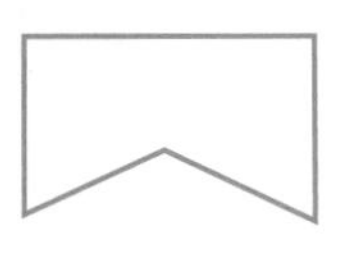 **13.** 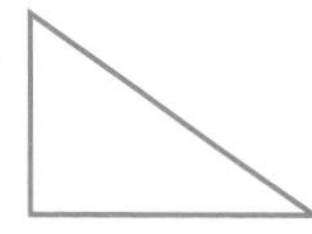 **14.**  **15.** 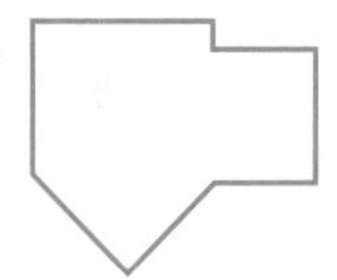

Use a straightedge to draw each figure.

16. triangle **17.** pentagon **18.** hexagon **19.** quadrilateral

Mixed Applications

20. Matias counted 8 sides on the STOP sign. What is another name for a polygon with 8 sides?

21. **WRITE ABOUT IT** Maggie drew the front of her house. She said that the shape was a pentagon since it had 5 angles. Was she correct? Explain.

Mixed Review

Write the number of faces found in each three-dimensional figure. (pages 196–199)

22. 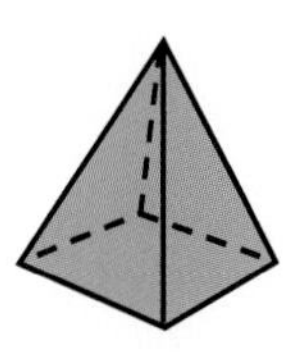 **23.** 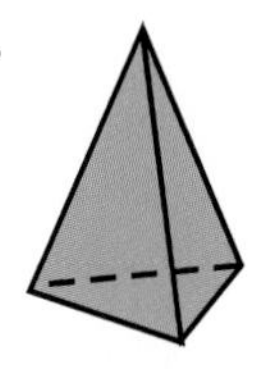 **24.** 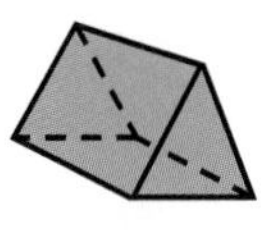 **25.** 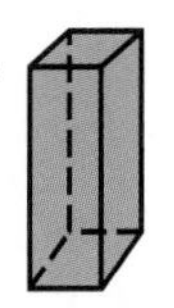

Use mental math to complete each equation. (pages 4–5)

26. $3 + 2 = \underline{?} - 2$ **27.** $9 - 4 = 3 + \underline{?}$ **28.** $3 \times 4 = 24 \div \underline{?}$ **29.** $32 \div 8 = \underline{?} \times 2$

30. $14 - 6 = \underline{?} + 4$ **31.** $56 \div \underline{?} = 4 \times 2$ **32.** $23 + \underline{?} = 5 \times 6$ **33.** $72 \div 9 = 2 \times \underline{?}$

MORE PRACTICE Student Handbook page H91

PART 1 Quadrilaterals

You will learn to classify and name quadrilaterals.

Why learn this? You will be able to name quadrilaterals in things you use every day.

WORD POWER
quadrilaterals

Many shapes are called **quadrilaterals** because they have 4 sides and 4 angles.

a.  **b.**  **c.**  **d.**  **e.**   **f.** 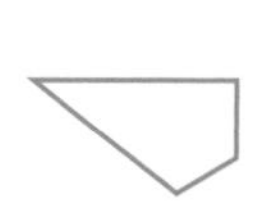

Talk About It

- Which quadrilaterals in the examples have 4 right angles? no right angles? acute and obtuse angles?
- Which quadrilaterals have exactly one pair of parallel sides? two pairs of parallel sides? no parallel sides?
- How can you find if a figure has right angles? parallel sides?

Quadrilaterals can be grouped and named by characteristics of their sides and angles. For each group, write a definition that makes sense to you. Share your definitions.

general quadrilaterals 

trapezoids 

parallelograms 

rectangles 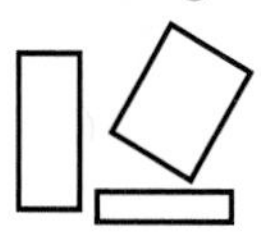

rhombuses 

squares 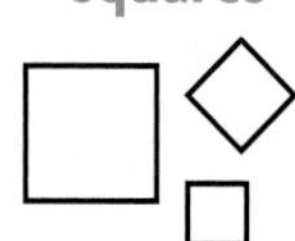

General quadrilaterals have 4 sides of different lengths and 4 angles. No sides are parallel.

Trapezoids have 2 sides that are parallel. They can have 2 acute and 2 obtuse angles.

Parallelograms have 2 pairs of parallel sides and 2 of the same size acute angles and 2 of the same size obtuse angles.

CRITICAL THINKING How are your definitions different from your classmates' definitions?

PRACTICE

Draw and name the quadrilateral.

1. Its opposite sides are parallel, and it has no right angles.
2. It has four sides of equal length and four right angles.
3. It has four sides of equal length. Its opposite sides are parallel. It has no right angles.
4. It has only one pair of parallel sides.

Name the kind of quadrilateral. Explain your choice.

5.

6.

7.

8.

9.

10. 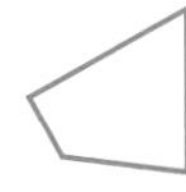

Choose the figure that does not belong. Explain.

11. a.  b.  c. 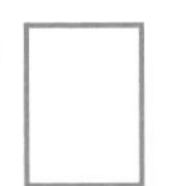 d. 

12. a. 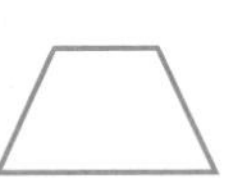 b.  c.  d. 

13. a.  b. c. 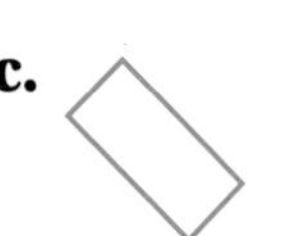 d. 

14. a. b. c. d.

A day at the ball park

Mixed Applications

15. Nefmar cut a figure from paper. It has 4 sides, 2 of which are parallel. There are no right angles. What is the figure?
16. Danny swims 2 laps on Monday, 5 laps on Tuesday, and 8 laps on Wednesday. If Danny follows this pattern, how many laps will he swim on Thursday?
17. Amber is at a baseball game and notices that the infield is a quadrilateral with four equal sides and four right angles. What is another name for the shape of a baseball diamond?
18. **WRITE ABOUT IT** Abby says that all parallelograms are quadrilaterals but not all quadrilaterals are parallelograms. Is she correct? Explain.

LESSON CONTINUES

PART 2 PROBLEM-SOLVING STRATEGY
Act It Out

THE PROBLEM Trace the right triangles and cut them out. Using all four right triangles, how many different quadrilaterals can you make?

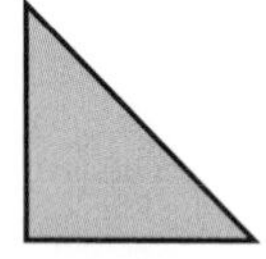 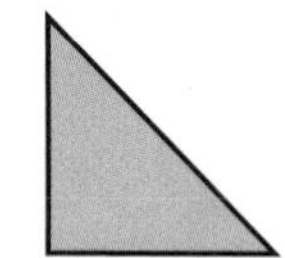 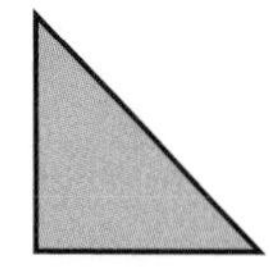 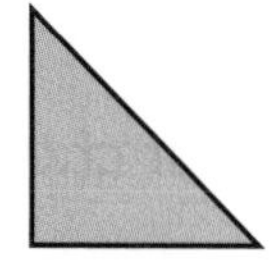

✓ Understand

- What are you asked to find?
- What information will you use?
- Is there any information you will not use? If so, what?

✓ Plan

- What strategy can you use to solve the problem?

  You can *act it out* to solve the problem.

✓ Solve

- How can you act out the problem?

  You can trace the four right triangles and cut them out. Then move them around to make quadrilaterals.

square

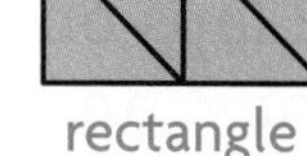
rectangle

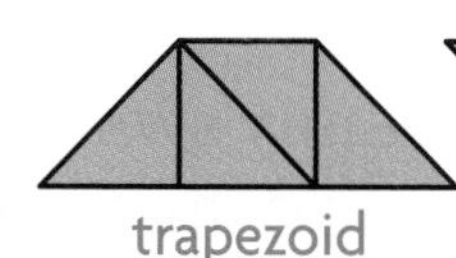
trapezoid

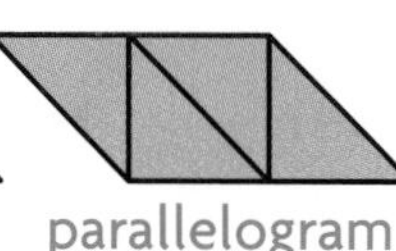
parallelogram

So, you can make 4 different quadrilaterals, a square, a rectangle, a trapezoid, and a parallelogram.

✓ Look Back

- How can you decide if your answer is reasonable?
- What other strategy could you use?

History Link

A German mathematician, David Hilbert (1862–1943), proved that any polygon can be transformed into any other polygon of equal area by cutting it into a number of pieces and putting the pieces together in another shape. Choose a polygon. How can you cut it apart and put it together to make a different polygon?

PRACTICE

CHOOSE  Paper/Pencil Calculator Hands-on Mental Math

Act it out to solve.

1. Trace and cut out the 4 puzzle pieces. Make a square. Then put the puzzle pieces together to make a triangle. Draw pictures of the triangle and square.

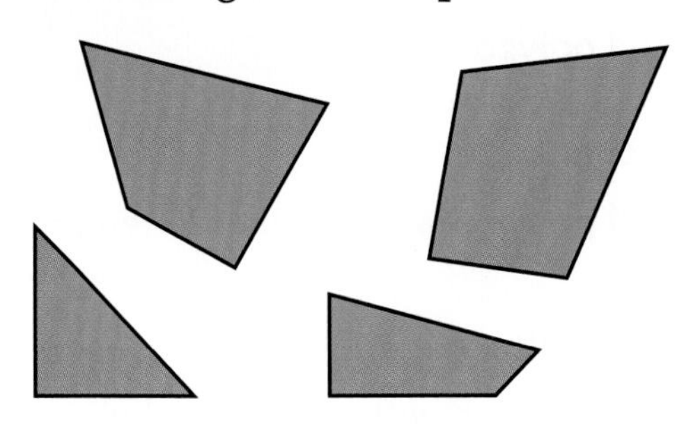

2. Susan, Mike, Stephanie, and Steven had a lemonade stand. At the end of the day they shared the earnings. They had 5 one-dollar bills, 1 quarter, 2 dimes, and 3 pennies. How much did each person receive?

3. Five students stood in a row. Bob was in the middle. Sadie stood next to Bob. Joel was at the right end. Tara stood between Bob and Joel. Where was Tom?

Mixed Applications

Solve.

CHOOSE A STRATEGY

- Guess and Check
- Draw a Diagram
- Work Backward
- Act It Out
- Find a Pattern

4. Ivan is at the World Showcase. He visits the display for France after Japan and before the United Kingdom. He visits the display for Morocco after Japan and before France. If France is next to the United Kingdom, in what order does Ivan visit the displays?

5. Olivia had some money in her purse. First, she spent $12 at the gift shop. Later that day her mother gave her $10 to buy lunch, but she spent only $6. At the end of the day, Olivia has $8. How much money did she have in her purse when she began her day?

6. Veronica's family plans to visit 14 places in Florida. On Tuesday they will visit twice as many places as they visited on Monday. Then they will still have 5 places left to see. How many places will they visit on Tuesday?

7. Pedro counted 12 flagpoles on each of two sides of the rectangular lake. If there are 4 flagpoles at each end of the lake, how many flagpoles are around the lake?

8. There were 145 people at the play on Friday and 189 people on Saturday. The theater seats 200 people. How many empty seats were there for those two nights?

9. The sum of two 2-digit numbers is 64. Their difference is 8. What are the numbers?

MORE PRACTICE Student Handbook page H92

Stretch a Shape

PURPOSE To practice identifying polygons and angles

YOU WILL NEED geoboard, rubber band, dot paper

With your geoboard and rubber band, form these polygons. Record them on dot paper for a partner to name.

- a 3-sided polygon with only 1 right angle
- a 3-sided polygon with 1 obtuse angle and 2 acute angles
- a 3-sided polygon with all sides different lengths
- a polygon with no right angles
- a 4-sided polygon with only 2 parallel lines

Line Designs

PURPOSE To practice using line segments to make artistic designs

YOU WILL NEED grid paper, pencil, ruler or straightedge

Copy on a sheet of paper the lines, points, and letters shown at the right. Draw line segments to connect matching letters. Write about your line design. Then, make a new design by changing the order of one set of letters.

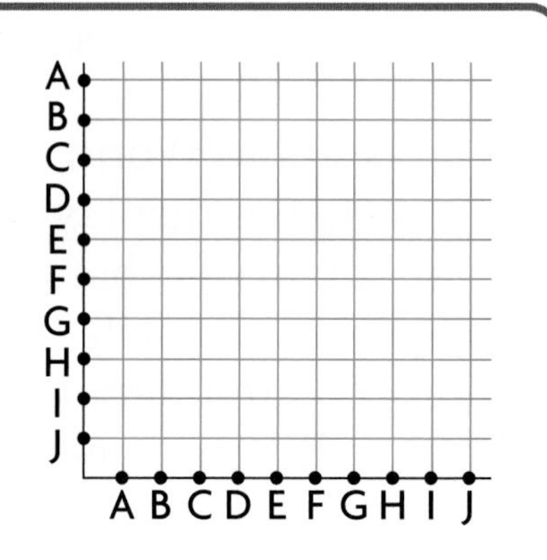

Tangram Puzzle

PURPOSE To practice making a square from seven polygons

YOU WILL NEED 7 tangram puzzle pieces

Fit the 7 pieces together to make a square.

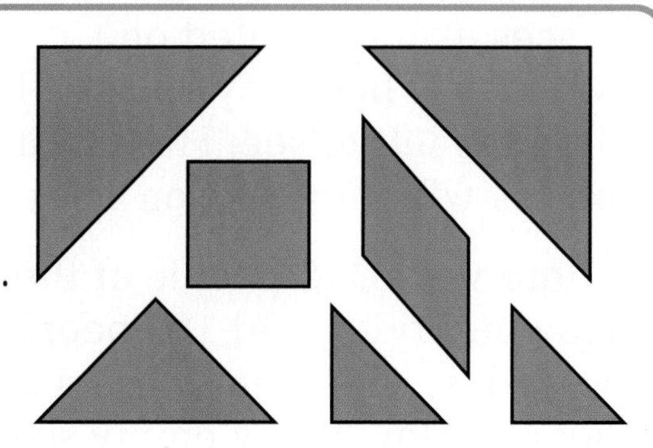

Challenge family members to make as many shapes as they can with the tangram puzzle.

CHAPTER 13

REVIEW

✓ CHECK UNDERSTANDING

VOCABULARY

1. A __?__ is a closed plane figure with straight sides. (page 218)

2. A __?__ is a four-sided polygon. (page 220)

Name the figure. Write *point, line, plane, line segment,* or *ray.* (pages 210–213)

3.

4. A

5.

6.

7. D C E

Write *intersecting, parallel,* or *perpendicular.* (pages 214–215)

8.

9.

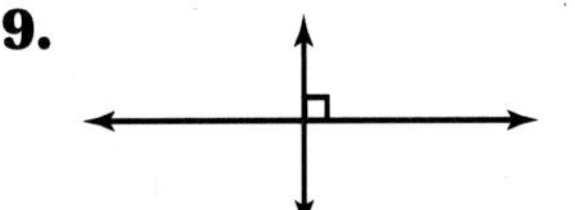

Write *right, acute,* or *obtuse.* (pages 212–213)

10.

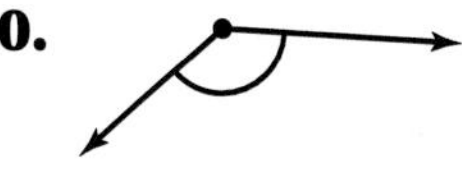

11.

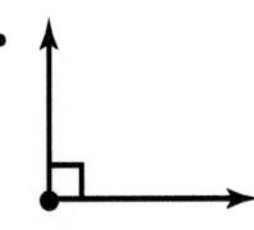

Use the drawing and a centimeter ruler for Exercises 12–15. (pages 216–217)

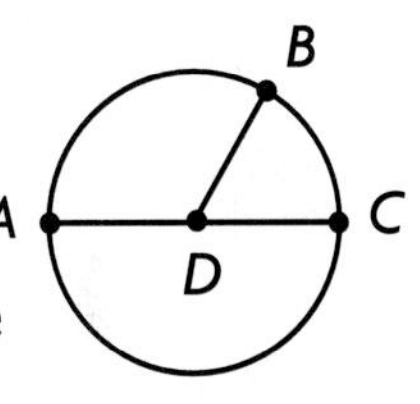

12. Point D is the __?__ of the circle.

13. AC is a __?__ of the circle.

14. DA is a __?__ of the circle.

15. The diameter of the circle measures __?__ cm.

✓ CHECK SKILLS

Name the polygon. Write *hexagon, quadrilateral,* or *triangle.* (pages 218–219)

16.

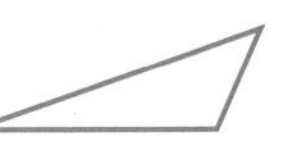

17.

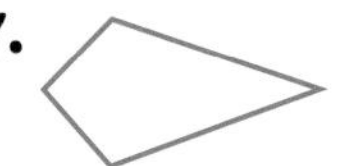

18.

Name the quadrilateral. Write *rectangle, rhombus,* or *trapezoid.* (pages 220–221)

19.

20.

21.

✓ CHECK PROBLEM SOLVING

Solve. (pages 222–223)

CHOOSE A STRATEGY

- Make a List
- Work Backward
- Draw a Diagram
- Act It Out

22. Show how you could slice a round pizza to serve 8 people. Use the labels *radius, diameter,* and *center* on your diagram.

23. Jo and 5 friends shared a box of pencils. Jo bought 2 extra pencils. Then he gave all 9 pencils to his sister. No pencils were left. How many pencils were in the box?

CHAPTER 14 PERIMETER AND AREA OF POLYGONS

DID YOU KNOW . . .

A tree-house builder in Seattle, Washington, built a 200-square foot tree house that was large enough to support fifty people.

It was built high up in a fir tree in a way that would cause no harm to the tree.

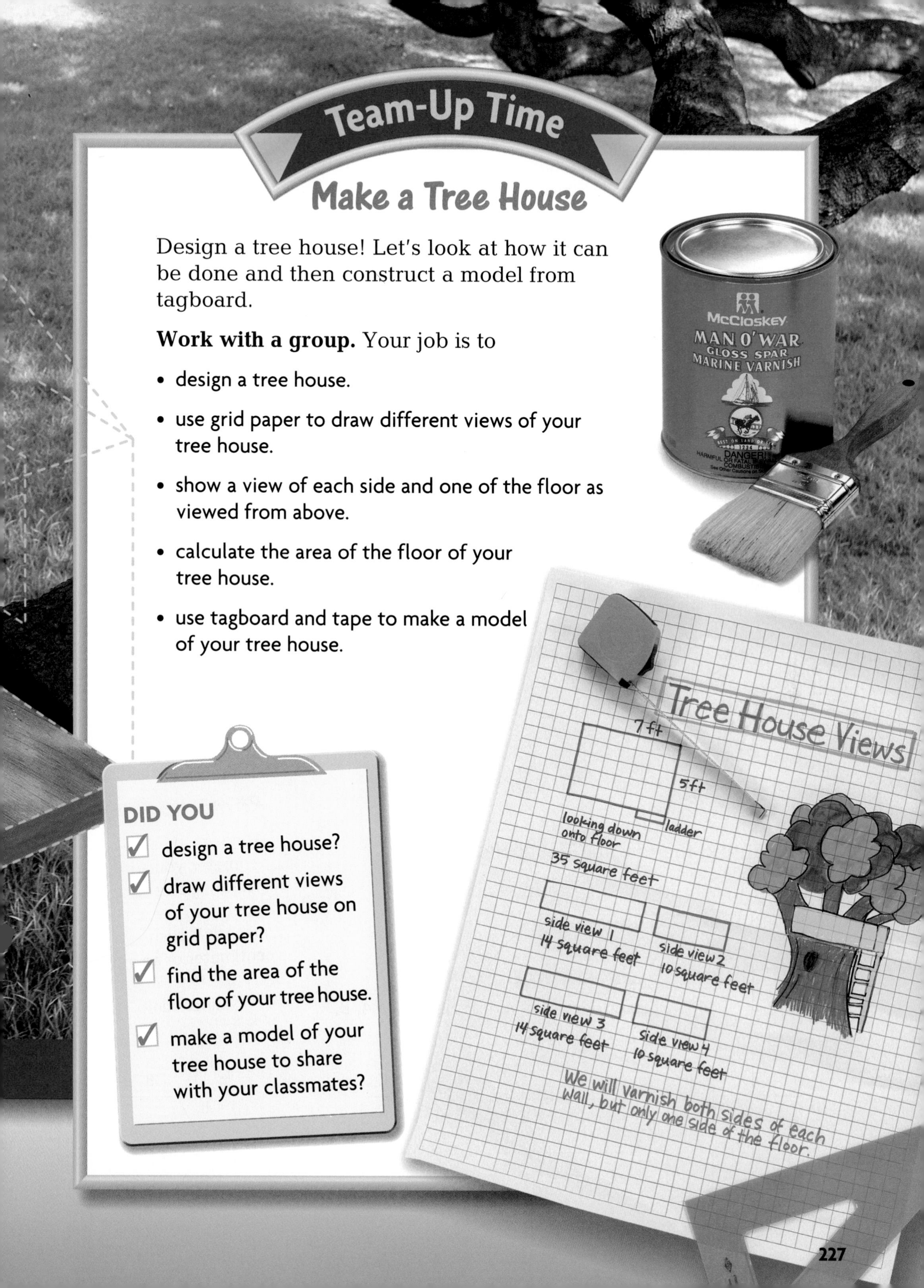

Team-Up Time

Make a Tree House

Design a tree house! Let's look at how it can be done and then construct a model from tagboard.

Work with a group. Your job is to

- design a tree house.
- use grid paper to draw different views of your tree house.
- show a view of each side and one of the floor as viewed from above.
- calculate the area of the floor of your tree house.
- use tagboard and tape to make a model of your tree house.

DID YOU

- ✓ design a tree house?
- ✓ draw different views of your tree house on grid paper?
- ✓ find the area of the floor of your tree house.
- ✓ make a model of your tree house to share with your classmates?

Finding Perimeter

You will learn how to find the perimeter of a figure.	**Why learn this?** You can figure out how many feet of lumber you would need to build a railing around your treehouse.	**WORD POWER** perimeter

Perimeter is the distance around a figure.

There are three ways to find perimeter.

Method A

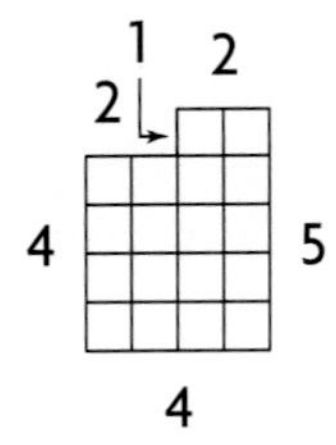

When the lengths of the sides are different, add the lengths of the sides.

Record:
$2 + 1 + 2 + 5 + 4 + 4 =$ 18 units

Method B

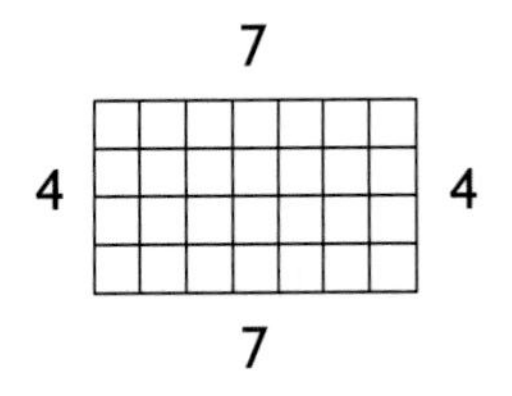

When two pairs of sides are the same length, multiply 2 times the length and 2 times the width. Then add the products.

Record:
$(2 \times 7) + (2 \times 4) =$?
$14 + 8 =$ 22 units

Method C

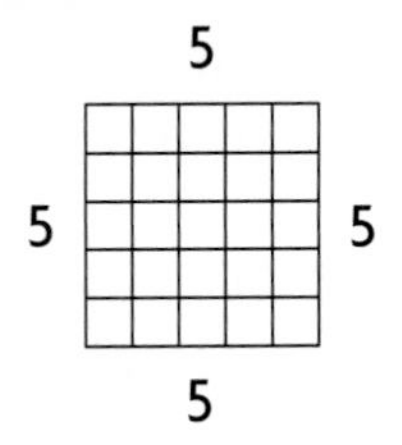

When all the sides are the same length, multiply the number of sides times the length of one side.

Record:
$4 \times 5 =$ 20 units
(4 = number of sides; 5 = length of one side)

Talk About It

- If you know the perimeter of a square, how can you find the length of each side?
- What unit would you use to measure the perimeter of your classroom?

REMEMBER: When you measure perimeter, you are measuring one dimension. Use a *linear unit,* such as a centimeter or an inch.

linear unit

Check Your Understanding

For Exercises 1–4, find the perimeter. Write the letter *A*, *B*, or *C* to show which method you used.

1.

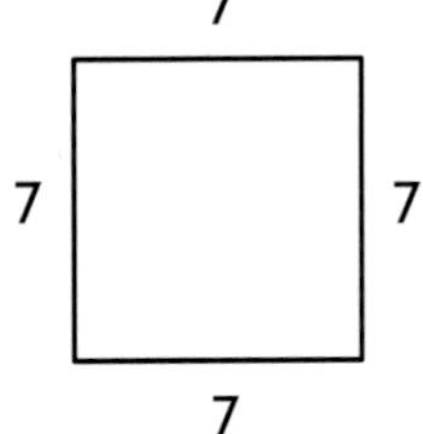

2.

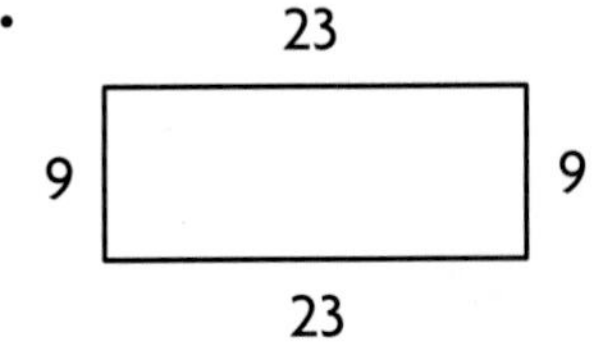

3.

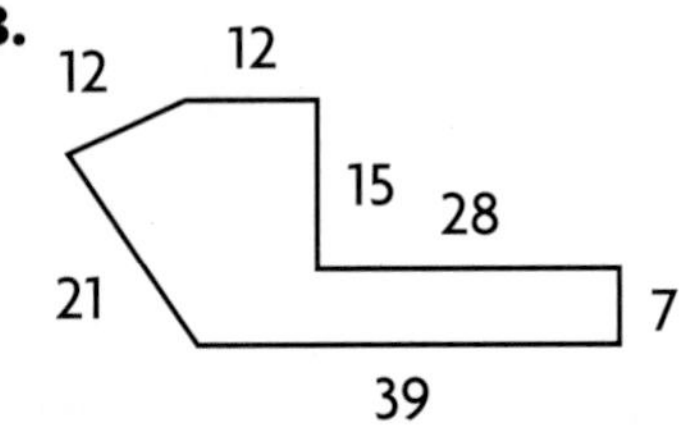

4.

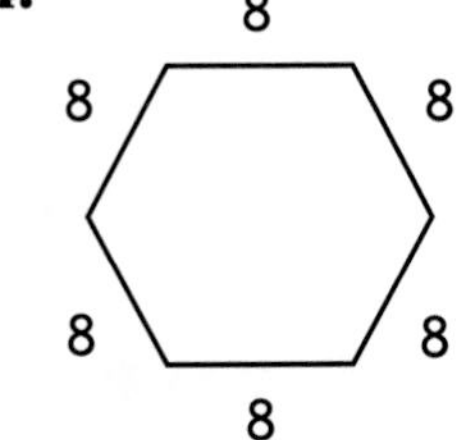

PRACTICE

Find the perimeter. Write the letter *A, B,* or *C* to show which method from page 228 you used.

5. 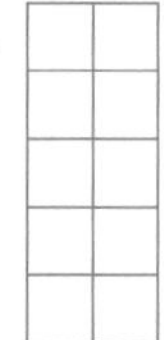

6. 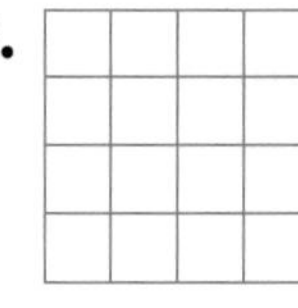

7. 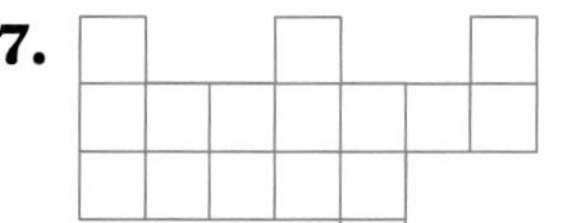

8. 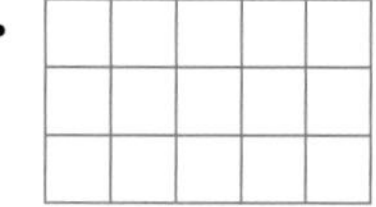

Find the perimeter.

9. 7 in. 7 in. 7 in. 7 in.

10. 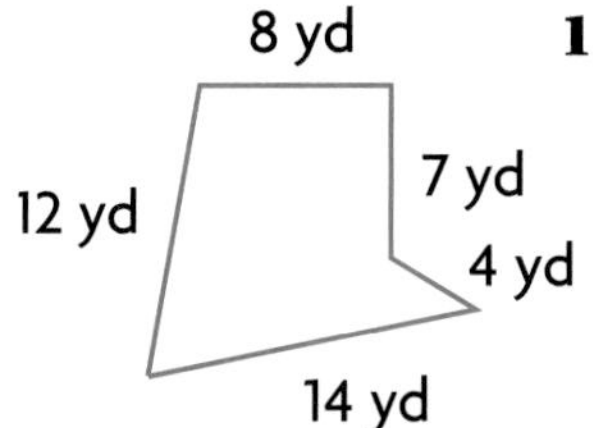

11. 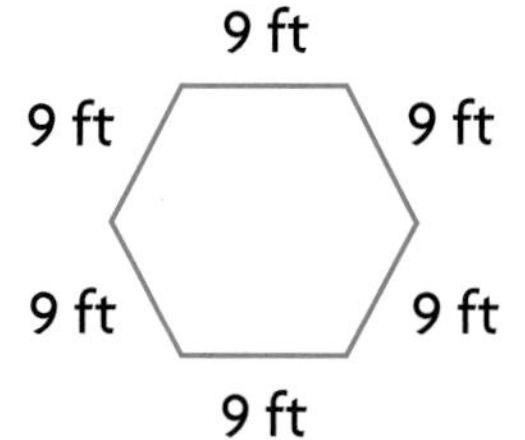

12. 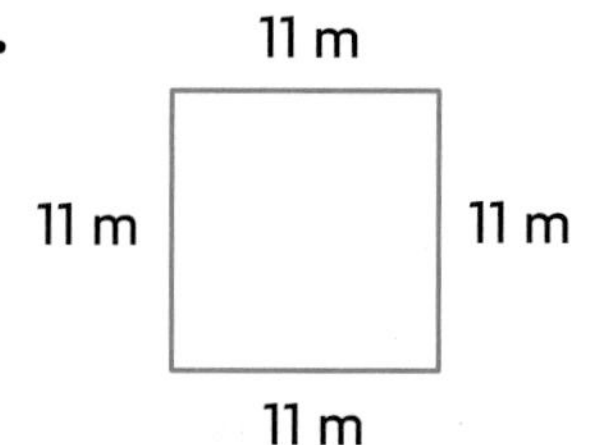

Use the floor plan to find the perimeter of each room. You may use a calculator.

13. Kitchen

14. Dining Room

15. Living Room

16. Family Room

17. Baths 1 and 2

18. Bedrooms 1, 2, and 3

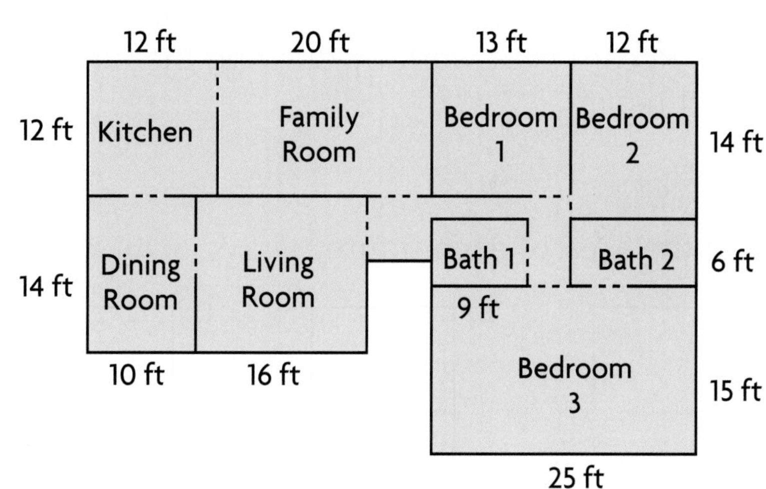

Mixed Applications

19. At recess Amy walked the perimeter of the playground 3 times. The playground is 25 meters long and 15 meters wide. How many meters did Amy walk?

20. **Write a problem** in which you need to find a perimeter.

Mixed Review

Write the value of each digit. (pages 88–89)

21. 451 **22.** 692 **23.** 807 **24.** 310 **25.** 409

Write each number in expanded form and written form. (pages 90–91)

26. 27 **27.** 139 **28.** 603 **29.** 2,385 **30.** 8,091

Exploring Area

You will investigate how to find the area of a flat surface.

Why learn this? You could tile a floor or cover a bulletin board.

WORD POWER
area

Explore

Area is the number of square units needed to cover a flat surface. Find the area in square units of each figure on the geoboard.

MATERIALS: geoboard, rubber bands, dot paper

Record

Describe how you found each area.

Now investigate how many different figures you can make that have an area of 2 square units. Record your work by drawing the figures on dot paper.

REMEMBER:
When you measure area, you use a *square unit.* One square unit is outlined on the geoboard.

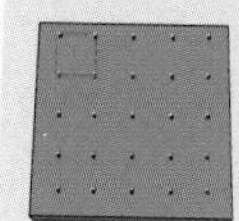

$= \frac{1}{2}$ unit

You can combine two $\frac{1}{2}$ units to make 1 unit.

Try This

Find the area of each figure.

A. 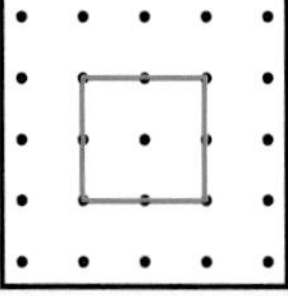

B. 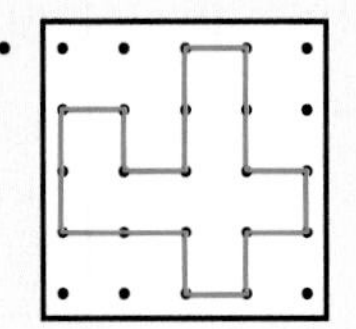

C. 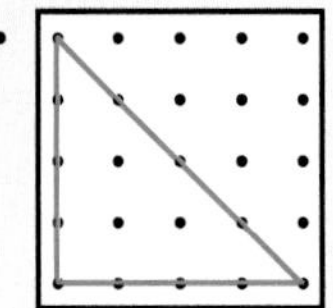

TALK ABOUT IT How did you find the area of each figure?

WRITE ABOUT IT How does the geoboard help you find area in square units?

Technology Link
E-Lab • Activity 14 Available on CD-ROM and the Internet at http://www.hbschool.com/elab

HANDS-ON PRACTICE

1. Use your geoboard to make as many different figures with an area of 4 square units as possible. Record your work on dot paper. Write the area in square units.

Applying What You Learned

Find the area.

2. 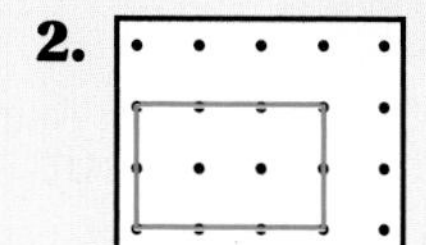

3. 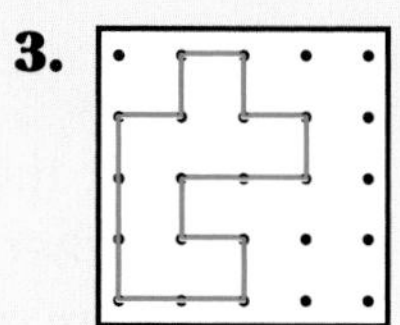

4. 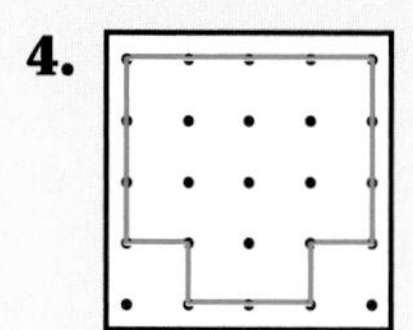

5. 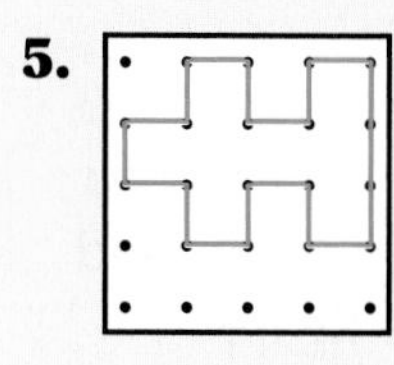

6. 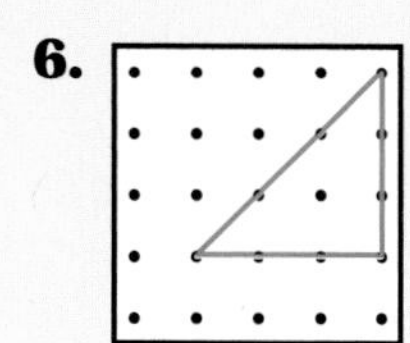

7. 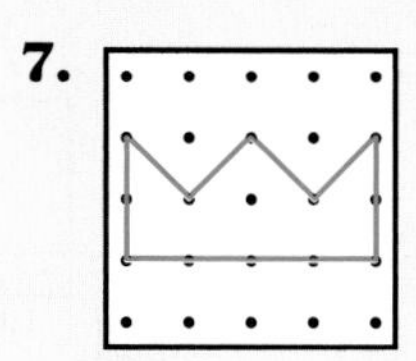

8. 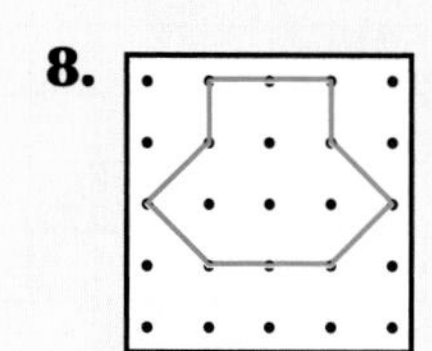

9. 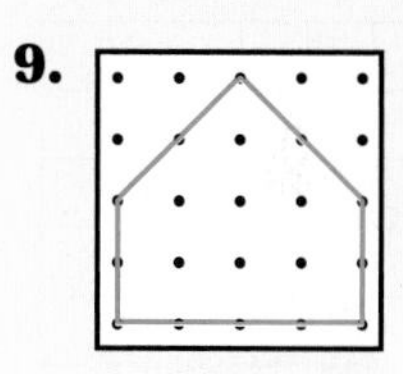

10. Which figures have the same area?

a. **b.** 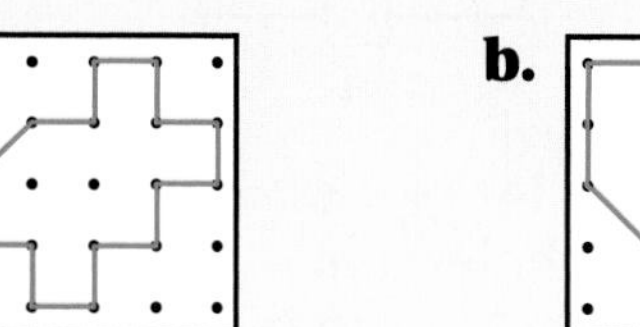

c. 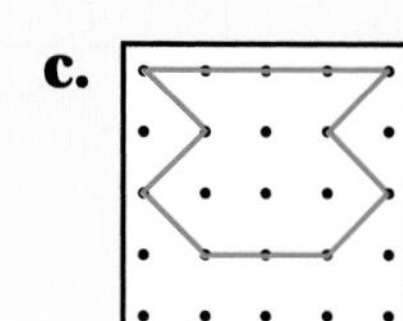

d. 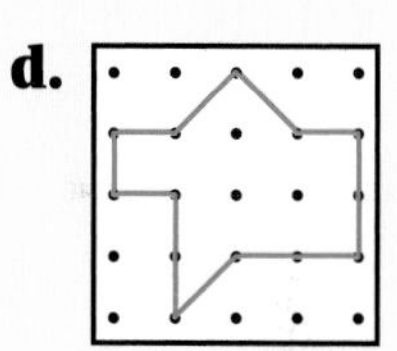

Mixed Applications

11. Marty's parents are buying carpet for his room. His floor space is 9 square yards. The carpet sells for $7 a square yard. How much will the carpet cost?

12. Kelsey is buying wallpaper border to put on the walls in her room. Her rectangular room is 13 feet long and 11 feet wide. How much border will Kelsey need?

13. Jon has 48 tiles to use in covering the kitchen floor. Each row will have 8 tiles. How many rows of tiles will there be?

14. **WRITE ABOUT IT** One bulletin board is rectangular-shaped. The other is square. Explain how 16 square photographs could cover the area of either one.

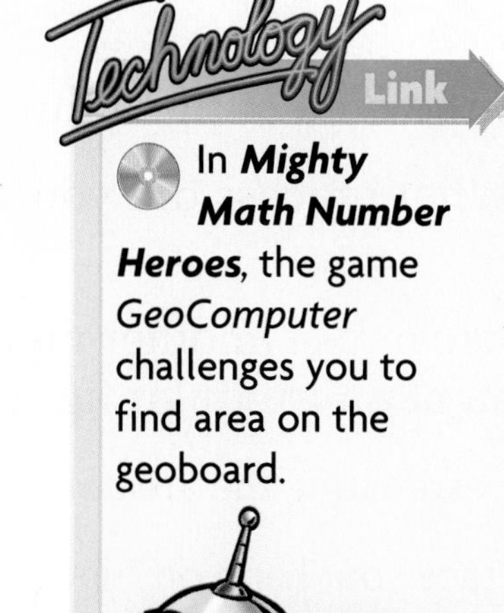

Technology Link

In ***Mighty Math Number Heroes***, the game *GeoComputer* challenges you to find area on the geoboard.

MORE PRACTICE Student Handbook page H93

Area of Irregular Figures

You will learn ways to find the area of irregular figures.

Why learn this? You can find the amount of paper or cloth needed to cover an irregular surface.

Find the area of the figure below.

MODEL

Step 1

Copy the figure onto 1-inch grid paper, and color the figure.

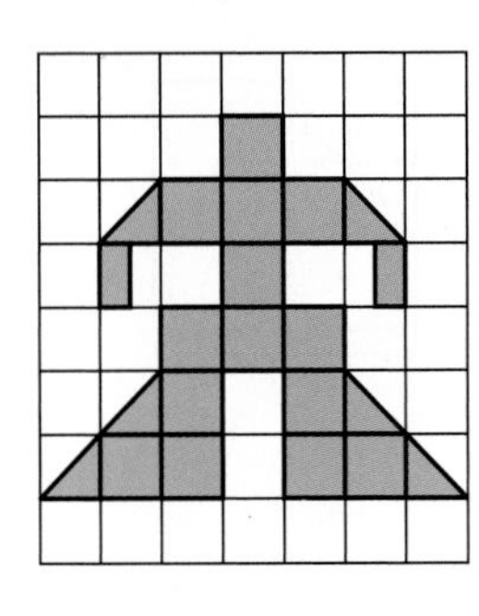

Step 2

Count the whole square units.

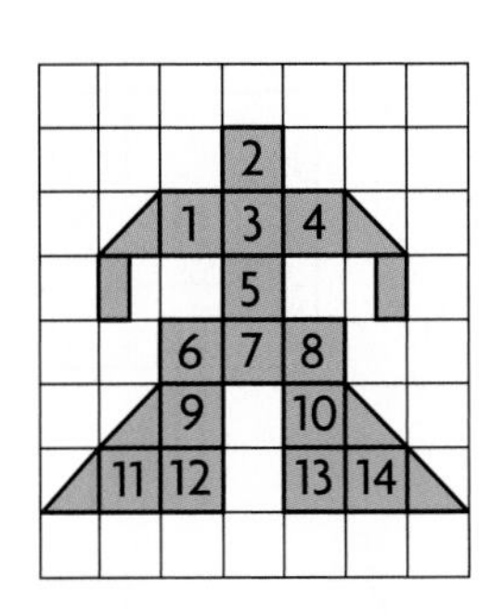

Record: 14 whole units

Step 3

Then count the parts of units, and put them together to make whole units. Find the sum of the square units.

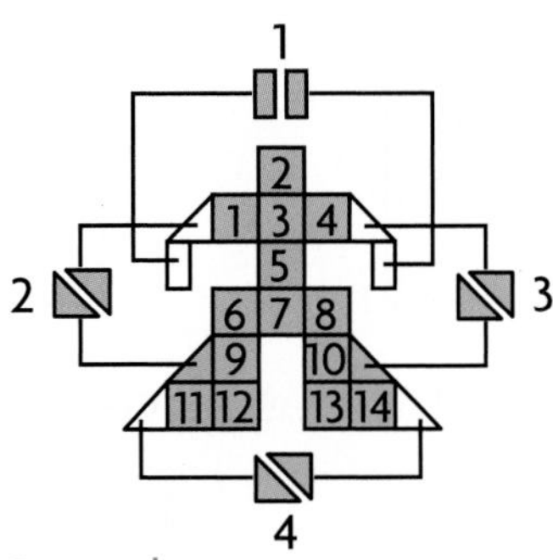

Record:
14 whole units + 4 units from parts = ? square units

So, the area of the figure is 18 square units.

- What process did you use to combine the $\frac{1}{2}$ units?

You can use another method to estimate the area of an irregular figure.

Try estimating the area of your handprint.

- Trace your hand on 1-inch grid paper. Shade the handprint.
- Outline the area that includes both partly shaded and fully shaded units. Count all the units outlined, and record the number.
- Subtract the fully shaded units from the total units outlined. Divide the number you get by 2.

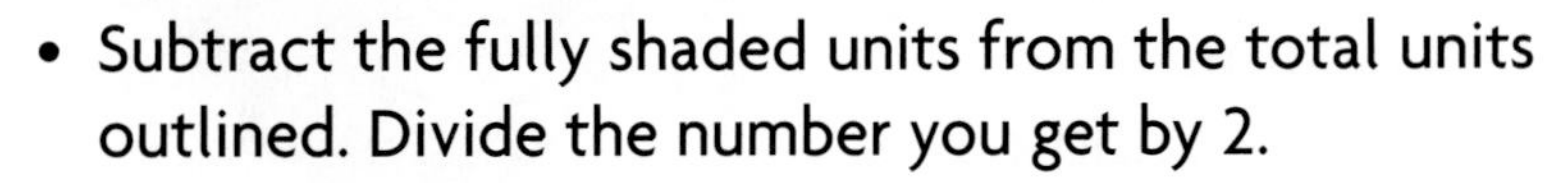

- Add the result to the number of fully shaded units.

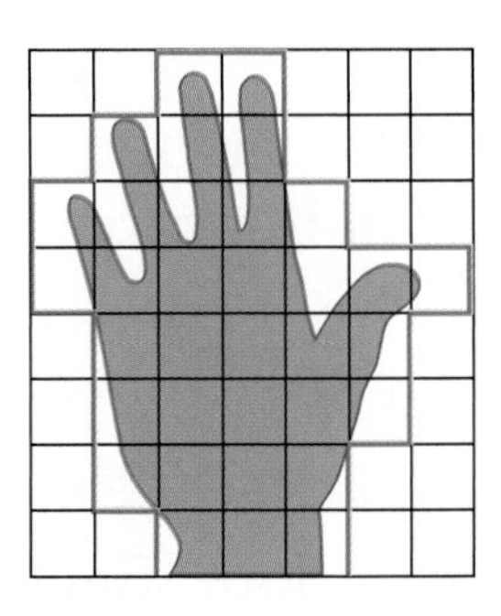

Record: 34 units in all − 10 fully shaded = 24 partially shaded

24 ÷ 2 = 12

12 + 10 = 22

Estimate is about 22 units.

PRACTICE

Copy the figure onto 1-inch grid paper. Find the area.

1. 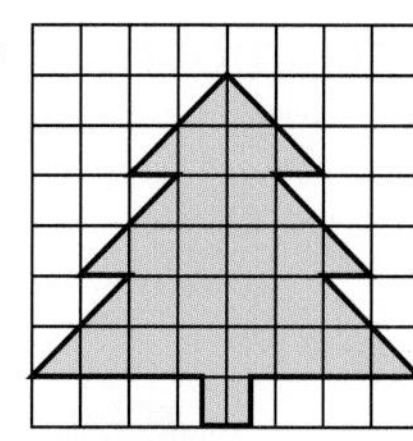

2. 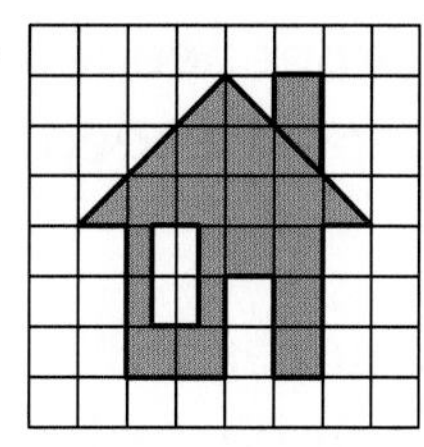

3. 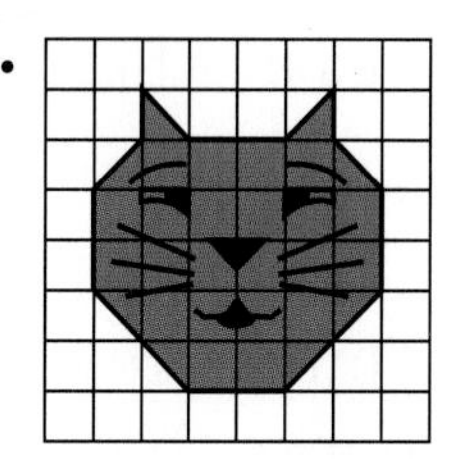

Copy the figure onto 1-inch grid paper. Estimate the area.

4. 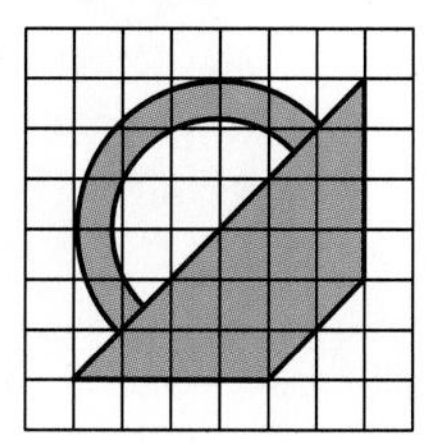

5. 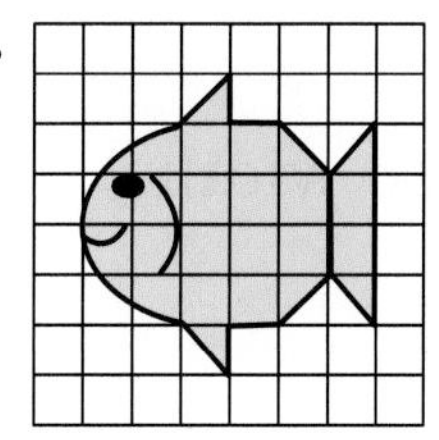

6. 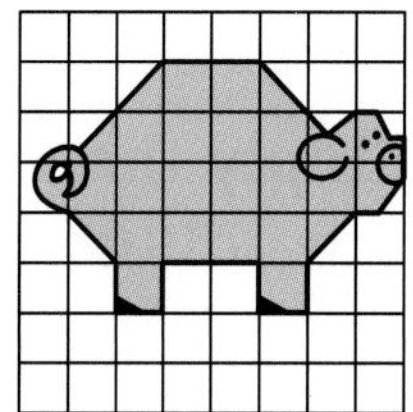

Mixed Applications

7. Yolanda's dad is buying fertilizer for the lawn. Each bag covers 5,000 square feet of lawn. Look at the drawing of the family's house and lawn. How many bags of fertilizer will Yolanda's dad need to buy?

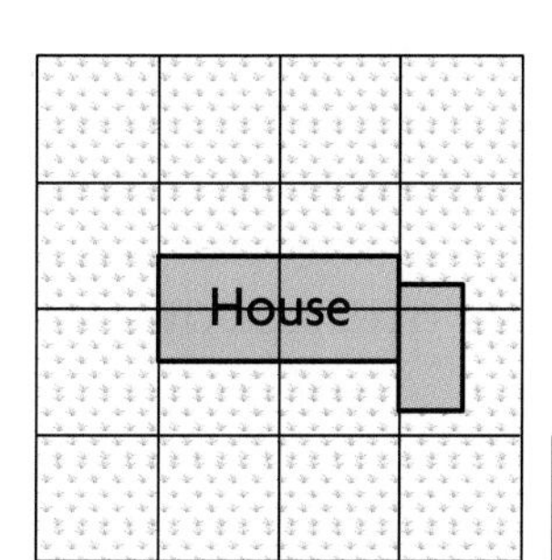

8. Will earns $9 for every lawn he mows. Each week he mows 3 lawns. How much does he earn in two weeks?

9. **WRITE ABOUT IT** How are the two methods of estimating the area of an irregular figure alike? How are they different?

Mixed Review

Write another name for each number and solve using mental math. (pages 92–93)

10.	**11.**	**12.**	**13.**	**14.**
900 +400	800 +300	5,000 +2,000	6,000 +7,000	8,400 +1,500

Write the name for each figure. (pages 210–211)

15. A•

16. C •——• D

17. ←•——•→ F G

18. 

Finding Area

You will learn to use multiplication to find the area of a flat, rectangular surface.	**Why learn this?** You can find the amount of carpet needed for a room or the amount of paper needed to cover a book.

Kevin and Tonya are using carpet squares to cover the floor of their clubhouse. Each carpet square covers 1 square foot. The floor is 9 feet long and 6 feet wide. How many carpet squares are needed?

You can multiply the length times the width to find the area of the floor.

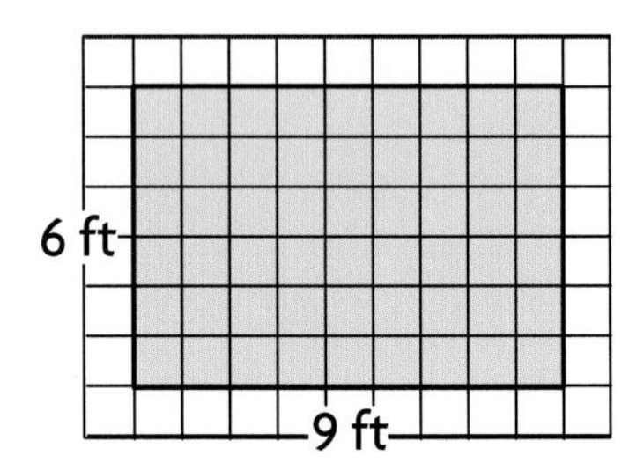

area (a) = length (l) × width (w)
__?__ sq ft = 6 ft by 9 ft
Record: 6 × 9 = 54, or 54 sq ft

So, 54 carpet squares are needed.

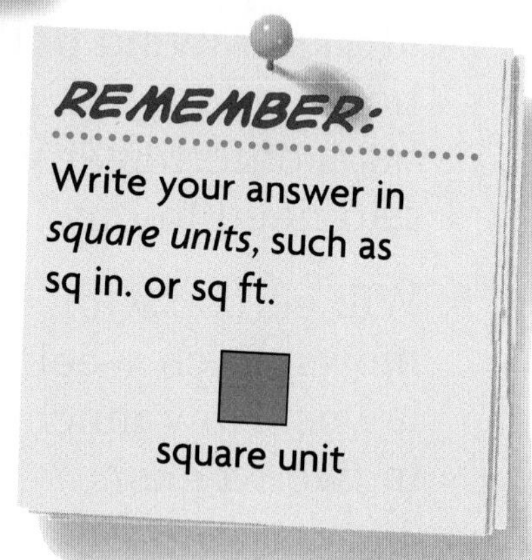

Talk About It

- How can you find the area by using an array?
- How does multiplication help you find area?
- How can you use this method to find the area of your desktop or tabletop?

Check Your Understanding

CRITICAL THINKING

Find the area and record, using measurement units.

Model	Record:
1. 9 in. by 7 in.	7 × 9 = __?__
2. 6 ft by 4 ft	4 × 6 = __?__

Model	Record:
3. 5 cm by 5 cm	5 × 5 = __?__
4. 8 m by 3 m	3 × 8 = __?__

PRACTICE

Find the area.

5.

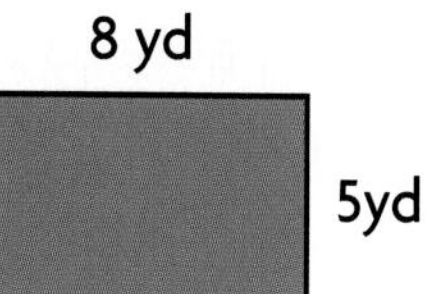

6.

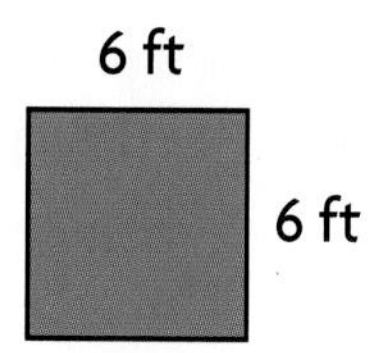

7.

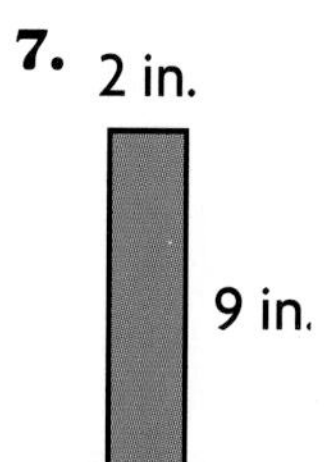

8.

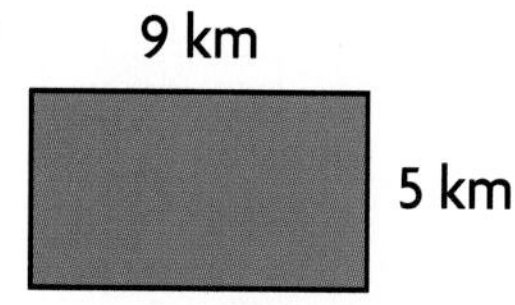

9.

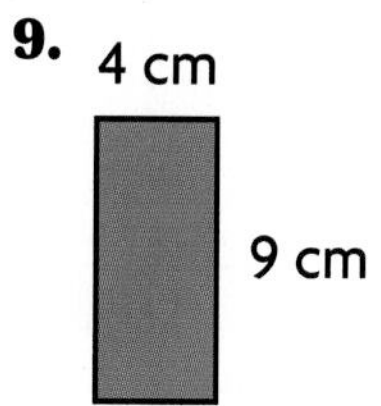

10.

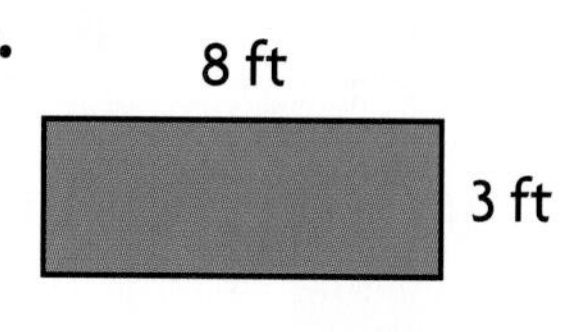

Write the letter of the rectangle that has the greater area.

11. a. 7 ft, 7 ft

b.

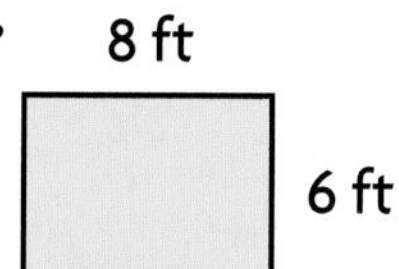

12. a.

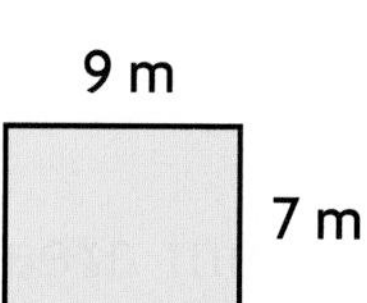

b. 8 m, 8 m

Mixed Applications

13. The Lowes are buying carpet for 4 rooms in their home. Two of the rooms need 16 square yards each. One needs 12 square yards. Another needs 20 square yards. What is the total amount of carpet needed?

14. Elena is making a mural for science class. It will be 6 feet long by 4 feet wide. How many square feet of paper does she need?

15. Mr. Kline used 120 sheets of colored paper to make book covers. He made 89 blue book covers. The rest were red. How many book covers were red?

16. **Write a problem** in which you need to find the area of a room in your home.

Mixed Review

Use the multiplication properties to solve. (pages 36–37)

17. $4 \times 0 = \underline{?}$ **18.** $1 \times 12 = \underline{?}$ **19.** $7 \times 5 = 5 \times \underline{?}$ **20.** $10 \times 0 = \underline{?}$

Tell whether each number is *cardinal, ordinal,* or *nominal.* (pages 72–73)

21. eighty-five **22.** (914) 675-1310 **23.** 3rd **24.** 2,689

PART 1 Relating Area and Perimeter

You will learn the relationship between area and perimeter.

Why learn this? You will be able to predict how changing the shape of a figure changes its area and perimeter.

Find the area and perimeter of each figure.

a. 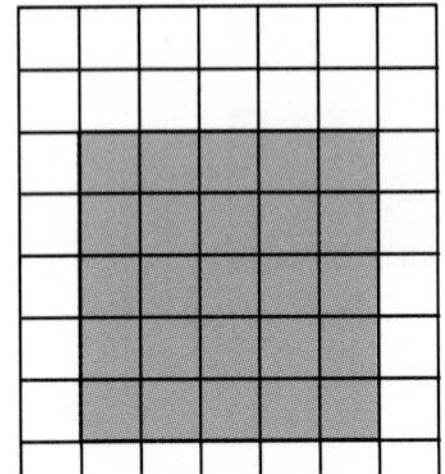

b. 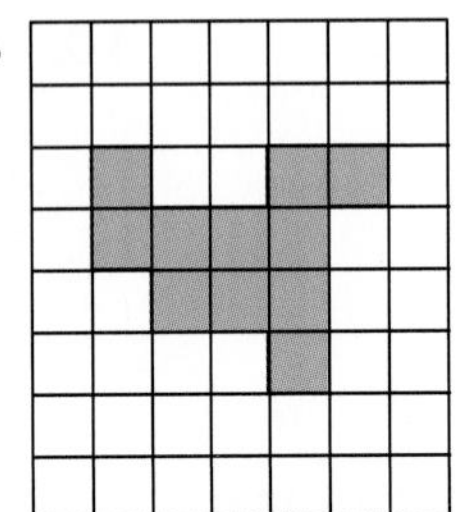

c. 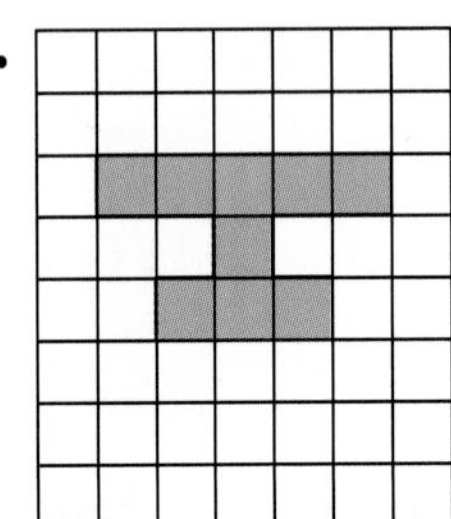

d. 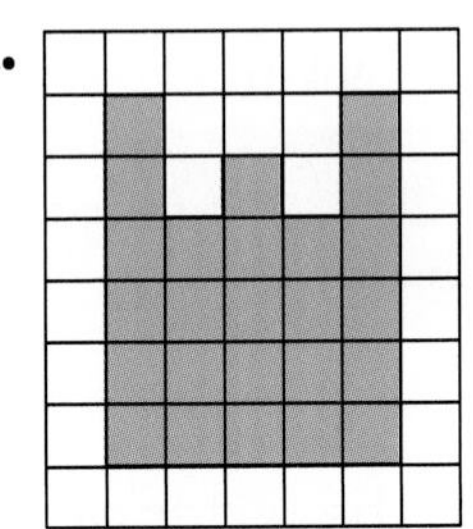

Talk About It

- Can figures with different areas have the same perimeter? Explain.
- Can figures with different perimeters have the same area? Explain.
- What happens to the perimeter as each figure's shape changes?

Check Your Understanding

MATERIALS: centimeter grid paper, centimeter ruler

1. Draw two figures that have different areas but the same perimeter.
2. Draw two figures that have different perimeters but the same area.
3. Draw as many different figures as you can that have an area of 8 square centimeters.
4. What is the perimeter of each figure in Exercise 3?
5. What units do you use to record area and perimeter?

Art Link

If you were designing the floor plan for a clubhouse, why would the relationship between area and perimeter be important?

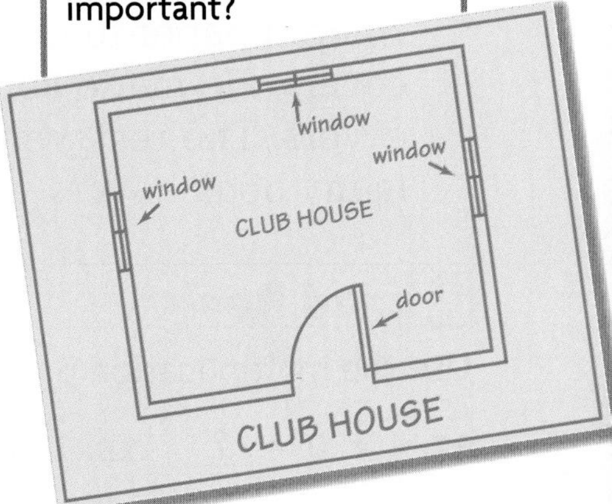

PRACTICE

Write the area and the perimeter.

6. 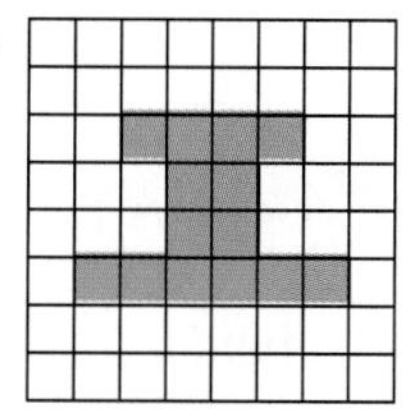
7. 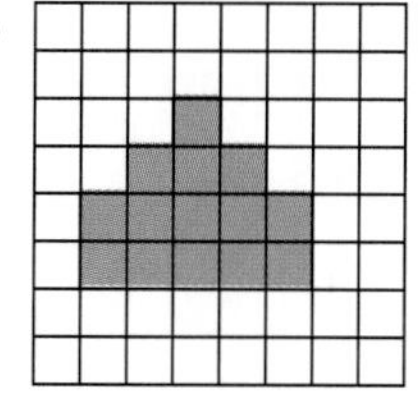
8. 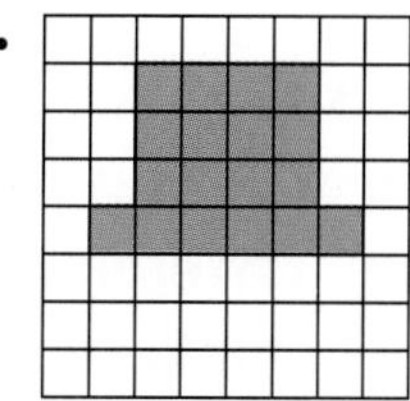
9. 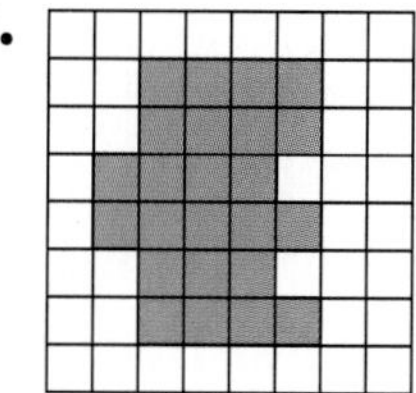

For each figure, draw another figure that has the same area but a different perimeter. You may wish to use grid paper.

10. 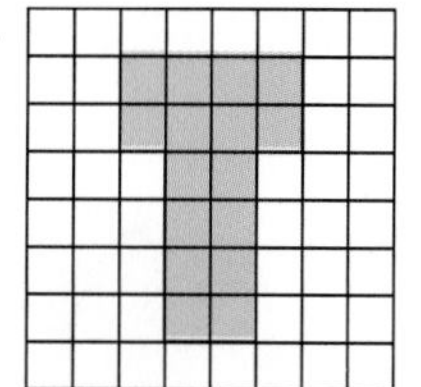
11. 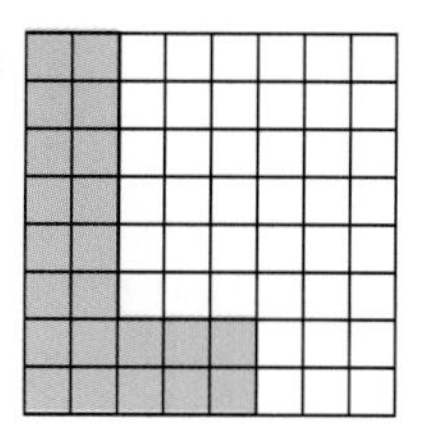
12. 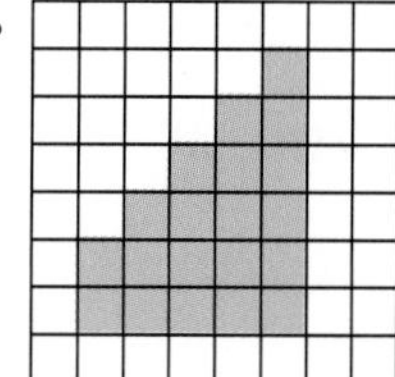 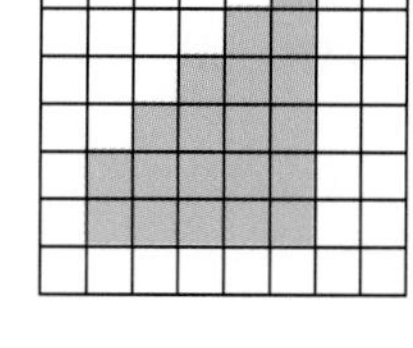
13. 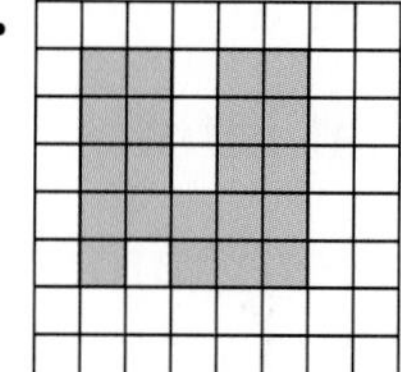 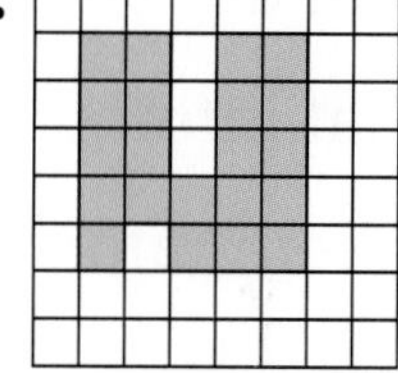

14. Which of the four figures below have the same area but different perimeters?

15. Which of the four figures below have the same perimeter but different areas?

a. 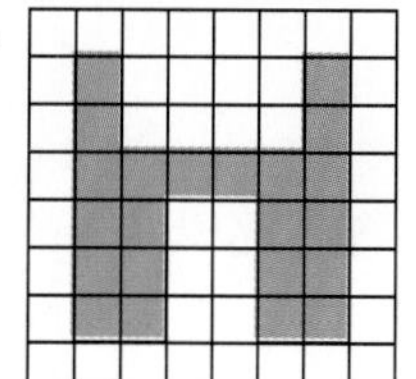
b. 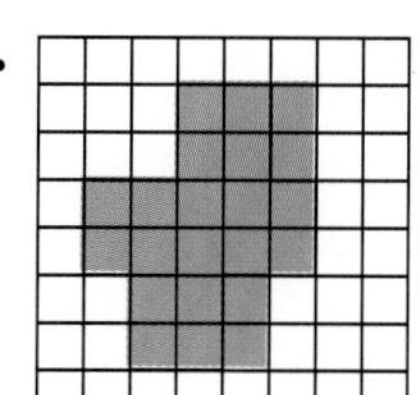
c. 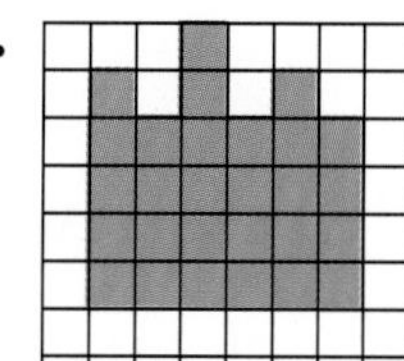
d. 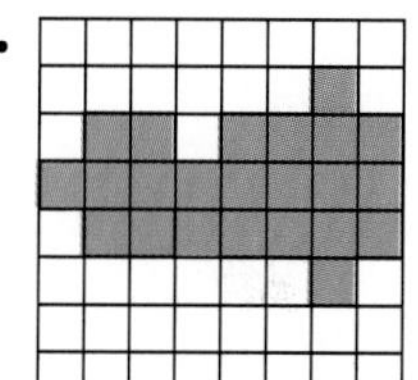

Mixed Applications

16. Janice decorated her room with 5 posters on each of 2 walls, and 3 posters on each of the other 2 walls. She paid $2 for each poster. How much did she spend for all the posters?

17. Samantha wants to know how many squares are in her quilt. The quilt is 6 squares long and 4 squares wide. How many squares are in her quilt?

18. The square floor of Ben's tree house is 6 feet on each side. What is the area of the floor? What is the perimeter?

19. The sum of two numbers is 64. One of the numbers is 3 times the other number. What are the two numbers?

20. **WRITE ABOUT IT** Explain how the quilt squares in Problem 17 could be arranged to make another quilt with the same area but a different perimeter.

LESSON CONTINUES

PART 2 PROBLEM-SOLVING STRATEGY
Draw a Diagram

THE PROBLEM Steven wants to make a rectangular pen with the greatest possible area for his rabbit. He has 24 feet of fencing. How many different shapes of rectangular pens could Steven make? Which shape would have the greatest area?

✓ Understand

- What are you asked to find?
- What information will you use?
- Is there information you will not use? If so, what?

✓ Plan

- What strategy can you use to solve the problem?

  You can *draw a diagram* to solve the problem.

✓ Solve

- How can diagrams help you solve the problem?

  You can draw a diagram of each shape with a perimeter of 24 feet that a rectangular pen could be. Then find the area of each one to see which one has the greatest area.

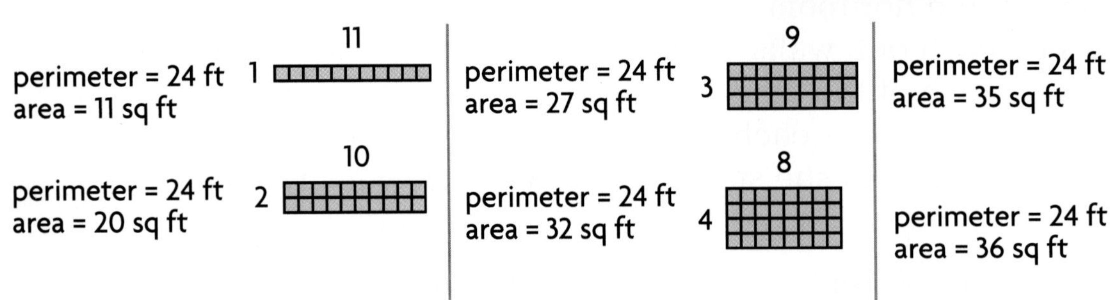

So, there are six possible shapes. A square 6 feet by 6 feet has the greatest area.

✓ Look Back

- How can you decide if your answer is reasonable?
- What other strategy could you use?

PRACTICE

CHOOSE Paper/Pencil Calculator Hands-on Mental Math

Draw a diagram to solve.

1. A farmer has 36 feet of wire to put around a garden. He wants to plant a garden with the greatest possible area. What is the greatest possible area that the farmer can make his garden?

2. Pablo spent half his money for a ticket to a football game. Then he spent half of the rest on a snack. He had $4 left. How much money did Pablo have at the start?

3. Drew has 72 feet of lumber to build a pen for his land turtles. Draw some of the shapes he could use. Which shape will give him the greatest area?

4. Nick, Amy, and Lisa are comparing their heights. At 52 inches, Nick is 6 inches taller than Amy. Amy is 3 inches shorter than Lisa. How tall is Lisa?

Mixed Applications

Solve.

CHOOSE A STRATEGY

- Act It Out
- Use a Table
- Draw a Diagram
- Guess and Check
- Make an Organized List
- Write a Number Sentence

5. The Clarks are comparing houses for sale. As the areas of the houses become greater, what happens to the prices? How much larger is House 4 than House 1? How much more is the price?

HOMES FOR SALE		
House	Area (in sq ft)	Price
House 1	1,200 sq ft	$ 85,000
House 2	1,600 sq ft	$ 90,000
House 3	2,000 sq ft	$105,000
House 4	2,100 sq ft	$110,000

6. Demi has 6 more stuffed animals than Marissa. The two girls have a total of 38 stuffed animals. How many does each girl have?

7. Alan has saved his allowance for the past 8 weeks. He gets $3 a week. How many more weeks will he have to save to buy a radio-controlled car for $42?

8. A gardener has 28 feet of fencing to put around a flower bed. What is the greatest possible area that the gardener can make his flower bed?

9. Morgan can't decide whether to paint her room pink, yellow, or blue. She can use either flat paint or glossy paint. What are all her choices?

MORE PRACTICE Student Handbook page H94

CULTURAL CONNECTION

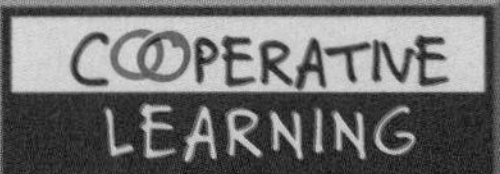

PLANNING A JAPANESE GARDEN

Ellen Takemoto's parents and grandparents own a large plant nursery near Novato, California. More than 100,000 people tour their gardens every year. Her grandparents decided to add a Japanese garden, a pond, and a tea house for visitors.

Ellen and her parents went to Japan to photograph gardens that were between 200 and 600 years old. Ellen's grandparents used the pictures to plan the garden.

In the diagram below, find the perimeter of the grounds for the Japanese garden, pond, and tea house.

CULTURAL LINK

For more than a thousand years, gardens in Japan have been planned around temples and palaces. People boating in the garden ponds can see many rare plants growing near the water and watch animals. Often musicians serenade the boaters from small islands in the ponds.

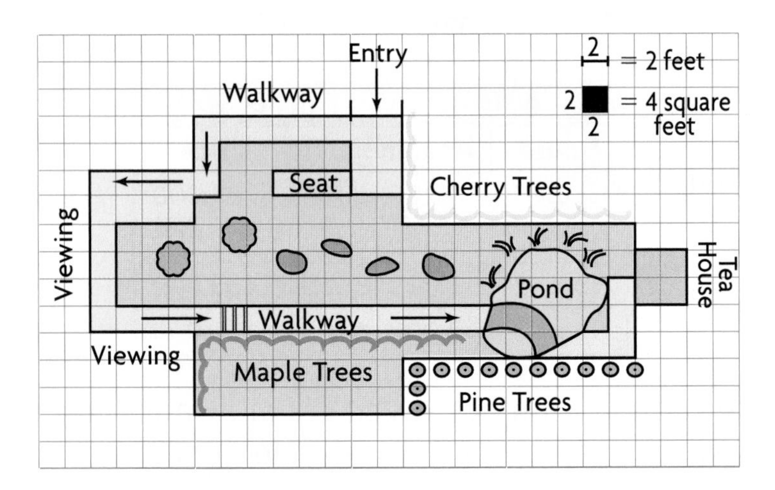

Work Together

1. Find the area of the garden, including the tea house. To check your work, form a different set of rectangles from the garden plan and find the area of the garden.

2. Using grid paper, design a vegetable garden with an area of 60 square feet. Draw a picture of your garden. Find the perimeter of the garden you designed.

3. Estimate the area of the pond.

CHAPTER 14

REVIEW

✓ CHECK UNDERSTANDING

VOCABULARY

1. The _?_ is the distance around a figure. (page 228)

2. The _?_ is the number of square units needed to cover a flat surface. (page 230)

Find the perimeter. (pages 228–229)

3. 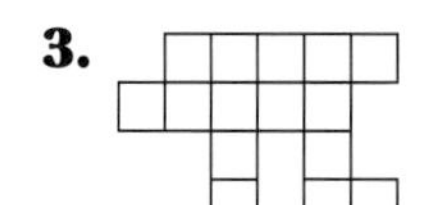

4. 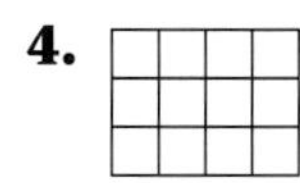

5. 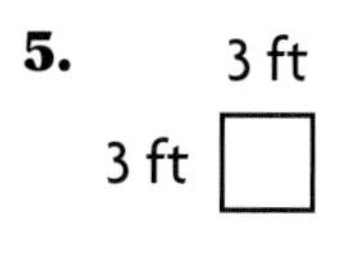

6. 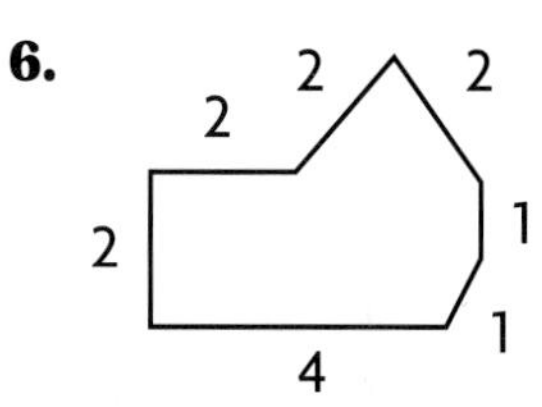

Find the area. (pages 230–235)

7. 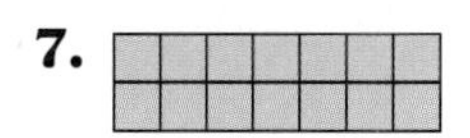

8. 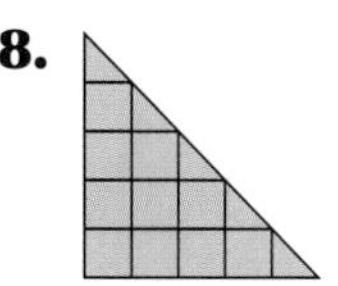

9. 7 cm, 7 cm

10. 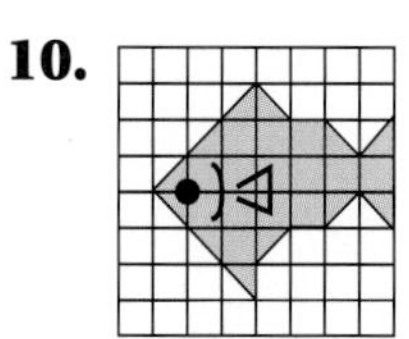

✓ CHECK SKILLS

Write the area and perimeter. (pages 236–237)

11. 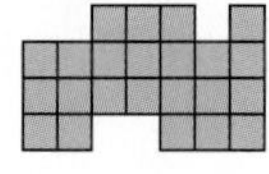

12. 5 in., 5 in.

13. 9 m, 4 m

14.

✓ CHECK PROBLEM SOLVING

Solve. (pages 238–239)

CHOOSE A STRATEGY

- Act It Out
- Draw a Diagram
- Guess and Check
- Write a Number Sentence

15. Mrs. Lee has 12 ft of fencing to make a pen for the class pet. What is the greatest possible area that the pen can be?

16. The new bathroom is 8 ft by 10 ft long. The shower will be 6 ft by 3 ft. What are the perimeter and area of the bathroom?

17. I am a number that is 19 ones and 9 tens greater than 389. What number am I?

18. The new house will be ready six months from March 17. In what month will the new house be ready?

GEOMETRY AND MOTION

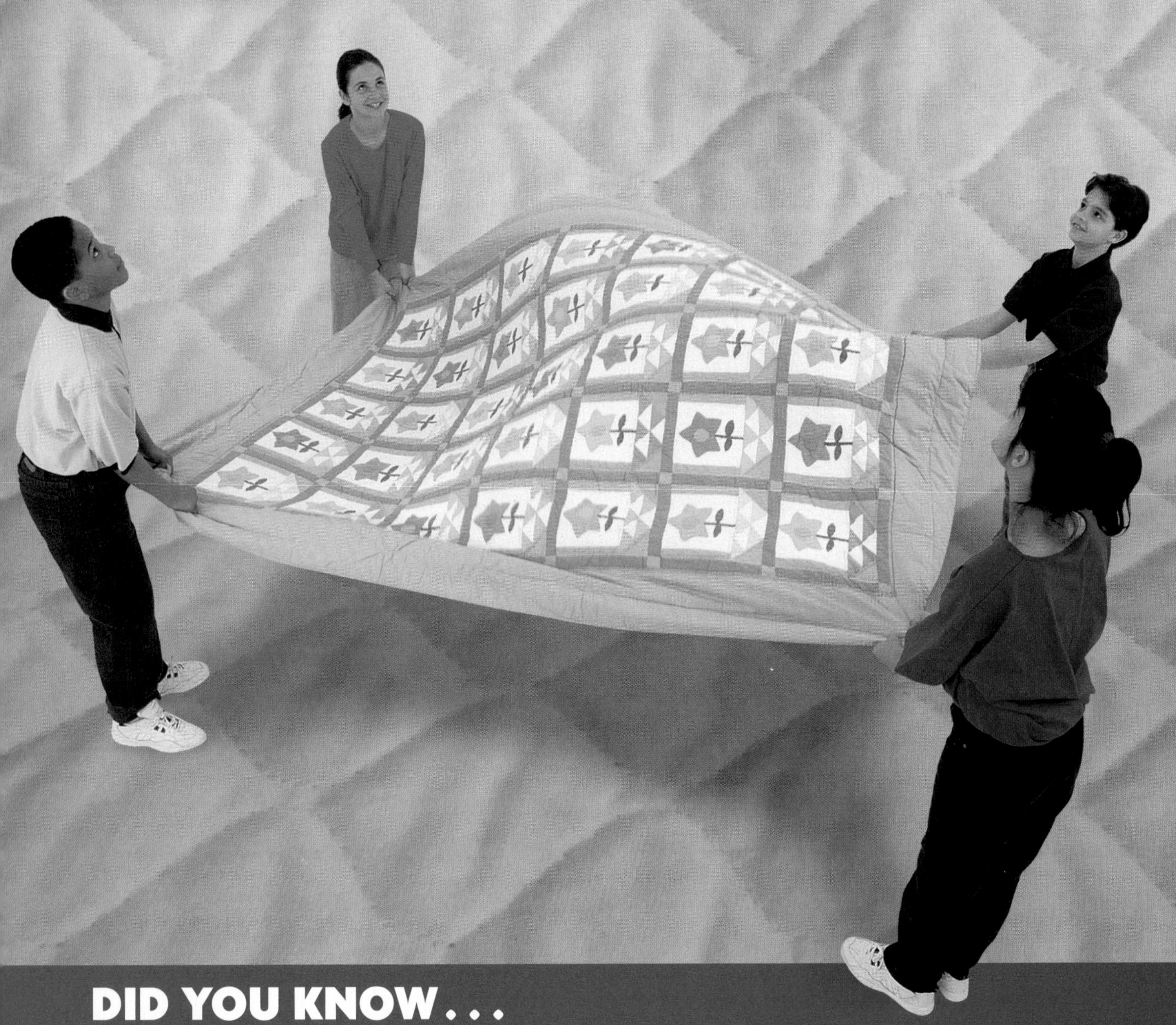

DID YOU KNOW . . .

The first American quilts were from Holland and England. Patchwork quilts later became popular in the United States.

Quilters often use geometric patterns to create beautiful designs.

Team-Up Time

Designing Quilt Patches

Patchwork quilts were made by pioneers to recycle bits of good cloth from items that were worn out. They often gave their designs names. Design at least two quilt squares and name them.

YOU WILL NEED squares of 6 in. by 6 in. colored paper, grid paper, scissors, glue

Work with a partner. Your job is to

- cut out 16 triangles and 16 squares from 6 in. by 6 in. squares. Use two colors.
- share pieces so that each person can have three or four colors to work with.
- make designs with your quilt pieces, and record and glue them on grid paper.
- name your designs.

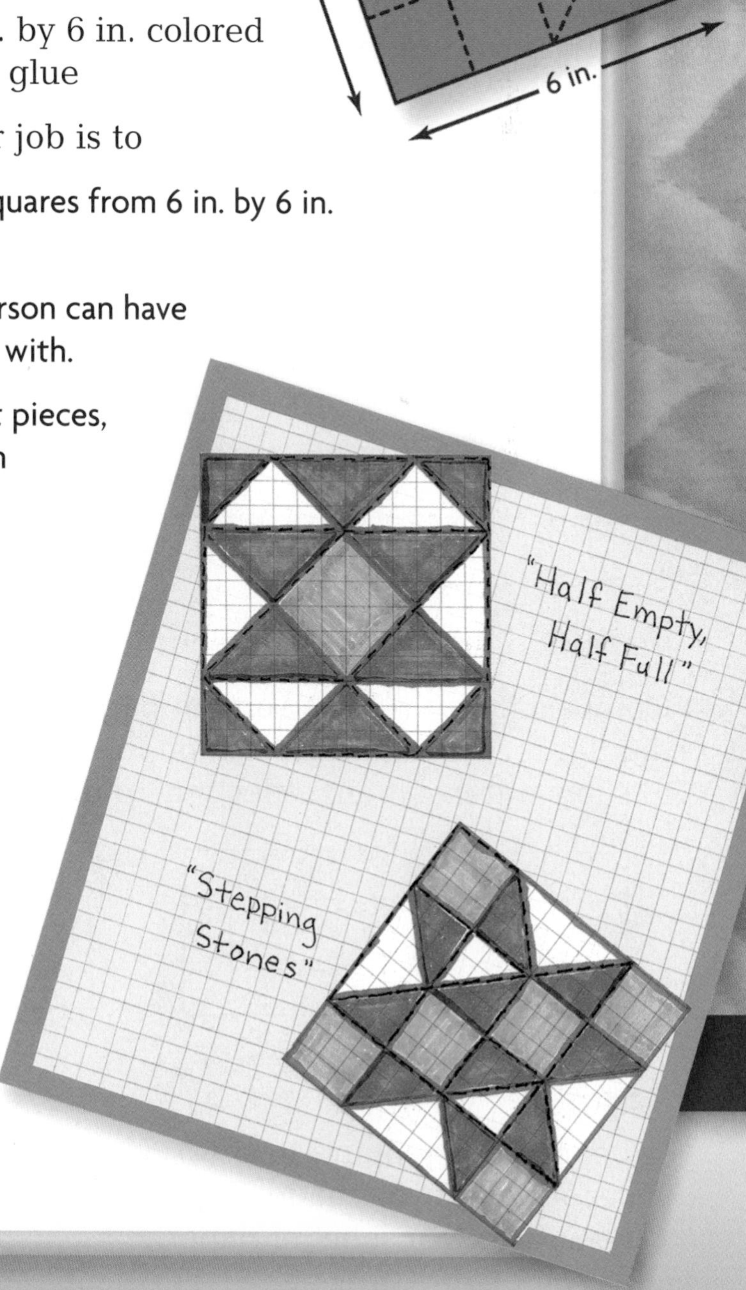

DID YOU

- ✓ design at least two quilt squares?
- ✓ record and glue the designs on grid paper?
- ✓ think of a descriptive name for each design?

Translations, Reflections, and Rotations

You will investigate what happens to a figure's size and shape when you slide, flip, or turn it.

Why learn this? You can make quilt designs by changing the positions of a square.

WORD POWER
transformations
translation
reflection
rotation

Transformations are different ways to move a figure. Three kinds of **transformations** are reflections, translations, and rotations.

A. When you *slide* a figure, it is a **translation**.	**B.** When you *flip* a figure over a line, it is a **reflection**.	**C.** When you *turn* a figure around a point or a vertex, it is a **rotation**.
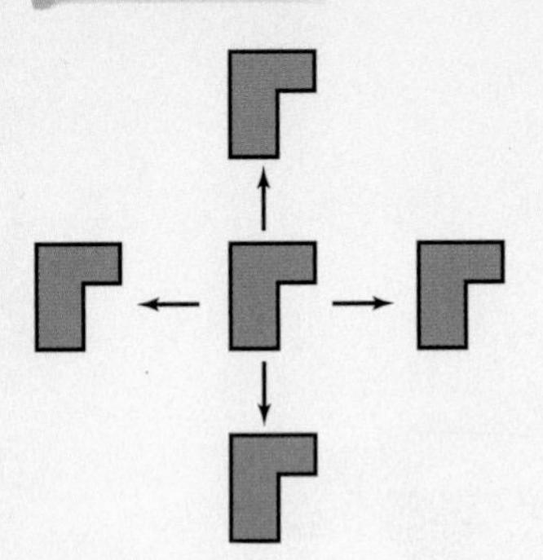	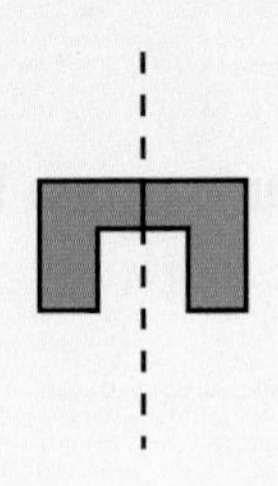	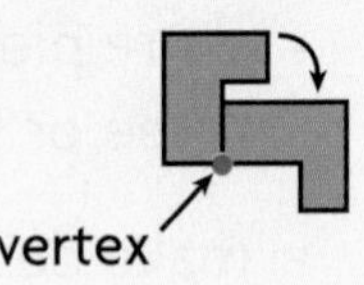

Explore

MATERIALS: dot paper, straightedge

Copy each figure below on dot paper. Cut out the figure. Move and trace it on the dot paper to show a translation, reflection, and rotation.

A. 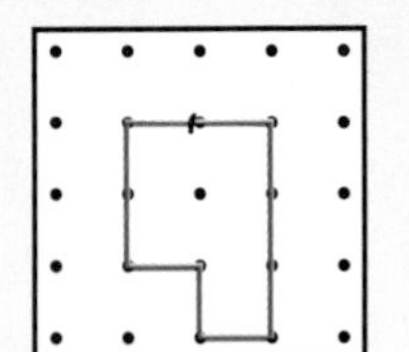 **B.** 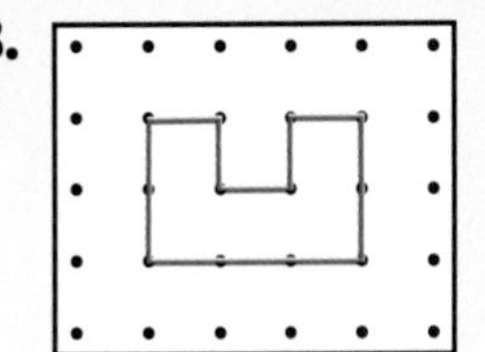 **C.** 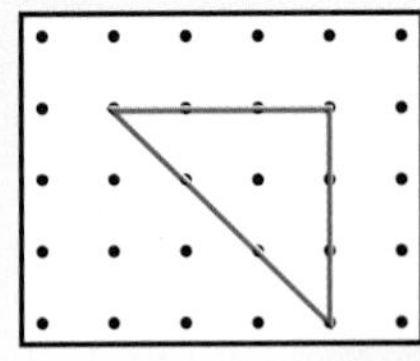

Record

Label each new figure to show the transformation you made. Tape or paste your figures to a sheet of paper.

Try This

Make a different figure on dot paper. Then draw it in a new position. Have a partner tell whether the transformation was a *translation*, *reflection*, or *rotation*.

TALK ABOUT IT When you move a figure, what do you notice about its size and shape?

WRITE ABOUT IT When you flip a figure over a line, how can you make sure the new figure is a reflection of the first figure?

HANDS-ON PRACTICE

Copy each figure on dot paper. Then draw figures for it to show a translation, reflection, and rotation.

1. 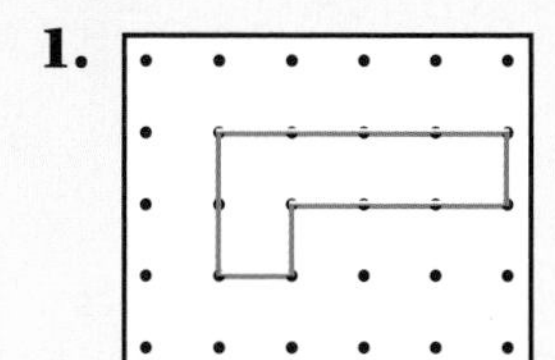

2. 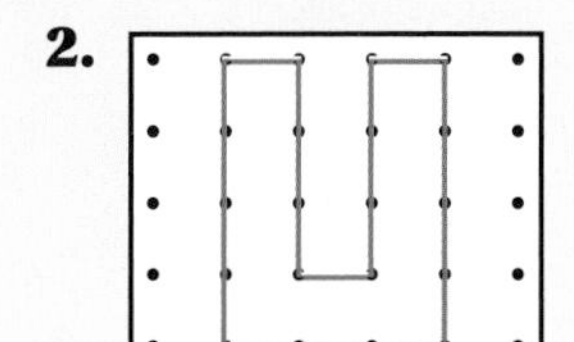

3. 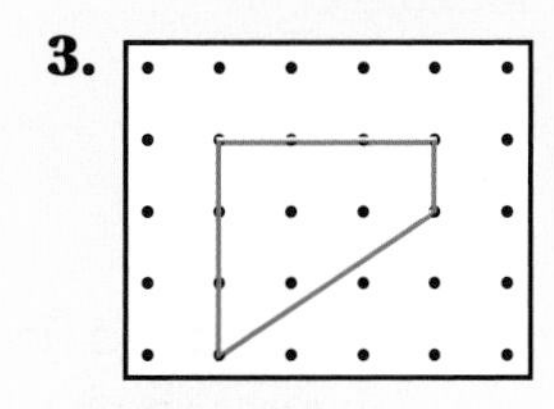

4. 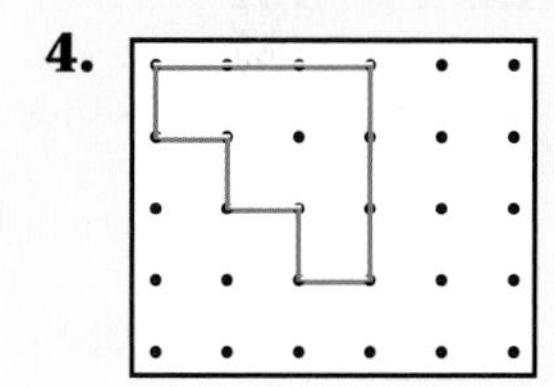

Applying What You Learned

Tell how each figure was moved. Write *translation, reflection,* or *rotation*.

5. 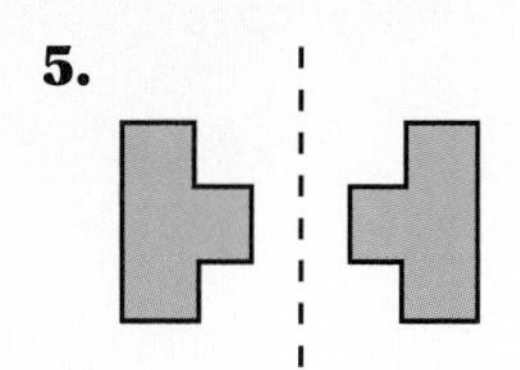

6. 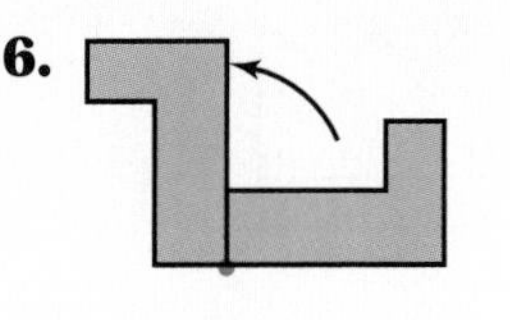

7. 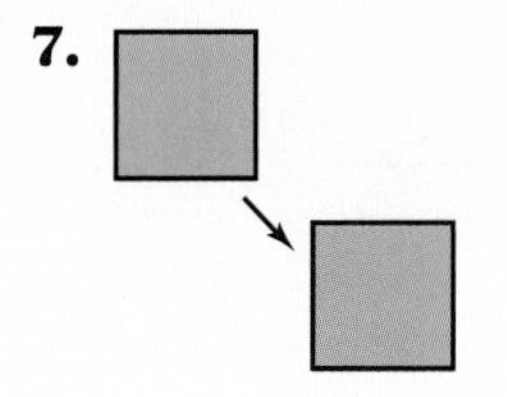

8. 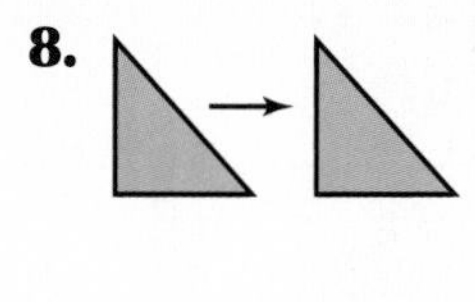

9. 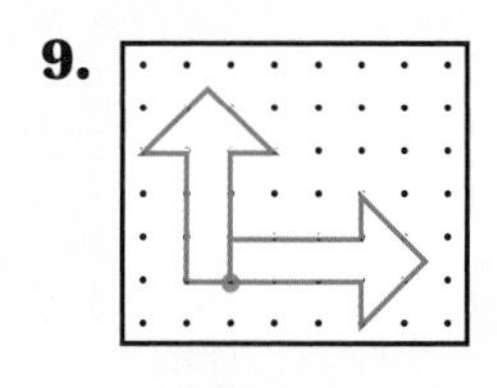

10. 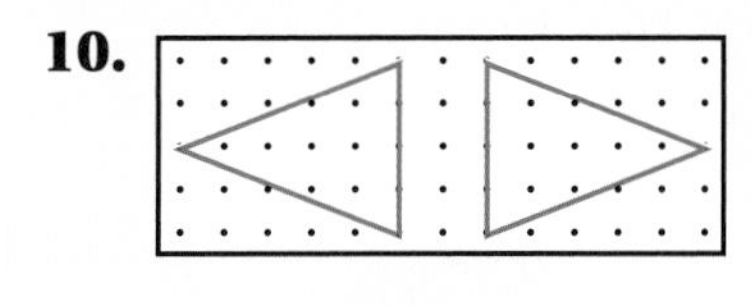

11. 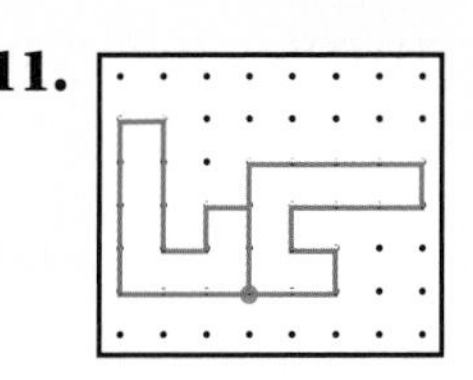

12. 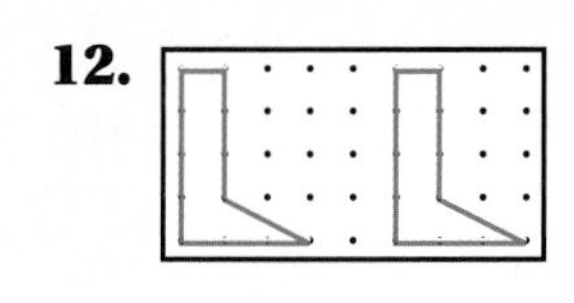

Mixed Applications

13. James made pancakes for breakfast. He flipped the pancakes three times. Did they end up on the same side as they began? Which word describes how the pancakes were moved: *translation*, *reflection*, or *rotation*?

14. **WRITE ABOUT IT** Look at yourself in a mirror. How is your reflection in a mirror like the transformation you have just learned about? Explain.

MORE PRACTICE Student Handbook page H94

Congruence

You will investigate, identify, make, and check congruent figures.

Why learn this? You can make copies of a figure and check to see if the copies have exactly the same size and shape.

WORD POWER
congruent figure

Explore

Congruent figures have the same size and shape. Use dot paper to show two figures that are congruent.

MATERIALS: dot paper, scissors

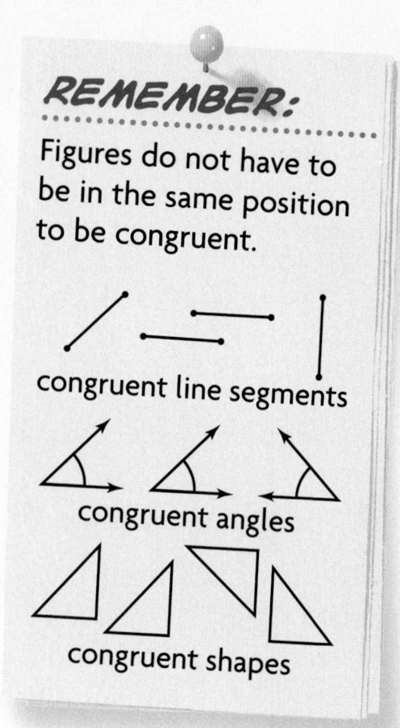

MODEL

Step 1

Draw these two figures on dot paper.

Step 2

Cut out the figures. Move the figures to check for congruency.

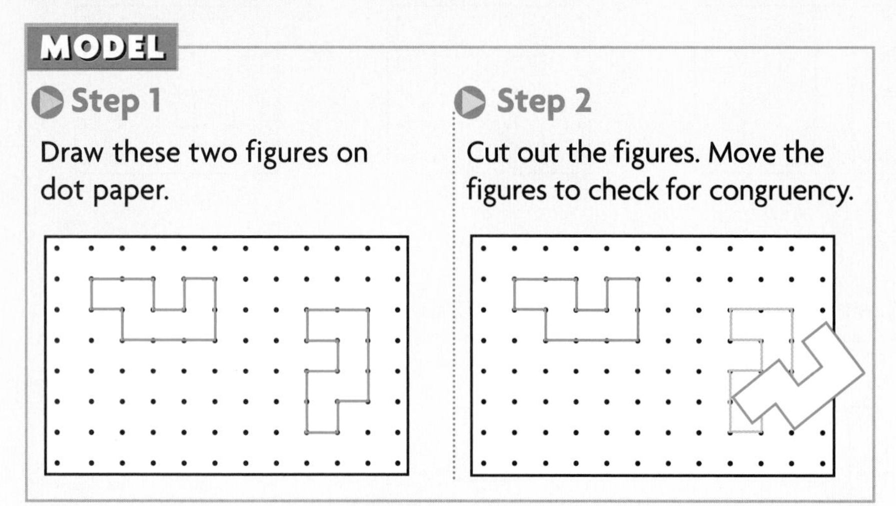

Record

Tape or paste the figures on a sheet of paper. Write to explain how you moved the figures to check to see if they were congruent.

Try This

Copy the figures on dot paper. Are they congruent?

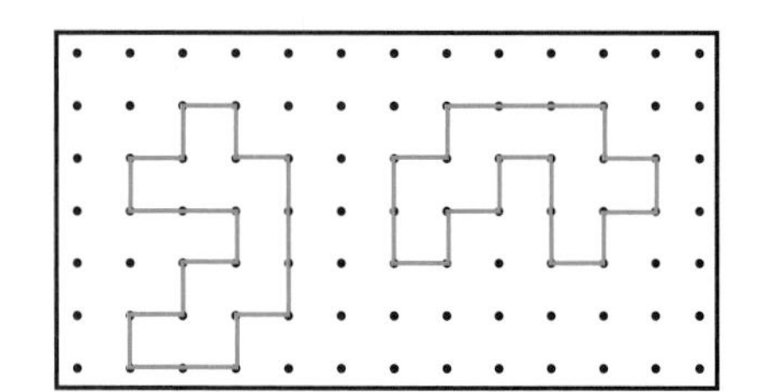

TALK ABOUT IT How did you transform the figures to see if they were congruent?

WRITE ABOUT IT Explain how you decided whether the figures were congruent.

HANDS-ON PRACTICE

Copy each pair of figures on dot paper. Cut out one in each pair, and move it to check for congruency. Write whether the pair is congruent.

1. 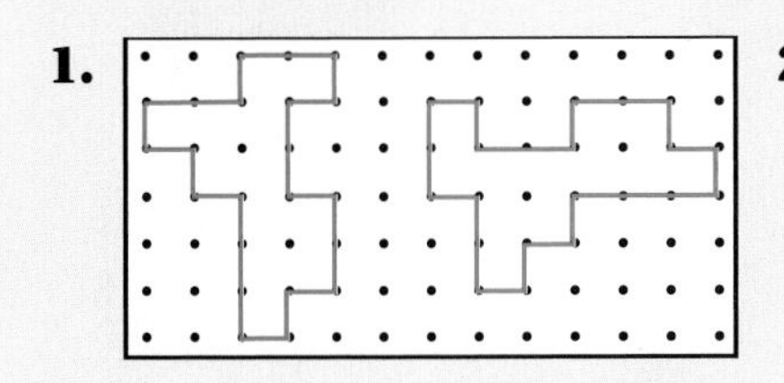

2. 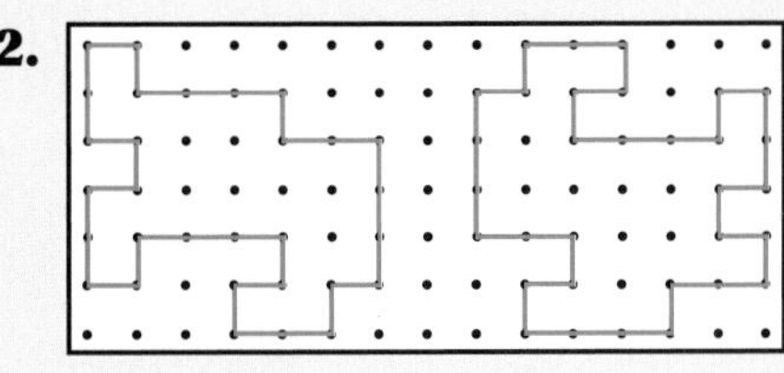

3. 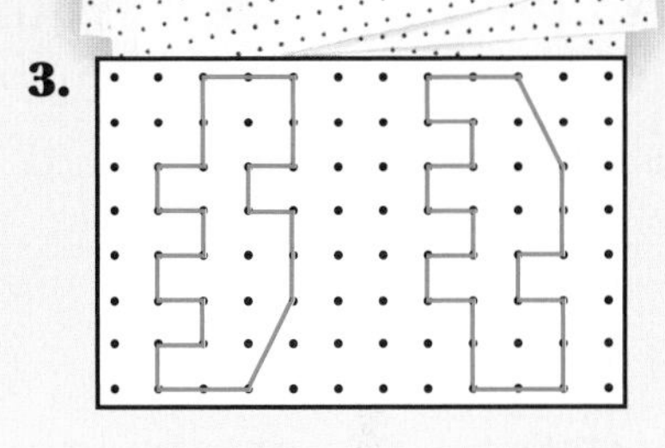

Applying What You Learned

Is each pair of figures congruent? Write *yes* or *no*.

4. 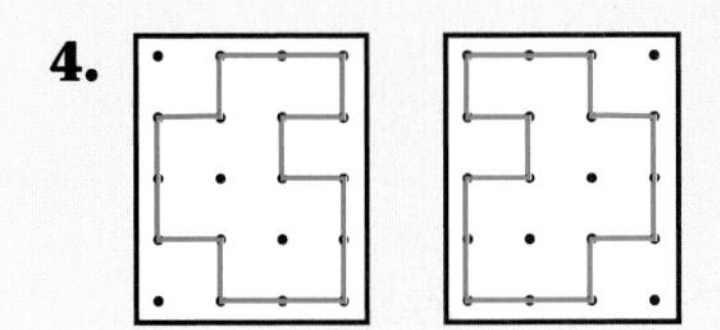

5. 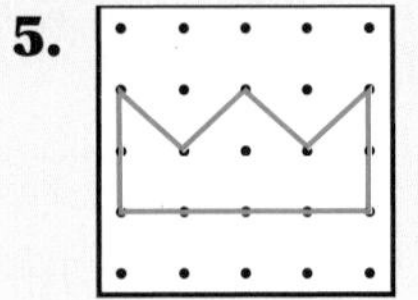 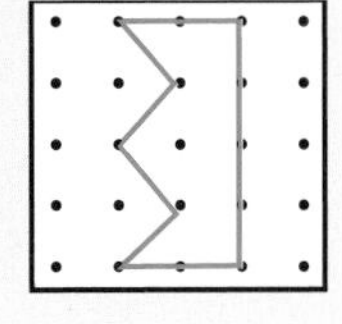

6. 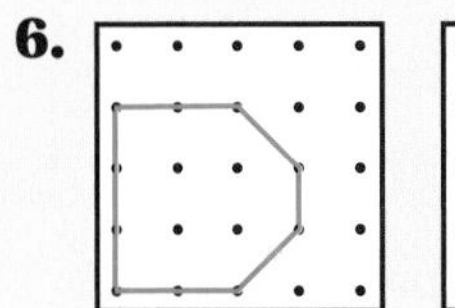 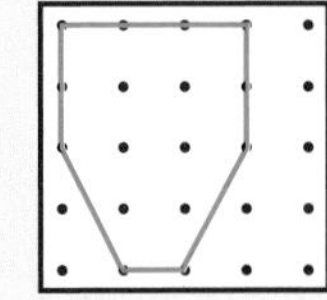

7. 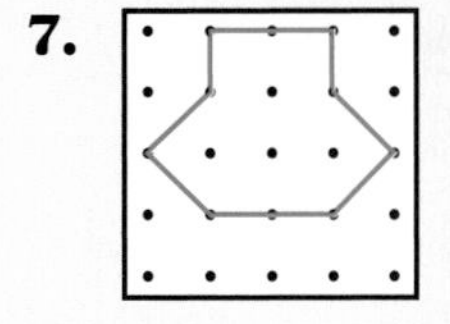 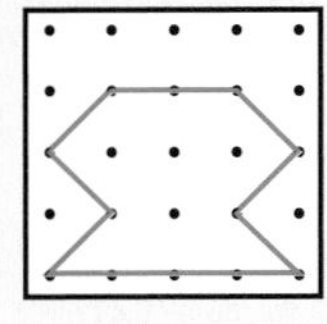

8. 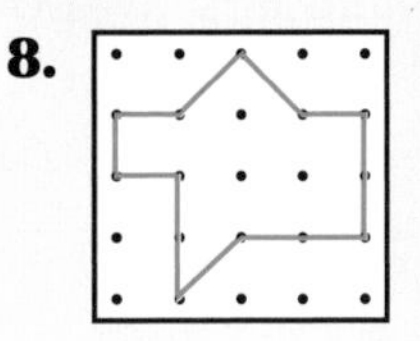 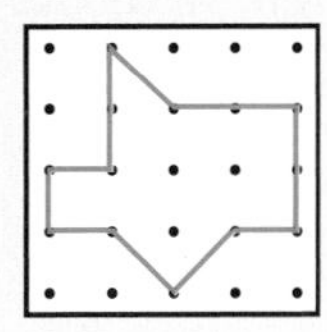

9. 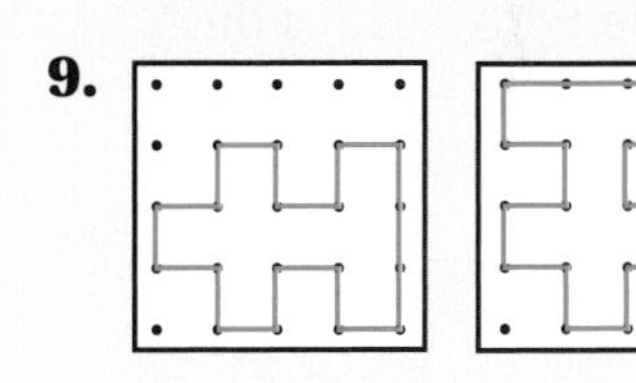

Mixed Applications

10. The pantry floor is 7 ft long and 5 ft wide. The laundry-room floor measures 5 ft by 7 ft. Are the floors congruent? How do you know?

11. Lydia bought tacks for $3, paper for $2, and stickers for $3. Later, Tom gave Lydia $2. Then Lydia had $5. How much money did Lydia have before she bought the supplies?

12. Mr. Jones has a number game for his class. When he says 7, the answer is 19. When he says 13, the answer is 25. When he says 21, the answer is 33. What is the answer when Mr. Jones says 35?

13. **WRITE ABOUT IT** Make a list of figures in your classroom that are congruent. Explain how you can check to make sure they are congruent.

PART 1 Two Kinds of Symmetry

You will investigate point symmetry and line symmetry in an object or a pattern.

Why learn this? You can find symmetrical objects and designs in nature and in art.

WORD POWER

point symmetry

A figure has **point symmetry** if it can be turned about a central point and still look the same in at least two different positions.

Explore

MATERIALS: paper, straightedge, scissors

You can make a model to show point symmetry.

MODEL

Step 1

On a sheet of paper, draw a triangle with equal sides. Cut it out.

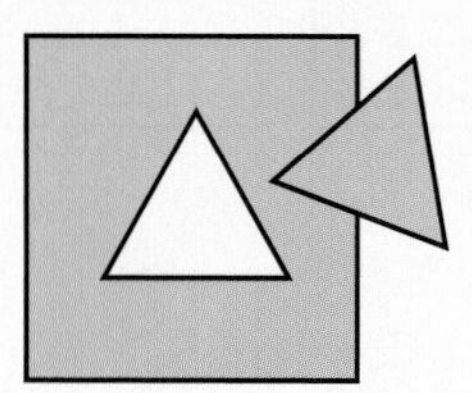

Step 2

Label the corners of the triangle with the numbers 1, 2, and 3.

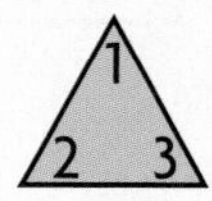

Step 3

Turn the triangle about its central point. How many different ways can the triangle fit back into the space in the paper?

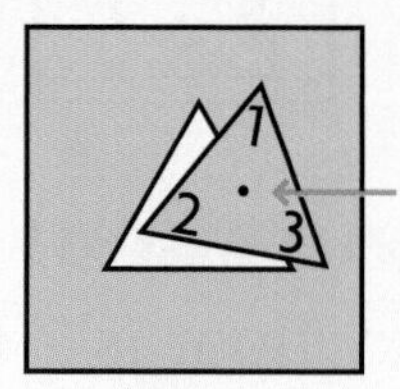

Label the central point.

Record

On a sheet of paper, trace and label the triangle after each turn.

Talk About It

- How many times did you turn the triangle?
- How do you know whether the triangle has point symmetry?

Technology Link

In ***Mighty Math Number Heroes***, the game called *Geocomputer* helps you make your own designs that have point symmetry.

Try This

Use a square. Follow steps like those for the triangle model to find out if the square has point symmetry.

TALK ABOUT IT How can you find out if the square has point symmetry?

WRITE ABOUT IT Does a Ferris wheel have point symmetry? How do you know?

HANDS-ON PRACTICE

Follow the steps in the model on page 248 to decide if each shape has point symmetry. Write *yes* or *no*.

1. 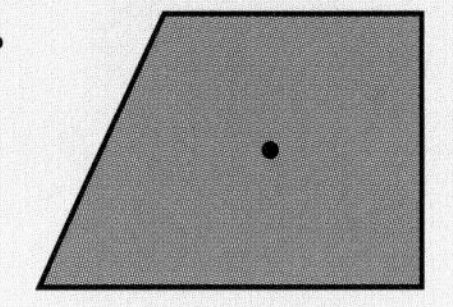

2. 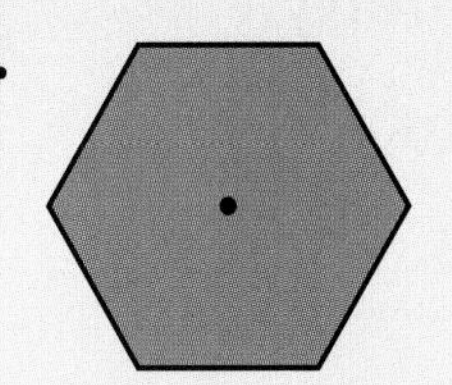

3. 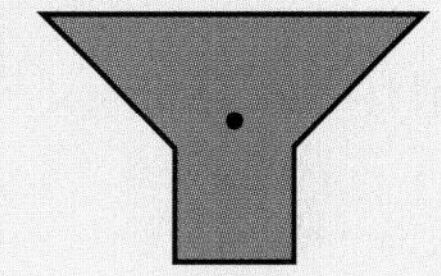

4. 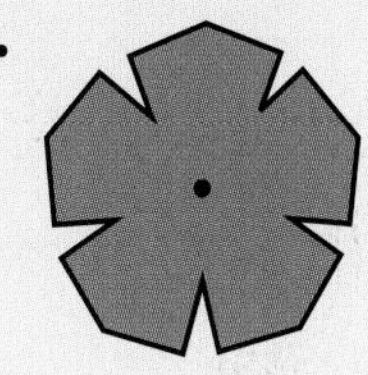

Applying What You Learned

Does each figure have point symmetry? Write *yes* or *no*.

5. 

6. 

7. 

8. 

9. 

10. 

11. 

12. 

Mixed Applications

13. Nick bought two magazines for $18.00. The difference in the cost of the magazines was $2.50. How much did each magazine cost?

14. The Ferris wheel at the fair has point symmetry. Draw a picture of a Ferris wheel. Label the wheel's central point.

15. This year, 2,089 students ran in the State College Fun Run. Last year, only 1,224 students ran in the event. How many more students ran this year?

16. **WRITE ABOUT IT** Name something that has point symmetry. Explain how you know it has point symmetry.

LESSON CONTINUES

PART 2 More About Symmetry

WORD POWER
line symmetry

Another kind of symmetry is **line symmetry**. A figure has line symmetry when it can be folded about a line so that its two parts are identical. When you unfold the figure, one side is a reflection of the other. A figure can have more than one line of symmetry.

REMEMBER:
You can use a mirror to test for line symmetry.

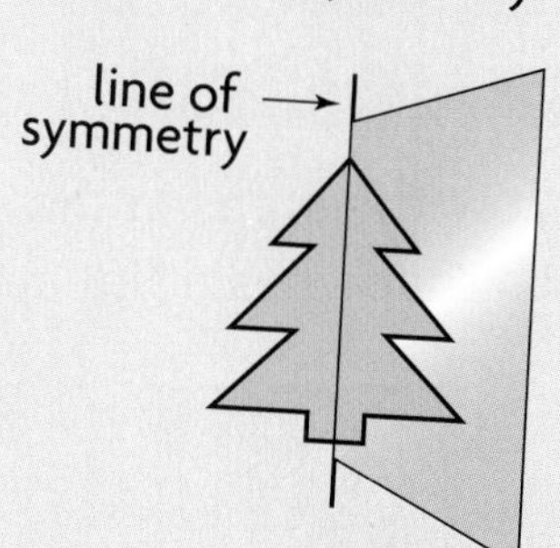

Explore

You can make a design to show line symmetry.

MATERIALS: dot paper, pattern blocks, crayons

MODEL

Step 1

Copy the left half of the design. Label the line of symmetry.

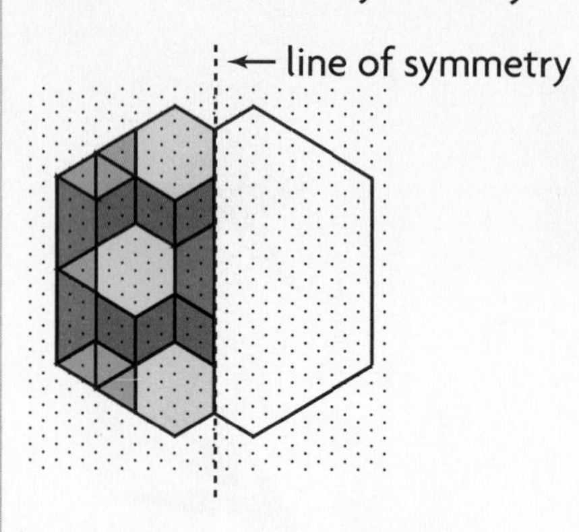

Step 2

Complete the design.

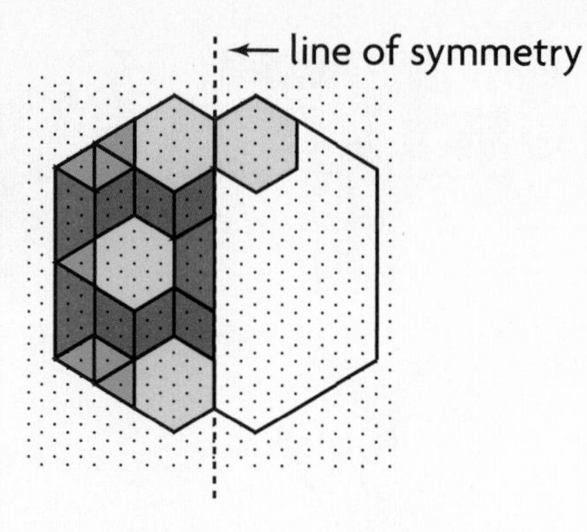

Record

Color the right half of the design to match the left half. Write to explain how you know your design shows line symmetry.

Science Link
The butterfly's shape shows line symmetry. Name another insect that has line symmetry.

Try This

Draw the first half of another design. Have a partner match your half to complete the design.

TALK ABOUT IT How many lines of symmetry does your new design have? How do you know?

Technology Link
E-Lab • Activity 15 Available on CD-ROM and the Internet at http://www.hbschool.com/elab

WRITE ABOUT IT How would you explain to a third grader the difference between line and point symmetry?

HANDS-ON PRACTICE

Complete the design to show line symmetry.

1. 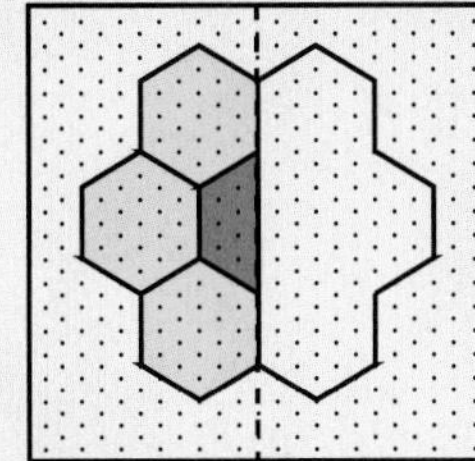

2. 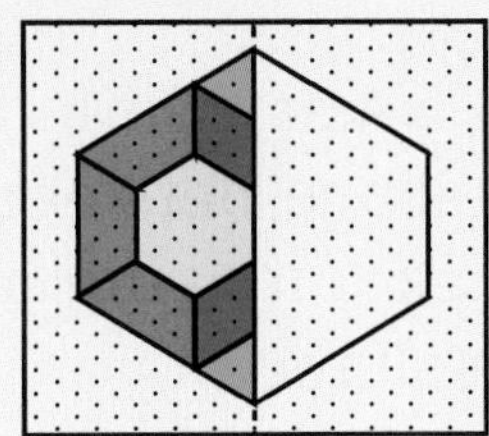

3. 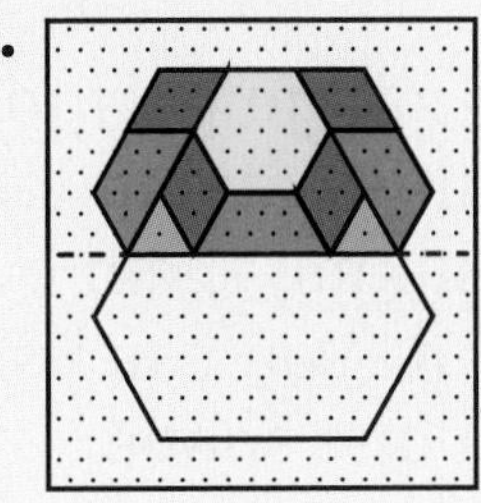

Applying What You Learned

Is the blue line a line of symmetry? Write *yes* or *no*.

4. 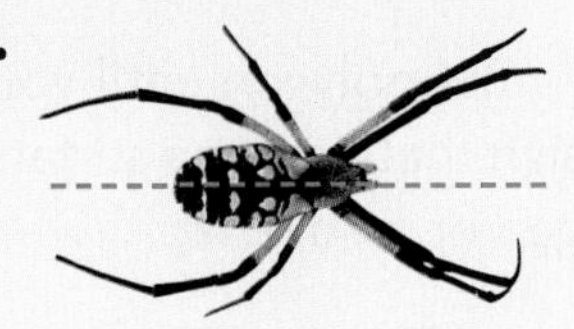

5. 

6. 

7. 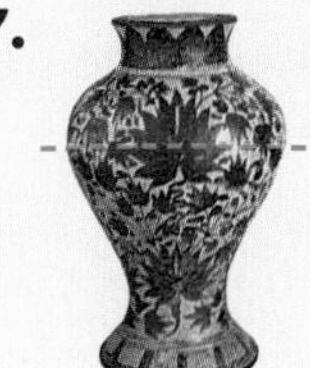

Copy each drawing. Then draw the other half of the figure to show that the figure has line symmetry.

8. 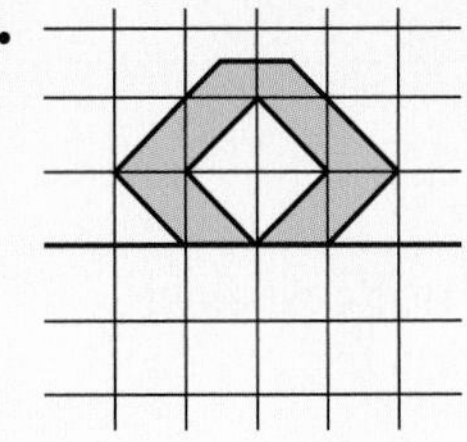

9. 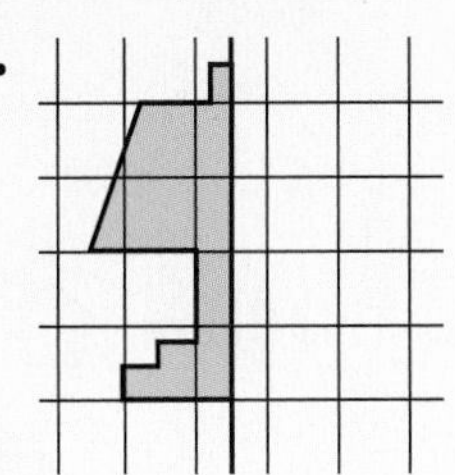

10. 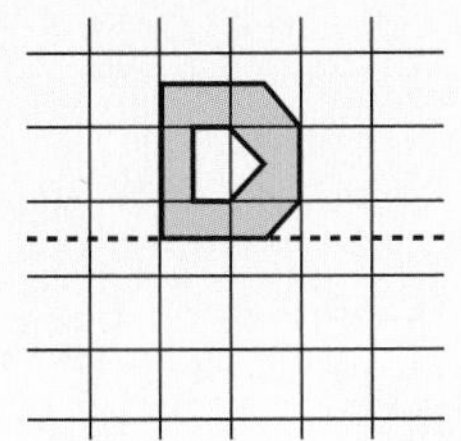

11. 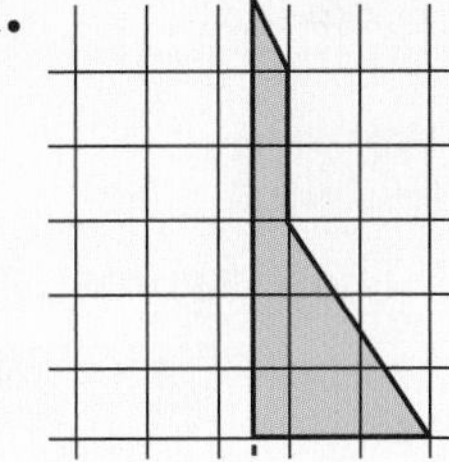

Mixed Applications

Use the table for Problems 12–13.

Possible Trips	Votes
Planetarium	4
Art Museum	14
Children's Theater	3
Zoo	6

12. Mr. Lovett's class is planning to take a field trip. Where do most of the students want to go?

13. How many more students voted for the Zoo than for the Children's Theater?

14. Dan drew a spider, a caterpillar, a butterfly, and a snail. Which of his drawings have line symmetry? How can Dan check his drawings for line symmetry?

15. Which letters of the alphabet have no symmetry?

A, B, C, D, E, F, G, H, I, J, K, L, M, N, O, P, Q, R, S, T, U, V, W, X, Y, Z

MORE PRACTICE Student Handbook page H95

Tessellations

You will learn to make a tessellation and determine whether or not a figure will tessellate.	Why learn this? You can recognize and make interesting designs that tessellate such as tile floors and clothing designs.	**WORD POWER** tessellation

You can arrange polygons so they cover a surface. If you do this without leaving any space between them or making them overlap, you are making a **tessellation**. You can use only one shape or more than one shape.

Are the shapes in the puzzle design congruent? How do you know?

MODEL

Step 1

Choose one polygon. Trace it.

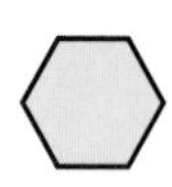

Step 2

Move the polygon to another position so that at least one of its sides touches. Make sure there are no overlaps. Trace it.

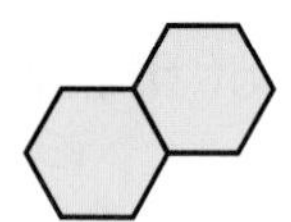

Step 3

Keep tracing the polygon until you make a design that covers a surface without a gap or an overlap.

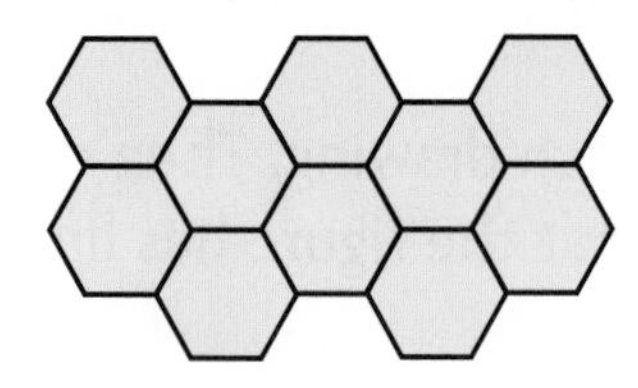

EXAMPLES

A. These figures  tesselate.

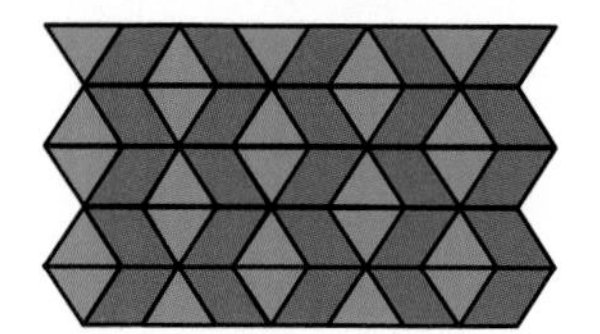

B. This figure does not tesselate.

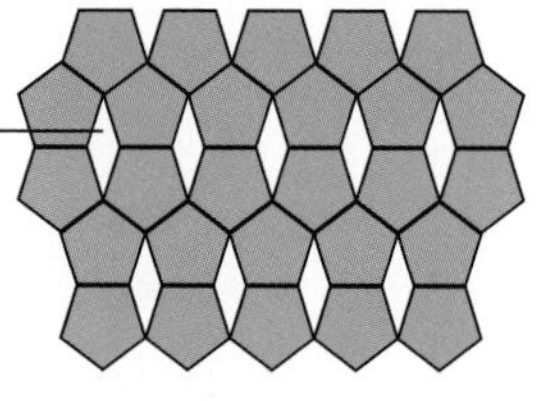

- What kinds of transformations do you see in Example A?

Check Your Understanding

1. Will this square  tessellate? How do you know?	**2.** Will these figures 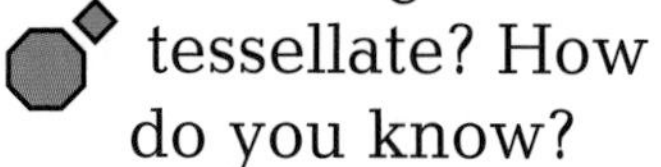 tessellate? How do you know?	**3.** Will this figure tessellate? How do you know?

PRACTICE

Follow the steps in the model on page 252 to decide whether the figure will tessellate. Write *yes* or *no*.

4. 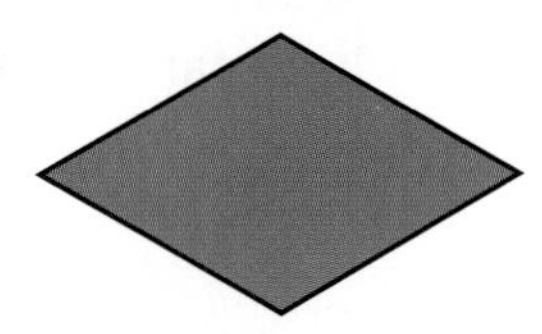

5. 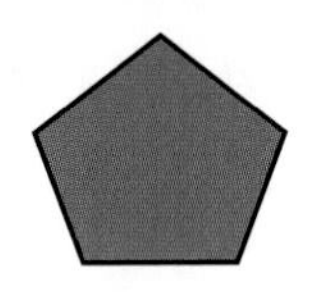

6. 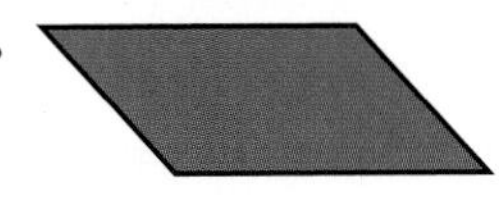

Will the figure tessellate? Write *yes* or *no*.

7. 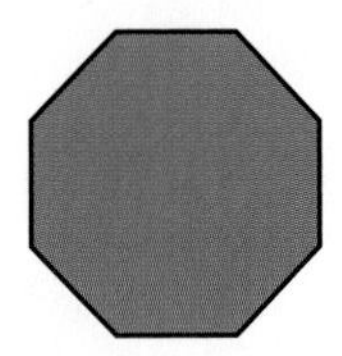

8. 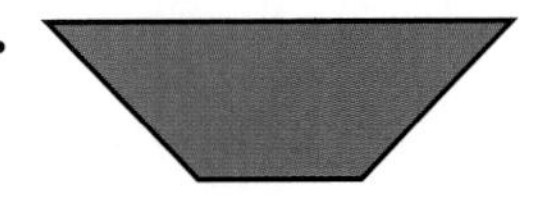

9. 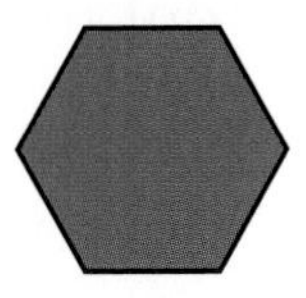

Write the names of the polygons that tessellate in each design.

10. 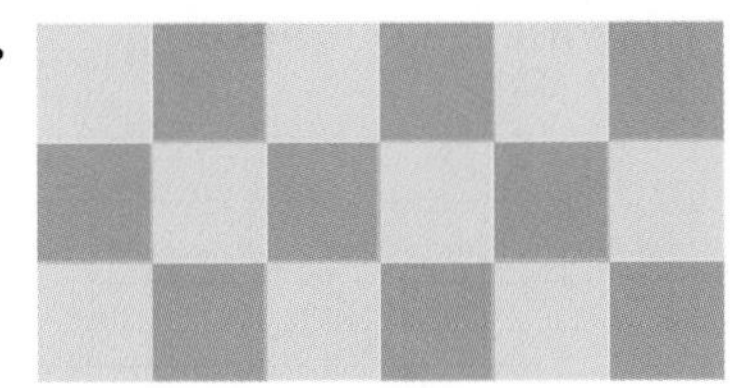

11. 

12. 

Mixed Applications

13. Use grid paper to make a tile design that will tessellate. Use two or more shapes in your design. Repeat your tile design to make a tessellation.

14. Chris bought 2 pounds of apples for $0.89 a pound and 3 oranges for $0.23 each. If he had $3.00, how much change did he receive?

Mixed Review

Write the time one hour later than the given time.
Use A.M. or P.M. **(pages 124–125)**

15. 10:14 A.M.   **16.** 9:45 P.M.   **17.** 11:33 A.M.   **18.** 11:42 A.M.

Use addition and subtraction to find the missing length. **(pages 18–19)**

19. 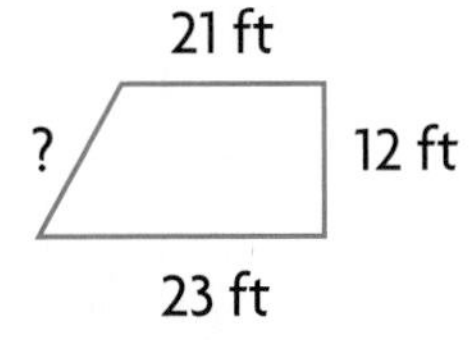

Perimeter = 72 ft

20. 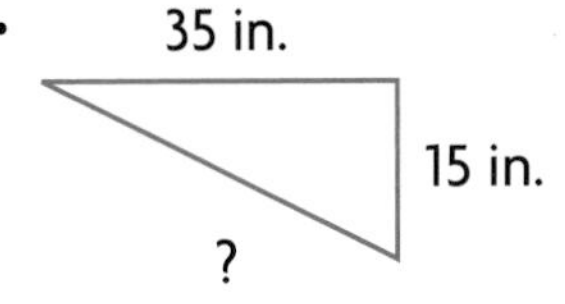

Perimeter = 90 in.

21. 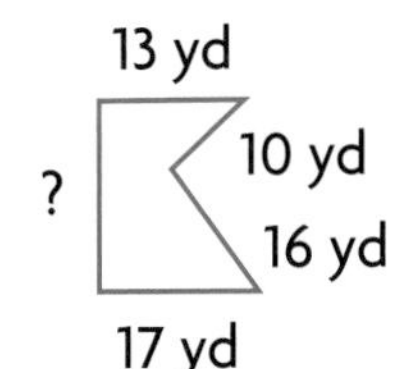

Perimeter = 71 yd

MORE PRACTICE Student Handbook page H95

PART 1

Changing Sizes of Shapes

You will learn that similar figures have the same shape but can have different sizes.

Why learn this? You can enlarge or reduce a shape or picture.

WORD POWER
similar

When you enlarge or reduce a figure, the second figure is **similar** to the first one. They have the same shape but may have different sizes.

Make a figure similar to this one. Use 1-inch grid paper. Your figure will be larger than this one.

MODEL

Step 1

Copy the figure one square at a time on your grid paper.

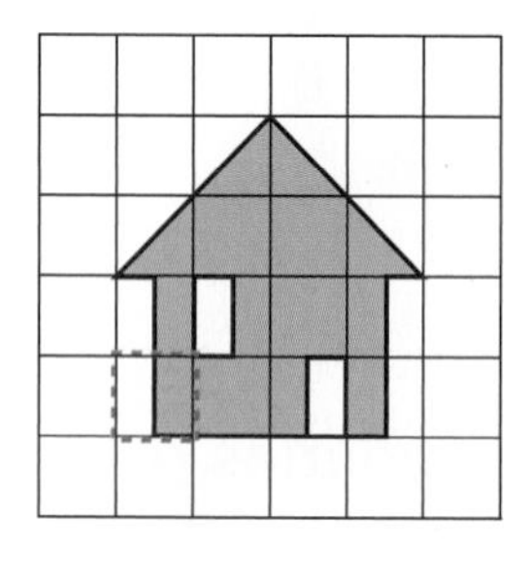

Step 2

For each square, count across and up to find the square to copy.

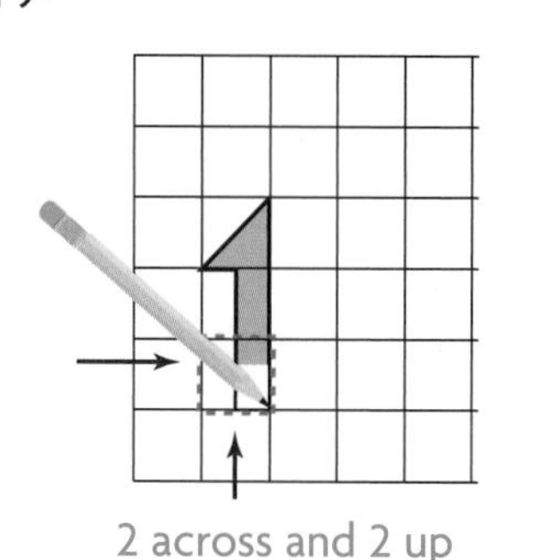

2 across and 2 up

Step 3

Copy the squares until the drawing is complete.

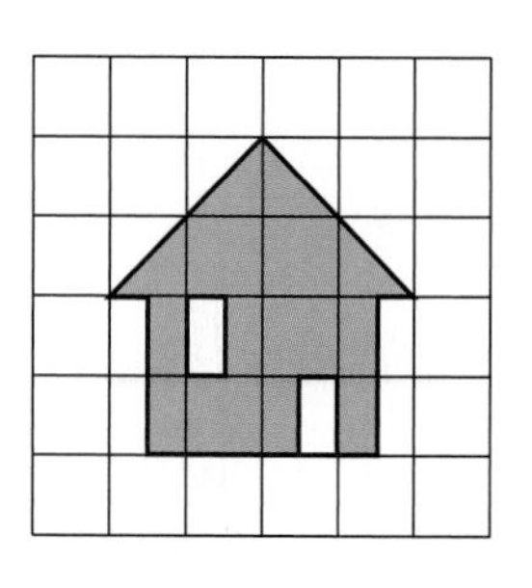

Talk About It

- How are the two figures alike? How are they different?
- Are the figures congruent? Explain.
- What will happen if you use smaller grid paper?

Check Your Understanding

Make similar figures. Explain how each is different from the one before it.

1. Copy this figure on 1-inch grid paper.

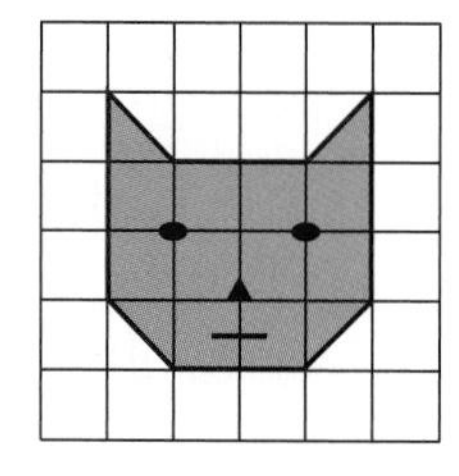

2. Copy this figure on 0.5 cm grid paper.

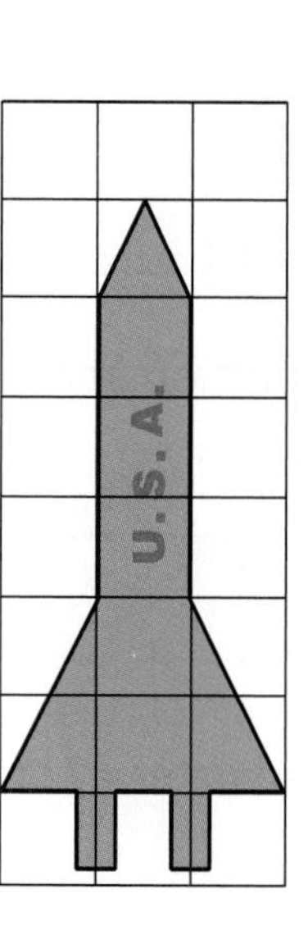

PRACTICE

Draw each figure larger on 1-inch grid paper.

3. 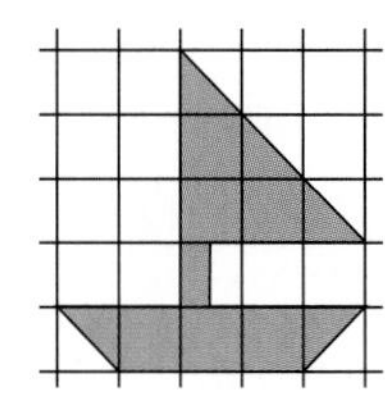

4. 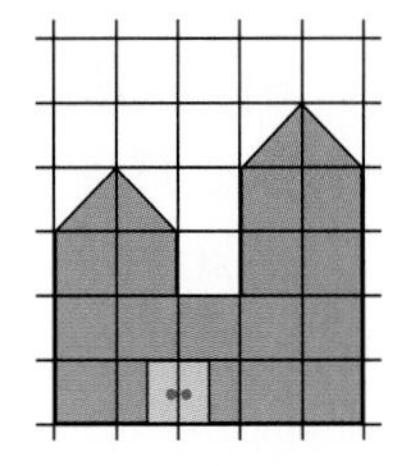

5. 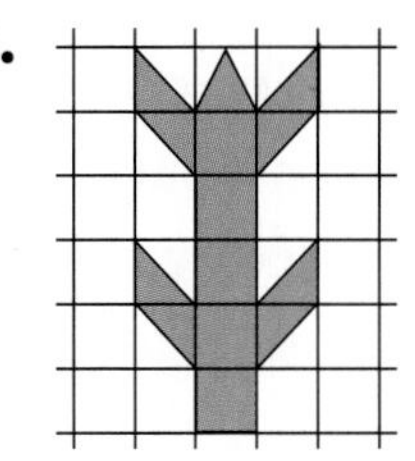

Draw the figure smaller on 0.5 cm grid paper.

6. 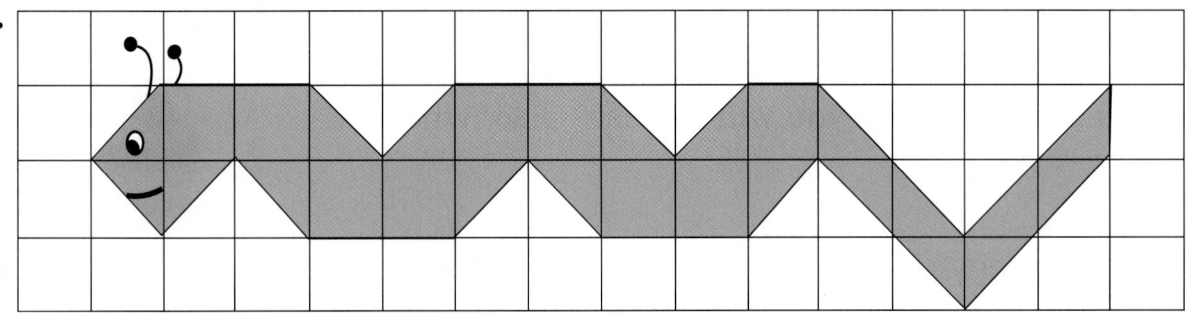

Tell whether each pair of figures is *similar, congruent*, or *both*.

7. 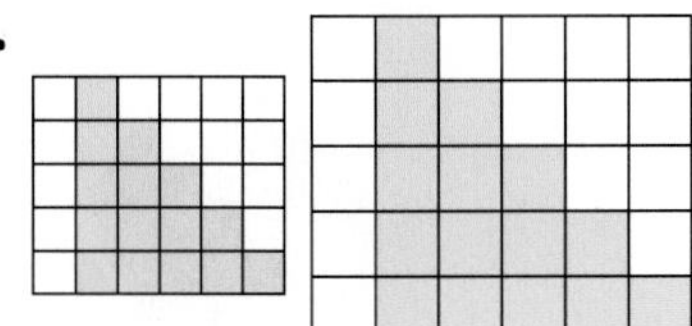

8. 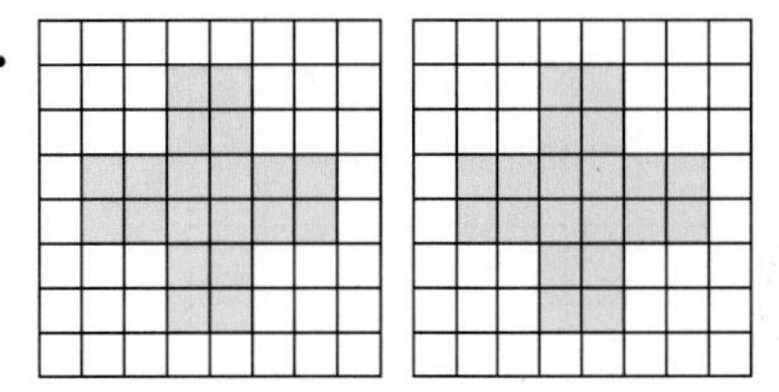

Mixed Applications

9. Draw a design on 1-inch grid paper. Have a partner draw it on 1-cm grid paper. Are the two figures similar? How do you know?

10. Each of the two scenes in the school play lasts 45 minutes. The play begins at 8:00 P.M. At what time does the play end?

11. Allison can take a trip in June, July, or August. She can go to the beach, the mountains, or the city. What choices does Allison have for her trip?

12. **WRITE ABOUT IT** Juan is looking at grasshoppers through a magnifying glass. He notices that the image of a small grasshopper looks different through the magnifying glass. How are the two images alike? How are they different?

LESSON CONTINUES

MORE PRACTICE Student Handbook pages H95–H96

PART 2 PROBLEM-SOLVING STRATEGY
Make a Model

THE PROBLEM **Suppose your group is in charge of making a bulletin board about a favorite book, *The Enormous Egg*. How can you draw a large picture of the dinosaur below for a bulletin board?**

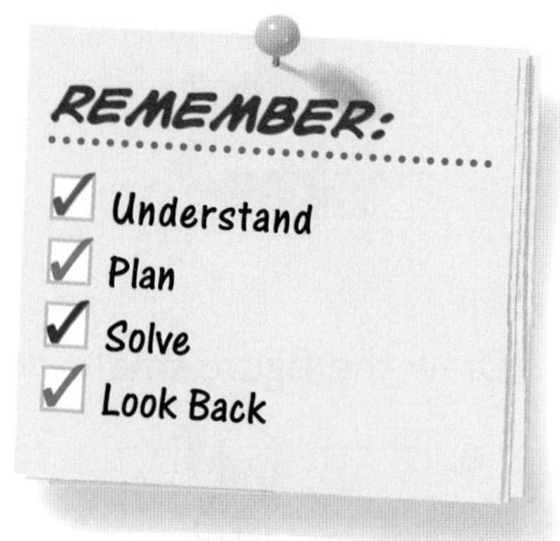

✓ Understand

- What are you asked to do?
- What information will you use?
- Is there information you will not use? If so, what?

✓ Plan

- What strategy can you use to solve the problem?

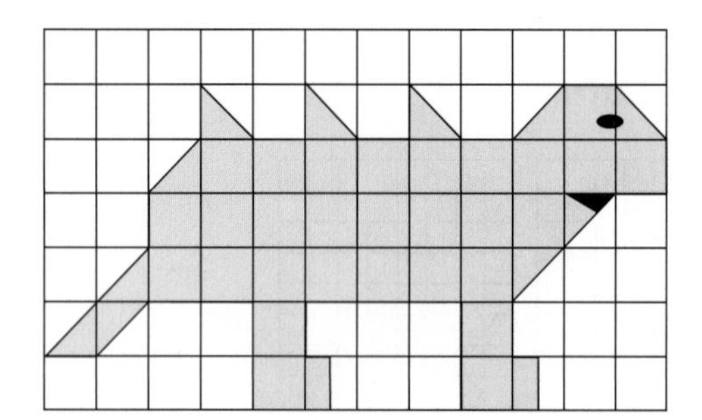

You can *make a model* of the dinosaur that is larger than but similar to the one shown here. Use larger grid paper to do this.

✓ Solve

- What model can you make to solve the problem?

You can use one-inch grid paper to enlarge the figure. Copy the picture, square by square, to make a larger picture.

✓ Look Back

- How can you decide if your picture is correct?
- What other strategy could you use?

PRACTICE

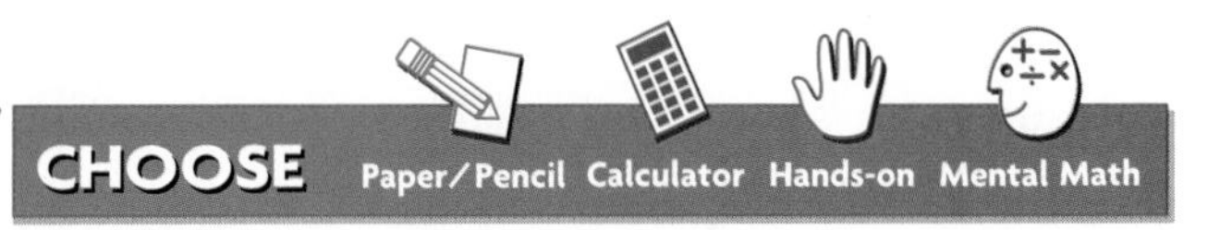

Make a model to solve.

1. Suppose you want to make a larger picture of the figure at the right to put on a poster. Use one-inch grid paper. Then copy the figure, square by square, to make a larger picture.

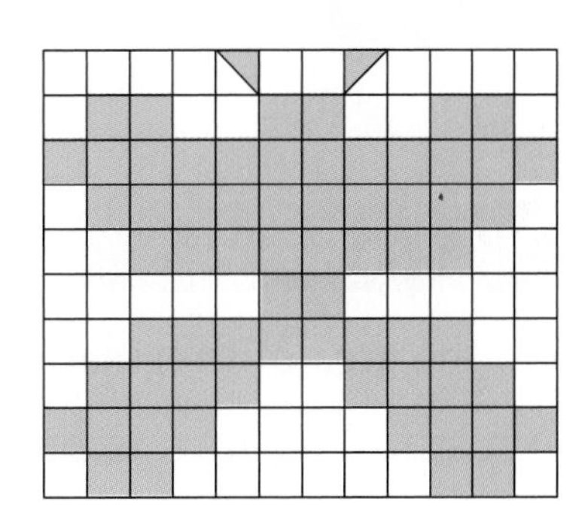

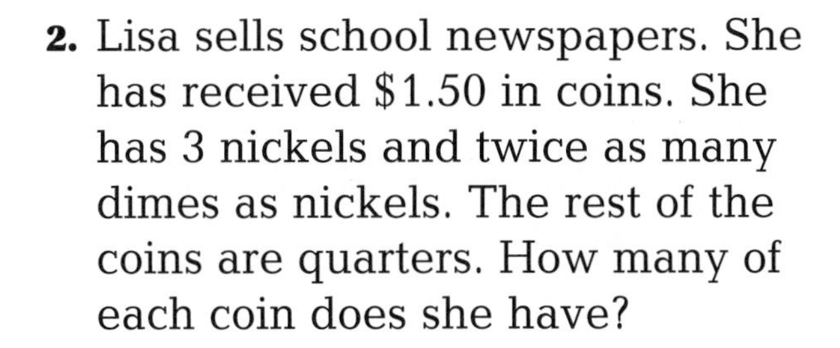

2. Lisa sells school newspapers. She has received $1.50 in coins. She has 3 nickels and twice as many dimes as nickels. The rest of the coins are quarters. How many of each coin does she have?

3. Ted and Kate want to fence in a rectangular part of their yard. They have 28 feet of fencing. What is the greatest possible area they can fence?

Mixed Applications

Solve.

CHOOSE A STRATEGY

- Make a Model
- Draw a Diagram
- Guess and Check
- Work Backward
- Make an Organized List
- Write a Number Sentence

4. Grant wants to enlarge the figure and put it on a sign. Copy the figure on one-inch grid paper to make a larger picture.

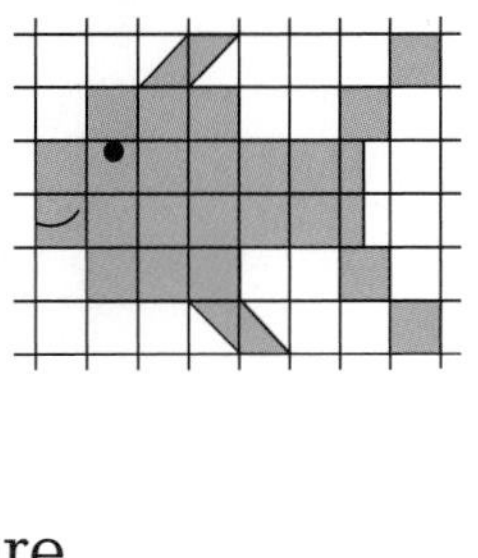

5. There are 7 players on the baseball team who can be on the all-star team. They have been given 56 tickets. Each player received the same number of tickets. How many tickets did each player receive?

6. At a concession stand, Luisa bought a drink for $0.75, a hot dog for $1.25, and 3 bags of peanuts for $0.30 each. She was given $2.10 in change. How much money did she have to start with?

7. For lunch Wendy can order a sandwich with chicken, tuna fish, or peanut butter. She can have the sandwich on white bread, wheat bread, rye bread, or a roll. How many choices does she have?

8. A 4-sided figure has a perimeter of 36 inches. What is the least area the figure can have? What is the greatest area?

9. The sum of two numbers is 23. Their difference is 5. What are the numbers?

MORE PRACTICE Student Handbook page H96

MATH FUN!

WEIRD AREAS

PURPOSE To find the area of irregular shapes

The area of each small square is one square unit.

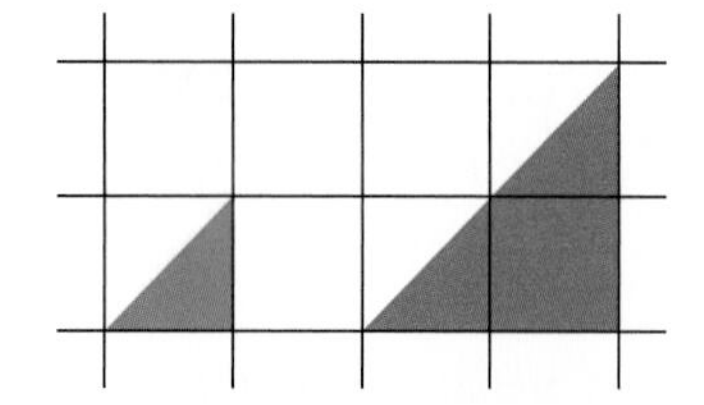

1. What is the area of the green triangle?
2. What is the area of the blue triangle?
3. Find the area of each figure in square units.

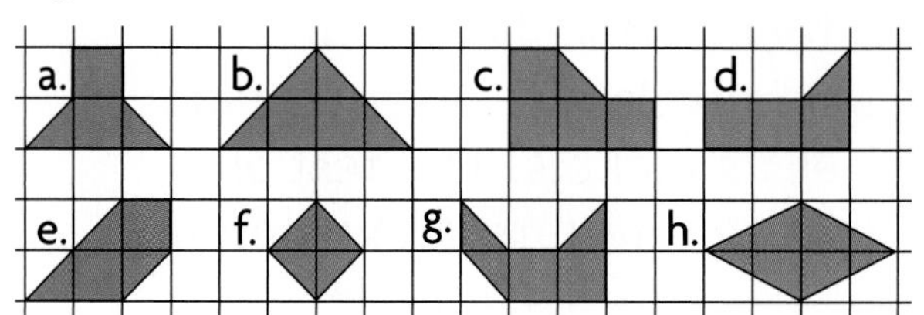

QUILT PUZZLES

PURPOSE To practice finding geometric patterns

Work with a partner. Look at the quilt pattern called Churn Dash. Find examples of translations, rotations, and reflections. Then find and draw examples of point symmetry and line symmetry.

Go to a library or a craft show to see other interesting quilt patterns.

Attribute Analogies

PURPOSE To use visual sense to finish the patterns

Think about how the first two figures are related. Then draw the figure that completes the sentence.

1. ○ is to ● as □ is to __?__.
2. ▲ is to △ as ▮ is to __?__.
3. ◈ is to ◆ as ◐ is to __?__.
4. ▣ is to ▣ as ◬ is to __?__.

CHAPTER 15

REVIEW

✓ CHECK UNDERSTANDING

VOCABULARY

1. Translations, reflections, and rotations are three kinds of _?_. (page 244)

2. Figures that have the same size and shape are _?_. (page 246)

3. Figures that have the same shape but may have different sizes are _?_. (page 254)

✓ CHECK SKILLS

Tell how each figure was moved. Write *translation, reflection*, or *rotation.* (pages 244–245)

4. 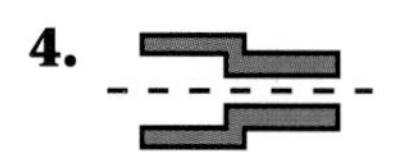

5.

Is each pair of figures congruent? Write *yes* or *no*. (pages 246–247)

6.

7.

Does each figure have *point* or *line* symmetry or *both*? (pages 248–251)

8. 

9. 

10. 

11. 

Will the figure tessellate? Write *yes* or *no*. (pages 252–253)

12. 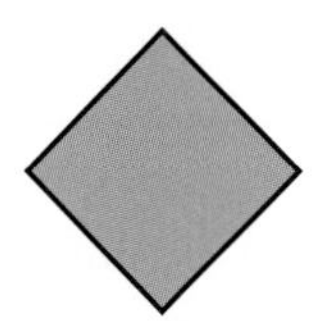

13. 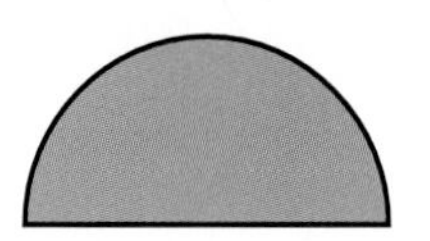

14. 

15. 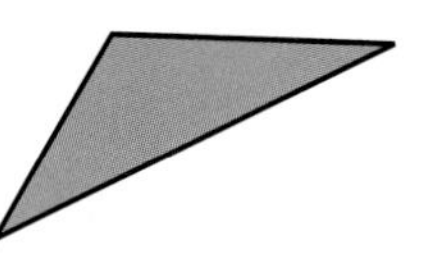

✓ CHECK PROBLEM SOLVING

Solve. (pages 256–257)

CHOOSE A STRATEGY

- Act It Out
- Draw a Diagram
- Guess and Check
- Make a Model

16. Tracy wants to design a five-pointed star using one pentagon and some triangles. How many triangles does Tracy need? How might the star look?

17. There are 69 people who work at the television station. There are twice as many women as men. How many of the workers are women? How many are men?

CHAPTERS 12–15

STUDY GUIDE & REVIEW

VOCABULARY CHECK

WORD BANK
area
congruent
perimeter
similar
vertex

Choose a term from the box to complete each sentence.

1. A ? is a place where three or more sides meet in a solid figure. (page 196)
2. The ? is the distance around a figure. (page 228)
3. The ? is the number of square units needed to cover a flat surface. (page 230)
4. Figures that have the same size and shape are ?. (page 246)
5. Figures that have the same shape but may have different sizes are ?. (page 254)

STUDY AND SOLVE

CHAPTER 12

EXAMPLE

Name the solid figure. Write the number of faces, edges, and vertices.

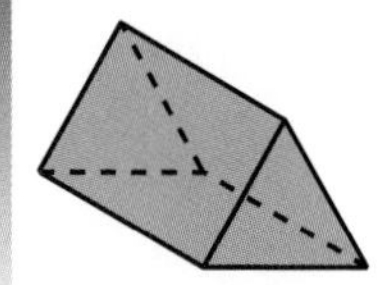

5 faces
9 edges
6 vertices

triangular prism

Name the solid figure. Write the plane figures that are its faces. (pages 196–197)

6. 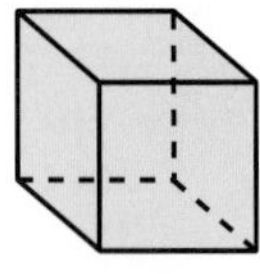

7. 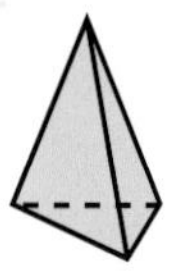

Name the solid figure. Write the number of faces, edges, and vertices. (pages 198–199)

8. 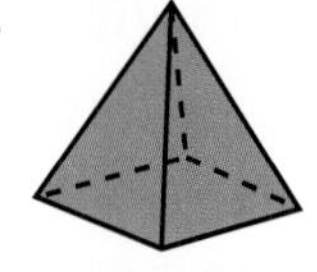

9. 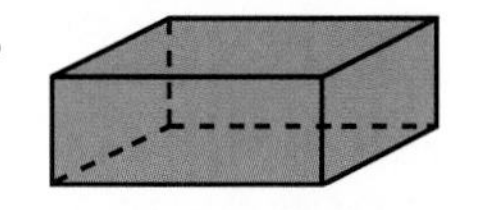

Solve. (pages 204–205)

10. Ms. Lopez's room has a globe, chalk, books, and a notebook. Sort the items into the three-dimensional shapes they suggest.

CHAPTER 13

Identify the figure. Write *point, line, line segment*, or *ray*. (pages 210–213)

11. ←——→

12. •——→

Write whether the lines are *intersecting, parallel*, or *perpendicular*. (pages 214–215)

13.

14. 

Identify each as a *right, acute,* or *obtuse* angle. (pages 212–213)

15. 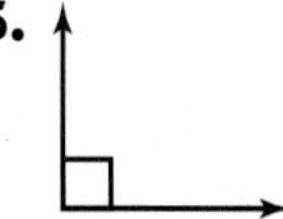

16. 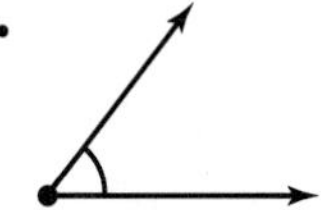

Name the polygon. Write *hexagon, octagon, pentagon,* or *triangle.* (pages 218–219)

17. 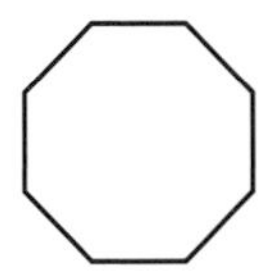

18. 

Name the quadrilateral. Write *rectangle, rhombus, square, trapezoid,* or *parallelogram.* (pages 220–221)

19. 

20. 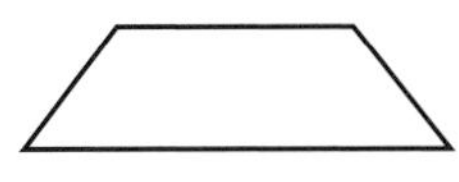

CHAPTER 14

EXAMPLE

Find the area and the perimeter.

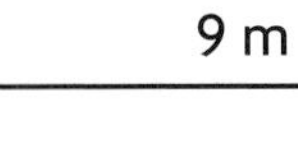

A = length × width

$A = 9 \times 4 = 36$

P = side + side + side + side

$P = 9 + 4 + 9 + 4 = 26$

Area = 36 sq m Perimeter = 26 m

Find the perimeter. (pages 228–229, 236–237)

21. 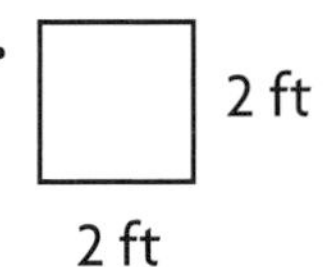

22. 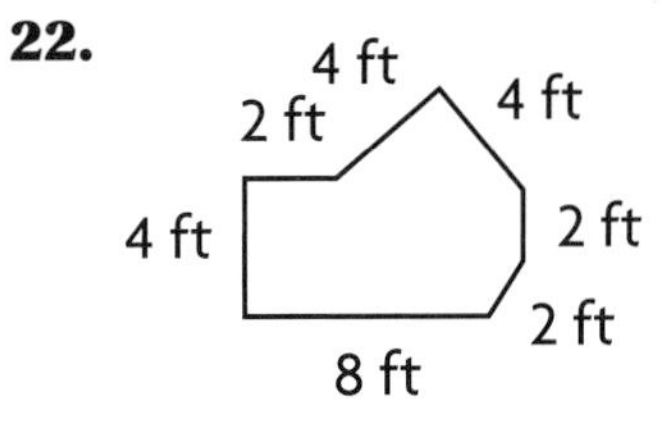

Find the area. (pages 230–237)

23. 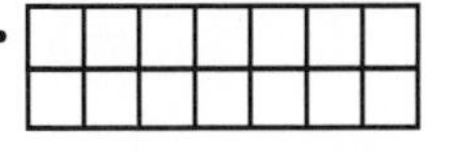

24. 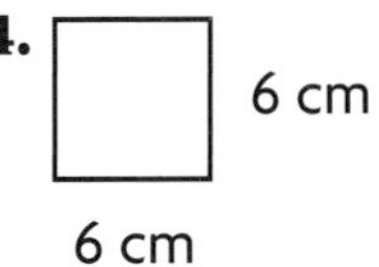

Solve. (pages 238–239)

25. Maria has 24 feet of wire to put around a garden. What is the greatest possible area that she can plant?

CHAPTER 15

EXAMPLE

Are these figures congruent?

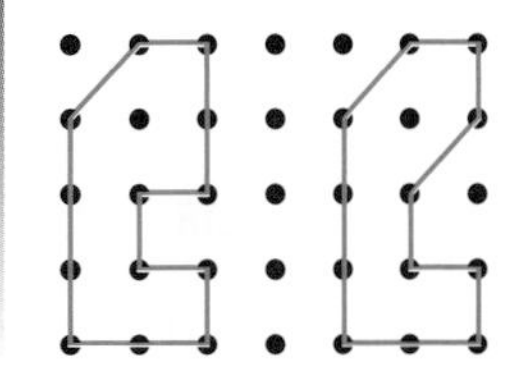

No. They have different shapes.

Is each pair of figures congruent? Write *yes* or *no.* (pages 246–247)

26. 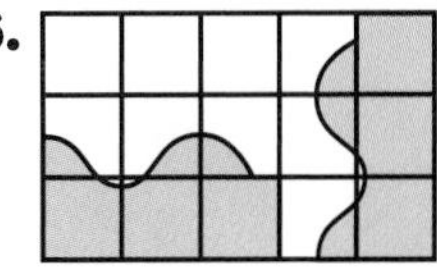

27. 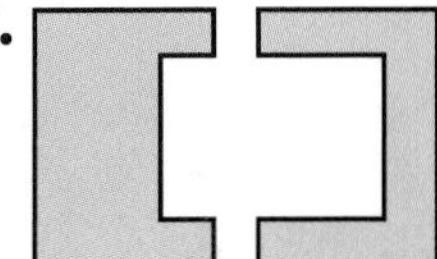

Does each figure have point symmetry, line symmetry, or both? (pages 248–251)

28. 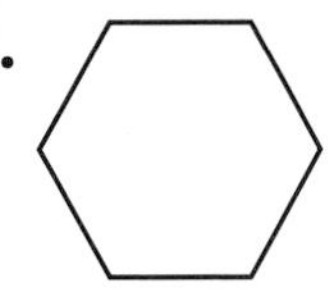

29. 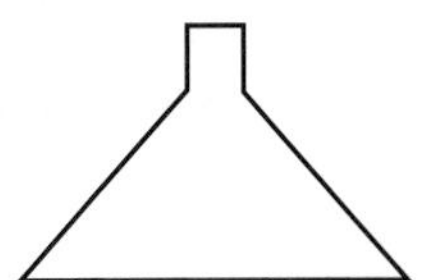

Solve. (pages 256–257)

30. Ahmad wants to draw an airplane 4 inches wide and twice as many inches long. How many square units of drawing paper will he need?

CHAPTERS 12–15

WHAT DID I LEARN?

WRITE ABOUT IT

1. Name two objects in your classroom that remind you of plane figures and two objects that remind you of solid figures. Explain your choices. (pages 192–193)

2. Use a straightedge to draw a quadrilateral and a hexagon. Explain how you know whether or not a figure is a polygon, and how you know you have drawn the named polygons. (pages 218–219)

3. Explain how to find the perimeter of the cover of your math book. Then find the perimeter. (pages 228–229)

4. Cut a triangle from dot paper. On another sheet of dot paper, trace the triangle and show

   a. a rotation.
   b. a reflection.
   c. a translation.

   Label and describe each figure. (pages 244–245)

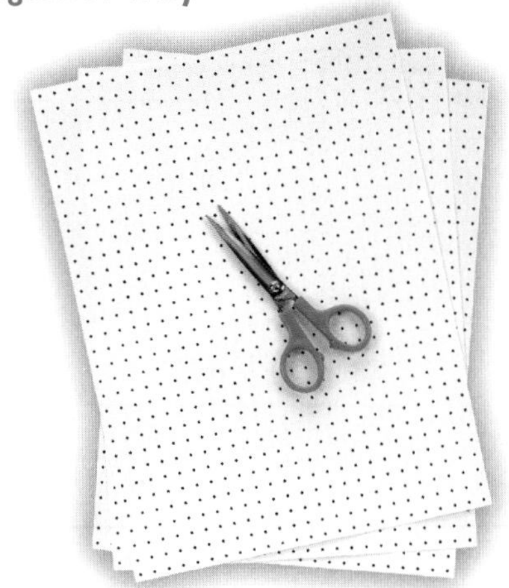

PERFORMANCE ASSESSMENT

Solve. Explain your method.

CHOOSE A STRATEGY

- **Act It Out** • **Make a Model** • **Draw a Diagram** • **Make an Organized List**

5. Joel has a box of cereal, a can of soup, an orange, an onion, a stick of butter, a roll of paper towels, a peach, and a box of crackers. Organize the items Joel bought according to their three-dimensional shapes. Explain why you organized them the way you did. (pages 204–205)

6. Marty has 4 right triangles. How many different quadrilaterals can he make? Name the quadrilaterals. (pages 222–223)

7. A class has 40 feet of rope to mark off a space. What is the greatest possible area the class can rope off? (pages 238–239)

8. Abe made this design. What figure did he start with? What move did he use to complete the design? (pages 256–257)

starting figure

CUMULATIVE REVIEW

Solve the problem. Then write the letter of the correct answer.

1. Matthew's back yard is 180 feet long and 60 feet wide. What is the perimeter?

A. 3 feet **B.** 120 feet
C. 240 feet **D.** 480 feet

(pages 6–7)

Round to the nearest thousand. Estimate the difference.

2. $5{,}009 - 1{,}941$

A. 3,000
B. 3,100
C. 4,000
D. 7,000 (pages 26–27)

3. $5 \times (2 \times 3) = \underline{?}$

A. 10 **B.** 30
C. 40 **D.** 60 (pages 40–41)

4. How many hundreds are in 8,641?

A. 1 hundred **B.** 4 hundreds
C. 6 hundreds **D.** 8 hundreds

(pages 78–79)

5. Mr. Visquel's anniversary is 2 months after May 2. His birthday is 4 days after his anniversary. What day is Mr. Visquel's birthday?

A. Mar 6 **B.** Jul 2
C. Jul 6 **D.** Aug 2 (pages 130–131)

For Problems 6–7, use the stem-and-leaf plot.

Stem	Leaves
3	5 6 7 8
4	1 2 4 5 5
5	0 2 3 4

Mighty Midgets Game Points

6. How many games did the Mighty Midgets play?

A. 3 games **B.** 10 games
C. 13 games **D.** 15 games

(pages 162–163)

7. What is the mode?

A. 35 **B.** 45
C. 50 **D.** 54 (pages 162–163)

8. Name the figure.

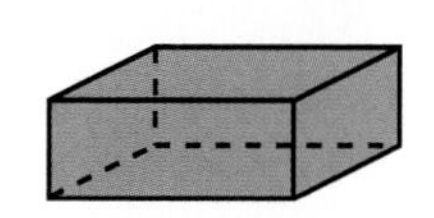

A. rectangular prism
B. rectangular pyramid
C. triangular prism
D. triangular pyramid

(pages 196–197)

9. Name the angle.

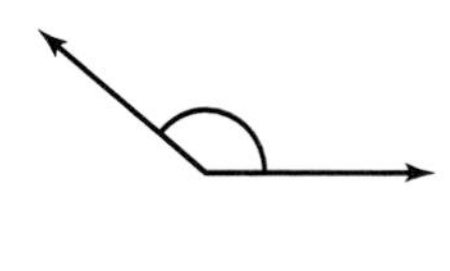

A. acute
B. obtuse
C. right
D. square (pages 212–213)

10. Lee's kitchen measures 8 feet by 9 feet. What is the area of the floor?

A. 63 sq ft **B.** 72 sq ft
C. 80 sq ft **D.** 89 sq ft

(pages 234–235)

MULTIPLYING BY ONE-DIGIT NUMBERS

DID YOU KNOW . . .

Some toys were invented by accident. Silly Putty® was invented when an experimenter was trying to make man-made rubber.

Making Jacob's Ladder Toys

A Jacob's Ladder is a series of wood blocks held together by ribbon. You can hold either end of a Jacob's Ladder, and a wood block will appear to "roll" to the other end.

Mr. Toma's class has decided to make Jacob's Ladder toys for children at the hospital. The students will make 16 of the toys in all. Make a chart that shows the materials that they will need.

Work with a partner to plan the project. Your job is to

- find out how much wood and ribbon to buy for 1 toy, 2 toys, and so on, to 16 toys.
- share your work with another group.

Materials for One Toy

- Two feet of wood molding, cut into
  12 2-inch pieces
- Five feet of narrow ribbon cut into
  6 8-inch pieces
  3 4-inch pieces

Number of Toys	1	2	3	4
Amount of Wood	2ft			
Amount of Ribbon	5ft			

DID YOU

- ✓ find out how much wood to buy for 1 to 16 toys?
- ✓ make a chart showing the materials needed for 1 to 16 toys?
- ✓ share your work with another group?

Multiplying by Multiples

You will learn to multiply by multiples of 10, 100, and 1,000.	**Why learn this?** You can quickly find an amount of money.	**WORD POWER** multiple

Suppose you want to find the total number of pennies in 7 rolls of pennies. You know that each roll has 50 pennies. How can you find the total?

You can multiply 7 and 50 to find the total. Think of 50 as a multiple of 10: 5 × 10, or 5 tens. A **multiple** is the product of a given number and another whole number.

$$\begin{array}{r} 50 \\ \times\ 7 \\ \hline 350 \end{array}$$

Think:
7 × 5 tens = 35 tens
35 tens = 35 × 10, or 350 pennies

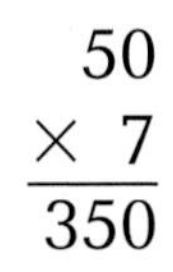

CRITICAL THINKING How does renaming 50 as 5 tens help you find the product?

Consumer Link

The Slinky® was invented to stop vibrating sounds on ships. It didn't work for that purpose, but it became popular as a toy. If 1 Slinky costs $10, how much do 8 of them cost?

You can use mental math to multiply greater numbers when you know the basic facts and the pattern of zeros.

EXAMPLES

A. 7 × 20 = 140
7 × 200 = 1,400
7 × 2,000 = 14,000

B. 5 × 80 = 400
5 × 800 = 4,000
5 × 8,000 = 40,000

You can use a calculator to find a product.

Press:

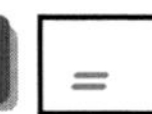

Display: = 140000.

Talk About It

- What basic facts are shown in Examples A and B?
- What pattern of zeros do you see in Example A?
- Why are there more zeros in the products in Example B?

Calculator Activities page H58

PRACTICE

Finish each pattern.

1. 2 × 40 = __?__
__?__ × 400 = 800
2 × __?__ = 8,000

2. __?__ × 30 = 120
4 × __?__ = 1,200
4 × 3,000 = __?__

3. 5 × 50 = __?__
__?__ × 500 = 2,500
5 × __?__ = 25,000

4. 7 × 50 = __?__
7 × __?__ = 3,500
__?__ × 5,000 = 35,000

5. __?__ × 60 = 120
2 × __?__ = 1,200
2 × 6,000 = __?__

6. 7 × 90 = __?__
__?__ × 900 = 6,300
7 × __?__ = 63,000

Use mental math and basic multiplication facts to find the product.

7. 5 × 20 = __?__ **8.** 7 × 300 = __?__ **9.** 6 × 1,000 = __?__

10. 8 × 5,000 = __?__ **11.** 4 × 50 = __?__ **12.** 9 × 400 = __?__

13. 60 × 7 **14.** 900 × 5 **15.** 400 × 4 **16.** 7,000 × 4 **17.** 5,000 × 6

Mixed Applications

18. Cole received a $20 bill from each of 4 family members for his birthday. How much money did he receive?

19. Cameron had $25.00. He spent $13.48 on a present for his mother. How much money does Cameron have left?

20. **Write a problem** about a store clerk who counts the money in her cash drawer. Be sure to use multiplication in your problem.

Cole's birthday gift

Mixed Review

Name the kind of quadrilateral. Explain your choice. (pages 220–221)

21. 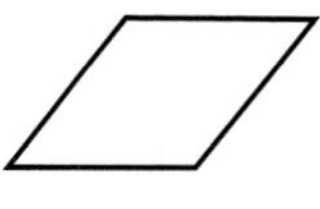
22. **23.** 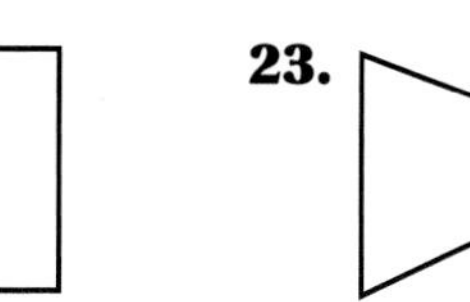
24. 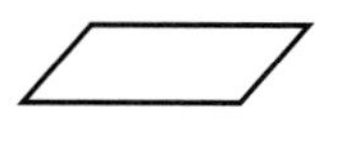
25. 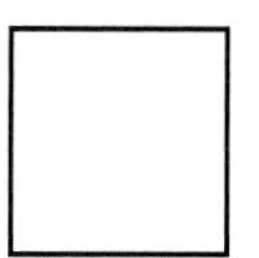

Write each number in two other ways. (pages 90–91)

26. two hundred sixty-five **27.** 5,806 **28.** 4,000 + 900 + 60 + 3

29. six hundred thirteen **30.** 16,420 **31.** 10,000 + 200 + 40 + 1

A Way to Multiply

You will investigate using equal groups of base-ten blocks to find products.

Why learn this? You will discover how to use multiplication to find a total. For example, you can find how much it costs to buy five packages of raisins.

Roger and his friends used 32 tokens per hour playing games at Video Land. How many tokens did they use in 4 hours?

Explore

Work together to make a model of the problem to find the product.

MATERIALS: base-ten blocks

MODEL

Step 1

Model 4 groups of 32.

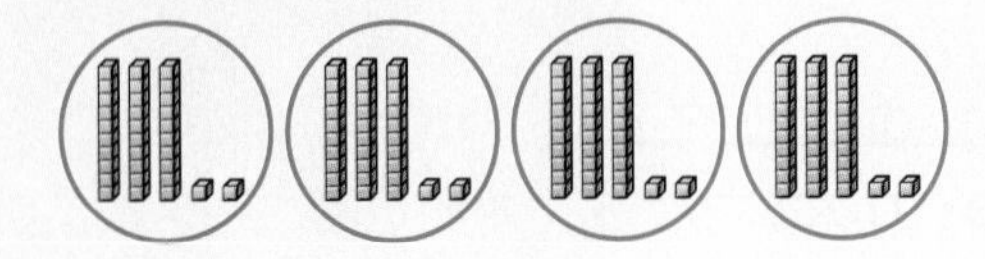

Step 2

Combine the groups.

Record

Explain in writing the method used to find the total number of tokens. Record the product, and answer the question.

Talk About It

- How did you find the total number of tokens?
- Did you have to regroup? Explain.

Try This

Make a model to show 43 tokens used each hour for 5 hours. Explain your method and record the product.

Technology Link

E-Lab • Activity 16 Available on CD-ROM and the Internet at http://www.hbschool.com/elab

Talk About It

- What model did you make to show the information in the problem?
- How did you find the product?

WRITE ABOUT IT How do your models show multiplication?

HANDS-ON PRACTICE

Use base-ten blocks. Find the product.

1. Mr. Wallace bought 7 boxes of paper for his office. Each box had 48 packages. How many packages did he buy?

2. The Ferrells rented 3 cartoons on Friday. Each one lasted 37 minutes. They watched all the cartoons. How many minutes did they watch them?

3. $\begin{array}{r} 26 \\ \times\ 4 \\ \hline \end{array}$

4. $\begin{array}{r} 37 \\ \times\ 5 \\ \hline \end{array}$

5. $\begin{array}{r} 29 \\ \times\ 6 \\ \hline \end{array}$

6. $\begin{array}{r} 53 \\ \times\ 2 \\ \hline \end{array}$

7. $\begin{array}{r} 35 \\ \times\ 8 \\ \hline \end{array}$

8. **WRITE ABOUT IT** Explain how to use base-ten blocks to find the product 2×28.

Mixed Applications

9. Each of the 24 students in Ms. Sherman's class checked out 3 books or videos from the media center. How many items did they check out in all?

10. Lauren and her family drove 124 miles to see a play. After the play, they drove another 55 miles to spend the night with friends. What was the total number of miles they drove?

11. Ray and his sister Mary Anne tape home movies. Ray has 4 times as many as Mary Anne. Mary Anne has 28. How many does Ray have?

12. Flicks Video rents 169 newer movies and 246 older movies every day. How many more older movies than newer movies does Flicks Video rent?

MORE PRACTICE Student Handbook page H96

Modeling Multiplication

You will learn to multiply by one-digit numbers, using two methods.

Why learn this? You can find the total of several groups, such as how many CDs are in three cases.

WORD POWER
partial product

Colleen has 3 cases of CDs. Each case has 24 CDs. How many CDs does she have?

One way to find the product is to use base-ten blocks.

MODEL

What is 3×24?

Step 1

Model 3 groups of 24.

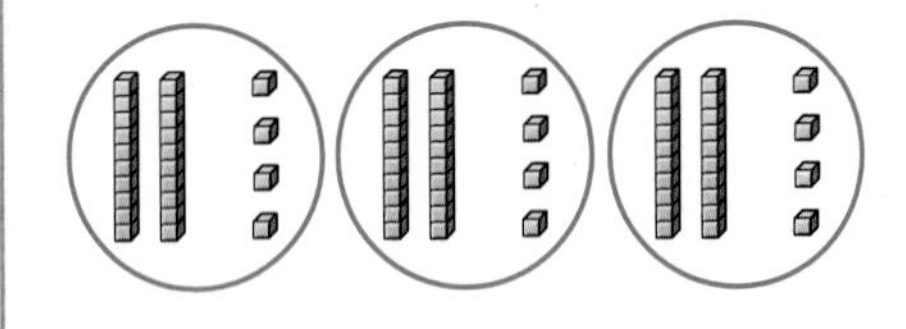

Step 2

Combine the ones.
$3 \times 4 = 12$ ones

Regroup 12 ones as 1 ten 2 ones.

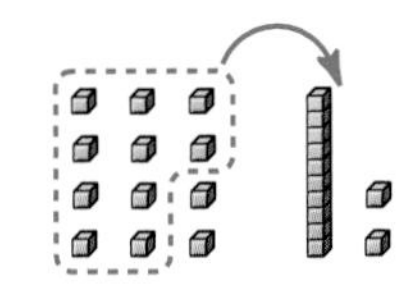

Step 3

Combine the tens.
$3 \times 2 = 6$ tens
6 tens + 1 ten = 7 tens

Record the total.

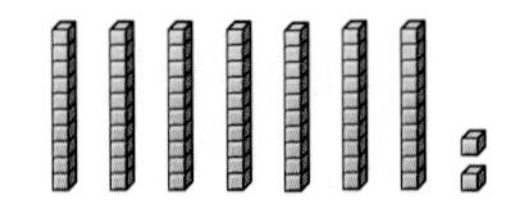

Record: 7 tens 2 ones, or 72

So, Colleen has 72 CDs.

Another way to find the product is to find partial products. To do this, multiply the ones and tens separately. Each product is called a **partial product**.

MODEL

What is 3×24?

Step 1

Think of 24 as 20 + 4.
Multiply the ones.

Record the product.

$$\begin{array}{r} 24 \\ \times\ 3 \\ \hline 12 \end{array}$$

← 3×4 ones, or $3 \times 4 = 12$

Step 2

Multiply the tens.

Record the product.

$$\begin{array}{r} 24 \\ \times\ 3 \\ \hline 12 \\ +60 \\ \hline \end{array}$$

← 3×2 tens, or $3 \times 20 = 60$

Step 3

Add the two partial products.

$$\begin{array}{r} 24 \\ \times\ 3 \\ \hline 12 \\ +60 \\ \hline 72 \end{array}$$

Talk About It

- How did renaming 24 as 20 + 4 help you find the product?
- What were the two partial products?

WRITE ABOUT IT Which method do you like better? Why?

PRACTICE

Use place-value mats and base-ten blocks to find the product.

1. 16×4
2. 41×3
3. 37×2
4. 25×6
5. 63×5

Find each product by using partial products.

6. 47×2
7. 73×9
8. 15×7
9. 65×4
10. 82×5

11. $2 \times 39 =$?
12. $3 \times 28 =$?
13. $7 \times 49 =$?
14. $4 \times 62 =$?

Mixed Applications

15. Casey has 345 trading cards. Mark has 269 more cards than Casey. How many cards does Mark have?

16. Kellin is a stamp collector. She has 4 full albums of stamps. Each album has 24 pages. How many pages of stamps does Kellin have?

17. The 8 girls in Emily's Girl Scout troop each sold 15 boxes of cookies. How many boxes did the troop sell?

18. **Write a problem** about the 16 students in Mr. Nelson's computer class. Be sure the problem uses multiplication.

Mixed Review

Tell whether each number is *cardinal, ordinal,* or *nominal.*
(pages 72–73)

19. fifty-four
20. 43rd
21. 12:00 noon
22. 55 feet

Write the number as you would say it with period names.
(pages 96–97)

23. 234,405
24. 53,001,126
25. 470,891,215

Recording Multiplication

You will learn a faster way to record multiplication by one-digit numbers.

Why learn this? You can figure out how many things are needed to finish a project.

Latasha wants to build two log cabins. She needs 156 craft sticks for each model of a log cabin. What is the total number of sticks Latasha needs?

You can multiply 2×156 to find the number of sticks Latasha needs.

Step 1

Multiply the ones.

2×6 ones = 12 ones

Regroup 12 ones as 1 ten 2 ones.

$$\begin{array}{r} {\scriptstyle 1} \\ 156 \\ \times \quad 2 \\ \hline 2 \end{array}$$

Record 12 ones. Place 2 in the ones place and 1 in the tens place.

Step 2

Multiply the tens.

2×5 tens = 10 tens

10 tens + 1 ten = 11 tens

Regroup 11 tens as 1 hundred 1 ten.

$$\begin{array}{r} {\scriptstyle 1\,1} \\ 156 \\ \times \quad 2 \\ \hline 12 \end{array}$$

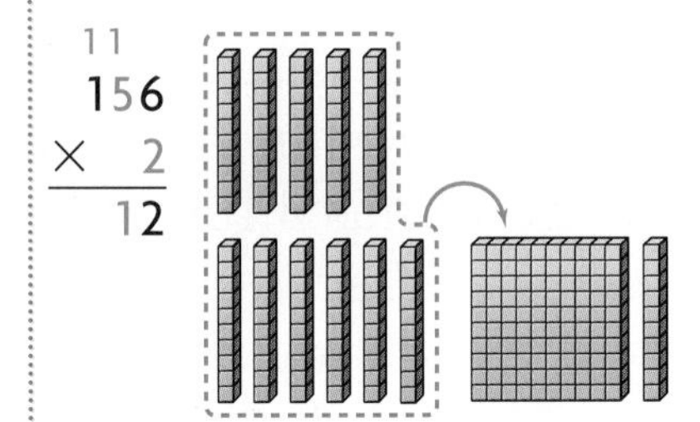

Record 11 tens. Place 1 in the tens place and 1 in the hundreds place.

Step 3

Multiply the hundreds.

2×1 hundred = 2 hundreds

Add the regrouped hundred.

2 hundreds + 1 hundred = 3 hundreds

$$\begin{array}{r} {\scriptstyle 1\,1} \\ 156 \\ \times \quad 2 \\ \hline 312 \end{array}$$

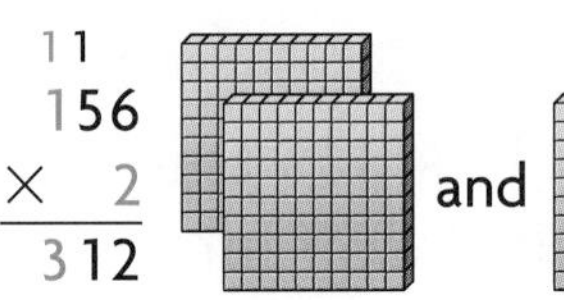

Record 3 in the hundreds place.

So, Latasha needs 312 craft sticks to build her models.

EXAMPLES

A. $\begin{array}{r} {\scriptstyle 1} \\ 104 \\ \times \quad 4 \\ \hline 416 \end{array}$

B. $\begin{array}{r} {\scriptstyle 1\,1} \\ 234 \\ \times \quad 3 \\ \hline 702 \end{array}$

C. $\begin{array}{r} {\scriptstyle 1} \\ 412 \\ \times \quad 5 \\ \hline 2{,}060 \end{array}$

- In Example A, how do you use the regrouped 1?

CRITICAL THINKING Why is it important to record the regrouping over the correct place-value position?

Social Studies Link

The original Conestoga wagons were covered wagons pulled by 6 horses. Many were used to carry heavy loads across the prairies of the United States. How many horses were needed to pull 125 Conestoga wagons?

PRACTICE

Multiply. Tell in which place-value positions you need to regroup.

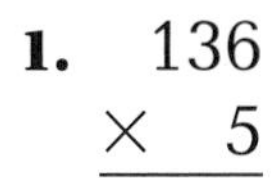

1. 136×5 **2.** 254×2 **3.** 142×6 **4.** 321×3 **5.** 246×4

Find the product.

6. 432×3 **7.** 516×2 **8.** 327×5 **9.** 618×4 **10.** 102×6

11. 875×2 **12.** 729×7 **13.** 214×9 **14.** 973×4 **15.** 806×5

Mixed Applications

16. While studying pioneers, each of the 114 fourth graders made a model of a Conestoga wagon. Each wagon had 4 wheels. How many wheels were needed for the project?

17. Ms. Lash bought 8 boxes of toothpicks for the Conestoga wagon project. Each box had 250 toothpicks. How many toothpicks did she buy?

18. The Oregon Trail was first used in 1805. In 1843, large groups of pioneers began using it. How many years had passed?

19. **Write a problem** about a project you've done that used multiplication.

Mixed Review

Write *one-dimensional, two-dimensional,* or *three-dimensional* to describe each figure. (pages 192–193)

20. 

21. 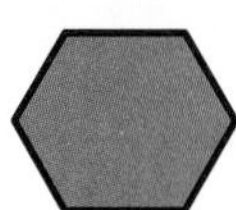

22. 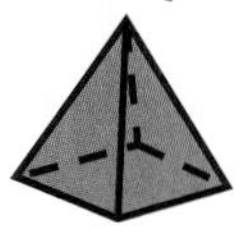

23.

What kind of angle is each? Write *right, acute,* or *obtuse.* (pages 212–213)

24. 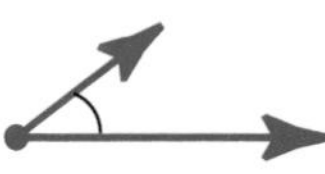

25. 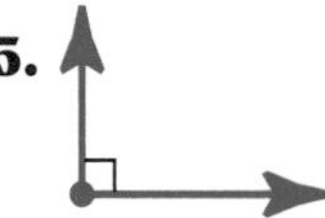

26. 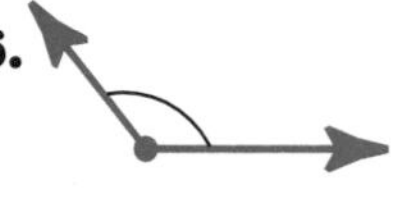

27. 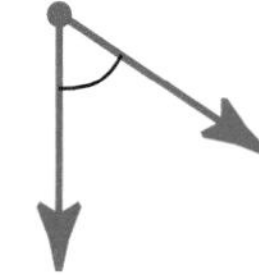

PART 1

Practicing Multiplication

You will learn to use whole numbers to multiply amounts of money.

Why learn this? You can find out if you have enough money to buy something.

Blank computer disks at Computer Warehouse are sold for \$3.95 a box. Ms. Jacques wants to buy 8 boxes of them for her class. How much will she have to pay?

You can multiply amounts of money as if you were multiplying whole numbers. Then you can write the product in dollars and cents.

MODEL

What is 8 × \$3.95?

Step 1

Write the problem, using whole numbers.

$$\begin{array}{r} 395 \\ \times \quad 8 \\ \hline \end{array}$$

Step 2

Multiply to find the product.

$$\begin{array}{r} {}^{7\,4} \\ 395 \\ \times \quad 8 \\ \hline 3160 \end{array}$$

Step 3

Write the product in dollars and cents.

The product is \$31.60.

So, Ms. Jacques needs \$31.60 to buy the computer disks.

EXAMPLES

A. $\begin{array}{r} \$2.74 \\ \times \quad 7 \\ \hline \end{array} \longrightarrow \begin{array}{r} {}^{5\,2} \\ 274 \\ \times \quad 7 \\ \hline 1918 \end{array} \longrightarrow \$19.18$

B. $\begin{array}{r} {}^{1} \\ \$4.03 \\ \times \quad 6 \\ \hline \$24.18 \end{array}$

Talk About It

- How is multiplying money like multiplying whole numbers?
- How is Example B different from Example A?
- How would you write the answer to Example B as a whole number?

Technology Link

In ***Mighty Math Calculating Crew***, the game *Superhero Superstore* challenges you to multiply money amounts.

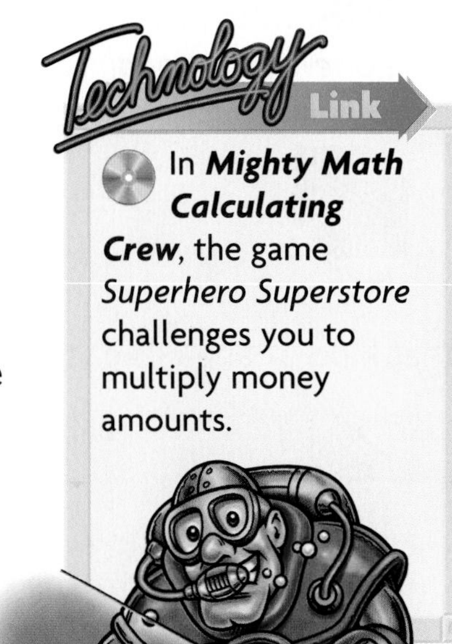

PRACTICE

Multiply, and record each product. Place the dollar sign and decimal point in it.

1. $\$1.82 \times 6$

2. $\$3.04 \times 3$

3. $\$8.41 \times 4$

4. $\$7.64 \times 5$

5. $\$5.23 \times 2$

6. $\$6.70 \times 9$

7. $\$2.05 \times 6$

8. $\$9.36 \times 7$

9. $\$4.07 \times 8$

10. $\$7.65 \times 4$

11. $\$2.08 \times 3$

12. $\$8.95 \times 8$

13. $2 \times \$3.14 = \underline{?}$

14. $5 \times \$4.02 = \underline{?}$

15. $3 \times \$7.56 = \underline{?}$

16. $7 \times \$6.80 = \underline{?}$

17. $4 \times \$8.35 = \underline{?}$

18. $6 \times \$9.42 = \underline{?}$

19. **WRITE ABOUT IT** When you multiply with money, how do you know where to place the dollar sign and decimal point in the product?

Mixed Applications

For Problems 20–22, use the table.

Price List	
Batteries (per set)	$2.79
Film (36 exposures)	$5.49
Audio tapes (per package)	$2.88
Headphones	$4.87

20. Nathan bought 2 rolls of film for his trip. How much did they cost in all? How many pictures can he take with them?

21. Dahlia decided to tape her favorite music. She bought 3 packages of audiotapes and 1 set of batteries. What was the total cost of these things?

22. **Write a problem** using the price list. Exchange with a classmate and solve.

Consumer Link

When trying to find the best value, consider the number of items in each package. Suppose a package of 4 batteries costs $2.79 and a package of 2 batteries costs $1.45. Would it be cheaper to buy 1 package of 4 batteries or 2 packages of 2 batteries?

PART 2 PROBLEM-SOLVING STRATEGY Write a Number Sentence

THE PROBLEM Ray likes to use his computer to find information on the Internet. Each hour on-line costs him $2.45. If he searches for 5 hours, what is the cost?

REMEMBER:
- ✓ Understand
- ✓ Plan
- ✓ Solve
- ✓ Look Back

✓ Understand

- What are you asked to find?
- What information will you use?
- Is there any information you will not use? If so, what?

✓ Plan

- What strategy can you use to find the answer?

You can *write a number sentence* to find the total cost of the on-line time. A number sentence can show how the facts in the problem are related.

Consumer Link

Computers use telephone lines to hook up to the Internet. Some customers are charged by the hour for their on-line time. One company charges $19.95 for Internet use each month. How much is this for 6 months?

✓ Solve

- How can you use the strategy to find the answer?

You can write a number sentence that uses n to stand for the product.

number of hours		**cost per hour**		**total cost of on-line time**
↓		↓		↓
5	×	$2.45	=	n

$$\begin{array}{r} \$2.45 \\ \times \quad 5 \\ \hline \$12.25 \end{array}$$

$$n = \$12.25$$

So, Ray needs $12.25 to pay for the cost of his time on the Internet.

✓ Look Back

- How can you decide if your answer is reasonable?
- What other strategy could you use?

PRACTICE

CHOOSE Paper/Pencil Calculator Hands-on Mental Math

Write a number sentence to solve.

1. Mary bought 3 books that cost \$9.75 each. How much did she spend?

2. Larry wants to buy 4 computer programs for \$36.25 each. How much money will he need?

3. Mr. Heath allows his computer class 25 minutes a day to try new computer programs. How many minutes is this in 5 days?

4. Jay's computer hard drive has 1,000 megabytes of memory. Ellen's has 810 megabytes. How much more memory does Jay's hard drive have than Ellen's?

Mixed Applications

Solve.

CHOOSE A STRATEGY

- Work Backward
- Write a Number Sentence
- Make an Organized List

5. Donna can buy either a color or a black-and-white printer. The printer can be ink-jet, dot matrix, or laser. List the different combinations Donna can buy.

6. There are 6 fourth-grade classrooms in Cowan Elementary School. Each room has 26 students. How many fourth graders attend the school?

7. Alana left her house at the time shown on the clock. She arrived at Ashlyn's house 15 minutes later. The girls spent 30 minutes eating lunch together. They took a 15-minute walk to the library after lunch. What time did the library clock show when the girls arrived?

8. Carey paid \$78.69 for a computer book, software, and speakers. Use the prices shown to find the cost of the speakers.

COMPUTERS MADE EASY by George Genius
\$18.99

\$28.95

9. A computer lab has 8 rows of computers. Each row has 4 computers. There are also 4 computers grouped in the center of the room. How many computers are in the lab?

10. Brittany mows lawns to earn money. She earns \$10.25 for every lawn she mows. So far, Brittany has mowed 7 lawns. How much money has she earned?

MORE PRACTICE Student Handbook page H97

CULTURAL CONNECTION

COOPERATIVE LEARNING

A Multiplication Machine

John Napier was a Scottish mathematician who lived from 1550 to 1617. One of his inventions, known as *Napier's Rods* or *Napier's Bones*, can be used to solve multiplication problems.

0	1	2	3	4	5	6	7	8	9
0/0	0/1	0/2	0/3	0/4	0/5	0/6	0/7	0/8	0/9
0/0	0/2	0/4	0/6	0/8	1/0	1/2	1/4	1/6	1/8
0/0	0/3	0/6	0/9	1/2	1/5	1/8	2/1	2/4	2/7
0/0	0/4	0/8	1/2	1/6	2/0	2/4	2/8	3/2	3/6
0/0	0/5	1/0	1/5	2/0	2/5	3/0	3/5	4/0	4/5
0/0	0/6	1/2	1/8	2/4	3/0	3/6	4/2	4/8	5/4
0/0	0/7	1/4	2/1	2/8	3/5	4/2	4/9	5/6	6/3
0/0	0/8	1/6	2/4	3/2	4/0	4/8	5/6	6/4	7/2
0/0	0/9	1/8	2/7	3/6	4/5	5/4	6/3	7/2	8/1

To solve 6 × 43 by using Napier's Rods, place the rods for 4 and 3 side by side. Look in the sixth row. Each diagonal represents a digit in the product. As you read from right to left, the ones digit of the product is 8. The tens digit is the sum of 4 and 1, or 5. The hundreds digit of the product is 2.

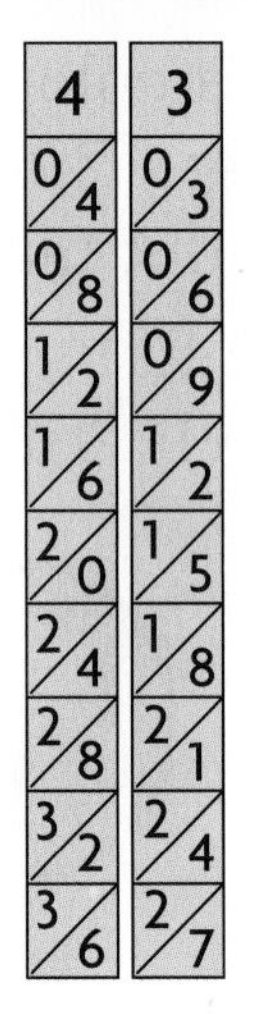

4	3
0/4	0/3
0/8	0/6
1/2	0/9
1/6	1/2
2/0	1/5
2/4	1/8
2/8	2/1
3/2	2/4
3/6	2/7

What is the purpose of the diagonal line in each square?

Work Together

1. Use 1-inch grid paper, a ruler, and a pencil to make a set of Napier's Rods as shown above. Cut out the set of Napier's Rods and put your initials on the back of each strip.
2. Use Napier's Rods to find the product 8 × 27. What happens in the tens place when the sum is greater than 9? Check the answer, using another multiplication method.
3. Multiply 7 × $3.45, using Napier's Rods. Check your answer by using another method.
4. **Write a word problem** involving multiplication. Use Napier's Rods to solve.

John Napier was born at Merchiston Castle, near Edinburgh, Scotland. Edinburgh is the capital of Scotland. Scotland is known for its ancient castles, highland scenery, and tartan plaids.

CHAPTER 16 REVIEW

✓ CHECK UNDERSTANDING

VOCABULARY

1. A _?_ is the product of a given number and another whole number. (page 266)

2. When the ones and tens are multiplied separately, each product is called a _?_. (page 270)

Use mental math and basic multiplication facts to find the product. (pages 266–267)

3. $6 \times 60 =$ _?_ **4.** $7 \times 900 =$ _?_ **5.** $3 \times 800 =$ _?_ **6.** $4 \times 5{,}000 =$ _?_

Find each product by using partial products. (pages 270–271)

7. $\begin{array}{r} 56 \\ \times\ 6 \\ \hline \end{array}$ **8.** $\begin{array}{r} 34 \\ \times\ 5 \\ \hline \end{array}$ **9.** $\begin{array}{r} 127 \\ \times\ 4 \\ \hline \end{array}$ **10.** $\begin{array}{r} 172 \\ \times\ 3 \\ \hline \end{array}$

✓ CHECK SKILLS

Find the product. (pages 272–275)

11. $\begin{array}{r} 16 \\ \times\ 5 \\ \hline \end{array}$ **12.** $\begin{array}{r} 73 \\ \times\ 2 \\ \hline \end{array}$ **13.** $\begin{array}{r} 42 \\ \times\ 7 \\ \hline \end{array}$ **14.** $\begin{array}{r} 66 \\ \times\ 6 \\ \hline \end{array}$

15. $\begin{array}{r} 45 \\ \times\ 3 \\ \hline \end{array}$ **16.** $\begin{array}{r} 128 \\ \times\ 9 \\ \hline \end{array}$ **17.** $\begin{array}{r} 143 \\ \times\ 8 \\ \hline \end{array}$ **18.** $\begin{array}{r} 427 \\ \times\ 3 \\ \hline \end{array}$

19. $312 \times 4 =$ _?_ **20.** $\$3.81 \times 5 =$ _?_ **21.** $\$2.92 \times 7 =$ _?_

✓ CHECK PROBLEM SOLVING

Solve. (pages 276–277)

CHOOSE A STRATEGY

- Act It Out
- Make a Model
- Guess and Check
- Write a Number Sentence

22. Fran's class collected 123 pounds of plastic, 356 pounds of newspaper, and 148 pounds of aluminum for recycling. How many pounds were collected?

23. The average American throws away 60 pounds of aluminum each month. How much aluminum is thrown away every 6 months?

CHAPTER 17 MULTIPLYING BY TWO-DIGIT NUMBERS

DID YOU KNOW...

The Tour de France is a famous bicycle race. It takes 28 days to complete, and travels through all areas of France.

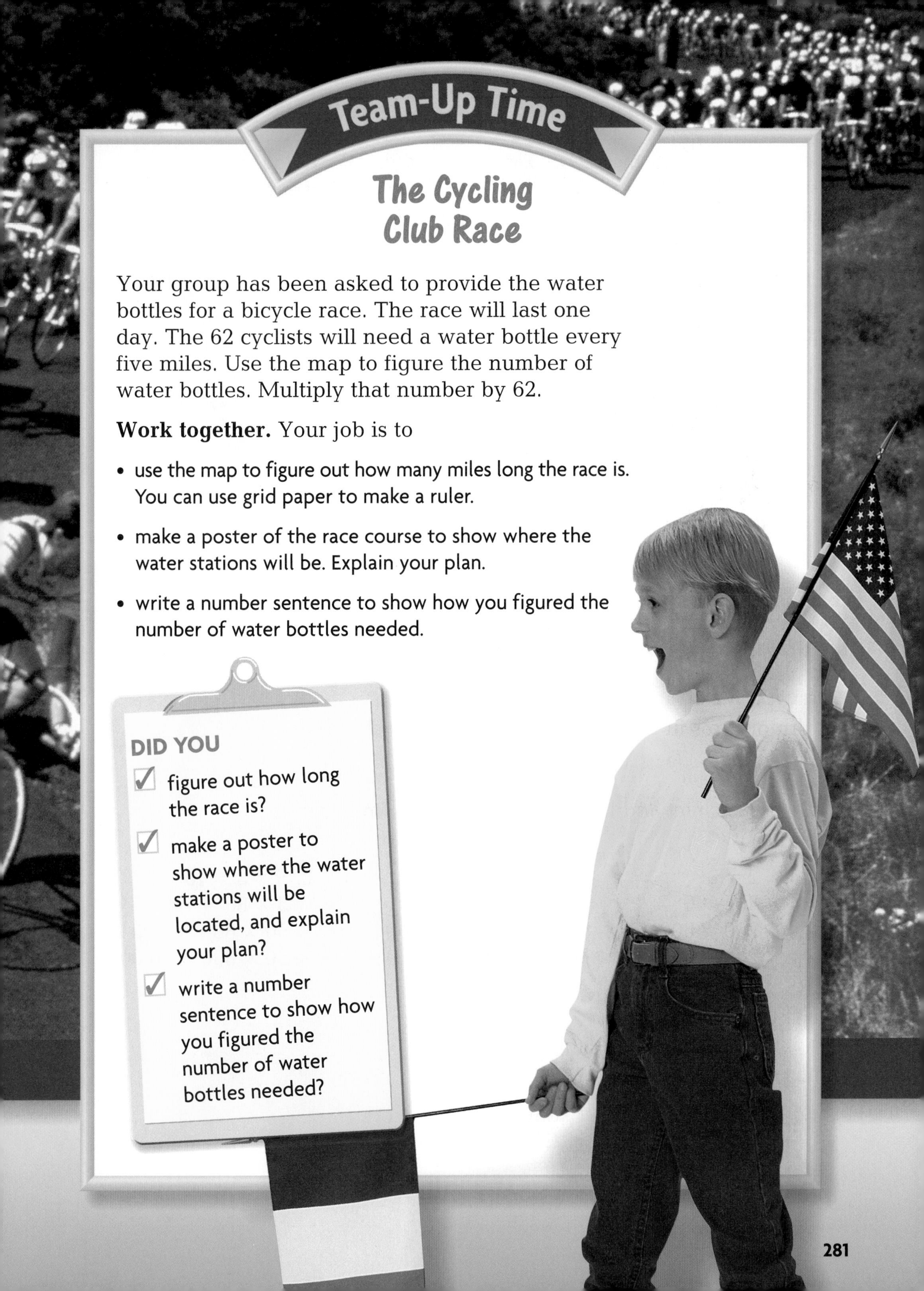

Team-Up Time

The Cycling Club Race

Your group has been asked to provide the water bottles for a bicycle race. The race will last one day. The 62 cyclists will need a water bottle every five miles. Use the map to figure the number of water bottles. Multiply that number by 62.

Work together. Your job is to

- use the map to figure out how many miles long the race is. You can use grid paper to make a ruler.
- make a poster of the race course to show where the water stations will be. Explain your plan.
- write a number sentence to show how you figured the number of water bottles needed.

DID YOU

- ✓ figure out how long the race is?
- ✓ make a poster to show where the water stations will be located, and explain your plan?
- ✓ write a number sentence to show how you figured the number of water bottles needed?

PART

1 Patterns with Multiples

You will learn to use mental math and basic facts to find the product of two-digit numbers.	**Why learn this?** You can find the number of things needed to build a design.

Each student has a grid with 20 spaces across and 20 spaces down. How many tiles does each student need to fill the grid with a design?

Multiply 20×20 to find the number of tiles in all.

Factors		Product	
2×2	=	4	**Think:** Use the basic fact 2×2.
20×2	=	40	Look for the pattern of zeros.
20×20	=	400	
one zero + one zero	=	two zeros	

So, each student needs 400 tiles to fill the grid with a design.

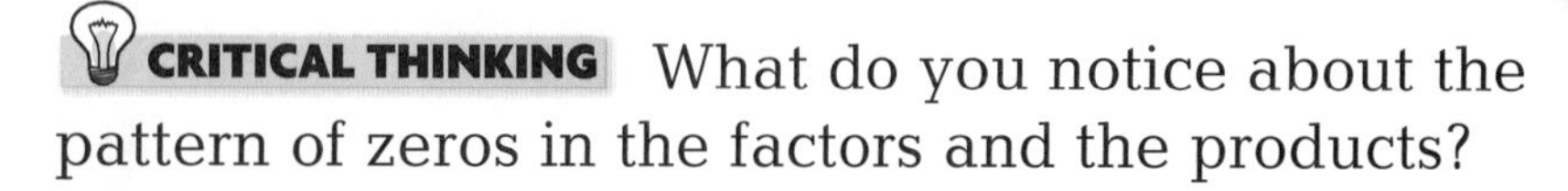

CRITICAL THINKING What do you notice about the pattern of zeros in the factors and the products?

EXAMPLES

Use a basic fact and the pattern of zeros to find the product.

A. $4 \times 2 = 8$
$4 \times 20 = 80$
$4 \times 200 = 800$
$4 \times 2{,}000 = 8{,}000$

B. $6 \times 4 = 24$
$6 \times 40 = 240$
$60 \times 40 = 2{,}400$
$60 \times 400 = 24{,}000$

C. $5 \times 8 = 40$
$5 \times 80 = 400$
$50 \times 80 = 4{,}000$
$50 \times 800 = 40{,}000$

Talk About It

- How can you use mental math to find the product?
- Why do the products in Example C have more zeros than the products in Example B?

PRACTICE

Copy and complete. Use a basic fact and the pattern of zeros to help you.

1. $3 \times 20 = n$
$3 \times 200 = n$
$3 \times 2{,}000 = n$

2. $7 \times 40 = n$
$70 \times 40 = n$
$70 \times 400 = n$

3. $9 \times 80 = n$
$90 \times 80 = n$
$900 \times 80 = n$

4. $5 \times 60 = n$
$50 \times 60 = n$
$50 \times 600 = n$

CULTURAL LINK

The first bicycle with pedals, the *velocipede,* was invented by a French mechanic in 1863. The velocipede was popular in England and France before it came to North America.

Use mental math and basic facts to find the product.

5. $6 \times 60 = n$ **6.** $2 \times 30 = n$ **7.** $50 \times 80 = n$

8. $4 \times 600 = n$ **9.** $40 \times 700 = n$ **10.** $10 \times 800 = n$

11. $60 \times 500 = n$ **12.** $40 \times 900 = n$ **13.** $70 \times 30 = n$

Find the product.

14. 40×6 **15.** 30×80 **16.** 700×3 **17.** 300×40 **18.** 200×50

19. 900×70 **20.** 700×20 **21.** $6{,}000 \times 50$ **22.** $90{,}000 \times 30$ **23.** $50{,}000 \times 80$

Mixed Applications

For Problems 24–26, use the graph.

24. How many bottles in all were collected from January to June?

25. How many more bottles were collected in March than in January and February together?

26. In February, the Pine Elementary students collected 10 times as many bottles as the Lake students collected. How many bottles did the Pine Elementary students collect?

27. **Write a problem** that can be solved by using a basic fact and the pattern of zeros.

MORE PRACTICE Student Handbook pages H97–H98

PART 2 PROBLEM-SOLVING STRATEGY

Find a Pattern

THE PROBLEM **The design on the wall of Mama's Pizza House needed 600 tiles to make. There are 20 students each making the same design. How many tiles will the students need in all?**

✓ Understand

- What are you asked to find?
- What information will you use?
- Is there any information that you will not use? If so, what?

✓ Plan

- What strategy can you use to solve the problem?

  You can *find a pattern* to decide how many tiles the students will need in all.

✓ Solve

- How can you use the strategy to solve the problem?

  You can use mental math and a pattern of zeros to find 20×600.

  Multiply. $20 \times 600 = n$ **Think:** $2 \times 6 = 12$ ← basic fact

$$20 \times 6 = 120$$
$$20 \times 60 = 1{,}200$$
$$20 \times 600 = 12{,}000$$

1 zero + 2 zeros = 3 zeros

So, the students will need 12,000 tiles in all.

✓ Look Back

- How can you decide if your answer is reasonable?
- What other strategy could you use?

CHOOSE Paper/Pencil Calculator Hands-on Mental Math

PRACTICE

Find a pattern to solve.

1. A recycling center collects about 900 cans a day. At this rate, about how many cans will it collect in 10 days?

2. Recycled paper is made into bags to be used at a grocery store. The bags come in packages of 80. How many bags are in 40 packages?

3. Eddie has a puzzle for his classmates. When he says 12, the answer is 24. When he says 15, the answer is 27. When he says 20, the answer is 32. What is the pattern?

4. The design around the room forms a pattern. Describe the figure that would be next in the pattern.

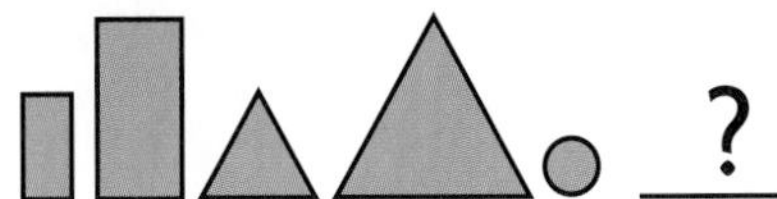

Mixed Applications

Solve.

CHOOSE A STRATEGY

- Act It Out
- Use a Table
- Work Backward
- Find a Pattern
- Write a Number Sentence

5. Each person in the United States throws away about 4 pounds of trash every day. About how many pounds of trash does a family of 4 throw away in 7 days?

6. On clean-up day, 36 people arrived at the school. The group was divided into 4 equal teams. How many people were on each team?

7. Jake and his family took a 30-minute drive to the park. They walked in the park for $1\frac{1}{2}$ hours and spent 30 minutes having lunch. They drove home the same way they came. They arrived home at 1:30 P.M. At what time did they leave home?

8. Robin washes 4 loads of laundry and uses the dryer for 2 hours. What is the energy cost of doing her laundry?

ENERGY COST OF APPLIANCES	
Appliance	**Cost for Use**
Electric dryer	$0.19 for 30 minutes
Electric washer	$0.11 per load

9. Mr. Yarko wanted to save money and fuel. He rode his bicycle to and from his job for 20 days. He lives 3 miles from his job. How many miles did he ride?

10. Frisky chewed 10 shoes one week, 8 shoes the next week and 6 shoes the third week. If this pattern continues, when will Frisky stop chewing shoes?

MORE PRACTICE Student Handbook page H98

Estimating Products with Multiples

You will learn to estimate products by rounding one or more factors.

Why learn this? It will help you make reasonable estimates of amounts.

Karen sold 43 gallons of lemonade during the summer. She used 12 lemons to make each gallon. About how many lemons did she use in all?

MODEL

Use estimation to find the product 12×43.

Step 1

Estimate.
Round each factor to the nearest ten.

$$\begin{array}{r} 43 \\ \times 12 \\ \hline \end{array} \rightarrow \begin{array}{r} 40 \\ \times 10 \\ \hline \end{array}$$

Step 2

Multiply.

$$\begin{array}{r} 40 \\ \times\ 10 \\ \hline 400 \end{array}$$

So, Karen used about 400 lemons in all.

REMEMBER:

To round a number:

- Find the digit in the place to be rounded.
- Look at the digit to its right.
- If that digit is *less than* 5, the digit being rounded remains the same.
- If the digit is *5 or more*, the digit being rounded is made greater by 1.

CRITICAL THINKING Explain how basic facts and patterns of zeros can help you find the product when you multiply by multiples of ten.

EXAMPLES

A.
$$\begin{array}{r} 73 \\ \times 42 \\ \hline \end{array} \rightarrow \begin{array}{r} 70 \\ \times\ 40 \\ \hline 2{,}800 \end{array}$$

B.
$$\begin{array}{r} \$254 \\ \times\ 65 \\ \hline \end{array} \rightarrow \begin{array}{r} 300 \\ \times\ 70 \\ \hline 21{,}000 \end{array} \rightarrow \$21{,}000$$

Talk About It

- Why are there more zeros in the product in Example B than in the product in Example A?
- How do rounding and multiplication help you estimate products?

Science Link

Lemon trees are covered with fruit all through the year. Workers can pick the fruit up to 10 times a year. About how many times will the lemons be picked in 25 years?

PRACTICE

Round each factor to the nearest ten. Estimate the product.

1. $\begin{array}{r} 18 \\ \times 29 \\ \hline \end{array}$ **2.** $\begin{array}{r} 12 \\ \times 45 \\ \hline \end{array}$ **3.** $\begin{array}{r} 37 \\ \times 22 \\ \hline \end{array}$ **4.** $\begin{array}{r} 56 \\ \times 43 \\ \hline \end{array}$ **5.** $\begin{array}{r} 78 \\ \times 36 \\ \hline \end{array}$ **6.** $\begin{array}{r} 64 \\ \times 67 \\ \hline \end{array}$

Round each factor. Estimate the product.

7. $\begin{array}{r} \$19 \\ \times \ 12 \\ \hline \end{array}$ **8.** $\begin{array}{r} 38 \\ \times 27 \\ \hline \end{array}$ **9.** $\begin{array}{r} \$548 \\ \times \quad 45 \\ \hline \end{array}$ **10.** $\begin{array}{r} 634 \\ \times \ 55 \\ \hline \end{array}$

11. $13 \times 85 = n$ **12.** $32 \times 61 = n$ **13.** $49 \times 24 = n$ **14.** $23 \times 219 = n$

15. $76 \times 852 = n$ **16.** $84 \times 497 = n$ **17.** $72 \times 419 = n$ **18.** $53 \times 794 = n$

Mixed Applications

19. Each person in the United States uses about 46 pounds of paper every month. Estimate the amount of paper used by each person in 1 year.

20. There are 60 packages of drawing paper in the art room. Each package has 200 sheets of paper. How many sheets of paper are there in all?

21. A store is having a sale on paper. If 1 package of 500 sheets is on sale for $4, how much would 2,000 sheets of paper cost?

22. **WRITE ABOUT IT** Explain how you used rounding to estimate the answer to Problem 19.

Mixed Review

Find the area. (pages 234–235)

23. 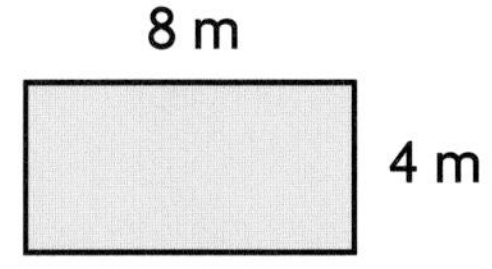

24. 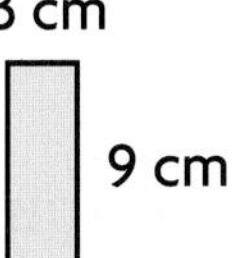

25. 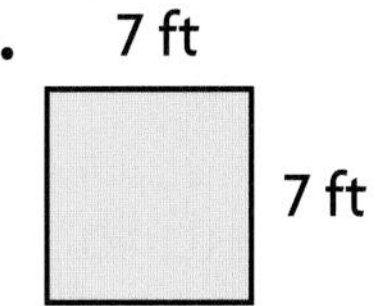

26. 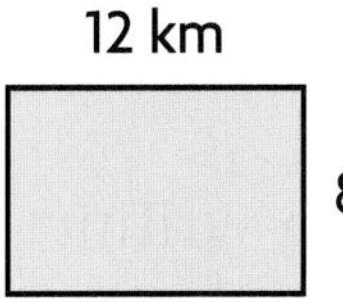

Write each number in standard form. (pages 96–97)

27. fourteen million, six hundred thirty thousand, seven hundred twenty-one

28. thirty-two million, eight hundred forty-one thousand, six hundred fifteen

29. twenty-nine million, seventy-five thousand, nine hundred ninety-nine

30. sixty million, four hundred fifty-five thousand, one hundred twenty-nine

Modeling Multiplication

You will investigate how to multiply two-digit numbers by making a model.

Why learn this? You can multiply a two-digit number by breaking it into smaller numbers.

Explore

Make a model that shows how to multiply 18 × 24. Find the product.

MATERIALS: grid paper

MODEL

What is 18 × 24?

Step 1

Outline a rectangle that is 18 units long and 24 units wide.

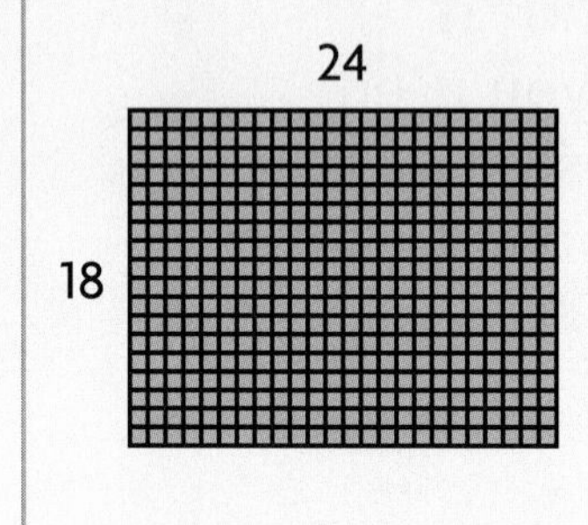

Step 2

Break apart the model to make rectangles whose factors are easy to multiply.

$$\begin{array}{r} 24 = 20 + 4 \\ \times 18 = 10 + 8 \\ \hline \end{array}$$

20 4
10 10
8 8
20 4

Step 3

Multiply. Add the partial products to find how many squares are in the model.

$8 \times 4 = n$

$8 \times 20 = n$

$10 \times 4 = n$

$10 \times 20 = n$

Record

Explain in writing how you found the number of squares in all. Write a number sentence for the multiplication.

Talk About It

- How can place value help you decide where to break apart the rectangle?
- How does breaking apart the model help you find the partial products?
- How does this method help you find the total number of squares?

E-Lab • Activity 17 Available on CD-ROM and the Internet at http://www.hbschool.com/elab

Try This

Make a model of the problem. Record the product.

$$\begin{array}{r} 45 \\ \times 37 \\ \hline \end{array}$$

TALK ABOUT IT How did you break apart the model?

WRITE ABOUT IT How does the model you made show multiplication?

Applying What You Learned

Use the model to find the product.

1.

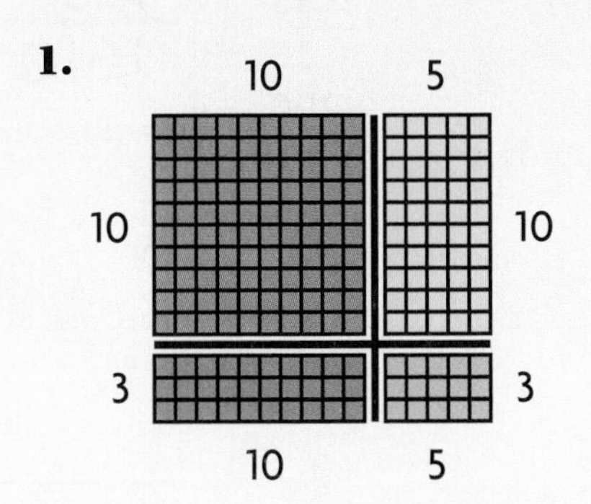

2.

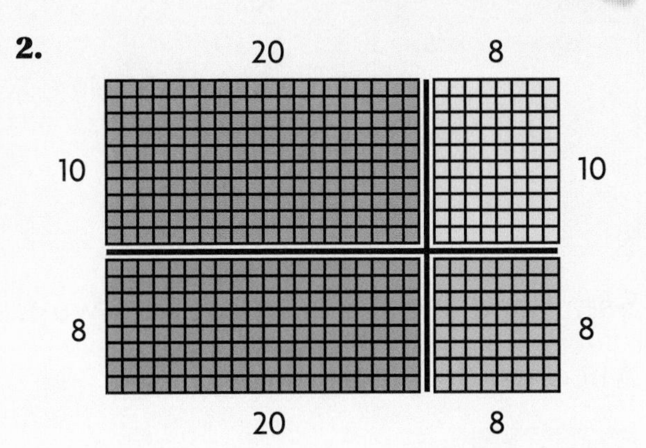

Make a model to find the product.

3. $\begin{array}{r} 16 \\ \times 15 \\ \hline \end{array}$ **4.** $\begin{array}{r} 19 \\ \times 12 \\ \hline \end{array}$ **5.** $\begin{array}{r} 22 \\ \times 18 \\ \hline \end{array}$ **6.** $\begin{array}{r} 21 \\ \times 14 \\ \hline \end{array}$ **7.** $\begin{array}{r} 26 \\ \times 21 \\ \hline \end{array}$

Mixed Applications

For Problems 8–10, use the table at the right.

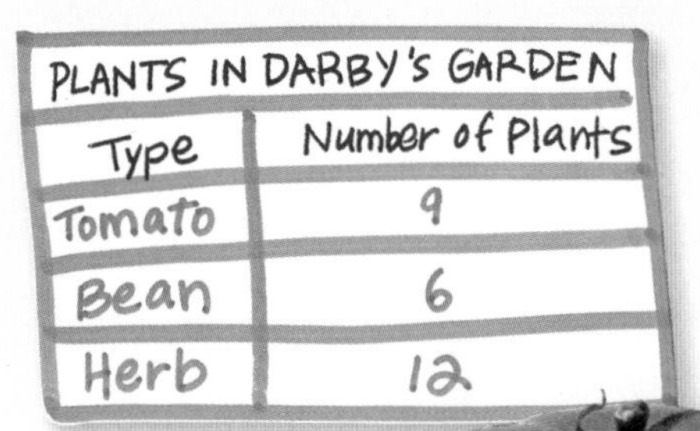

PLANTS IN DARBY'S GARDEN

Type	Number of Plants
Tomato	9
Bean	6
Herb	12

8. Darryll's garden has 15 times as many rows of bean plants as Darby's garden. Both gardens have 3 plants in each row. How many bean plants are in Darryll's garden?

9. Darby picked 3 tomatoes from each of her tomato plants. How many tomatoes did she pick in all?

10. Mr. McGregor has 9 times as many herb plants as Darby. How many herb plants does Mr. McGregor have?

Recording Multiplication

You will learn to multiply by two-digit numbers.	**Why learn this?** You can find the product by using a shorter way.

Look at the way Sam found $35 \times 46 = n$.

Sam

$$\begin{array}{r} 46 \\ \times 35 \\ \hline 30 \\ 200 \\ 180 \\ 1,200 \\ \hline 1,610 \end{array}$$

MODEL

What is 35×46?

Step 1

$$\begin{array}{r} 46 \\ \times 35 \\ \hline 30 \end{array} \leftarrow 5 \times 6 = 30$$

Step 2

$$\begin{array}{r} 46 \\ \times 35 \\ \hline 30 \\ 200 \end{array} \leftarrow 5 \times 40 = 200$$

Step 3

$$\begin{array}{r} 46 \\ \times 35 \\ \hline 30 \\ 200 \\ 180 \end{array} \leftarrow 30 \times 6 = 180$$

Step 4

$$\begin{array}{r} 46 \\ \times 35 \\ \hline 30 \\ 200 \\ 180 \\ +1,200 \\ \hline 1,610 \end{array} \leftarrow 30 \times 40 = 1,200$$

Sam used the partial-products way.

Alice used a shorter way.

Alice

$$\begin{array}{r} 46 \\ \times 35 \\ \hline 230 \\ 1,380 \\ \hline 1,610 \end{array}$$

MODEL

What is 35×46?

Step 1

Think of 35 as 3 tens and 5 ones. Multiply the 5 ones.

$$\begin{array}{r} {}^{3} \\ 46 \\ \times 35 \\ \hline 230 \end{array} \leftarrow 5 \times 46 = 230$$

Think:

Step 2

Multiply by 3 tens, or 30.

$$\begin{array}{r} {}^{1} \\ 46 \\ \times 35 \\ \hline 230 \\ +1,380 \end{array} \leftarrow 30 \times 46 = 1,380$$

Think:

Step 3

Add the products.

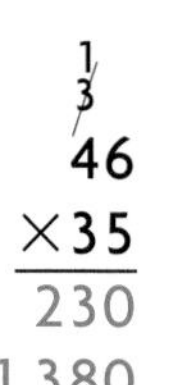

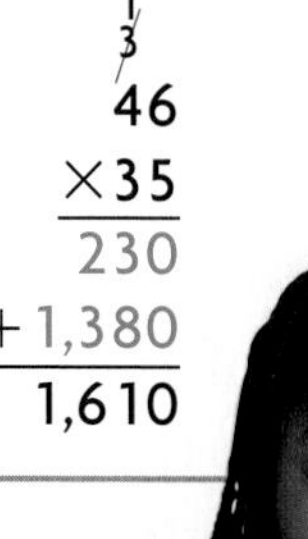

$$\begin{array}{r} {}^{1} \\ 46 \\ \times 35 \\ \hline 230 \\ +1,380 \\ \hline 1,610 \end{array}$$

Talk About It

- Why is the order in which you multiply the digits important?
- How is Sam's method like the break-apart method on page 288?
- Why is Alice's way shorter?

PRACTICE

Find the product.

1. $\begin{array}{r} 55 \\ \times 46 \\ \hline \end{array}$
2. $\begin{array}{r} 78 \\ \times 25 \\ \hline \end{array}$
3. $\begin{array}{r} \$74 \\ \times\ 53 \\ \hline \end{array}$
4. $\begin{array}{r} 92 \\ \times 31 \\ \hline \end{array}$
5. $\begin{array}{r} 63 \\ \times 48 \\ \hline \end{array}$
6. $\begin{array}{r} 29 \\ \times 18 \\ \hline \end{array}$
7. $\begin{array}{r} 65 \\ \times 34 \\ \hline \end{array}$
8. $\begin{array}{r} \$57 \\ \times\ 68 \\ \hline \end{array}$
9. $\begin{array}{r} 86 \\ \times 54 \\ \hline \end{array}$
10. $\begin{array}{r} 69 \\ \times 42 \\ \hline \end{array}$
11. $\begin{array}{r} \$61 \\ \times\ 39 \\ \hline \end{array}$
12. $\begin{array}{r} 98 \\ \times 72 \\ \hline \end{array}$

13. $14 \times 84 = n$
14. $39 \times 56 = n$
15. $25 \times 62 = n$
16. $34 \times 16 = n$
17. $91 \times 24 = n$
18. $83 \times 45 = n$

Mixed Applications

For Problems 19–20, use the table at the right.

PAPER FOR RECYCLING

Class	Pounds Collected
Ms. Bell	34
Miss Katz	42
Mr. Linden	36
Mrs. Hart	45

19. For one week the fourth-grade classes at Bay View School collected paper for recycling. How many pounds in all did the classes collect that week?

20. Each class collected the same amount of paper for 8 weeks. How many pounds of paper did all the classes collect?

21. **WRITE ABOUT IT** When you multiply a two-digit number by a two-digit number, what is the greatest number of digits you can have in the product? Explain.

Mixed Review

Write the elapsed time. (pages 124–125)

22. **start:** 11:00 A.M. **end:** 12:30 P.M.
23. **start:** 3:15 P.M. **end:** 6:30 P.M.
24. **start:** 10:45 P.M. **end:** 3:45 A.M.

Find the perimeter. (pages 228–229)

25. 5 ft, 3 ft

26. 6 m, 6 m

27. 9 cm, 14 cm

28. 20 yd, 40 yd

Practicing Multiplication

You will learn more about multiplying by two-digit numbers.	**Why learn this?** You can find how many things when there are too many to count.

Marty's family has 32 rows of trees in its orange grove. Each row has 136 orange trees. How many trees does Marty's family own?

Multiply 32 × 136 to find how many orange trees Marty's family owns.

Estimate. $30 \times 100 = 3{,}000$

MODEL

What is 32 × 136?

Step 1

Multiply by the ones.

$$\begin{array}{r} {}^{1} \\ 136 \\ \times\ 32 \\ \hline 272 \end{array} \leftarrow 2 \times 136$$

Step 2

Multiply by the tens.

$$\begin{array}{r} {}^{1\,1} \\ \not{1} \\ 136 \\ \times\ 32 \\ \hline 272 \\ +4{,}080 \end{array} \leftarrow 30 \times 136$$

Step 3

Add the products.

$$\begin{array}{r} {}^{1\,1} \\ \not{1} \\ 136 \\ \times\ 32 \\ \hline 272 \\ +4{,}080 \\ \hline 4{,}352 \end{array}$$

So, Marty's family owns 4,352 orange trees.

EXAMPLES

A.

$$\begin{array}{r} {}^{1} \\ 204 \\ \times\ 41 \\ \hline 204 \\ +8{,}160 \\ \hline 8{,}364 \end{array} \begin{array}{l} \\ \\ \\ \leftarrow 1 \times 204 \\ \leftarrow 40 \times 204 \\ \\ \end{array}$$

B.

$$\begin{array}{r} {}^{1\ \ 1} \\ \not{1} \\ 3{,}405 \\ \times\ \ 32 \\ \hline 6{,}810 \\ +102{,}150 \\ \hline 108{,}960 \end{array} \begin{array}{l} \\ \\ \\ \\ \leftarrow 2 \times 3{,}405 \\ \leftarrow 30 \times 3{,}405 \\ \\ \end{array}$$

Science Link

An orange is a citrus fruit that contains juice and vitamin C. If you drink a 12-ounce glass of juice each day, how many ounces will you drink in 30 days?

Talk About It

- What do you do with the regrouped digit in a multiplication problem?
- In Examples A and B, what happens to the regrouped digit when there is a zero in the factor?

PRACTICE

Find the product.

1. 119×13

2. $\$602 \times 24$

3. 421×72

4. 359×25

5. 215×38

6. $\$9.72 \times 63$

7. 748×45

8. $\$6.29 \times 92$

9. 814×67

10. 569×53

11. $1,735 \times 41$

12. $\$4,627 \times 15$

13. $3,904 \times 86$

14. $\$70.95 \times 34$

15. $9,750 \times 47$

16. $62 \times 198 = n$ **17.** $17 \times 543 = n$ **18.** $32 \times 1,947 = n$ **19.** $28 \times 5,284 = n$

Mixed Applications

20. There are 24 watercoolers in the building. Each cooler holds 30 gallons of water. How many gallons of water do all the coolers hold?

21. A bottle for a home watercooler holds 12 gallons of water. How many gallons of water do 4 bottles hold?

22. Grace buys a ten-gallon water bottle for $5.49. How much does Grace pay for 8 water bottles?

23. Sam starts his shower at 6:45 A.M. He finishes 20 minutes later. At what time does he finish?

24. Each time a person takes a bath, 50 gallons of water are used. Ray takes 1 bath each day. Does Ray use more than or less than 300 gallons of water in a week?

25. **Write a problem** using large numbers that can be solved by using multiplication.

Mixed Review

Compare the numbers. Write the comparisons using $<$, $>$, or $=$. (pages 106–107)

26. 37 ● 49 **27.** 98 ● 89 **28.** 441 ● 441 **29.** 206 ● 260

Write *true* or *false* for each statement. Rewrite false statements to make them true. (pages 94–95)

30. There are exactly 10 hundreds in 10,000.

31. There are exactly 10 thousands in 100,000.

MATH FUN!

Product Patterns

PURPOSE To practice multiplication

YOU WILL NEED number cards (1–5), calculator

Arrange number cards 1–5 as factors that can be multiplied to find the largest and the smallest possible products.

Check your answer with the calculator.

What other multiplication problems can you make with the digits 1–5?

- How does putting the digits in different places change the product?

Challenge your family to find a product that is greater than 1,000 and less than 10,000.

SECRET MESSAGE

PURPOSE To practice multiplication

YOU WILL NEED paper and pencil

Multiply. Match the product to the letter in the code box. Copy the problems and boxes. Place the letter in the box above each problem to show a message.

?	?	?	?	?	?	?	?	? !
49 ×36	36 ×28	92 ×34	71 ×19	34 ×45	65 ×44	42 ×31	75 ×53	52 ×36

CODE:

Product	Letter
1,008	A
1,302	F
1,349	H
1,530	I
1,764	M
1,872	N
2,860	S
3,128	T
3,975	U

Make up another message and code it by using multiplication.

Calculator Challenge

PURPOSE To use a calculator to multiply

YOU WILL NEED calculator

Find the greatest whole number which, when multiplied by itself, has a product less than or equal to the number given. Use a calculator.

1. 1,290 **2.** 14,400

3. 7,564 **4.** 49,284

5. 12,400 **6.** 279,833

CHAPTER 17

REVIEW

✓ CHECK UNDERSTANDING

Use mental math and basic facts to find the product. (pages 282–283)

1. $40 \times 600 = n$ **2.** $50 \times 700 = n$ **3.** $20 \times 800 = n$ **4.** $90 \times 300 = n$

Round each factor. Estimate the product. (pages 286–287)

5. 23×14 **6.** 62×25 **7.** 357×42 **8.** 192×33

✓ CHECK SKILLS

Find the product. (pages 290–293)

9. 46×51 **10.** 78×42 **11.** 92×37 **12.** 56×26

13. 139×23 **14.** 524×68 **15.** 283×74 **16.** 605×43

17. $53 \times 261 = n$ **18.** $45 \times 813 = n$ **19.** $87 \times 469 = n$ **20.** $39 \times 572 = n$

21. $29 \times 616 = n$ **22.** $79 \times 424 = n$ **23.** $32 \times 149 = n$ **24.** $42 \times 299 = n$

✓ CHECK PROBLEM SOLVING

Solve. (pages 284–285)

CHOOSE A STRATEGY

- Find a Pattern
- Act It Out
- Work Backward
- Write a Number Sentence

25. The team is giving away 106 books of game tickets. Each book has 24 tickets. How many game tickets in all is the team giving away?

26. The Corner Pizza House cuts its party-size pizza into 16 equal slices. What is the least number of cuts that can be made across the pizza?

27. Martin's youth group collected 60 boxes of canned goods for a food drive. Each box held 90 cans. How many cans of food did the youth group collect?

28. The Baseball Shop had 27 cases of baseball cards. Each case had 480 cards. How many baseball cards were there in all?

DIVIDING BY ONE-DIGIT NUMBERS

RECIPE	SERVES	USES
ZUCCHINI STEW	8	3 ZUCCHINI
ZUCCHINI PATTIES	4	6 ZUCCHINI
CALICO STUFFED ZUCCHINI	6	3 ZUCCHINI
CHOCOLATE ZUCCHINI CAKE	8	4 ZUCCHINI
ZUCCHINI SWEET BREAD	8	3 ZUCCHINI
ZUCCHINI COOKIES	8	1 ZUCCHINI

DID YOU KNOW . . .

The word *zucchini* comes from *zucchino,* which is Italian for *small squash.*

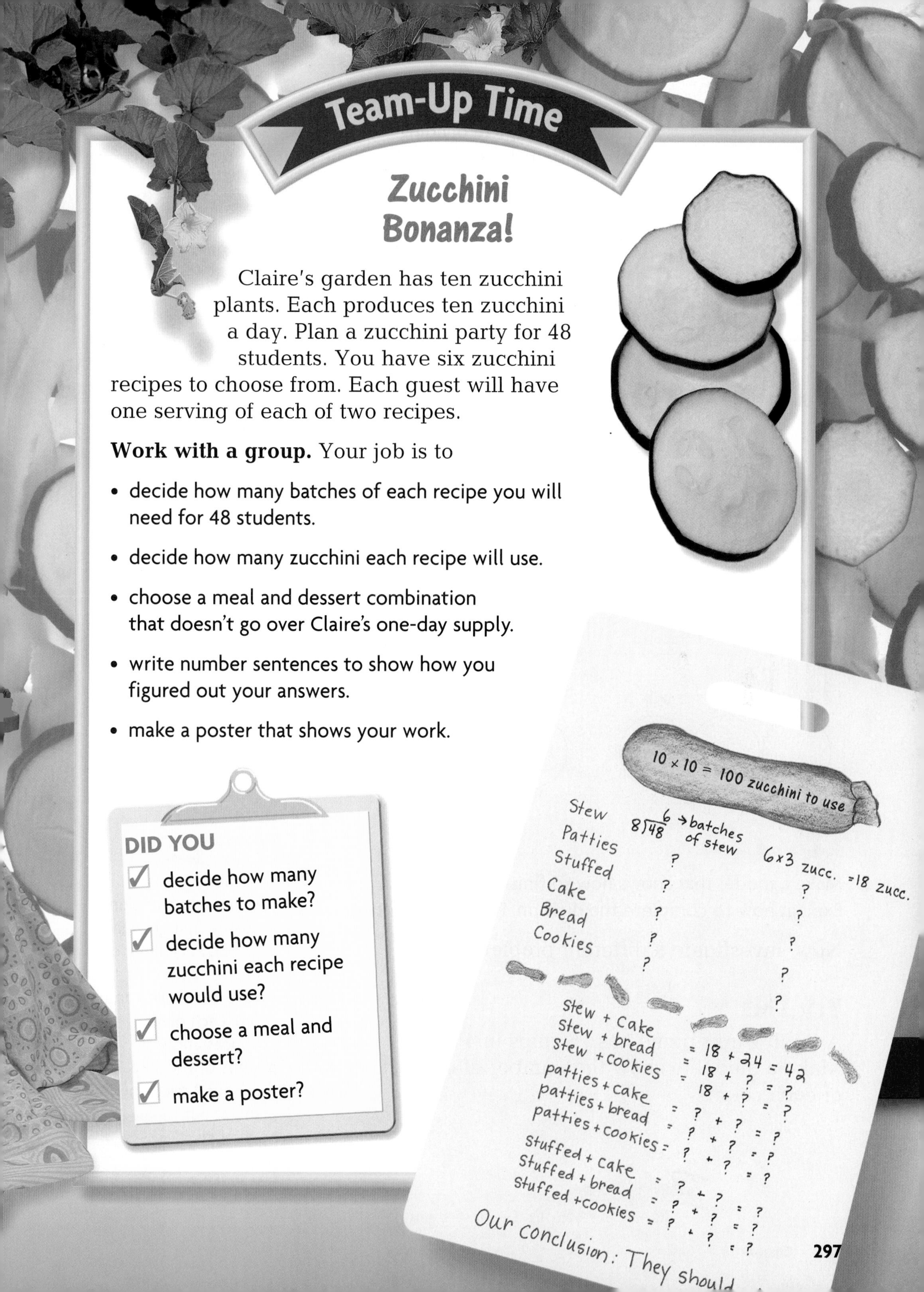

Team-Up Time

Zucchini Bonanza!

Claire's garden has ten zucchini plants. Each produces ten zucchini a day. Plan a zucchini party for 48 students. You have six zucchini recipes to choose from. Each guest will have one serving of each of two recipes.

Work with a group. Your job is to

- decide how many batches of each recipe you will need for 48 students.
- decide how many zucchini each recipe will use.
- choose a meal and dessert combination that doesn't go over Claire's one-day supply.
- write number sentences to show how you figured out your answers.
- make a poster that shows your work.

DID YOU

- ✓ decide how many batches to make?
- ✓ decide how many zucchini each recipe would use?
- ✓ choose a meal and dessert?
- ✓ make a poster?

Modeling Division

You will investigate dividing by one-digit numbers using base-ten blocks.

Why learn this? You can show how to share items equally among friends.

Divide. $48 \div 3 = n$

Explore

Make a model to show how many in each group.

MATERIALS: base-ten blocks

MODEL

What is $48 \div 3$?

Step 1

Draw 3 circles. Show 48 as 4 tens 8 ones.

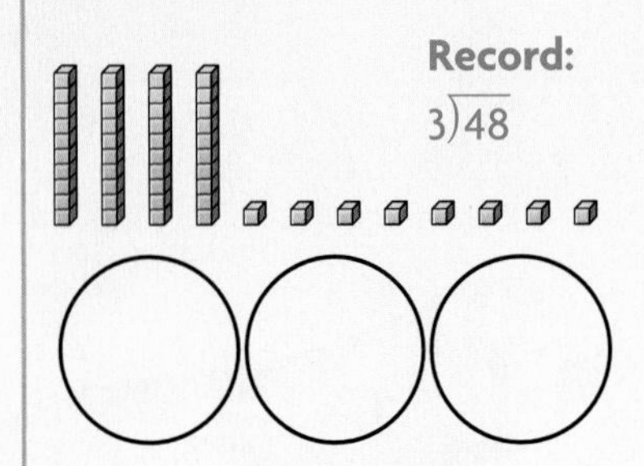

Record:

3)48

Step 2

Place an equal number of tens into each circle.

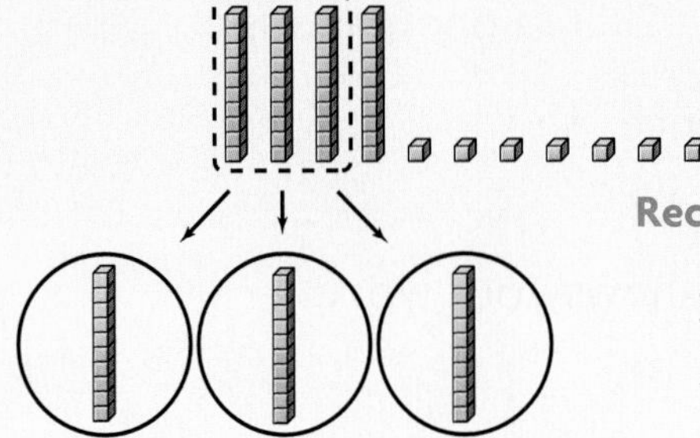

Record:

```
   1   ← 1 ten in each group
3)48
 -3    ← 3 tens used
  1    ← 1 ten left
```

Record

Make a model that shows how to finish the problem. Explain how to complete the division. Record the answer.

Now, investigate a different problem.

Try This

A tiddlywinks game has 76 chips in 4 colors. Make a model to show the number of chips of each color.

Science Link

Squashes such as zucchini and pumpkins probably first grew in America. Zucchini grows for about 2 months before it is picked and eaten. Each plant produces about 9 pounds of zucchini. If there are 9 zucchini on 1 plant, about how much does each one weigh?

E-Lab • Activity 18 Available on CD-ROM and the Internet at http://www.hbschool.com/elab

Talk About It

- What model did you make to represent the problem?
- How did you find how many in each group?

WRITE ABOUT IT Write about an experience you had dividing or sharing something. Tell how you were able to divide it.

HANDS-ON PRACTICE

Use base-ten blocks to model and record each problem.

1. A checkerboard has an equal number of red squares and black squares. There are 64 squares in all. How many squares are red?

2. The game of Chinese checkers uses 72 marbles in 6 different colors. How many marbles of each color are there?

Make a model and solve.

3. $65 \div 5 = \underline{?}$ **4.** $36 \div 2 = \underline{?}$ **5.** $96 \div 6 = \underline{?}$ **6.** $57 \div 3 = \underline{?}$

7. $98 \div 7 = \underline{?}$ **8.** $45 \div 3 = \underline{?}$ **9.** $34 \div 2 = \underline{?}$ **10.** $48 \div 4 = \underline{?}$

Mixed Applications

For Problems 11–15, use the table.

DOMINO GAME	
Number of Players	Total Number of Dominoes Needed
3	27
4	28
5	25

11. Each player receives the same number of dominoes. How many dominoes does each player get in a game with 3 players? 4 players?

12. Three friends are playing one game of dominoes in Ms. Hunter's class, and four friends are playing one game of dominoes in Mr. Hane's class. How many dominoes are being used in all?

13. If Ms. José has 50 dominoes, can she have 2 games of dominoes going on at the same time? If so, how many players would be in each game?

14. Miss Hyden holds a domino match every Friday. She has 2 games with 4 students playing and 3 games with 3 students playing. How many dominoes does she need for all the games?

15. Dominoes come 64 to a box. If Miss Hyden has 3 boxes of dominoes, how many dominoes does Miss Hyden have?

MORE PRACTICE Student Handbook page H99

Dividing with Remainders

You will learn to use multiplication facts to divide even when there are leftovers.

Why learn this? You can quickly find out if you can divide evenly or if you will have leftovers.

WORD POWER
remainder

Sometimes when you divide, a number is not evenly divided. There will be a **remainder**, or an amount left over.

Divide. $37 \div 5 = n$ (37 ← dividend, 5 ← divisor, n ← quotient)

divisor → $5\overline{)37}$ ← dividend; n ← quotient

Think of the multiplication facts that have 5 as a factor and their products.

$37 \div 5 = n$, $5 \times n = 37$

Since there is not a product 37 when you multiply by 5, think of the multiplication facts that have 5 as a factor and the products between 30 and 40.

REMEMBER:

$5 \times 0 = 0$	$5 \times 5 = 25$
$5 \times 1 = 5$	$5 \times 6 = 30$
$5 \times 2 = 10$	$5 \times 7 = 35$
$5 \times 3 = 15$	$5 \times 8 = 40$
$5 \times 4 = 20$	$5 \times 9 = 45$

All the products of 5 have a 0 or 5 in the ones place.

MODEL

What is $37 \div 5$?

Step 1

$5\overline{)37}$ with quotient 7

Since $5 \times 7 = 35$, use 7 as the quotient.

Step 2

$5\overline{)37}$ with quotient 7 r2; -35; 2 ← remainder

Multiply. $5 \times 7 = 35$
Subtract. $37 - 35 = 2$
Compare. $2 < 5$

Write the remainder next to the quotient.

Step 3

Check the quotient by multiplying.

7 ← quotient
$\times$ 5 ← divisor
35
$+$ 2 ← Add the remainder.
37 ← dividend

So, the quotient is correct.

So, $37 \div 5 = 7$ r2.

EXAMPLES

A. $5\overline{)23}$ = 4 r3; -20; 3. The remainder is 3.

B. $2\overline{)17}$ = 8 r1; -16; 1. The remainder is 1.

REMEMBER:

$2 \times 0 = 0$	$2 \times 5 = 10$
$2 \times 1 = 2$	$2 \times 6 = 12$
$2 \times 2 = 4$	$2 \times 7 = 14$
$2 \times 3 = 6$	$2 \times 8 = 16$
$2 \times 4 = 8$	$2 \times 9 = 18$

All the products of 2 end with an even number.

- Why do you think the words "left over" or "remainder" are used in division?

Calculator Activities page H60

Talk About It

- How do you know when there will be a remainder in a division problem?
- What do you notice about the products when you multiply by 5? by 2?
- How can you quickly tell if you can divide a number by 2 or 5 with no remainder?

Find the quotient. Check by multiplying.

1. $4\overline{)18}$ **2.** $6\overline{)21}$ **3.** $5\overline{)31}$ **4.** $3\overline{)20}$ **5.** $2\overline{)15}$

6. $4\overline{)33}$ **7.** $8\overline{)45}$ **8.** $3\overline{)23}$ **9.** $7\overline{)52}$ **10.** $9\overline{)24}$

11. $7\overline{)69}$ **12.** $8\overline{)53}$ **13.** $3\overline{)28}$ **14.** $7\overline{)58}$ **15.** $6\overline{)32}$

Mixed Applications

16. Lucinda, Rowena, and Celia each have 12 jacks. How many jacks do they have in all?

17. Harriet, Michelle, Sharon and Lupida shared 72 jacks. How many jacks did each girl have?

18. Marilyn bought 5 packages of jacks. There were 25 jacks in each package. How many jacks were there in all?

19. **WRITE ABOUT IT** If 3 girls get more jacks and divide them evenly, would there ever be more than 2 left over? Explain how you know.

Mixed Review

Finish each pattern. (pages 266–267)

20. $3 \times 40 = \underline{?}$
$\underline{?} \times 400 = 1{,}200$
$3 \times \underline{?} = 12{,}000$

21. $\underline{?} \times 20 = 140$
$7 \times \underline{?} = 1{,}400$
$7 \times 2{,}000 = \underline{?}$

22. $6 \times 50 = \underline{?}$
$6 \times \underline{?} = 3{,}000$
$\underline{?} \times 5{,}000 = 30{,}000$

For Exercises 23–25 use the drawing at the right. (pages 216–217)

23. Name the center of the circle.

24. Name each radius.

25. Name the diameter.

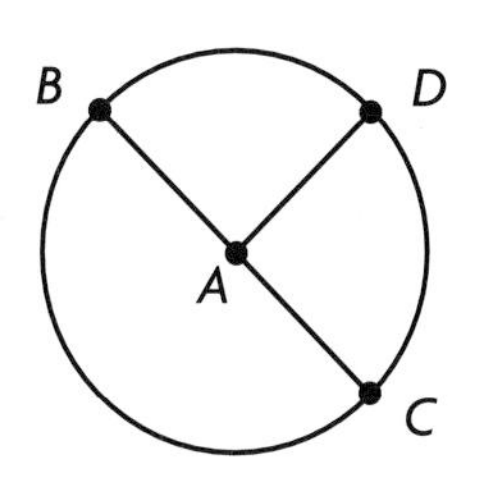

Division Procedures

You will learn to divide by one-digit divisors.	**Why learn this?** You can solve problems that require finding how many groups or how many in each group.

Bonnie's Bakery donated 65 cookies for a fair at the Senior Center. The senior citizens will put 3 cookies in each bag. How many bags will the senior citizens need for the cookies?

Divide. $65 \div 3 = n$ (65 ← dividend, 3 ← divisor, n ← quotient)

divisor → $3\overline{)65}$ ← dividend, with n ← quotient above

MODEL

What is 65 ÷ 3?

Step 1

Divide the 6 tens. $3\overline{)6}$

Think: $3 \times 2 = 6$

$$\begin{array}{r} 2 \\ 3\overline{)65} \\ -6 \\ \hline 0 \end{array}$$

Multiply. 3×2
Subtract. $6 - 6$
Compare. $0 < 3$

Step 2

Bring down the ones. Divide. $3\overline{)5}$

Think: $3 \times 1 = 3$

$$\begin{array}{r} 21 \text{ r2} \\ 3\overline{)65} \\ -6\downarrow \\ \hline 05 \\ -3 \\ \hline 2 \end{array}$$

Multiply. 3×1
Subtract. $5 - 3$
Compare. $2 < 3$

Write the remainder next to the quotient.

Step 3

Check the quotient by multiplying.

$$\begin{array}{r} 21 \\ \times 3 \\ \hline 63 \\ +2 \\ \hline 65 \end{array}$$

21 ← quotient
× 3 ← divisor
+ 2 ← Add the remainder.
65 ← dividend

So, the quotient is correct.

So, the senior citizens will need 21 bags for the cookies. There will be 2 cookies left over.

EXAMPLES

A.
$$\begin{array}{r} 32 \\ 3\overline{)96} \\ -9\downarrow \\ \hline 06 \\ -6 \\ \hline 0 \end{array}$$

B.
$$\begin{array}{r} 15 \\ 4\overline{)60} \\ -4\downarrow \\ \hline 20 \\ -20 \\ \hline 0 \end{array}$$

C.
$$\begin{array}{r} 12 \text{ r3} \\ 7\overline{)87} \\ -7\downarrow \\ \hline 17 \\ -14 \\ \hline 3 \end{array}$$

Talk About It 

- When you divide, why must the remainder be less than the divisor?
- Why do you have to use both multiplication and addition to check the answer in Example C?

Social Studies Link

A bazaar is a place where goods are sold or traded. One bazaar has 75 booths on 3 streets. There is an equal number on each street. How many booths are on one street?

PRACTICE

Find the quotient. Check by multiplying.

1. $2\overline{)46}$ **2.** $4\overline{)84}$ **3.** $5\overline{)76}$ **4.** $3\overline{)68}$

5. $6\overline{)75}$ **6.** $8\overline{)93}$ **7.** $7\overline{)91}$ **8.** $4\overline{)73}$

9. $5\overline{)96}$ **10.** $3\overline{)92}$ **11.** $9\overline{)97}$ **12.** $7\overline{)89}$

Mixed Applications

For Problems 13–15, use the price list.

BAKE SALE PRICE LIST

Cookie	Price
peanut butter	\$0.10
chocolate chip	\$0.14
decorated	\$0.15

13. Juanita sold 36 cookies. She sold the same number of each kind of cookie. How many of each kind of cookie did she sell?

14. Jane sold 8 peanut butter cookies, 9 chocolate chip cookies, and 6 decorated cookies. How much money did Jane make at the bake sale?

15. The students volunteered to bake cookies for the bake sale. If each of 6 students baked 12 of each type of cookie, how many cookies did they bake for the bake sale?

16. Holly's mother baked 36 chocolate cookies, 48 peanut butter cookies, and 60 decorated cookies. How many cookies did she bake in all?

Mixed Review

Write the numbers in order from the least to the greatest. (pages 112–113)

17. 550, 502, 520 **18.** 696, 966, 690 **19.** 423, 324, 243

Round each factor to nearest ten. Estimate the product. (pages 286–287)

20. 36×23 **21.** 47×35 **22.** 59×42 **23.** 65×57

MORE PRACTICE Student Handbook page H99

PART 1 Placing the First Digit in the Quotient

You will learn to use place value to place the first digit in the quotient and to decide what each digit should be.

Why learn this? You can quickly decide how many digits will be in a quotient.

Davion and Brandi are dividing 253 sheets of colored tissue paper equally among 4 groups to use in art class. How many sheets of tissue paper will each group get?

Divide. $253 \div 4 = n$ $\quad 4\overline{)253}$

MODEL

What is $253 \div 4$?

Step 1

Decide where to place the first digit in the quotient.

$$\begin{array}{r} \text{x} \\ 4\overline{)253} \end{array}$$

$2 < 4$.
There are not enough hundreds.

$$\begin{array}{r} \blacksquare \\ 4\overline{)253} \end{array}$$

$25 > 4$
Use 25 tens. Place the first digit in the tens place.

Step 2

Divide the tens. $4\overline{)25}$

Think: $4 \times 6 = 24$

$$\begin{array}{r} 6 \\ 4\overline{)253} \\ -24 \\ \hline 1 \end{array}$$

Multiply. 4×6
Subtract. $25 - 24$
Compare. $1 < 4$

Step 3

Bring down the ones. Divide. $4\overline{)13}$

Think: $4 \times 3 = 12$

$$\begin{array}{r} 63 \text{ r1} \\ 4\overline{)253}\phantom{\text{ r1}} \\ -24\phantom{\text{ r1}} \\ \hline 13\phantom{\text{ r1}} \\ -12\phantom{\text{ r1}} \\ \hline 1\phantom{\text{ r1}} \end{array}$$

Multiply. 4×3
Subtract. $13 - 12$
Compare. $1 < 4$

So, each group will get 63 sheets of paper. There will be 1 sheet left over.

EXAMPLES

A. $7\overline{)94}$ **B.** $4\overline{)38}$ **C.** $2\overline{)356}$ **D.** $8\overline{)29}$

Talk About It

Look at Examples A–D.

- Where will the first digit be placed in each quotient?
- How many digits will be in each quotient?

Art Link

Papier-mâché is a mixture of newspaper dipped in flour-and-water paste. It takes 150 sheets of paper to make 6 small figures. How many sheets of newspaper are used for each figure?

PRACTICE

Copy each problem. Draw a box where the first digit in the quotient should be placed.

1. $6\overline{)38}$ **2.** $4\overline{)81}$ **3.** $2\overline{)195}$ **4.** $5\overline{)85}$

5. $3\overline{)225}$ **6.** $8\overline{)807}$ **7.** $9\overline{)873}$ **8.** $6\overline{)951}$

Find the quotient. Check by multiplying.

9. $3\overline{)29}$ **10.** $2\overline{)87}$ **11.** $4\overline{)189}$ **12.** $6\overline{)378}$

13. $5\overline{)254}$ **14.** $7\overline{)873}$ **15.** $7\overline{)563}$ **16.** $3\overline{)801}$

17. $9\overline{)462}$ **18.** $5\overline{)694}$ **19.** $6\overline{)969}$ **20.** $8\overline{)765}$

Mixed Applications

For Problems 21–23, use the line graph.

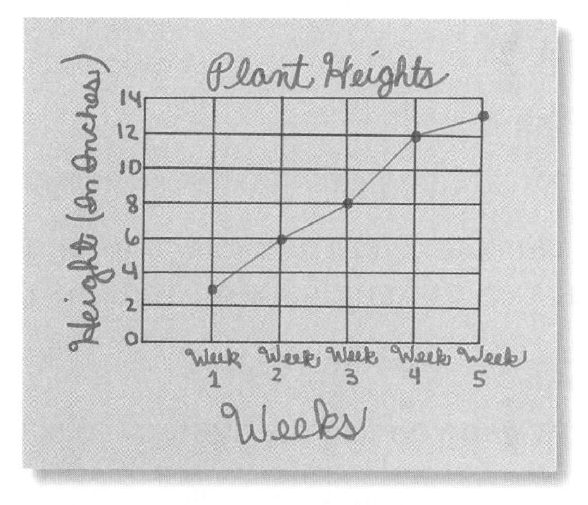

21. Rodney grew plants for his science fair project. He measured the height of his plants each week. How tall were the plants on the third week?

22. How much did Rodney's plant grow between the second and fourth week?

23. Rodney made a graph to show how his plants grew each week. How much taller were Rodney's plants on the fifth week than on the first week?

24. Art class begins 1 hour and 40 minutes after science class. Science class starts at 12:30 P.M. At what time does art class begin?

25. In an art class, there are 14 tables with 4 work stations at each table. If all the stations are being used by students, how many students are in the art class?

26. Cindy bought decorations for her art project. She bought glitter for \$1.49, lace for \$1.89, and paint for \$2.30. How much change did she receive from \$6.00?

27. Some students took a total of 144 pictures in a photography class. Each of 6 students took the same number of pictures. How many pictures did each student take?

28. **Write a problem** with a one-digit divisor, a two-digit dividend, a two-digit quotient, and a remainder of 1.

MORE PRACTICE Student Handbook page H100

PART 2 PROBLEM-SOLVING STRATEGY
Guess and Check

THE PROBLEM **There are 81 students visiting a museum. When they are placed in equal groups to tour the museum, 3 students are left over. How many groups are formed? How many students are in each group?**

REMEMBER:
- ✓ Understand
- ✓ Plan
- ✓ Solve
- ✓ Look Back

✓ Understand

- What are you asked to find out?
- What information will you use?
- Is there any information you will not use? If so, what?

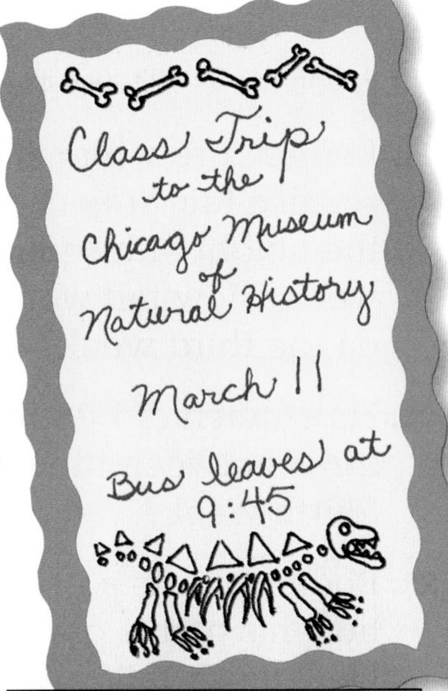

✓ Plan

- What strategy can you use to solve the problem?

You can use *guess and check* to find the number of groups and the number of students in each group.

✓ Solve

- How can you use the strategy to solve the problem?

If you don't know how to solve a problem, you can guess the answer and then check to see if the guess is correct.

Guess 8 groups.	Check.
10 r1 8)81 −8 01 − 0 1	8 groups 10 in each group Remainder of 1 does not check.

Guess 7 groups.	Check.
11 r4 7)81 −7 11 − 7 4	7 groups 11 in each group Remainder of 4 does not check.

Guess 6 groups.	Check.
13 r3 6)81 −6 21 −18 3	6 groups 13 in each group Remainder of 3 checks.

So, there are 6 groups with 13 students in each group, and 3 students left over.

✓ Look Back

- How can you decide if your answer is reasonable?
- What other strategy could you use?

PRACTICE

CHOOSE Paper/Pencil Calculator Hands-on Mental Math

Use guess and check to solve.

1. There were 86 students touring the museum. After equal groups were formed, 1 student was left over. How many groups were formed? How many students are in each group?

2. Mary Ellen spent $16.50 at the museum gift shop. She bought 2 birthday gifts. One of the gifts cost $2.50 more than the other. How much was each gift?

3. There are 79 people in a room with fewer than 10 paintings. In the center of the room, 2 people are talking. All the others are standing in equal groups. Each group is in front of a painting. How many paintings are in the room? How many people are in front of each painting?

4. There are 35 clay pots in a room. An equal number of pots are displayed on tables, and 2 pots are standing on the floor. There are fewer than 10 tables. How many tables are there? How many pots are on each table?

Mixed Applications

Solve.

CHOOSE A STRATEGY

- **Guess and Check**
- **Find a Pattern**
- **Write a Number Sentence**
- **Make a Table**

5. On the first day of a new exhibit, 50 people came to the museum. The second day, 60 people came, and the third day, 80 people came. The fourth day, there were 110 people. If this pattern goes on, how many people will visit the new exhibit on the fifth day it is open?

6. In which of the four classes do the campers spend the most time? the least time?

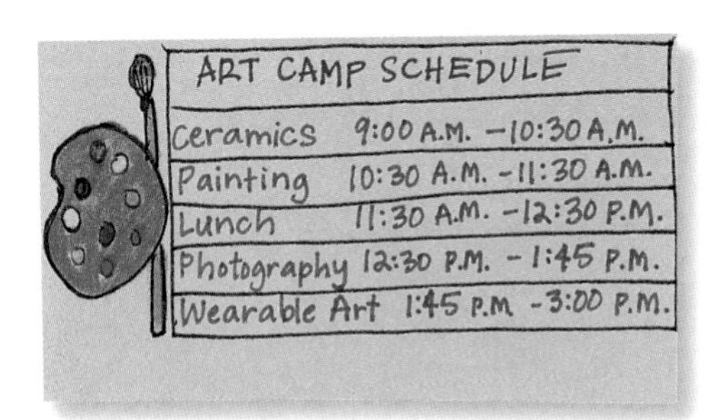

ART CAMP SCHEDULE	
Ceramics	9:00 A.M. – 10:30 A.M.
Painting	10:30 A.M. – 11:30 A.M.
Lunch	11:30 A.M. – 12:30 P.M.
Photography	12:30 P.M. – 1:45 P.M.
Wearable Art	1:45 P.M. – 3:00 P.M.

7. The campers at art camp are having an art show. They sent out 400 invitations to the show. Only 127 of those invited said they will attend. How many invited people will not attend the art show?

8. The leather-works class begins 45 minutes after lunch ends. Lunch ends at 12:30 P.M. What time does the leather-works class begin?

MORE PRACTICE Student Handbook page H100

Dividing Three-Digit Numbers

You will learn to divide a three-digit number by a one-digit number.

Why learn this? You can find the number of people in each group when groups are divided equally.

Midway Intermediate School is sending 175 students to a concert by bus. The school ordered 4 buses. How many students can ride on each bus?

Divide. $175 \div 4 = n$

MODEL

What is $175 \div 4$?

Step 1

Decide where to place the first digit in the quotient.

Think: $1 < 4$

```
   x
4)175
```
There are not enough hundreds.

```
   ■
4)175
```
$17 > 4$
Use 17 tens. Place the first digit in the tens place.

Step 2

Divide the tens. $4\overline{)17}$

Think: $4 \times 4 = 16$

```
   4
4)175
 -16
   1
```
Multiply. 4×4
Subtract. $17 - 16$
Compare. $1 < 4$

Step 3

Bring down the ones. Divide. $4\overline{)15}$

Think: $4 \times 3 = 12$

```
   43 r3
4)175
 -16
   15
  -12
    3
```
Multiply. 4×3
Subtract. $15 - 12$
Compare. $3 < 4$

The remainder is 3.

Step 4

Check the quotient by multiplying.

```
   1
   43  ← quotient
 ×  4  ← divisor
  172     Add the
 +  3  ← remainder.
  175  ← dividend
```

So, the quotient is correct.

So, 43 students can ride on 4 buses, with 1 more student on each of 3 buses.

EXAMPLES

A.
```
   37 r4        Check.
5)189              3
 -15               37
  39             ×  5
 -35              185
   4             +  4
                  189
```

B.
```
   193 r1       Check.
2)387              1
 -2               193
  18             ×  2
 -18              386
   07            +  1
  - 6             387
    1
```

C.
```
   170 r2       Check.
4)682              2
 -4               170
  28             ×  4
 -28              680
   02            +  2
  - 0             682
    2
```

- Why are there three digits in the quotients of Examples B and C?

PRACTICE

Copy each problem. Draw a box where the first digit in the quotient should be placed.

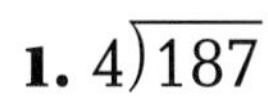

1. $4\overline{)187}$ **2.** $2\overline{)453}$ **3.** $5\overline{)692}$ **4.** $3\overline{)270}$

5. $6\overline{)987}$ **6.** $4\overline{)934}$ **7.** $7\overline{)241}$ **8.** $9\overline{)709}$

Find the quotient. Check by multiplying.

9. $3\overline{)141}$ **10.** $4\overline{)506}$ **11.** $2\overline{)837}$ **12.** $7\overline{)659}$

13. $6\overline{)285}$ **14.** $7\overline{)224}$ **15.** $9\overline{)530}$ **16.** $4\overline{)617}$

17. $186 \div 3 = n$ **18.** $247 \div 8 = n$ **19.** $372 \div 6 = n$ **20.** $546 \div 5 = n$

Mixed Applications

21. The Science Center has a movie theater that seats 45 people. There are 110 students at the Science Center. Will all of them be able to watch the movie in 2 showings? Explain.

22. The movie *Weather or Not* was shown 6 times during the day. Each of the 45 seats was used at each showing. How many people saw the movie?

23. The movie *Clues to the Past* was seen by 228 students in one day. The same number of students saw each of the 6 showings. How many students saw the movie at each showing?

24. **Write a problem** that can be solved by dividing a three-digit dividend that has a remainder.

Mixed Review

Use the Grouping Property to solve each problem. (pages 40–41)

25. $(3 \times 3) \times 2 = \underline{?}$ **26.** $2 \times (2 \times 3) = \underline{?}$

27. $(5 \times 2) \times 3 = \underline{?}$ **28.** $(2 \times 4) \times 3 = \underline{?}$

Write the fact family for each set of numbers. (pages 52–53)

29. 3, 6, 18 **30.** 2, 4, 8

31. 4, 5, 20 **32.** 4, 6, 24

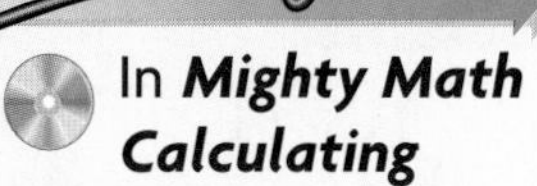

In ***Mighty Math Calculating Crew,*** the game *Intergalactic Trader* challenges you to divide 3-digit by 1-digit numbers.

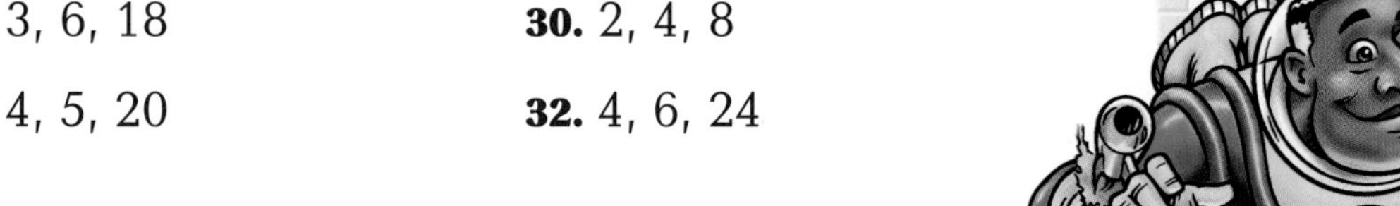

Practicing Division

You will learn to find a three-digit quotient.

Why learn this? You can find amounts each person collected from totals donated.

LaTika collected 371 pairs of new socks for 3 homeless shelters. She divided the socks equally among the 3 shelters. How many pairs of socks will each homeless shelter receive?

Divide. $371 \div 3 = n$

MODEL

What is $371 \div 3$?

Step 1

Decide where to place the first digit in the quotient.

```
  ■     3 = 3
3)371   You can divide
        3 hundreds by 3.
```

Step 2

Divide the hundreds. $3\overline{)3}$

Think: $3 \times 1 = 3$

```
   1
3)371   Multiply. 3 × 1
 -3     Subtract. 3 − 3
  0     Compare. 0 < 3
```

Step 3

Bring down the tens. Divide. $3\overline{)7}$

```
   12
3)371
 -3↓    Multiply. 3 × 2
  07    Subtract. 7 − 6
  -6    Compare. 1 < 3
   1
```

Step 4

Bring down the ones. Divide. $3\overline{)11}$

```
   123 r2
3)371      Multiply.
 -3        3 × 3
  07       Subtract.
  -6↓      11 − 9
   11      Compare.
  - 9      2 < 3
    2
```

So, each homeless shelter will receive 123 pairs of socks. There will be 2 extra pairs of socks.

- Why must you bring down the 1 one in Step 4 before you can divide again?

EXAMPLES

A.
```
   106 r1
3)319
 -3
  019
  -18
    1
```

B.
```
   154 r2
4)618
 -4
  21
 -20
   18
  -16
    2
```

C.
```
   105 r6
9)951
 -9
  05
 - 0
  51
 -45
   6
```

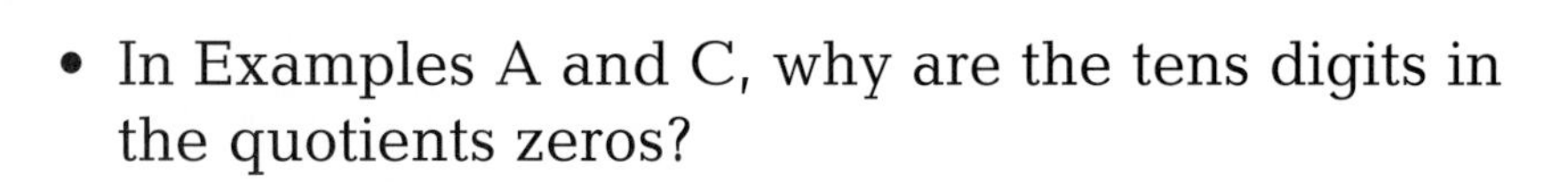

- In Examples A and C, why are the tens digits in the quotients zeros?

PRACTICE

Find the quotient. Check by multiplying.

1. $2\overline{)212}$ **2.** $5\overline{)658}$ **3.** $4\overline{)873}$ **4.** $3\overline{)905}$

5. $4\overline{)736}$ **6.** $7\overline{)502}$ **7.** $3\overline{)298}$ **8.** $5\overline{)697}$

9. $369 \div 6 = n$ **10.** $865 \div 8 = n$ **11.** $672 \div 5 = n$ **12.** $831 \div 9 = n$

13. $751 \div 8 = n$ **14.** $509 \div 2 = n$ **15.** $498 \div 7 = n$ **16.** $915 \div 4 = n$

Mixed Applications

For Problems 17–20, use the graph.

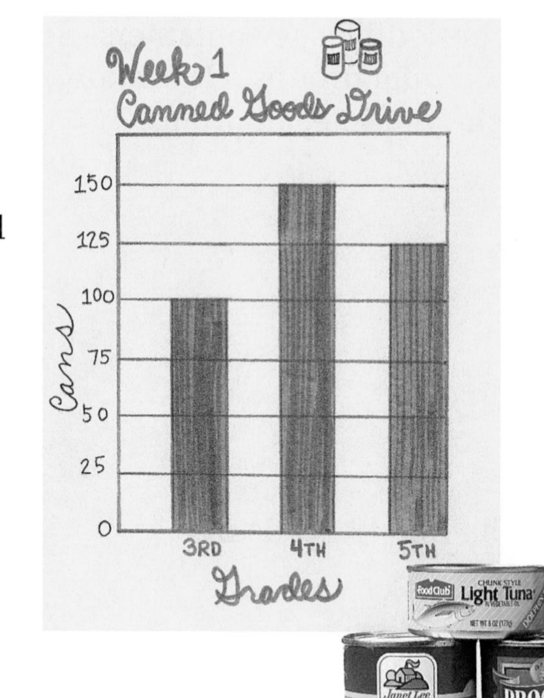

17. How many more cans will the third, fourth, and fifth grades have to collect to meet their goal of collecting 1,000 cans?

18. The 4 third–grade classes each collected the same number of cans. How many cans did each class collect?

19. Four classes from the fourth grade collected canned goods. One class collected 39 cans, and each of the other 3 classes collected the same number of cans. How many cans did each of the 3 other classes collect?

20. **Write a problem** using division and the information in the graph.

Mixed Review

Find the product. (pages 282–283)

21. 30×5 **22.** 40×20 **23.** 80×50 **24.** 600×3 **25.** 500×50

Find the difference. (pages 22–23)

26. $300 - 189$ **27.** $900 - 456$ **28.** $7{,}000 - 472$ **29.** $1{,}450 - 894$ **30.** $2{,}004 - 741$

CULTURAL CONNECTION

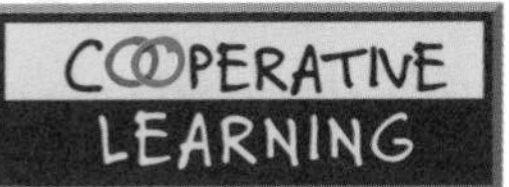

Growing Better Plants

Danesha read about George Washington Carver's experiments with plants and soil improvement. For her spring science project, she decided to study how to grow better plants. Danesha planted 215 seeds in recycled plastic containers. She divided the seeds into 5 equal groups. How many seeds did she put in each group?

$215 \div 5 = \underline{\ ?\ }$

$$\begin{array}{r} 43 \\ 5\overline{)215} \\ \underline{-20} \\ 15 \\ \underline{-15} \\ 0 \end{array}$$

So, Danesha put 43 seeds in each group.

CULTURAL LINK

George Washington Carver helped poor farmers enrich their soil after years of just growing cotton had made the soil poor. By planting peanuts or sweet potatoes, farmers could put rich nutrients back into the soil. Carver developed 118 useful products using the sweet potato, including flour, starch, sugar, molasses, vinegar, ink, dye, and glue. He developed more than 300 uses for the peanut, including cream, cookies, cheese, bleach, shoe polish, 30 dyes, and a substitute for coffee.

Work Together

1. Danesha decided to use 130 ounces of water over 4 weeks for her experiment. How many ounces of water would she give each of the 5 groups?

2. At the end of the project, Danesha had 200 plants. She chose 78 plants and divided them into 6 equal groups for 6 neighbors. How many plants did each neighbor receive?

3. Danesha planted some of the plants that were left in pots and the rest in rows in her garden. First she put 8 plants in each row. How many rows did she plant? How many plants were put in pots?

4. There were 20 tables in the auditorium for the science-project displays. Each table was 8 feet long. Every student was given 4 feet for a display. How many students could set up displays in the auditorium?

CHAPTER 18

REVIEW

✓ CHECK UNDERSTANDING

1. **VOCABULARY** A _?_ is an amount left over when you divide. (page 300)

Tell if each can be evenly divided by 2, by 5, or by neither. (pages 300–301)

2. 45 **3.** 60 **4.** 84 **5.** 53

Draw a box where the first digit in the quotient should be placed. Write the number of digits. (pages 304–305)

6. $3\overline{)89}$ **7.** $7\overline{)69}$ **8.** $4\overline{)92}$ **9.** $2\overline{)750}$

✓ CHECK SKILLS

Find the quotient. Check by multiplying. (pages 302–305, 308–311)

10. $3\overline{)87}$ **11.** $2\overline{)85}$ **12.** $6\overline{)94}$ **13.** $4\overline{)62}$

14. $5\overline{)72}$ **15.** $4\overline{)98}$ **16.** $7\overline{)89}$ **17.** $5\overline{)62}$

18. $3\overline{)815}$ **19.** $5\overline{)282}$ **20.** $7\overline{)427}$ **21.** $9\overline{)881}$

22. $613 \div 5 = n$ **23.** $244 \div 5 = n$ **24.** $826 \div 2 = n$ **25.** $197 \div 5 = n$

✓ CHECK PROBLEM SOLVING

Solve. (pages 306–307)

CHOOSE A STRATEGY

- Act It Out
- Guess and Check
- Make a Model
- Write a Number Sentence

26. The Sweet Shoppe has 4 jars of candy. It takes 96 pieces of candy to fill all the jars. How many pieces will fit in each jar?

27. Mrs. McGill dips chocolates for the Sweet Shoppe. She works 38 days every 2 months. How many days a month is this?

28. After 118 people are equally placed in Red Cross classes, there are 6 people left over. How many classes will the Red Cross teach?

29. Maria has 87 boxes of beads. Each box has 125 beads. How many beads does Maria have in all?

30. There are 477 candies in a five-pound bag. How many candies are in 3 five-pound bags?

31. Matt tosses a number cube labeled with numbers 1–6. What is the probability that it will land on 3?

CHAPTER 19 MORE ABOUT DIVIDING BY ONE-DIGIT NUMBERS

DID YOU KNOW . . .

In India there are many spring festivals that feature kites. One is held on January 14th. It celebrates the return of warmer weather.

Team-Up Time

Celebrating Spring with Kites

Each classroom at Benito Juarez School has been given $25 by the PTA to create an activity for the Spring Arts Festival. Mr. Chu's class has decided to have a kite-making booth.

Work with a partner. Your job is to

- find out how many kites you can make from one package of tissue paper.
- find how many packages of sticks you will need.
- decide if you are within Mr. Chu's budget.
- write number sentences to show all your calculations.

MAKING YOUR OWN KITE

Each kite uses a piece of paper that measures 18 inches by nine inches. One sheet of tissue paper is 20 inches by 28 inches. There are 20 sheets of tissue paper in a package.

Each kite uses 3 split bamboo sticks. One package contains 27 sticks. The sticks will not need to be cut.

Follow these steps to make a kite:

- Use glue to attach the tissue paper to the split bamboo frame.
- Use thread to tie the sticks together.
- Use string to bend the wings and make the bridle.
- Use crepe paper streamers to make your kite tail.
- Decorate your kite with colored markers.

DID YOU

- ✓ find the number of kites you can make with one package of tissue paper?
- ✓ find how many packages of sticks you will need?
- ✓ find the total cost of the materials?
- ✓ write number sentences for your calculations?

Order Form

Quantity	Item	price
1	white glue	$0.75
1	spool heavy thread	$1.25
1	large ball of kite string	$1.50
3	rolls streamers	$0.50
1	pkg tissue paper	$4.00
1	pkg split bamboo sticks	$2.00
1	pkg colored markers	$1.75

Division Patterns to Estimate

You will learn to use mental math and patterns of zeros to estimate quotients.

Why learn this? You can find about how many people can sit in each section of seats at a sports event.

Each of the 4 sections of seats at the kite festival can seat the same number of people. The 4 sections can seat 8,240 people in all. About how many seats are in each section?

REMEMBER:

Read: 8,240 divided by 4

Round: 8,240 to the nearest 1,000 is 8,000.

Divide. $8{,}240 \div 4$ $\quad 4\overline{)8{,}240}$

$\downarrow$

Estimate. $8{,}000 \div 4 = n$

Use the basic fact $8 \div 4$ and a pattern of zeros to estimate the quotient.

$8 \div 4 = 2$
$80 \div 4 = 20$
$800 \div 4 = 200$
$8{,}000 \div 4 = 2{,}000$

three zeros **three zeros**

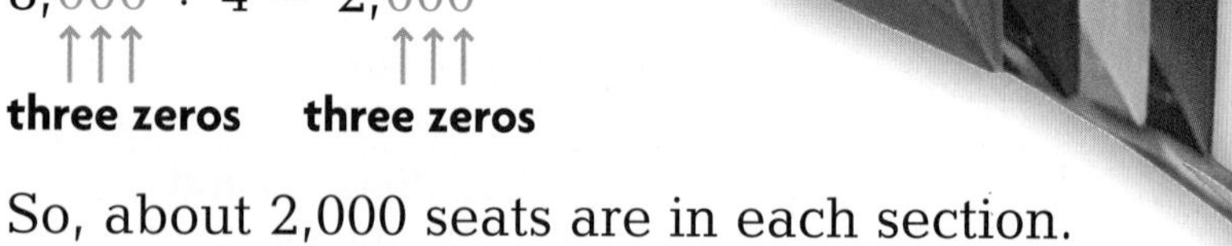

Let's go fly a kite!

So, about 2,000 seats are in each section.

As the number of zeros in the dividend increases, what happens to the number of zeros in the quotient?

EXAMPLES

A. $9 \div 3 = 3$
$90 \div 3 = 30$
$900 \div 3 = 300$
$9{,}000 \div 3 = 3{,}000$

B. $12 \div 2 = 6$
$120 \div 2 = 60$
$1{,}200 \div 2 = 600$
$12{,}000 \div 2 = 6{,}000$

C. $30 \div 6 = 5$
$300 \div 6 = 50$
$3{,}000 \div 6 = 500$
$30{,}000 \div 6 = 5{,}000$

Talk About It

- What difference do you see in the pattern of zeros in Examples A, B, and C?
- In Example C, why is there one less zero in each quotient than in each dividend?
- How can you use division patterns to estimate quotients?

PRACTICE

Copy and complete. Use a basic fact and a pattern of zeros to help you.

1. $180 \div n = 90$
$1{,}800 \div 2 = n$
$n \div 2 = 9{,}000$

2. $560 \div 7 = n$
$5{,}600 \div n = 800$
$n \div 7 = 8{,}000$

3. $n \div 6 = 70$
$4{,}200 \div 6 = n$
$42{,}000 \div n = 7{,}000$

4. $200 \div n = 40$
$2{,}000 \div 5 = n$
$n \div 5 = 4{,}000$

Find the quotient.

5. $2\overline{)140}$ **6.** $7\overline{)2{,}100}$ **7.** $3\overline{)9{,}000}$ **8.** $9\overline{)540}$ **9.** $6\overline{)42{,}000}$

10. $5\overline{)25{,}000}$ **11.** $8\overline{)6{,}400}$ **12.** $6\overline{)120}$ **13.** $4\overline{)16{,}000}$ **14.** $8\overline{)4{,}000}$

Estimate. Use a pattern of zeros to find the quotient.

15. $3{,}613 \div 4 = n$ **16.** $492 \div 7 = n$ **17.** $24{,}375 \div 3 = n$ **18.** $2{,}711 \div 9 = n$

19. $844 \div 8 = n$ **20.** $3{,}157 \div 8 = n$ **21.** $12{,}087 \div 2 = n$ **22.** $3{,}032 \div 6 = n$

Mixed Applications

For Problems 23–24, use the sign at the right.

23. Tennis balls come 3 to a can. How many cans are there at the Best Sports Shop?

24. How many more basketballs and baseballs together are there than golf balls in the Best Sports Shop?

25. Myra's basketball team sold 47 boxes of chocolate bars. Each box had 24 chocolate bars. How many chocolate bars did the team sell in all?

26. **Write a problem** using division that can be solved by using a basic fact and a pattern of zeros.

Mixed Review

Round to the nearest *ten, hundred,* and *thousand.* (pages 26–27)

27. 1,879 **28.** 3,067 **29.** 5,552

Write the time, using A.M. or P.M. (pages 122–123)

30. when school starts **31.** when you have lunch **32.** when you go to bed

Zeros in Division

You will learn how to divide when a zero is in the dividend or in the quotient.

Why learn this? You can find the right number of things in each group by placing the digits in the correct place.

A postal carrier makes 432 stops in 4 hours. How many stops is this every hour?

Estimate. $400 \div 4 = 100$

MODEL

What is $432 \div 4$?

Step 1

Decide where to place the first digit in the quotient.

Think: You *can* divide 4 hundreds by 4.

$4\overline{)432}$ (box above the 4)

Step 2

Divide the hundreds.

$4\overline{)4}$

Think: $4 \times n = 4$

```
   1
4)432
 -4
  0
```

Multiply. 4×1
Subtract. $4 - 4$
Compare. $0 < 4$

Step 3

Bring down the tens.

Divide. $4\overline{)3}$

Think: Since $4 > 3$, write a zero in the quotient.

```
   10
4)432
 -4↓
  03
  -0
   3
```

Step 4

Bring down the ones.

Divide. $4\overline{)32}$

Think: $4 \times n = 32$

```
  108
4)432
 -4
  03
  -0↓
   32
  -32
    0
```

Multiply. 4×8
Subtract. $32 - 32$
Compare. $0 < 4$

So, the postal carrier makes 108 stops every hour.

EXAMPLES

A.

```
  102 r2
8)818
 -8↓
  01
  -0↓
   18
  -16
    2
```

B.

```
   $1.30
6 )$7.80
   -6↓
    18
   -18↓
     00
     -0
      0
```

C.

```
  114 r6
7)804
 -7↓
  10
  -7↓
   34
  -28
    6
```

Talk About It

- What would happen in Example A if you did not write a zero in the tens place?

- How can you decide how many digits will be in the quotient?

PRACTICE

Write the number of digits in each quotient.

1. $8\overline{)818}$ **2.** $6\overline{)510}$ **3.** $3\overline{)207}$ **4.** $4\overline{)600}$

Find the quotient.

5. $3\overline{)420}$ **6.** $9\overline{)502}$ **7.** $6\overline{)362}$ **8.** $4\overline{)723}$

9. $8\overline{)825}$ **10.** $5\overline{)740}$ **11.** $7\overline{)880}$ **12.** $3\overline{)421}$

13. $7\overline{)636}$ **14.** $4\overline{)481}$ **15.** $6\overline{)243}$ **16.** $2\overline{)340}$

Mixed Applications

For Problems 17–18, use the table at the right.

SHIPPING COSTS	
1 lb – 5 lb	$0.74 lb
6 lb – 10 lb	$0.69 lb
11 lb – 15 lb	$0.57 lb
16 lb – 20 lb	$0.49 lb

17. Manuel mailed 3 boxes. One box weighed 5 pounds. Another box weighed 7 pounds, and the third box weighed 18 pounds. How much did it cost Manuel to send the boxes?

18. Sandra has $7.00. Does she have enough money to mail a box that weighs 13 pounds? How much will it cost to mail the box?

19. Speedy Delivery shipped 630 boxes in 5 days. It shipped the same number of boxes each day. How many boxes were shipped each day?

20. Labels come 500 to a box. The mail room bought 8 boxes in May and 6 boxes in July. How many labels is this in all?

21. **WRITE ABOUT IT** Explain what would happen if you did not place a zero in the quotient when one is needed.

Mixed Review

Use mental math and basic multiplication facts to find the product. (pages 266–267)

22. $800 \times 7 = \underline{?}$ **23.** $40 \times 6 = \underline{?}$ **24.** $7{,}000 \times 5 = \underline{?}$

Use mental math to complete each equation. (pages 4–5)

25. $25 - 13 = 10 + \underline{?}$ **26.** $9 + 5 = 20 - \underline{?}$ **27.** $15 - 6 = 2 + \underline{?}$

Practicing Division

You will learn to divide amounts of money.

Why learn this? You can find the amount of money one item costs.

Ellen spent $9.90 at a book fair. She bought 6 books. Each book was the same price. How much did Ellen spend for each book?

Divide amounts of money the same as you divide whole numbers. Line up the dollar sign and decimal point.

MODEL

What is $9.90 ÷ 6?

Step 1

Divide the hundreds. 6)9

Think: $6 \times n = 6$

```
    1
6)$9.90
  -6
   3
```

Multiply. 6 × 1
Subtract. 9 − 6
Compare. 3 < 6

Step 2

Bring down the tens. Divide. 6)39

Think: $6 \times n = 36$

```
    1 6
6)$9.90
  -6
   39
  -36
    3
```

Multiply. 6 × 6
Subtract. 39 − 36
Compare. 3 < 6

Step 3

Bring down the ones. Divide. 6)30

Think: $6 \times n = 30$

```
    1 65
6)$9.90
  -6
   39
  -36
    30
   -30
     0
```

Multiply. 6 × 5
Subtract. 30 − 30
Compare. 0 < 6

Step 4

Write the quotient with a dollar sign and a decimal point.

165 ⟶ $1.65, or

```
  $1.65
6)$9.90
```

So, Ellen spent $1.65 for each book.

EXAMPLES

A.

```
     $2.04
7)$14.28
  -14
    02
    -0
    28
   -28
     0
```

B.

```
    $2.26
4)$9.04
  -8
   10
   -8
   24
  -24
    0
```

C.

```
    $1.75
4)$7.00
  -4
   30
  -28
   20
  -20
    0
```

- Why is it important to keep the digits in the quotient in the correct place-value position?

PRACTICE

Find the quotient. Place the dollar sign and decimal point in the quotient.

1. $4\overline{)\$4.20}$
2. $3\overline{)\$8.76}$
3. $6\overline{)\$7.44}$
4. $8\overline{)\$7.04}$
5. $2\overline{)\$6.28}$
6. $5\overline{)\$8.90}$
7. $7\overline{)\$6.44}$
8. $9\overline{)\$9.81}$
9. $3\overline{)\$8.52}$
10. $5\overline{)\$7.75}$
11. $4\overline{)\$23.60}$
12. $2\overline{)\$38.92}$
13. $6\overline{)\$52.14}$
14. $8\overline{)\$40.88}$
15. $9\overline{)\$61.47}$
16. $7\overline{)\$27.37}$
17. $3\overline{)\$45.06}$
18. $4\overline{)\$80.52}$
19. $6\overline{)\$34.38}$
20. $5\overline{)\$78.10}$

Mixed Applications

For Problems 21–23, use the table at the right.

DRIED FRUIT	
Fruit	Cost
1 lb raisins	$0.97
1 lb bananas	$1.49
1 lb coconut	$2.36
1 lb apples	$3.24

21. Marty needs to buy 3 pounds of bananas and 2 pounds of coconut for a dessert. He has $10.00. Does he have enough money? How much money does Marty need in all?

22. Holly's mother bought 1 pound of each fruit on the list to make trail mix. How much did she spend on dried fruit?

23. A hiking club buys 42 pounds of dried apples for a trip. How much does the hiking club spend on apples?

24. The Corner Store buys barrels of dried bananas. Each barrel has 345 pounds of bananas. The store puts 5 pounds of bananas in each bag. How many bags can the Corner Store fill?

25. **WRITE ABOUT IT** Why is it important to keep the digits in the correct place-value position when you are dividing money?

Mixed Review

Tell whether each number is *cardinal, ordinal,* or *nominal.* (pages 72–73)

26. your age
27. favorite TV channel
28. your place in line

Find the product. (pages 272–273)

29. 238×6
30. 456×9
31. 522×4
32. 618×7

MORE PRACTICE Student Handbook page H101

PART

1 Meaning of the Remainder

You will learn to understand the meaning of the remainder.	**Why learn this?** You can decide how to interpret an amount that is left over.

When you solve a division problem that has a remainder, the way you interpret the remainder depends on the situation.

Portia and Preston are building birdhouses to sell.

Problem	Division	Interpretation
They need 248 brackets for their birdhouses. The brackets come 6 to a package. How many packages will they need to buy? Since 41 packages are not enough, they need to buy 42 packages of brackets.	$\begin{array}{r} 41 \text{ r}2 \\ 6\overline{)248} \\ -24 \\ \hline 08 \\ -6 \\ \hline 2 \end{array}$	Round the quotient to the next greater whole number.
For the birdhouses, they will buy a total of 250 feet of lumber. Then, they will cut the lumber into 3-foot pieces. How many 3-foot pieces will they have? The remainder is not enough for another 3-foot piece. So, they will have a total of 83 pieces.	$\begin{array}{r} 83 \text{ r}1 \\ 3\overline{)250} \\ -24 \\ \hline 10 \\ -9 \\ \hline 1 \end{array}$	Drop the remainder.
Portia has packaged birdseed to sell. She divided 125 pounds of birdseed into 2-pound bags. How many bags of birdseed does she have? How much birdseed will be left over? She has 62 bags to sell with 1 pound left over.	$\begin{array}{r} 62 \text{ r}1 \\ 2\overline{)125} \\ -12 \\ \hline 05 \\ -4 \\ \hline 1 \end{array}$	Use the remainder as part of your answer.

Talk About It

- Why is it important to consider both the quotient and the remainder when you are solving a division problem?
- How do you know what to do with the remainder?

Calculator Activities page H60

PRACTICE

Solve. Tell how you interpret the meaning of the remainder.

1. Alex has 428 bird stamps in a collection. She can fit 8 stamps on a page. How many pages does she need?

2. Beth is making bows for the pet store. It takes 5 yards of ribbon to make a bow. She has 127 yards. How many bows can Beth make?

3. Mrs. Murphy stuffs her pillows with 3 pounds of duck feathers. She has 67 pounds of feathers. How many pillows can she stuff? How many pounds of feathers will be left over?

4. Georgie's Bird Palace keeps 4 parakeets to a cage. It has 270 parakeets in all. How many cages are needed?

Mixed Applications

For Problems 5–7 and 9, use the table at the right.

5. The Westside Bird-Watchers Club went hiking on Saturday. They recorded the number of birds they spotted. How many birds in all did they see on Saturday?

6. The Westside Bird-Watchers Club spotted wrens and warblers. How many more wrens than warblers did they see?

7. Pedro went bird-watching again on Sunday. He spotted 3 times as many warblers on Sunday as the club spotted on Saturday. How many warblers did Pedro see on Sunday?

8. The first week, 1,000 pizzas were sold. In the second week, 1,250 pizzas were sold. In the third week, 1,500 pizzas were sold. If this pattern continues, how many pizzas will be sold in the fourth week?

9. **Write a problem** that can be solved by using division. Use information from the table.

BIRDS SPOTTED ON SATURDAY

KIND	HOW MANY
Eagles	2
Wrens	126
Sparrows	39
Warblers	76

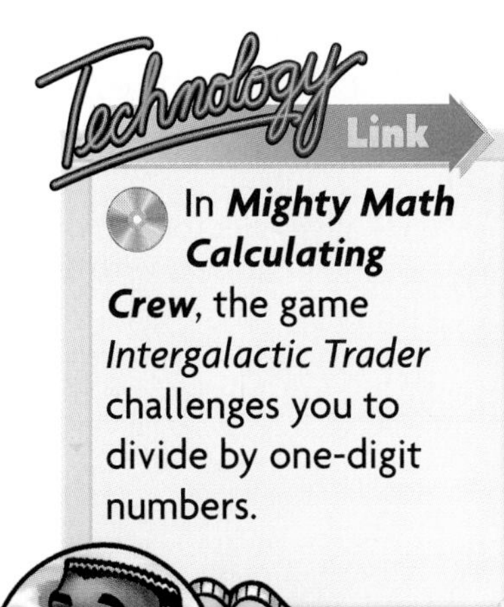

Technology Link

In ***Mighty Math Calculating Crew***, the game *Intergalactic Trader* challenges you to divide by one-digit numbers.

LESSON CONTINUES

PART 2 PROBLEM-SOLVING
Account for All Possibilities

THE PROBLEM **Hector has about 120 minutes before dinner to deliver his 20 wrapping-paper orders. It takes him about 9 minutes to deliver an order. How many orders can Hector deliver? How can Hector plan to use the time he has?**

✓ Understand

- What are you asked to find?
- What information will you use?
- Is there any information you will not use? If so, what?

✓ Plan

- What plan can you make to solve the problem?

You can account for all the possible ways Hector can use the time he has to make his deliveries. Then, decide what is the best way to use the time.

✓ Solve

- How can you solve the problem?

You can divide to find the number of orders Hector can deliver in 120 minutes. Then plan the best way to deliver the orders.

$$\begin{array}{r} 13\text{ r}3 \\ 9\overline{)120} \\ -9 \\ \hline 30 \\ -27 \\ \hline 3 \end{array}$$

Hector can deliver 13 orders with 3 minutes left over. If Hector delivers 13 orders, he will have time left before dinner.

or

$$9\overline{)120} \quad 13\text{ r}3 \rightarrow 14$$

$$\begin{array}{r} 14 \\ \times\ 9 \\ \hline 126 \end{array}$$

If Hector delivers 14 orders, it will take 126 minutes, and he may be late for dinner.

So, Hector's best plan is to deliver the 13 orders, so that he will have 3 minutes left over to return home for dinner.

✓ Look Back

- How can you decide if your answer is reasonable?
- What is another way to solve the problem?

PRACTICE

CHOOSE Paper/Pencil Calculator Hands-on Mental Math

Solve. Account for all the possibilities.

1. Robyn has a 137-page book to read for school. She has 8 nights to read the book. How many pages should Robyn read each night? How can Robyn use the time she has?

2. Carol collected 142 baskets. She wants to hang an equal number of baskets on each of 3 walls in her kitchen. How many baskets can she hang on each wall? How can she best use the space she has?

3. Josh has 300 pounds of paper to recycle in 7 boxes. How many pounds is this for each box? How can Josh best use the boxes he has?

4. Luke baby-sits for a neighbor. Last month he earned $57.00. He worked for 6 days. How much did Luke earn each day?

Mixed Applications

Solve.

CHOOSE A STRATEGY

- **Use a Table**
- **Work Backward**
- **Write a Number Sentence**
- **Find a Pattern**

5. Stevie guessed that there are about 3,000 books in the Reading Room. Is his estimate close? How many books are there in all?

6. The South Branch Public Library has 1,030 mystery books. How many more mystery books does it have than the Reading Room?

READING ROOM BOOKS

Type	Number
mystery	637
sports	492
animal stories	541
funny stories	829
adventure	703

7. Mr. Harrison knows that there are 5 times as many sports books at the store as there are in the Reading Room. How many sports books are there at the book store?

8. The Reading Room is ordering 6 new shelves to hold the funny stories. An equal number of books will be placed on each shelf. How many books will there be on each shelf?

9. Lucy collected 2 pennies on Monday, 4 pennies on Tuesday, and 8 pennies on Wednesday. If this pattern continues, how many pennies will she collect on Sunday?

10. José has $156.67 in the bank. This month he deposited $25.00 and withdrew $10.00. Then his parents deposited $45.00. How much money did José have at the beginning of the month?

MORE PRACTICE Student Handbook page H102

Finding the Average

You will investigate finding the average of a set of numbers.

Why learn this? You can average sets of numbers, such as grades.

WORD POWER
average
mean

An **average**, or a **mean**, is one way to find a number that best represents all the numbers in a set. You can use unit cubes to find the average.

Use the data from the table. What was the average number of baskets scored by Julio?

MODEL

What is the average of 2, 6, 5, 4, and 3?

Step 1

Use unit cubes. Make stacks of cubes to model the number of points scored by Julio each day.

Mon | Tue | Wed | Thu | Fri

Step 2

Arrange the stacks in order from the shortest to the tallest.

Step 3

To find the average, make the 5 stacks equal.

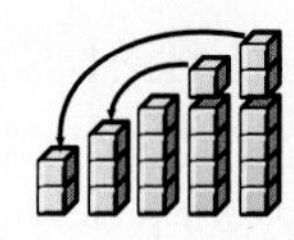

Notice that

- each equal stack has 4 cubes in it. The average is 4.
- the average falls between the least and the greatest numbers.

So, the average number of baskets scored was 4.

The median is the middle number in an ordered series of numbers.

Example
2, 3, 4, 5, 6
median

Explore

Use unit cubes and the data in the table at the right to find the average number of students in fourth-grade clubs.

MATERIALS: unit cubes

FOURTH-GRADE CLUBS	
Club	**Number of Students**
Drama	6
Art	4
Music	5
Spanish	9

Record

Find the average number of students in fourth-grade clubs. Draw a picture to show how you got your answer.

Technology Link
E-Lab • Activity 19 Available on CD-ROM and the Internet at http://www.hbschool.com/elab

CRITICAL THINKING Can the average of a set of numbers ever be greater than the greatest number in the set? Explain.

Try This

Mr. Henri wanted to find the average number of art projects in three rooms. He counted 7 projects in one room, 9 in another room, and 11 in another room. Use unit cubes and draw a picture to show the average number of art projects that Mr. Henri counted in each room.

TALK ABOUT IT How did you use the cubes to find the average?

WRITE ABOUT IT Explain how finding an average is like dividing to find equal groups.

HANDS-ON PRACTICE

Find the average of each set of numbers by using unit cubes.

1. 8, 9, 11, 15, 17

2. 4, 7, 12, 13, 14, 16

3. 5, 10, 18, 19

4. 12, 14, 16, 18

5. 9, 13, 15, 15, 18

6. 21, 24, 27

Mixed Applications

For Problems 7–9, use the table at the right.

Number of Books Read

Name	Total Number Read
Andy	65
Marsha	51
Jennifer	47
Tasha	28
Quentin	21

7. Mrs. Jasper made a chart to show the 5 students who read the most books in her class for the year. How many books did these students read in all?

8. Marsha loves to read. How many more books did Marsha read than Tasha?

9. The librarian gives prizes for every 5 books read. How many prizes can Andy get?

10. Sharonda has a book with 125 pages to read. If she reads 8 pages a night, can she read her book in 2 weeks? Explain.

MORE PRACTICE Student Handbook page H102

Choosing the Operation

You will learn that addition, subtraction, multiplication, and division are used to solve different kinds of problems.

Why learn this? You can choose the correct operation to solve a problem.

Number relationships in a problem can help you decide whether to add, subtract, multiply, or divide.

Add	• Joining groups of different sizes
Subtract	• Taking away or comparing groups
Multiply	• Joining equal-sized groups
Divide	• Separating into equal-sized groups • Finding how many in each group

Study the problems. Use the chart to help you choose the operation needed to solve each problem.

The Smith family is planning a family reunion.

A. There will be 384 relatives attending the reunion. Each table seats 8 people. How many tables will the Smith family need?

B. Jimmy Smith drove 1,452 miles to the reunion. Sharon Smith drove 967 miles to the reunion. How many more miles did Jimmy Smith drive than Sharon Smith?

C. The food for the reunion picnic includes 24 pounds of hot dogs, 35 pounds of hamburger, and 67 pounds of chicken. How many pounds of meat is this in all?

D. The reunion committee has bought 25 packages of paper plates. Each package has 16 plates. Will there be enough plates for the Smith family?

- What are you asked to find in each of the problems A–D? What facts are given?

Check Your Understanding

1. Work with a partner to solve problems A–D. What operation did you use?
2. What other step do you need in order to solve Problem D?

PRACTICE

Solve. Name the operation you used.

3. Mr. Smith drives 26 miles round trip to work. He makes this trip 22 times a month. How many miles does he drive a month?

4. Tim Smith is writing a book. His book will have 500 pages. He has written 272 pages. How many more pages does Tim have to write?

5. There will be a talent show during the Smith family reunion. The show will last 102 minutes. If each act lasts 6 minutes, how many acts will be in the talent show?

6. Carlotta is selling pictures of the Smith family reunion. Each picture costs $4.85. If 68 family members each buy one picture, how much money will Carlotta get?

Mixed Applications

For Problems 7–8, use the table at the right.

7. A truck travels from Salt Lake City to Denver. The trip takes 8 hours one way. How many miles does the truck travel in one hour?

ROAD MILEAGE TO DENVER, COLORADO			
City	Miles	City	Miles
Dallas, TX	797	Chicago, IL	1,017
Salt Lake City, UT	496	Phoenix, AZ	904

8. Larry lives in Chicago. He drives to Denver twice a month. How many miles is this round trip each month?

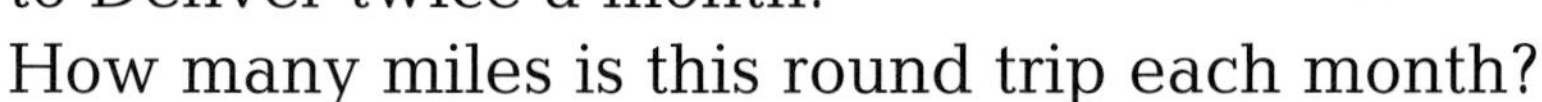

9. A bus going to Denver leaves Salt Lake City at 7:15 A.M. The trip takes $11\frac{1}{2}$ hours. At what time will the bus arrive in Denver?

10. **WRITE ABOUT IT** Explain how you know what operation to use when solving a problem.

Mixed Review

Round each factor. Estimate the product. (pages 286–287)

11. $22 \times 51 = n$ **12.** $84 \times 68 = n$ **13.** $74 \times 19 = n$ **14.** $187 \times 81 = n$

What kind of line relationship is each? Write *intersecting, parallel*, or *perpendicular*. (pages 214–215)

15. 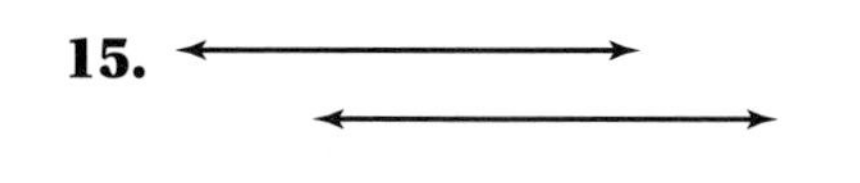

16. 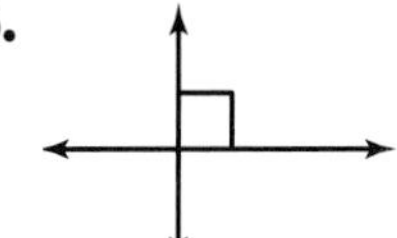

17. 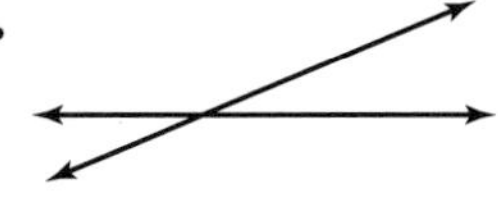

MORE PRACTICE Student Handbook page H102

MATH FUN!

JACKS

PURPOSE To practice division

YOU WILL NEED 20 connecting cubes or other small objects; spinner labeled 2, 3, 5, 10; small rubber ball

Play with a partner. The first player puts out between 10 and 20 cubes. The second player spins a number and decides if the number of cubes can be divided evenly by that number.

Then the second player tosses up the ball and tries to pick up the cubes in groups equal to the number on the spinner.

If the prediction was correct, the player scores the same number of points as the divisor.

Switch roles and play again. The first player to score 35 points wins.

Number Puzzles

PURPOSE To practice multiplication and division

From the eight numbers below, find four pairs of factors with a product of 180. You may use a calculator.

30, 2, 5, 90, 4, 36, 6, 45

From the ten numbers below, find five pairs of numbers with a quotient of 24.

7, 72, 4, 6, 96, 120, 144, 5, 3, 168

Challenge your family to figure out these number puzzles.

GREATEST QUOTIENT

PURPOSE To practice division

YOU WILL NEED paper and pencil, number cards (0-9)

Play in groups of four or five. Draw a division symbol on your paper with one blank for the divisor and three blanks for the dividend.

Shuffle the cards and lay them face down on the table. One player draws a number card. All players write that number in one of the blank positions on their paper. Return the card to the table.

Continue in the same way until all blanks are filled. The player with the largest quotient gets 1 point. The first player to earn 5 points wins the game.

Player 1 $5\overline{)647}$

Player 2 $4\overline{)756}$

CHAPTER 19 REVIEW

✓ CHECK UNDERSTANDING

1. **VOCABULARY** The __?__ is one way to find a number that best represents all the numbers in a set. (page 326)

Estimate. Use a pattern of zeros to find the quotient. (pages 316–317)

2. $615 \div 3 = n$
3. $3{,}869 \div 8 = n$
4. $16{,}235 \div 4 = n$
5. $24{,}798 \div 5 = n$

Solve. Tell how you interpret the remainder. (pages 322–323)

6. Debbie needs 109 stars. There are 8 stars in a package. How many packages does she need?
7. Mr. Neil made 148 cards for 6 classes. He gave each class the same number of cards. How many cards did each class receive?

Solve. Name the operation you used. (pages 328–329)

8. The box factory gave away 620 sheets of poster board. Larry's class used 286 sheets. How many sheets are left?
9. Andrea cut 54 pieces of ribbon. Each piece was 12 inches long. How many inches is this altogether?

✓ CHECK SKILLS

Find the quotient. (pages 318–321)

10. $4\overline{)435}$
11. $6\overline{)\$8.10}$
12. $6\overline{)365}$
13. $9\overline{)504}$
14. $6\overline{)330}$
15. $8\overline{)481}$
16. $8\overline{)\$9.60}$
17. $5\overline{)527}$

✓ CHECK PROBLEM SOLVING

Solve. (pages 324–325)

CHOOSE A STRATEGY

- **Find a Pattern**
- **Work Backward**
- **Write a Number Sentence**
- **Make a Model**

18. Jerrika saved 123 birthday cards in 6 years. About how many cards is this each year?
19. Kerry spent $15.45 on 3 pounds of turkey. How much did the turkey cost for each pound?
20. A fisherman has 6 boxes. He caught 255 lobsters. How many lobsters can he put in each box? How can the fisherman best use the boxes?
21. Cherry mailed 4 small boxes and 1 large box. The postage was $23.48. The large box cost $5.36 to ship. What was the cost of each small box?

CHAPTERS 16–19

STUDY GUIDE & REVIEW

VOCABULARY CHECK

WORD BANK
- average, or mean
- multiple
- partial product
- remainder

Choose a term from the box to complete each sentence.

1. A _?_ is the product of a given number and another whole number. (page 266)

2. When the ones and tens are multiplied separately, each product is called a _?_. (page 270)

3. A _?_ is an amount left over when you divide. (page 300)

4. The _?_ is one number that best represents all numbers in a set. (page 326)

STUDY AND SOLVE

CHAPTER 16

EXAMPLE

```
   1
 945
×  2
1,890
```

1. Multiply the ones. Regroup.
2. Multiply the tens. Add the regrouped ten.
3. Multiply the hundreds.

Use mental math and basic multiplication facts to find the product. (pages 266–267)

5. $6 \times 800 = \underline{?}$ **6.** $4 \times 3,000 = \underline{?}$

Find the product. (pages 270–275)

7. 25×7 **8.** 46×5

9. 79×8 **10.** 621×3

11. $\$2.82 \times 6$ **12.** 576×4

Solve. (pages 276–277)

13. The fourth grade has 4 classes with 25 students in each class. How many fourth-grade students are there in all?

14. Maria bought 3 notebooks for $2.99 each. How much did she spend?

CHAPTER 17

EXAMPLE

```
    1 1
  $5.23
×    75
  26.15
+366.10
$392.25
```

1. Multiply. $5.23 × 5
2. Multiply. $5.23 × 70
3. Add the partial products.

Use mental math and basic facts to solve. (pages 282–283)

15. $2 \times 900 = n$ **16.** $80 \times 40 = n$

17. $40 \times 700 = n$ **18.** $50 \times 800 = n$

Round each factor to its greatest place-value position. Estimate the product. (pages 286–287)

19. $\begin{array}{r} 12 \\ \times 77 \\ \hline \end{array}$

20. $\begin{array}{r} 783 \\ \times\ 41 \\ \hline \end{array}$

21. $\$581 \times 17 = n$

22. $813 \times 87 = n$

Find the product. (pages 290–293)

23. $\begin{array}{r} 57 \\ \times 18 \\ \hline \end{array}$

24. $\begin{array}{r} 36 \\ \times 42 \\ \hline \end{array}$

25. $\begin{array}{r} 188 \\ \times\ 29 \\ \hline \end{array}$

26. $\begin{array}{r} 470 \\ \times\ 62 \\ \hline \end{array}$

27. $\$216 \times 29 = n$

28. $479 \times 81 = n$

Solve. (pages 284–285)

29. Ms. Boatman has 27 students in her class. Last month each student worked 12 hours as a volunteer. How many hours did the students work in all?

30. Each week, Mr. Montoya travels 230 miles to and from his job. How many miles does he travel in 16 weeks?

CHAPTER 18

EXAMPLE

$$\begin{array}{r} 21 \text{ r}2 \\ 3\overline{)65} \\ -6 \\ \hline 05 \\ -\ 3 \\ \hline 2 \end{array}$$

1. Divide.
2. Multiply.
3. Subtract.
4. Compare remainder with quotient.
5. Bring down.
6. Repeat as needed.

Find the quotient. (pages 300–305, 308–311)

31. $4\overline{)60}$

32. $6\overline{)76}$

33. $3\overline{)48}$

34. $5\overline{)79}$

35. $439 \div 9 = n$

36. $198 \div 7 = n$

Solve. (pages 306–307)

37. During the past 6 months, 252 customers had a satellite dish installed. How many customers is this each month?

CHAPTER 19

EXAMPLE

$$\begin{array}{r} 108 \text{ r}5 \\ 8\overline{)869} \\ -8 \\ \hline 06 \\ -\ 0 \\ \hline 69 \\ -64 \\ \hline 5 \end{array}$$

1. Divide.
2. Multiply.
3. Subtract.
4. Compare remainder with quotient.
5. Bring down.
6. Repeat as needed.

Find the quotient. (pages 318–321)

38. $5\overline{)525}$

39. $6\overline{)655}$

40. $7\overline{)\$7.28}$

41. $4\overline{)\$1.84}$

42. $838 \div 8 = n$

43. $508 \div 9 = n$

Solve. Tell how you interpret the remainder. (pages 322–323)

44. Rebecca has 86 pictures to put into a photo album. She can fit 4 pictures on a page. How many pages does she need?

CHAPTERS 16–19

WHAT DID I LEARN?

WRITE ABOUT IT

1. Explain the pattern you see in this group of problems. Then explain how to use mental math and basic facts to find the products and name the products.

   $4 \times 7 = \underline{?}$
   $4 \times 70 = \underline{?}$
   $4 \times 700 = \underline{?}$
   $4 \times 7{,}000 = \underline{?}$

   (pages 266–267)

2. Show each step as you find the product 24×36. (pages 290–291)

3. Explain each step as you find these quotients.

   $4\overline{)35}$ $4\overline{)93}$

   Explain how you know when there will be a remainder in a division problem. (pages 300–303)

4. Explain each step as you find the quotient $\$38.25 \div 5 = n$. (pages 320–321)

PERFORMANCE ASSESSMENT

Solve. Explain your method.

CHOOSE A STRATEGY

• Find a Pattern • Act It Out • Make a Model • Draw a Picture • Write a Number Sentence

5. Ryan worked 8 hours and Becky worked 10 hours. They each earned $4.00 an hour. Together they earned exactly enough money for 6 hockey sticks. How much did each hockey stick cost? (pages 276–277)

6. When Rosa says 5, the answer is 100. When she says 60, the answer is 1,200. When she says 700, the answer is 14,000. What is the pattern? How did you find the pattern? (pages 284–285)

7. Mr. Miller took 75 students on a trip. After he put the students in equal groups, there were 5 students left over. How many groups were formed? How many students were in each group? (pages 306–307)

8. Kimi wants to serve milk and cookies to 20 children. She has six 64-ounce bottles of milk and 7 dozen chocolate chip cookies. Kimi has cups that hold 8 ounces. How many cups of milk will each child get? How can she best share the milk? (pages 324–325)

CUMULATIVE REVIEW

Solve the problem. Then write the letter of the correct answer. (pages 6–7)

1. $\begin{array}{r} 688 \\ +454 \\ \hline \end{array}$

A. 234 **B.** 1,032 **C.** 1,042 **D.** 1,142

2. $\begin{array}{r} 8,001 \\ -3,469 \\ \hline \end{array}$

A. 4,532
B. 4,642
C. 5,468
D. 11,470 (pages 22–23)

3. Bill has 30 marbles. He has twice as many red marbles as blue marbles and he has 6 green marbles. How many red marbles does he have?

A. 8 **B.** 10
C. 16 **D.** 24 (pages 80–81)

4. What is the probability of pulling a green marble if all the marbles in Problem 3 are put into a bag?

A. $\frac{6}{30}$, or $\frac{1}{5}$ **B.** $\frac{16}{30}$, or $\frac{8}{15}$
C. $\frac{24}{30}$, or $\frac{4}{5}$ **D.** $\frac{30}{6}$, or $\frac{5}{1}$ (pages 178–179)

5. Eggs are packed 12 to a box. How many eggs are in 144 boxes?

A. 12 eggs **B.** 132 eggs
C. 156 eggs **D.** 1,728 eggs

(pages 292–293)

Order the numbers from the least to the greatest. (pages 112–113)

6. 6,043; 6,041; 6,139

A. 6,139; 6,043; 6,041
B. 6,139; 6,041; 6,043
C. 6,041; 6,043; 6,139
D. 6,043; 6,041; 6,139

7. It is __?__ that you will spin an even number.
(pages 172–173)

A. certain **B.** impossible
C. likely **D.** unlikely

8. Which is a line segment?

A. 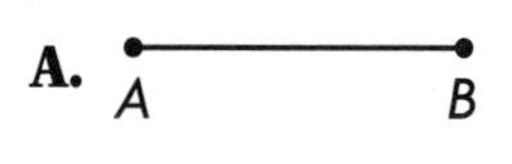

B. 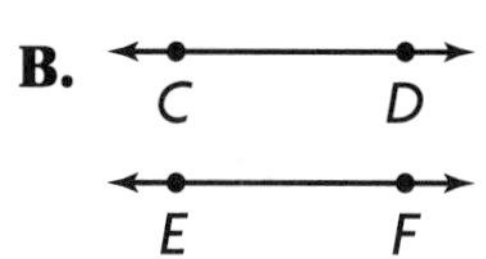

C. G H

D. 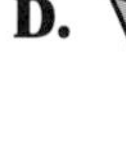 

(pages 210–211)

9. What is the area of a rectangle that has a length of 15 meters and a width of 10 meters?

A. 5 sq m **B.** 25 sq m
C. 50 sq m **D.** 150 sq m

(pages 234–235)

10. $\begin{array}{r} 546 \\ \times\ 23 \\ \hline \end{array}$

A. 523 **B.** 569
C. 11,308 **D.** 12,558

(pages 290–291)

11. Dinner at a restaurant is $26.40 for a family of 4. Each person spends the same amount. What is the cost for each person?
(pages 320–321)

A. $6.60 **B.** $7.40
C. $8.00 **D.** $9.50

CHAPTER 20 UNDERSTANDING FRACTIONS

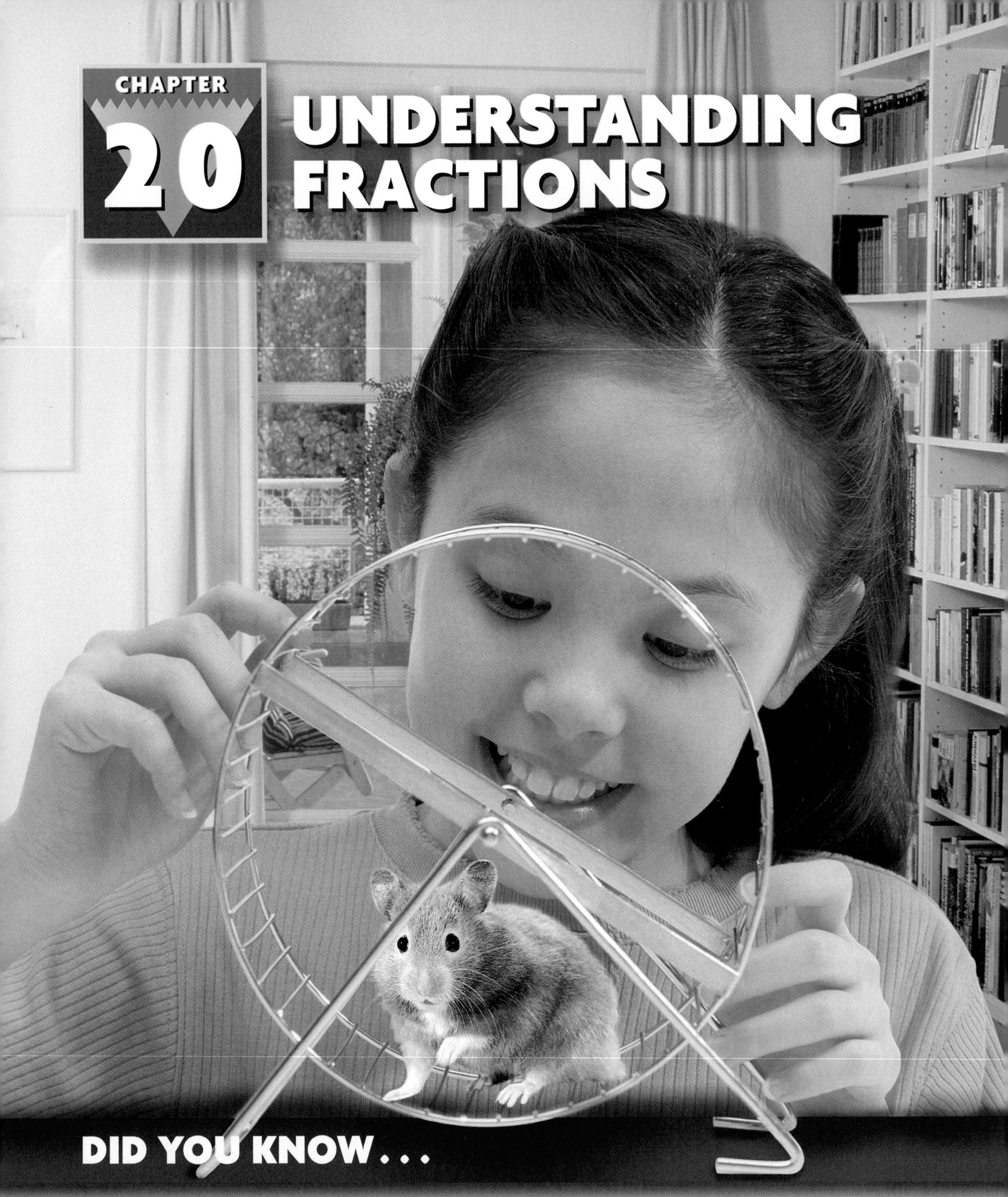

DID YOU KNOW . . .

The name hamster means to hoard or hide away. Hamsters use cheek-pouches to collect large amounts of food.

They are nocturnal or night animals and so they tuck away the food for a midday snack.

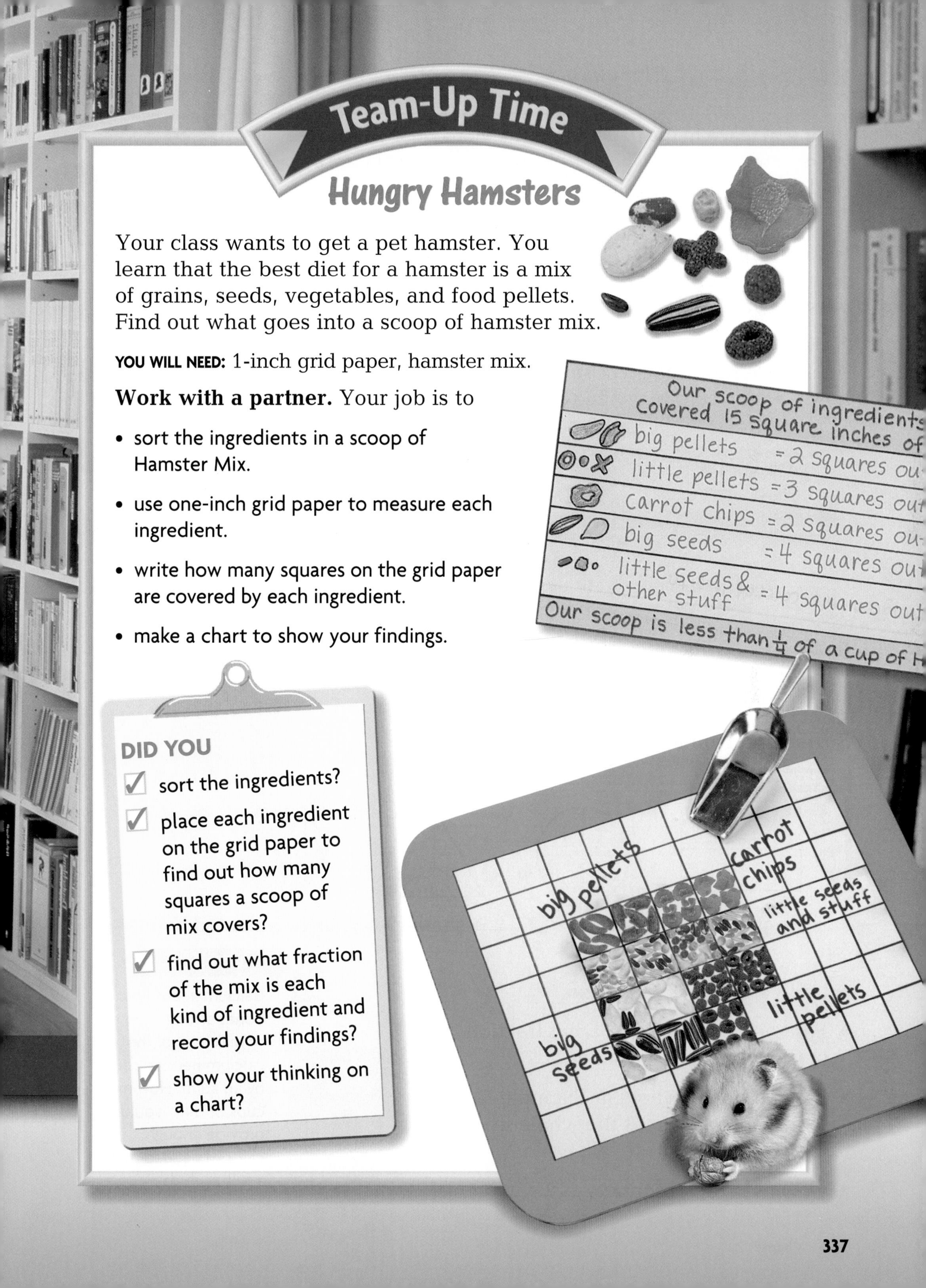

Team-Up Time

Hungry Hamsters

Your class wants to get a pet hamster. You learn that the best diet for a hamster is a mix of grains, seeds, vegetables, and food pellets. Find out what goes into a scoop of hamster mix.

YOU WILL NEED: 1-inch grid paper, hamster mix.

Work with a partner. Your job is to

- sort the ingredients in a scoop of Hamster Mix.
- use one-inch grid paper to measure each ingredient.
- write how many squares on the grid paper are covered by each ingredient.
- make a chart to show your findings.

DID YOU

- ✓ sort the ingredients?
- ✓ place each ingredient on the grid paper to find out how many squares a scoop of mix covers?
- ✓ find out what fraction of the mix is each kind of ingredient and record your findings?
- ✓ show your thinking on a chart?

Fractions: Part of a Whole

You will learn to use fractions to represent part of a whole and to read and write fractions.

Why learn this? You will use fractions when you share a snack with someone or mix food for a pet.

WORD POWER
fraction

Mike, Conner, and Nicole shared a sub sandwich equally. What fraction of the sandwich did each person eat?

A **fraction** is a number that names a part of a whole. The whole represents 1. Use fraction bars to show how 1 whole can be divided into 3 equal parts.

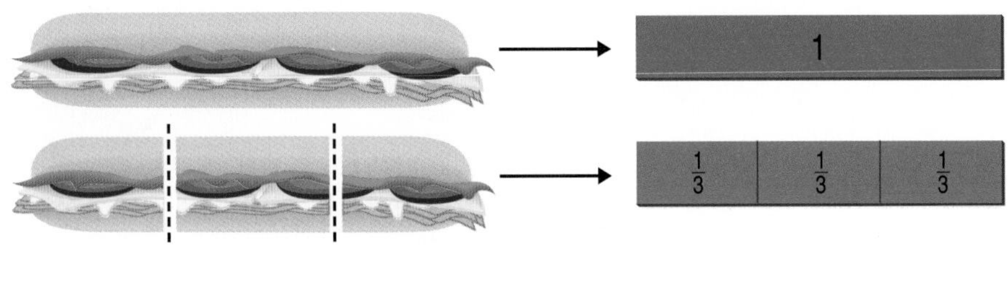

each person's part ⟶ $\mathbf{1}$ ⟵ numerator
total equal parts ⟶ $\mathbf{3}$ ⟵ denominator

Read: one third
one out of three
one divided by three

Write: $\frac{1}{3}$

So, each person ate $\frac{1}{3}$ of the sub sandwich.

REMEMBER:

The **numerator** is the number above the bar in a fraction. It tells how many parts are being considered.

The **denominator** is the number below the bar. It tells the total number of equal parts.

EXAMPLES

A. $\frac{1}{2}$ | $\frac{1}{2}$

$\frac{1}{2}$ is shaded.

B.

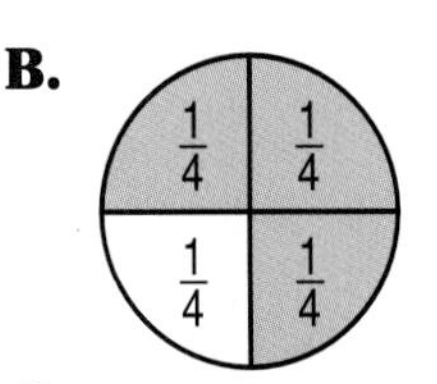

$\frac{3}{4}$ is shaded.

C.

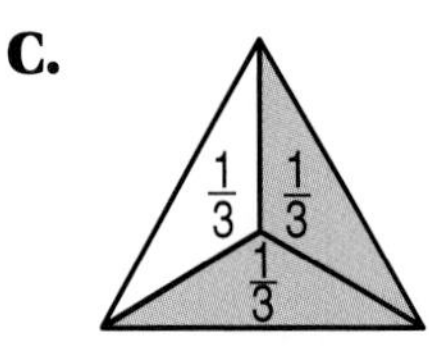

$\frac{2}{3}$ is shaded.

D.

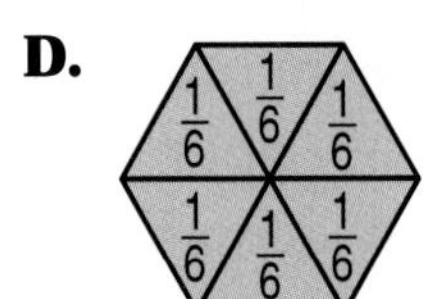

$\frac{6}{6}$, or 1, is shaded.

Talk About It

- For each example, tell what fraction of the whole is not shaded.
- If $\frac{6}{6}$ names the whole in Example D, what fraction names the whole in the other examples?
- How can you describe $\frac{1}{3}$ as 1 divided by 3?

Health Link

Calcium keeps your bones strong. One cup of milk has $\frac{1}{3}$ of the calcium needed daily by an adult. How many cups of milk would provide enough calcium needed by an adult each day?

PRACTICE

Copy and complete the table.

	Model	Write	Read
		$\frac{1}{2}$	one half, one out of two, one divided by two
1.		?	?
2.	?	$\frac{2}{3}$	?
3.	?	?	three fifths, three out of five, three divided by five
4.		?	?

What fraction is shaded? What fraction is not shaded?

5. 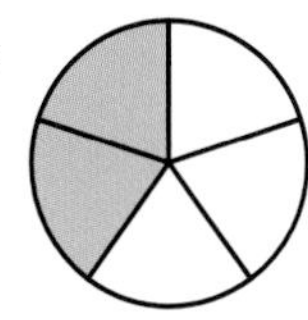

6. 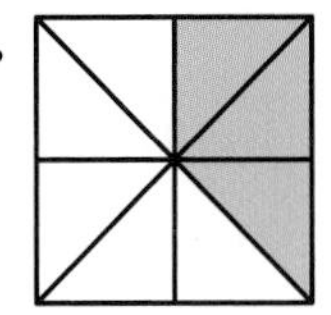

7. 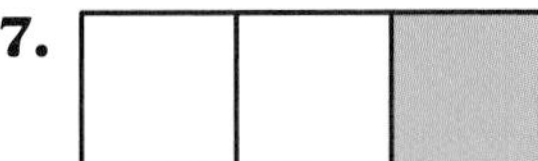

8. 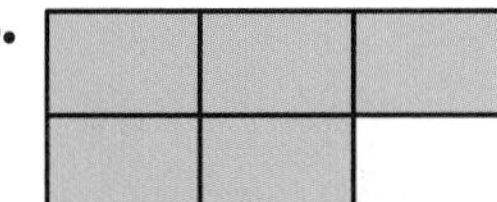

Draw a picture and shade part of it to show the fraction.

9. $\frac{1}{3}$ **10.** $\frac{3}{5}$ **11.** $\frac{2}{3}$ **12.** $\frac{4}{6}$ **13.** $\frac{6}{8}$

For Exercises 14–17, use the figure at the right.

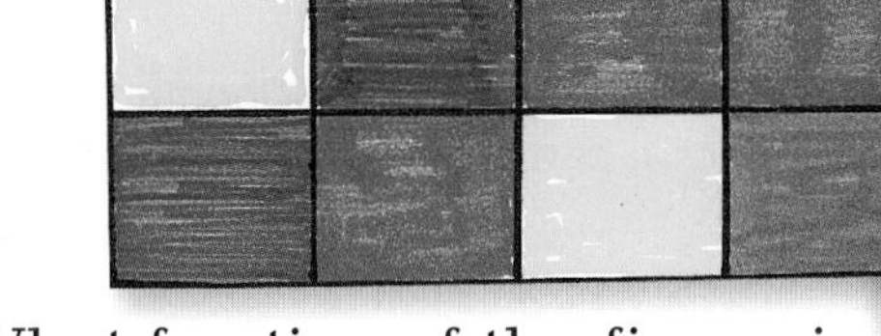

14. What fraction of the figure is red?

15. What fraction of the figure is not blue?

16. What fraction of the figure is not yellow or red?

17. What fraction of the figure is red, blue, yellow, or green?

Mixed Applications

18. Three friends ordered one sub sandwich for $2.69 and 3 small fruit drinks for $0.89 each. What was the total bill for these items?

19. **WRITE ABOUT IT** Explain why it is possible that $\frac{1}{2}$ of your allowance is more than $\frac{1}{2}$ of your friend's allowance.

Mixed Review

Find the quotient. (pages 310–311)

20. $3\overline{)168}$ **21.** $5\overline{)320}$ **22.** $4\overline{)292}$ **23.** $7\overline{)609}$

Write the time as it would appear on a digital clock. (pages 120–121)

24. five minutes past one **25.** ten minutes before nine **26.** two-thirty

MORE PRACTICE Student Handbook page H102

Fractions: Part of a Group

You will learn to use fractions to represent part of a group and to read and write fractions.

Why learn this? You will use fractions when you share a plate of cookies, or a box of crayons with someone.

Sonia put cookies on two plates. Each plate has 6 cookies. What fraction of the cookies on each plate are chocolate?

A fraction can also name a part of a group. Use counters to show the cookies.

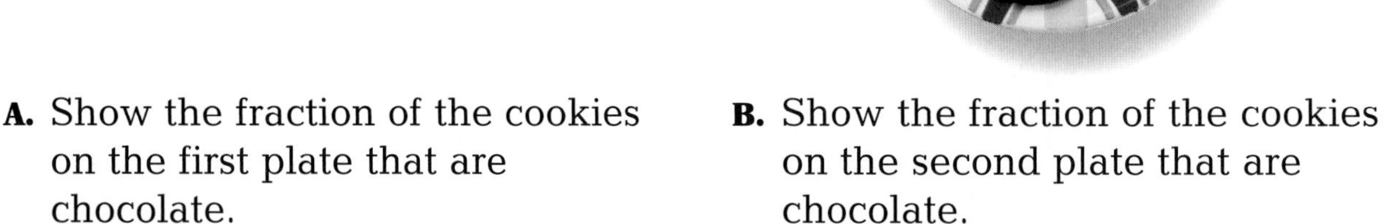

A. Show the fraction of the cookies on the first plate that are chocolate.

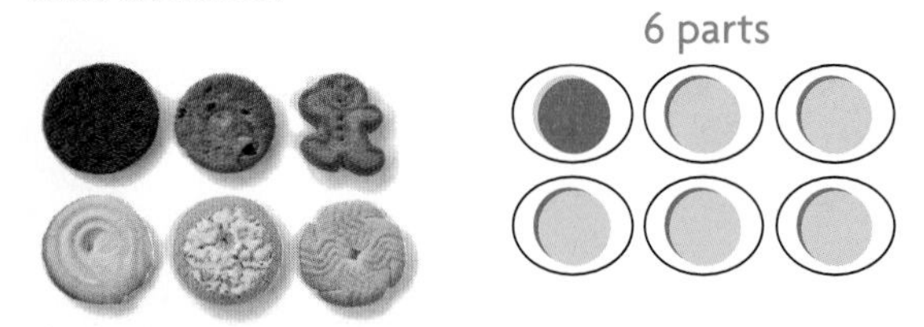

part chocolate — **1** — numerator
number of equal parts — **6** — denominator

Read: one sixth
one out of six
one divided by six

Write: $\frac{1}{6}$

So, $\frac{1}{6}$ of the cookies on the first plate are chocolate.

B. Show the fraction of the cookies on the second plate that are chocolate.

part chocolate — **1** — numerator
number of equal parts — **3** — denominator

Read: one third
one out of three
one divided by three

Write: $\frac{1}{3}$

So, $\frac{1}{3}$ of the cookies on the second plate are chocolate.

Talk About It

- For each example, tell how many parts are chocolate and how many equal parts there are.
- Draw a picture that shows 6 cookies in 2 equal parts. Write a fraction to represent the cookies that are raisin.
- How would you show $\frac{0}{5}$ of a group?

CRITICAL THINKING How is part of a group different from part of a whole? Explain.

Technology Link

In ***Mighty Math Number Heroes***, the game *Fraction Fireworks* challenges you to make fireworks to compare fractions.

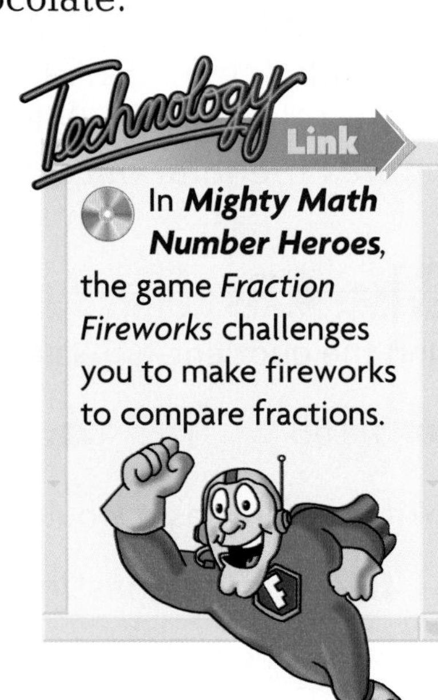

PRACTICE

What fraction of the parts is shaded? What fraction is not shaded?

1. 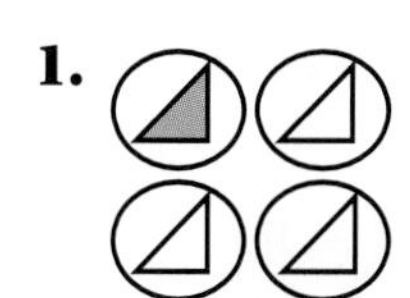
2. 
3. 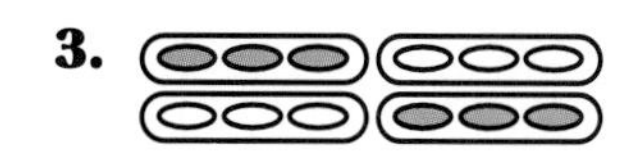
4. 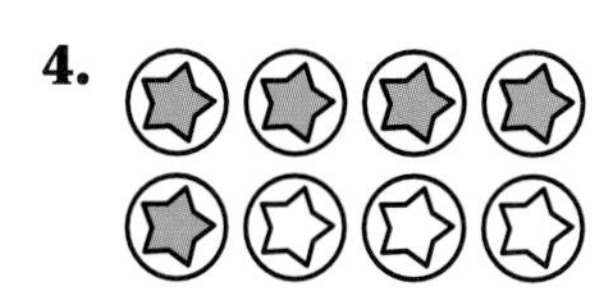
5. 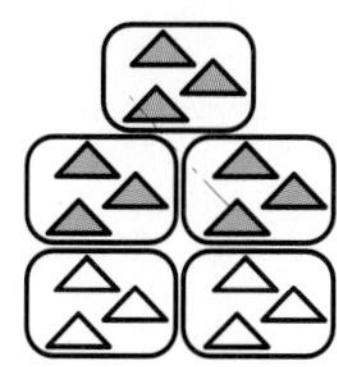
6. 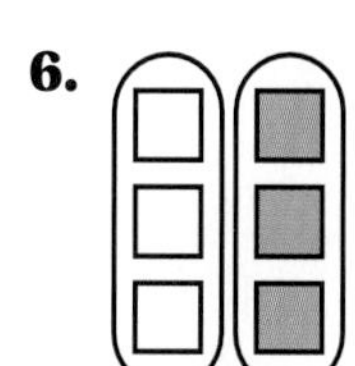
7. 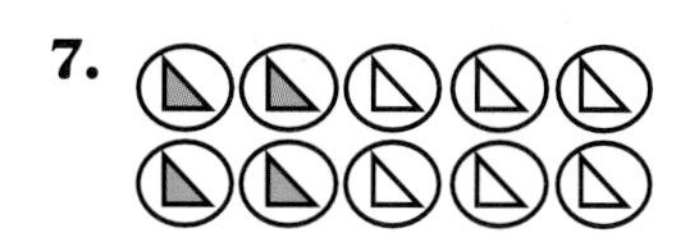
8. 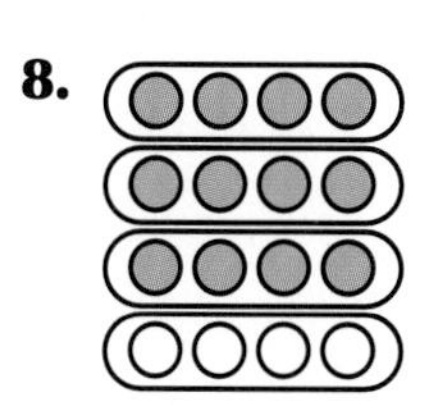

Draw the picture and shade 1 part. Write the fraction for the shaded part.

9. 5 circles
   5 parts
10. 9 stars
    3 parts
11. 4 squares
    4 parts
12. 6 triangles
    2 parts

Mixed Applications

13. Ms. Webber is buying fruit drinks for a class party. The drinks come in six-packs. She plans to have enough drinks for 3 students to share a six-pack. What fraction of a six-pack does each student drink?

14. How much money can Drew save by buying one box of a dozen eggs for $0.96 rather than 2 boxes of a half-dozen eggs for $0.59 each?

15. If 2 cups of flour are used to make 24 cookies, how many cookies can be made with 4 cups of flour?

16. **Write a problem** for which you need to name a fraction. Use the 8 bags of fruit snacks that come in a box as your groups.

Mixed Review

Write the greatest place-value position in which the digits differ. Write the greater number. (pages 106–107)

17. 76; 72
18. 365; 384
19. 2,189; 2,275
20. 408; 395

Write the area and the perimeter of each shaded figure. (pages 236–237)

21. 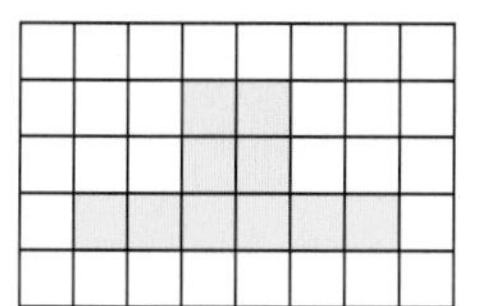
22. 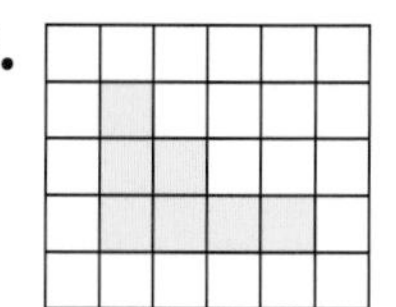
23. 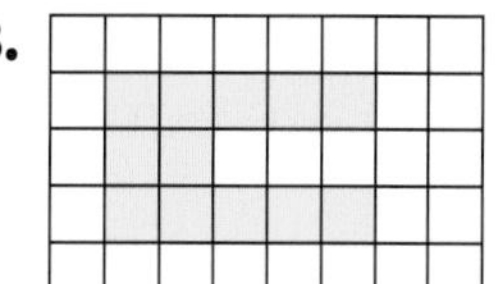
24. 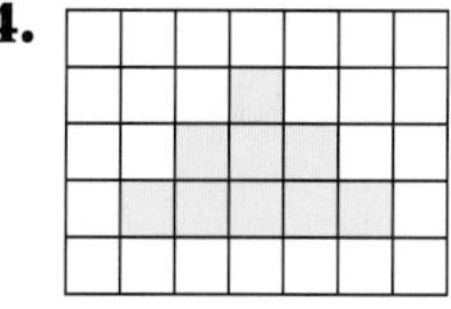

Equivalent Fractions

You will investigate equivalent fractions.

Why learn this? You can recognize that two fractional parts name the same amount.

WORD POWER

equivalent fraction

Fractions that name the same amount are called **equivalent fractions**.

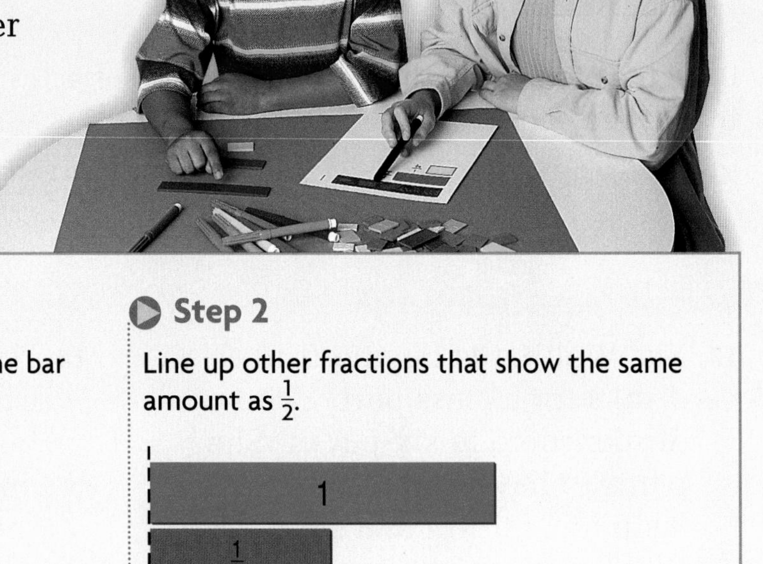

Explore

Use fraction bars to model other fractions that name $\frac{1}{2}$.

MATERIALS: fraction bars

MODEL

Step 1

Start with the bar for 1. Then line up the bar for $\frac{1}{2}$.

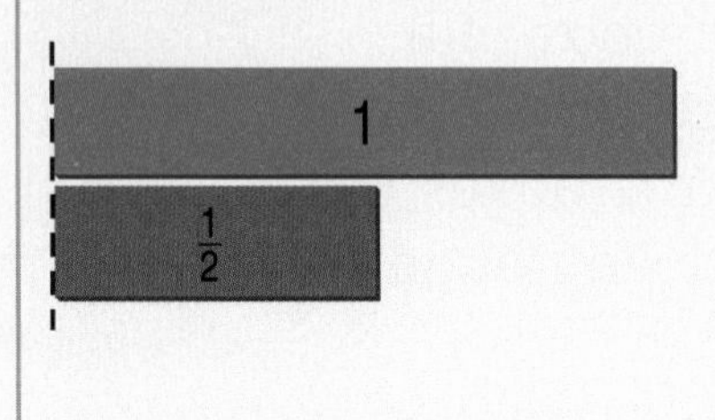

Step 2

Line up other fractions that show the same amount as $\frac{1}{2}$.

1

$\frac{1}{2}$

$\frac{1}{4}$ ← $\frac{1}{4}$

Record

Draw a picture of each model and record the fractions.

Now, investigate finding equivalent fractions.

Try This

Find an equivalent fraction for each.

$\frac{3}{4}$ $\frac{8}{12}$ $\frac{1}{6}$ $\frac{4}{8}$

WRITE ABOUT IT Explain how to draw a model to decide whether $\frac{1}{2}$ and $\frac{6}{10}$ are equivalent.

Calculator Activities page H64

HANDS-ON PRACTICE

Use fraction bars to model an equivalent fraction for each. Draw a picture of each model and record the fractions.

1. 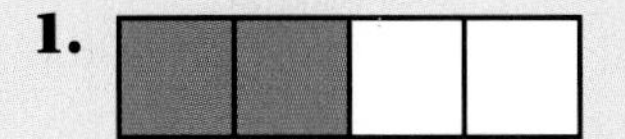

2.

3.

4.

Applying What You Learned

Find an equivalent fraction. Use fraction bars.

5. $\frac{1}{3} = \frac{?}{6}$ **6.** $\frac{1}{5} = \frac{?}{10}$ **7.** $\frac{1}{2} = \frac{?}{6}$ **8.** $\frac{2}{4} = \frac{?}{8}$

9. $\frac{1}{2}$ **10.** $\frac{2}{3}$ **11.** $\frac{4}{5}$ **12.** $\frac{3}{3}$ **13.** $\frac{2}{6}$ **14.** $\frac{5}{10}$

15. $\frac{9}{12}$ **16.** $\frac{1}{4}$ **17.** $\frac{6}{12}$ **18.** $\frac{6}{6}$ **19.** $\frac{3}{5}$ **20.** $\frac{4}{12}$

Mixed Applications

For Problems 22–24, use the menu at the right.

21. Mr. and Mrs. Black had lunch with a friend. The 3 of them split the bill equally. What fraction of the bill did Mr. and Mrs. Black owe?

22. Althea and Marcie ordered 2 grilled cheese sandwiches and 2 bottles of spring water. Will $5.00 be enough money to pay the bill? Explain.

23. Don has $3.00 to spend for lunch. Name at least two combinations of items he can buy.

24. Sue and Dan each ordered a grilled cheese sandwich and spring water. The tax on their order is 6¢ for every dollar spent. How much do they owe?

25. Mr. Allen bought a six-pack of apple juice. Sandra, Tom, and Mrs. Allen each drank 1 can. Mr. Allen drank 2 cans. What fraction of the six-pack was left?

26. **Write a problem** about some friends who split a loaf of bread served at their table for lunch. Use fractions in your problem.

PART 1

Comparing and Ordering Fractions

You will learn to compare and order fractions.

Why learn this? You will be able to compare fractional amounts when cooking or building something.

You can compare fractions by using fraction bars.

A. Compare $\frac{2}{8}$ and $\frac{3}{8}$.

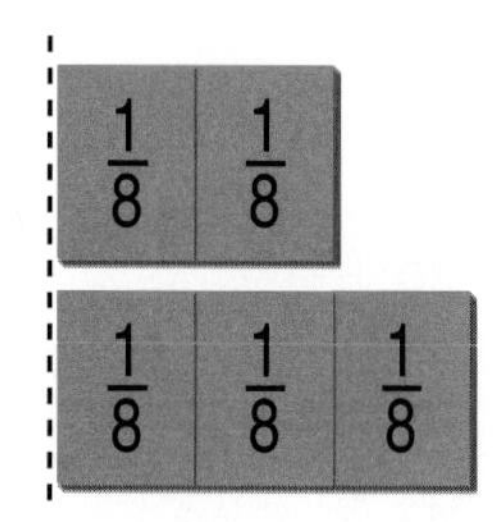

Record: $\frac{2}{8} < \frac{3}{8}$, or $\frac{3}{8} > \frac{2}{8}$

B. Compare $\frac{3}{5}$ and $\frac{3}{6}$.

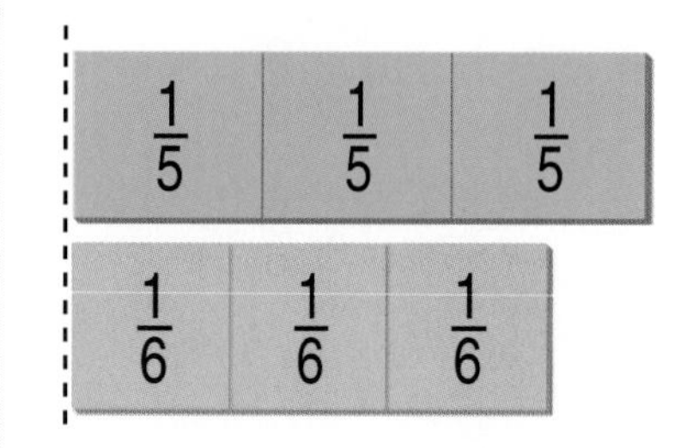

Record: $\frac{3}{5} > \frac{3}{6}$, or $\frac{3}{6} < \frac{3}{5}$

Science Link

Sleep allows your body to save energy and repair itself. Young children need to sleep about $\frac{1}{2}$ of each day. Teenagers need to sleep $\frac{1}{3}$ of a day. Which age group needs more sleep?

Talk About It

- How can you compare fractions that have the same denominators such as $\frac{3}{7}$ and $\frac{2}{7}$?
- How can you compare fractions that have the same numerators but different denominators, such as $\frac{2}{5}$ and $\frac{2}{4}$?

You can put fractions in order by using fraction bars. Order $\frac{3}{8}$, $\frac{1}{4}$, and $\frac{2}{3}$ from greatest to least.

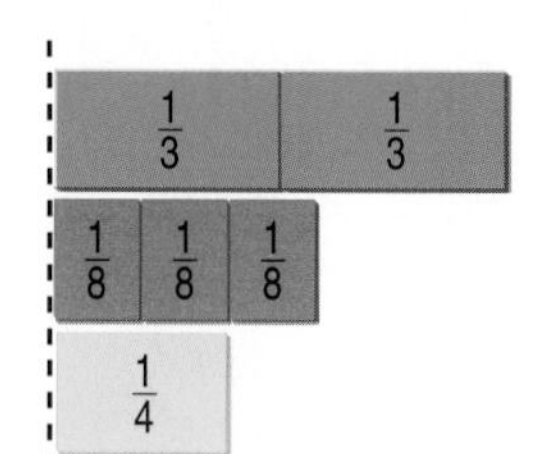

Record: $\frac{2}{3} > \frac{3}{8} > \frac{1}{4}$

So, the fractions from greatest to least are $\frac{2}{3}$, $\frac{3}{8}$, and $\frac{1}{4}$.

Check Your Understanding

Write the fraction for each model. Then compare, using $<$, $>$, or $=$.

1. 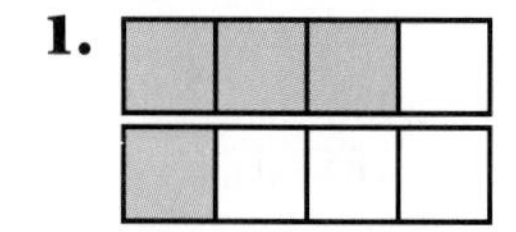

2. 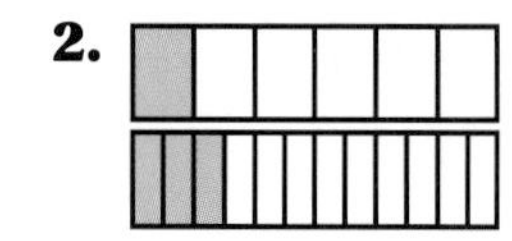

3. 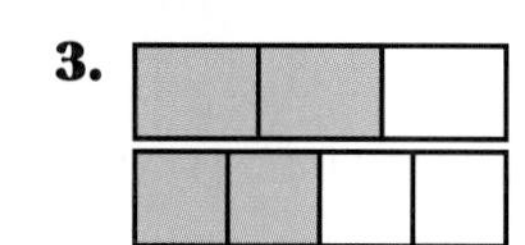

4.

PRACTICE

Write the fraction for each model.
Then compare, using $<$, $>$, or $=$.

5. 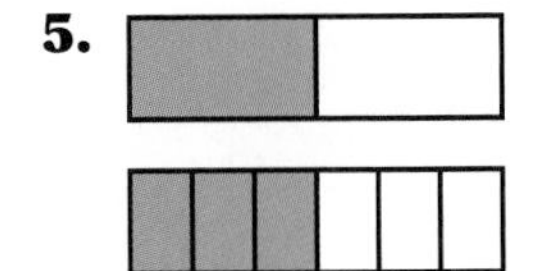

6. 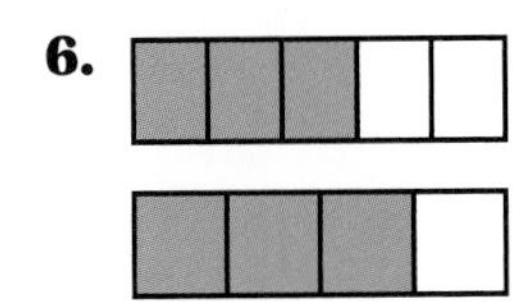

7. 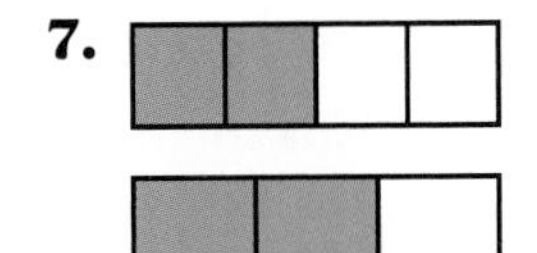

8. 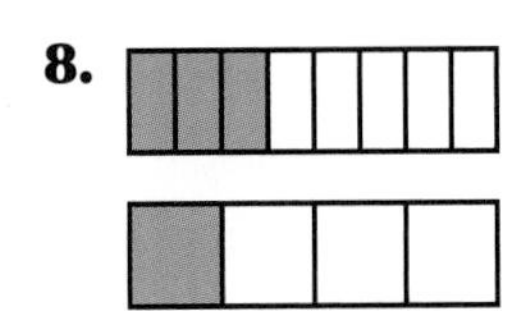

Compare the fractions. Write $<$, $>$, or $=$. Use fraction bars.

9. $\frac{2}{5} \bullet \frac{1}{5}$ **10.** $\frac{1}{4} \bullet \frac{3}{4}$ **11.** $\frac{7}{8} \bullet \frac{3}{8}$ **12.** $\frac{2}{6} \bullet \frac{1}{3}$

13. $\frac{2}{4} \bullet \frac{1}{2}$ **14.** $\frac{3}{4} \bullet \frac{3}{5}$ **15.** $\frac{5}{8} \bullet \frac{5}{6}$ **16.** $\frac{3}{10} \bullet \frac{3}{4}$

Use fraction bars to order each set of fractions from greatest to least.

17. $\frac{1}{4}, \frac{3}{4}, \frac{2}{4}$ **18.** $\frac{2}{6}, \frac{1}{12}, \frac{3}{4}$ **19.** $\frac{1}{2}, \frac{1}{4}, \frac{1}{3}$ **20.** $\frac{3}{10}, \frac{4}{5}, \frac{2}{5}$

Use fraction bars to order each set of fractions from least to greatest.

21. $\frac{3}{4}, \frac{3}{5}, \frac{3}{6}$ **22.** $\frac{7}{8}, \frac{1}{4}, \frac{5}{8}$ **23.** $\frac{3}{6}, \frac{2}{12}, \frac{2}{3}$ **24.** $\frac{1}{8}, \frac{9}{12}, \frac{2}{4}$

Mixed Applications

For Problems 25–30, use the price list. You may use fraction bars.

PRICE LIST

Item	Price
$\frac{1}{3}$ pound almonds	$1.95
$\frac{1}{2}$ pound cashews	$3.15
$\frac{1}{4}$ pound deluxe mix	$1.35

25. Darrin bought each of the items listed. Does he have enough money left over from $9.00 to buy another $\frac{1}{2}$ pound of cashews? How much does he have left over?

26. If Linda buys $\frac{1}{2}$ pound of the deluxe mix, will she pay more or less than $1.35?

27. Candace bought $\frac{1}{3}$ pound of almonds, and Michael bought $\frac{1}{2}$ pound. Who bought more almonds, Candace or Michael?

28. If Julio buys $3.50 worth of cashews, will he have more or less than $\frac{1}{2}$ pound of cashews?

29. If Karen buys $1.95 worth of almonds, will she have more or less than $\frac{1}{2}$ pound of almonds?

30. **Write a problem** using the fractions in the price list.

PART 2 PROBLEM-SOLVING STRATEGY
Make a Model

THE PROBLEM Amanda is making punch for the class party. The recipe calls for $\frac{2}{3}$ gallon of orange juice, $\frac{1}{2}$ gallon of pineapple juice, and $\frac{3}{4}$ gallon of lemonade. List the ingredients in order from least to greatest.

✓ Understand

- What are you asked to do?
- What information will you use?
- Is there information you will not use? If so, what?

✓ Plan

- What strategy can you use to solve the problem?

  You can *make a model* by using fraction bars.

✓ Solve

- What model can you make to solve the problem?

  Line up the fraction bars for $\frac{1}{2}$, $\frac{2}{3}$, and $\frac{3}{4}$. One of the $\frac{1}{2}$ bars is the smallest, the two $\frac{1}{3}$ bars are next, and the three $\frac{1}{4}$ bars are the largest. The model shows that $\frac{1}{2} < \frac{2}{3} < \frac{3}{4}$.

  So, the list of ingredients in order from least to greatest is pineapple juice, orange juice, and lemonade.

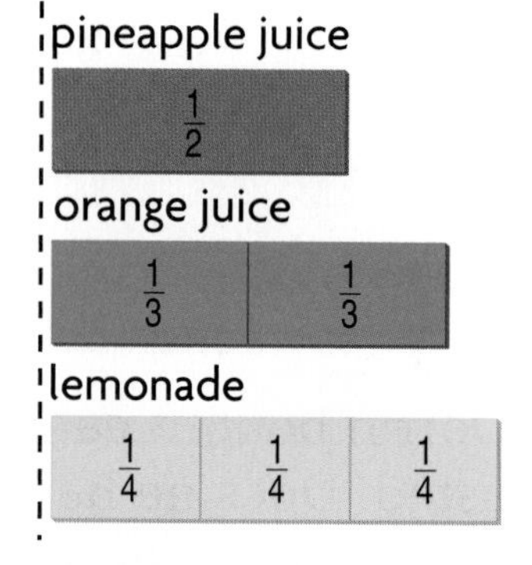

✓ Look Back

- How can you determine if your model is correct?
- What other strategy could you use?

CHOOSE Paper/Pencil Calculator Hands-on Mental Math

PRACTICE

Make a model to solve.

1. Suppose Amanda had $\frac{2}{3}$ gallon of orange juice, $\frac{1}{2}$ gallon of pineapple juice, and $\frac{1}{4}$ gallon of lemonade. What would the list of ingredients be in order from least to greatest?

2. Roger is helping his mom make spaghetti sauce. He measures $\frac{1}{2}$ teaspoon of basil, $\frac{3}{4}$ teaspoon of oregano, and $\frac{1}{3}$ teaspoon of pepper. List the ingredients in order from greatest to least.

3. Candy is making a design with 16 tiles. The 4 corner tiles are red, and the rest of the outside border tiles are blue. She puts 4 green tiles in the middle. Show what Candy's design might look like.

4. A spinner has 12 equal sections. Two of the sections are blue, 3 sections are yellow, 2 sections are red, and 5 sections are green. What two colors together cover $\frac{2}{3}$ of the spinner?

Mixed Applications

Solve.

CHOOSE A STRATEGY

- Make a Model
- Work Backward
- Use a Table
- Write a Number Sentence
- Make an Organized List

5. Stephanie used a recipe calling for $\frac{1}{2}$ cup of apples, $\frac{3}{4}$ cup of water, and $\frac{1}{8}$ cup of honey. List the ingredients in order from the greatest amount to the least.

6. Kurt baked 3 dozen corn muffins and 4 dozen bran muffins for the Boy Scout Breakfast. How many muffins did he bake?

7. When Jon got home from school, there were 8 cupcakes on the table. Jon had taken 12 cupcakes to school that morning. During the day his brother and sister each ate 2 cupcakes. How many cupcakes were on the table that morning?

8. Hal's birthday cake can be either a yellow cake or a chocolate cake. The frosting can be either lemon, chocolate, or strawberry. List the choices Hal has for his birthday cake.

9. Which assembly will be the longest? the shortest?

Assembly Schedule	
Kindergarten and First Grade	8:45– 9:15
Second and Third Grade	9:30–10:15
Fourth and Fifth Grade	10:30–11:20

MORE PRACTICE Student Handbook page H103

Mixed Numbers

You will learn to identify, read, and write mixed numbers and to rename fractions greater than 1 as mixed numbers.	Why learn this? You will use mixed numbers to name amounts made up of wholes and parts.	WORD POWER mixed number

A **mixed number** is made up of a whole number and a fraction. Look at the fraction bars that represent two and one fourth granola bars.

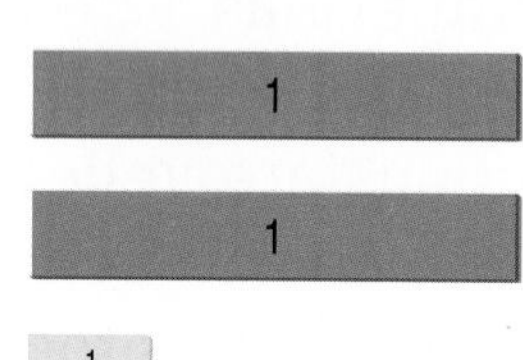

Read: two and one fourth

Write: $2\frac{1}{4}$

- Which fraction bars represent the whole-number part? the fraction part?

A. one and one fourth

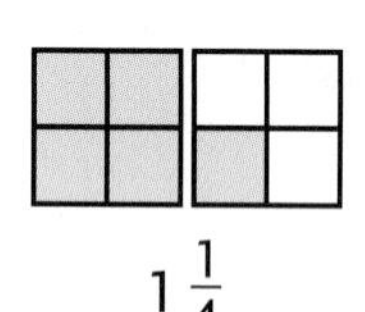

$1\frac{1}{4}$

B. two and two thirds

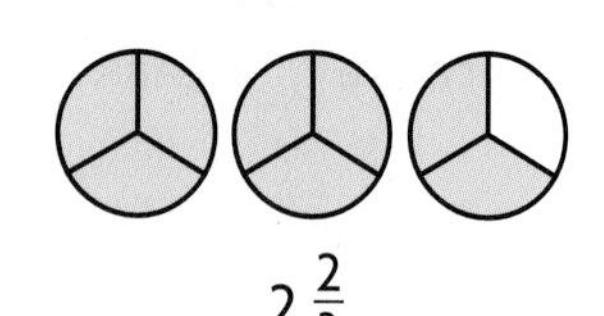

$2\frac{2}{3}$

C. three and one sixth

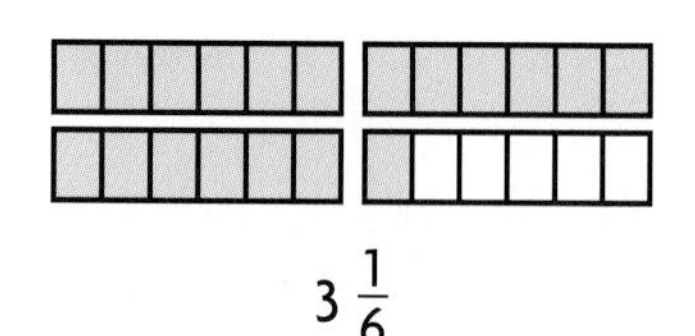

$3\frac{1}{6}$

You can rename a fraction as a mixed number when the numerator is greater than the denominator.

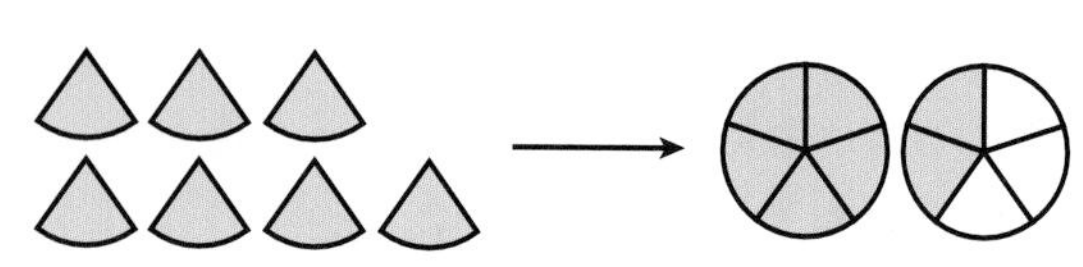

$\frac{7}{5} \longrightarrow \frac{5}{5}$, or $1 + \frac{2}{5} = 1\frac{2}{5}$

Check Your Understanding

CRITICAL THINKING

Write a mixed number for each picture.

1. 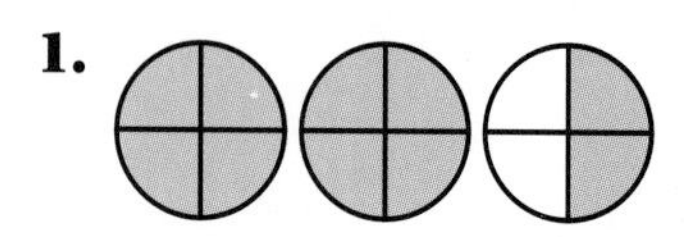

2. 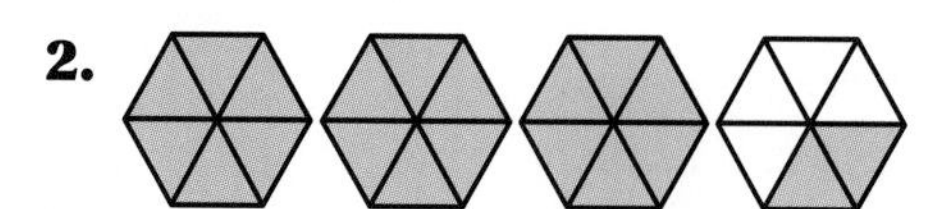

3. 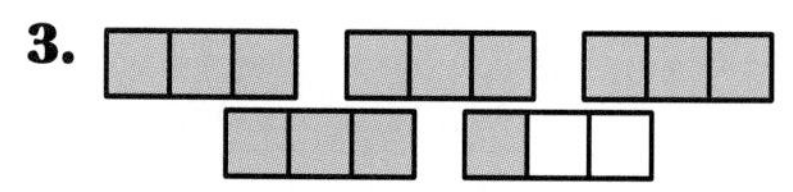

Rename each fraction as a mixed number. You may wish to draw a picture.

4. $\frac{4}{3}$ **5.** $\frac{11}{5}$ **6.** $\frac{13}{4}$ **7.** $\frac{19}{6}$ **8.** $\frac{5}{2}$

Calculator Activities, page H65

PRACTICE

For Exercises 9–12, use the figures at the right.

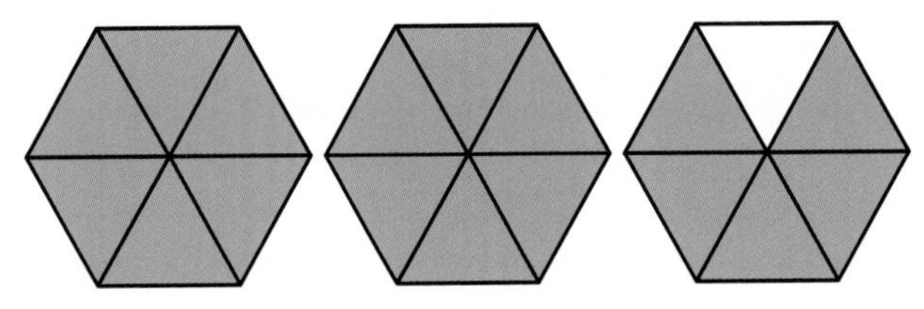

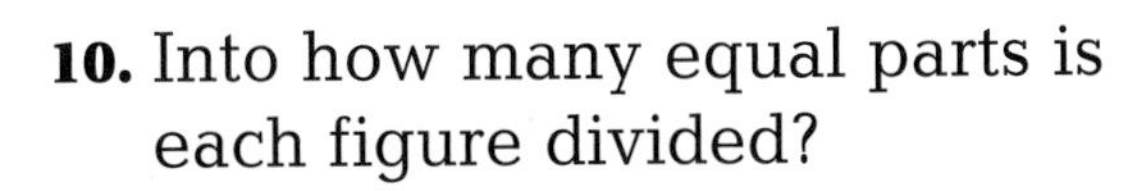

9. How many whole figures are shaded?

10. Into how many equal parts is each figure divided?

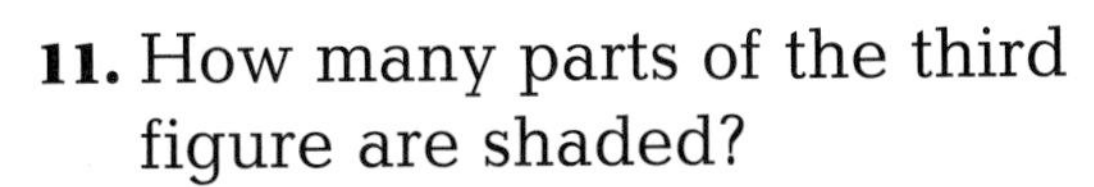

11. How many parts of the third figure are shaded?

12. What fraction and mixed number can you write for the picture?

Write a mixed number for each picture.

13. 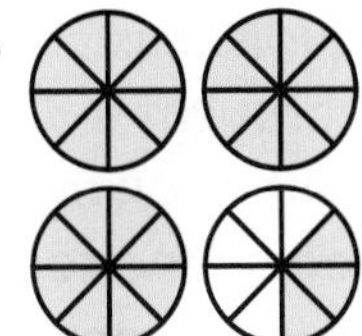

14. 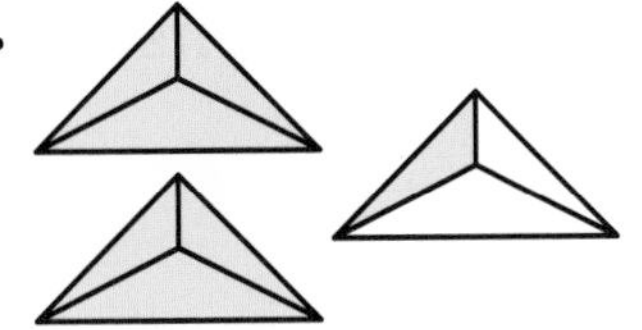

15. 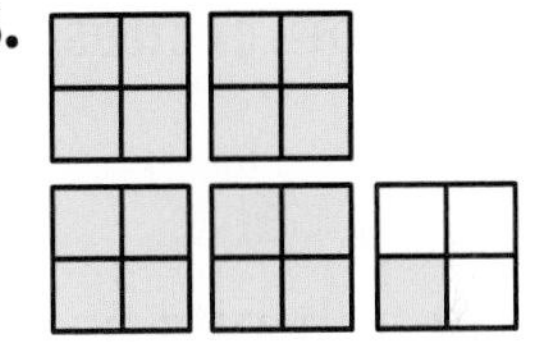

Rename each fraction as a mixed number. You may wish to draw a picture.

16. $\frac{5}{2}$ 17. $\frac{10}{3}$ 18. $\frac{9}{8}$ 19. $\frac{15}{4}$ 20. $\frac{11}{6}$

Mixed Applications

21. At snack time, Tim drank $\frac{1}{2}$ cup of juice, and Cory drank $\frac{3}{4}$ cup of juice. Who drank more juice?

22. A cup holds 8 ounces of liquid. Mary used 24 ounces of milk to make waffles. How many cups of milk did she use?

23. Eric ate $\frac{4}{3}$ of the pizza. Draw a picture to show how much of the pizza Eric ate.

24. **WRITE ABOUT IT** How can you tell when a fraction names a number greater than 1?

Mixed Review

Find the product. (pages 290–293)

25. 16×22 26. 57×18 27. 74×53 28. 31×92 29. 188×29

Are the figures congruent? Write *yes* or *no*. (pages 246–247)

30. 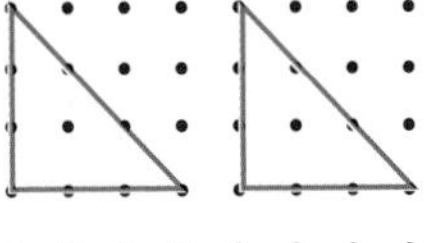

31. 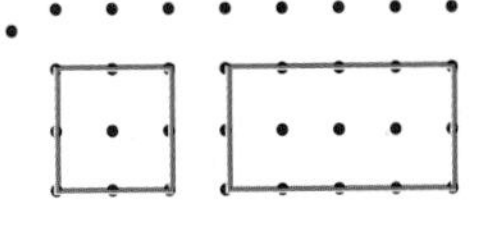

32. 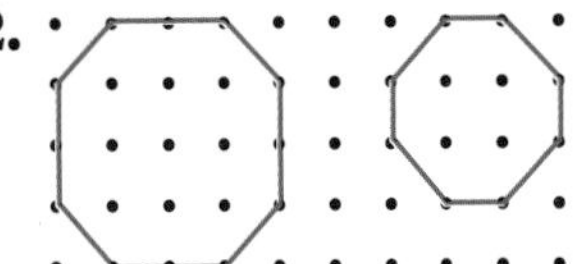

33. 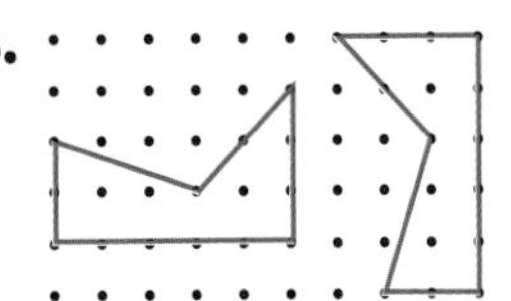

CULTURAL CONNECTION

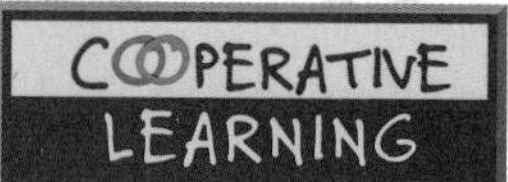

A Game of Dish

Melanie and her class were studying the Iroquois culture in New York State. Their project included Iroquois sports and games. The class played one of the games, called Dish. Dish is played with peach or plum pits, painted dark on one side and light on the other. The pits are shaken and tossed. What are the possible outcomes if you play with three pits?

CULTURAL LINK

The game of Dish had several variations. It was traditionally played after a feast at the New Year's festival every year. At an Iroquois feast, everyone brought a dish to the public cooking place, filled it, and took it home to eat in peace. Afterward, the game of Dish was played for two days in the Council House by teams of pairs.

Work Together

1. If two peach pits are tossed, the possibilities are DD, DL, LD, and LL. What fraction of the outcomes have at least one dark side up? at least one light side up? both dark sides up? both light sides up?

2. These are the possible outcomes when the game is played with four peach pits.

   DDDD LLLL LDDL DLDD

   DDDL LLLD DLLD DDLD

   DDLL LLDD DLDL LDLL

   DLLL LDDD LDLD LLDL

   What fraction of the outcomes have 4 L's? 4 D's?

3. What fraction of the outcomes have 1 L and 3 D's? Draw a model or use fraction bars to find an equivalent fraction.

4. Compare the number of outcomes containing dark sides, from zero to four. Name the fractions.

CHAPTER 20 REVIEW

✓ CHECK UNDERSTANDING

VOCABULARY

1. Fractions that name the same amount are called __?__. (page 342)

2. A __?__ number is made up of a whole number and a fraction. (page 348)

Draw the picture and shade 1 part. Write the fraction for the shaded part. (pages 338–339)

3. 6 triangles
   3 parts

4. 6 squares
   6 parts

5. 8 circles
   4 parts

6. 3 stars
   3 parts

✓ CHECK SKILLS

What fraction is shaded? What fraction is not shaded? (pages 338–341)

7. 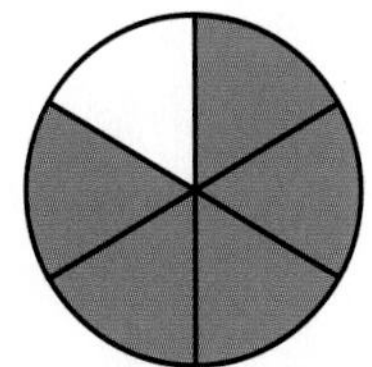

8. 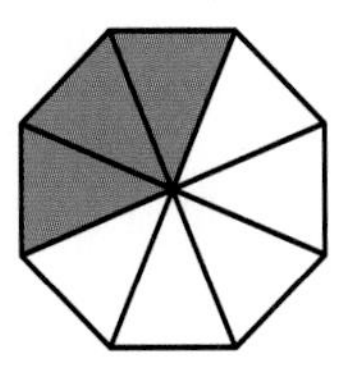

9. 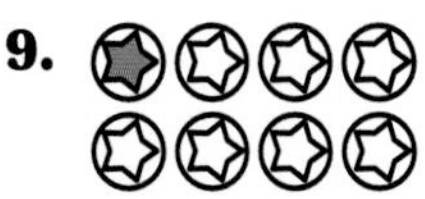

10. 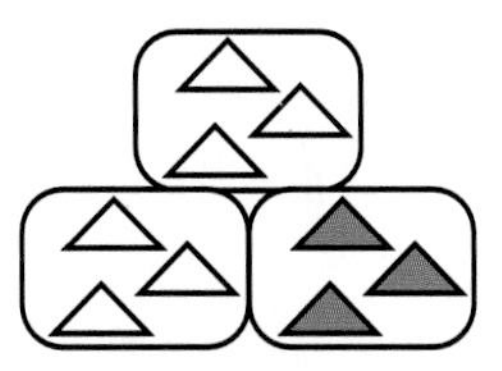

Use fraction bars for Exercises 11–14.

Compare using $<$, $>$, or $=$. (pages 344–345)

11. $\frac{4}{8}$ ● $\frac{2}{8}$

12. $\frac{3}{6}$ ● $\frac{6}{12}$

Order each set of fractions from least to greatest. (pages 344–345)

13. $\frac{5}{8}, \frac{6}{8}, \frac{3}{8}$

14. $\frac{2}{4}, \frac{3}{8}, \frac{4}{6}$

Write a mixed number for each picture. (pages 348–349)

15. 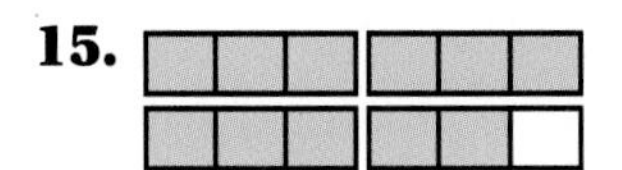

16. 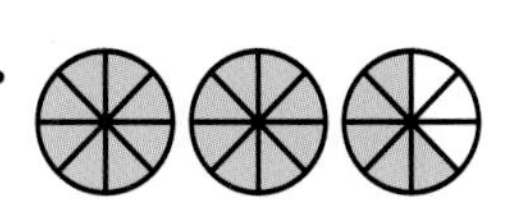

Rename each fraction as a mixed number. (pages 348–349)

17. $\frac{8}{3}$

18. $\frac{3}{2}$

✓ CHECK PROBLEM SOLVING

Solve. (pages 346–347)

CHOOSE A STRATEGY

- Act It Out
- Guess and Check
- Make a Model
- Draw a Diagram

19. Mrs. Wong left home at 8:30 A.M. She drove for 5 hr and 40 min to go to Lake City. At what time did she reach Lake City?

20. Mrs. Ruiz made one dozen muffins for her 3 sons to share equally. What fraction of the muffins will each boy receive?

CHAPTER 21

ADDING AND SUBTRACTING FRACTIONS

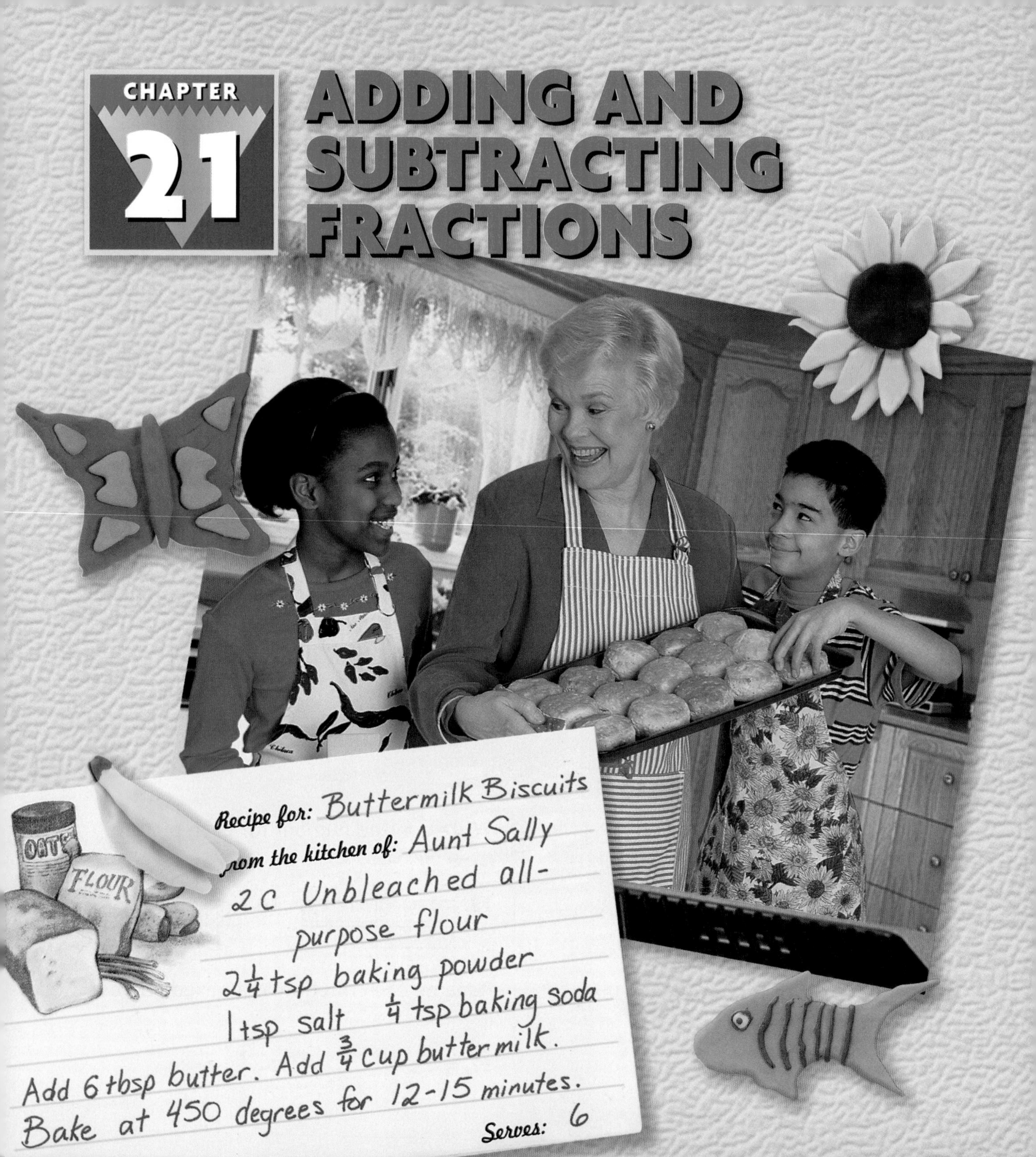

DID YOU KNOW . . .

Baking soda is used to make cookies and cakes rise while baking. When it combines with the acid in buttermilk, yogurt, or molasses, baking soda makes gas bubbles. It reacts when wet, so always mix the dry ingredients first.

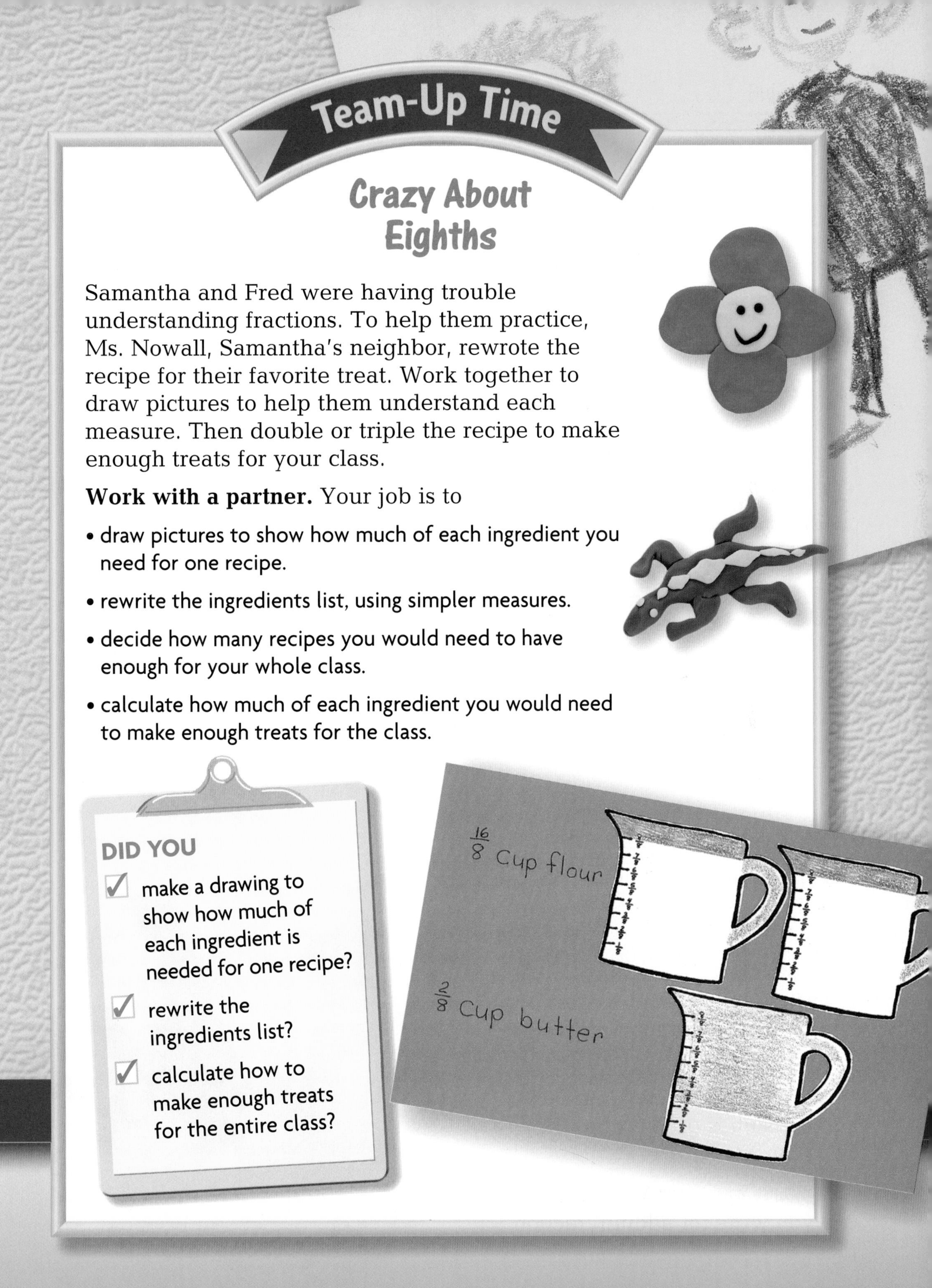

Team-Up Time

Crazy About Eighths

Samantha and Fred were having trouble understanding fractions. To help them practice, Ms. Nowall, Samantha's neighbor, rewrote the recipe for their favorite treat. Work together to draw pictures to help them understand each measure. Then double or triple the recipe to make enough treats for your class.

Work with a partner. Your job is to

- draw pictures to show how much of each ingredient you need for one recipe.
- rewrite the ingredients list, using simpler measures.
- decide how many recipes you would need to have enough for your whole class.
- calculate how much of each ingredient you would need to make enough treats for the class.

DID YOU

- ✓ make a drawing to show how much of each ingredient is needed for one recipe?
- ✓ rewrite the ingredients list?
- ✓ calculate how to make enough treats for the entire class?

Adding Like Fractions

You will investigate adding fractions with the same denominators.

Why learn this? You can add fractional amounts of ingredients when you are cooking something.

Explore

You can use fraction bars to add fractions.

MATERIALS: fraction bars

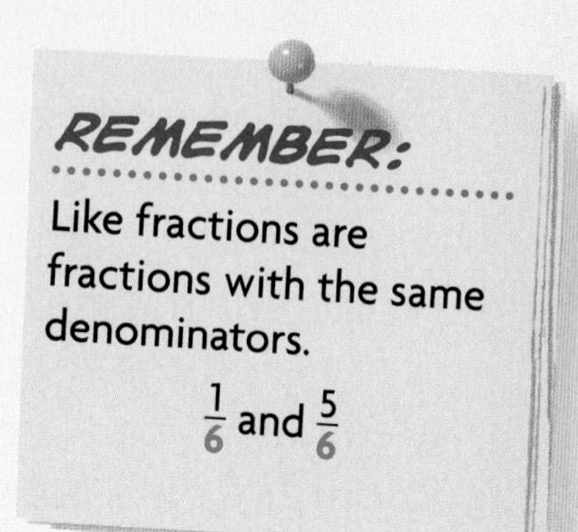

MODEL

Find the sum of $\frac{2}{8}$ and $\frac{5}{8}$. Is the sum greater than or less than 1?

Step 1

Line up 2 of the $\frac{1}{8}$ bars next to the bar for 1.

1	
$\frac{1}{8}$	$\frac{1}{8}$

Step 2

Line up 5 more $\frac{1}{8}$ bars. Count the $\frac{1}{8}$ bars.

1						
$\frac{1}{8}$	$\frac{1}{8}$	$\frac{1}{8}$	$\frac{1}{8}$	$\frac{1}{8}$	$\frac{1}{8}$	$\frac{1}{8}$

Record

Trace the fraction bars on a sheet of paper. Record an addition number sentence for the model.

Try This

Find the sum of $\frac{3}{5}$ and $\frac{3}{5}$. Make a model and record by writing a number sentence.

TALK ABOUT IT How do you know when a sum is greater than 1 or less than 1?

WRITE ABOUT IT What rule can you write for adding fraction pieces?

HANDS-ON PRACTICE

Use fraction bars to find the sum. Draw the bars and write the number sentence.

1. $\frac{3}{8} + \frac{3}{8} = n$ **2.** $\frac{1}{5} + \frac{2}{5} = n$ **3.** $\frac{2}{6} + \frac{5}{6} = n$

4. $\frac{4}{10} + \frac{3}{10} = n$ **5.** $\frac{2}{3} + \frac{1}{3} = n$ **6.** $\frac{6}{12} + \frac{7}{12} = n$

Applying What You Learned

Write the letter of the number sentence for each model. Find the sum.

7.

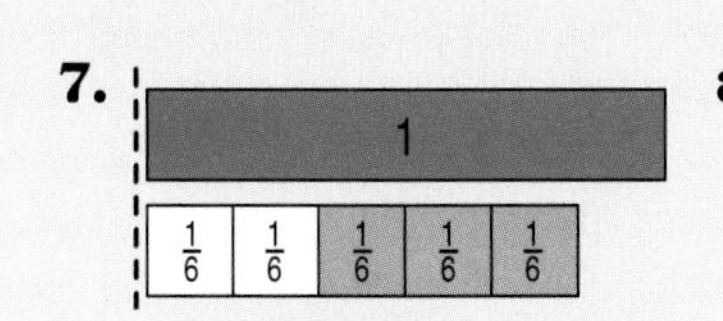

8. 1 | 1/5 1/5 1/5 1/5

9. 1 | 1/2 1/2

10. 1 | 1/8 1/8 1/8 1/8 1/8

a. $\frac{3}{5} + \frac{1}{5} = n$

b. $\frac{2}{6} + \frac{3}{6} = n$

c. $\frac{1}{8} + \frac{4}{8} = n$

d. $\frac{1}{2} + \frac{1}{2} = n$

11.

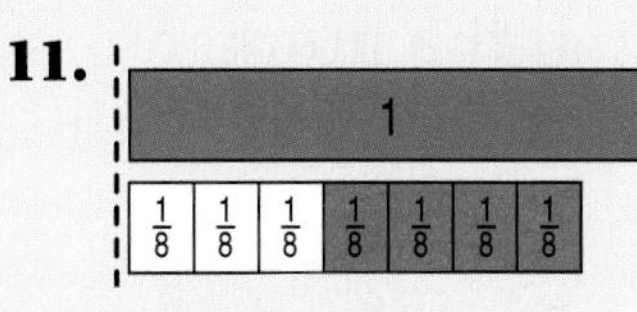

12.

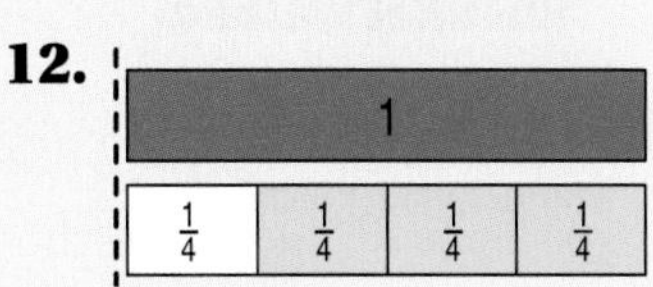

13.

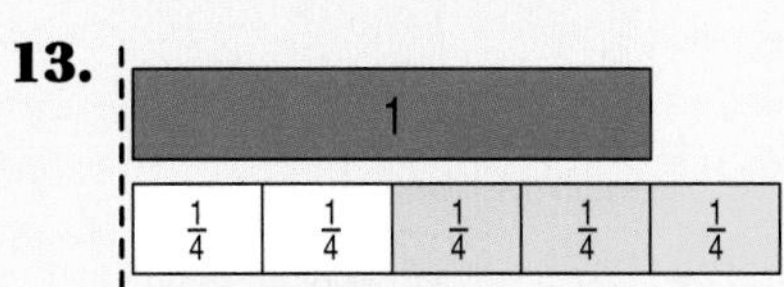

14.

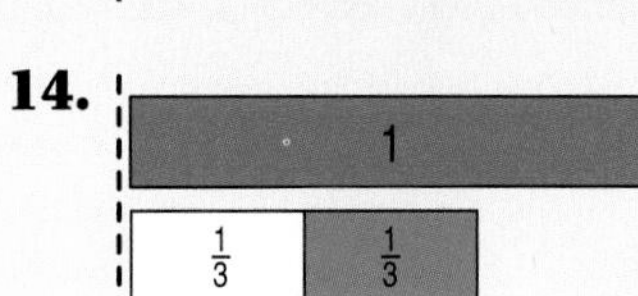

a. $\frac{2}{4} + \frac{3}{4} = n$

b. $\frac{1}{3} + \frac{1}{3} = n$

c. $\frac{1}{4} + \frac{3}{4} = n$

d. $\frac{3}{8} + \frac{4}{8} = n$

Mixed Applications

15. Twelve Boy Scouts went to camp. Four boys slept in one tent, and three slept in another tent. The rest of the group slept in a cabin. What fraction of the group slept in tents?

16. A group of Girl Scouts went hiking. The scouts hiked $\frac{3}{10}$ of the trail in the morning and $\frac{2}{10}$ of the trail in the afternoon. What part of the trail did they hike?

17. Leslie's picture has a white border of $\frac{1}{8}$ inch wide around it. A second colored border of $\frac{3}{8}$ inch goes around the white border. How wide is the border around Leslie's picture?

18. **Write a problem** about adding two fractions of an inch with like denominators.

MORE PRACTICE Student Handbook page H104

More About Adding Like Fractions

You will learn to add fractions with the same denominators.	**Why learn this?** You can find the sum of two or more fractional measures, such as parts of an hour or parts of a mile.

Rachael walked $\frac{1}{4}$ mile to Lisa's house. Then the two girls walked together $\frac{2}{4}$ mile to school. How far did Rachael walk?

You can add fractions with like denominators by adding the numerators. Use the folded-paper model to solve the problem.

Distance to Lisa's House		Distance to School		Total distance Rachael walked	
$\frac{1}{4}$	+	$\frac{2}{4}$	=	$\frac{?}{4}$	← Add the numerators.
$\frac{1}{4}$	+	$\frac{2}{4}$	=	$\frac{3}{4}$	← Place the sum of the numerators over the same denominator.

So, Rachael walked $\frac{3}{4}$ mile.

- Is the sum greater than or less than 1 mile?

____

Complete the table.

Addends	Sum	Reading the Problem	Reading the Sum
$\frac{2}{5} + \frac{1}{5}$	$\frac{?}{5}$	two fifths plus one fifth	three fifths
$\frac{2}{10} + \frac{7}{10}$	$\frac{?}{?}$	?	?
$\frac{3}{8} + \frac{6}{8}$	$\frac{?}{?}$	?	?
$\frac{2}{6} + \frac{5}{6}$	$\frac{?}{?}$	?	?

Talk About It

- If you read each number sentence aloud, what words are repeated?
- How do you know when a sum is greater than 1?

CRITICAL THINKING Why do you add only the numerators when adding like fractions?

PRACTICE

Write a number sentence for each problem and then find the sum.

1. six eighths plus one eighth

2. four ninths plus four ninths

3. five tenths plus six tenths

4. three twelfths plus seven twelfths

Find the sum.

5. $\frac{3}{5} + \frac{1}{5} = n$

6. $\frac{6}{10} + \frac{3}{10} = n$

7. $\frac{4}{8} + \frac{3}{8} = n$

8. $\frac{2}{7} + \frac{2}{7} = n$

9. $\frac{1}{6} + \frac{4}{6} = n$

10. $\frac{2}{3} + \frac{2}{3} = n$

Mixed Applications

11. On Monday, Marion rode her bicycle $\frac{1}{4}$ hour before school and $\frac{2}{4}$ hour after school. What fraction of an hour did Marion ride her bicycle on Monday?

12. It took Rona 15 minutes to run from her house to the park. She spent 35 minutes at the park. Then it took her 25 minutes to walk home. How long was Rona gone?

13. Ms. Segal added $\frac{3}{8}$ inch ribbon to the hem of a skirt. The hem was already $\frac{5}{8}$ inch wide. How wide was the hem after Ms. Segal added the ribbon?

14. **WRITE ABOUT IT** Explain why the denominators are not added when finding the sum of two fractions.

Mixed Review

Find the product. (pages 272–273)

15. 184×2

16. 315×3

17. 524×5

18. 408×4

19. 697×3

Name each polygon. Tell the number of sides and angles. (pages 218–219)

20. 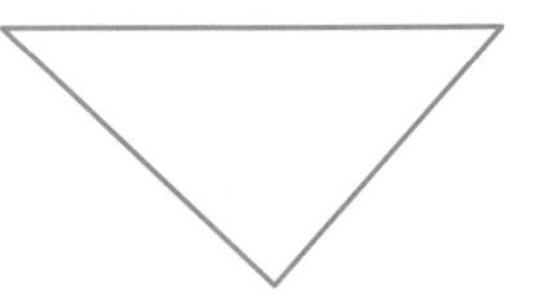

21. 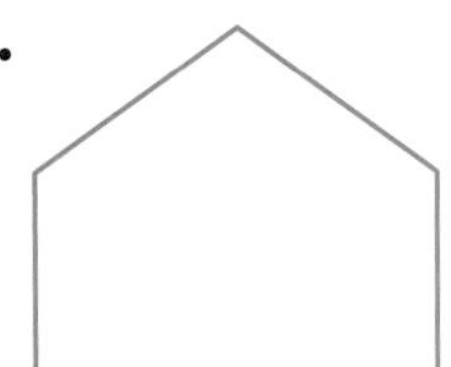

22. 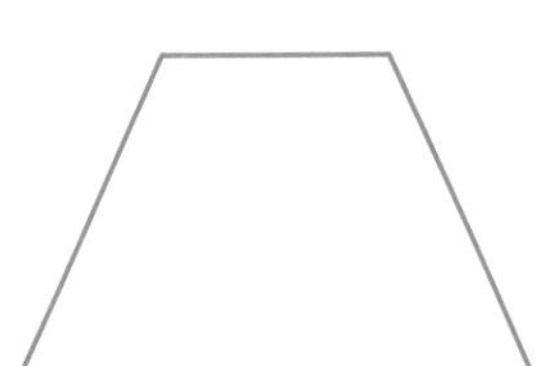

23. 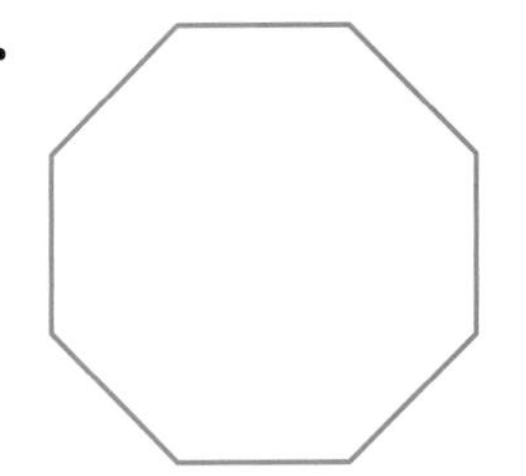

PART 1 Subtracting Like Fractions

You will investigate subtracting fractions with the same denominators.

Why learn this? You can find the difference of two measures, such as fractions of a cup.

There are two ways to use fraction bars to subtract fractions.

What is $\frac{5}{6} - \frac{4}{6}$?

A. Take away bars.

Line up 5 of the $\frac{1}{6}$ bars. Take away 4 of the $\frac{1}{6}$ bars. Count the $\frac{1}{6}$ bars left.

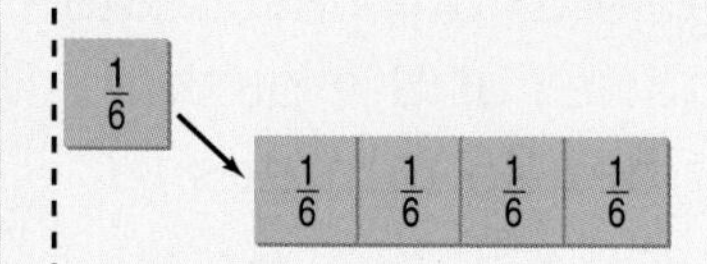

So, $\frac{5}{6} - \frac{4}{6} = \frac{1}{6}$.

B. Compare two bars.

Line up 5 of the $\frac{1}{6}$ bars. Then line up 4 of the $\frac{1}{6}$ bars. Compare the $\frac{5}{6}$ and $\frac{4}{6}$ bars. Count the difference.

1/6 1/6 1/6 1/6 1/6
1/6 1/6 1/6 1/6

So, $\frac{5}{6} - \frac{4}{6} = \frac{1}{6}$.

Talk About It

- In Example A, why are some of the fraction bars taken away? What fraction is modeled by the fraction bars that are left?
- In Example B, what is the difference of the two fractions being compared?

Explore

Find the difference of $\frac{7}{8}$ and $\frac{4}{8}$.

MATERIALS: fraction bars

Record

Trace the fraction bars on a sheet of paper. Use the take-away and compare models shown in A. and B. above. Record a subtraction number sentence for each model.

Now, investigate using paper folding to subtract fractions.

Try This

Find the difference of $\frac{3}{4}$ and $\frac{2}{4}$. Fold and shade paper that has been divided into fourths. Record by drawing a picture and writing a number sentence.

TALK ABOUT IT In your folded-paper model, how did you show the difference?

WRITE ABOUT IT What rule can you write for subtracting like fraction bars or like pieces with paper folding?

HANDS-ON PRACTICE

Use fraction bars or paper folding to find the difference. Draw a picture and write the number sentence.

1. $\frac{7}{8} - \frac{2}{8} = n$ **2.** $\frac{8}{10} - \frac{1}{10} = n$ **3.** $\frac{5}{6} - \frac{4}{6} = n$

4. $\frac{4}{5} - \frac{2}{5} = n$ **5.** $\frac{7}{12} - \frac{3}{12} = n$ **6.** $\frac{3}{4} - \frac{1}{4} = n$

7. $\frac{4}{6} - \frac{1}{6} = n$ **8.** $\frac{6}{10} - \frac{3}{10} = n$ **9.** $\frac{4}{8} - \frac{3}{8} = n$

Write the letter of the number sentence for each model. Find the difference.

10. 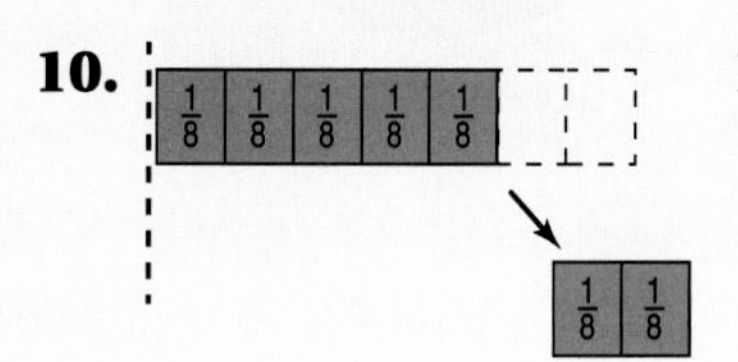

11. 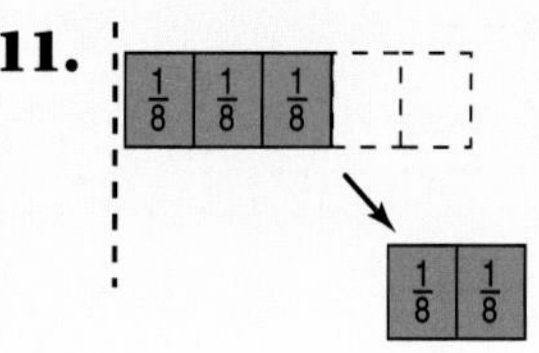

12. 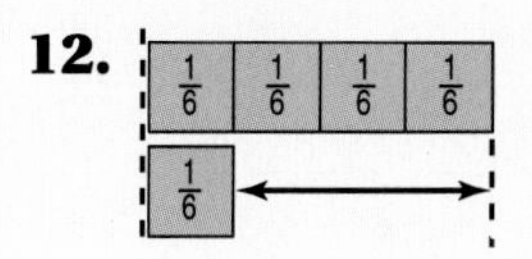

13. 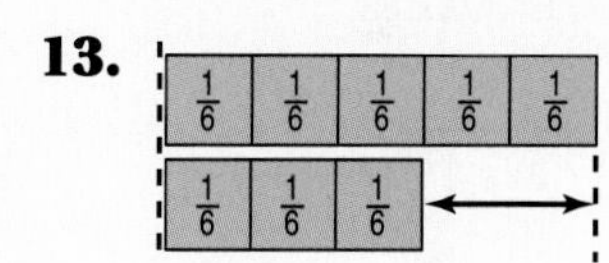

a. $\frac{5}{6} - \frac{3}{6} = n$ **b.** $\frac{5}{8} - \frac{2}{8} = n$ **c.** $\frac{7}{8} - \frac{2}{8} = n$ **d.** $\frac{4}{6} - \frac{1}{6} = n$

Mixed Applications

14. Wesley made two batches of pancakes using this recipe. How much pancake mix did he use? How much milk did he use?

15. Ling measured $\frac{2}{3}$ cup milk to add to her pancake mix. When she read the recipe again, she saw she had poured too much milk. How much extra milk did Ling measure?

LESSON CONTINUES

MORE PRACTICE Student Handbook page H105

PART 2 PROBLEM-SOLVING STRATEGY Make a Model

THE PROBLEM Tasha and Julio each ate $\frac{3}{8}$ of a large pizza. What fraction of the pizza was left?

REMEMBER:
- ✓ Understand
- ✓ Plan
- ✓ Solve
- ✓ Look Back

✓ Understand

- What are you asked to do?
- What information will you use?
- Is there information you will not use? If so, what?

✓ Plan

- What strategy can you use to solve the problem?

  You can *make a model* to find how much of the pizza was eaten and how much was left.

✓ Solve

- What model can you make to solve the problem?

  You can use fraction circles to make a model of the pizza.

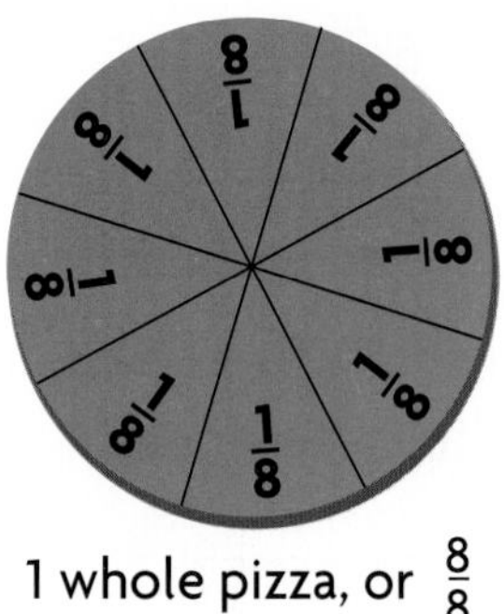

1 whole pizza, or $\frac{8}{8}$

MODEL

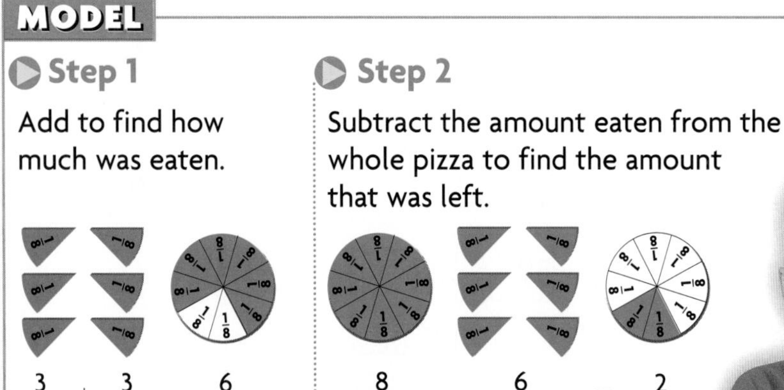

Step 1

Add to find how much was eaten.

$\frac{3}{8} + \frac{3}{8} = \frac{6}{8}$

Step 2

Subtract the amount eaten from the whole pizza to find the amount that was left.

$\frac{8}{8} - \frac{6}{8} = \frac{2}{8}$

So, $\frac{2}{8}$ of the pizza was left.

✓ Look Back

- How can you decide if your answer is reasonable?
- What other strategy could you use?

PRACTICE

CHOOSE Paper/Pencil Calculator Hands-on Mental Math

Make a model to solve.

1. Suppose Tasha and Julio each ate $\frac{2}{8}$ of a large pizza. What fraction of the pizza would be left?

2. Ms. Marder baked a peach pie. Her son and daughter each ate $\frac{1}{8}$ of the pie. What fraction of the peach pie was left?

3. In a group of 10 students, $\frac{3}{10}$ of the group voted to present their reports on Monday, $\frac{2}{10}$ voted to present them on Tuesday. The rest of the group voted to present their reports on Wednesday. What fraction of the group voted to present their reports on Wednesday?

4. Daniel had homework in English, math, and science. He spent $\frac{1}{6}$ of his time doing English and $\frac{1}{6}$ of his time doing science. He spent the rest of his time doing math. What fraction of the time did Daniel spend doing math?

Mixed Applications

Solve.

CHOOSE A STRATEGY

- **Act It Out**
- **Use a Table**
- **Guess and Check**
- **Work Backward**
- **Make a Model**
- **Make an Organized List**

5. The winner of the raffle will be the person whose name is drawn from among 100 cards. The probability of a 4th grader winning is $\frac{1}{10}$. How many cards have the name of a 4th grader?

6. The cheerleaders spend $\frac{1}{4}$ of their time practicing cheers, and $\frac{1}{4}$ of their time learning dance steps. They spend the rest of their time tumbling. What fraction of the their time are they tumbling?

7. There are 45 students in band class. An equal number of students play woodwinds and brass. Only half the number of students who play woodwinds or brass are in percussion. How many students play in each of the three groups of the band?

8. Some friends are ordering a pizza. It can be either thin crust or deep dish, with either ham, mushroom, or sausage as a topping. What are the choices of pizza?

9. The clock shows the time Mario left the baseball field. His team had played for 1 hour. After playing, he spent 20 minutes talking with friends. He had arrived at the baseball field 15 minutes early. What time did he arrive at the field?

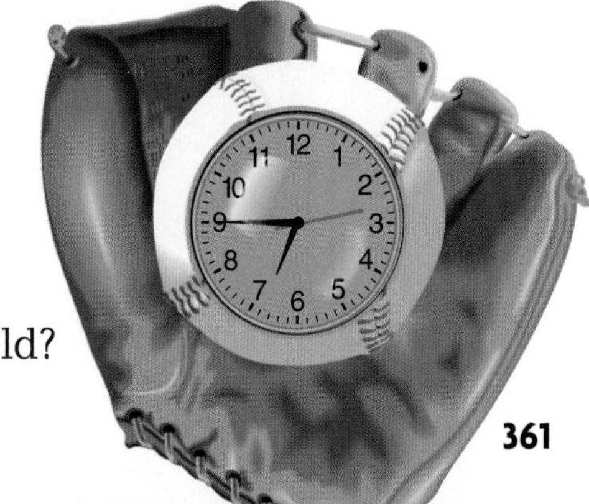

MORE PRACTICE Student Handbook page H105

Adding Mixed Numbers

You will learn to add mixed numbers.

Why learn this? You can find the total of two amounts, such as two amounts of sugar or two lengths of string.

Tim is making a string-art design. He needs $2\frac{2}{4}$ feet of red string and $1\frac{1}{4}$ feet of blue string. How many feet of string does Tim need in all?

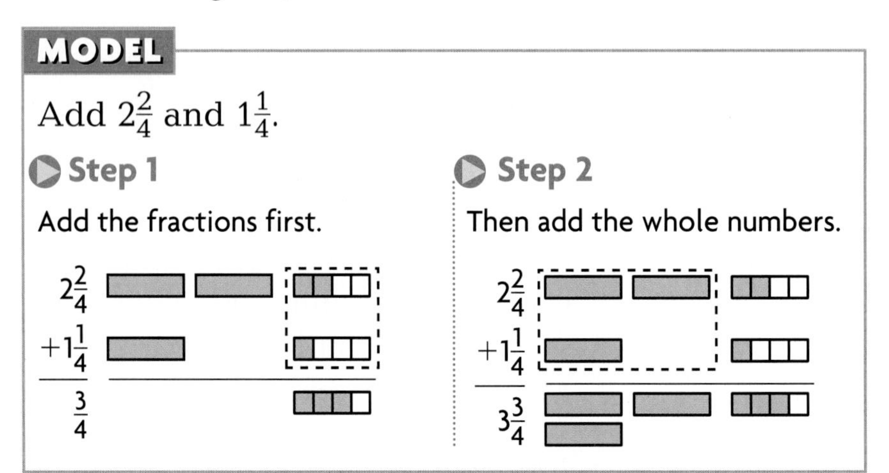

Art Link

Line art uses lines to make designs. With string and nails, Lynn made a dinosaur. If Lynn used $3\frac{1}{2}$ ft of dark green string and $8\frac{1}{2}$ ft of light green string to make the dinosaur, how much string did she use altogether?

So, Tim needs $3\frac{3}{4}$ feet of string in all.

Talk About It

- How did you add the fractions?
- How many whole fraction bars are shown in the sum?

REMEMBER:

You can write an addition problem vertically or horizontally.

$$\begin{array}{r} 2\frac{2}{4} \\ +\ 1\frac{1}{4} \\ \hline 3\frac{3}{4} \end{array} \quad \text{or } 2\frac{2}{4} + 1\frac{1}{4} = 3\frac{3}{4}$$

EXAMPLES

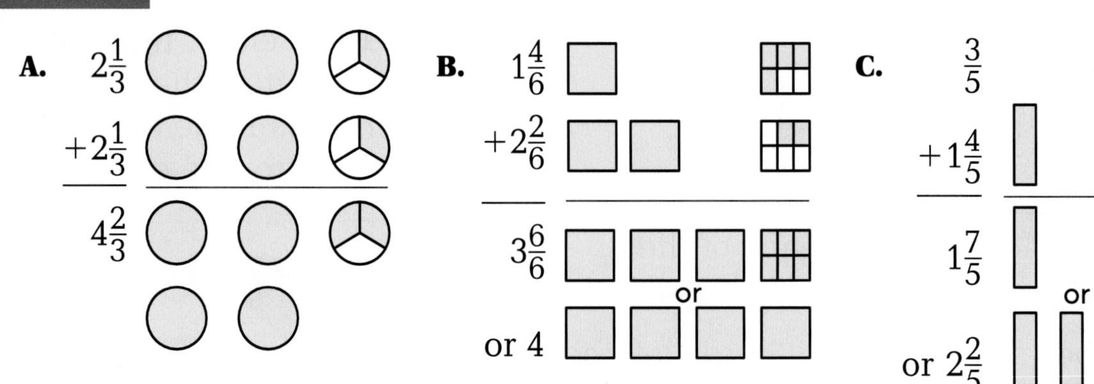

CRITICAL THINKING Why do you need to rename the sums in Examples B and C?

PRACTICE

Find the sum.

1. $2\frac{1}{4}$ + $3\frac{3}{4}$

2. $4\frac{3}{5}$ + $1\frac{3}{5}$

Find the sum. You may wish to draw a picture.

3. $3\frac{1}{3} + 2\frac{1}{3}$

4. $4\frac{3}{5} + 1\frac{1}{5}$

5. $5\frac{1}{4} + 1\frac{2}{4}$

6. $7\frac{1}{6} + 2\frac{4}{6}$

7. $6\frac{3}{12} + 5\frac{4}{12}$

8. $8\frac{1}{6} + 1\frac{5}{6}$

9. $5\frac{3}{10} + 3\frac{8}{10}$

10. $7\frac{2}{9} + 4\frac{8}{9}$

11. $2\frac{6}{10} + 4\frac{3}{10} = n$

12. $5\frac{3}{8} + 1\frac{5}{8} = n$

13. $6\frac{6}{12} + 9\frac{7}{12} = n$

Mixed Applications

14. Chelsea and Shelly are making a curtain for their puppet theater. Each girl cuts out a piece of cloth that is $2\frac{1}{3}$ feet wide. If they put the two pieces of cloth together, how wide is the curtain?

15. Chelsea and Shelly worked for 45 minutes on Monday and for 1 hour 20 minutes on Tuesday. How much time did they work in the two days?

16. The puppet theater stage is 42 inches high and 36 inches wide. What is the perimeter of the theater stage?

17. **Write a problem** in which you add 2 mixed numbers and need to rename the sum.

Mixed Review

Round each factor. Estimate the product. (pages 286–287)

18. 17×23

19. 18×36

20. 54×25

21. $\$37 \times 28$

22. $\$275 \times 12$

Rename each fraction as a mixed number. You may wish to draw a picture. (pages 348–349)

23. $\frac{3}{2}$

24. $\frac{7}{4}$

25. $\frac{13}{6}$

26. $\frac{13}{5}$

27. $\frac{11}{3}$

Subtracting Mixed Numbers

You will learn to subtract mixed numbers.

Why learn this? You can find the difference of two amounts, such as two lengths of rope or two amounts of flour.

Sharon needs $1\frac{1}{4}$ cups of flour to make biscuits. She has $2\frac{3}{4}$ cups of flour. How much flour will Sharon have left?

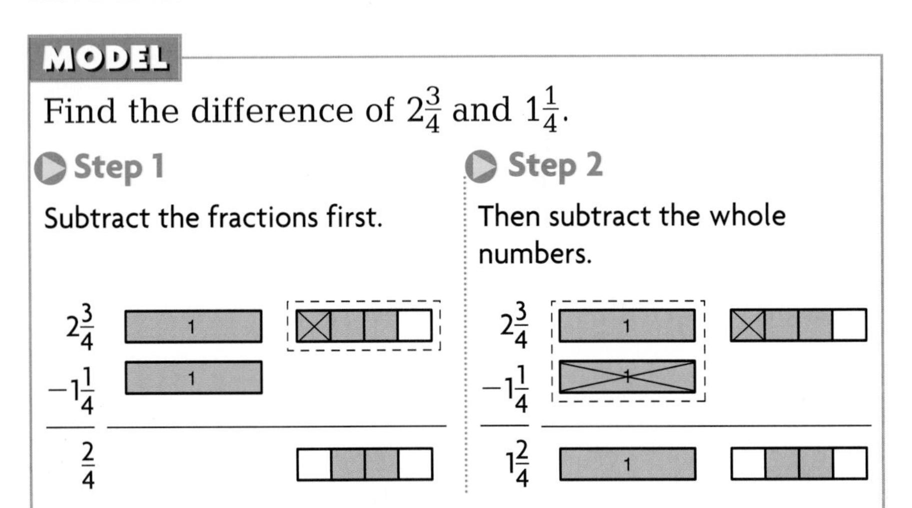

In ***Mighty Math Calculating Crew***, the game *Nautical Number Line* challenges you to add and subtract fractions on a number line.

So, Sharon will have $1\frac{2}{4}$ cups of flour left.

Talk About It

- How did you subtract the fractions?
- How can you use the models to find the amount that is left?

Check Your Understanding

Find the difference.

1. $2\frac{3}{5} - 1\frac{1}{5}$

2. $2\frac{5}{6} - 1\frac{3}{6}$

Find the difference. You may use fraction models or draw a picture.

3. $3\frac{2}{4} - 2\frac{1}{4} = n$

4. $2\frac{3}{6} - 1\frac{2}{6} = n$

5. $4\frac{5}{8} - 2\frac{2}{8} = n$

PRACTICE

Find the difference.

6. $4\frac{3}{4}$ $- 1\frac{1}{4}$

7. $3\frac{5}{6}$ $- 2\frac{2}{6}$

Find the difference. You may wish to draw a picture.

8. $3\frac{5}{6} - 1\frac{4}{6}$

9. $5\frac{4}{5} - 1\frac{2}{5}$

10. $6\frac{5}{8} - 3\frac{2}{8}$

11. $8\frac{7}{10} - 4\frac{3}{10}$

12. $10\frac{7}{8} - 5\frac{1}{8}$

13. $8\frac{9}{10} - 5\frac{3}{10}$

14. $7\frac{7}{8} - 4\frac{5}{8}$

15. $9\frac{11}{12} - 2\frac{8}{12}$

16. $8\frac{3}{5} - 4\frac{1}{5} = n$

17. $7\frac{3}{8} - 5\frac{2}{8} = n$

18. $9\frac{7}{9} - 3\frac{4}{9} = n$

Mixed Applications

For Problems 19–21, use the table.

Costume	Fabric Needed
Cowboy	$3\frac{1}{4}$ yards
Ballerina	$1\frac{1}{4}$ yards
Lion	$2\frac{3}{4}$ yards

19. How much more fabric is needed to make a cowboy costume than a ballerina costume?

20. Ms. Jenkins is making a lion costume and a ballerina costume. How much fabric will she need?

21. **Write a problem** using the information in the table which can be solved by adding or subtracting fractions.

Mixed Review

Find the elapsed time. (pages 124–125)

22.

Start A.M.

End P.M.

23.

Start P.M.

End P.M.

Find the quotient. (pages 318–319)

24. $5\overline{)260}$

25. $6\overline{)425}$

26. $7\overline{)634}$

27. $9\overline{)380}$

MORE PRACTICE Student Handbook page H106

MATH FUN!

How Many Out of How Many?

PURPOSE To find the number of fractional parts of a set

YOU WILL NEED paper and pencil

Study the shapes shown. How many are there in all?

Write a fraction to tell how many of the group are

1. red.

2. not blue.

3. green or purple.

4. yellow or triangular.

Number Puzzles

PURPOSE To use fraction bars to model addition problems

YOU WILL NEED fraction bars

Use fraction bars to model an addition problem with each mixed number as the sum. Use numbers less than 1 as addends.

1. $1\frac{3}{8}$

2. $1\frac{5}{12}$

3. $1\frac{5}{7}$

4. $1\frac{7}{9}$

5. $1\frac{2}{5}$

6. $1\frac{4}{6}$

7. $1\frac{4}{11}$

8. $1\frac{4}{10}$

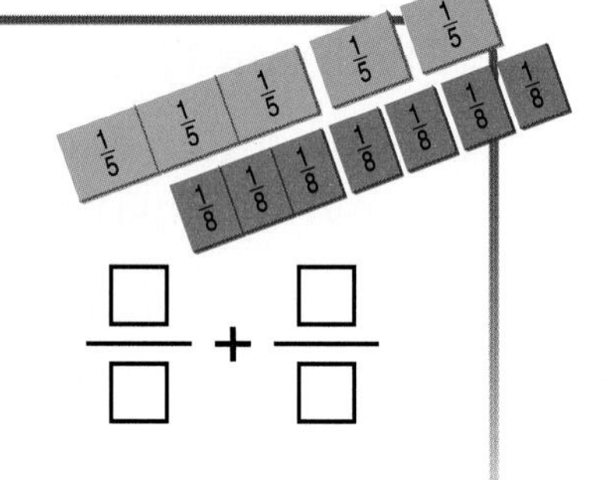

MAKING HUMMUS

PURPOSE To use fractions to measure ingredients

YOU WILL NEED hummus recipe

Hummus (hum′ əs) is a traditional Arabic dip that is often served in Middle Eastern countries. To make hummus, combine the following ingredients in a food processor or blender. Make into a smooth paste. You can use pieces of pita bread to scoop up the dip.

HUMMUS

- 16 oz (2 cups) drained, canned chick-peas. Save $\frac{1}{4}$ cup of the liquid.
- $\frac{1}{4}$ cup lemon juice
- $\frac{2}{3}$ cup toasted sesame seeds
- 2 teaspoons sesame oil
- 1 small garlic clove

Make hummus for your family to taste. Serves 10.

CHAPTER 21 REVIEW

✓ CHECK UNDERSTANDING

Write the letter of the number sentence for each model.
Find the sum or difference. (pages 354–359)

1. 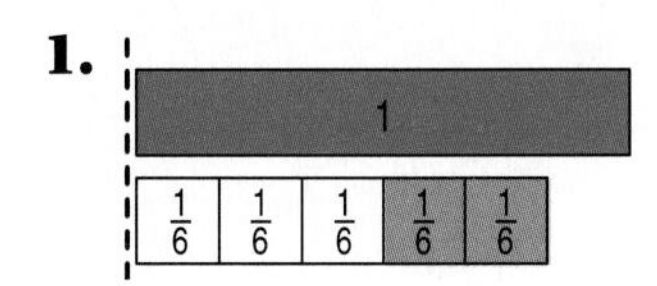

2. 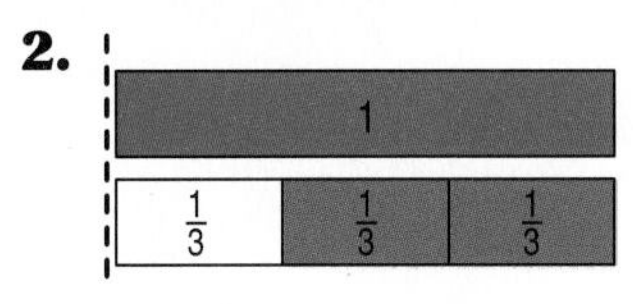

3. 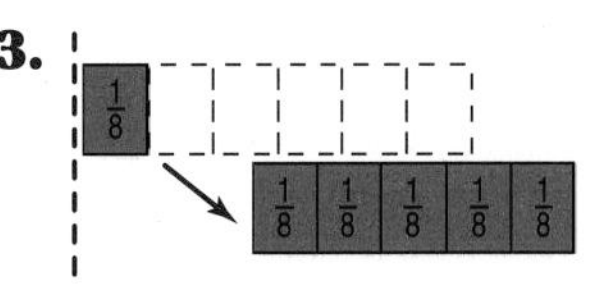

4. 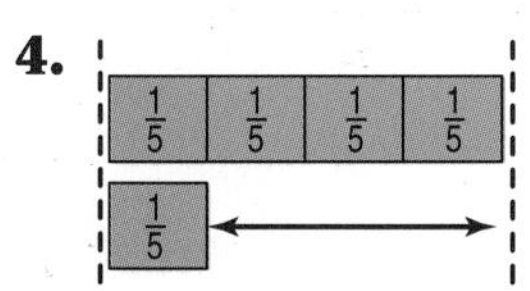

a. $\frac{1}{3} + \frac{2}{3} = \underline{\ ?\ }$ b. $\frac{3}{6} + \frac{2}{6} = \underline{\ ?\ }$ c. $\frac{4}{5} - \frac{1}{5} = \underline{\ ?\ }$ d. $\frac{6}{8} - \frac{5}{8} = \underline{\ ?\ }$

Complete the table. (pages 356–357)

	Addends	Sum	Reading the Problem	Reading the Sum
5.	$\frac{2}{6} + \frac{3}{6}$	$\frac{5}{6}$	?	five sixths
6.	$\frac{1}{8} + \frac{6}{8}$	$\frac{?}{?}$	one eighth plus six eighths	seven eighths
7.	$\frac{3}{5} + \frac{4}{5}$	$\frac{?}{?}$	?	?

✓ CHECK SKILLS

Find the sum or difference. You may use fraction bars or folded paper. (pages 354–359 and 362-365)

8. $\frac{1}{5} + \frac{2}{5} = n$ 9. $\frac{5}{6} - \frac{2}{6} = n$ 10. $\frac{2}{3} - \frac{1}{3} = n$ 11. $\frac{3}{8} + \frac{6}{8} = n$

12. $\frac{7}{10} - \frac{4}{10} = n$ 13. $\frac{3}{12} + \frac{8}{12} = n$ 14. $\frac{4}{5} + \frac{1}{5} = n$ 15. $\frac{3}{4} - \frac{1}{4} = n$

16. $3\frac{2}{4} + 1\frac{1}{4}$ 17. $5\frac{3}{6} - 3\frac{2}{6}$ 18. $2\frac{1}{5} + 3\frac{3}{5}$ 19. $6\frac{2}{10} + 4\frac{5}{10}$ 20. $7\frac{5}{8} - 4\frac{2}{8}$

✓ CHECK PROBLEM SOLVING

Solve. (pages 360–361)

CHOOSE A STRATEGY

- Work Backward
- Draw a Diagram
- Guess and Check
- Make a Model
- Act It Out

21. Melissa and Jason each ate $\frac{2}{6}$ of the apples. What fraction of the apples are left?

22. A spinner has 8 equal parts. Two of them are red, 1 is blue, 1 is orange, 1 is green, and 3 are yellow. Which two colors together cover more than $\frac{1}{2}$ of the spinner?

CHAPTER 22

UNDERSTANDING DECIMALS

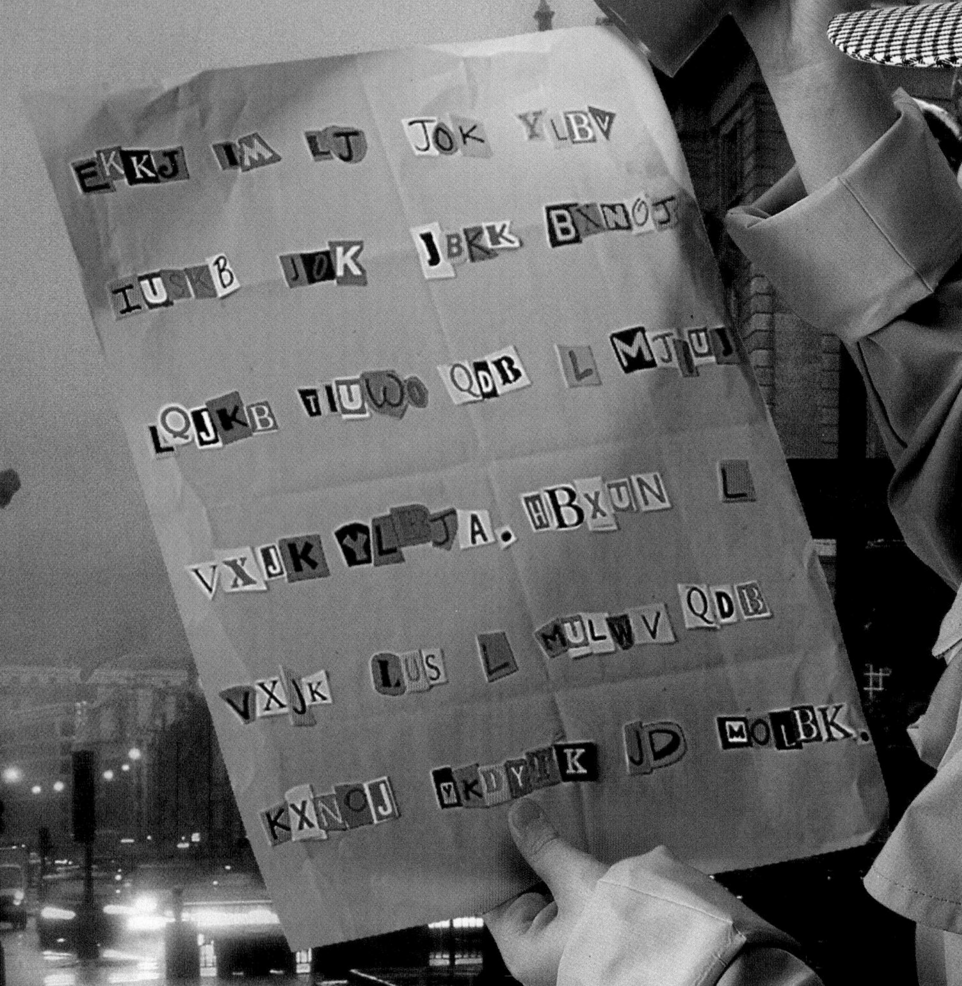

DID YOU KNOW...

Cryptography comes from a Greek work krypto which means hidden. A cryptogram is a coded message or a hidden message.

Some Egyptians (in 1900 B.C.) used codes in their messages that were written in hieroglyphics.

Team-Up Time

Crack the Code!

Do you know which letters are used most often in the English language? If you do, it will help you crack this code. The message has exactly 100 letters, so you can use data about letter use to help you solve the code.

Work with a partner. Your job is to

- analyze the Code Cracker's Handbook and find out which 5 letters are used most frequently in the English language.
- make a tally chart to show how often the letters in the code appear.
- analyze the first word in the code. Use the Code Cracker's Handbook to help you guess the real letter behind each coded letter.

CODE CRACKER'S HANDBOOK

Number of times each letter would appear in 100 letters of text in the English language:

- **A** 7 out of 100 or $\frac{7}{100}$ or 0.07
- **B** 1 out of 100 or $\frac{1}{100}$ or 0.01
- **C** 3 out of 100 or $\frac{3}{100}$ or 0.03
- **D** 4 out of 100 or $\frac{4}{100}$ or 0.04
- **E** 13 out of 100 or $\frac{13}{100}$ or 0.13
- **F** 3 out of 100 or $\frac{3}{100}$ or 0.03
- **G** 2 out of 100 or $\frac{2}{100}$ or 0.02
- **H** 3 out of 100 or $\frac{3}{100}$ or 0.03
- **I** 7 out of 100 or $\frac{7}{100}$ or 0.07
- **J** almost 0
- **K** 1 out of 100 or $\frac{1}{100}$ or 0.01
- **L** 4 out of 100 or $\frac{4}{100}$ or 0.04
- **M** 3 out of 100 or $\frac{3}{100}$ or 0.03
- **N** 8 out of 100 or $\frac{8}{100}$ or 0.08
- **O** 8 out of 100 or $\frac{8}{100}$ or 0.08
- **P** 3 out of 100 or $\frac{3}{100}$ or 0.03
- **Q** almost 0
- **R** 8 out of 100 or $\frac{8}{100}$ or 0.08
- **S** 6 out of 100 or $\frac{6}{100}$ or 0.06
- **T** 9 out of 100 or $\frac{9}{100}$ or 0.09
- **U** 3 out of 100 or $\frac{3}{100}$ or 0.03
- **V** 2 out of 100 or $\frac{2}{100}$ or 0.02
- **W** 2 out of 100 or $\frac{2}{100}$ or 0.02
- **X** almost 0
- **Y** 2 out of 100 or $\frac{2}{100}$ or 0.02
- **Z** almost 0

DID YOU

- ✓ find the 5 letters which appear most often in the English language and write the frequency they appear as a decimal?
- ✓ count how many times each coded letter appears in the message?
- ✓ figure out the first letter in the code?

R

E

Relating Fractions and Decimals

You will learn to read and write fractions and decimal parts of a whole.	Why learn this? You can use fractions or decimals to name an amount less than 1.	WORD POWER decimal

A **decimal** is a number that uses place value and a decimal point to show a value less than one, such as tenths and hundredths.

Tricia scoring a run in Saturday's game

Tricia was at bat 10 times. She had 6 hits. In how many of her times at bat did she have a hit?

Write the answer as a fraction or a decimal.

Model	Fraction	Decimal
	Write: $\frac{6}{10}$ **Read:** six tenths	**Write:** 0.6 **Read:** six tenths

So, Tricia hit the ball $\frac{6}{10}$, or 0.6, of her times at bat.

Darla's team has scored 100 runs so far this year. Darla scored 14 of the runs. What fraction and decimal can you write to show how many of the team's runs were scored by Darla?

Model	Fraction	Decimal
	Write: $\frac{14}{100}$ **Read:** fourteen hundredths	**Write:** 0.14 **Read:** fourteen hundredths

So, Darla scored $\frac{14}{100}$, or 0.14, of the team's runs.

CRITICAL THINKING How is the model showing tenths different from the model showing hundredths?

Talk About It

- How are fractions and decimals alike?
- What decimal can you write to show $\frac{2}{10}$? to show $\frac{25}{100}$?

Language Link

Julius Caesar was a Roman Emperor (100–44 B.C.). He made up a cryptogram, or secret code, by shifting some alphabet letters a set amount. Copy 100 letters in a paragraph. Use A's in the place of B's and B's in the place of C's. Write as a decimal the frequency the letters A and B appear in your paragraph. Ask a classmate to read and decode the paragraph.

Calculator Activities page H63

PRACTICE

Write the decimal for the part that is shaded.

1. 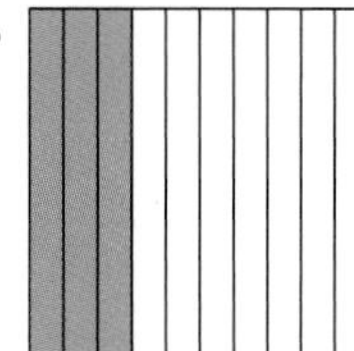

2. 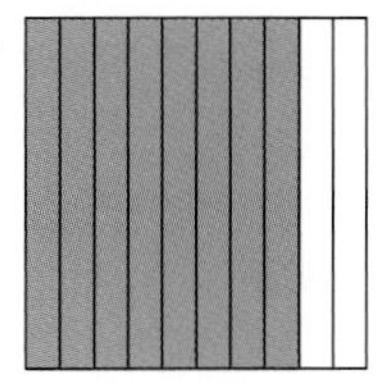

3. 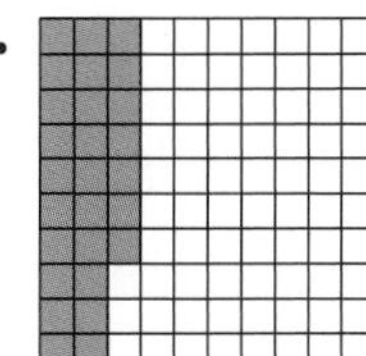

4. 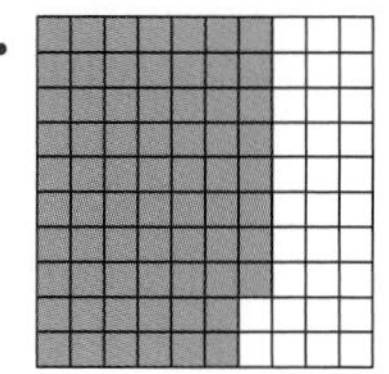

Write each fraction as a decimal.

5. $\frac{5}{10}$ **6.** $\frac{9}{10}$ **7.** $\frac{34}{100}$ **8.** $\frac{75}{100}$ **9.** $\frac{2}{10}$ **10.** $\frac{99}{100}$

Write each decimal as a fraction.

11. 0.1 **12.** 0.4 **13.** 0.18 **14.** 0.44 **15.** 0.7 **16.** 0.86

Mixed Applications

17. Madison played computer games for 10 minutes. She played Tetris® for 2 minutes and chess for 8 minutes. Write a fraction and a decimal that show how long she played Tetris®.

18. Sonia's survey showed that 77 out of 100 people like going to the movies better than going to a football game. Write a fraction and a decimal that show Sonia's results.

19. Bill bought two pens for $0.59 each and a notebook for $1.29. How much change did he receive from a $5.00 bill?

20. **WRITE ABOUT IT** Explain how you would use a model and a decimal to show $\frac{6}{10}$.

Mixed Review

What fraction is shaded? What fraction is not shaded?
(pages 338–339)

21. 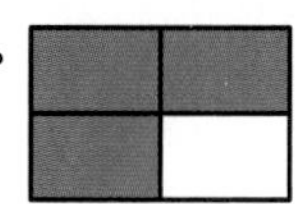

22. 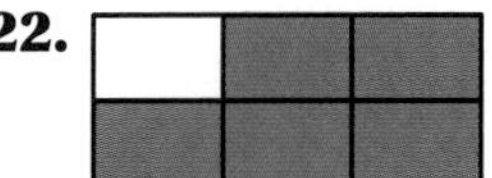

23. 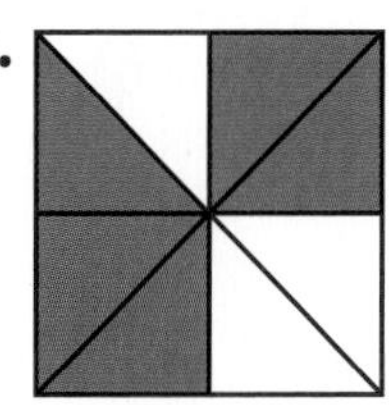

24. 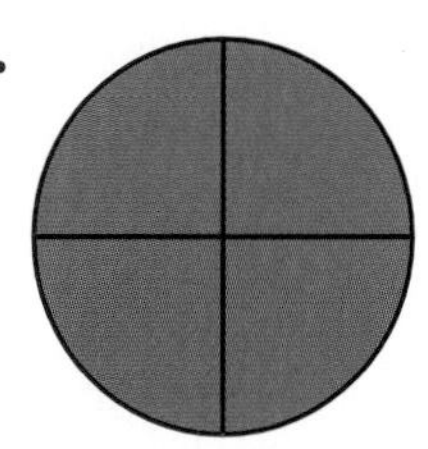

Find the quotient. Check by multiplying. (pages 310–311)

25. $5\overline{)248}$ **26.** $6\overline{)351}$ **27.** $4\overline{)824}$ **28.** $2\overline{)457}$ **29.** $7\overline{)229}$ **30.** $5\overline{)619}$

Tenths and Hundredths

You will learn how to read and write money and decimal amounts.

Why learn this? You can understand how coins and dollars are related to decimals.

Decimal numbers can be modeled using money.

1 dollar

\$1.00

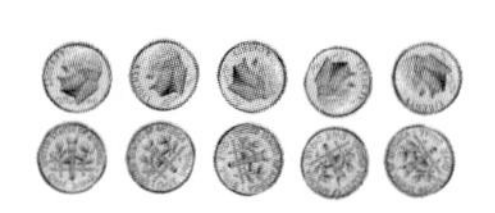

10 dimes = 1 dollar

1 dime = $\frac{1}{10}$, or 0.1 dollar

\$0.10

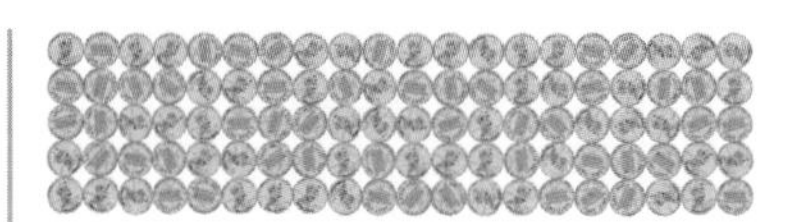

100 pennies = 1 dollar

1 penny = $\frac{1}{100}$, or 0.01 dollar

\$0.01

REMEMBER:

Place the decimal point between the ones and the tenths.

decimal point

0.1

A zero is used to show there are no ones.

CRITICAL THINKING Which coin represents one tenth of a dollar? one hundredth of a dollar?

____

Decimal numbers can be modeled using decimal squares.

This square represents one whole, or 1.
Read: one
Write: 1, or 1.0

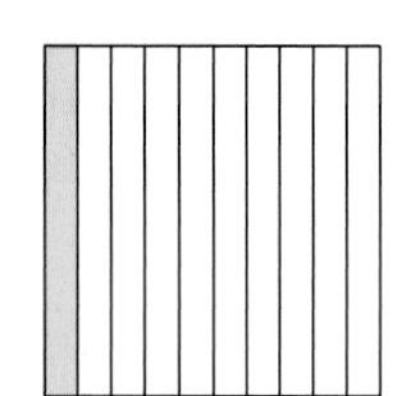

This whole is divided into 10 equal parts. One part is shaded.
Read: one tenth
Write: 0.1

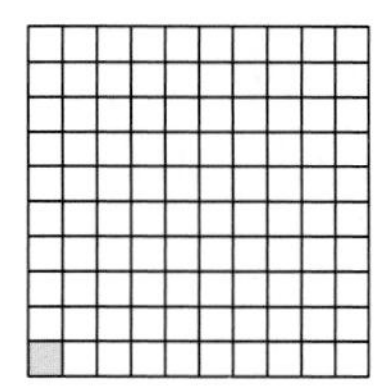

This whole is divided into 100 equal parts. One part is shaded.
Read: one hundredth
Write: 0.01

Talk About It

- What do you notice about the size of the models that represent one whole, one tenth, and one hundredth?
- How can you use decimal models to show 0.3? to show 0.36?
- Which model would you use to show $\frac{9}{10}$ of a dollar? Explain.

PRACTICE

Write the amount as a fraction of a dollar, a decimal, and a money amount.

1. 14 pennies **2.** 29 pennies **3.** 8 dimes **4.** 10 dimes

5. 42 pennies **6.** 6 dimes **7.** 84 pennies **8.** 99 pennies

Write the decimal and the decimal name for the shaded part of each model.

9. 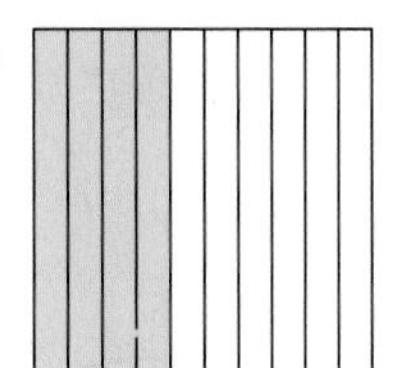
10. 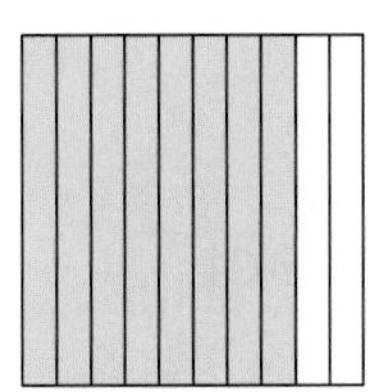
11. 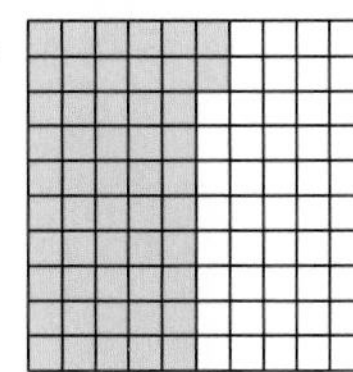
12. 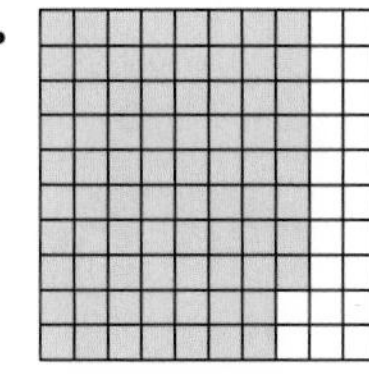

13. 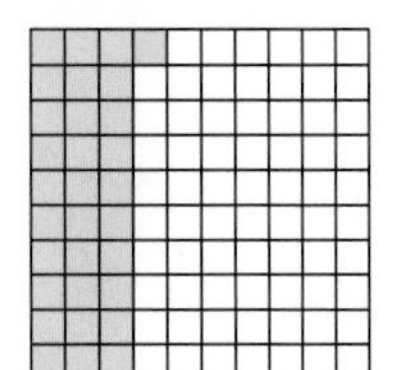
14. 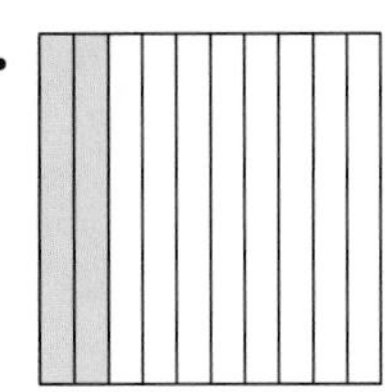
15. 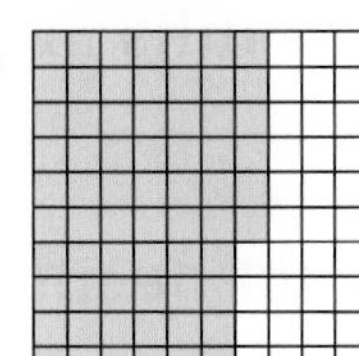
16. 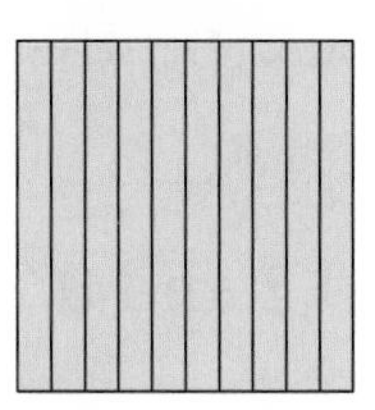

Mixed Applications

17. Ross gave the cashier at the snack bar $\frac{7}{10}$ of a dollar. How many dimes is that? How many pennies?

18. Chelsea has 89 pennies in a penny jar. What is that amount as a fraction? as a decimal? as a money amount?

19. Alan made a spinner for a game with 2 red sections, 2 yellow sections, and 2 blue sections. What is the probability that he will spin yellow?

20. **Write a problem** using decimals in tenths or hundredths.

Draw a picture and shade part of it to show the fraction. (pages 338–339)

21. $\frac{2}{5}$ **22.** $\frac{3}{6}$ **23.** $\frac{2}{8}$ **24.** $\frac{1}{4}$ **25.** $\frac{2}{3}$

Choose an operation to use. Then solve. (pages 62–63)

26. The art show has 68 paintings and 49 pieces of jewelry. How many items are in the show?

27. John paid $36.98 for a ring and $89.50 for a watch. How much more did he pay for the watch than the ring?

Equivalent Decimals

You will investigate equivalent decimals.

Why learn this? You can use equivalent decimals when you are counting change for a dollar.

WORD POWER
equivalent decimals

Equivalent decimals are different names for the same amount.

REMEMBER:
Equivalent fractions are different names for the same amount.

$\frac{2}{4} = \frac{1}{2}$

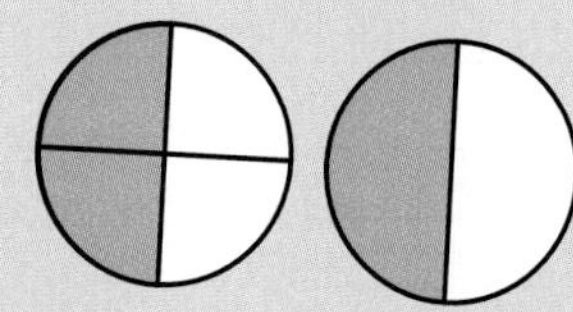

Explore

Use models and paper folding to find equivalent decimals.

MATERIALS: tenths and hundredths models

MODEL

Are 0.2 and 0.20 equivalent decimals?

Step 1

Shade 0.2 of the tenths model and 0.20 of the hundredths model.

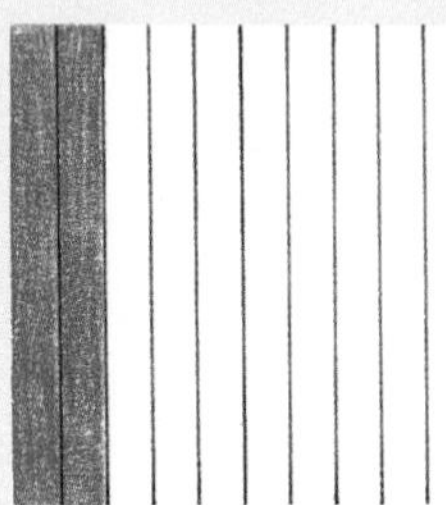

two tenths
2 out of 10

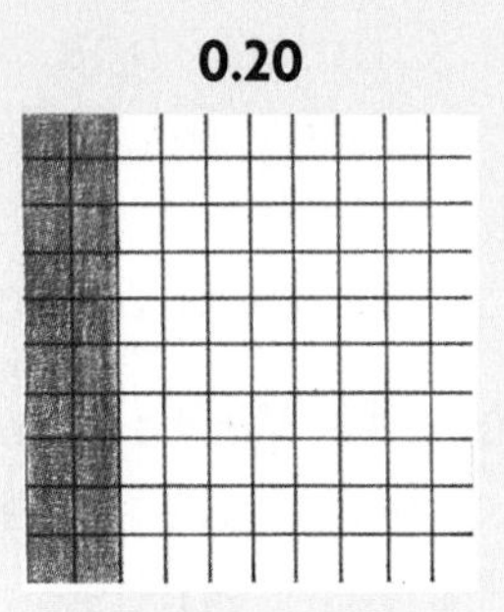

twenty hundredths
20 out of 100

Step 2

Fold 0.2 of the tenths model and 0.20 of the hundredths model. Then compare the two models.

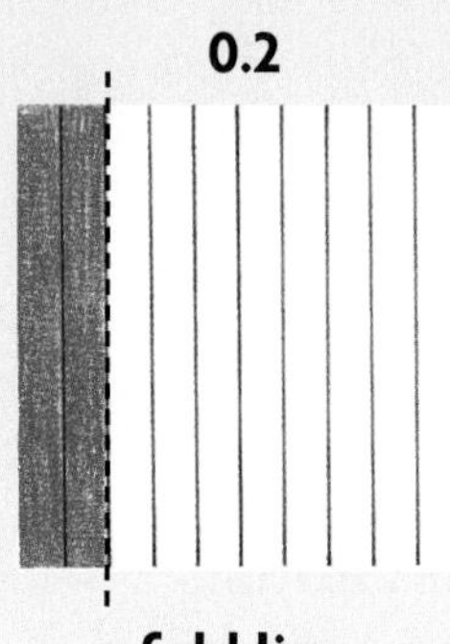

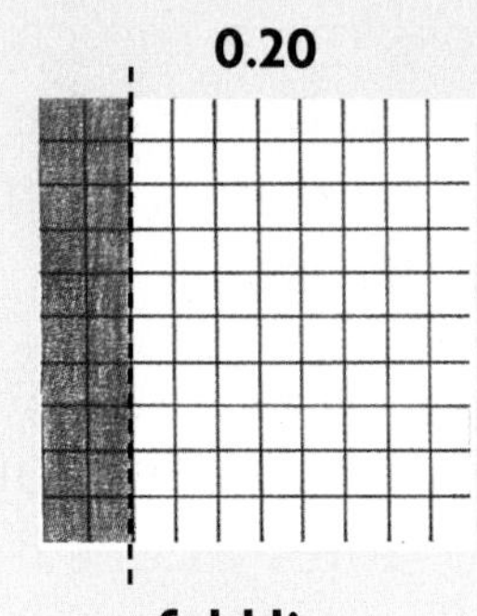

Record

Explain how you used the models to decide whether 0.2 and 0.20 are equivalent.

Talk About It

- How much did you fold in each of the models?
- How can you use paper folding to show that 0.4 and 0.50 are not equivalent?

Technology Link
E-Lab • Activity 22 Available on CD-ROM and the Internet at http://www.hbschool.com/elab

Now, investigate shading decimal models to find other equivalent decimals.

Try This

Find all the equivalent decimals that you can by using the tenths and hundredths models.

TALK ABOUT IT What equivalent decimals did you find?

- Look at the pattern. How do you know two decimal numbers are equivalent without paper folding?

WRITE ABOUT IT Explain how you know you have found all the possible equivalent decimals for the models.

HANDS-ON PRACTICE

Write an equivalent decimal for each. You may wish to use decimal models.

1. 0.8 **2.** 0.3 **3.** 0.90 **4.** 0.5 **5.** 0.10

6. 0.1 **7.** 0.40 **8.** 0.2 **9.** 0.60 **10.** 0.7

Applying What You Learned

Are the two decimals equivalent? Write *yes* or *no*.

11. 0.6 and 0.60 **12.** 0.06 and 0.6 **13.** 0.4 and 0.04

14. 0.8 and 0.80 **15.** 0.70 and 0.7 **16.** 0.9 and 0.90

Mixed Applications

17. Glenn said that $0.80 is 80 hundredths of a dollar. Kim said that $0.80 is 8 tenths of a dollar. Who was correct?

18. Erin's family plants a garden on 0.5 acre of their land. Write an equivalent decimal for this amount of land.

19. The area of a floor is 20 square yards. The length of the floor is 5 yards. What is the width of the floor?

20. Laura's class took a field trip to the science museum. They arrived there at 10:15 A.M. and left 4 hours 30 minutes later. At what time did they leave?

MORE PRACTICE Student Handbook page H107

Comparing and Ordering

You will learn to compare and order decimals.

Why learn this? You can compare times, such as those used in a race.

At the 1996 Olympics, Brad Bridgewater won the gold medal in the 200-meter backstroke by 0.46 of a second. Amy Van Dyken won the gold medal in the 50-meter freestyle by 0.03 of a second. Who won by the greater number of seconds?

You can use a place-value chart to compare the numbers.

Ones	Tenths	Hundredths
0 .	4	6
0 .	0	3

- First, line up the decimal points.
- Begin with the digits on the left.
- Compare the digits in each place.
- There are no ones, so compare the tenths.
- Since 4 > 0, 0.46 is greater than 0.03.

So, Brad won by the greater number of seconds.

- How does a place-value chart help you compare decimals?

You can use a decimal number line to order numbers.

- This number line shows decimals from 0 to 1.0.
- The large ticks show the tenths and are labeled 0.1, 0.2, 0.3, and so on.
- The small ticks, in between the tenths, show the hundredths such as 0.73 and 0.87.

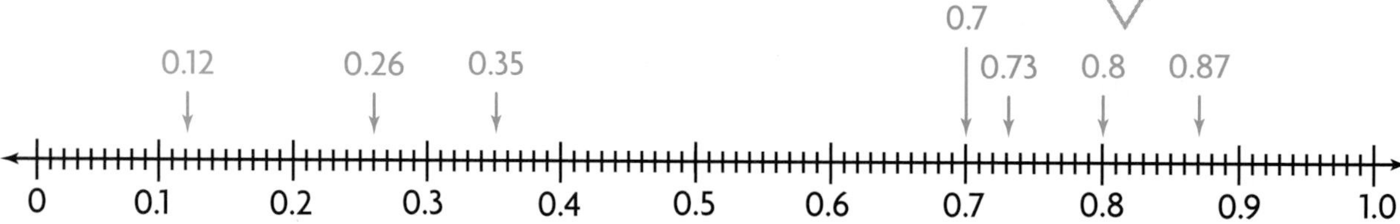

Suppose you want to order 0.26, 0.35, and 0.12 from least to greatest. Locate the decimals on the number line. The numbers from least to greatest are 0.12, 0.26, and 0.35.

Talk About It

- How does a number line help you order decimals?
- Are 0.2 and 0.20 at the same place on a number line? Explain.

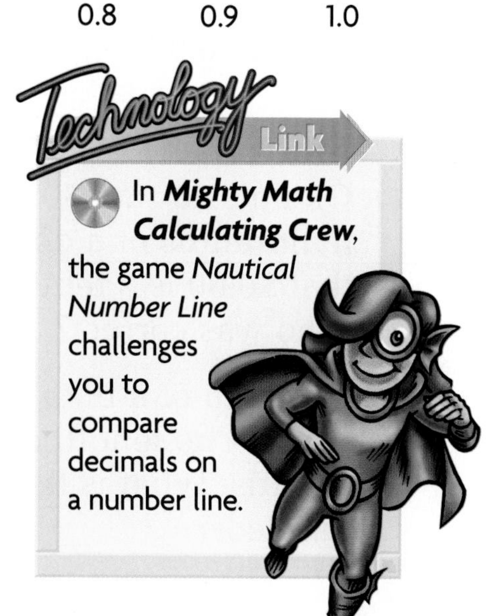

In ***Mighty Math Calculating Crew***, the game *Nautical Number Line* challenges you to compare decimals on a number line.

PRACTICE

Tell which number is greater.

1. 0.95
   0.85
2. 0.2
   0.5
3. 0.8
   0.81
4. 0.5
   0.25
5. 0.03
   0.30
6. 0.20
   0.2
7. 0.50
   0.55
8. 0.8
   0.18
9. 0.01
   0.11
10. 0.79
    0.7
11. 0.14
    0.41
12. 0.29
    0.26
13. 0.60
    0.06
14. 0.26
    0.6
15. 0.52
    0.53

Use the number line to order the decimals from greatest to least.

0 0.1 0.2 0.3 0.4 0.5 0.6 0.7 0.8 0.9 1.0

16. 0.87, 0.78, 0.80, 0.08
17. 0.3, 0.2, 0.03, 0.02, 0.32
18. 0.6, 0.46, 0.64, 0.06, 0.4
19. 0.25, 0.5, 0.15, 0.10, 0.2
20. 0.17, 0.71, 0.07, 0.7, 0.01
21. 0.11, 0.09, 0.23, 0.13, 0.29

Mixed Applications

22. Kelly has \$0.50. Frank has \$0.56, Jay has \$0.65, Ruth has \$0.60, and Leigh has \$0.26. Write the amounts in order from least to greatest.
23. Sue beat Josh in the race by 0.48 seconds. She beat Amy by 0.36 seconds. Who came in first? second? third?
24. On vacation, the Reed family took 5 rolls of 36-photo film and 3 rolls of 24-photo film. How many photos did they take?
25. **WRITE ABOUT IT** Name a situation in which you would need to order decimal numbers.

Mixed Review

Is the blue line a line of symmetry? Write *yes* or *no*. (pages 250–251)

26. 

27. 

28. 

29. 

Copy each problem. Draw a ■ where the first digit in the quotient should be placed. (pages 304–305)

30. $6\overline{)39}$
31. $4\overline{)72}$
32. $7\overline{)201}$
33. $5\overline{)847}$
34. $3\overline{)296}$

MORE PRACTICE Student Handbook page H107

PART
1 Mixed Decimals

You will learn how to read and write mixed decimals.	Why learn this? You can understand how to use decimal numbers or money amounts greater than 1.	WORD POWER mixed decimal

The swim club is selling candy to raise money. There are 10 candy bars in each box. Joshua has 5 boxes and 4 bars to sell. How can you write the amount as a mixed decimal?

A **mixed decimal** is a number that is made up of a whole number and a decimal.

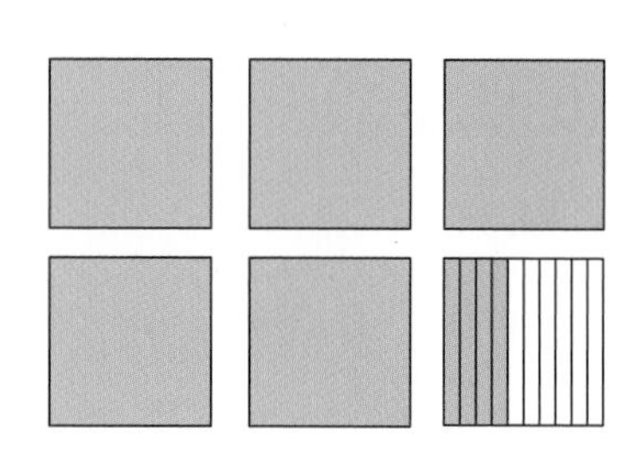

5 and $\frac{4}{10}$ boxes are being sold.

Read: five and four tenths
Write: 5.4

So, Joshua has 5.4 boxes to sell.

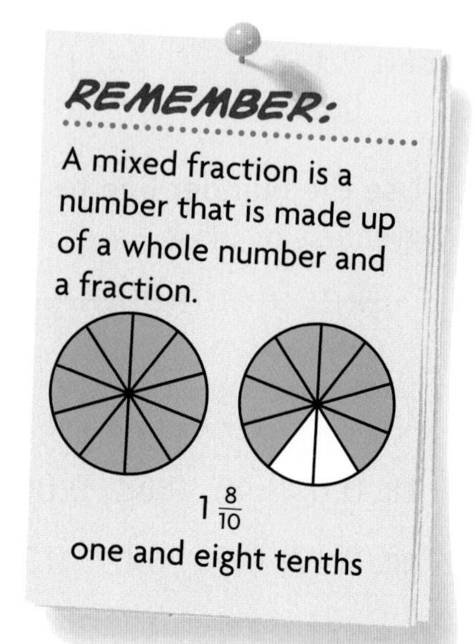

Talk About It

- How do the decimal models show 5 boxes?
- How does the decimal model show 4 bars?

Make models to show equivalent mixed decimals.

1.2

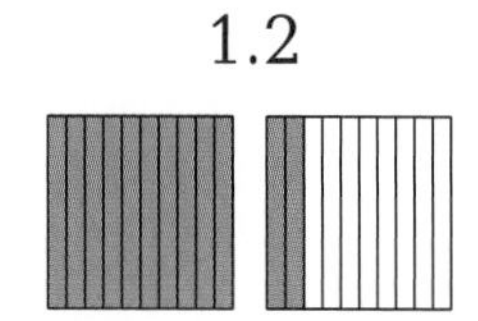

Read: one and two tenths
Write: $1\frac{2}{10} = 1.2$

1.20

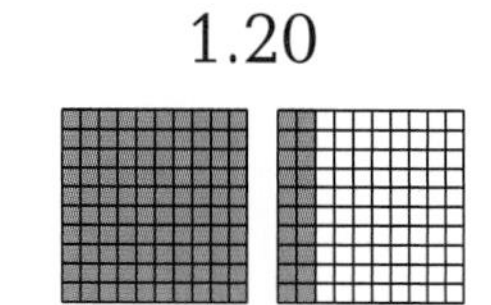

Read: one and twenty hundredths
Write: $1\frac{20}{100} = 1.20$

- How do these models show that 1.2 and 1.20 are equivalent?

CRITICAL THINKING How can you use models to show an equivalent mixed decimal for 1.5?

Consumer Link

When you shop, you use mixed decimals. A dollar sign and a decimal point are used for mixed decimals, such as $3.45. Name a mixed decimal you have used.

PRACTICE

Write a mixed decimal for each model.

1. 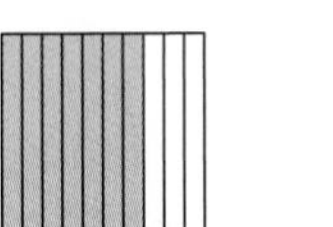

2. 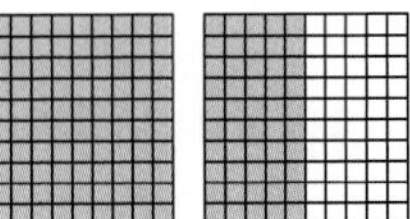

3. 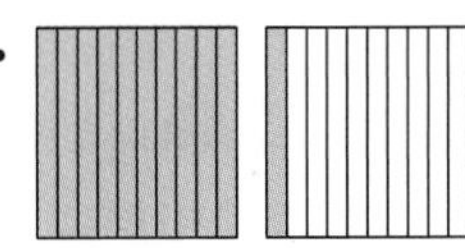

Write two equivalent mixed decimals for each model.

4. 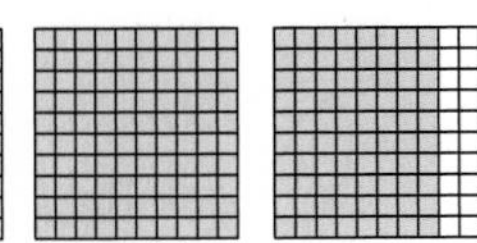

5. 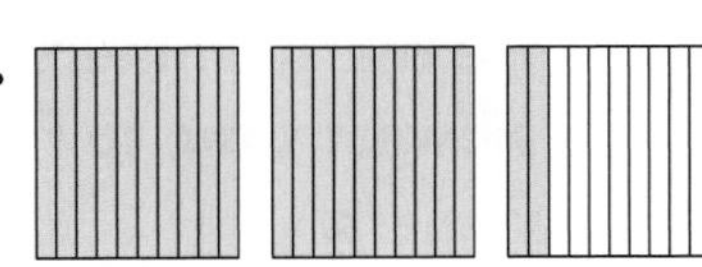

Write each mixed number as a mixed decimal.

6. $3\frac{2}{10}$ **7.** $1\frac{4}{10}$ **8.** $5\frac{5}{100}$ **9.** $4\frac{1}{10}$ **10.** $6\frac{3}{100}$

11. $1\frac{1}{100}$ **12.** $9\frac{99}{100}$ **13.** $15\frac{9}{10}$ **14.** $29\frac{18}{100}$ **15.** $17\frac{89}{100}$

Write each mixed decimal as a mixed number.

16. 3.3 **17.** 6.84 **18.** 9.25 **19.** 11.1

Write an equivalent mixed decimal for each. You may wish to use decimal models.

20. 3.80 **21.** 4.2 **22.** 1.10 **23.** 9.60

Mixed Applications

24. To build a doghouse, Tim bought 2 boards that were each 2.5 meters long. The boards cost $1.35 per meter. How many meters of lumber did Tim buy? How much did Tim spend for the boards?

25. Mike and Tonya went to the grocery store to buy milk and cheese. The price of milk was $0.39 more than the price of cheese. The cheese cost $2.49. What was the price of the milk?

26. Price's basketball team has scored 10 points so far. Price has scored 4 of these points. Write a fraction and an equivalent decimal to show Price's part of the team's points.

27. **WRITE ABOUT IT** At the gymnastics meet, Tony noticed that two athletes had scores of 9.70 and 9.7. Which gymnast received the higher score? Explain.

MORE PRACTICE Student Handbook page H107

PART 2 PROBLEM-SOLVING STRATEGY
Make a Table

THE PROBLEM During the 1996 Olympics, Jingyi Le of China swam the women's 50-meter freestyle race in 24.90 seconds. Amy Van Dyken of the United States swam it in 24.87 seconds. Sandra Volker of Germany swam it in 25.14 seconds. Arrange the swimmers' times from the fastest time to the slowest time to find the gold, silver, and bronze medal winners.

REMEMBER:
- ✓ Understand
- ✓ Plan
- ✓ Solve
- ✓ Look Back

✓ Understand
- What are you asked to find?
- What information will you use?
- Is there any information you will not use? If so, what?

✓ Plan
- What strategy can you use to solve the problem?

You can *make a table* to arrange the swimmers' times in order from fastest to slowest.

✓ Solve
- How can you solve this problem?

Compare the times. Then, *make a table* arranging the times in order from least to greatest.

Swimmer	Time
Amy Van Dyken, United States	24.87 seconds
Jingyi Le, China	24.90 seconds
Sandra Volker, Germany	25.14 seconds

So, Amy Van Dyken won the gold medal, Jingyi Le won the silver medal, and Sandra Volker won the bronze medal.

✓ Look Back
- How can you decide if your answer is reasonable?
- What other strategy could you use?

Sports Link

In some sporting events, such as swimming, where speed is so important, the least decimal number shows the winner. Name a sport in which the greatest decimal number shows the winner.

PRACTICE

CHOOSE Paper/Pencil Calculator Hands-on Mental Math

Make a table to solve.

1. At the gymnastics competition, Jody scored 9.85, Beth scored 9.70, and Michelle scored 9.82. If first place goes to the athlete with the highest score, who finished in first place? second place? third place?

2. The three athletes with the longest jumps advance to the finals. Which of the following athletes advanced to the finals? Jim jumped 24.40 ft; Tom, 25.35 ft; Price, 26.00 ft; Dan, 25.55 ft; Will, 27.15 ft; and Mike, 22.83 ft.

3. Saul kept track of the amount of money he spent for meals on the class trip. On Monday, he spent $4.98 for breakfast, $5.17 for lunch, and $6.12 for dinner. On Tuesday, he spent $6.25 for breakfast, $6.35 for lunch, and $6.50 for dinner. Did he spend the most for breakfast, lunch, or dinner in the two days?

4. In a survey of 40 fourth graders, 15 students said basketball was their favorite sport, 5 said football, 9 said baseball, and 11 said ice hockey. According to the survey, which sport is the fourth graders' favorite? second-favorite? third-favorite?

Mixed Applications

Solve.

CHOOSE A STRATEGY

- Make a Table
- Find a Pattern
- Work Backward
- Write a Number Sentence
- Use a Table
- Guess and Check

5. It is 63 days until Valerie's birthday. How many weeks is it until her birthday? If today is January 10, in what month is Valerie's birthday?

6. At the swim meet, Mark swam the race in 32.80 seconds, David swam it in 38.70 seconds, and Carlos swam it in 37.25 seconds. Who came in first? second? third?

7. Sandy went to the museum with her family. Her mother bought 2 adult tickets and 3 child tickets. Each adult ticket cost $1 more than a child ticket. If her mother paid a total of $22 for the tickets, how much was 1 adult ticket? one child ticket?

8. The train takes 55 minutes from Mr. Link's station to the Loop. At what time will he arrive in the Loop if he takes Train A? Train B?

CHICAGO-LOOP TRAIN SCHEDULE	
Train	**Departure**
A	7:15 A.M.
B	8:05 A.M.

MORE PRACTICE Student Handbook page H107

CULTURAL CONNECTION

COOPERATIVE LEARNING

CELEBRATING KWANZAA

Daniel and his family celebrate Kwanzaa, an African American holiday that begins on December 26 and lasts for seven days. Daniel looked at a cookbook with 20 recipes to pick 5 favorites to make for the Kwanzaa feast. What fraction of the recipes did Daniel choose? Write the fraction as a decimal.

Work Together

1. Daniel found several recipes that used similar ingredients. Cornbread, sweet potatoes, and peach cobbler called for cinnamon. The amounts were $\frac{1}{4}$, $\frac{1}{2}$, and $\frac{3}{4}$ teaspoons. Model these amounts on decimal squares and write each as a fraction in hundredths. Then write each as a decimal.

2. When Daniel shopped, he learned that a pound of red beans costs 67¢. A pound of sweet potatoes costs 89¢, and a pound of kale costs 72¢. Write these numbers as fractions of a dollar and as decimals.

3. Daniel baked two pans of cornbread ahead of time to decide which recipe he liked better. He cut each pan into 10 servings. His family ate 0.4 from one pan and 0.5 from the other. Which amount is greater? Write an equivalent decimal for each amount.

4. Daniel's brother went to buy the cinnamon. He found that cinnamon comes in containers with 8.75 ounces, 2.37 ounces, 1.87 ounces, and 0.90 ounce. Use a place-value chart or a number line to order these containers by size. Write the amounts in order from least to greatest.

CULTURAL LINK

Cornmeal is an important ingredient in many traditional recipes used to celebrate African American culture. Cornmeal is used in cornbread, corn sticks, corn muffins, corn fritters, and hush puppies. Hush puppies are a combination of cornmeal, flour, eggs, milk, and seasoning, fried and served warm. According to legend, the name developed when an outdoor cook threw one of the puffed balls to hungry dogs, yelling, "Hush, puppies!"

CHAPTER 22

REVIEW

✓ CHECK UNDERSTANDING

VOCABULARY

1. A __?__ is a number that uses place value and a decimal point to show a value less than one, such as tenths and hundredths. (page 370)

2. Different names for the same amount, such as 0.4 and 0.40, are __?__. (page 374)

3. A number that is made up of a whole number and a decimal is a __?__. (page 378)

Write the decimal for the part that is shaded. (pages 370–371, 378–379)

4. 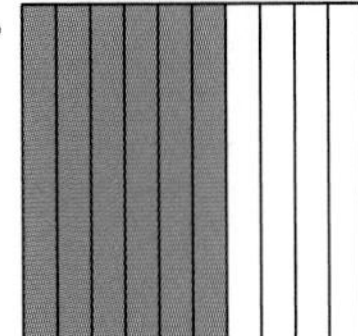

5. 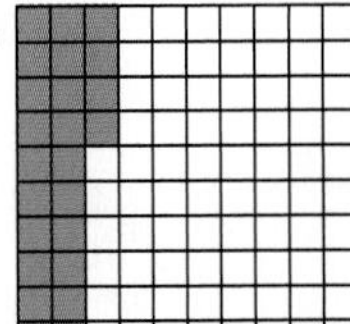

6. 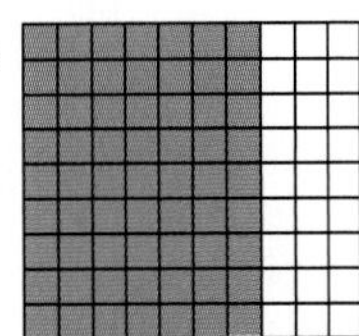

7. 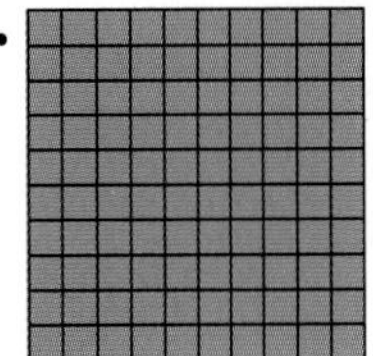 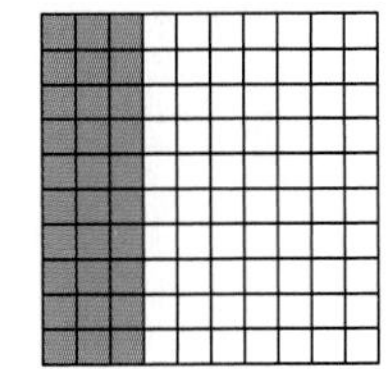

✓ CHECK SKILLS

Tell which number is greater. (pages 376–377)

8. 0.39
0.3

9. 0.12
0.21

10. 0.47
0.44

11. 0.8
0.09

12. 0.6
0.16

Order the decimals from greatest to least. You may use a number line to help you. (pages 376–377)

13. 0.5, 0.9, 0.7, 0.2

14. 0.06, 0.40, 0.04, 0.60

15. 0.7, 0.67, 0.76, 0.07, 0.6

✓ CHECK PROBLEM SOLVING

Solve. (pages 380–381)

CHOOSE A STRATEGY

- Act It Out
- Draw a Picture
- Make a Model
- Make a Table

16. Becky bought school supplies. She received $0.25 change. How many different ways can you show $0.25 with coins?

17. Tom ran the race in 5.36 minutes, Roy ran it in 4.47 minutes, Greg in 4.72 minutes, and Louis in 5.14 minutes. In what order did the boys finish the race?

ADDING AND SUBTRACTING DECIMALS

DID YOU KNOW . . .

Meteorologists are scientists who study Earth's atmosphere. They watch how and at what speed the air moves in space. They also predict temperature and weather system changes.

Team-Up Time

Weather Watch

Ms. Watson's class members record daily precipitation (rain and snow) in inches for every month of the school year. One foot of snow is the same as one inch of rain. Here are the data for three years.

Work with a partner. Your job is to

- find the total precipitation for each school year.
- find the wettest month of each school year.
- find the difference in total inches of precipitation between the average at Mt. Waialeale and each of the years at the school.
- find the difference in total inches of precipitation between the average at Death Valley and each of the years at the school.
- report your findings to the class.

DID YOU

- ✓ find the total precipitation for each year?
- ✓ find the wettest month of each school year?
- ✓ find the difference in total precipitation between the rainiest and driest places on Earth and each of the years at the school?
- ✓ report your findings to the class?

Ms. Watson's Weather Watchers

Precipitation in inches

	1995	1996	1997
Sept	3.3	3.8	2.9
Oct	4.1	4.0	4.5
Nov	3.2	3.1	3.8
Dec	3.0	3.3	3.6
Jan	3.8	3.5	3.7
Feb	4.2	4.0	4.1
Mar	3.2	3.5	3.2
Apr	3.6	3.5	3.7
May	2.8	3.0	3.1

Modeling Addition and Subtraction

You will investigate how to use models to add and subtract decimals.

Why learn this? You can add and subtract measurements or money amounts.

You can use decimal squares to model addition and subtraction of decimals.

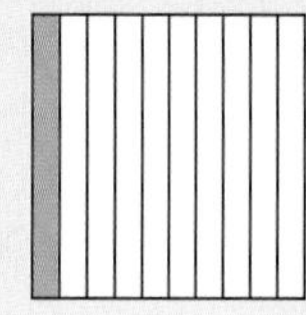

0.1
tenths model

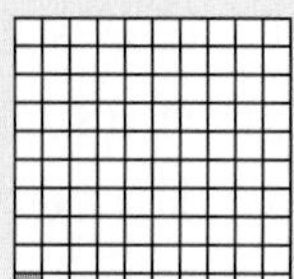

0.01
hundredths model

MODEL

A. Add. $0.6 + 0.2 = n$

Step 1

Shade 0.6 of the whole decimal square red. Cut out the shaded part.

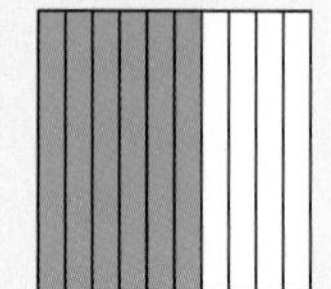

Step 2

Then shade 0.2 of the remaining part of the square blue. Cut out the shaded part. Combine the parts to find the sum.

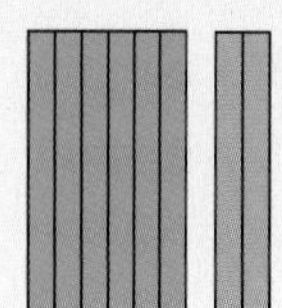

$0.6 + 0.2 = 0.8$

B. Add. $0.45 + 0.55 = n$

Step 1

Shade 0.45 of the whole decimal square red. Cut out the shaded part.

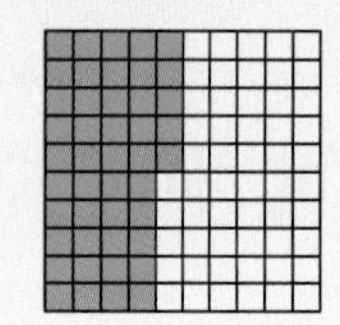

Step 2

Then shade 0.55 of the remaining part of the square blue. Cut out the shaded part. Combine the parts to find the sum.

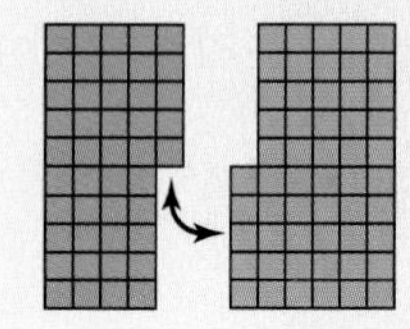

Notice that $0.05 + 0.05 = 0.10$, or 0.1.

So, $0.45 + 0.55 = 1.00$, or 1.

Talk About It

- How do the red and blue parts together compare with a whole decimal square in the tenths model? in the hundredths model?
- What two addition sentences can you name from the tenths model? from the hundredths model?

Explore

Use decimal squares to subtract decimals.

MATERIALS: decimal squares, red marker

Technology Link

E-Lab • Activity 23 Available on CD-ROM and the Internet at http://www.hbschool.com/elab

EXAMPLES

A. Subtract. $0.7 - 0.2 = n$

Shade 0.7 of the whole decimal square red. Cut out the shaded part.

Then cut away 0.2 of the shaded part of the square. Count to find what is left.

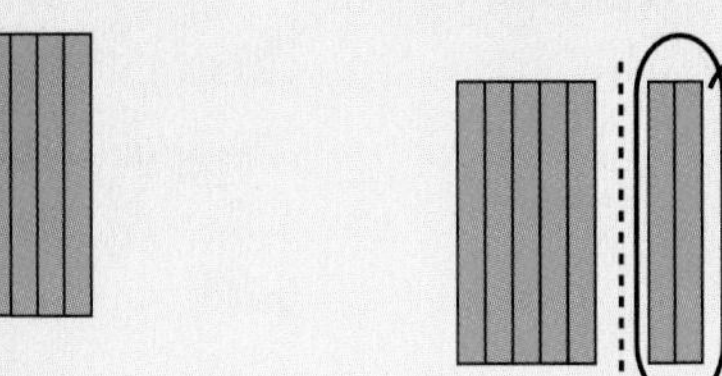

B. Subtract. $0.65 - 0.30 = n$

Shade 0.65 of the whole decimal square red. Cut out the shaded part.

Then cut away 0.30 of the shaded part of the square. Count to find what is left.

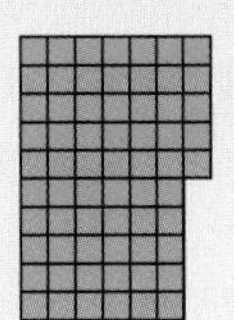

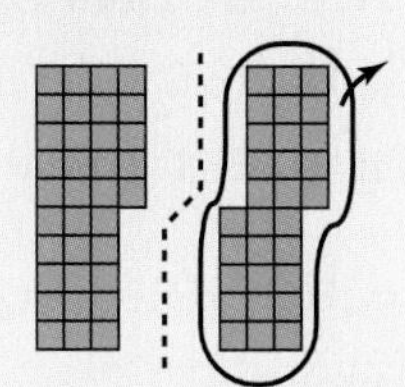

Record

Use decimal squares to model the problems. Tape or paste the parts to a sheet of paper. Write a number sentence for each problem.

- Why can you model subtraction by using only one color for your shading?

Now, investigate how to use decimal squares to find sums and differences.

A rainy day

Try This

Use decimal squares to find the sum or difference.

A. $0.7 + 0.6 = n$ **B.** $1.00 - 0.49 = n$

TALK ABOUT IT In Example A, is the sum greater than or less than 1 whole? Explain.

WRITE ABOUT IT How can you use a decimal square to find the difference in Example B?

HANDS-ON PRACTICE

Use decimal squares to find the sum or difference.

1. $0.3 + 0.4 = n$ **2.** $0.8 - 0.3 = n$ **3.** $0.65 - 0.22 = n$ **4.** $0.53 + 0.27 = n$

Mixed Applications

5. Curt ran 0.45 km on Monday and 0.75 km on Tuesday. How far did he run in the two days?

6. Shelby measured the rainfall for two days. On Saturday it rained 0.6 cm, and on Sunday it rained 0.4 cm. How much more did it rain on Saturday?

MORE PRACTICE Student Handbook page H108

Adding Decimals

You will learn to find decimal sums greater than 1.	**Why learn this?** You can add decimal measures.

Three weeks ago Lucy's sunflower was 0.85 meters tall. It has grown 0.45 meters. How tall is Lucy's sunflower now?

Use decimal squares to add.

MODEL

What is 0.85 + 0.45?

Step 1

Shade 0.85 red and 0.45 blue.

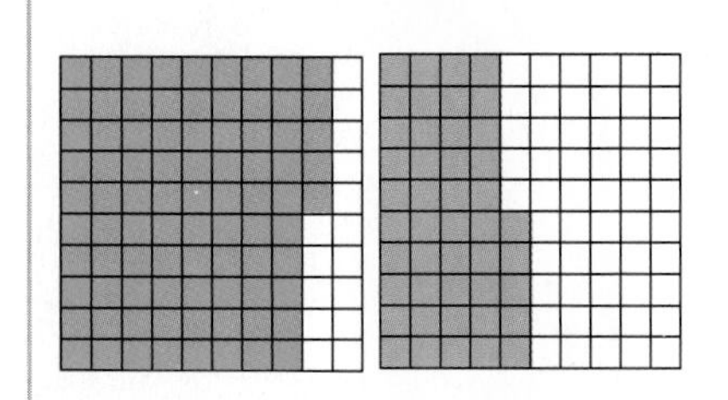

Step 2

Put the red and blue parts together.

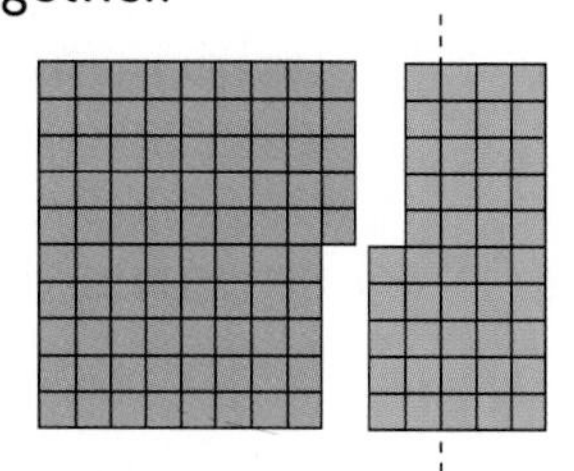

Step 3

Find the sum.

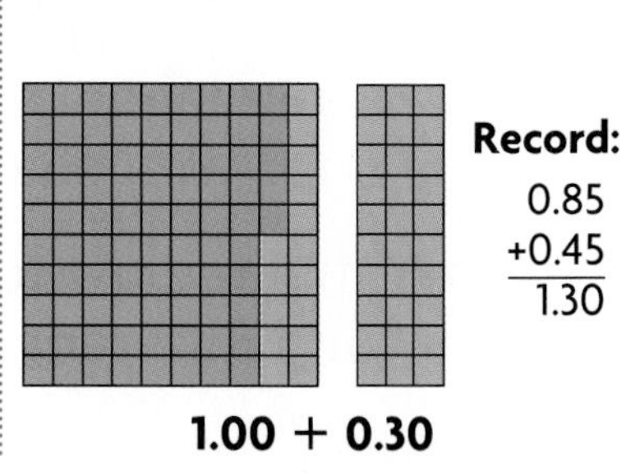

Record:

$$\begin{array}{r} 0.85 \\ +0.45 \\ \hline 1.30 \end{array}$$

1.00 + 0.30

So, Lucy's sunflower is 1.30, or 1.3, meters tall.

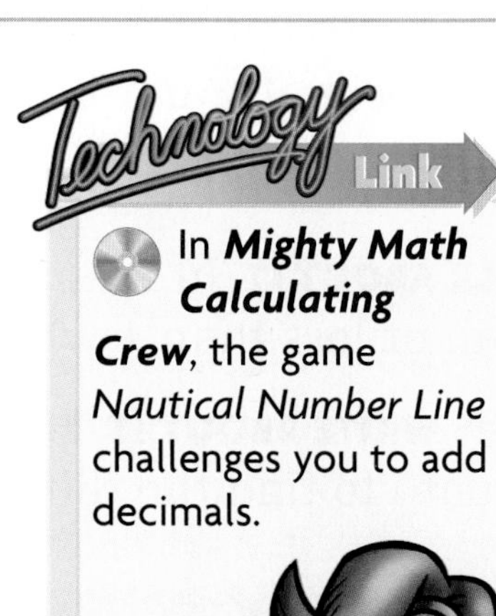

In ***Mighty Math Calculating Crew***, the game *Nautical Number Line* challenges you to add decimals.

Talk About It

- How do you know the sum is greater than 1?
- How many hundredths greater than 1 is 0.85 + 0.45?
- Could the sum be expressed as 1.3? Why or why not?

EXAMPLES

A.	**B.**	**C.**	**D.**
$\begin{array}{r} ^{1} \\ 0.4 \\ +0.9 \\ \hline 1.3 \end{array}$	$\begin{array}{r} 0.41 \\ +0.36 \\ \hline 0.77 \end{array}$	$\begin{array}{r} ^{1} \\ 0.26 \\ +0.54 \\ \hline 0.80 \end{array}$	$\begin{array}{r} ^{1} \\ 0.52 \\ +0.56 \\ \hline 1.08 \end{array}$

- How do you know if you need to regroup when adding decimals?

WRITE ABOUT IT How are adding decimals and adding whole numbers different?

PRACTICE

Write the letter of the model that matches each problem. Solve.

A. 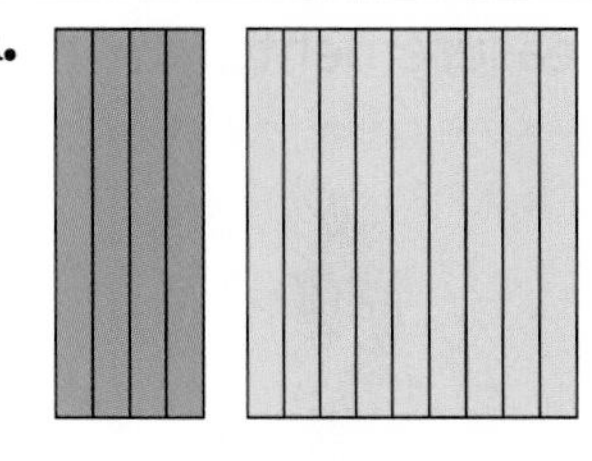

B. 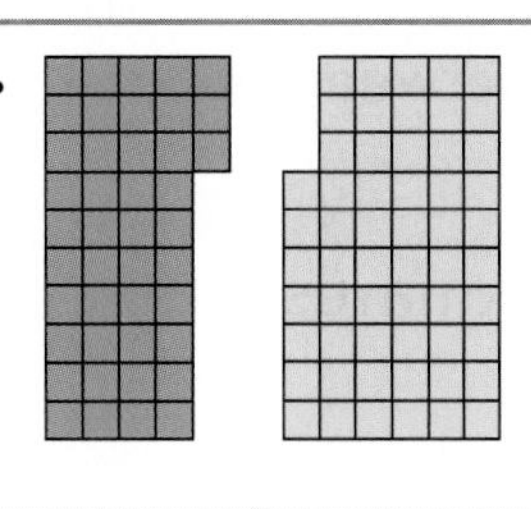

C. 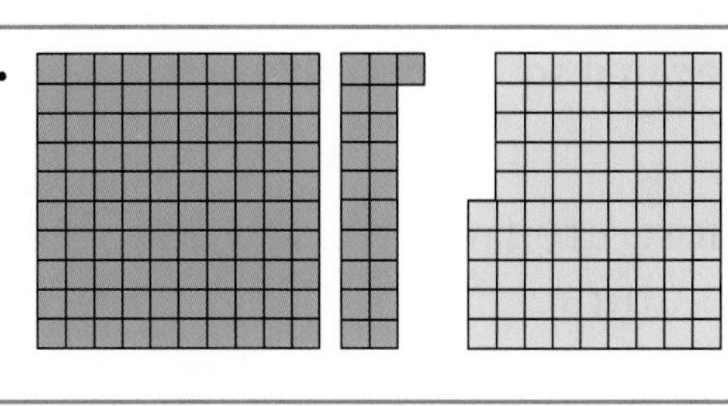

1. $1.21 + 0.85 = n$ **2.** $0.4 + 0.9 = n$ **3.** $0.43 + 0.57 = n$

Find the sum.

4. $\begin{array}{r} 0.7 \\ +0.5 \\ \hline \end{array}$ **5.** $\begin{array}{r} 0.77 \\ +0.21 \\ \hline \end{array}$ **6.** $\begin{array}{r} 0.36 \\ +0.28 \\ \hline \end{array}$ **7.** $\begin{array}{r} 0.61 \\ +0.69 \\ \hline \end{array}$ **8.** $\begin{array}{r} 0.49 \\ +0.22 \\ \hline \end{array}$

9. $\begin{array}{r} 0.30 \\ +0.72 \\ \hline \end{array}$ **10.** $\begin{array}{r} 0.7 \\ +0.8 \\ \hline \end{array}$ **11.** $\begin{array}{r} 0.73 \\ +0.49 \\ \hline \end{array}$ **12.** $\begin{array}{r} 1.91 \\ +1.70 \\ \hline \end{array}$ **13.** $\begin{array}{r} 1.88 \\ +0.67 \\ \hline \end{array}$

Mixed Applications

14. Three teammates ran in a relay race. Their times were 1.45 minutes, 1.15 minutes, and 1.34 minutes. What was their total time?

15. Maria baby-sat from 4:30 P.M. until 9:30 P.M. She earned $2 per hour. How long did she baby-sit? How much did she earn?

16. A turkey sandwich with cheese and tomatoes costs $2.75. Without the cheese and tomatoes, it costs $2.35. The cheese costs $0.25. How much do the tomatoes cost?

17. **Write a problem** using the decimals 1.5 and 2.4.

Mixed Review

Copy and complete. Use a basic fact and a pattern of zeros. (pages 316–317)

18. $240 \div n = 40$
$2{,}400 \div 6 = n$
$n \div 6 = 4{,}000$

19. $360 \div n = 60$
$3{,}600 \div 6 = n$
$n \div 6 = 6{,}000$

20. $560 \div n = 70$
$5{,}600 \div 8 = n$
$n \div 8 = 7{,}000$

21. $810 \div n = 90$
$8{,}100 \div 9 = n$
$n \div 9 = 9{,}000$

Use mental math and basic multiplication facts to find the product. (pages 266–267)

22. $8 \times 300 = n$ **23.** $5 \times 7{,}000 = n$ **24.** $8 \times 8{,}000 = n$

MORE PRACTICE Student Handbook page H108

Subtracting Decimals

You will learn that you can use decimal squares to subtract.

Why learn this? You can find the difference between two decimal measurements.

There are two ways to use decimal squares to subtract.

A. Take-Away Model

What is 1.2 − 0.7?

Shade 1.2 of the whole decimal squares. Cut out the shaded part. Then cut away 0.7 of the shaded part. Count to find the difference.

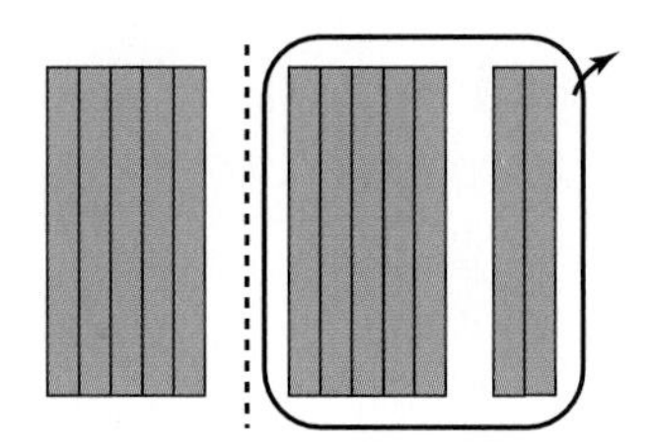

So, 1.2 − 0.7 = 0.5.

B. Comparison Model

What is 0.80 − 0.30?

Shade 0.80 of one decimal square and 0.30 of a second decimal square. Cut out the shaded parts. Line them up and compare. Count to find the difference.

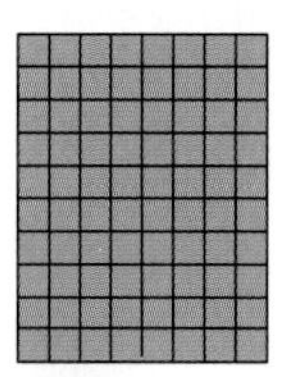

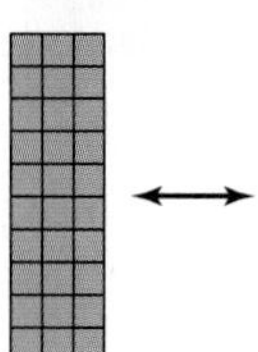

So, 0.80 − 0.30 = 0.50.

Talk About It

- How are the take-away model and the comparison model alike? How are they different?
- How can you use the take-away model to show 0.65 − 0.42?

Social Studies Link

The Statue of Liberty, in New York City Harbor, is 1.1 miles by ferryboat and 6.4 miles by car from the Empire State Building. How far is the Statue of Liberty from the Empire State Building?

EXAMPLES

A.
$$\begin{array}{r} \scriptstyle 0\ 18 \\ \not{1}.\not{8} \\ -0.9 \\ \hline 0.9 \end{array}$$

B.
$$\begin{array}{r} \scriptstyle 3\ 10 \\ 1.\not{4}\not{0} \\ -0.31 \\ \hline 1.09 \end{array}$$

C.
$$\begin{array}{r} \scriptstyle 0\ 16 \\ \not{1}.\not{6}2 \\ -0.72 \\ \hline 0.90 \end{array}$$

D.
$$\begin{array}{r} \scriptstyle 7\ 11 \\ 0.\not{8}\not{1} \\ -0.52 \\ \hline 0.29 \end{array}$$

E.
$$\begin{array}{r} \scriptstyle 11 \\ \scriptstyle 1\ \not{1}\ 13 \\ \not{2}.\not{2}\not{3} \\ -1.69 \\ \hline 0.54 \end{array}$$

CRITICAL THINKING How is regrouping to subtract decimals like regrouping whole numbers?

Calculator Activities, page H66

PRACTICE

Write the letter of the model that matches each problem. Solve.

A. 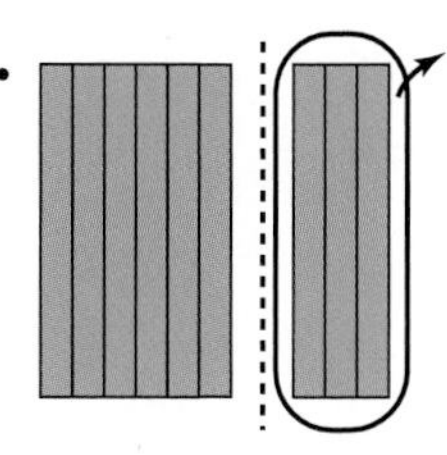

B. 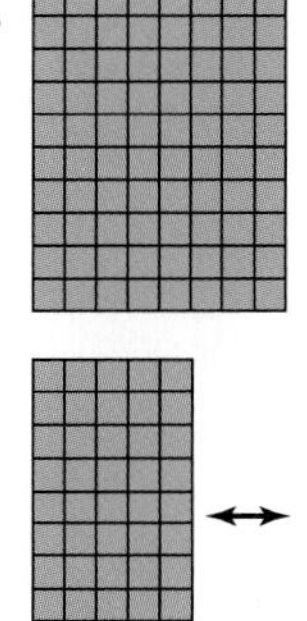

C. 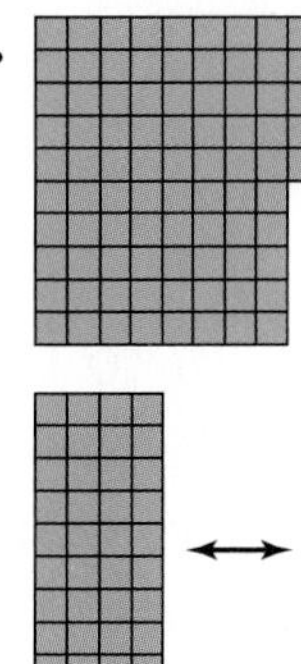

D. 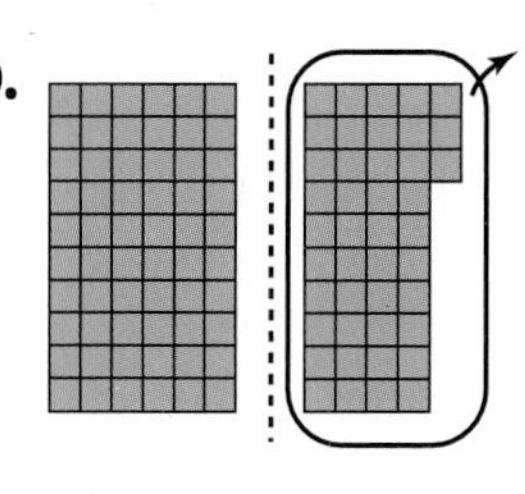

1. $1.03 - 0.43 = n$ **2.** $0.9 - 0.3 = n$ **3.** $0.85 - 0.40 = n$ **4.** $0.80 - 0.50 = n$

Find the difference.

5. $\begin{array}{r} 0.7 \\ -0.4 \\ \hline \end{array}$ **6.** $\begin{array}{r} 0.91 \\ -0.61 \\ \hline \end{array}$ **7.** $\begin{array}{r} 1.4 \\ -0.8 \\ \hline \end{array}$ **8.** $\begin{array}{r} 1.30 \\ -0.40 \\ \hline \end{array}$ **9.** $\begin{array}{r} 1.01 \\ -0.25 \\ \hline \end{array}$

10. $\begin{array}{r} 1.00 \\ -0.91 \\ \hline \end{array}$ **11.** $\begin{array}{r} 1.44 \\ -0.58 \\ \hline \end{array}$ **12.** $\begin{array}{r} 1.89 \\ -0.98 \\ \hline \end{array}$ **13.** $\begin{array}{r} 1.11 \\ -0.49 \\ \hline \end{array}$ **14.** $\begin{array}{r} 1.53 \\ -0.85 \\ \hline \end{array}$

Mixed Applications

15. The tallest player on the basketball team is 1.84 meters tall. The shortest player is 1.57 meters tall. What is their difference in height?

16. **Write a problem** using this information: Bob rode 1.50 miles. Terry rode 1.25 miles.

Mixed Review

Is each pair of figures congruent? Write *yes* or *no*.
(pages 246–247)

17. 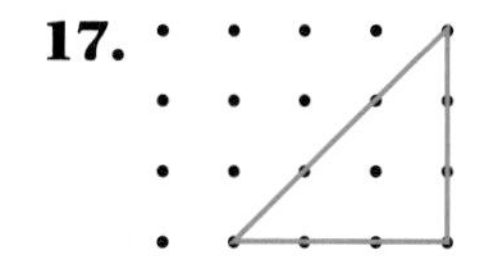 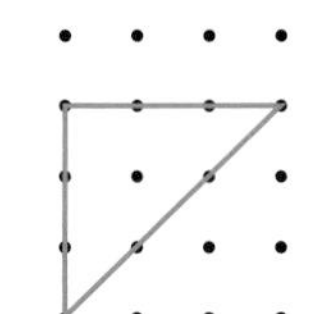

18. 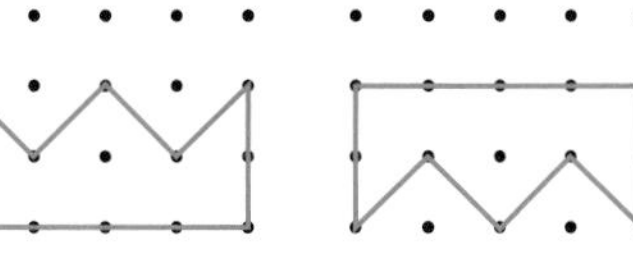 

19. 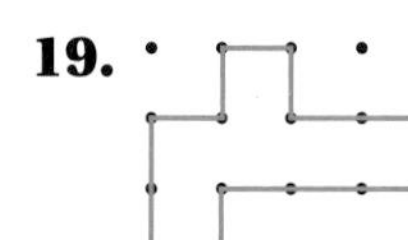 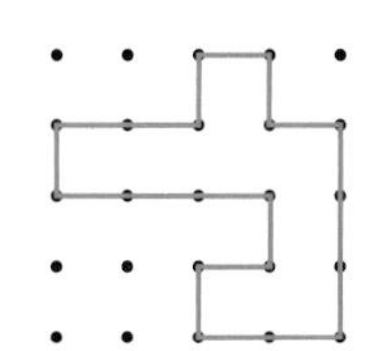

Find the sum. You may wish to draw a picture. (pages 362–363)

20. $\begin{array}{r} 1\frac{2}{4} \\ +2\frac{1}{4} \\ \hline \end{array}$ **21.** $\begin{array}{r} 5\frac{2}{6} \\ +2\frac{3}{6} \\ \hline \end{array}$ **22.** $\begin{array}{r} 4\frac{4}{10} \\ +3\frac{7}{10} \\ \hline \end{array}$ **23.** $\begin{array}{r} 2\frac{5}{8} \\ +6\frac{4}{8} \\ \hline \end{array}$ **24.** $\begin{array}{r} 7\frac{4}{9} \\ +5\frac{6}{9} \\ \hline \end{array}$

PART

1 Using Decimals

You will learn that you can add and subtract decimals to solve problems.

Why learn this? You can find out how far you have ridden on a bicycle.

Nicholas rode his bicycle 1.4 km to the pond and 0.52 km to the store. Danny rode his bicycle 1.33 km to the library and 1.2 km to the playground. How far did each ride?

Use place value to add and subtract decimals the same way you add and subtract whole numbers.

Nicholas

Ones	Tenths	Hundredths
1 .	4	0
+0 .	5	2
1 .	9	2

Danny

Ones	Tenths	Hundredths
1 .	3	3
+1 .	2	0
2 .	5	3

Use 0 to name an equivalent decimal.

So, Nicholas rode 1.92 km and Danny rode 2.53 km.

How much farther did Danny ride than Nicholas?
$2.53 - 1.92 = n$

Ones	Tenths	Hundredths
1 ~~2~~ .	15 ~~5~~	3
−1 .	9	2
0 .	6	1

Regroup 2.5 as 1 one and 15 tenths.

So, Danny rode 0.61 km farther than Nicholas.

CRITICAL THINKING Why should you keep the digits in the same column?

EXAMPLES

A.
```
  0.50
+1.00
  1.50
```

B.
```
   1
  0.52
+0.60
  1.12
```

C.
```
  0 10
  1̸.0̸4
−0.50
  0.54
```

• How can using equivalent decimals help you add and subtract?

REMEMBER:

Equivalent decimals are different names for the same amount.

0.2 is equivalent to 0.20.

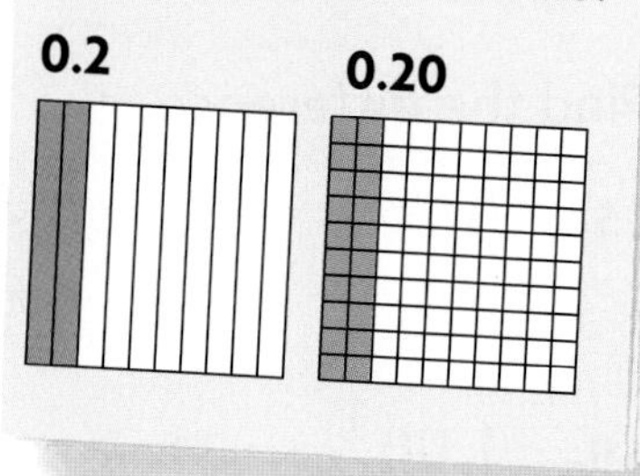

History Link

The high-wheeler bicycle of the 1860's had a large wheel that measured 1.5 meters. Many bicycles today have wheels that measure 0.70 meters. How much larger was the wheel on the high-wheeler?

Calculator Activities, page H62

PRACTICE

Find the sum.

1. $\begin{array}{r} 0.4 \\ +0.2 \\ \hline \end{array}$
2. $\begin{array}{r} 0.80 \\ +0.15 \\ \hline \end{array}$
3. $\begin{array}{r} 0.93 \\ +0.70 \\ \hline \end{array}$
4. $\begin{array}{r} 1.32 \\ +0.54 \\ \hline \end{array}$
5. $\begin{array}{r} 1.74 \\ +0.60 \\ \hline \end{array}$
6. $\begin{array}{r} 0.5 \\ +0.5 \\ \hline \end{array}$
7. $\begin{array}{r} 1.73 \\ +0.27 \\ \hline \end{array}$
8. $\begin{array}{r} 3.94 \\ +1.57 \\ \hline \end{array}$
9. $\begin{array}{r} 4.20 \\ +1.89 \\ \hline \end{array}$
10. $\begin{array}{r} 6.99 \\ +2.09 \\ \hline \end{array}$

Find the difference.

11. $\begin{array}{r} 0.9 \\ -0.6 \\ \hline \end{array}$
12. $\begin{array}{r} 0.8 \\ -0.7 \\ \hline \end{array}$
13. $\begin{array}{r} 0.85 \\ -0.50 \\ \hline \end{array}$
14. $\begin{array}{r} 0.40 \\ -0.29 \\ \hline \end{array}$
15. $\begin{array}{r} 1.50 \\ -0.08 \\ \hline \end{array}$
16. $\begin{array}{r} 1.28 \\ -0.19 \\ \hline \end{array}$
17. $\begin{array}{r} 1.32 \\ -0.41 \\ \hline \end{array}$
18. $\begin{array}{r} 3.08 \\ -1.39 \\ \hline \end{array}$
19. $\begin{array}{r} 5.60 \\ -2.59 \\ \hline \end{array}$
20. $\begin{array}{r} 6.42 \\ -2.26 \\ \hline \end{array}$

Find the sum or difference.

21. $0.52 + 0.6 = n$
22. $2.32 - 1.6 = n$
23. $1.1 + 0.90 = n$
24. $3.02 - 1.71 = n$
25. $0.9 + 2.25 = n$
26. $2.51 - 0.8 = n$

Mixed Applications

27. Ashley rides her bike 1.6 km to school. Lauren rides her bike 0.9 km to school. How much farther does Ashley ride her bike to school?

28. Louis is walking to the ball field, which is 1.4 km from his home. He has walked 0.8 km. How much farther must he walk?

29. Alex went to the store with \$10.00. He bought milk, bread, and eggs. He had \$5.98 when he left the store. The milk was \$1.49 and the eggs were \$0.89. How much was the bread?

30. David's baseball bat measures 1.05 meters in length. Rick's bat measures 0.98 meters in length. How much longer is David's baseball bat?

31. Richard scored 2 home runs in the baseball game. How many feet did Richard run to score the 2 home runs?

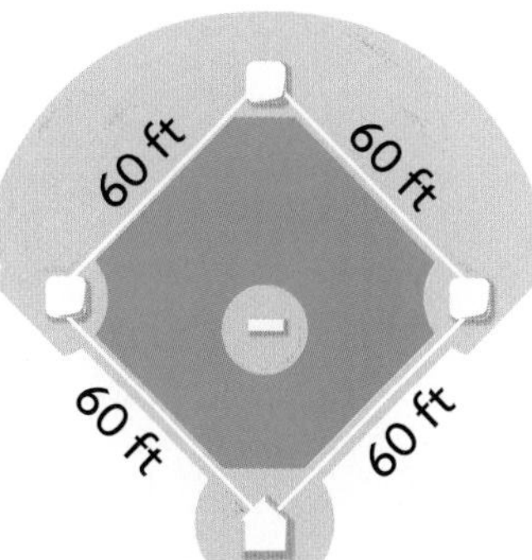

32. **Write a problem** about adding or subtracting decimals. Use two scores from a gymnastics meet.

LESSON CONTINUES

PART 2 **PROBLEM-SOLVING STRATEGY**

Write a Number Sentence

THE PROBLEM Mike is getting ready for a school track meet. He ran 1.4 miles on Tuesday, 2.35 miles on Thursday, and 3.2 miles on Saturday. How many miles did he run on those three days?

REMEMBER:
- ✓ Understand
- ✓ Plan
- ✓ Solve
- ✓ Look Back

✓ Understand

- What are you asked to find?
- What information will you use?
- Is there any information you will not use? If so, what?

✓ Plan

- What strategy can you use to solve the problem?

Since you know how far Mike ran each day, you can *write a number sentence* that will show the facts in the problem.

✓ Solve

- What number sentence can you write?

miles run on Tuesday		miles run on Thursday		miles run on Saturday		
1.4	+	2.35	+	3.2	=	n

$$\begin{array}{r} 1.40 \\ 2.35 \\ +3.20 \\ \hline 6.95 \end{array}$$

So, Mike ran 6.95 miles in the three days.

✓ Look Back

- How can you decide if your answer is reasonable?
- What other strategy can you use?

PRACTICE

CHOOSE Paper/Pencil Calculator Hands-on Mental Math

Write a number sentence to solve.

1. Suppose Mike ran 1.85 miles on Tuesday, 2.55 miles on Thursday, and 3.6 miles on Saturday. How many miles did he run on those three days?

2. Nadia scored 8.70 in the first gymnastics event, 9.0 in the second event, and 8.65 in the third event. How many points does she have in all?

3. This season Alana scored 12 points in each of 3 basketball games. She scored 14 points in each of 2 games. In the rest of the games, she scored a total of 42 points. How many points in all did Alana score during the season?

4. Don practiced football for 24 hours last week. He practiced for the same number of hours each day for 6 days. For how many hours did he practice each day?

Mixed Applications

Solve.

CHOOSE A STRATEGY

- **Guess and Check**
- **Make a Model**
- **Make a Table**
- **Find a Pattern**
- **Write a Number Sentence**

5. Mario spent $25.50 on two shirts. One of the shirts was $3.50 more than the other. How much was each shirt?

6. In the arena, there are 40 sections of seats. Each section has about 400 seats. About how many seats are in the arena?

7. At the 100-meter-run competition, Allan's time was 12.25 seconds. Carl's time was 12.05 seconds, and Bob's time was 12.17 seconds. First place went to the runner with the shortest time. Which runner was first? second? third?

8. The fourth grade held an election for class officers. Alicia received $\frac{1}{10}$ of the vote. Michelle received $\frac{3}{10}$ of the vote. The rest of the fourth grade voted for Tony. What fraction of the fourth grade voted for Tony?

9. Gregory has $74.99 saved to buy a bicycle. How much more money does Gregory need in order to buy a 10-speed bicycle? a 15-speed? an 18-speed?

MORE PRACTICE Student Handbook page H108

Estimating Sums and Differences by Rounding

You will learn that you can estimate decimal amounts.

Why learn this? You can round to estimate when you add or subtract decimals.

James wants to ride his bicycle 10 miles per week. He rode 1.6 miles on Monday, 1.4 miles on Tuesday, and 2.3 miles on Wednesday. About how many miles has James ridden so far this week?

Estimate by rounding to the nearest whole number.

$$\begin{array}{rcr} 1.6 & \rightarrow & 2.0 \\ 1.4 & \rightarrow & 1.0 \\ +2.3 & \rightarrow & +2.0 \\ \hline & & 5.0 \end{array}$$

- Line up the decimal points.
- Look at the digit to the right of the whole number.
- If the digit in the tenths place is 5 or more, round to the next higher whole number.

So, James has ridden about 5 miles so far this week.

To round whole numbers:

- find the digit to be rounded.
- look at the digit to the right.
- if the digit is less than 5, the digit stays the same.
- if the digit is more than 5, the digit being rounded is increased by 1.

Talk About It

- Why is 1.6 rounded to the next higher whole number, but 1.4 is rounded to the same whole number?
- Name some situations in which you might use an estimate.

Sara swam the race in 28.42 seconds. Julie swam it in 28.59 seconds. To the nearest tenth of a second, about how much faster was Sara?

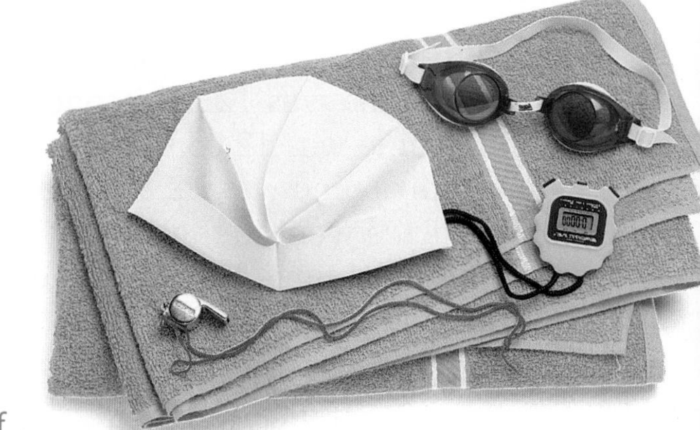

You can estimate by rounding to the nearest tenth.

$$\begin{array}{rcr} 28.59 & \rightarrow & 28.6 \\ -28.42 & \rightarrow & -28.4 \\ \hline & & 0.2 \end{array}$$

- Line up the decimal points.
- Look at the digit to the right of the tenths place.
- If the digit in the hundredths place is 5 or more, round to the next tenths digit.

So, Sara was about 0.2 of a second faster.

- Why was 28.59 rounded to 28.6 and 28.42 rounded to 28.4?

Calculator Activities, page H67

PRACTICE

Estimate the sum or difference by rounding to the nearest whole number.

1. $\begin{array}{r} 1.7 \\ +1.2 \\ \hline \end{array}$
2. $\begin{array}{r} 1.2 \\ +0.9 \\ \hline \end{array}$
3. $\begin{array}{r} 1.9 \\ -1.1 \\ \hline \end{array}$
4. $\begin{array}{r} 2.8 \\ -1.2 \\ \hline \end{array}$
5. $\begin{array}{r} 2.3 \\ +2.8 \\ \hline \end{array}$
6. $\begin{array}{r} 3.1 \\ -1.8 \\ \hline \end{array}$
7. $\begin{array}{r} 5.9 \\ -2.4 \\ \hline \end{array}$
8. $\begin{array}{r} 1.8 \\ 1.3 \\ +2.9 \\ \hline \end{array}$
9. $\begin{array}{r} 2.3 \\ 0.7 \\ +3.8 \\ \hline \end{array}$
10. $\begin{array}{r} 1.5 \\ 4.2 \\ +3.6 \\ \hline \end{array}$

Estimate the sum or difference by rounding to the nearest tenth.

11. $\begin{array}{r} 1.82 \\ -1.56 \\ \hline \end{array}$
12. $\begin{array}{r} 1.39 \\ -0.87 \\ \hline \end{array}$
13. $\begin{array}{r} 1.07 \\ +1.54 \\ \hline \end{array}$
14. $\begin{array}{r} 2.49 \\ +2.53 \\ \hline \end{array}$
15. $\begin{array}{r} 3.05 \\ -1.92 \\ \hline \end{array}$

Mixed Applications

For Problems 16, 18, and 20, use the table.

Mead Park Bike Trails	
North Trail	1.8 miles
South Trail	2.4 miles
East Trail	1.2 miles
West Trail	0.9 mile

16. Heather rode the North and South trails. Nicole rode the East and West trails. About how many more miles did Heather ride than Nicole?

17. Pamela bought a bike helmet for \$18.29 and a backpack for \$9.95. How much change did she receive from \$30.00?

18. Tim and his brother rode all four bike trails. To the nearest mile, how far did they ride?

19. Lauren rode the trails in half the time it took Tyler. Tyler rode the trails in 46 minutes. How long did it take Lauren to ride the trails?

20. **Write a problem** using the information in the table.

Mixed Review

Find the quotient. Place the dollar sign and decimal point in the quotient. (pages 320–321)

21. $6\overline{)\$5.10}$
22. $4\overline{)\$4.36}$
23. $2\overline{)\$9.32}$
24. $8\overline{)\$54.64}$
25. $5\overline{)\$28.65}$

Find the sum. (pages 356–357)

26. $\frac{2}{9} + \frac{3}{9} = n$
27. $\frac{4}{10} + \frac{6}{10} = n$
28. $\frac{3}{5} + \frac{3}{5} = n$

MORE PRACTICE Student Handbook page H109

MATH FUN!

Pattern Puzzlers

PURPOSE To practice adding and subtracting decimals and money

YOU WILL NEED paper and pencil

Copy the pattern and fill in the blanks on your own paper. The first three numbers in each pattern should give you the hint you need. Will you add or subtract?

4.08, 4.16, 4.24, ____, ____, ____

3.14, 3.28, 3.42, ____, ____, ____

0.60, 0.80, 1.20, ____, ____, ____

1.92, 1.82, 1.72, ____, ____, ____

5.88, 5.83, 5.78, ____, ____, ____

Make up pattern puzzlers for your family members to solve.

HIGH FIVE

PURPOSE To practice adding and subtracting decimals

YOU WILL NEED 1 number cube

Play with a partner. For each round, draw three blanks on a sheet of paper. Take turns rolling a cube 3 times and filling in the blanks to make the largest decimal you can.

The winner of the round is the player with the higher number. Calculate the number of points the winner gets by finding the difference between the players' scores. At the end of five rounds, add all your scores. High score wins the game.

Decimal Maze

PURPOSE To practice estimating decimal sums and adding decimals

YOU WILL NEED calculator

Start at the entrance to the maze. Find a path whose sum is 59.23. Use estimation to find a reasonable path. Then use a calculator to add decimals along the way. Copy the maze, and mark your path. You can move forward only. You cannot pass through the same box twice.

Enter →	1.81	3.26	9.15	1.28	
	8.76	3.99	4.87	6.79	
	7.21	1.08	5.84	7.16	
	8.22	7.73	2.82	9.92	→ Exit 59.23

CHAPTER 23

REVIEW

✓ CHECK UNDERSTANDING

Write the letter of the model that matches each problem. Solve. (pages 386–391)

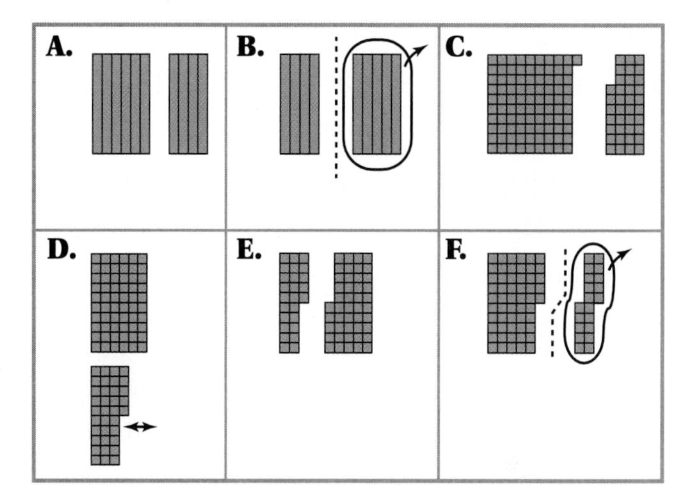

1. $0.9 - 0.5 = n$
2. $0.25 + 0.45 = n$
3. $0.6 + 0.4 = n$
4. $0.60 - 0.35 = n$
5. $0.91 + 0.37 = n$
6. $0.75 - 0.20 = n$

✓ CHECK SKILLS

Find the sum or difference. (pages 388–393)

7. $\begin{array}{r} 0.7 \\ +0.6 \\ \hline \end{array}$
8. $\begin{array}{r} 0.12 \\ +0.59 \\ \hline \end{array}$
9. $\begin{array}{r} 1.21 \\ -0.38 \\ \hline \end{array}$
10. $\begin{array}{r} 0.39 \\ +1.04 \\ \hline \end{array}$
11. $\begin{array}{r} 0.47 \\ -0.16 \\ \hline \end{array}$

12. $0.71 + 0.8 = n$
13. $2.56 - 1.5 = n$
14. $1.4 + 0.70 = n$

Estimate the sum or difference by rounding to the nearest whole number. (pages 396–397)

15. $\begin{array}{r} 1.2 \\ +0.7 \\ \hline \end{array}$
16. $\begin{array}{r} 1.9 \\ -1.1 \\ \hline \end{array}$
17. $\begin{array}{r} 1.8 \\ +0.9 \\ \hline \end{array}$
18. $\begin{array}{r} 1.5 \\ +1.6 \\ \hline \end{array}$
19. $\begin{array}{r} 3.1 \\ -0.8 \\ \hline \end{array}$

✓ CHECK PROBLEM SOLVING

Solve. (pages 394–395)

CHOOSE A STRATEGY

- **Act It Out**
- **Draw a Picture**
- **Make a Model**
- **Write a Number Sentence**

20. Mrs. Long walked 1 mile on Monday. On Tuesday she walked 0.3 mile less. How far did she walk on Tuesday?

21. Nate rode his bike 2.4 miles on Saturday and 3.6 miles on Sunday. How many miles did he ride his bike on those two days?

22. Joshua caught the bus at 7:15 A.M. He was on the bus for 55 minutes. At what time did he arrive at school?

23. Sara found two seeds. One was 0.9 cm long. The other was 0.5 cm long. How much longer was the first seed?

CHAPTERS 20–23

STUDY GUIDE & REVIEW

VOCABULARY CHECK

Choose a term from the box to complete each sentence.

WORD BANK

- decimal
- equivalent decimals
- equivalent fractions
- fraction
- mixed decimal
- mixed number

1. A number that names part of a whole or part of a group is a __?__. (pages 338, 340)
2. Fractions that name the same amount are called __?__. (page 342)
3. A __?__ is made up of a whole number and a fraction. (page 348)
4. A __?__ is a number that uses place value and a decimal point to show a value less than one. (page 370)
5. Different names for the same amount, such as 0.4 and 0.40, are __?__. (page 374)
6. A number that is made up of a whole number and a decimal is a __?__. (page 378)

STUDY AND SOLVE

CHAPTER 20

EXAMPLE

Compare the fractions. Use $<$, $>$, or $=$ for each ●.

Use fraction bars to decide whether they are equal.

$\frac{1}{2}$		
$\frac{1}{6}$	$\frac{1}{6}$	$\frac{1}{6}$

$\frac{3}{6}$ ● $\frac{1}{2}$

$\frac{3}{6} = \frac{1}{2}$

What fraction is shaded? (pages 338–341)

7. 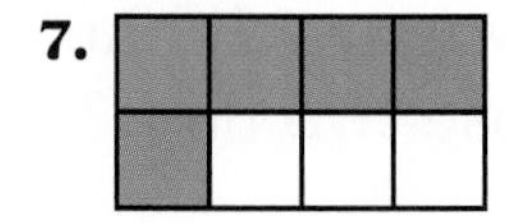

8. 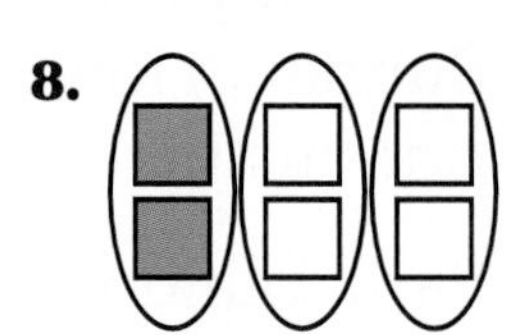

Compare the fractions. Use $<$, $>$, or $=$ for each ●. Use fraction bars. (pages 344–345)

9. $\frac{3}{5}$ ● $\frac{4}{5}$

10. $\frac{2}{3}$ ● $\frac{2}{4}$

Use fraction bars to order the fractions from least to greatest. (pages 344–345)

11. $\frac{1}{2}, \frac{4}{6}, \frac{1}{3}$

12. $\frac{2}{6}, \frac{1}{12}, \frac{3}{4}$

Write a mixed number for each picture. (pages 348–349)

13. 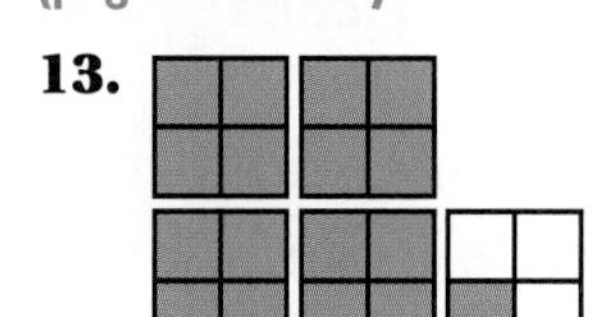

14. 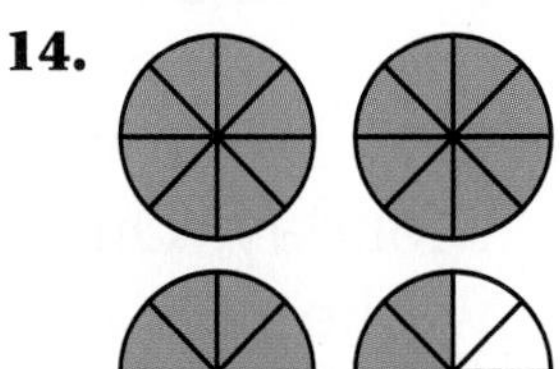
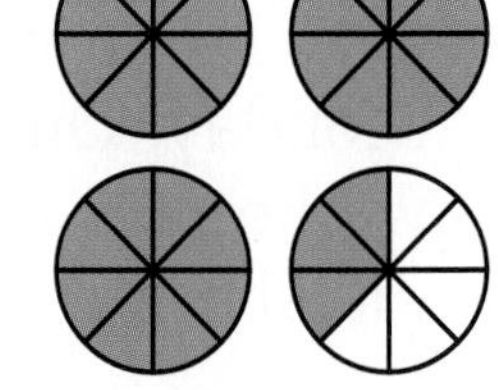

Rename each fraction as a mixed number. (pages 348–349)

15. $\frac{11}{4}$

16. $\frac{7}{2}$

CHAPTER 21

EXAMPLE

$$\begin{array}{r} 2\frac{1}{6} \\ +3\frac{4}{6} \\ \hline 5\frac{5}{6} \end{array}$$

1. Add fractions.
2. Add whole numbers.

Write a number sentence and find the sum. (pages 354–355)

17. five sixths plus two sixths

Find the sum or difference. Use fraction bars or folded paper. (pages 354–359, 362-365)

18. $\frac{3}{4} + \frac{1}{4} = n$

19. $\frac{7}{10} - \frac{4}{10} = n$

20. $\begin{array}{r} 4\frac{5}{8} \\ -3\frac{2}{8} \\ \hline \end{array}$

21. $\begin{array}{r} 1\frac{2}{7} \\ +7\frac{3}{7} \\ \hline \end{array}$

Solve. (pages 360–361)

22. Andre and Maria each ate $\frac{3}{8}$ of an apple pie. How much of the pie was left?

CHAPTER 22

EXAMPLE

Order the decimals 0.71, 0.78, 0.65, 0.6 from the least to the greatest.

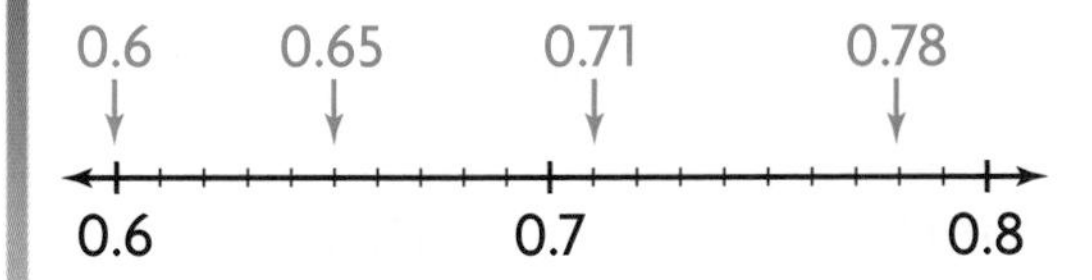

Locate the decimals on the number line. The numbers from least to greatest are 0.6, 0.65, 0.71, 0.78.

Tell which number is greater. (pages 376–377)

23. 0.02
0.1

24. 0.30
0.03

Order the decimals from greatest to least. Use a number line. (pages 376–377)

25. 0.5, 0.05, 0.55, 0.61, 0.16

Write each mixed number as a decimal. (pages 378–379)

26. $8\frac{9}{100}$

27. $16\frac{3}{10}$

Solve. (pages 380–381)

28. Janet swam three laps of the pool in 4.47 minutes. Cy swam that distance in 4.7 minutes. Whose time was shorter?

CHAPTER 23

EXAMPLE

$1.32 - 0.46 = n$

$$\begin{array}{r} \overset{0\ 12\ 12}{\not{1}.\not{3}2} \\ -0.46 \\ \hline 0.86 \end{array}$$

1. Line up decimal points.
2. Subtract as with whole numbers.
$n = 0.86$

Find the sum or difference. (pages 386–391)

29. $\begin{array}{r} 0.29 \\ +1.06 \\ \hline \end{array}$

30. $\begin{array}{r} 2.40 \\ -1.47 \\ \hline \end{array}$

Estimate the sum or difference by rounding to the nearest whole number. (pages 396–397)

31. $\begin{array}{r} 1.1 \\ +0.8 \\ \hline \end{array}$

32. $\begin{array}{r} 3.2 \\ -1.9 \\ \hline \end{array}$

Solve. (pages 394–395)

33. David ran 4.8 miles one day and 5.5 the next. How much farther did he run on Day 2?

CHAPTERS 20–23

WHAT DID I LEARN?

WRITE ABOUT IT

1. Use fraction bars to order these fractions from least to greatest. Draw a picture to show how you ordered them.

   $\frac{3}{4}$ $\frac{1}{2}$ $\frac{5}{8}$ (pages 342–343)

2. Explain each step as you find these sums.

   $\frac{3}{8} + \frac{4}{8} = n$ $\quad 3\frac{2}{6} + 4\frac{5}{6} = n$

   (pages 356–357, 362–363)

3. Use the number line on page 376 or a place-value chart to order these numbers from greatest to least. Explain your method.

   0.33, 0.3, 0.39, 0.13

   (pages 376–377)

4. Show each step as you estimate the sum or difference by rounding to the nearest tenth.

   $\begin{array}{r} 2.06 \\ +1.72 \\ \hline \end{array}$ $\quad \begin{array}{r} 1.77 \\ -1.25 \\ \hline \end{array}$ (pages 396–397)

✓ PERFORMANCE ASSESSMENT

Solve. Explain your method.

CHOOSE A STRATEGY

- **Make a Table** • **Act It Out** • **Make a Model** • **Draw a Picture** • **Write a Number Sentence**

5. Lynn ran $\frac{1}{4}$ mile, Darrin ran $\frac{4}{12}$ mile, and Jed ran $\frac{3}{6}$ mile. Show the distances they ran. Order from the greatest to the least. Who ran the farthest? (pages 346–347)

6. White Bluff received 1.78 inches of rain. Plains City received 2.14 inches. Milltown received 1.62 inches. River Bend received 2.09 inches. Which town received the most rain? the least? What is the difference between the greatest and least amounts? (pages 380–381)

7. The results of a survey showed that $\frac{3}{10}$ of the students like comedies, $\frac{2}{10}$ like dramas, and $\frac{1}{10}$ like nature shows. The rest like cartoons. What fraction of the group likes cartoons? (pages 360–361)

8. Jean swam 25 meters in 16.26 seconds on Monday. On Tuesday, she swam 25 meters in 15.94 seconds. On Wednesday, she swam 25 meters in 16.56 seconds. What is the difference between her fastest and her slowest time? (pages 394–395)

CUMULATIVE REVIEW

Solve the problem. Then write the letter of the correct answer.

1. Round $58.45 to the nearest dollar.

A. $58.00 **B.** $58.40
C. $58.50 **D.** $59.00

(pages 10–11)

2. One book has 254 pages. Another has 165 pages. How many more pages does the first book have?

A. 89 pages **B.** 99 pages
C. 111 pages **D.** 419 pages

(pages 28–29)

3. What is the name of the ordered pair shown on the grid?

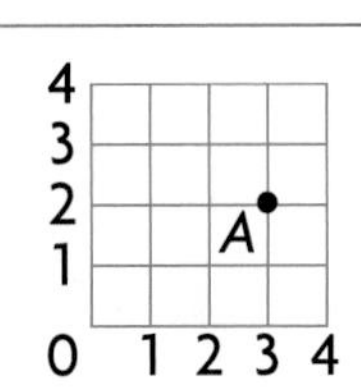

A. (2,0) **B.** (2,3)
C. (3,0) **D.** (3,2)

(pages 74–75)

4. What time is shown on the clock?

A. 4:12 and 9 sec
B. 2:43 and 45 sec
C. 2:23 and 45 sec
D. 2:23 and 9 sec

(pages 120–121)

5. How many vertices does this solid figure have?

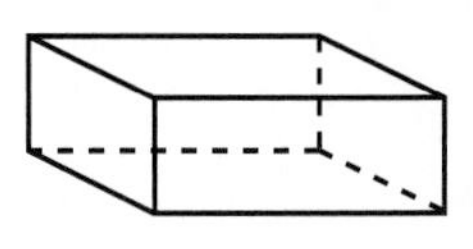

A. 6 **B.** 8
C. 10 **D.** 12

(pages 198–199)

6. $\begin{array}{r} 365 \\ \times\ 49 \\ \hline \end{array}$

A. 316
B. 414
C. 15,145
D. 17,885

(pages 290–293)

7. $6\overline{)606}$

A. 10 r6
B. 11
C. 101
D. 3,636

(pages 308–309)

8. Compare the fractions. Choose $<$, $>$, or $=$ for the ●.

$\frac{2}{4}$ ● $\frac{4}{8}$

A. $>$ **B.** $<$
C. $-$ **D.** $=$

(pages 344–345)

9. Choose the decimal that equals $7\frac{7}{100}$.

A. 0.77 **B.** 7.07
C. 7.7 **D.** 7.700

(pages 378–379)

10. Harry had a rope that measured 5.6 meters in length. He needs 4.07 meters. How much rope will be left over?

A. 1.53 m **B.** 1.63 m
C. 2.36 m **D.** 7.67 m

(pages 390–391)

CHAPTER 24

MEASUREMENT: CUSTOMARY UNITS

DID YOU KNOW . . .

Building bricks come in many colors and surface textures. Most are made from fired clay or a rock called shale.

They are made to be the same size and shape and measure about 8 in. long by 4 in. wide by $2\frac{1}{2}$ in. high.

Planning a Brick Border

Someone has donated 120 used bricks to your classroom to help your class make a wall for a garden. The wall will be 20 feet long and 1 foot high. If each brick is 8 in. long, 4 in. wide, and $2\frac{1}{2}$ in. high, will you have enough bricks? What brick design will you use? Why?

Work with a group. Your job is to

- try different brick designs and choose two.
- find out how many bricks you will need to make the wall using each design.
- make a poster showing the two different designs, telling the number of bricks needed for each, and explaining why or why not each design should be used.

We can make a 12 by 12 section of wall with $4\frac{1}{2}$ bricks. This wall is $2\frac{1}{2}$ inches thick. 20 feet of this wall would use up 90 bricks.

12 = 8 + 4

4 + 4 + 4

DID YOU

- ✓ try different brick designs for the wall and find the number of bricks needed for each?
- ✓ explain why one design may be better or more appealing than the other?
- ✓ make a poster showing the two designs and explain your choice?

Linear Measures

You will learn to measure length in customary units.	**Why learn this?** You can measure the length of a garden wall, your height, or the distance from your home to a friend's home.

WORD POWER
- linear
- inch (in.)
- foot (ft)
- yard (yd)
- mile (mi)

In the United States we usually use the customary system of measurement. **Linear** units measure in one direction, such as length, width, height, or distance.

An **inch** is about the length of your thumb from the first knuckle to the tip.

1 in.

A **foot** is about the height of a cat.

1 ft

A **yard** is about the length of a baseball bat.

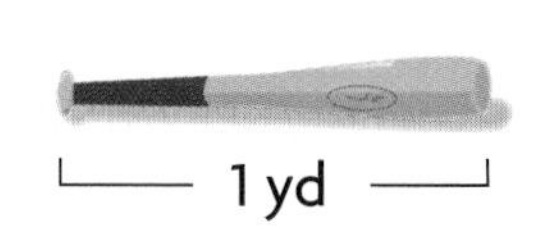

1 yd

A **mile** is about the distance you can walk in 20 minutes.

1 mi

- How can you decide what linear unit to use?

To find length to the nearest inch, line one end of the object at 0 and look on the ruler for the whole number that is nearest to the length of the object.

So, the string is 2 in. to the nearest in.

- What tools can you use to find linear measures?

Check Your Understanding

Choose the reasonable unit of measure. Write *in., ft, yd,* or *mi.*

1. The length of a pencil is about 5 _?_.

2. A man's height is about 6 _?_.

3. The length of a football field is 100 _?_.

Use a ruler to measure the length of each ribbon to the nearest inch.

4. 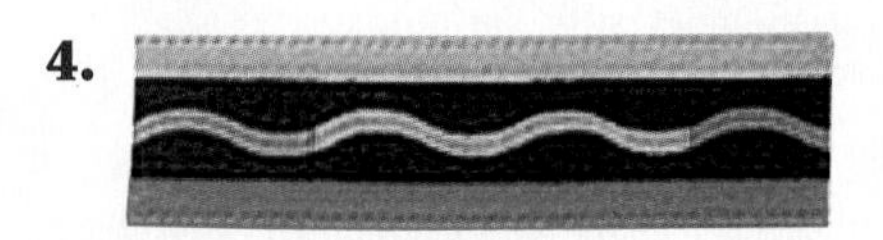

5. 

6. 

PRACTICE

Choose the reasonable unit of measure. Write *in., ft, yd,* or *mi.*

7. The distance from my home to the library is 4 _?_.

8. The height of my desk is about 2 _?_.

9. The cloth used to make the dress is 3 _?_.

10. The length of the classroom is 15 _?_.

11. The width of my room is 12 _?_ .

12. The length of a goldfish is about 3 _?_.

Use a ruler to measure the length of each string to the nearest inch.

13.

14.

Name the longer measurement.

15. 400 mi or 400 yd

16. 11 in. or 11 ft

17. 8 yd or 8 mi

Mixed Applications

18. Lucinda walked around the park for two hours. Which linear unit of measure would you use to describe the distance that she walked?

19. Ms. Almon wants to measure the length of the playground. Would it be more reasonable to find the length in feet, using a 12-inch ruler, or in yards, using a yardstick?

20. The Nile, which is 4,160 miles long, is the longest river in the world. The Missouri River is 2,714 miles long. How many miles longer is the Nile River than the Missouri River?

21. **Write a problem** about something in your classroom that can be measured. Ask what linear measure should be used.

Mixed Review

Find the sum. **(pages 388–389)**

22. $\begin{array}{r} 0.6 \\ +0.8 \\ \hline \end{array}$

23. $\begin{array}{r} 3.5 \\ +4.9 \\ \hline \end{array}$

24. $\begin{array}{r} 0.81 \\ +0.37 \\ \hline \end{array}$

25. $\begin{array}{r} 1.15 \\ +1.70 \\ \hline \end{array}$

26. $\begin{array}{r} 1.92 \\ +0.69 \\ \hline \end{array}$

Rename each fraction as a mixed number. You may wish to draw a picture. **(pages 348–349)**

27. $\frac{7}{5}$

28. $\frac{9}{2}$

29. $\frac{8}{3}$

30. $\frac{14}{4}$

31. $\frac{13}{6}$

MORE PRACTICE Student Handbook page H109

PART 1

Changing Units

You will learn how to change units of measure by multiplying and dividing.

Why learn this? You can change units of measure from small units to large units, or large units to small units.

Tranh and his classmates are decorating the bulletin board for Open House. Tranh is using a yardstick to find the *length* of the bulletin board in yards. The border they want to use is measured in feet. How many feet of border does Tranh need for the top and bottom of the bulletin board?

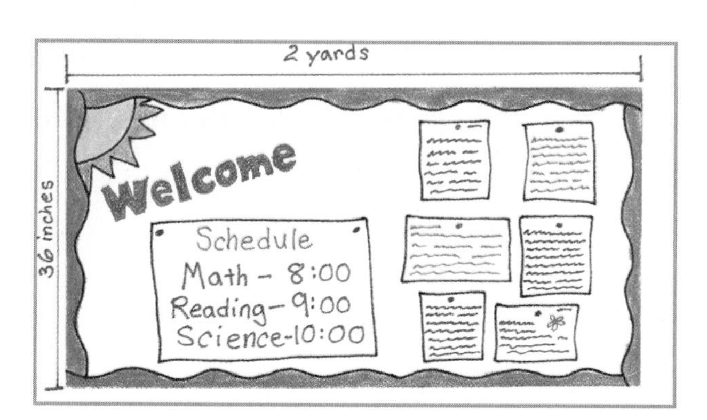

When you change larger units to smaller units, you multiply.

The length of the top *and* the bottom is 4 yards. ⟶	number of yd		number of ft in 1 yd		total ft
	4	×	3	=	*n*

Since $4 \times 3 = 12$, they need 12 ft of border.

Customary Units for Linear Measures		
12 inches (in.)	=	1 foot (ft)
3 feet	=	1 yard (yd)
5,280 feet	=	1 mile (mi)
1,760 yards	=	1 mile

Latoya is measuring the *width* of the bulletin board. The width is 36 in. How many feet of border does Latoya need for each side of the bulletin board?

You can use a calculator when changing units. When you change smaller units to larger units, you divide.

number of in.		number of in. in 1 ft		total ft
36	÷	12	=	*n*

Press:

Since $36 \div 12 = 3$, she needs 3 ft of border for each side of the bulletin board.

CULTURAL LINK

In ancient Egypt, people used some units that were based on parts of the body. Scientists have found evidence of a unit called the *cubit* carved in pieces of wood and stone as early as 3000 B.C.

Check Your Understanding

Write *multiply* or *divide* to tell how to change the unit.

1. yards to feet

2. feet to miles

3. inches to feet

4. miles to feet

PRACTICE

Choose a word from the box that makes each sentence true.

inches multiply miles feet divide yards

5. When you change feet to inches you _?_.
6. When you change inches to yards you _?_.
7. When you change miles to yards you _?_.
8. There are 5,280 _?_ in 1 mile.
9. There are 9 feet in 3 _?_.
10. There are 72 _?_ in 6 feet.

Change the unit. You may use a calculator.

11. 36 in. = _?_ ft
12. 7,040 yd = _?_ mi
13. 2 mi = _?_ ft
14. 5 yd = _?_ ft
15. 60 in. = _?_ ft
16. 9 yd = _?_ ft
17. 4 mi = _?_ ft
18. 8 ft = _?_ in.
19. 1,200 ft = _?_ yd

Mixed Applications

20. Sam walks 850 yd from his house to his friend's house. If he walks home, will he have walked a mile? How do you know?
21. A sewing pattern calls for 3 yd of fabric. Felicia already has 10 ft of fabric. Does she have enough fabric to use? Explain.

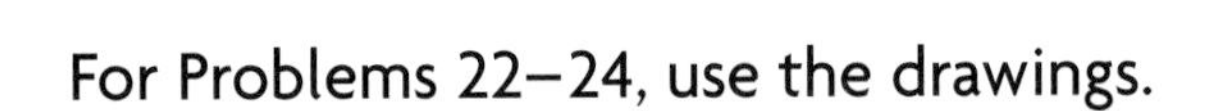

For Problems 22–24, use the drawings.

22. What is the perimeter of Rusty's doghouse in yards? in inches?
23. What is the perimeter of Max's doghouse in feet? in inches?
24. What is the difference in the perimeters of Rusty's doghouse and Max's doghouse in inches? in feet? in yards?

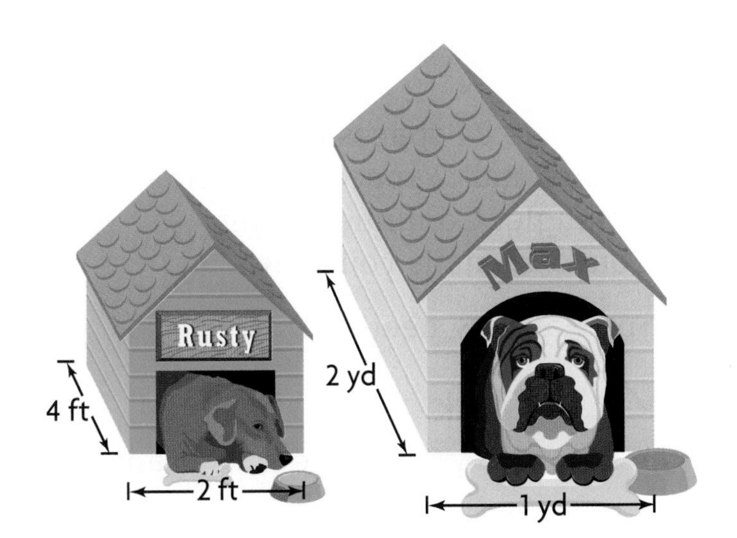

25. **WRITE ABOUT IT** Explain when to use multiplication and when to use division when changing units.

MORE PRACTICE Student Handbook page H109

PART 2 PROBLEM-SOLVING STRATEGY
Draw a Diagram

THE PROBLEM Matthew likes to paint models. He is making a rack for hanging his paintbrushes. He uses a 2-ft piece of wood to make the rack. He will hammer a nail every 2 in. beginning 2 in. from the left end. He will not put nails on the ends. How many nails will he need?

✓ Understand

- What are you asked to do?
- What information will you use?
- Is there information you will not use? If so, what?

✓ Plan

- What strategy can you use to solve the problem?

  You can *draw a diagram* to find how many nails are needed.

✓ Solve

- How can drawing a diagram help you solve this problem?

2 in.

1 square = 1 inch

Draw a diagram of the rack on grid paper. Have each square represent 1 in. Change the 2-ft piece of wood from ft to in. Multiply $2 \times 12 = 24$. So, 2 ft = 24 in. Draw the rectangle 24 spaces long and 2 spaces wide. Draw the first nail 2 spaces from the left edge of the rectangle. Continue to draw nails every 2 spaces. Count the nails you drew.

So, Matthew needs 11 nails.

✓ Look Back

- How can you decide if your answer is reasonable?
- What other strategy could you use?

PRACTICE

CHOOSE Paper/Pencil Calculator Hands-on Mental Math

Draw a diagram to solve.

1. Matthew decides to use a 3-ft piece of wood. He hammers a nail every 3 in. beginning 3 in. from the left end. He does not put a nail on either end of the rack. How many nails does he need?

2. Ed's backyard is 14 yd along the back fence. He plants a bush every 6 ft beginning 6 ft from the left corner, without any bushes on the ends. How many bushes does he plant?

3. A bulletin board is 3 ft wide. Ms. Huang places a star every 4 in. beginning 4 in. from the left end. She does not place a star on either end. How many stars does she place across the board?

4. What is the greatest number of slices of bread you can get by using 12 cuts to slice a loaf of bread?

Mixed Applications

Solve.

CHOOSE A STRATEGY

- Act It Out
- Draw a Diagram
- Find a Pattern
- Work Backward
- Write a Number Sentence

5. Abby collects stamps. She has two books of stamps. One book has 5 more pages than the other. If she has 49 pages of stamps in all, how many pages are in each book?

6. Sam rode his bicycle 3.8 mi on Monday, 2.7 mi on Wednesday, and 1.5 mi on Friday. How far did Sam ride his bicycle on those three days?

7. A meeting hall is 9 yd long. Every 3 ft there is a chair along the wall. There are no chairs in the corners of the room. How many chairs are along one wall?

8. Describe the figure that would come next in this pattern.

9. Ashley ran one mile in 11 minutes 30.25 seconds. Nancy ran one mile in 12 minutes 29 seconds. April ran one mile in 11 minutes 30.85 seconds. Arrange the students' times from the fastest to the slowest. Who came in first? second? third?

10. Josh has 6 coins that equal $0.95. Which 6 coins does he have?

MORE PRACTICE Student Handbook page H109

Fractions in Measurements

You will learn to measure length to the nearest whole unit, or nearest fraction of a unit.

Why learn this? You can measure something when its length falls between two units on the ruler.

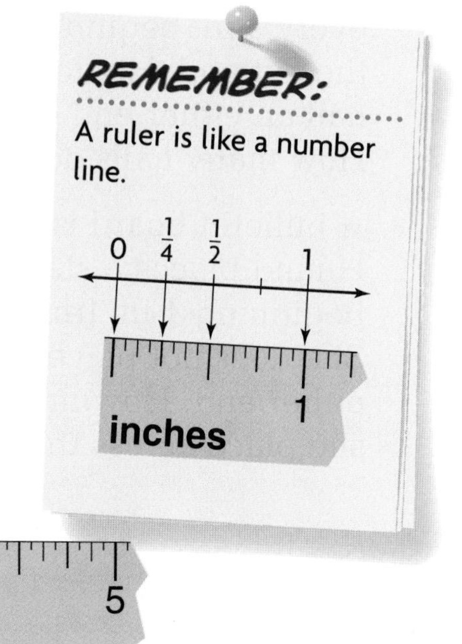

Sometimes the length of an object is not in whole units. You can round the measurement to the nearest whole unit or to the nearest fraction of a unit.

Find the length of each object to the nearest inch, $\frac{1}{2}$ inch, and $\frac{1}{4}$ inch.

A. To find the length of the pencil to the nearest in., look for the whole number that is nearest to its length.

So, the pencil is 4 in. long to the nearest in.

B. To find the length of the stick to the nearest $\frac{1}{2}$ in., look for the $\frac{1}{2}$-in. mark that is nearest to the stick's length.

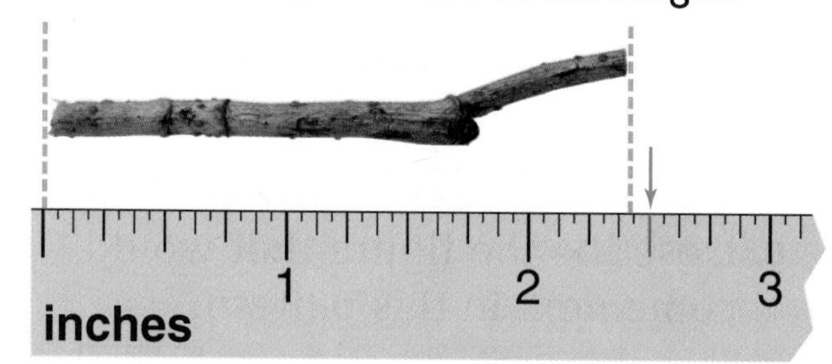

So, the stick is $2\frac{1}{2}$ in. long to the nearest $\frac{1}{2}$ in.

C. To find the length of the paper clip to the nearest $\frac{1}{4}$ in., look for the $\frac{1}{4}$-in. mark that is nearest to the paper clip's length.

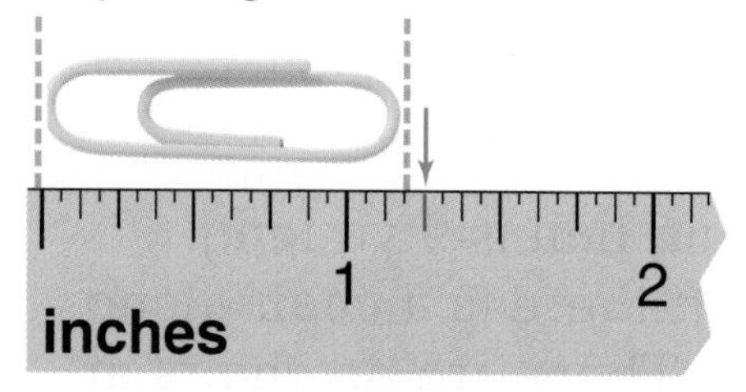

So, the paper clip is $1\frac{1}{4}$ in. long to the nearest $\frac{1}{4}$ in.

- How do you know where to find the $\frac{1}{2}$-in. marks on the ruler? the $\frac{1}{4}$-in. marks?

Check Your Understanding

Measure the length to the nearest $\frac{1}{2}$ in.

1. ORANGE

Measure the length to the nearest $\frac{1}{4}$ in.

2.

PRACTICE

Measure the length to the nearest $\frac{1}{2}$ in.

3.

4.

Measure the length of each item to the nearest $\frac{1}{4}$ in.

5.

6.

7.

Mixed Applications

For Problems 8–9, use the flower chart.

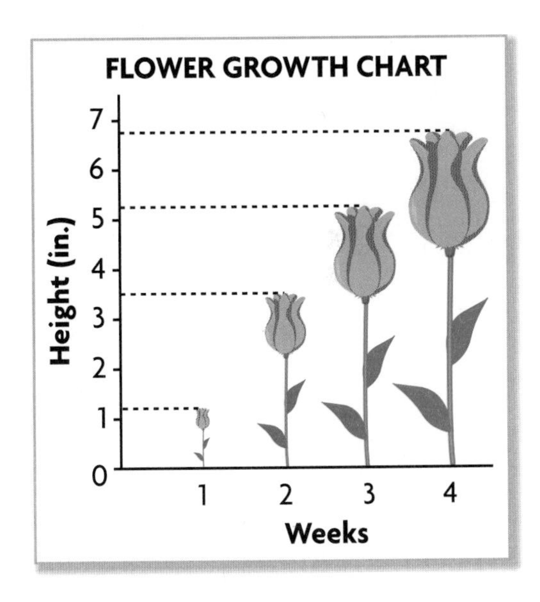

8. To the nearest inch, how tall was the flower in Week 3? Week 4?

9. Did the flower grow more between Weeks 1 and 2 or between Weeks 3 and 4?

10. Linda bought a package of flower seeds for \$1.89. She also bought gloves for \$3.99 and a small shovel for \$2.25. Did she receive enough change from \$10.00 to buy another package of seeds? How much change did she receive?

11. **WRITE ABOUT IT** Explain what it means to measure to the nearest in., $\frac{1}{2}$ in., or $\frac{1}{4}$ in.

Mixed Review

Find the product. (pages 292–293)

12. $13 \times 705 = n$ **13.** $74 \times 893 = n$ **14.** $97 \times 848 = n$ **15.** $45 \times 2{,}079 = n$

Find the difference. (pages 364–365)

16. $7\frac{2}{6} - 2\frac{1}{6} = n$ **17.** $11\frac{6}{8} - 5\frac{3}{8} = n$ **18.** $6\frac{3}{4} - 2\frac{2}{4} = n$

Capacity

You will investigate how capacity is measured in customary units.

Why learn this? You can decide which customary units to use to measure liquids.

WORD POWER
capacity
cup (c)
pint (pt)
quart (qt)
gallon (gal)

Capacity is the amount a container can hold when filled. The customary units for measuring capacity are **cup (c)**, **pint (pt)**, **quart (qt)**, and **gallon (gal)**.

Customary Units for Measuring Liquids	
1 cup (c)	
1 pint (pt)	= 2 cups
1 quart (qt)	= 2 pints
1 gallon (gal)	= 4 quarts

Explore

How many cups does it take to fill a 1-quart container?

MATERIALS: empty school-lunch milk cartons, 1-cup container, 1-quart container, 1-gallon container, water

MODEL

Step 1

Fill a milk carton with water. Find how many cups are in the milk carton.

Step 2

Pour milk cartons full of water into a 1-quart container to find how many cups are in a quart.

Record

Write how many milk cartons of water are in a cup. Then write how many cups of water are in a quart.

Now, investigate the capacity of a gallon container.

Try This

Use milk cartons to fill a gallon container with water. Since 1 milk carton is equivalent to 1 cup, record your answer in cups.

Technology Link
E-Lab • Activity 24 Available on CD-ROM and the Internet at http://www.hbschool.com/elab

Talk About It

- How can you use a calculator to change units of capacity?
- What equivalent units can you name for gallons?
- What unit would you use to measure water in a bucket? lemonade in a glass? water in a cooking pot?

WRITE ABOUT IT Show how two different containers can have the same capacity.

Consumer Link

Many recipes call for measuring liquids by the teaspoon (t), tablespoon (tbsp), and fluid ounce (fl oz). There are 3 t in 1 tbsp. One recipe calls for 4 tbsp of water. How many t is that?

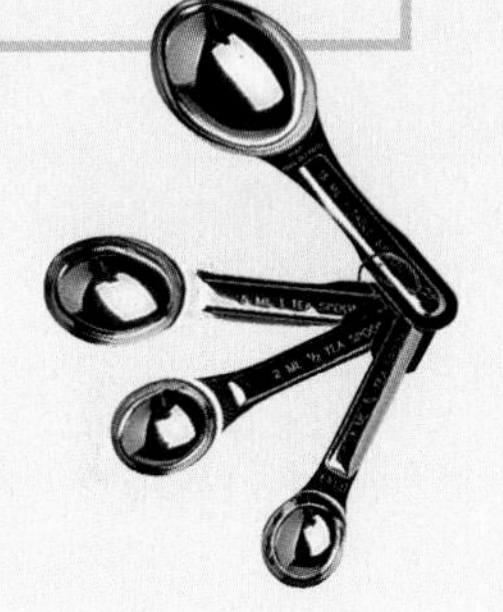

HANDS-ON PRACTICE

For Problems 1–2, use measuring containers.

1. How many cups fill 3 pint containers?

2. How many pints fill a gallon container?

Applying What You Learned

Write the letter of the reasonable unit.

3.

a. gal **b.** qt

4.

a. qt **b.** gal

5.

a. c **b.** gal

Write the equivalent measurement.

6. 6 c = __?__ pt

7. 2 qt = __?__ pt

8. 1 qt = __?__ c

9. 3 gal = __?__ qt

10. 8 c = __?__ qt

11. 8 qt = __?__ gal

Mixed Applications

For Problems 12–14, use the recipe.

Fruit Punch
1 qt apple juice
1 qt pineapple juice
1 pt orange juice

12. What is the total number of cups in the fruit punch? the total number of pints?

13. If the recipe were doubled, would there be enough cups for 30 students? Explain.

14. **Write a problem** about capacity using the recipe.

MORE PRACTICE Student Handbook page H110

Weight

You will learn how weight is measured in customary units.	**Why learn this?** You will know which customary units to use to find how much things weigh.	**WORD POWER** ounce (oz) pound (lb) ton (T)

The customary units for measuring weight are **ounce (oz)**, **pound (lb)**, and **ton (T)**.

1 slice of bread weighs about 1 oz.

1 loaf of bread weighs about 1 lb.

1 bread truck weighs about 1 T.

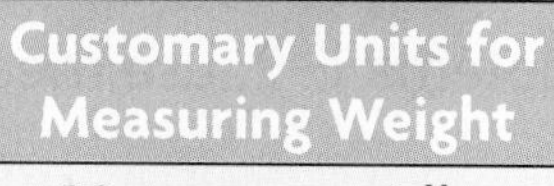

Customary Units for Measuring Weight		
16 oz	=	1 lb
2,000 lb	=	1 T

Talk About It

- What is something that weighs an ounce or less?
- What is something that weighs about a pound?
- What is something that weighs about a ton?
- How can you change pounds to ounces? pounds to tons?

You can use a calculator to change units.

EXAMPLES

A. 3 T = ___?___ lb

Since 2,000 lb are in 1 T, multiply by 2,000.

Press:        

3 × 2 0 0 0 = | = 6000.

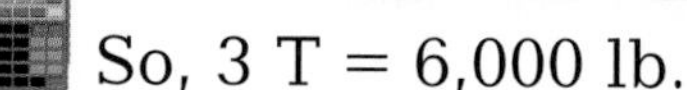

So, 3 T = 6,000 lb.

B. 64 oz = ___?___ lb

Since 16 oz are in 1 lb, divide by 16.

Press: 6 4 ÷ 1 6 = | = 4.

So, 64 oz = 4 lb.

- What buttons can you press to change 5 lb to oz?

Calculator Activities, page H62

PRACTICE

Choose a reasonable unit of measure. Write *oz*, *lb*, or *T*.

1. 

2. 

3. 

Choose the more reasonable measurement.

4. 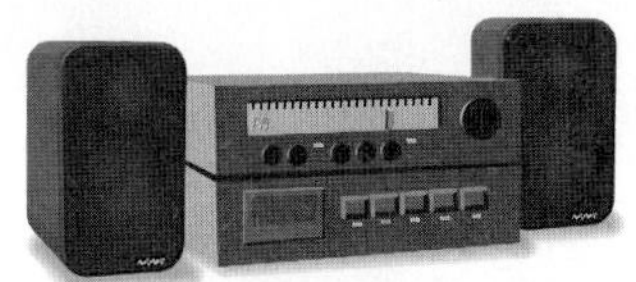

15 oz or 15 lb

5. 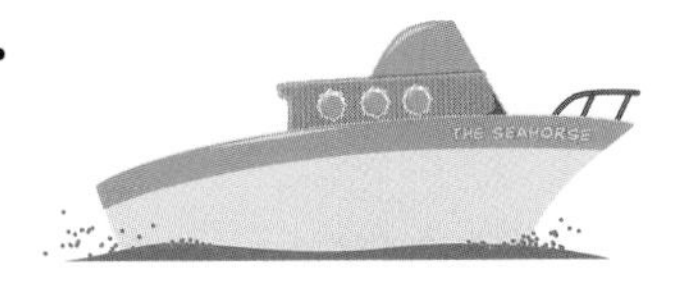

3 lb or 3 T

6. 

14 oz or 14 lb

Write the equivalent measurement. You may use a calculator.

7. 3 lb = __?__ oz

8. 5 T = __?__ lb

9. 128 oz = __?__ lb

10. 18,000 lb = __?__ T

11. 14 lb = __?__ oz

12. 15 T = __?__ lb

Mixed Applications

13. Rose is carrying 5 paperback books. Each book weighs about 4 oz. Is the total weight of the books more or less than 1 lb? Explain.

14. A truckload of 50 televisions is being delivered to a store. Each television weighs 80 lb. How many tons do the televisions weigh?

15. Which weighs more, 42 oz of sugar or 3 lb of flour? Which weighs less, 2,500 lb of sand or a 1-T truck?

16. **WRITE ABOUT IT** Tell how to decide if the weight of something should be given in ounces, pounds, or tons.

Mixed Review

Find the sum. You may wish to draw a picture. (pages 362–363)

17. $2\frac{1}{4} + 3\frac{2}{4}$

18. $6\frac{3}{8} + 2\frac{1}{8}$

19. $4\frac{5}{9} + 5\frac{2}{9}$

20. $8\frac{5}{7} + 1\frac{2}{7}$

Write each decimal as a fraction. (pages 370–371)

21. 0.3 **22.** 0.25 **23.** 0.7 **24.** 0.39 **25.** 0.87

MORE PRACTICE Student Handbook page H110

CULTURAL CONNECTION

COOPERATIVE LEARNING

Pick a Peck of Apples

Stefan and Anna helped their Aunt Ulla and Uncle Guenter pick apples in Ohio. Their aunt wanted to sell some apples at a fruit stand and keep some for cooking special dishes at a celebration.

Apples are measured by the capacity of their containers in customary units of dry measure. Look at the chart and tell how to change pints to quarts, quarts to pecks, and pecks to bushels.

Customary Units for Dry Measure
1 quart (qt) = 2 pints (pt)
1 peck (pk) = 8 quarts
1 bushel (bu) = 32 quarts

CULTURAL LINK

The custom in Germany and several other European countries is for the birthday person to give a party, prepare food and entertainment, and invite others.

Work Together

1. Stefan picked 1 peck of apples, while Anna picked 14 pints. Change the amount to the same unit and compare who picked more.

2. Uncle Guenter picked 20 pecks before he ran out of bushel baskets. How many bushels had he picked? Which operation is used to change a smaller unit to a larger unit?

3. Aunt Ulla invited her relatives to her birthday party. She was preparing to serve sliced apples with cinnamon sugar, apfel kuchen (cake), apfel streudel (pastry), and apfelsaft (apple juice). Choose the reasonable unit to measure the amount of apples she will need to serve 20 family members: 1 pint, 1 quart, 1 peck, or 1 bushel.

4. Write the equivalent measure in pints for each unit: quart, peck, and bushel. What operation did you use?

CHAPTER 24

REVIEW

✓ CHECK UNDERSTANDING

VOCABULARY

1. Units that measure in one direction, such as length, width, height, or distance, are called __?__ units. (page 406)

2. The amount a container can hold when filled is its __?__. (page 414)

Use a ruler to measure the length to the nearest $\frac{1}{4}$ inch. (pages 412–413)

3. 

4. 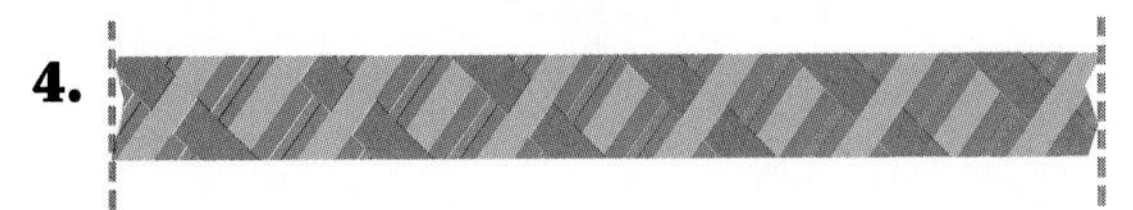

✓ CHECK SKILLS

Choose the reasonable unit of measure. Write *in., ft, yd,* or *mi.* (pages 406–407)

5. The length of a hammer is about 1 __?__.

6. The width of the book is 8 __?__.

Choose the more reasonable measurement. (pages 414–417)

7. 

T or lb

8. 

qt or gal

9. 

c or qt

Write the equivalent measurement. You may use a calculator. (pages 408–409, 414–417)

10. 2 yd = __?__ ft

11. 48 in. = __?__ ft

12. 6 c = __?__ pt

13. 80 oz = __?__ lb

✓ CHECK PROBLEM SOLVING

Solve. (pages 410–411)

CHOOSE A STRATEGY

- **Work Backward**
- **Draw a Diagram**
- **Guess and Check**
- **Write a Number Sentence**

14. Juan, Young, and Tina are comparing their heights. At 54 in., Juan is 6 in. taller than Tina. Tina is 3 in. shorter than Young. How tall is Young?

15. Tom made chili sauce to freeze. He made enough sauce to fill six 2-qt freezer bags. How many gallons of sauce will he freeze?

CHAPTER 25 MEASUREMENT: METRIC UNITS

DID YOU KNOW...

Bamboo is a plant that has been used for food, shelter, medicine and making musical instruments.

Some kinds of bamboo grow between 45 cm and one meter per day. It sometimes grows to be about 30 meters tall.

Pampering Plants

Your class has decided to grow some plants from seeds in peat pots, but your classroom is drafty when the door is open. To keep a constant warm temperature for the developing seedlings, you decide to make a small greenhouse.

YOU WILL NEED: metersticks, 1-cm dowels, plastic sheeting, glue and nails, small hammer, pipe calculator (optional)

Work with a group. Your job is to

- calculate how many meters of dowel you need to make a greenhouse frame that is 44 cm long, 28 cm wide, and 16 cm in height.
- calculate how much plastic sheeting you need.
- measure the materials.
- make a greenhouse, using your calculations.

Miniature Greenhouse

1. Glue and nail wood frame together
2. Cut pipe and glue on top of roof supports
3. Glue plastic sheeting to supports, and tape with cloth tape. Tape roof sheeting to ventilation pipe; tape back side of pipe to frame.
4. Open a hole in sheeting at both short sides to uncover the pipe.

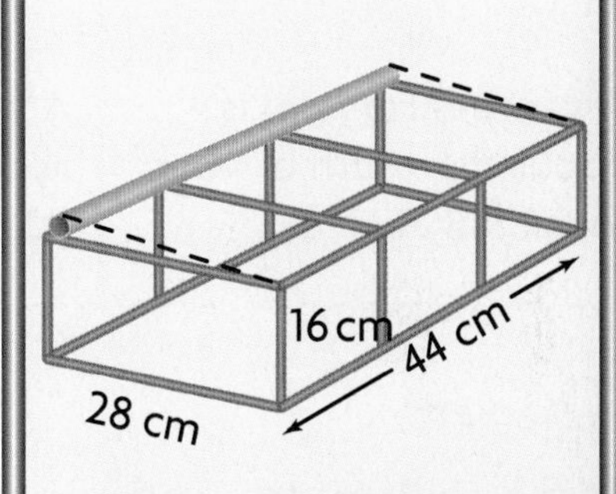

DID YOU

- ✓ figure out how many meters of dowel you need?
- ✓ figure out how much plastic sheeting you need?
- ✓ make a greenhouse?
- ✓ share your project with the class?

Linear Measures

You will investigate how to measure length in metric units.

Why learn this? You can decide which metric unit to use to measure objects.

WORD POWER
centimeter (cm)
decimeter (dm)
meter (m)

You can use metric units to measure length or distance.

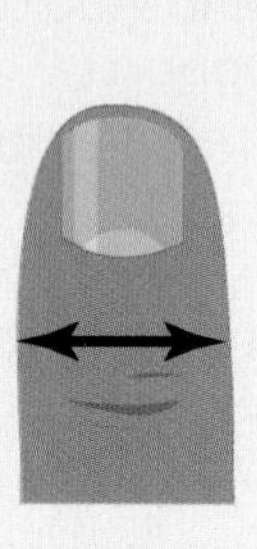

1 cm

A **centimeter (cm)** is about the width of your index finger.

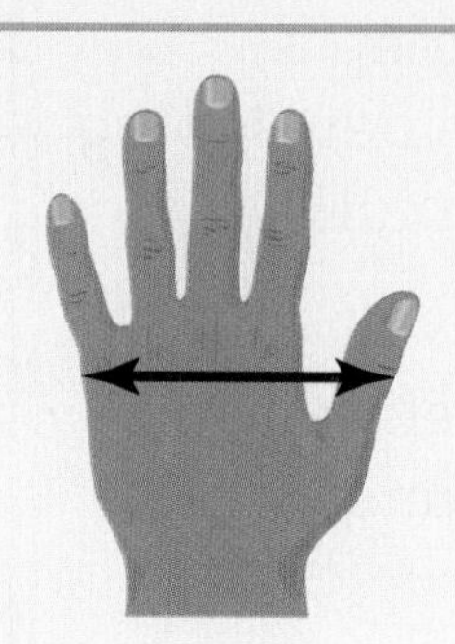

1 dm
10 cm = 1 dm

A **decimeter (dm)** is about the width of an adult's hand.

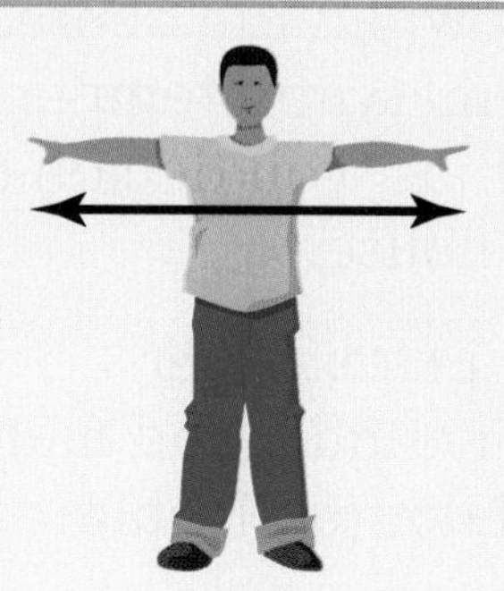

1 m
10 dm = 1 m
100 cm = 1 m

A **meter (m)** is about the distance from one hand to the other when you stretch out your arms.

Explore

Name, estimate, and measure the lengths of ten objects in your classroom. Use centimeter, decimeter, and meter units of measure.

MATERIALS: centimeter ruler, meterstick

REMEMBER:
Linear units measure in one direction, such as length, width, height, or distance.

Record

Make a table to record the estimates and measurements to the nearest cm, dm, or m.

	Object	Unit of Measure	Estimate	Measurement
	book	cm	30 cm	28 cm
1.				
2.				
3.				

Talk About It

- How did you estimate the length of each object?
- How did you decide what unit of measure to use for each object?
- How did you use the centimeter ruler or meterstick to measure each object?

Now, measure your math book.

Try This

Choose a unit of measure. Record all the linear measurements of your math book to the nearest cm or dm.

TALK ABOUT IT What parts of your math book did you measure? Did you and your classmates get the same measurements? If not, why not?

HANDS-ON PRACTICE

Use a centimeter ruler or a meterstick to measure each thing. Write the measurement and unit of measure you used.

1. height of a classmate **2.** length of a stapler **3.** length of classroom

Applying What You Learned

Choose the most reasonable measurement. Write *a*, *b*, or *c*.

4.  length of a car **a.** 4 cm **b.** 4 dm **c.** 4 m

5.  length of a bat **a.** 1 cm **b.** 1 dm **c.** 1 m

6. length of a leaf **a.** 5 cm **b.** 5 dm **c.** 5 m

Mixed Applications

7. Ricardo's pencil is 14 cm long. Trisha's pencil is 1 dm long. Who has the longer pencil? How much longer?

8. The height of Polly's plant is 3 times the height of Marcia's plant. Marcia's plant is 14 cm high. How high is Polly's plant?

9. Sam's bedroom is 4 m long. How many cm long is his bedroom?

10. **WRITE ABOUT IT** How are a centimeter, a decimeter, and a meter related?

MORE PRACTICE Student Handbook page H110

Decimals and Metric Measures

You will learn how meters, decimeters, and centimeters are related.

Why learn this? You can use a meterstick and record lengths in decimals.

You can use a meterstick to model decimal numbers.

meter

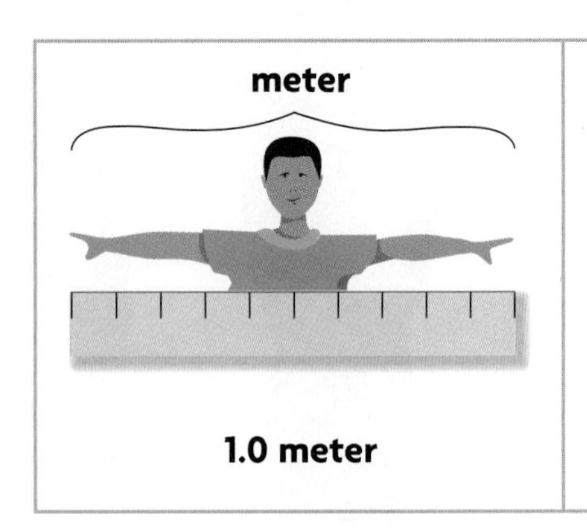

1.0 meter

decimeter
***Deci* means "tenths."**

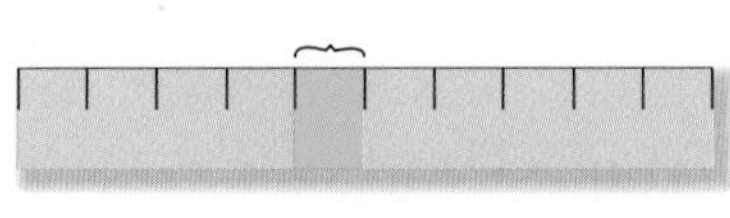

1 decimeter = 0.1, or $\frac{1}{10}$, meter

centimeter
***Centi* means "hundredths."**

1 centimeter = 0.01, or $\frac{1}{100}$, meter

Talk About It

- How many decimeters equal 1 meter? centimeters equal 1 meter?
- What part of a meter equals 1 decimeter? equals 1 centimeter?
- What is another name for 0.3 meters on the meterstick? for 0.06 meters on the meterstick?

Sports Link

In the 1996 Olympics, France's Jean Galfione, Russia's Igor Trandenkov, and Germany's Andrei Tivontchik tied with a pole-vault height record of 5.92 meters. What is this height in centimeters?

Check Your Understanding

Copy the table. Fill in the missing measures. You may use a meterstick to help you.

	METRIC LINEAR UNITS		
	Meter	Decimeter	Centimeter
1.	?	10	?
2.	2	?	?
3.	?	4	?
4.	?	?	10
5.	?	?	9
6.	?	?	30
7.	3	?	?
8.	?	?	400

PRACTICE

Write the missing unit. Use a meterstick to help you.

9. 4 __?__ = 40 cm　　**10.** 0.85 __?__ = 85 cm

11. 0.6 __?__ = 6 dm　　**12.** 7 __?__ = 70 cm

13. 0.03 __?__ = 3 cm　　**14.** 2 __?__ = 20 dm

15. 3 __?__ = 30 dm　　**16.** 0.25 __?__ = 25 cm

Write the decimal number. Use a meterstick to help you.

17. 5 dm = __?__ m　　**18.** 4 cm = __?__ m

19. 50 cm = __?__ m　　**20.** 2 dm = __?__ m

21. 80 cm = __?__ m　　**22.** 60 cm = __?__ m

23. Jan's shoe measures 21 cm in length. Is her shoe longer or shorter than 2 dm? What is her shoe's measurement in m?

24. Haley and Alison are knitting blankets. Haley's blanket is 4 times as long as Alison's blanket. Alison's blanket is 3 dm long. How much longer than 1 m is Haley's blanket?

25. Mary needs 118 cm of ribbon. She has one piece of ribbon 76 cm and another piece 38 cm. Does she have enough ribbon? Explain.

26. **Write a problem** about measuring something in your desk in cm. Then write that measurement in dm or m.

Find the sum. (pages 356–357)

27. $\frac{1}{6} + \frac{2}{6} = $ __?__　　**28.** $\frac{3}{8} + \frac{2}{8} = $ __?__　　**29.** $\frac{7}{10} + \frac{6}{10} = $ __?__　　**30.** $\frac{3}{4} + \frac{2}{4} = $ __?__

31. $\frac{4}{7} + \frac{3}{7} = $ __?__　　**32.** $\frac{1}{5} + \frac{2}{5} = $ __?__　　**33.** $\frac{7}{9} + \frac{3}{9} = $ __?__　　**34.** $\frac{5}{12} + \frac{7}{12} = $ __?__

Are the two decimals equivalent? Write *yes* or *no*. (pages 374–375)

35. 0.4 and 0.40　　**36.** 0.7 and 0.07　　**37.** 0.9 and 0.09　　**38.** 0.1 and 0.10

39. 0.5 and 0.05　　**40.** 0.2 and 0.20　　**41.** 0.80 and 0.8　　**42.** 0.30 and 0.03

43. 0.60 and 0.6　　**44.** 0.4 and 0.04　　**45.** 0.70 and 0.7　　**46.** 0.50 and 0.05

PART 1

Changing Units

You will learn how to change metric units of measure by multiplying.	**Why learn this?** You can change large units of measure to smaller units of measure.

Nicky bought a new fishing pole that is 2 meters long. How many decimeters long is his fishing pole?

Equivalent Measures		
10 centimeters	=	1 decimeter
10 decimeters	=	1 meter
100 centimeters	=	1 meter

When you change larger units to smaller units, you multiply. So, after the change, the number of units is greater.

length of fishing pole in meters		number of decimeters in 1 meter		number of decimeters in all
2	×	10	=	20

So, Nicky's fishing pole is 20 decimeters long.

How many centimeters long is his fishing pole?

length of fishing pole in meters		number of centimeters in 1 meter		number of centimeters in all
2	×	100	=	200

So, Nicky's fishing pole is 200 centimeters long.

- If you change 4 meters to centimeters, does the number of units become greater or less? How much greater or less?

Check Your Understanding

Write the equivalent measurement. You may use a calculator. Example: 3 m = ? dm

1. 4 m = ? dm

2. 3 m = ? cm

3. 4 dm = ? cm

4. 3 dm = ? cm

PRACTICE

Would you multiply each by 10 or by 100 to change the larger units to the smaller units? Write × *10* or × *100*.

5. 8 m = ? cm **6.** 9 m = ? dm **7.** 3 m = ? cm

8. 5 dm = ? cm **9.** 10 dm = ? cm **10.** 1 m = ? dm

11. 6 m = ? cm **12.** 4 m = ? dm **13.** 7 dm = ? cm

Fill in the missing measures. You may use a calculator.

	Meters	Decimeters	Centimeters
14.	6	60	?
15.	?	150	1,500
16.	8	80	?
17.	25	?	2,500
18.	?	20	200
19.	9	?	900

Science Link

The Kitt Peak National Observatory has the largest solar telescope in the world. Three mirrors are used. One of the mirrors is 146 m deep inside a mountain. How many decimeters deep is the mirror?

Write the equivalent measurement. You may use a calculator.

20. 4 m = ? cm **21.** 35 m = ? dm

22. 7 dm = ? cm **23.** 10 m = ? dm

24. 10 m = ? cm **25.** 10 dm = ? cm

Mixed Applications

For Problems 26–30, use the floor plan and measurements of Corey's room.

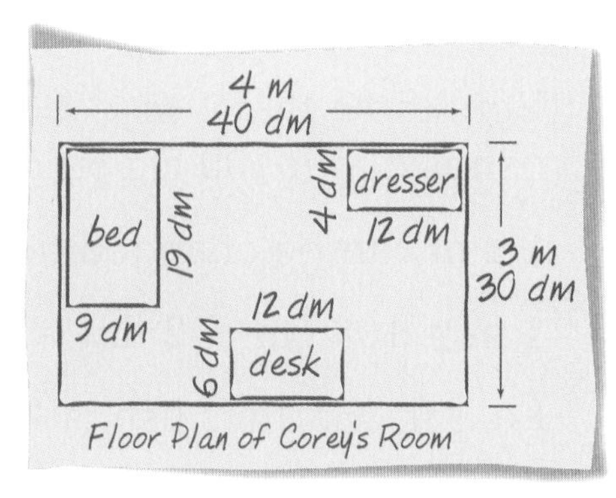

26. Corey's room is 40 decimeters long. How many decimeters are there between her bed and her dresser?

27. What is the perimeter of Corey's room in meters?

28. Corey's bed has a dust ruffle all the way around it. How long is the ruffle?

29. Corey's desk is 6 decimeters wide. How many centimeters wide is her desk?

30. **Write a problem** using the floor plan of Corey's room.

PART 2

PROBLEM-SOLVING STRATEGY
Solve a Simpler Problem

THE PROBLEM Mr. Martin and Nicky went fishing. They rented a boat for two days. Mr. Martin caught a fish that is 1.2 meters long. How many centimeters long was Mr. Martin's fish?

✓ Understand

- What are you asked to find?
- What information will you use?
- Is there any information you will not use? If so, what?

✓ Plan

- What strategy can you use to solve the problem?

  You can *solve a simpler problem* by using simpler numbers first and then by using the same steps to solve the problem.

✓ Solve

- How can you solve this problem?

  To use simpler numbers, round the decimal to the nearest whole number.

  1.2 rounds to 1.

  You know that 1 m = 100 cm, so Mr. Martin's fish is *about* 100 cm long.

  1.2 m can be changed to 1 m and 2 dm.

  1 m = 100 cm 2 dm = 20 cm 100 + 20 = 120

  So, Mr. Martin's fish is 120 cm long.

A day at the lake

✓ Look Back

- How can you decide if your answer is reasonable?
- What other strategy could you use?

PRACTICE

CHOOSE Paper/Pencil Calculator Hands-on Mental Math

Solve a simpler problem.

1. Ms. Martin caught a fish that is 1.1 meters long. How many centimeters long is Ms. Martin's fish?

2. Frances has $4.20 in nickels. How many nickels does she have?

3. Ed's height is 13 decimeters. Nicki's height is 1.2 meters. Who is taller? How many decimeters taller?

4. A square area is 12 feet on each side. Around the area are posts and wire. There is a post every 12 inches and a post at every corner. How many posts are there in all?

Mixed Applications

Solve.

CHOOSE A STRATEGY

- Make an Organized List
- Solve a Simpler Problem
- Find a Pattern
- Write a Number Sentence
- Work Backward
- Guess and Check

5. There are 45 people and one guide going deep-sea fishing. An equal number of people will be in each boat, except for one, which will also carry the guide. There will be more than 5 boats. How many boats will there be?

6. The Clarks arrived home at 4:00 P.M. They spent $3\frac{1}{2}$ hours fishing, 30 minutes eating lunch, 45 minutes driving to the fish camp, and 45 minutes driving home. At what time did they leave their house to go fishing?

7. Mark's desk is 1.3 meters long. How many centimeters long is Mark's desk?

8. Rhonda and Mitch caught a total of 18 fish. Rhonda caught 4 more fish than Mitch. How many fish did each catch?

9. The Davidsons rented a fishing boat for 3 hours. They rented 2 fishing poles and bought bait they could use to catch the fish. How much did they spend?

Sunrise Fish Camp

Boat Rental	$35/hour
Fishing Pole Rental	$4.25/day
Bait	$5.75

10. Sonia and Mike work as guides on the boats. They each work every other day. If Sonia works on Sunday, who will work on the Sunday at the beginning of the fourth week?

11. A group can go canoeing either for a half day or for a full day. They can rent one, two, or three canoes. How many different choices do they have?

MORE PRACTICE Student Handbook page H111

Capacity

You will learn how capacity is measured in metric units.	Why learn this? You can decide which metric units to use to measure liquids.	WORD POWER milliliter (mL) liter (L)

A **milliliter (mL)** and a **liter (L)** are metric units of capacity.

REMEMBER:
Capacity is the amount a container can hold when filled.

This table will help you understand the metric units that are used to measure liquids. How many mL does it take to fill a 2-L container?

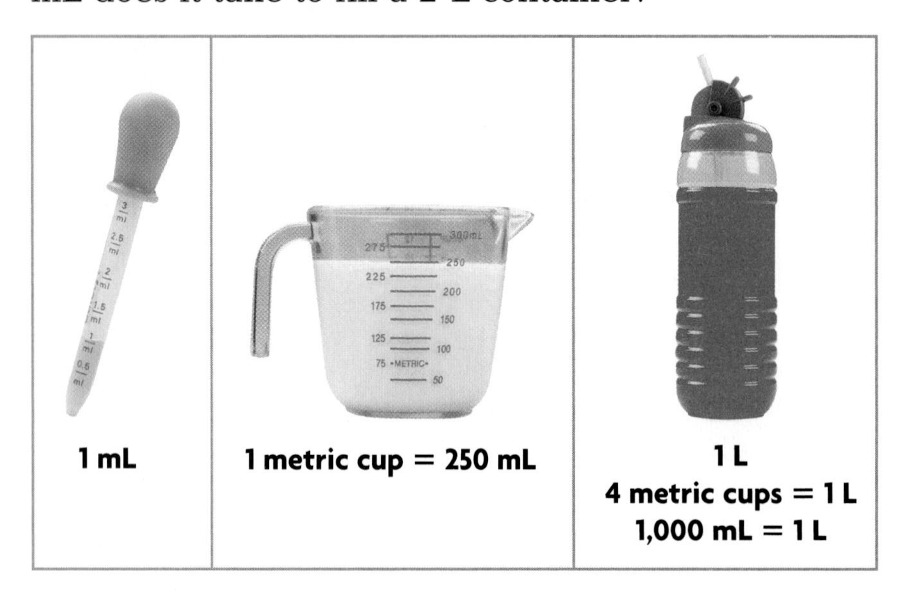

1 mL	1 metric cup = 250 mL	1 L 4 metric cups = 1 L 1,000 mL = 1 L

Since 1,000 mL equals 1 L, it takes 2,000 mL of liquid to fill a 2-L container.

- What are two things that are measured in milliliters? in liters?

Consumer Link

A can of soft drink has the capacity of 340 mL. About how many liters of soft drink are in a six-pack of soft drinks?

Check Your Understanding

Choose the reasonable unit of measure. Write *mL* or *L*.

1.

2.

Write the equivalent measurement.

3. 3 L = ? mL **4.** 6 L = ? mL **5.** 4,000 mL = ? L

6. 12 metric cups = ? L **7.** 5 L = ? mL **8.** 10 L = ? mL

PRACTICE

Choose the reasonable unit of measure. Write *mL, metric cup,* or *L.*

9. a bucket of water **10.** a glass of orange juice **11.** a gas tank in a car

12. a bottle of shampoo **13.** a bowl of soup **14.** water in a pool

15. juice in a punch bowl **16.** a measuring spoon **17.** a raindrop

Choose the most reasonable measurement.

18. 

a. 25 mL
b. 250 mL
c. 25 L

19. 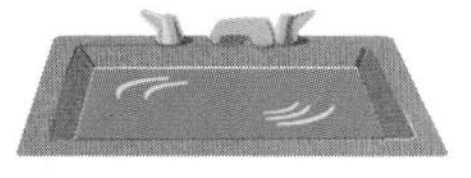

a. 5 mL
b. 500 mL
c. 5 L

20. 

a. 6 mL
b. 600 mL
c. 6 L

21. 

a. 2 mL
b. 20 mL
c. 2 L

22. 

a. 12 mL
b. 120 mL
c. 12 L

Mixed Applications

23. Eric drinks 4 glasses of water each day. There are 300 mL of water in each glass. Anna drinks 1 L of water each day. Who drinks more water? How much more?

24. A 1-L bottle of soda sells for $0.59 and a 2-L bottle of soda sells for $1.15. Marcia bought three 1-L bottles and two 2-L bottles. How much change did she get from $5.00?

25. During a camping trip, 4 friends each drank 750 mL of water. How many liters of water did they drink altogether?

26. **Write a problem** using this information: a large canteen holds 2 L of water.

Mixed Review

Find the quotient. Check by multiplying. (pages 320–321)

27. $7\overline{)\$39.90}$ **28.** $9\overline{)\$21.33}$ **29.** $8\overline{)\$25.20}$ **30.** $7\overline{)\$27.44}$ **31.** $5\overline{)\$78.15}$

32. $6\overline{)\$26.28}$ **33.** $4\overline{)\$27.72}$ **34.** $9\overline{)\$42.84}$ **35.** $6\overline{)\$34.86}$ **36.** $5\overline{)\$56.60}$

Tell which number is greater. (pages 376–377)

37. 0.4, 0.5 **38.** 0.87, 0.97 **39.** 0.52, 0.5 **40.** 0.7, 0.68 **41.** 0.9, 0.91

42. 0.86, 0.68 **43.** 0.7, 0.73 **44.** 0.34, 0.4 **45.** 0.15, 0.5 **46.** 0.56, 0.60

MORE PRACTICE Student Handbook page H111

Mass

You will investigate how to measure the mass of objects in metric units.

Why learn this? You will know which metric units to use to find the mass of objects.

WORD POWER
mass
gram (g)
kilogram (kg)

Matter is what all objects are made of. **Mass** is the amount of matter in an object. A **gram (g)** and a **kilogram (kg)** are metric units of mass.

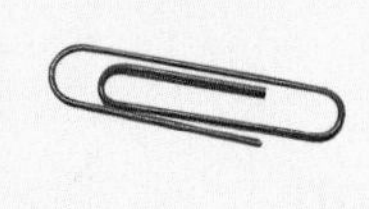

1 gram (g)

The mass of a dollar bill or a large paper clip is about 1 gram.

1 kilogram (kg)
1,000 grams (g) = 1 kilogram (kg)

The mass of a baseball bat is about 1 kilogram.

Explore

Choose three small objects in your desk. Estimate the mass of each object. Use a simple balance and large paper clips to find the mass of each object in grams. One large paper clip has a mass of about 1 gram.

MATERIALS: simple balance, large paper clips

Record

Make a table to record the measurements.

	Object	Estimate	Measurement
	penny	2 g	3 g
1.			
2.			
3.			

Explain how to put the items you measured in order from the least mass to the greatest mass.

E-Lab • Activity 25 Available on CD-ROM and the Internet at http://www.hbschool.com/elab

Talk About It

- Name two objects in your classroom that have about the same mass.
- About how many large paper clips have a mass of 1 kg?

Now, investigate the mass of other objects.

Science Link

A larger object does not always have a greater mass than a smaller object. A brick has a greater mass than a pillow. Name two other objects whose mass does not reflect their size.

Try This

Choose two objects, such as a bar of soap and a chalkboard eraser. Estimate the mass of each object. Then use a simple balance to compare the mass of the two objects.

WRITE ABOUT IT What do you notice about the size of each object and its mass?

Applying What You Learned

Choose the reasonable unit. Write *g* or *kg*.

1. 

2. 

3. 

4. 

5. 

Choose the more reasonable measurement.

6. 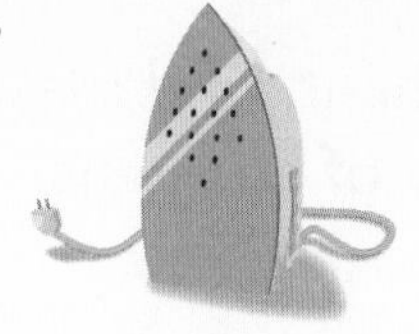

1 g or 1 kg

7. 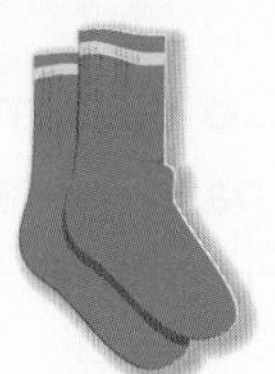

20 g or 200 g

8. 

10 g or 10 kg

9. 

10 kg or 1,000 kg

Mixed Applications

10. One loaf of bread has a mass of 448 grams. What is the mass of 4 loaves of bread? Is that more or less than 2 kilograms?

11. Linda needs 1 kilogram of flour. She already has 275 grams of flour. How much more flour does she need?

12. There are 45 calories in one slice of bread. Mauricio ate 3 slices of bread. How many more slices of bread does he need to eat in order to reach 180 calories?

13. **Write a problem** using this information: A whole-grain bar has 90 calories, 5 grams of fat, and 7 grams of sugar.

ANCIENT MEASURES

Name	Length in cm	Length in dm

PURPOSE To compare metric and nonstandard units of length

YOU WILL NEED metric ruler or meterstick, paper and pencil

A unit of length called a *cubit* was used in ancient Egypt. A cubit is the length of a man's forearm, from the tip of the elbow to the tip of the middle finger.

Work with a group. Measure each other's forearms in centimeters and decimeters. Record your results in a table.

Whose cubit is longest? Whose cubit is shortest? Order the lengths you have measured from the least to the greatest.

METRIC MATCH

PURPOSE To develop benchmarks for measuring and comparing metric units of capacity

YOU WILL NEED 6 empty containers, such as milk cartons, soda bottles, and juice cans; metric measuring cup; water

Work with a partner. Estimate the capacity of each container. Line up the containers from the least to the greatest capacity. Now, test your estimates. Find the capacity of each container by carefully measuring the water each can hold. Compare your predictions with your findings.

Go on a metric hunt. Find the mass or capacity of different containers in your kitchen.

Equivalents

PURPOSE To develop benchmark conversions between customary and metric units of measure

YOU WILL NEED metersticks and inch rulers, pencil and paper

Work with a partner. Choose five objects to measure. Make a table like the one shown. Record your findings.

Object	Estimate cm or dm	Actual cm or dm	Estimate in. or ft	Actual in. or ft

Study your findings. About how many centimeters make an inch? About how many centimeters make a foot?

CHAPTER 25

REVIEW

✓ CHECK UNDERSTANDING

VOCABULARY

1. The amount of matter in an object is its _?_. (page 432)

2. A _?_ is about the width of an adult's hand. (page 422)

3. The distance from one hand to the other when you stretch out your arms is about a _?_. (page 422)

4. A _?_ is about the width of your index finger. (page 422)

5. A drop of water is about one _?_. (page 430)

6. A capacity of 1,000 mL is equivalent to 1 _?_. (page 430)

7. A kilogram is equivalent to 1,000 _?_. (page 432)

Choose the more reasonable measurement. (pages 422–423, 430–433)

8. 

5 cm or 5 dm

9. 

40 mL or 40 L

10. 

2 mL or 2 L

11. 

300 g or 300 kg

✓ CHECK SKILLS

Write the equivalent measurement. (pages 424–427, 430–433)

12. 4 dm = _?_ m **13.** 5 m = _?_ cm **14.** 3 L = _?_ mL **15.** 1,000 g = _?_ kg

16. 2 L = _?_ mL **17.** 2,000 g = _?_ kg **18.** 100 cm = _?_ m **19.** 100 dm = _?_ m

✓ CHECK PROBLEM SOLVING

Solve. (pages 428–429)

CHOOSE A STRATEGY

- Act It Out
- Draw a Picture
- Make a Model
- Solve a Simpler Problem

20. Lisa had 20 sq ft of soil for flowers. She put 2 buttercups and 3 tulips in each square foot. How many of each kind of flower did she need?

21. Each of 6 thirsty workers drank 500 mL of water. How many liters of water in all did the workers drink?

CHAPTER 26

MORE ABOUT MEASUREMENT

DID YOU KNOW . . .

A ropes course is an obstacle course with cables, ropes, beams, and platforms hung from 2 to 30 feet off the ground. It encourages people to reach their goals.

Team-Up Time

Our Obstacle Course

Design an obstacle course with your class and then time your team with a stopwatch.

Work with a group. Your job is to

- plan an obstacle for your classroom's obstacle course.
- set up your obstacle and measure the length of the whole course.
- take turns running the course, being the obstacle attendant, timing the others on your team, and recording each person's time.
- add up the total time for your team.

Our group's times

Thalia	3 min 23.61 sec
Andrew	2 min 47.38 sec
Aylin	3 min 01.27 sec
Sam	3 min 42.02 sec
	11 min 114.28 sec

60 sec = 1 min
114.28 sec = 1 min 54.28 sec

So, our total time is 12 min 54.28

DID YOU

- ✓ contribute an obstacle to the classroom obstacle course?
- ✓ take turns running, timing, and recording others' times on the whole course?
- ✓ add up the total time for your team?

Time as a Fraction

You will learn to explain time by using fractions of an hour or fractions of a year.	**Why learn this?** You can describe time in different ways.

Janine and Penny are meeting at the mall at 10:30. What is another way to say 10:30?

When the minute hand on a clock points to the six, it shows 30 minutes, or $\frac{1}{2}$, past the hour.

So, half past ten is another way to say 10:30.

You can also use quarter hours to tell time.

A.

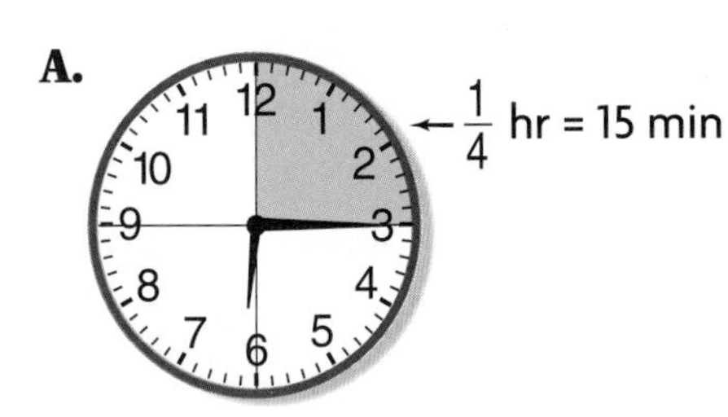

This clock shows 6:15, or a quarter past six.

B.

This clock shows 5:45, or a quarter to six.

- Why does it make sense to tell time by using halves and quarters?

Sports Link

At the National Unicycle Convention, children can compete in a unicycle obstacle course. A fast fourth grader can finish the obstacle course in $\frac{1}{2}$ to $\frac{3}{4}$ of an hour. How many minutes is that?

Fractions of a year can be used to describe longer amounts of time. Some people who work in large companies meet four times per year. These are called quarterly meetings.

JANUARY
FEBRUARY
MARCH

Sun	Mon	Tue	Wed	Thu	Fri	Sat
	1	2	3	4	5	6
7	8	9	10	11	12	13
14	15	16	17	18	19	20
21	22	23	24	25	26	27
28	29	30	31			

APRIL
MAY
JUNE

Sun	Mon	Tue	Wed	Thu	Fri	Sat
		1	2	3	4	5
6	7	8	9	10	11	12
13	14	15	16	17	18	19
20	21	22	23	24	25	26
27	28	29	30			

JULY
AUGUST
SEPTEMBER

Sun	Mon	Tue	Wed	Thu	Fri	Sat
			1	2	3	4
5	6	7	8	9	10	11
12	13	14	15	16	17	18
19	20	21	22	23	24	25
26	27	28	29	30		

OCTOBER
NOVEMBER
DECEMBER

Sun	Mon	Tue	Wed	Thu	Fri	Sat
			1	2	3	4
5	6	7	8	9	10	11
12	13	14	15	16	17	18
19	20	21	22	23	24	25
26	27	28	29	30	31	

Talk About It

- How many months long is $\frac{1}{4}$ of a year?
- What is something that happens every quarter year?

CRITICAL THINKING Why is a meeting that is held four times per year called a quarterly meeting?

PRACTICE

Write each time in a different way.

1. 1:30 **2.** 4:15 **3.** 9:45 **4.** 12:45

5. a quarter past eight **6.** half past two **7.** a quarter to five **8.** half past five

Use *a quarter* or *half* to express the time shown.

9. 

10. 

11. 

12. 

13. 

14. 

15. 

16. 

Mixed Applications

17. Roy's lunch time begins at a quarter to twelve. It ends 30 minutes later. How can you use *a quarter* or *half* to express the time that Roy's lunch ends?

18. The Fun and Games Company had a quarterly meeting at the end of March. When will its next three quarterly meetings be?

19. The school fair begins on October 20. It ends two weeks later. There are 31 days in October. On what date does the fair end?

20. **WRITE ABOUT IT** It is 6:55 P.M. Sandi needs to bake a cake for $\frac{1}{2}$ hour. She is leaving her house at a quarter past seven. Does Sandi have time to bake the cake? Explain.

Mixed Review

Find the product. (pages 292–293)

21. $15 \times 324 = n$ **22.** $21 \times 137 = n$ **23.** $11 \times 901 = n$ **24.** $22 \times 426 = n$

Find the quotient. Check by multiplying. (pages 308–311)

25. $6\overline{)336}$ **26.** $7\overline{)441}$ **27.** $9\overline{)891}$ **28.** $4\overline{)716}$ **29.** $3\overline{)972}$

MORE PRACTICE Student Handbook page H112

PART 1 Choosing Customary or Metric Units

You will learn to compare customary and metric units of measure.	**Why learn this?** You can decide which units are more practical to use.

Raquel wants to frame a picture her sister painted. She measured the picture's perimeter once using inches and once using centimeters. Is the number of inch units or the number of centimeter units greater?

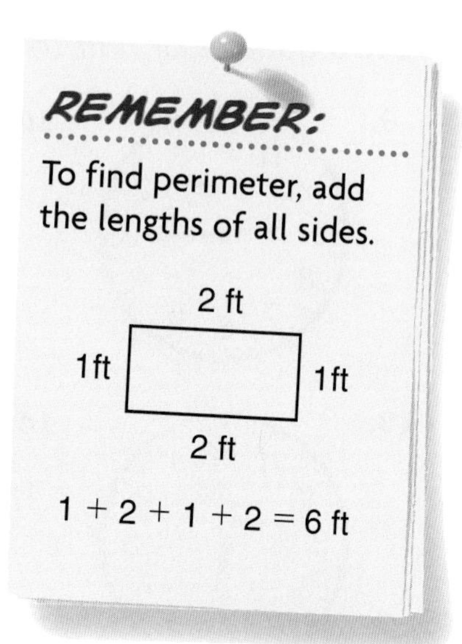

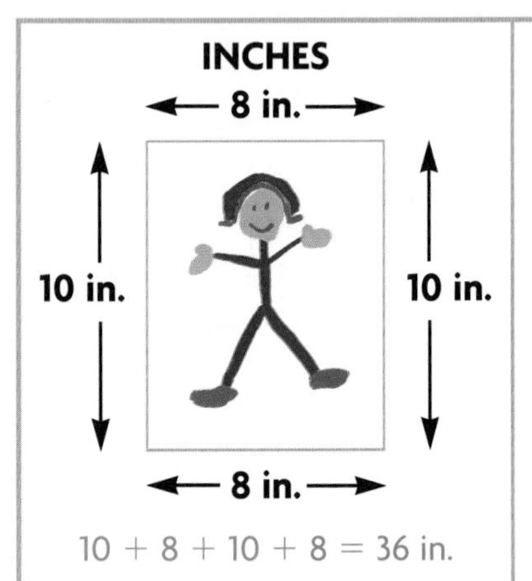

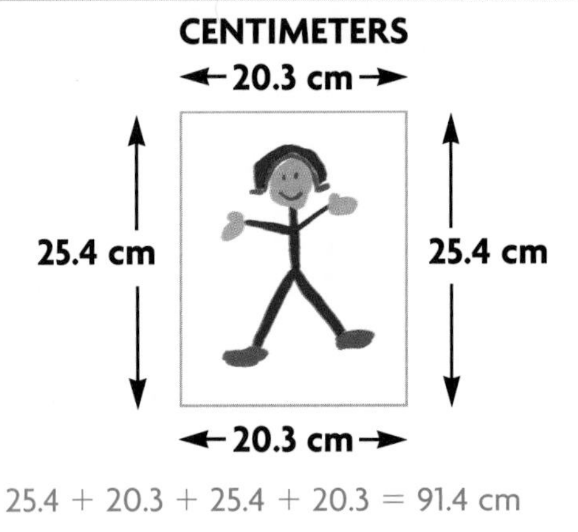

Since $91.4 > 36$, the number of centimeter units is greater. The perimeters are the same.

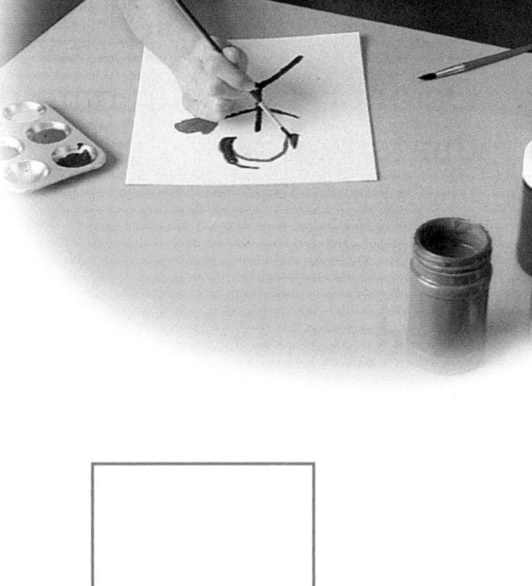

Talk About It

- Why is the number of centimeter units greater than the number of inch units?
- If you used decimeters, would the number be greater than or less than the number of inches? Explain.

CRITICAL THINKING In this example, does it make more sense to measure with inches or with centimeters? Explain.

Check Your Understanding

Use a ruler.

1. What is the perimeter of this square in inches? in centimeters?

PRACTICE

Find the perimeter of each figure in customary and metric units.

2. 

3. 

Choose the most reasonable measure for what is shown.

4. 

a. 2 cm **b.** 2 in.

5. 

a. 6 cm **b.** 6 in.

6. 

a. 4 cm **b.** 4 in.

7. 

a. 1.5 cm **b.** 1.5 in.

Mixed Applications

8. Selena walked $2\frac{1}{4}$ miles to school. After school she walked $\frac{1}{4}$ mile during track practice. She walked $1\frac{1}{4}$ miles to her friend's house and $\frac{1}{4}$ mile home. How many miles did Selena walk?

9. Ernest is getting his lunches ready for the week. He has 45 baby carrots that he wants to divide evenly in 7 containers. How many baby carrots will be in each container? How many will be left over?

10. Linda's pencil is 6 inches long. Mandy's is 6 centimeters long. Whose pencil is longer? Explain.

11. Shane studied from 3:15 to 4:45 and from 7:30 to 8:45. For how long did he study?

12. **WRITE ABOUT IT** Would you use centimeters or inches to measure the width of your finger? Explain.

MORE PRACTICE Student Handbook page H112

PART 2 PROBLEM-SOLVING STRATEGY
Write a Number Sentence

THE PROBLEM Jesse wants to build a fence around a vegetable garden. The garden is a rectangle 36 feet long and 24 feet wide. Fencing is sold by the yard. What is the perimeter of the garden in yards?

✓ Understand

- What are you asked to find?
- What information will you use?
- Is there information you will not use? If so, what?

✓ Plan

- What strategy can you use to solve the problem?

  You can *write a number sentence* to find the perimeter of the garden in yards.

✓ Solve

- What number sentence can you write to solve the problem?

  Add to find the perimeter in feet.

$$36 + 36 + 24 + 24 = 120$$

  Divide by 3 to find the number of yards.

$$3\overline{)120}\ \ 40$$

So, the perimeter of the garden is 40 yards.

✓ Look Back

- How can you determine if your answer is reasonable?
- What other strategy could you use?

PRACTICE

CHOOSE Paper/Pencil Calculator Hands-on Mental Math

Write a number sentence to solve.

1. Jan is using wood to put a fence around a rose garden. The garden is square and measures 12 feet on each side. What is the perimeter of the garden in yards?

2. Rick needs enough ribbon to put around a picture that has 2 sides 20 centimeters long and 2 sides 40 centimeters long. How many meters of ribbon does he need?

3. Ms. Mavis took the 27 students in her class to a health fair. The class was divided into 3 equal groups. At the fair, 2 groups had their pulses taken. How many students had their pulses taken?

4. Ira wants four CDs that cost $15 each. He has a coupon for $5 off the price of one CD. What is the total price Ira will pay for all four CDs?

Mixed Applications

Solve.

CHOOSE A STRATEGY

- Act It Out
- Draw a Diagram
- Make a Graph
- Make an Organized List
- Write a Number Sentence

5. Ernie folded a sheet of paper in half several times. When he opened it up, it showed 16 squares. How many times did Ernie fold the paper?

6. Rosie had 3 stickers. Then she and 5 friends divided a pack of stickers. Rosie gave all her 9 stickers to her sister. She had no stickers left. How many stickers were in the pack?

7. Mark has 3 T-shirts: a red one, a blue one, and a green one. He also has 3 pairs of shorts. The colors of the shorts are yellow, white, and black. How many different combinations of T-shirts and shorts can he wear?

8. Mr. Nellis made a 5-foot square border around the flagpole at school. He planted flowers in each corner of the square. Then he planted flowers 1 foot apart along each side of the square. How many flowers did he plant in all?

9. Abby, Bess, and Chris competed in the events at field day. The scoreboard shows how many points each had at the end of the day. Who scored the most points? Who scored the least?

FIELD EVENTS

Competitor	Score
Abby	3,125
Bess	3,135
Chris	3,120

MORE PRACTICE Student Handbook page H113

Temperature

You will learn to read thermometers and compare the difference in degrees of temperatures.

Why learn this? You can determine how hot or cold something is.

WORD POWER
degrees Fahrenheit (°F)
degrees Celsius (°C)

Degrees Fahrenheit (°F) are customary units for measuring temperature. This is a Fahrenheit thermometer. It shows room temperature at 68°F.

Some temperatures are less than 0°F. The lowest temperature on this thermometer, ⁻10°F, is read as ten degrees below zero.

To find the difference between degrees, subtract the lesser number of degrees from the greater number of degrees. Or, on this thermometer, you can count each mark as 5°.

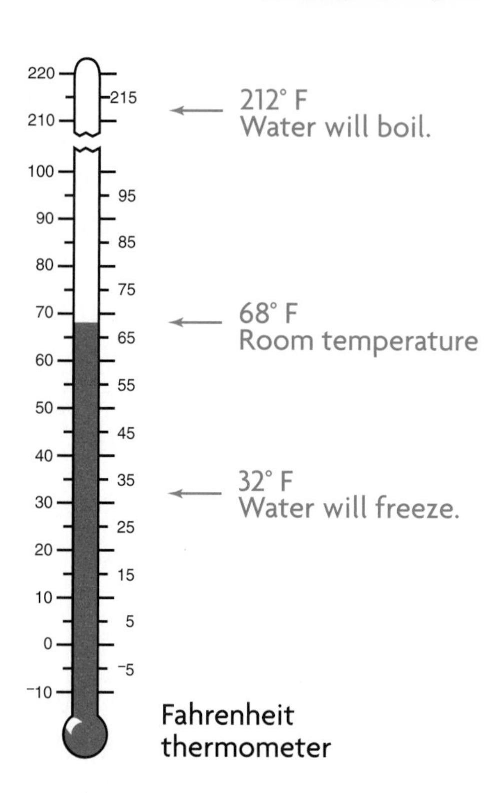

Fahrenheit thermometer

Talk About It

- Why might you need to know the temperature outside?
- Which is warmer, 75°F or 50°F? How many degrees difference is there?

The greater the number of degrees, the warmer something is.

Degrees Celsius (°C) are metric units for measuring temperature. This is a Celsius thermometer. It shows room temperature at 20°C.

- What is the difference in degrees Celsius between the temperatures at which water freezes and boils?

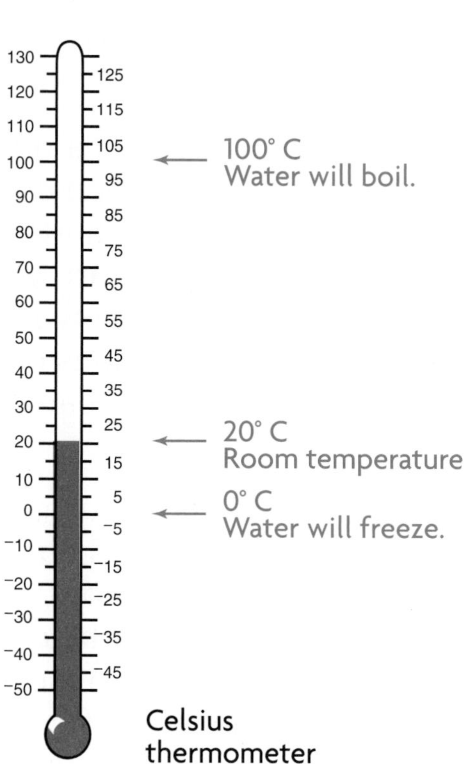

Celsius thermometer

Check Your Understanding

Use the thermometers. Find the difference.

1. 45°F and 90°F

2. ⁻5°F and 20°F

3. ⁻35°C and 15°C

4. 40°C and 115°C

PRACTICE

Use the thermometers on page 444. Find the difference between the two temperatures.

5. Fahrenheit room temperature and temperature at which water boils

6. Celsius room temperature and temperature at which water boils

7. Fahrenheit temperature at which water freezes and boils

8. Celsius room temperature and temperature at which water freezes

9. 5°F and ⁻10°F

10. 0°C and ⁻45°C

Use the thermometer to answer the question.

11. 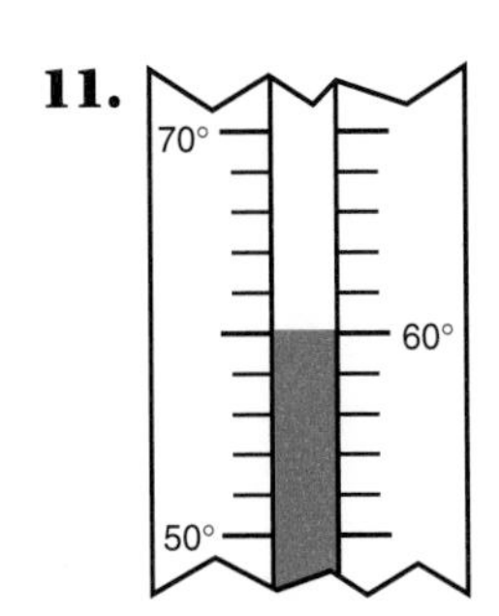

The temperature at night is shown. The temperature during the day was 85°F. What is the difference between the two temperatures?

12. 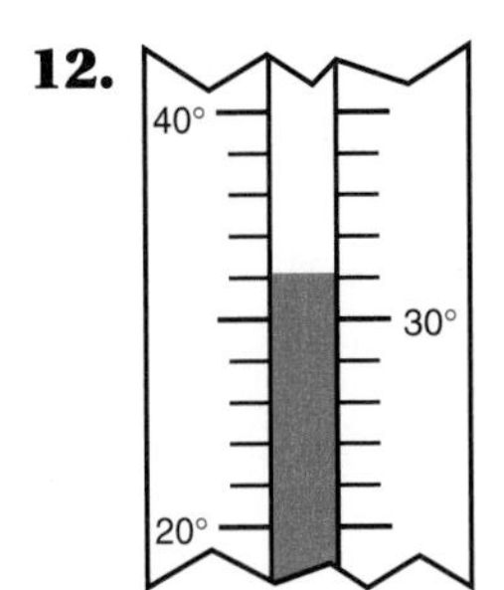

The temperature outside is shown. The water in the swimming pool is 24°C. What is the difference between the two temperatures?

Mixed Applications

13. At sunrise the temperature was 72°F. At noon it was 19 degrees warmer. Then it cooled off 12 degrees in the evening. What was the evening temperature?

14. **Write a problem** that compares the difference in degrees between two temperatures.

Mixed Review

Copy the Venn diagram. Place the numbers where they belong. (pages 114–115)

15. 70, 110, 80, 50, 125, 25, 95, 200

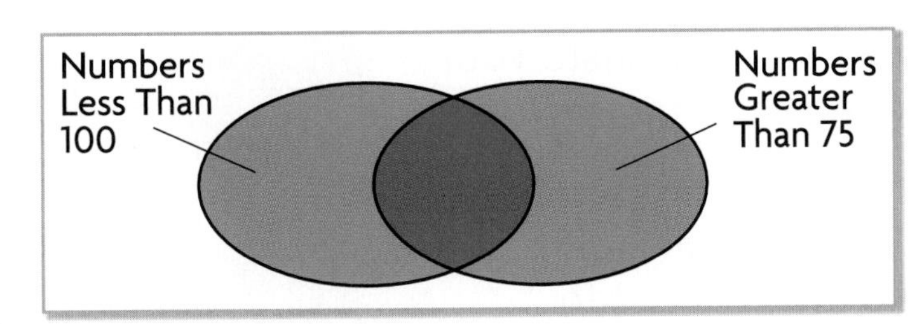

Choose an operation to use. Then solve. (pages 62–63)

16. Marian does 2 chores each day. How many chores does she do in 7 days?

17. There are 18 books on 3 shelves in Clay's room. How many books are on each shelf?

Making Equal Areas

You will investigate making equal areas with pattern-block shapes.

Why learn this? You can see that equal areas can have different shapes.

Explore

Use pattern-block shapes to make equal areas.

MATERIALS: pattern-block shapes; yellow, red, blue, and green markers; scissors

Cut out the pattern-block shapes. Color the hexagons yellow, the trapezoids red, the rhombuses blue, and the triangles green.

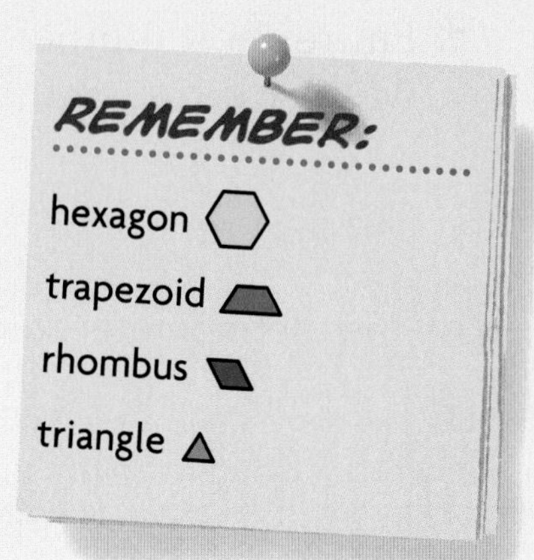

The ⬡ represents the whole. Use the other shapes to model $\frac{1}{2}$.

MODEL

How can you model $\frac{1}{2}$ of the whole?

Step 1

Draw a line dividing the hexagon in half.

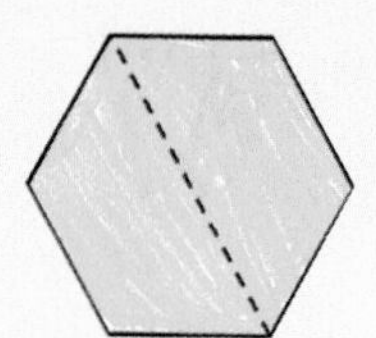

Step 2

Use any combination of the pattern-block shapes to cover exactly $\frac{1}{2}$ of the hexagon.

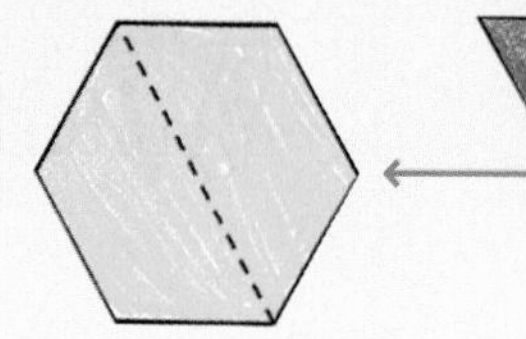

Record

Find two other ways to model $\frac{1}{2}$ of the hexagon. Tape or paste your models to a piece of paper.

TALK ABOUT IT How do you know the combinations of blocks have areas equal to $\frac{1}{2}$ of the hexagon?

Technology Link

E-Lab • Activity 26 Available on CD-ROM and the Internet at http://www.hbschool.com/elab

WRITE ABOUT IT What other shapes can you make that represent the same area as the hexagon?

Now, investigate making other areas with pattern-block shapes.

Try This

Use [trapezoid] as the whole. Make different models to show $\frac{2}{3}$. Draw your models on a piece of paper.

TALK ABOUT IT How do you know that your models show $\frac{2}{3}$?

WRITE ABOUT IT Explain how to make different shapes with equal areas.

HANDS-ON PRACTICE

Use pattern-block shapes to model each area.

1. Use [rhombus] as the whole. Model $\frac{1}{2}$.
2. Use [hexagon] as the whole. Model $\frac{1}{3}$.
3. Use [trapezoid] as the whole. Model $\frac{1}{3}$.
4. Use [hexagon] as the whole. Model $\frac{1}{6}$.
5. Use [hexagon] as the whole. Model $\frac{2}{3}$.
6. Use [trapezoid] as the whole. Model $\frac{2}{3}$.

Mixed Applications

7. Sandra is making a tile design. She has some [triangle] and some [rhombus]. How can Sandra use some of each shape to make a hexagon?
8. Ed and Ray have 3 [triangle], 3 [trapezoid], and 4 [rhombus] altogether. How can they use these pieces to make two shapes with equal areas?
9. Lucy is making friendship bracelets. She uses 25 beads in each bracelet. If Lucy wants to make bracelets for 11 friends, how many beads will she need?
10. Mr. Fox needs to buy 570 cans of soda for the school dance. Soda costs $2 for each six-pack. How many six-packs should Mr. Fox buy? How much money will he spend?
11. Tai spent $3.75 to see a movie and $9.97 for school supplies. Then Sue gave her $4.00. Now Tai has $10.28. How much money did she start with?
12. Drew saw two snakes. One snake was 35.6 centimeters long and the other snake was 17.9 centimeters long. What is the difference between the lengths of the two snakes?

MORE PRACTICE Student Handbook page H113

CULTURAL CONNECTION

COOPERATIVE LEARNING

PLANNING A TRIP TO PUERTO RICO

Luis and Juanita are traveling to San Juan, Puerto Rico, with their mother to visit their grandparents. Their grandfather has promised to take them snorkeling.

Before Juanita and Luis packed, they studied the weather report in the newspaper so they would know what clothes to pack. Look at the table below. What is the difference between the average daytime temperature in New York City and that in San Juan, Puerto Rico, in October? What type of clothing should they pack?

AVERAGE DAYTIME TEMPERATURE IN OCTOBER	
New York, New York	54° F
San Juan, Puerto Rico	80° F

Work Together

Juanita and Luis' schedule on traveling day is shown on these clocks. Give the time for each clock in at least two different ways.

1. Board the plane.

2. Arrive in San Juan.

3. Arrive at grandparents' house.

4. How much time passed from when Luis and Juanita boarded the plane to when they arrived at their grandparents' house?

CULTURAL LINK

Puerto Rico is one of the largest islands that lies between Florida and South America. A large part of the island is farmland. The leading crops harvested are sugar cane, coffee, and several kinds of fruit. Sugar cane is a tall grass plant that stores sugar in its stalks. After the stalks are gathered from the fields, the stalks are crushed and hot water is added to make a sugary juice. Sugar crystals come from this juice.

CHAPTER 26

REVIEW

✓ CHECK UNDERSTANDING

1. VOCABULARY __?__ and __?__ are units for measuring temperature. (page 444)

Choose the most reasonable measure for what is shown. (pages 440–441)

2. 

a. 3.5 cm **b.** 3.5 in.

3. 

a. 2.5 cm **b.** 2.5 in.

4. 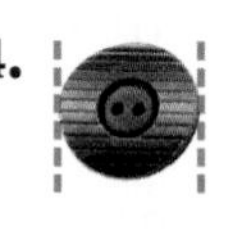

a. 1 cm **b.** 1 in.

5. 

a. 5 cm **b.** 5 in.

✓ CHECK SKILLS

Write each time in a different way. (pages 438–440)

6. 5:15 **7.** 10:45 **8.** half past nine **9.** a quarter to two

Use the thermometer to answer the question. (pages 444–445)

10. The temperature at 5:00 A.M. is shown. At 3:00 P.M. the temperature was 53°F. What is the difference between the two temperatures?

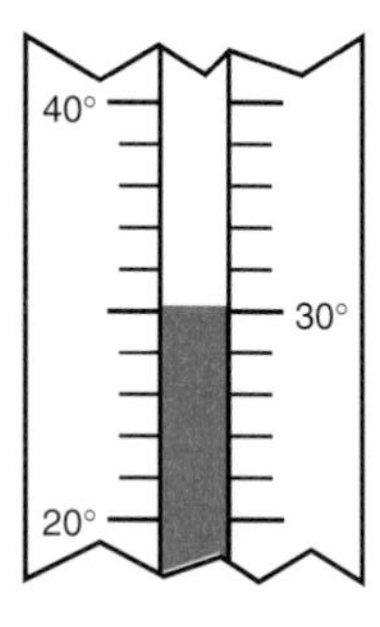

11. The temperature at the beach was 27°C. The temperature at Julia's house is shown. What is the difference between the two temperatures?

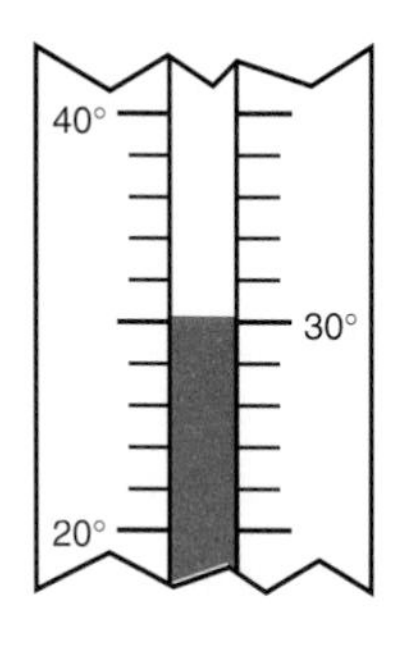

✓ CHECK PROBLEM SOLVING

Solve. (pages 442–443)

CHOOSE A STRATEGY

- Work Backward
- Act It Out
- Draw a Diagram
- Write a Number Sentence

12. Fred and Michael are comparing their heights. Fred is 4 feet tall. Michael is 49 inches tall. Who is taller? Explain.

13. Carol has 4 ▲, 3 ▰, and 2 ▲. How can she use these pieces to make two shapes with equal areas?

CHAPTERS 24–26

STUDY GUIDE & REVIEW

VOCABULARY CHECK

WORD BANK
capacity
degrees Celsius
degrees Fahrenheit
linear
mass

Choose a term from the box to complete each sentence.

1. Units that measure in one direction, such as length, width, height, or distance, are called __?__ units. (page 406)
2. The amount a container can hold when filled is its __?__. (page 414)
3. The amount of matter in an object is its __?__. (page 432)
4. The units for measuring temperature are __?__ and __?__. (page 444)

STUDY AND SOLVE

CHAPTER 24

EXAMPLE

3 ft = __?__ in.

12 in. = 1 ft, so 3 × 12 = 36

3 ft = 36 in.

Use a ruler to measure the length to the nearest $\frac{1}{4}$ inch. (pages 412–413)

5.

Choose the reasonable unit of measure. Write *in., ft, yd,* or *mi.* (pages 406–407)

6. A writing pen is about 5 __?__ long.
7. The distance from home to the grocery store is about 1 __?__ .

Choose the more reasonable measurement. (pages 414–417)

8. 

qt or gal

9. 
oz or lb

Write the equivalent measurement. You may use a calculator. (pages 408–409, 414–417)

10. 3 yd = __?__ ft
11. 2 mi = __?__ ft
12. 8 qt = __?__ gal
13. 4 pt = __?__ c
14. 3 lb = __?__ oz
15. 3 T = __?__ lb

Solve. (pages 414–415)

16. Stella made 10 pints of apple butter. How many quart jars will she need for the apple butter?

CHAPTER 25

EXAMPLE

4 dm = __?__ cm

1 dm = 10 cm, so $4 \times 10 = 40$

4 dm = 40 cm

Use a ruler to measure the length to the nearest centimeter. (pages 422–423)

17. ————————————

Choose the reasonable unit of measure. Write *m, dm, cm, L, mL,* or *g.*
(pages 422–423, 430–433)

18. What is the width of your index finger? 1 __?__

19. What is the distance between hands of outstretched arms? 1 __?__

20. What is the capacity of a sport drink bottle? 1 __?__

21. What is the mass of a large paper clip? 1 __?__

Choose the more reasonable measurement. (pages 430–433)

22. 

23. 

340 mL or 340 L   1,500 g or 1,500 kg

Write the equivalent measurement.
(pages 424–427, 430–433)

24. 400 cm = __?__ m

25. 3 cm = __?__ dm

26. 1 kg = __?__ g

Solve. (pages 424–427, 430–431)

27. A pair of scissors is 20 cm in length. How many meters in length are the scissors?

28. A team drank 16 L of sport drink. How many mL is this?

CHAPTER 26

EXAMPLE

Write the time in a different way.

10:30   half past ten

Write the time in a different way.
(pages 438–440)

29. 2:15   **30.** half past twelve

Choose the more reasonable measure.
(pages 440–441)

31. ——————————————

7 in. or 7 cm

Read the thermometers. Use < or > to compare the numbers of degrees. Find the difference. (pages 444–445)

32. 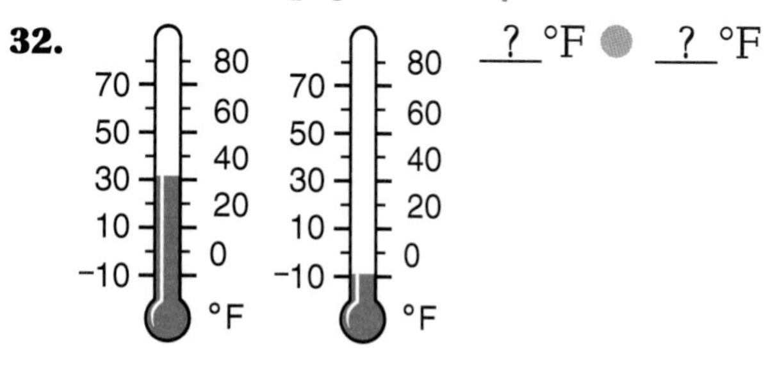

__?__ °F ● __?__ °F

Solve. (pages 442–443)

33. Emil is buying fencing. He needs enough for 2 50-foot sides and 2 100-foot sides. How many yards of fence does he need?

CHAPTERS 24–26

WHAT DID I LEARN?

WRITE ABOUT IT

1. Name or draw pictures of two objects that could be measured in ounces, two objects that could be measured in pounds, and two objects that could be measured in tons. (pages 416–417)

2. Explain a strategy you would use to solve this problem. Then solve the problem.

   The space between the windows in Jessica's room is 2.3 meters. Jessica wants to put a bookshelf between the windows. How many centimeters long can the board be? (pages 428–429)

3. Explain a strategy you would use to solve this problem. Then solve the problem.

   Ross needs enough fencing to build a pen for his dog. The pen will be 18 feet by 30 feet. Fencing is sold by the yard. How many yards of fencing does Ross need? (pages 440–441)

✓ PERFORMANCE ASSESSMENT

Solve. Explain your method.

CHOOSE A STRATEGY

- Solve a Simpler Problem
- Make a Model
- Draw a Picture
- Act It Out
- Draw a Diagram
- Write a Number Sentence

4. Ruben made a birthday cake that is 14 in. long. He is putting 1 candle every 2 in. in a single row on the cake. He does not put a candle on either end of the cake. How many candles are on the cake? (pages 410–411)

5. Lily is buying paper to wrap a gift. Paper on a roll is 140 cm long. Paper in a flat package is 1.8 m long. The width of the paper is the same. Should Lily buy the roll or the flat package to get more paper? (pages 428–429)

6. Lucia's rabbit pen is 12 ft long and 9 ft wide. Wire screen sells for $2.25 a yard. How many yards of screen will she need for the perimeter of the pen? How much will Lucia have to pay for the screen in all? (pages 442–443)

CUMULATIVE REVIEW

Solve the problem. Then write the letter of the correct answer.

1. $\begin{array}{r} 7{,}564 \\ +2{,}958 \\ \hline \end{array}$

A. 4,606
B. 9,412
C. 10,412
D. 10,522 (pages 6–7)

2. What digit shows hundreds in 4,657?

A. 4 **B.** 5
C. 6 **D.** 7 (pages 78–79)

3. What is the ending time?

start time: 6:45 P.M.
elapsed time: 40 minutes

A. 6:15 P.M. **B.** 6:50 P.M.
C. 7:15 P.M. **D.** 7:25 P.M.
(pages 124–125)

For Problems 4–5, use the spinner.

4. It is __?__ that you will spin an odd number.

A. unlikely **B.** likely
C. impossible **D.** certain
(pages 174–175)

5. What is the probability of spinning a 14?

A. $\frac{1}{14}$ **B.** $\frac{1}{8}$
C. $\frac{2}{14}$ **D.** $\frac{2}{8}$
(pages 178–179)

6. Figures that have the same shape but may have a different size are __?__.

A. congruent **B.** transformations
C. similar **D.** tessellations
(page 254)

7. $\begin{array}{r} 436 \\ \times\ 58 \\ \hline \end{array}$

A. 378
B. 494
C. 23,748
D. 25,288 (pages 290–293)

8. $5\overline{)517}$

A. 13 r2 **B.** 101 r2
C. 103 r2 **D.** 2,585 (pages 318–321)

9. $4\frac{4}{5} - 2\frac{1}{5} = n$

A. $\frac{13}{1}$ **B.** $2\frac{3}{1}$
C. $2\frac{3}{5}$ **D.** $6\frac{5}{5}$, or 7 (pages 364–365)

10. $\begin{array}{r} 2.54 \\ +0.68 \\ \hline \end{array}$

A. 0.03
B. 1.86
C. 2.12
D. 3.22 (pages 388–389)

11. Choose the reasonable measure for the height of a basketball goal.

A. 10 ft **B.** 10 in.
C. 10 mi **D.** 10 yd (pages 406–407)

12. Compare the temperatures.
0°C ● 10°C

A. $>$ **B.** $<$
C. $=$ **D.** $-$ (pages 444–445)

DIVIDING BY TWO-DIGIT NUMBERS

DID YOU KNOW...

June 14th is Flag Day. Flag Day was celebrated for many years before the day became a national holiday on August 3, 1949.

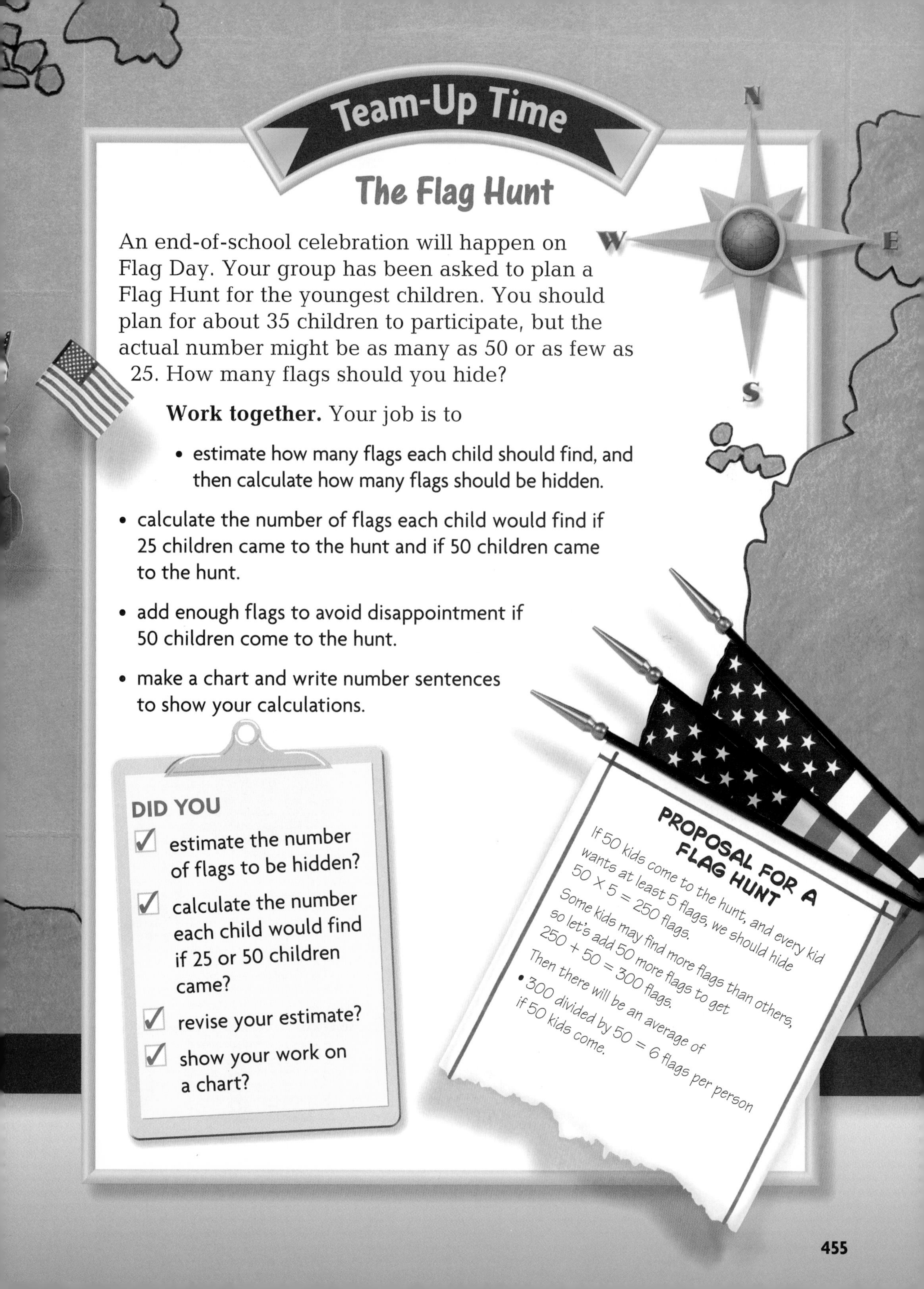

Team-Up Time

The Flag Hunt

An end-of-school celebration will happen on Flag Day. Your group has been asked to plan a Flag Hunt for the youngest children. You should plan for about 35 children to participate, but the actual number might be as many as 50 or as few as 25. How many flags should you hide?

Work together. Your job is to

- estimate how many flags each child should find, and then calculate how many flags should be hidden.
- calculate the number of flags each child would find if 25 children came to the hunt and if 50 children came to the hunt.
- add enough flags to avoid disappointment if 50 children come to the hunt.
- make a chart and write number sentences to show your calculations.

Division Patterns to Estimate

You will learn to use multiples of 10 and a pattern of zeros to estimate quotients.

Why learn this? You can estimate when buying things that come in groups.

Elaine hid 34 flags for the Flag Hunt. There are 11 children searching for flags. About how many flags can each child find?

You can use multiples of 10 to estimate the quotient of 34 ÷ 11. Since 11 is close to 10, use 10 as the divisor. Round the dividend to the nearest number that can be easily divided by 10.

$34 \div 11 = n$
↓ ↓ ↓
$30 \div 10 = 3$

So, each child can find about 3 flags.

A. $57 \div 19 = n$ → $60 \div 20 = 3$

B. $411 \div 82 = n$ → $400 \div 80 = 5$

C. $722 \div 89 = n$ → $720 \div 90 = 8$

Science Link

Elephants eat for 19 hours each day. They eat at least 250 pounds of food. About how many pounds of food does an elephant eat in one hour?

Talk About It

- Why do you change the divisor to a multiple of 10?
- What basic facts can help you find the quotients for Examples A, B, and C?

A pattern of zeros and basic facts can help you find quotients.

Talk About It

- What basic fact helps you find the quotients in the table at the right?
- How does the pattern of zeros help you decide the number of zeros in the quotient?
- How many zeros will be in the quotient of 900,000 ÷ 30?

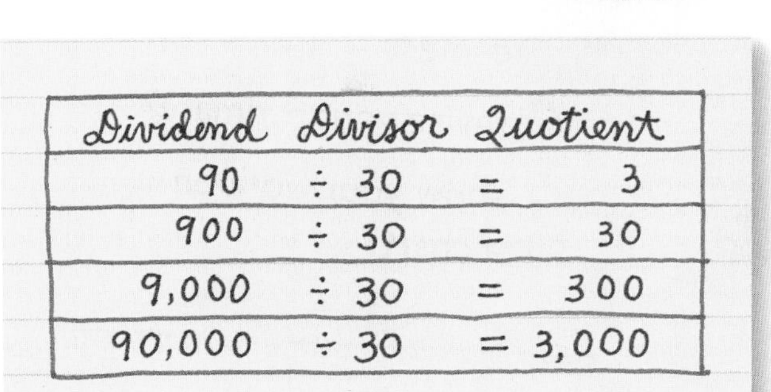

Dividend	Divisor	Quotient
90	÷ 30	= 3
900	÷ 30	= 30
9,000	÷ 30	= 300
90,000	÷ 30	= 3,000

PRACTICE

Write the numbers you would use to estimate the quotients. Then write the estimate.

1. $59 \div 12 = n$
2. $398 \div 23 = n$
3. $493 \div 72 = n$
4. $355 \div 37 = n$
5. $635 \div 81 = n$
6. $920 \div 32 = n$

Write the basic fact that helps you find the quotient.

7. $71 \div 11 = n$
8. $243 \div 79 = n$
9. $148 \div 33 = n$
10. $82 \div 21 = n$
11. $298 \div 57 = n$
12. $814 \div 92 = n$

Complete the table.

	Dividend	Divisor	Quotient
13.	80	÷ 20	= ?
14.	?	÷ 20	= 40
15.	8,000	÷ 20	= ?
16.	?	÷ 20	= 4,000

	Dividend	Divisor	Quotient
17.	60	÷ 30	= ?
18.	?	÷ 30	= 20
19.	?	÷ 30	= 200
20.	60,000	÷ 30	= ?

Mixed Applications

21. Kerry went to the science center at 9:15 A.M. She stayed there for 5 hours 55 minutes. When did she leave the science center?

22. The video store rents about 28 videos each hour. The store is open 12 hours each day. How many videos does the store rent in a month with 30 days?

23. On the first day of basketball tryouts, 103 girls showed up. There will be about 12 girls on each team. About how many teams will there be?

24. **WRITE ABOUT IT** Explain how you can use multiples of 10 and a pattern of zeros to estimate quotients.

Mixed Review

Find the quotient. Check by multiplying. (pages 308–309)

25. $4\overline{)169}$
26. $7\overline{)508}$
27. $6\overline{)894}$
28. $8\overline{)715}$

What fraction of the parts is shaded? What fraction is not shaded? (pages 340–341)

29. 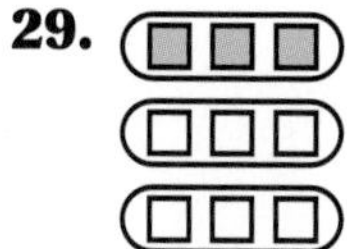

30. 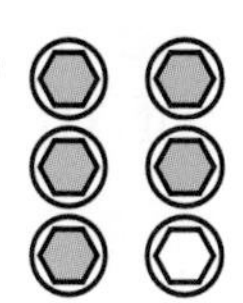

31. 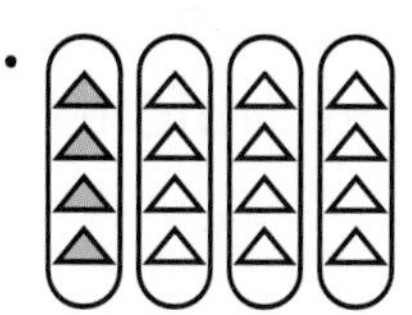

Dividing by Tens

You will learn to divide by multiples of 10.

Why learn this? You can round to the nearest 10 to estimate quotients.

Brianna is giving blankets to homeless shelters. Her school collected 454 blankets. The blankets are to be divided evenly among 50 shelters. How many blankets will each shelter get?

REMEMBER:

All the products of multiples of 10 have a zero in the ones place.

×	2	4	6	8	10
20	40	80	120	160	200
30	60	120	180	240	300
40	80	160	240	320	400
50	100	200	300	400	500

MODEL

What is $454 \div 50$?

Step 1

Decide where to place the first digit in the quotient.

no $50\overline{)454}$ (x over the 4) — You *cannot* divide 4 by 50. There are not enough hundreds.

no $50\overline{)454}$ (xx over the 45) — You *cannot* divide 45 by 50. There are not enough tens.

yes $50\overline{)454}$ (xx■ over the 454) — You *can* divide 454 by 50. There are enough ones.

So, place the first digit in the ones place.

Step 2

Estimate. Use multiples of 10.

Think: $450 \div 50 = 9$

Divide. Write the 9 in the ones place of the quotient.

$$\begin{array}{r} 9 \text{ r4} \\ 50\overline{)454} \\ -450 \\ \hline 4 \end{array}$$

Multiply. 50×9
Subtract. $454 - 450$
Compare. $4 < 50$
Write the remainder next to the quotient.

So, each shelter will get 9 blankets with 4 left over.

EXAMPLES

A.
$$\begin{array}{r} 3 \text{ r4} \\ 30\overline{)94} \\ -90 \\ \hline 4 \end{array}$$

B.
$$\begin{array}{r} 6 \text{ r5} \\ 60\overline{)365} \\ -360 \\ \hline 5 \end{array}$$

C.
$$\begin{array}{r} 7 \\ 40\overline{)280} \\ -280 \\ \hline 0 \end{array}$$

- In Example C, what do you notice about the dividend when you divide by multiples of 10 and there is no remainder?

CRITICAL THINKING Explain how you can use the multiplication table to divide by multiples of 10.

PRACTICE

Copy each problem. Draw a box where the first digit in the quotient should be placed.

1. $20\overline{)65}$ **2.** $30\overline{)908}$ **3.** $80\overline{)421}$ **4.** $70\overline{)364}$

5. $60\overline{)617}$ **6.** $40\overline{)823}$ **7.** $50\overline{)209}$ **8.** $90\overline{)795}$

9. $80\overline{)932}$ **10.** $20\overline{)195}$ **11.** $60\overline{)522}$ **12.** $30\overline{)301}$

Find the quotient.

13. $30\overline{)678}$ **14.** $40\overline{)969}$ **15.** $70\overline{)436}$ **16.** $20\overline{)785}$

17. $90\overline{)907}$ **18.** $60\overline{)491}$ **19.** $50\overline{)357}$ **20.** $80\overline{)738}$

21. $40\overline{)853}$ **22.** $90\overline{)547}$ **23.** $80\overline{)335}$ **24.** $50\overline{)734}$

Mixed Applications

25. During one month, 30 volunteers worked 750 hours at a homeless shelter. Each of these volunteers worked the same number of hours. How many hours did each of these volunteers work at the homeless shelter?

26. The 40 members of the Outing Club made 285 birdhouses. Each member made the same number of birdhouses. The club mother made 5 birdhouses. How many birdhouses did each member make?

27. There are 40 members in the Civics Club. Each member has been asked to find old books. If each member finds 20 books, how many books will they have in all?

28. **WRITE ABOUT IT** Record a number sentence that has a divisor that is a multiple of 10, a three-digit dividend, a one-digit quotient, and a remainder of 3. Explain why you used each number.

Mixed Review

Find the quotient. (pages 318–319)

29. $7\overline{)630}$ **30.** $5\overline{)504}$ **31.** $8\overline{)600}$ **32.** $4\overline{)809}$ **33.** $6\overline{)720}$

Find the product. (pages 282–283)

34. 30×5 **35.** 40×20 **36.** 600×3 **37.** 700×50 **38.** 500×80

MORE PRACTICE Student Handbook page H114

Modeling Division

You will investigate dividing with two-digit divisors.

Why learn this? You can make equal groups of things to be shared, such as a snack for your class.

You can make a model to divide with two-digit divisors.

MODEL

What is 64 ÷ 21?

Step 1

To divide 64 by 21, start by showing 64 as 6 tens 4 ones.

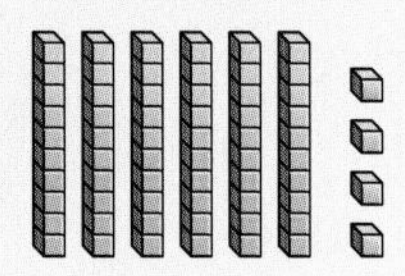

Record:

$21\overline{)64}$

Step 2

Estimate. 64 ÷ 21 = *n*

Think: 60 ÷ 20 = 3

Try to make 3 groups of 21.

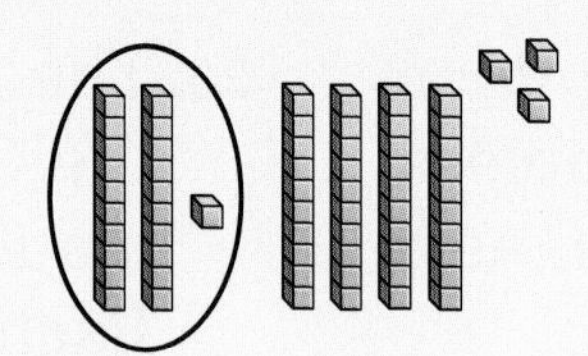

Record:

$$\begin{array}{r} 3 \\ 21\overline{)64} \end{array}$$

Step 3

Make 3 groups of 21. Count how many ones are left over.

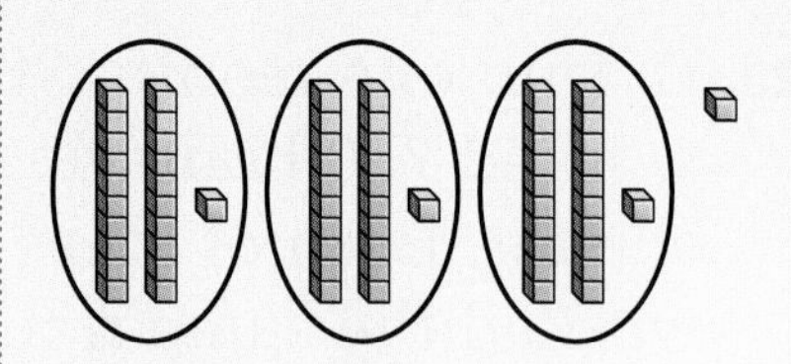

Record:

$$\begin{array}{r} 3 \text{ r}1 \\ 21\overline{)64} \\ -63 \\ \hline 1 \end{array}$$

Multiply. 3 × 21
Subtract. 64 − 63
Compare. 1 < 21

So, 64 ÷ 21 = 3 r1.

Talk About It

- What is the divisor in the model?
- What do the three groups in Step 3 represent?
- How can you check the quotient?

Explore

Find the quotient of 89 ÷ 29.

MATERIALS: base-ten blocks

Record

Draw a picture of your solution, as shown in Step 3 of the model. Record a division number sentence for the picture.

E-Lab • Activity 27 Available on CD-ROM and the Internet at http://www.hbschool.com/elab

Now, investigate how to find the quotient of a three-digit dividend divided by a two-digit divisor.

Try This

Find the quotient of 129 ÷ 18. Draw a picture of your solution, and record a division number sentence for the picture.

TALK ABOUT IT How does an estimate help you find the quotient?

WRITE ABOUT IT Write the steps you can follow when dividing by a two-digit divisor.

HANDS-ON PRACTICE

Make a model and find the quotient.

1. $23\overline{)95}$ **2.** $32\overline{)98}$ **3.** $18\overline{)129}$

4. $25\overline{)152}$ **5.** $31\overline{)167}$ **6.** $14\overline{)156}$

7. 89 ÷ 21 = ? **8.** 108 ÷ 35 = ? **9.** 132 ÷ 16 = ?

Applying What You Learned

Use the model to complete the number sentence.

10.

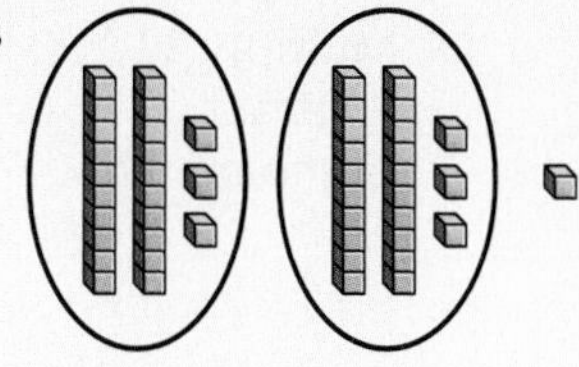

47 ÷ 23 = ?

11.

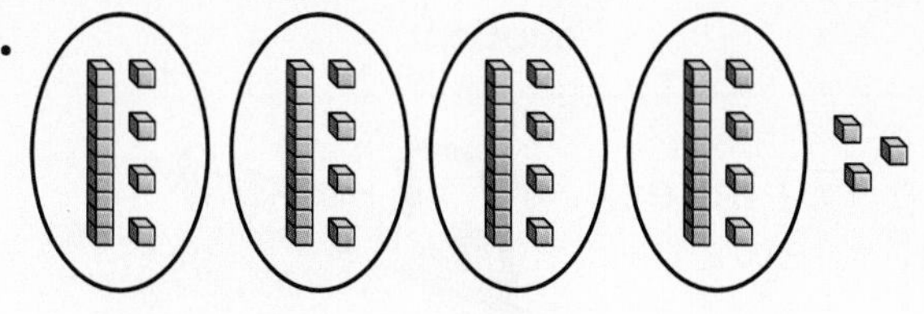

59 ÷ 14 = ?

Mixed Applications

12. Elizabeth wants to buy a stereo that costs $130. She can save $12 each week. Will she be able to buy the stereo in 10 weeks? Explain.

13. There are 156 parking spaces in front of Duane's school. They are arranged in 12 rows with the same number of parking spaces in each row. How many parking spaces are in each row?

MORE PRACTICE Student Handbook page H114

PART

1 Division Procedures

You will learn to divide by two-digit divisors.

Why learn this? You can divide large numbers without a calculator.

The Kurtz family is planning a 182-mile bicycle trip. Each day they will ride 17 miles. How many days will it take the Kurtzes to ride the whole distance?

Divide. $182 \div 17 = n$ $\quad 17\overline{)182}$

Estimate. **Think:** $180 \div 20 = 9$

MODEL

What is $182 \div 17$?

Step 1

Decide where to place the first digit in the quotient.

no $17\overline{)182}$ (x over the 1) — You *cannot* divide 1 by 17. There are not enough hundreds.

yes $17\overline{)182}$ (x■ over the 18) — You *can* divide 18 by 17. There are enough tens.

So, place the first digit in the tens place.

Step 2

Divide the tens. $17\overline{)18}$

Think: $17 \times n = 17$

Write a 1 in the tens place in the quotient.

$$\begin{array}{r} 1 \\ 17\overline{)182} \\ -17\downarrow \\ \hline 12 \end{array}$$

Multiply. 17×1
Subtract. $18 - 17$
Compare. $12 < 17$

Step 3

Divide the ones. $17\overline{)12}$

Think: Since $17 > 12$, write a zero in the ones place in the quotient.

$$\begin{array}{r} 10 \text{ r}12 \\ 17\overline{)182} \\ -17\downarrow \\ \hline 12 \\ -0 \\ \hline 12 \end{array}$$

Multiply. 17×0
Subtract. $12 - 0$
Compare. $12 < 17$

Write the remainder in the quotient.

It will take 10 days for the Kurtzes to ride 170 miles, with 12 more miles to ride on the eleventh day.

So, it will take them 11 days to ride the whole distance.

- What would happen in Step 3 if you did not write a zero in the ones place?

CRITICAL THINKING How can you check the answer by multiplying?

Technology Link

In ***Mighty Math Number Heroes***, the game *Quizzo* challenges you to solve puzzles by using what you are learning about two-digit division.

To use a calculator to check the quotient, multiply the quotient by the divisor. Then add the remainder. The answer you get should be the same as the dividend.

Press:

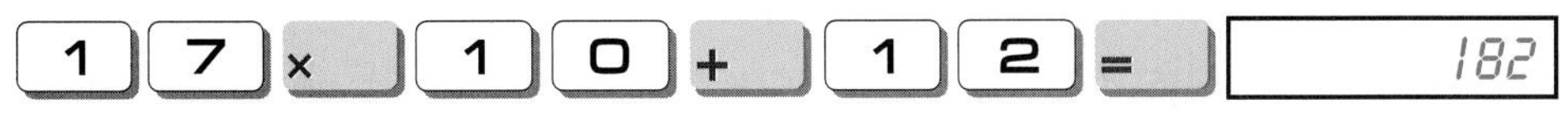

PRACTICE

Write the missing numbers for each problem.

1.
```
    1■ r2
18)236
  -1■
    56
   -■4
     2
```

2.
```
    21 r■
23)487
  -■6
    ■7
   -23
     4
```

3.
```
    ■4 r9
35)849
  -70
   14■
  -14■
     9
```

Find the quotient. Check by multiplying.

4. $16\overline{)195}$ **5.** $18\overline{)124}$ **6.** $21\overline{)468}$ **7.** $25\overline{)187}$

8. $45\overline{)379}$ **9.** $36\overline{)395}$ **10.** $27\overline{)580}$ **11.** $42\overline{)807}$

12. $56\overline{)621}$ **13.** $24\overline{)943}$ **14.** $47\overline{)762}$ **15.** $51\overline{)689}$

Mixed Applications

For Problems 16–19, use the table.

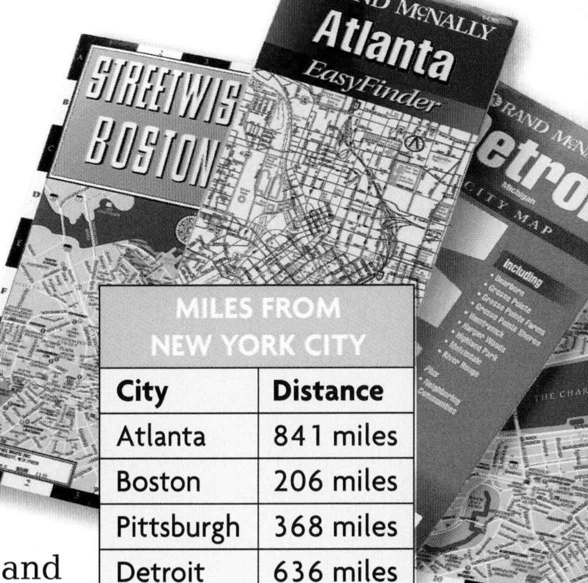

MILES FROM NEW YORK CITY	
City	**Distance**
Atlanta	841 miles
Boston	206 miles
Pittsburgh	368 miles
Detroit	636 miles

16. Daniel's family drove from New York City to Boston. They drove about 50 miles per hour. How many hours did it take to make the trip?

17. The Cooper family spent 12 hours driving to Detroit from New York City. They traveled the same number of miles each hour. How many miles did they drive each hour?

18. Mr. Higby drove from New York to Boston and back. Then he drove from New York to Detroit and back. How many miles did he drive in all?

19. **Write a problem** that can be solved by dividing. Use the information in the table.

PART 2 PROBLEM-SOLVING STRATEGY
Write a Number Sentence

THE PROBLEM **Phyllis and Chris like to play Frisbee®. Phyllis can throw her Frisbee a distance of 375 inches. Chris can throw his Frisbee a distance of 31 feet. What is the distance in feet that Phyllis can throw her Frisbee? Who can throw the Frisbee farther?**

✓ Understand

- What are you asked to find?
- What information will you use?
- Is there any information you will not use? If so, what?

Plan

- What strategy can you use to solve the problem?

  You can *write a number sentence* to change inches to feet.

✓ Solve

- What number sentence can you write to solve the problem?

  Since Phyllis threw her Frisbee 375 inches, divide 375 by 12 to find the distance in feet.

  $375 \div 12 = 31 \text{ r}3$

  ↑ The remainder is part of the answer. It tells how many extra inches there are.

So, Phyllis can throw her Frisbee a distance of 31 feet 3 inches. Compared to Chris's throw of 31 feet, Phyllis can throw the Frisbee farther.

Phyllis

375 in. ÷ 12 in. = n ft

$$\begin{array}{r} 31 \text{ r}3 \\ 12\overline{)375} \\ -36 \\ \hline 15 \\ -12 \\ \hline 3 \end{array}$$

✓ Look Back

- How can you determine if your answer is reasonable?
- What other strategy could you use?

PRACTICE

CHOOSE Paper/Pencil Calculator Hands-on Mental Math

Write a number sentence to solve.

1. What if Phyllis threw her Frisbee 350 inches and Chris threw his Frisbee 30 feet? What is the distance in feet that Phyllis threw her Frisbee? Who threw the Frisbee farther?

2. Mark won a computer game in 12 minutes. Peter won the game in 700 seconds. How many minutes did it take Peter to win the game? Who won the game faster?

3. Monday was Kevin's birthday. He was 11 years old. On Monday Rachel was 130 months old. How many years old is Rachel? Who is older, Kevin or Rachel?

4. The Park Forest Health Club lets people work out on the bicycle for 25 minutes at a time. The club is open 16 hours per day. How many people can use the bicycle in one day? How many extra minutes are there?

Mixed Applications

Solve.

CHOOSE A STRATEGY

- **Make a Model**
- **Guess and Check**
- **Work Backward**
- **Make a Graph**
- **Write a Number Sentence**

5. Dennis needs the following ingredients to make cookies: $\frac{1}{2}$ cup sugar, $\frac{1}{8}$ cup margarine, and $\frac{3}{4}$ cup nuts. Order these ingredients from the least to the greatest.

6. Kurt and Vicki spent the day canoeing. They traveled about 3 miles each hour. They went 15 miles in all. They stopped for 1 hour to eat lunch. About how long were they gone?

7. Jenna had $1.50 in her pocket when she got home from the football game. The ticket for the game cost $3.50, and she spent $1.75 on food. Then Julie gave $0.75 to Jenna. How much money did Jenna have when she left home?

8. Randy kept track of the temperature on the day he went hiking. Between which two times did the temperature change the most? Was it an increase or a decrease?

Temperature	
Time	Degrees Fahrenheit
8:00 A.M.	65°F
11:00 A.M.	74°F
2:00 P.M.	82°F
5:00 P.M.	76°F

9. James weighs 25 pounds more than Rick. Together they weigh 165 pounds. How much does each boy weigh?

MORE PRACTICE Student Handbook page H114

Correcting Quotients

You will learn to correct the quotient when the estimate is too high or too low.

Why learn this? You can correct the first digit of the quotient before moving on to the other digits.

Ms. Ray's class had a car wash. She and her 27 students washed a total of 244 cars. Each student washed an equal number of cars. Ms. Ray washed the extra cars. How many cars did each student wash? How many did Ms. Ray wash?

Our class car wash

Since 27 students washed the cars, divide 244 cars by 27 students.

Divide. $244 \div 27 = n \quad 27\overline{)244}$

Estimate. $240 \div 30 = 8$

Try 8.

$$\begin{array}{r} 8 \\ 27\overline{)244} \\ -216 \\ \hline 28 \end{array}$$

Since $28 > 27$, the estimate is too low.

Try 9.

$$\begin{array}{r} 9\text{ r}1 \\ 27\overline{)244} \\ -243 \\ \hline 1 \end{array}$$

So, each student washed 9 cars. Ms. Ray washed 1 car.

EXAMPLE

Divide. $321 \div 54 = n \quad 54\overline{)321}$

Estimate. $300 \div 50 = 6$

Try 6.

$$\begin{array}{r} 6 \\ 54\overline{)321} \\ -324 \\ \hline \end{array}$$

Since $324 > 321$, the estimate is too high.

Try 5.

$$\begin{array}{r} 5\text{ r}51 \\ 54\overline{)321} \\ -270 \\ \hline 51 \end{array}$$

Talk About It

- How do you know when an estimated quotient is too low? too high?
- What can you do to correct an estimate that is too low? too high?
- How do you know when an estimated quotient is correct?

Social Studies Link

The Appalachian National Scenic Trail is 2,000 miles long. It is the longest hiking trail in the United States. If you hiked 11 miles every day, how long would it take to hike 900 miles?

PRACTICE

Write *too high, too low,* or *just right* for each estimate. Find the quotient.

1. $18\overline{)164}$ estimate 8
2. $32\overline{)265}$ estimate 9
3. $27\overline{)184}$ estimate 6
4. $41\overline{)276}$ estimate 7
5. $64\overline{)355}$ estimate 6
6. $62\overline{)325}$ estimate 5
7. $74\overline{)275}$ estimate 4
8. $25\overline{)214}$ estimate 7
9. $69\overline{)551}$ estimate 8
10. $65\overline{)422}$ estimate 6
11. $79\overline{)718}$ estimate 9
12. $36\overline{)324}$ estimate 8
13. $59\overline{)296}$ estimate 5
14. $81\overline{)477}$ estimate 6
15. $34\overline{)124}$ estimate 4
16. $44\overline{)196}$ estimate 5

Mixed Applications

17. In Sid's first two turns in a board game, he moved 5 spaces forward and 2 back. Jon moved 6 spaces forward and 1 back. Who is ahead in the game? How far ahead is he?

18. Evan has 125 nickels. Each nickel wrapper holds 40 nickels. How many nickel wrappers can he fill? How much money will be left over?

19. Paul is packing 140 math books in boxes. Each box can hold 16 books. Will Paul be able to pack all the books in 9 boxes? Explain.

20. **WRITE ABOUT IT** Explain how to correct a quotient when the estimate is too small or too large.

Mixed Review

Write each fraction as a decimal. (pages 370–371)

21. $\frac{6}{10}$
22. $\frac{4}{10}$
23. $\frac{25}{100}$
24. $\frac{90}{100}$
25. $\frac{5}{100}$
26. $\frac{9}{10}$
27. $\frac{1}{100}$
28. $\frac{6}{100}$
29. $\frac{3}{10}$
30. $\frac{3}{100}$

Multiply, and record each product. Place the dollar sign and decimal point in it. (pages 274–275)

31. $2.75 × 3
32. $4.02 × 6
33. $7.18 × 4
34. $3.96 × 5
35. $6.21 × 4
36. $5.90 × 7
37. $3.03 × 8
38. $2.16 × 5

MATH FUN!

Close Quotients

PURPOSE To estimate quotients

YOU WILL NEED spinner labeled with tens from 10–90, 5 index cards, calculator

Play with a partner.

Each player writes one 3-digit number on each of five index cards.

Combine the index cards, shuffle them, and place them face down on a table.

Draw a card and spin for a divisor. Estimate the quotient to the nearest ten. Record. Then calculate the exact quotient. The player with the closer estimate wins a point.

Shuffle the cards and play again. The first player to earn 5 points wins the game.

Money Everywhere!

PURPOSE To find division patterns

YOU WILL NEED paper and pencil

Copy and complete the table. Show how many bills equal each value in the first column. Then describe the patterns shown in your table.

Total Value	Number of Bills		
	$10	$20	$50
$100			
$1,000			
$10,000			
$100,000			

Calculator Trick

PURPOSE To use a calculator to divide

YOU WILL NEED calculator, paper and pencil

On a calculator, enter a six-digit number in which the last three digits are a repeat of the first three digits (Example: 289,289). Then follow these steps using your calculator. (Do not clear between steps.)

1. 

2. 

3. 

What number is in the display? Try this with numbers you make up. Does it always work?

Amaze your family by teaching them this trick!

CHAPTER 27

REVIEW

✓ CHECK UNDERSTANDING

Write the basic fact that helps you find the quotient. **(pages 456–457)**

1. $317 \div 37 = n$ **2.** $452 \div 53 = n$ **3.** $556 \div 81 = n$

Copy each problem. Draw a box where the first digit in the quotient should be placed. **(pages 458–459)**

4. $30\overline{)61}$ **5.** $70\overline{)165}$ **6.** $20\overline{)909}$ **7.** $60\overline{)612}$

✓ CHECK SKILLS

Find the quotient. **(pages 458–459)**

8. $50\overline{)667}$ **9.** $30\overline{)249}$ **10.** $90\overline{)634}$ **11.** $70\overline{)395}$

12. $80\overline{)307}$ **13.** $60\overline{)811}$ **14.** $40\overline{)116}$ **15.** $20\overline{)718}$

Find the quotient. Check by multiplying. **(pages 462–463)**

16. $22\overline{)315}$ **17.** $16\overline{)414}$ **18.** $34\overline{)287}$ **19.** $41\overline{)693}$

20. $24\overline{)834}$ **21.** $96\overline{)528}$ **22.** $34\overline{)889}$ **23.** $57\overline{)768}$

Write *too high, too low,* or *just right* for each estimate. Find the quotient. **(pages 466–467)**

24. $\begin{array}{r} 6 \\ 16\overline{)124} \end{array}$ **25.** $\begin{array}{r} 6 \\ 86\overline{)537} \end{array}$ **26.** $\begin{array}{r} 4 \\ 62\overline{)242} \end{array}$ **27.** $\begin{array}{r} 5 \\ 83\overline{)403} \end{array}$

28. $\begin{array}{r} 5 \\ 51\overline{)249} \end{array}$ **29.** $\begin{array}{r} 9 \\ 25\overline{)271} \end{array}$ **30.** $\begin{array}{r} 9 \\ 37\overline{)355} \end{array}$ **31.** $\begin{array}{r} 8 \\ 59\overline{)475} \end{array}$

✓ CHECK PROBLEM SOLVING

Solve. **(pages 464–465)**

CHOOSE A STRATEGY

- **Make a Model**
- **Guess and Check**
- **Work Backward**
- **Write a Number Sentence**

32. Fred has a swimming pool that is 32 feet long. Robin has a pool that is 390 inches long. How many feet long is Robin's pool? Whose pool is longer, Fred's or Robin's?

33. There are 75 students trying out for the school choir. There are 19 more girls than boys. How many girls are trying out for the choir? how many boys?

CHAPTER 28 FRACTIONS AND DECIMALS IN CIRCLE GRAPHS

DID YOU KNOW . . .

Ice cream was invented in China around 200 B.C. A soft milk and rice mixture was packed in snow and made solid. The United States is now the ice cream capital of the world. U.S. citizens eat about 23 quarts per year.

Team-Up Time

Our Class Favorites

Do you know what your classmates like best? Guessing isn't the same as finding the facts. You can know all your class's favorites by taking a survey. Then make a chart to show the results.

Work with a group. Your job is to

- choose one of the survey categories shown, or think of your own.
- record your classmates' responses, using a tally sheet.
- make a graph to summarize the responses.
- write at least two facts about your data, using fractions and decimals.

SURVEY CATEGORIES

favorite school lunch
favorite sport
favorite toy
favorite television commercial
favorite book
favorite restaurant

What Is the Favorite Ice Cream Flavor In Our Class?

Number of students surveyed: 32

Vanilla
Chocolate
Chocolate chip
Cookies & cream
Strawberry
Pistachio
Other

Van. Choc. Choc. Ch. C&C Straw. pistac. other

Facts About Our Graph

1. Seven people in our class like chocolate best.
2. More people like cookies & cream than any other flavor.
3. Four people like a different flavor. Their favorite is not on the graph.

DID YOU

- ✓ choose a category for your survey?
- ✓ record your classmates' responses?
- ✓ make a graph to summarize the responses?
- ✓ write at least two facts about your data, using fractions and decimals?

Making a Circle Graph

You will investigate making a circle graph.

Why learn this? You can make a circle graph to show data you collect.

WORD POWER
circle graph

A **circle graph** is a graph in the shape of a circle. It shows data as a whole made up of different parts.

EXAMPLES

A.

VEGETABLES IN A GARDEN
Carrots
Lettuce

This circle graph shows a garden that is $\frac{1}{2}$ carrots and $\frac{1}{2}$ lettuce.

B.

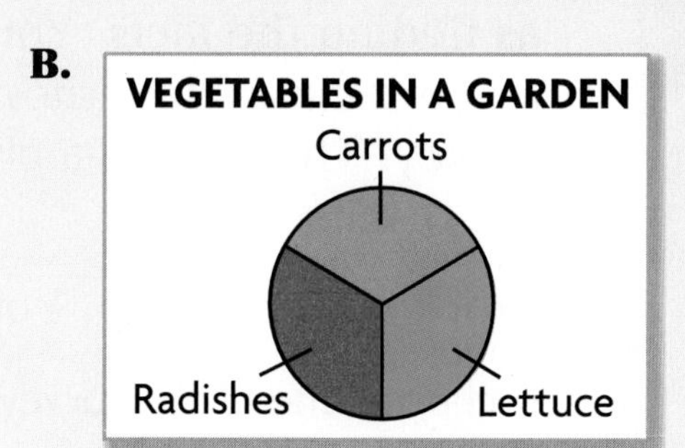

This circle graph shows a garden that is $\frac{1}{3}$ carrots, $\frac{1}{3}$ lettuce, and $\frac{1}{3}$ radishes.

Notice that

- each circle shows the whole garden.
- each part of the circle represents a fraction of the garden and is labeled.

Explore

MATERIALS: fraction-circle pieces

Sid and Martha are planting a flower garden. It will be $\frac{1}{2}$ daisies, $\frac{1}{4}$ marigolds, and $\frac{1}{4}$ tulips. Using fraction-circle pieces, make a circle graph to show their garden.

Record

Draw the circle graph by tracing each fraction-circle piece. Color each part of the graph a different color. Title the graph and label each part.

Technology Link
E-Lab • Activity 28 Available on CD-ROM and the Internet at http://www.hbschool.com/elab

TALK ABOUT IT What does the whole circle stand for? Which part shows the largest amount? the smallest amount?

Try This

Make a circle graph to show a garden that is $\frac{1}{3}$ tomatoes, $\frac{1}{2}$ onions, and $\frac{1}{6}$ squash. Draw the circle graph by tracing each fraction-circle piece. Color each part a different color.

WRITE ABOUT IT How do you know the unequal parts of this circle graph add up to a whole?

HANDS-ON PRACTICE

Use fraction-circle pieces to make each circle graph. Draw the circle graph by tracing the pieces. Title the graph and label each part.

1. a family that is $\frac{1}{2}$ boys and $\frac{1}{2}$ girls
2. a farm that is $\frac{1}{3}$ cows, $\frac{1}{3}$ pigs, and $\frac{1}{3}$ chickens
3. a meal that is $\frac{1}{2}$ chicken, $\frac{1}{4}$ peas, and $\frac{1}{4}$ rice
4. a pizza that is $\frac{1}{2}$ pepperoni, $\frac{1}{3}$ olives, and $\frac{1}{6}$ onions
5. a fair that is $\frac{1}{5}$ rides, $\frac{1}{5}$ games, $\frac{1}{5}$ shows, $\frac{1}{5}$ food stands, and $\frac{1}{5}$ picnic areas
6. a playground that is $\frac{1}{6}$ basketball courts, $\frac{1}{6}$ jungle gyms, and $\frac{2}{3}$ ball fields

Mixed Applications

7. Vinnie's garden has 4 rows of vegetable plants, with 8 plants in each row. Calvin's garden has 6 rows of vegetable plants, with 6 plants in each row. How many more plants are in Calvin's garden than in Vinnie's garden?
8. Luis bought 2 green peppers for \$0.39 each, 2 bags of carrots for \$0.99 a bag, and 3 bunches of radishes for \$0.79 a bunch. How much change did Luis get back from \$10.00?
9. Allison and Marnie are counting their change. Allison has 13 quarters, 2 dimes, 5 nickels, and 8 pennies. Marnie has 9 quarters, 9 dimes, 4 nickels, and 6 pennies. Who has more money? Explain.

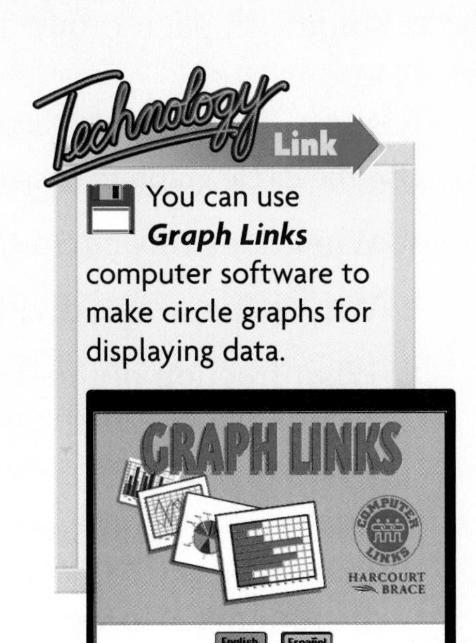

MORE PRACTICE Student Handbook page H115

Fractions in Circle Graphs

You will learn to identify fractions shown in circle graphs.

Why learn this? You can compare the amounts shown in a circle graph.

There are 4 groups of singers in the Sunridge Community Chorus. Each group of singers represents a part of the chorus.

A circle graph shows how parts are related to one another. This circle graph shows the different groups of singers in the Sunridge Community Chorus.

THE 36 MEMBERS OF THE SUNRIDGE COMMUNITY CHORUS

Soprano
Bass
Alto
Tenor

Talk About It

- What does the whole circle stand for?
- What fraction represents the whole chorus?
- What fraction of chorus members are alto? bass? soprano? tenor?
- How does the part of the chorus that sings soprano compare with the part of the chorus that sings alto?
- What would the graph look like if the number of singers in each group was the same?

Check Your Understanding

Use the circle graph to answer the questions.

1. What does this circle graph show?
2. Why is the graph divided into fifths?
3. What fraction of the 25 students chose chocolate? strawberry? vanilla?
4. Which ice cream flavor was chosen by the least number of students? How can you tell?

PRACTICE

For Problems 5–10, use the circle graphs.

FAVORITE PIE CHOICES OF 24 STUDENTS

Blueberry
Cherry
Peach
Apple

5. What fraction of the 24 students chose apple pie?
6. What fraction of the 24 students chose peach pie?
7. What fraction represents all the students in the survey?
8. Which grade has the least number of members on the swim team?
9. What fraction of the swim team is in grade 4? in grade 5? in grade 6?
10. What fraction represents all the students on the swim team?

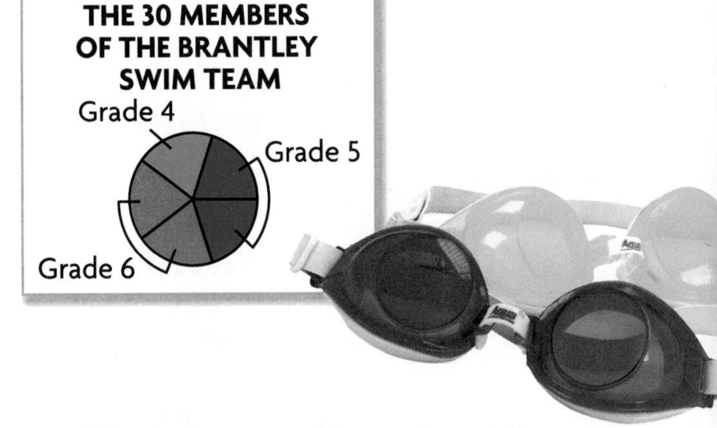

Mixed Applications

11. Suzanne wants to bake cookies for 180 people. Each box of cookie mix makes 36 cookies. How many boxes of cookie mix does Suzanne need to buy?

12. **Write a problem** about the circle graph.

13. Mr. Black is going hiking on the Appalachian Trail. He will hike 11 miles each day. How many days will it take Mr. Black to hike 230 miles?

Mixed Review

Use mental math and basic multiplication facts to find the product. (pages 266–267)

14. $4 \times 30 = $?
15. $6 \times 200 = $?
16. $7 \times 6{,}000 = $?

Find the area. (pages 234–235)

17. 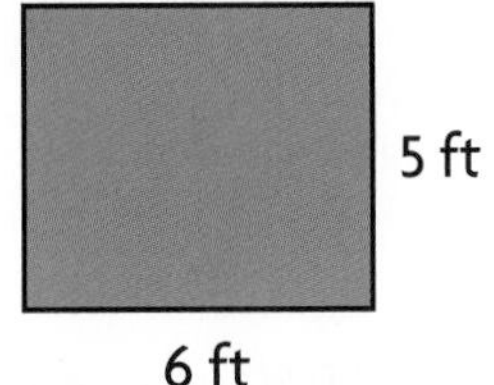

18. 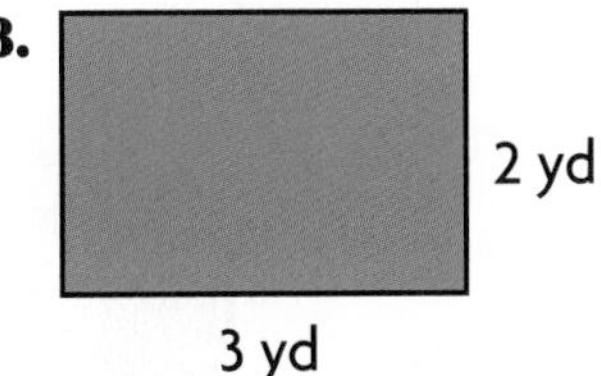

19. 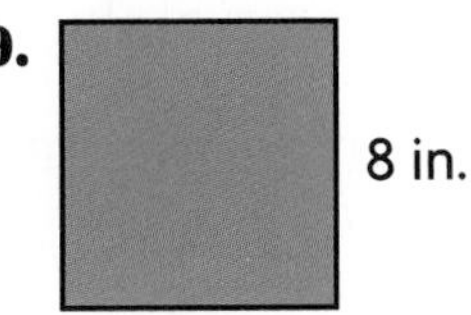

PART
1 Decimals in Circle Graphs

You will learn to arrange data in a circle graph and show the parts as decimals.

Why learn this? You can show data on a circle graph by using decimals or fractions.

Of 10 students, 5 said math was their favorite subject, 2 said science, and 3 said reading.

MODEL

How can you make a circle graph to show these data?

Step 1

Use a circle with 10 equal parts to stand for the 10 students.

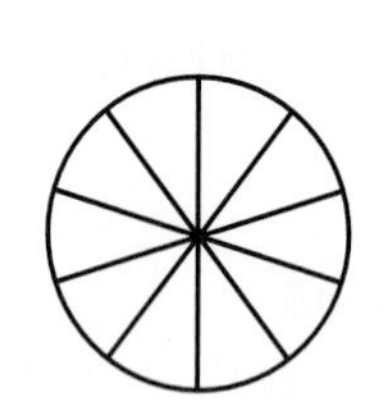

Step 2

Shade 5 parts purple to show the students who chose math, 2 parts red to show the students who chose science, and 3 parts teal to show the students who chose reading.

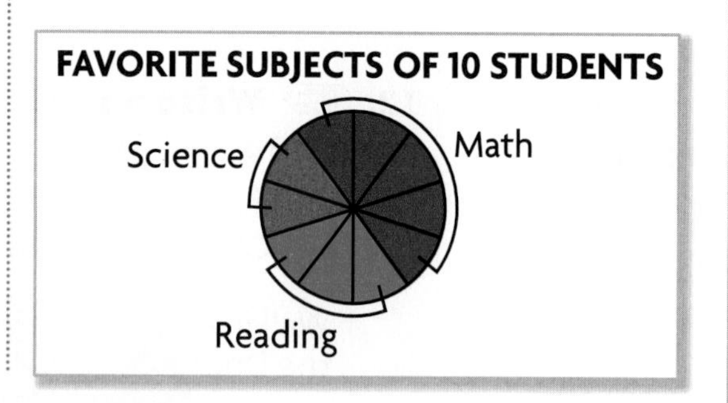

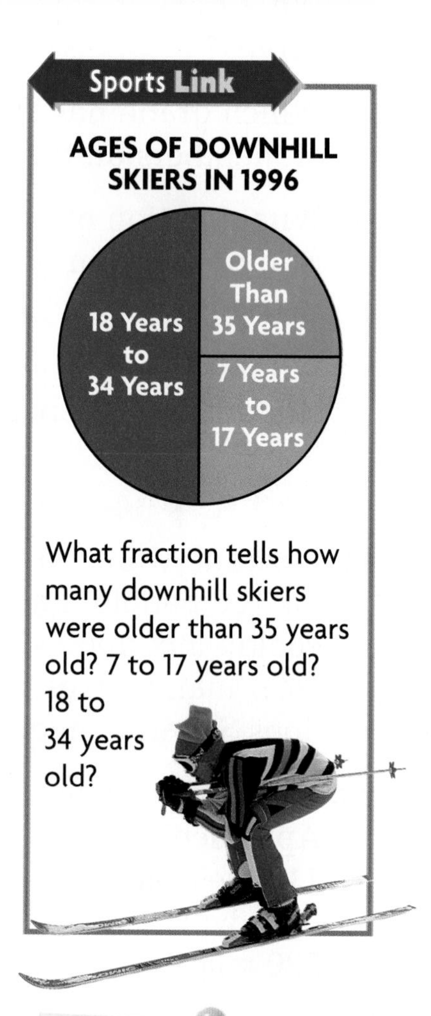

What fraction tells how many downhill skiers were older than 35 years old? 7 to 17 years old? 18 to 34 years old?

Talk About It

- What does the whole circle graph show?
- What fraction tells how many of the students chose math? chose reading? chose science?
- What decimal tells how many of the students chose math? chose reading? chose science?

REMEMBER:

Decimals can be written as fractions.

$0.1 = \frac{1}{10}$

$0.4 = \frac{4}{10}$

Since every fraction can be named as a decimal, all circle-graph data can be represented as decimals.

- What fraction represents each part of the circle graph?
- What is the sum of the decimals that represent the 3 parts of the circle graph?

The decimal 0.25 represents each of these parts of the circle graph.

The decimal 0.50 represents this part of the circle graph.

PRACTICE

For Problems 1–6, use the circle graphs.

1. What does the whole circle graph show?
2. What decimal tells how many classes painted desks? picked up litter? pulled weeds? planted flowers?
3. What is the sum of the four decimals?

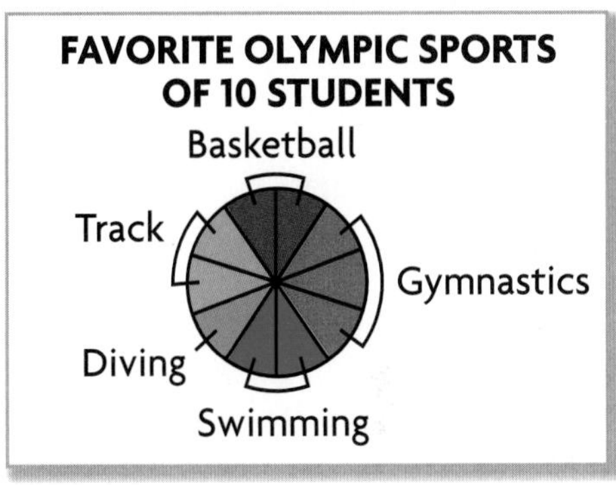

4. What decimal tells how many students chose diving? chose gymnastics?
5. What decimal tells how many students chose track and basketball?
6. What is the sum of the decimals that represent the 5 parts of the graph?

Show the following data on a circle graph.

7. There were 10 students who were asked what was their favorite type of book. Of the students, 4 said fiction, 4 said biography, and 2 said mystery. Write each part as a decimal.
8. There are 4 birds in the pet shop. Of the birds, 2 are green, 1 is white, and 1 is gray. Write each part as a fraction and a decimal.

Mixed Applications

9. Terry pulled weeds on the playground for 20 minutes, near the chorus room for 20 minutes, and near the office for 30 minutes. Did she spend more or less than 1 hour pulling weeds?
10. There are 5 flower seeds in each package of seeds. If 6 students each plant 2 packages of flower seeds, how many seeds will they plant in all?
11. Ernesto had perfect attendance this school year. He was in school 6 hours each day for 180 days. How many hours is that?
12. In 3 weeks, Jo walked for a total of 315 minutes. She walked an equal number of minutes each day. How long did she walk each day?
13. Jeremy painted 5 rows of desks, with 5 desks in each row. It took him 10 minutes to paint each desk. How many minutes did it take him to paint all the desks?
14. **Write a problem** about data that can be shown in a circle graph divided into 10 equal parts.

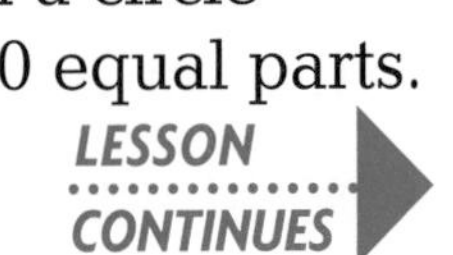

MORE PRACTICE Student Handbook page H116

PART 2 PROBLEM-SOLVING STRATEGY Make a Graph

THE PROBLEM Tasha and Patti asked 10 students in their classes to vote whether they liked popcorn, candy, or fruit as a snack at the movies. The vote in Tasha's class was 6 popcorn, 4 candy, and 0 fruit. The vote in Patti's class was 6 popcorn, 2 candy, and 2 fruit. Which class had a larger part who liked popcorn? candy? fruit?

REMEMBER:
- ✓ Understand
- ✓ Plan
- ✓ Solve
- ✓ Look Back

✓ Understand

- What are you asked to find?
- What information will you use?
- Is there any information you will not use? If so, what?

✓ Plan

- What strategy can you use to solve the problem?

You can *make a graph*.

Since the circle stands for 1 whole, divide each circle into 10 parts to show the 10 votes.

✓ Solve

- What graphs can you make to solve the problem?

Think:	Compare:	Tasha's Class		Patti's Class
$\frac{6}{10} = 0.6$	Popcorn	0.6	=	0.6
$\frac{4}{10} = 0.4$	Candy	0.4	>	0.2
$\frac{2}{10} = 0.2$	Fruit	0	<	0.2

Make two circle graphs. Show the data collected from Tasha's class in one and from Patti's class in the other. Name each choice as a decimal part of the whole. Compare the data in the two graphs.

So, each class had the same part who liked popcorn. Tasha's class had a larger part who liked candy. Patti's class had a larger part who liked fruit.

✓ Look Back

- How can you decide if your answer is reasonable?
- What other strategy could you use?

PRACTICE

CHOOSE Paper/Pencil Calculator Hands-on Mental Math

Make a graph to solve.

1. The vote in Mark's class was 5 popcorn, 3 candy, and 2 fruit. The vote in Juan's class was 6 popcorn, 4 candy, and 0 fruit. Which class had a larger part who liked popcorn? candy? fruit?

2. Tim asked 10 friends to name their favorite sport. Of his friends, 4 chose football, 4 chose baseball, and 2 chose golf. What decimal tells how many friends chose football? baseball? golf?

3. Lee makes soup that is $\frac{1}{2}$ milk, $\frac{1}{4}$ onions, and $\frac{1}{4}$ potatoes. What decimal represents the amount of milk? of onions? of potatoes?

4. Kelly spends 4 months in art classes during a 10-month period. Doug spends 3 months in art classes during a 5-month period. Who spends a larger part of his or her time in art classes?

Mixed Applications

Solve.

CHOOSE A STRATEGY

• Find a Pattern • Draw a Diagram • Act It Out • Write a Number Sentence • Make a Graph

5. Ms. Vier teaches art to 300 students. Each student will finish 10 projects in her class. How many projects will be done in all?

6. Of the 10 Media Club members, 6 are in fifth, 3 are in fourth, and 1 is in third grade. What decimals tell how many are in each grade?

7. Michele had 16 rolls of 50 pennies each. She traded the pennies for quarters. How many quarters did Michele get? How much money did she have?

8. Alex has 24 feet of fencing to put around a rectangular garden. Draw some shapes Alex can make. Which shape has the greatest area?

9. Dee watered a row of plants in her garden. She skipped the first plant, watered the second plant, skipped the next 5 plants, and watered the last plant. How many plants were in the row?

10. Each day for lunch, Ray spends the amount shown. How much does he spend for lunch in 5 days?

11. Corey has 864 ribbons to give to 24 classes. Each class will get the same number of ribbons. How many ribbons will each class get?

12. Mitzy bought 7 stickers in April, 14 in May, and 28 in June. If this pattern continues, how many stickers will she buy in August?

MORE PRACTICE Student Handbook page H116

Choosing Graphs to Represent Data

You will learn to match a graph with the data it shows.

Why learn this? You can judge whether a graph correctly shows the data.

Bill and Joe went to the county fair. They spent $\frac{1}{4}$ of the time eating, $\frac{1}{4}$ of the time playing games, and $\frac{1}{2}$ of the time on rides. Which graph describes how Bill and Joe spent their time at the county fair?

On the bumper car ride with Joe!

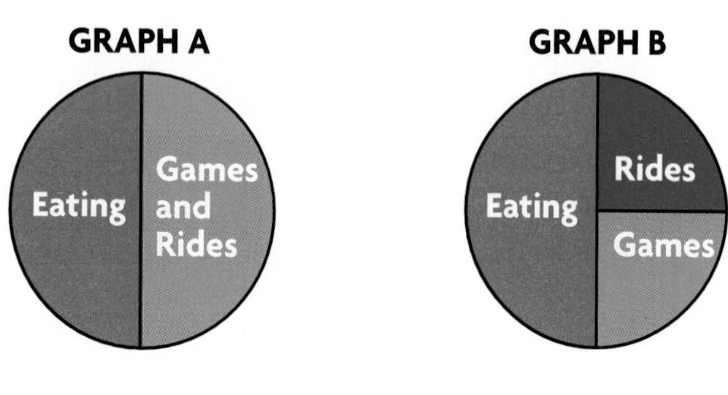

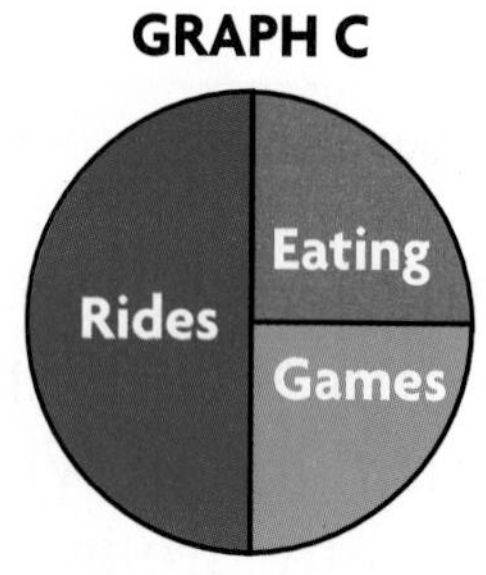

Graph A shows $\frac{1}{2}$ of the time eating and $\frac{1}{2}$ of the time on games and rides.

Graph B shows $\frac{1}{2}$ of the time eating, $\frac{1}{4}$ of the time on rides, and $\frac{1}{4}$ of the time playing games.

Graph C shows $\frac{1}{4}$ of the time eating, $\frac{1}{4}$ of the time playing games, and $\frac{1}{2}$ of the time on rides.

So, Graph C describes how Bill and Joe spent their time at the county fair.

Social Studies Link

In 1850 about $\frac{1}{2}$ of all work in the United States was done by animals, about $\frac{1}{8}$ by people, and about $\frac{3}{8}$ by machines. Draw a graph that shows these data.

Talk About It

- Why does Graph C show how Bill and Joe spent their time at the county fair, but Graph B does not?
- Would Graph C be correct if *Eating* and *Games* were switched? Explain.

PRACTICE

Match the graph with the set of data it describes.

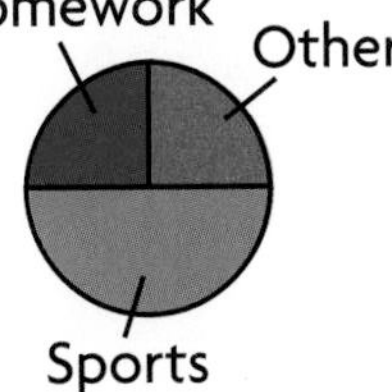

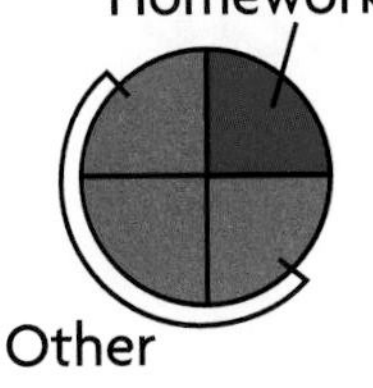

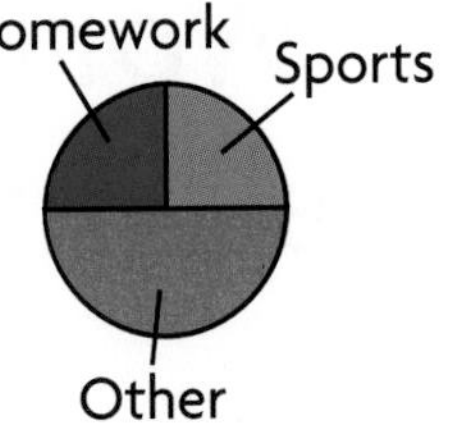

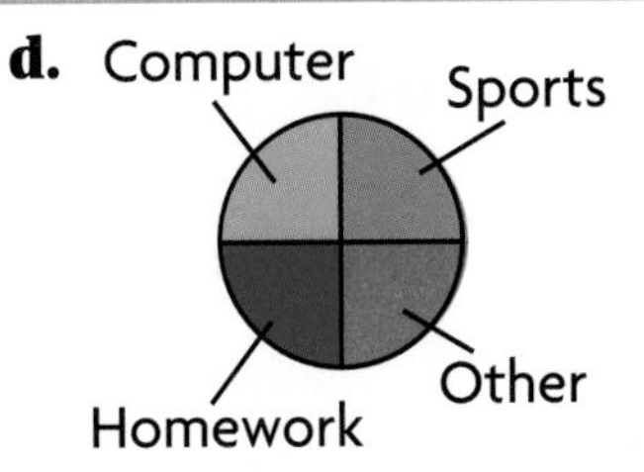

1. $\frac{1}{4}$ homework
   $\frac{3}{4}$ other

2. $\frac{1}{4}$ homework
   $\frac{1}{4}$ other
   $\frac{1}{2}$ sports

3. $\frac{1}{4}$ homework
   $\frac{1}{4}$ sports
   $\frac{1}{4}$ other
   $\frac{1}{4}$ computer

4. $\frac{1}{4}$ homework
   $\frac{1}{4}$ sports
   $\frac{1}{2}$ other

Mixed Applications

For Problems 5–8, use the circle graph.

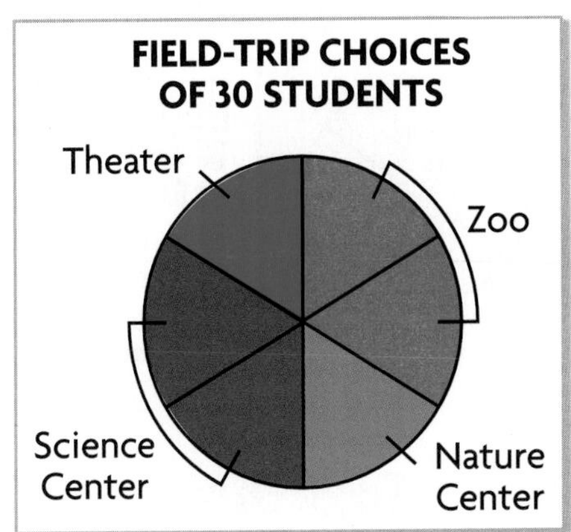

5. What does the whole circle stand for?
6. What fraction represents the whole circle?
7. What fraction of students chose the nature center? the science center? the theater? the zoo?
8. **WRITE ABOUT IT** How would the graph change if no one chose the theater, 10 chose the science center, 10 chose the nature center, and 10 chose the zoo?

Mixed Review

Write the numbers in order from the greatest to the least. (pages 112–113)

9. 635; 563; 653
10. 1,275; 1,752; 1,527
11. 2,105; 1,205; 1,502
12. 409; 490; 419
13. 5,298; 5,289; 5,270
14. 9,101; 9,111; 9,001

Find the product. (page 272–273)

15. 315×3
16. 425×6
17. 207×5
18. 631×7
19. 572×8

CULTURAL CONNECTION

COOPERATIVE LEARNING

Parts of the World That Form a Whole Nation

Ms. Trammel's fourth-grade students marked a world map to show where their ancestors had lived. They wanted to learn more about the places where their families had come from. They set aside a week for a United Nations fair. Study the circle graph to see the areas of the world where the students' families had lived. Make as many statements as you can to describe what the graph shows.

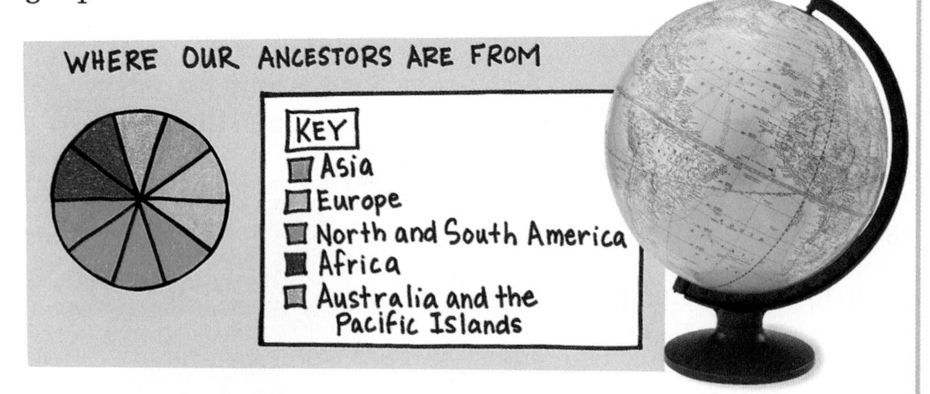

CULTURAL LINK

The Statue of Liberty in New York Harbor is a symbol of freedom for people who have come from other countries to live in the United States. The statue was a gift from the people of France. This statue of a woman is one of the largest statues in the world. It is 151 feet 1 inch tall and weighs 254 metric tons.

Work Together

1. Use the circle graph to write the fraction of the students' families who came from each area of the world.

2. The students formed groups to study areas of the world. Each group had 2 hours to present its information to the class. Amy's group studied Asia. Make a circle graph to show how the group divided its time. (HINT: Each 15 minutes equals $\frac{1}{8}$ of the circle.)

15 minutes:	Show slides of Korea.
15 minutes:	Teach the class how to play a Thai game with a ball.
30 minutes:	Fold paper animals with Japanese origami patterns.
15 minutes:	Read a Chinese folktale play.
15 minutes:	Practice eating peanuts with chopsticks and taste Asian foods.
15 minutes:	Tell about interesting facts and customs of different Asian countries.
15 minutes:	End with Question-and-Answer time.

CHAPTER 28 REVIEW

✓ CHECK UNDERSTANDING

1. **VOCABULARY** A _?_ is a graph that shows data as a whole made up of different parts. **(page 472)**

For Problems 2–5, use the circle graph. **(pages 474–475)**

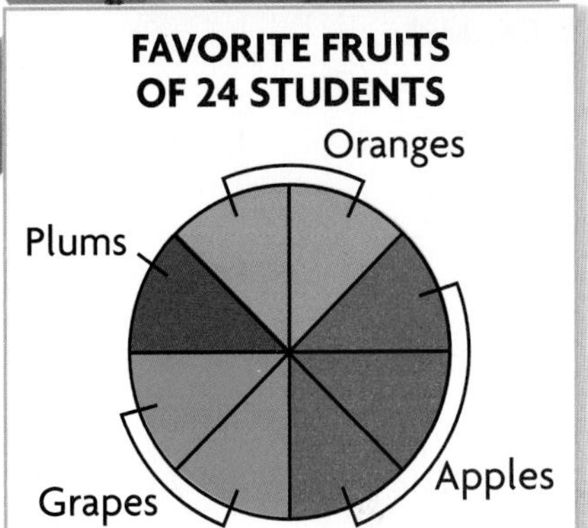

2. What does the whole circle stand for?
3. What fraction of the students chose apples? grapes? plums? oranges?
4. Which fruit was chosen by the greatest number of children? by the least number of children?
5. How does the part of the students who chose grapes compare with the part who chose oranges?

✓ CHECK SKILLS

Match the graph with the set of data it describes. **(pages 480–481)**

a.

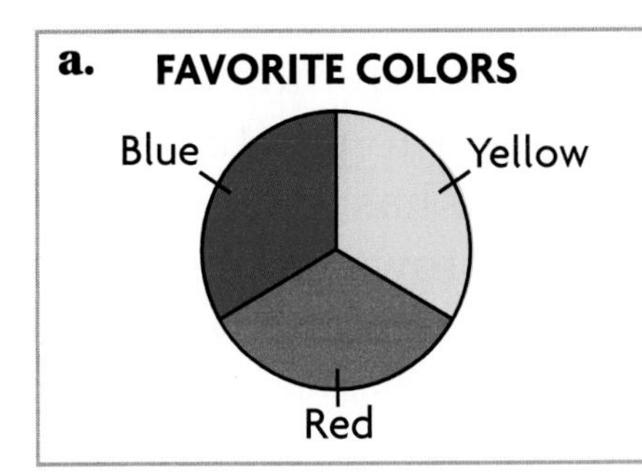

b.

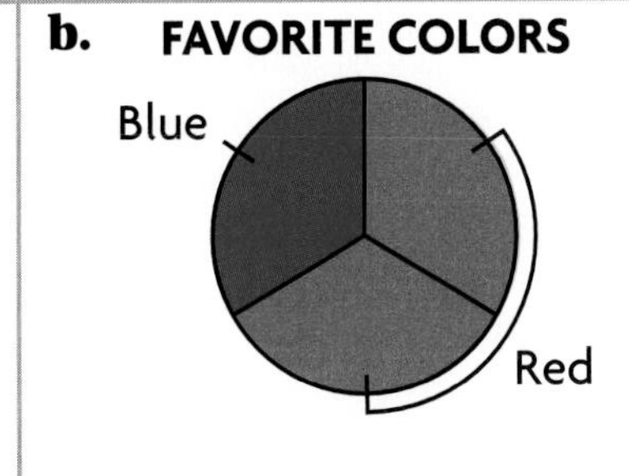

c.

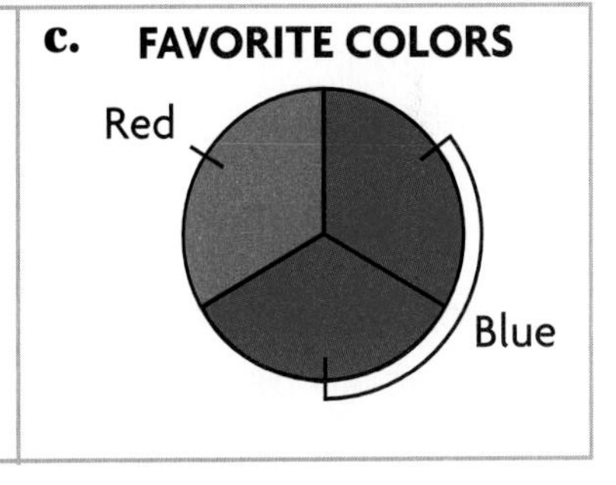

6. $\frac{1}{3}$ red, $\frac{2}{3}$ blue
7. $\frac{1}{3}$ red, $\frac{1}{3}$ blue, $\frac{1}{3}$ yellow
8. $\frac{1}{3}$ blue, $\frac{2}{3}$ red

✓ CHECK PROBLEM SOLVING

Solve. **(pages 478–479)**

CHOOSE A STRATEGY

- **Find a Pattern**
- **Make a Graph**
- **Write a Number Sentence**

9. There were 10 students who were asked in what month they were born. Of the students, 5 said in May, 2 said in February, and 3 said in July. What decimal tells how many were born in May? in February? in July?

10. Carlos runs 3 miles a day. He runs 5 days every week. How many miles does he run in one week? How many miles does he run in one year? (HINT: There are 52 weeks in a year.)

CHAPTERS 27–28 STUDY GUIDE & REVIEW

STUDY AND SOLVE

CHAPTER 27

EXAMPLE

$$\begin{array}{r} 29 \text{ r}2 \\ 12\overline{)350} \\ -24 \\ \hline 110 \\ -108 \\ \hline 2 \end{array}$$

1. Divide.
2. Multiply.
3. Subtract.
4. Compare.
5. Bring down.
6. Repeat as needed.

Write the numbers you would use to estimate the quotients. Then write the estimate. (pages 456–457)

1. $154 \div 32 = n$ **2.** $249 \div 13 = n$

3. $118 \div 64 = n$ **4.** $279 \div 73 = n$

Write the basic fact that helps you find the quotient. (pages 456–457)

5. $183 \div 61 = n$ **6.** $199 \div 48 = n$

7. $274 \div 32 = n$ **8.** $238 \div 39 = n$

Draw a box where the first digit in the quotient should be placed. (pages 458–459)

9. $40\overline{)144}$ **10.** $60\overline{)219}$

11. $30\overline{)387}$ **12.** $50\overline{)752}$

Find the quotient. (pages 458–459)

13. $80\overline{)245}$ **14.** $40\overline{)286}$

15. $60\overline{)565}$ **16.** $20\overline{)117}$

17. $70\overline{)136}$ **18.** $50\overline{)451}$

Find the quotient. Check by multiplying. (pages 462–463)

19. $45\overline{)225}$ **20.** $32\overline{)58}$

21. $79\overline{)188}$ **22.** $13\overline{)199}$

23. $47\overline{)251}$ **24.** $16\overline{)386}$

Write *too high, too low,* or *just right* for each estimate. Find the quotient. (pages 466–467)

25. $\begin{array}{r} 6 \\ 61\overline{)364} \end{array}$ **26.** $\begin{array}{r} 5 \\ 29\overline{)147} \end{array}$

27. $\begin{array}{r} 8 \\ 22\overline{)163} \end{array}$ **28.** $\begin{array}{r} 6 \\ 17\overline{)124} \end{array}$

Solve. (pages 464–465)

29. Mr. Diego is planting tomato plants. He wants to put 15 plants in each row. He has 137 plants. How many full rows can he plant? How many plants will he have left?

30. Soda comes 24 cans to a case. Mini Mart has 220 cans. How many cases is this? How many cans are left over?

CHAPTER 28

EXAMPLE

What data are represented on the circle graph?

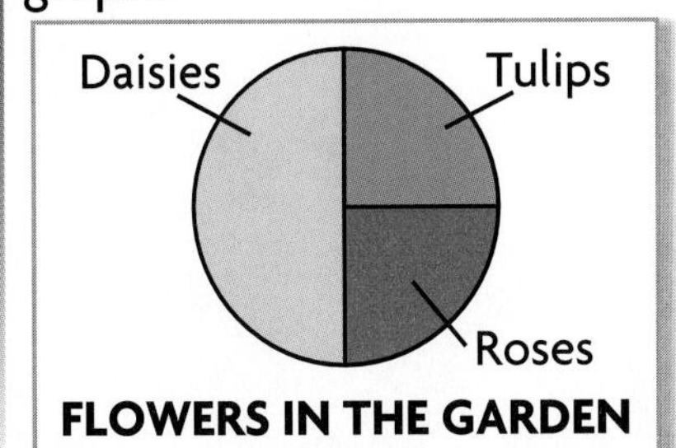

$\frac{1}{2}$ daisies,

$\frac{1}{4}$ tulips,

$\frac{1}{4}$ roses

For Problems 31–35, use the circle graph below. (pages 474–475)

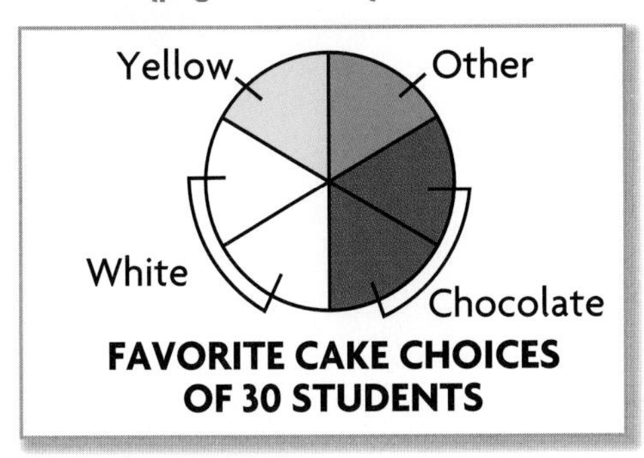

31. What does the whole circle represent?

32. What fraction of the students chose chocolate cake?

33. What fraction of the students chose yellow cake?

34. Which flavor of cake was chosen by the same fraction of students as chocolate?

35. What fraction represents all the students in the survey?

For Problems 36–38, use the circle graph. (pages 476–477)

36. What decimal represents the part of the students whose favorite snack is pretzels?

37. Which two snacks did the same number of students choose?

38. What decimal represents the sum of the three favorite snacks?

Solve. (pages 478–479)

39. Kelly asked 10 friends to choose their favorite subject. Of her friends, 4 chose math, 3 chose science, 2 chose music, and 1 chose art. What decimal tells the part that chose science?

40. There are 10 dogs in a pet shop. Of the dogs, 2 are brown, 3 are black, 4 are white, and 1 is gray. What fraction tells the part of the dogs that are white?

CHAPTERS 27–28

WHAT DID I LEARN?

WRITE ABOUT IT

1. Explain a strategy you would use to solve this problem. Then solve the problem.

   Rick and Cindy are baking cookies for the school fair. Each batch of cookies bakes for 18 minutes. How many batches of cookies can they finish baking in two hours? How many extra minutes are there? (pages 464–465)

2. Explain how to use the circle graph of Favorite Olympic Sports on page 477 to answer these questions.
   - What decimal tells how many students chose basketball?
   - What decimal tells how many students chose swimming or diving? (pages 476–477)

PERFORMANCE ASSESSMENT

Solve. Explain your method.

CHOOSE A STRATEGY

- Find a Pattern
- Act It Out
- Make a Model
- Draw a Picture
- Write a Number Sentence

3. Nick's scout troop ate 270 doughnuts at a meeting. They probably will eat about the same amount at the next meeting. Nick ordered 23 dozen doughnuts. Is this more than 270? Did Nick make a good decision? Explain. (pages 464–465)

4. Kim asked 10 students what they ate for lunch. Of the students, 2 ate pizza, 4 ate spaghetti, 1 ate sandwiches, and 3 ate fish sticks. Make a graph to show the information Kim collected. Which food was eaten by the most? by the fewest? What decimal represents the part of the students that ate pizza? (pages 476–477)

CUMULATIVE REVIEW

Solve the problem. Then write the letter of the correct answer.

1. $\begin{array}{r} 8{,}000 \\ -2{,}516 \\ \hline \end{array}$

   A. 5,484
   B. 5,594
   C. 6,594
   D. 10,516 (pages 20–23)

2. Compare. 3,899 ● 3,901

   A. $>$ B. $<$
   C. $=$ D. $-$ (pages 104–107)

For Problems 3–4, use the stem-and-leaf plot.

Stem	Leaves
1	7 8 9 0
2	0 2 4 5 6 6 6
3	0 1 2 2

Swim Class Size

3. What is the largest class size?

   A. 2 B. 9
   C. 17 D. 32

4. What is the median?

   A. 8 B. 24
   C. 25 D. 26 (pages 162–163)

5. What is the area of a rectangle with a length of 10 m and a width of 8 m?

   A. 2 sq m B. 18 sq m
   C. 36 sq m D. 80 sq m (pages 234–235)

6. $\begin{array}{r} 567 \\ \times\ 24 \\ \hline \end{array}$

   A. 13,608
   B. 12,288
   C. 591
   D. 543 (pages 290–293)

7. $4\frac{3}{7} + 2\frac{2}{7} = n$

   A. $n = 2\frac{1}{7}$
   B. $n = 3\frac{5}{7}$
   C. $n = 6\frac{3}{7}$
   D. $n = 6\frac{5}{7}$ (pages 362–363)

8. $\begin{array}{r} 3.45 \\ -1.67 \\ \hline \end{array}$

   A. 0.0178
   B. 1.78
   C. 2.68
   D. 5.12 (pages 390–393)

For Problems 9–10, write the equivalent measurement.

9. 2 c = __?__ pt

   A. 8 B. 6
   C. 4 D. 1 (pages 414–415)

10. 300 cm = __?__ m

    A. 0.3 B. 3
    C. 30 D. 30,000 (pages 424–427)

11. $42\overline{)888}$

    A. 2 r48
    B. 20 r48
    C. 21 r6
    D. 37,296 (pages 462–463)

12. A __?__ graph is a graph that shows data that are parts of a whole.

    A. line B. double-bar
    C. circle D. bar (pages 472–473)

STUDENT HANDBOOK

1 Intervention Lessons H2

Before you begin a new topic, it often helps to review things that you learned earlier. These lessons will help you get ready to learn new topics in math.

2 Extension Lessons H36

You can challenge yourself to learn new and interesting things when you try these Extension lessons.

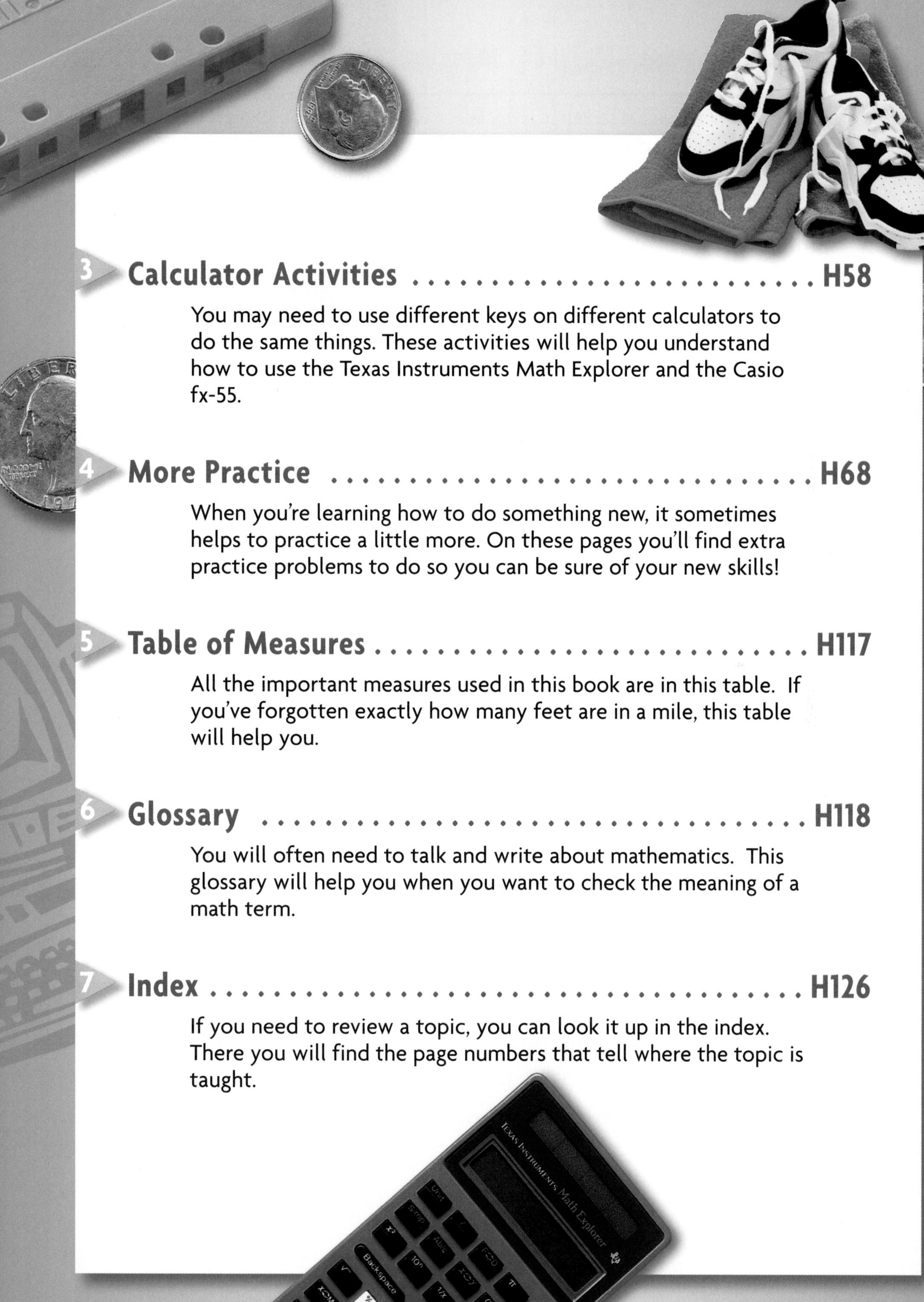

Adding Three-Digit Numbers

You will learn how to use base-ten blocks and regrouping to add.	**Why learn this?** You can add large numbers, such as the number of miles your family might drive on a vacation.

John's family took a vacation. His dad drove 166 miles on Monday and 157 miles on Tuesday. How many miles did John's dad drive in all?

MODEL

Find 166 + 157 = ?.

Step 1

Add the ones. 6 + 7 = 13 ones

Regroup. 13 ones = 1 ten 3 ones

$$\begin{array}{r} \scriptstyle 1 \\ 166 \\ +157 \\ \hline 3 \end{array}$$

Record the sum of the ones as 3. Place the regrouped 1 ten in the tens column.

Step 2

Add the tens. 1 + 6 + 5 = 12 tens

Regroup. 12 tens = 1 hundred 2 tens

Add the hundreds.

$$\begin{array}{r} \scriptstyle 1\,1 \\ 166 \\ +157 \\ \hline 323 \end{array}$$

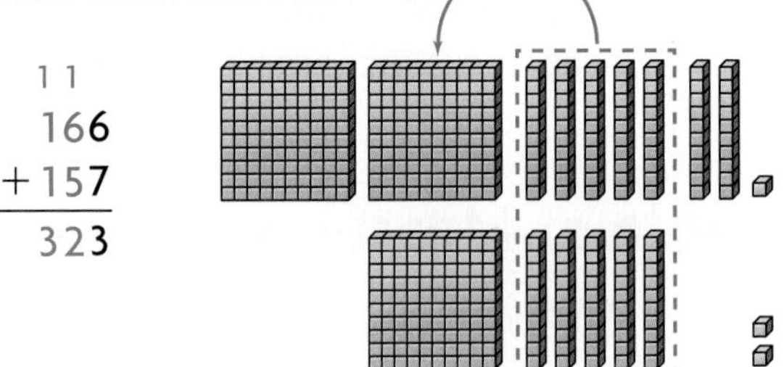

Record the sum of the tens as 2. Place the regrouped 1 hundred in the hundreds column. The sum of the hundreds, or 3, is placed in the hundreds place.

So, John's dad drove 323 miles in all.

You can add without using base-ten blocks.

Step 1

Add the ones.

7 + 8 = 15 ones

Regroup 15 ones as 1 ten 5 ones.

$$\begin{array}{r} \scriptstyle 1 \\ 447 \\ +678 \\ \hline 5 \end{array}$$

Step 2

Add the tens.

1 + 4 + 7 = 12 tens

Regroup 12 tens as 1 hundred 2 tens.

$$\begin{array}{r} \scriptstyle 1\,1 \\ 447 \\ +678 \\ \hline 25 \end{array}$$

Step 3

Add the hundreds.

1 + 4 + 6 = 11 hundreds

Regroup 11 hundreds as 1 thousand 1 hundred.

$$\begin{array}{r} \scriptstyle 1\,1 \\ 447 \\ +678 \\ \hline 1{,}125 \end{array}$$

Talk About It

- In Step 1, how do you know how many ones to record in the ones column?
- What happens to the 12 tens in Step 2?
- What operation can you use to check the sum in Step 3? Explain.

PRACTICE

You may wish to use base-ten blocks to model. Then find the sum.

1. $\begin{array}{r} 148 \\ +235 \\ \hline \end{array}$ **2.** $\begin{array}{r} 364 \\ +165 \\ \hline \end{array}$ **3.** $\begin{array}{r} 245 \\ +132 \\ \hline \end{array}$ **4.** $\begin{array}{r} 256 \\ +374 \\ \hline \end{array}$

Find the sum.

5. $\begin{array}{r} 547 \\ +325 \\ \hline \end{array}$ **6.** $\begin{array}{r} 826 \\ +171 \\ \hline \end{array}$ **7.** $\begin{array}{r} 746 \\ +185 \\ \hline \end{array}$ **8.** $\begin{array}{r} 485 \\ +497 \\ \hline \end{array}$

9. $\begin{array}{r} 239 \\ +470 \\ \hline \end{array}$ **10.** $\begin{array}{r} 218 \\ +659 \\ \hline \end{array}$ **11.** $\begin{array}{r} 198 \\ +701 \\ \hline \end{array}$ **12.** $\begin{array}{r} 367 \\ +533 \\ \hline \end{array}$

13. $\begin{array}{r} 618 \\ +243 \\ \hline \end{array}$ **14.** $\begin{array}{r} 735 \\ +194 \\ \hline \end{array}$ **15.** $\begin{array}{r} 831 \\ +349 \\ \hline \end{array}$ **16.** $\begin{array}{r} 673 \\ +538 \\ \hline \end{array}$

17. $\begin{array}{r} 489 \\ +516 \\ \hline \end{array}$ **18.** $\begin{array}{r} 369 \\ +847 \\ \hline \end{array}$ **19.** $\begin{array}{r} 522 \\ +879 \\ \hline \end{array}$ **20.** $\begin{array}{r} 157 \\ +963 \\ \hline \end{array}$

Mixed Applications

21. There are 178 students who eat during the first lunch period. There are 263 students who eat during the second lunch period. In all, how many students eat during these periods?

22. Kyle scored 685 points in one video game. He scored 497 points in another. What is the total number of points that he scored in the two games?

23. There are 247 books in one bookcase in the library. That is 100 more books than in another bookcase. How many books are in the second bookcase?

24. Mr. Tully's class has 346 cans and 96 bottles for recycling. Ms. Largo's class has 327 cans and 131 bottles. Which class has more cans and bottles? How many more?

Subtracting Three-Digit Numbers

You will learn to use base-ten blocks and regrouping to subtract.

Why learn this? You can use subtraction when you have lost count of what you have given away.

Tom had 315 basketball cards. He gave some to Tony. Now Tom has 185 cards. How many cards did he give to Tony?

You can use a diagram to help you understand what the problem is asking.

To find how many cards Tom gave to Tony, subtract the number Tom has now from the number he first had.

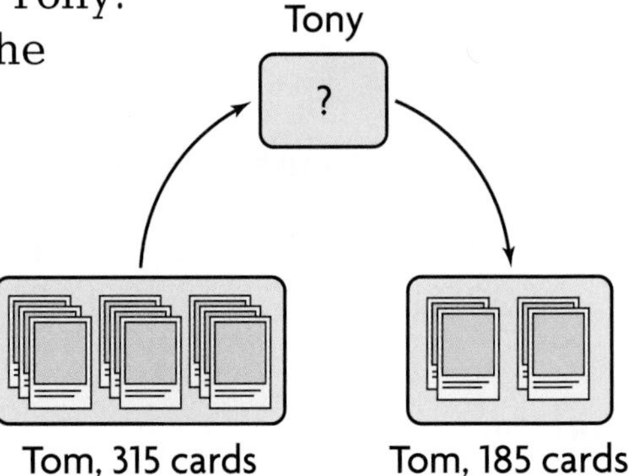

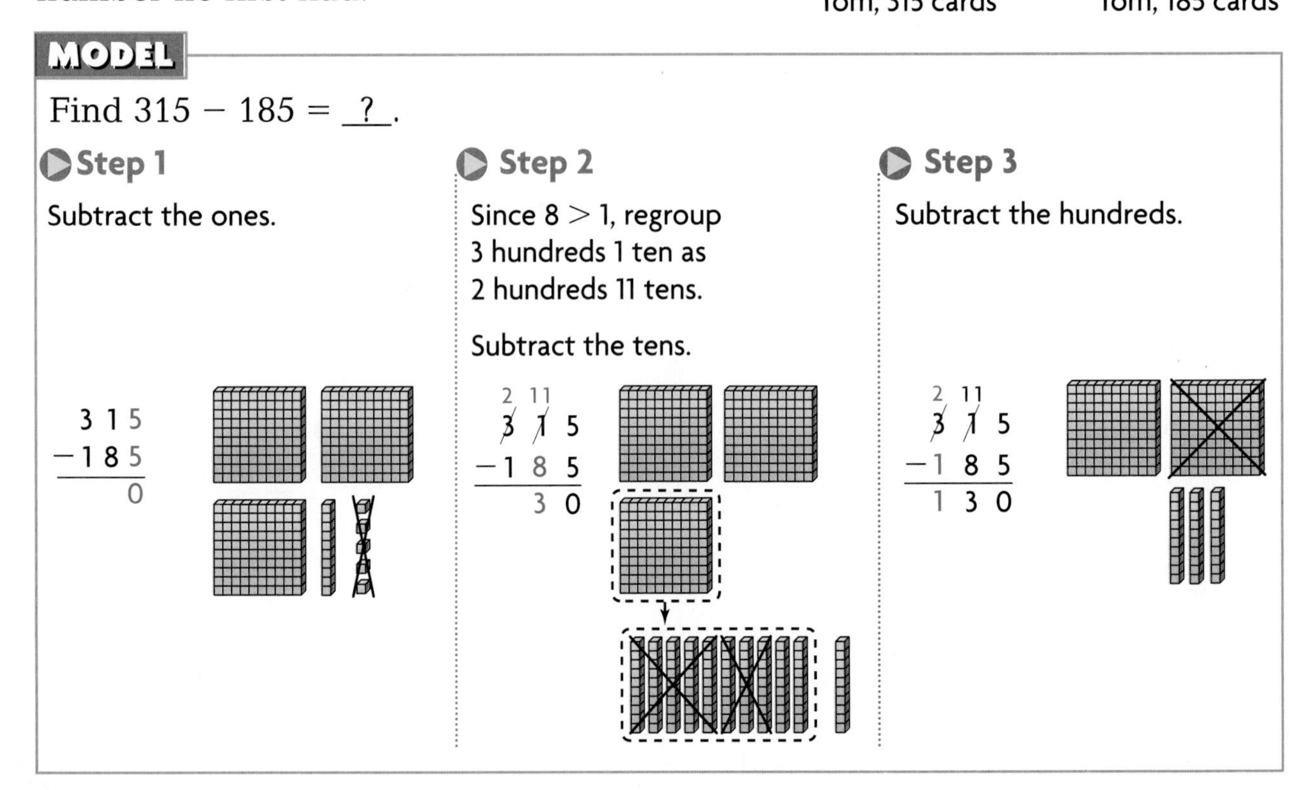

So, Tom gave 130 cards to Tony.

Talk About It

- Why do you need to regroup 300 as 2 hundreds 11 tens in Step 2?
- How can you use addition to check your answer?
- In Step 1 why aren't the tens regrouped to subtract the ones?

PRACTICE

Solve. You may wish to use base-ten blocks.

1. $\begin{array}{r} 243 \\ -156 \\ \hline \end{array}$ **2.** $\begin{array}{r} 412 \\ -252 \\ \hline \end{array}$ **3.** $\begin{array}{r} 324 \\ -156 \\ \hline \end{array}$ **4.** $\begin{array}{r} 832 \\ -429 \\ \hline \end{array}$

Find the difference.

5. $\begin{array}{r} 624 \\ -381 \\ \hline \end{array}$ **6.** $\begin{array}{r} 487 \\ -296 \\ \hline \end{array}$ **7.** $\begin{array}{r} 532 \\ -\ 84 \\ \hline \end{array}$ **8.** $\begin{array}{r} 713 \\ -547 \\ \hline \end{array}$

9. $\begin{array}{r} 379 \\ -286 \\ \hline \end{array}$ **10.** $\begin{array}{r} 563 \\ -357 \\ \hline \end{array}$ **11.** $\begin{array}{r} 641 \\ -559 \\ \hline \end{array}$ **12.** $\begin{array}{r} 834 \\ -\ 45 \\ \hline \end{array}$

13. $\begin{array}{r} 475 \\ -286 \\ \hline \end{array}$ **14.** $\begin{array}{r} 377 \\ -168 \\ \hline \end{array}$ **15.** $\begin{array}{r} 991 \\ -766 \\ \hline \end{array}$ **16.** $\begin{array}{r} 483 \\ -144 \\ \hline \end{array}$

Mixed Applications

17. Jake is saving to buy a new bicycle. He has already saved $85. He earned $47 mowing lawns. How much money does Jake have for his bicycle?

18. During one week, 234 tickets to a baseball game were sold. The next week, 179 tickets were sold. How many more tickets were sold in the first week than in the second week?

19. Marcy and Daniel collect baseball cards. Marcy has 215 cards. She has 89 more cards than Daniel. How many cards does Daniel have?

20. Jeff has 461 sports cards. There are 212 baseball cards, and 122 football cards. The rest are basketball cards. How many basketball cards does Jeff have?

21. Marliss sells food at the games. Friday night she sold 188 hamburgers and 169 hot dogs. Saturday night she sold 224 hamburgers and 146 hot dogs. On which night did she sell more hamburgers and hot dogs? How many more?

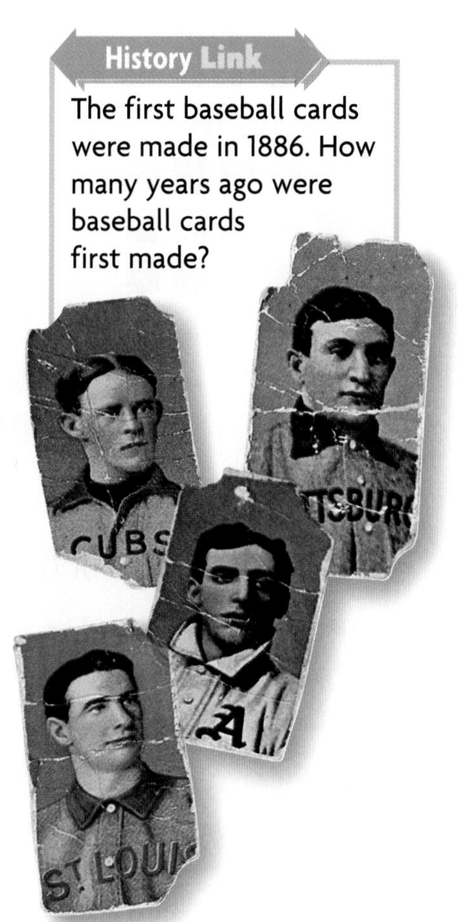

Understanding Multiplication

You will learn that you can multiply to find the total when there are a number of equal groups.

Why learn this? You can quickly find a total number, such as how many wheels are on 5 cars.

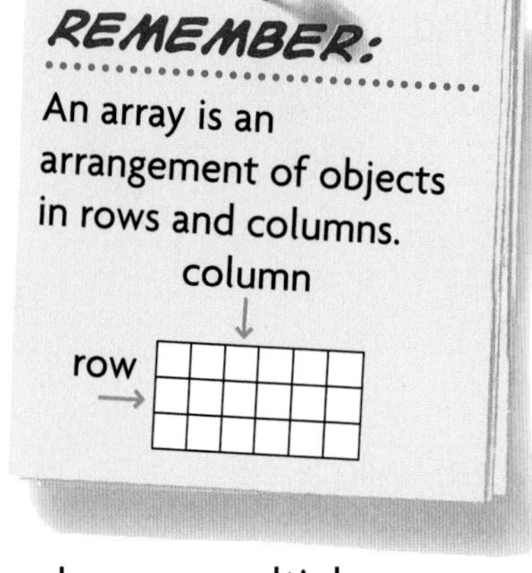

Jason's dad has 5 cars. Jason is polishing the hubcaps on the wheels. How many wheels are on 5 cars?

What are some ways to find out?

- Count by fours. 4, 8, 12, 16, 20
- Add. $4 + 4 + 4 + 4 + 4 = 20$
- Multiply. $5 \times 4 = 20$ or

$$\begin{array}{r} 4 \\ \times 5 \\ \hline 20 \end{array}$$

4 ← factor, ×5 ← factor — the numbers you multiply

20 ← product ← the answer

So, there are 20 wheels on 5 cars.

- How are addition and multiplication alike? How are they different?

You can make an array with tiles to help you multiply.

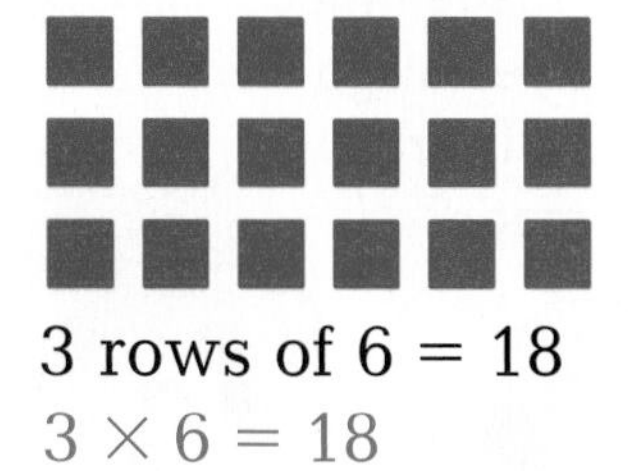

3 rows of 6 = 18

$3 \times 6 = 18$

6 rows of 3 = 18

$6 \times 3 = 18$

Talk About It

- How are 3 rows of 6 like 6 rows of 3?
- How does the order of factors change the product? Give an example that explains your thinking.

CRITICAL THINKING What is another way to group 4 rows of 9 tiles?

CULTURAL LINK

The largest single automobile plant in the world is the Volkswagenwerk in Wolfsburg, Germany. It has 60,000 workers and can make 4 thousand cars every week. How many cars can they make in 4 weeks?

PRACTICE

Show how to count, add, and multiply to solve each problem.

1. Ramon has 3 bags of marbles. There are 5 marbles in each bag. How many marbles does Ramon have?

2. Henry has 2 boxes of crayons. Each box has 8 crayons. How many crayons does Henry have?

Use the array to solve each number sentence.

3. $7 + 7 + 7 = \underline{?}$
$3 \times 7 = \underline{?}$

4. $4 + 4 + 4 + 4 = \underline{?}$
$4 \times 4 = \underline{?}$

Draw an array and find the product.

5. 5 rows of 2 **6.** 3 rows of 4 **7.** 5 rows of 6 **8.** 2 rows of 7

Find the product.

9. $4 \times 3 = \underline{?}$ **10.** $9 \times 3 = \underline{?}$ **11.** $4 \times 8 = \underline{?}$ **12.** $2 \times 9 = \underline{?}$

13. $3 \times 3 = \underline{?}$ **14.** $8 \times 3 = \underline{?}$ **15.** $4 \times 2 = \underline{?}$ **16.** $8 \times 2 = \underline{?}$

17. $3 \times 2 = \underline{?}$ **18.** $3 \times 6 = \underline{?}$ **19.** $6 \times 2 = \underline{?}$ **20.** $1 \times 2 = \underline{?}$

21. $3 \times 1 = \underline{?}$ **22.** $4 \times 4 = \underline{?}$ **23.** $8 \times 4 = \underline{?}$ **24.** $4 \times 9 = \underline{?}$

25. $3 \times 4 = \underline{?}$ **26.** $3 \times 9 = \underline{?}$ **27.** $1 \times 4 = \underline{?}$ **28.** $6 \times 4 = \underline{?}$

Mixed Applications

29. Tommy has 6 pencils in each of his 2 pencil cases. He also has 5 extra pencils in his desk. How many pencils does Tommy have?

30. Kimberly bought balloons for $1.75, party hats for $2.25, and whistles for $2.50. How much did Kimberly spend?

31. Larry has 3 red cars in a box. He has 4 times as many blue cars. How many blue cars does Larry have?

32. Julie spent $7.50 at the craft store. Maria spent $4.75 less than Julie. How much did Maria spend?

33. Suzanne made 3 bracelets. She put 5 red beads and 4 blue beads on each bracelet. How many beads did she use?

34. **WRITE ABOUT IT** Explain how to arrange 24 tiles to show 3 equal rows and then 4 equal rows.

Concept of Division

You will learn that in division you find the number of groups or the number in each group.

Why learn this? You can find how many things each person will receive when you share them equally with your classmates.

You can use division to find how many equal groups there are.

Suppose 20 students are running a relay race. There are 5 runners on each team. How many teams are there?

20	÷	5	=	4
↑		↑		↑
number of students		number on each team		number of teams

So, there are 4 teams of 5 runners each.

- Explain how this problem shows how many equal groups there are.

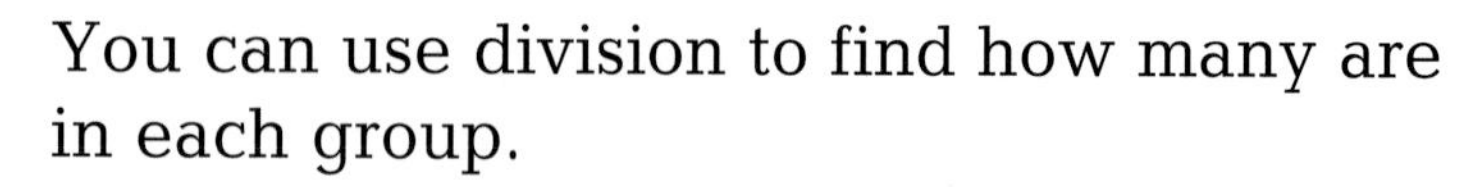

You can use division to find how many are in each group.

Suppose 12 students are playing volleyball. How many players are on each of the 2 teams?

12	÷	2	=	6
↑		↑		↑
number of students		number of teams		number on each team

So, there are 6 players on each of the 2 teams.

- Explain how this problem shows how many are in each group.

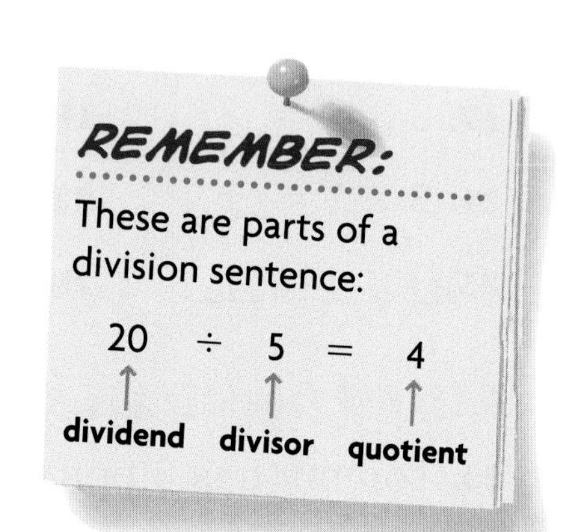

Check Your Understanding

1. Work with a partner. Write one division problem to find how many equal groups there are. Write one problem to find how many are in each group.
2. Explain how each problem shows each kind of division.

PRACTICE

Write *a* or *b* to tell how division is being used. Solve.

a. to find how many equal groups there are
b. to find how many are in each group

3. Ms. Clark has 27 students in her class. There are 9 computers for them to share. How many students will share each computer?

4. There are 18 students in the computer center. There are 2 students at each computer. How many computers are in the center?

5. There are 42 boys and girls signed up for basketball teams. Each team will have 7 members. How many teams will there be?

6. There are 81 cheerleaders in teams at the workshop. There are 9 cheerleaders on each team. How many teams are there?

7. Mr. Riggins has 36 books in his classroom library. Each of 4 shelves has the same number of books. How many books are on each shelf?

8. Ms. Jenkins has 28 ribbons to give to the winners of the art contest. She will give out the same number of ribbons in each of 4 classes. How many ribbons will she give out in each class?

Mixed Applications

9. There are 8 tables in the school library. There are 3 students sitting at each table. What is the total number of students sitting at the tables?

10. There were 18 students from class 4-A who made the honor roll, 14 students from class 4-B, and 16 students from class 4-C. How many students made the honor roll?

11. There are 5 more fifth graders than fourth graders in the lunchroom. There are 12 fourth graders in the lunchroom. What is the total number of fourth graders and fifth graders in the lunchroom?

12. **Write a problem** that uses the numbers 5 and 10 and that asks how many equal groups there are. Use the numbers 2 and 10 to write a problem that asks how many are in each group.

Value of a Digit

You will learn that the place-value position tells the value of each digit.	**Why learn this?** You can understand the value of numbers you use every day.

You can use base-ten blocks to help you understand the value of each digit.

Hundreds	Tens	Ones
(1 hundred block)	(1 ten block)	(1 one block)

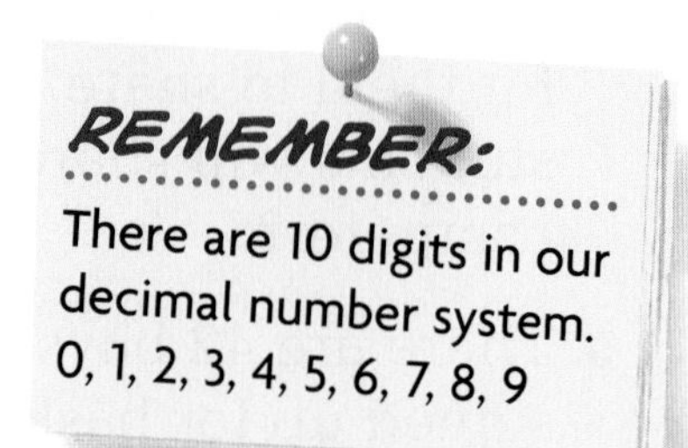

Talk About It

- How many ones are in 1 ten? in 1 hundred?
- How many tens are in 1 hundred?

Digits are used to make all numbers.

Dianne's Girl Scout troop sold 345 boxes of cookies.

How can you show 345 with base-ten blocks? What is the value of each digit?

Hundreds	Tens	Ones
3 hundreds $3 \times 100 = 300$	4 tens $4 \times 10 = 40$	5 ones $5 \times 1 = 5$

← The place-value position tells the value of each digit.

So, $345 = 300 + 40 + 5$.

Talk About It

- How would you show 789 with base-ten blocks?
- What number is $400 + 20 + 6$?

CRITICAL THINKING How can you use place value to find the value of each digit in the number 621?

History Link

The Girl Scouts organization was founded by Juliette Gordon Low in 1912. A Junior Girl Scout in grades 4-6 can earn up to 109 badges. How does place value help you understand the number 109?

PRACTICE

Write the number shown by the base-ten blocks.

1.

2.

3.

Record how many hundreds, tens, and ones.
You may wish to model with base-ten blocks.

4. 294	**5.** 168	**6.** 712	**7.** 956	**8.** 583	**9.** 347
10. 114	**11.** 369	**12.** 687	**13.** 447	**14.** 203	**15.** 850
16. 609	**17.** 821	**18.** 360	**19.** 593	**20.** 107	**21.** 424

Write the value of the blue digit.

22. 684	**23.** 276	**24.** 392	**25.** 439
26. 157	**27.** 815	**28.** 961	**29.** 748
30. 370	**31.** 141	**32.** 529	**33.** 653
34. 802	**35.** 968	**36.** 326	**37.** 421

Mixed Applications

38. Name the number that has four tens, twice as many ones as tens, and two fewer hundreds than ones.

39. There are 249 people attending the band concert. There are 45 band members. How many people are at the concert in all?

40. There are 98 people watching the Little League play-offs. There are 56 Little League players. How many people are at the play-offs?

41. There are 4 fourth-grade classes at Oaks Elementary. There are 23 students in each class. How many fourth-grade students are there?

42. Emily goes to dance class 4 days each week. Each class is 30 minutes long. For how long does Emily have dance class each week?

43. **WRITE ABOUT IT** Explain how place value helps you find the value of each digit in the number 346.

Relating Ones, Tens, and Hundreds

You will learn how multiples of 10 help you understand place value and money.

Why learn this? You can use what you know about place value to understand money amounts.

Each place-value position is ten times greater than the place to its right.

Thousands	Hundreds	Tens	Ones
$10 \times 100 = 1{,}000$	$10 \times 10 = 100$	$10 \times 1 = 10$	$1 \times 1 = 1$
1 thousand = 10 hundreds or 100 tens or 1,000 ones	1 hundred = 10 tens or 100 ones	1 ten = 10 ones	1 one

- How many ones are in 1 ten? How many tens are in 1 hundred? How many hundreds are in 1 thousand?

So, each block is ten times larger than the one to its right.

You can use what you know about place value to understand relationships among some coins and bills.

EXAMPLES

10 dollars = 100 dimes or 1,000 pennies

1 dollar = 10 dimes or 100 pennies

1 dime = 10 pennies

1 penny

Notice that

➩ each money amount is ten times greater than the one to its right.

- How many pennies equal 1 dime? How many dimes equal $1? How many one-dollar bills equal $10?

CRITICAL THINKING How are place-value and money relationships alike? How are they different?

PRACTICE

Answer each question.

1. How many [cube] in [thousands cube]?
2. How many [tens rod] in [thousands cube]?
3. How many [hundreds flat] in [thousands cube]?
4. How many [tens rod] in [hundreds flat]?
5. How many [dime] in [one-dollar bill]?
6. How many [dime] in [ten-dollar bill]?
7. How many [penny] in [one-dollar bill]?
8. How many [penny] in [ten-dollar bill]?

Write *true* or *false* for each statement. Rewrite false statements to make them true.

9. There are 10 ones in 100.
10. There are 10 hundreds in 1,000.
11. There are 10 thousands in 100.
12. There are 1,000 ones in 1,000.
13. There are 10 tens in 100.
14. There are 100 hundreds in 1,000.
15. There are 10 dimes in $1.
16. There are 100 pennies in $10.
17. There are 10 one-dollar bills in $10.
18. There are 1,000 pennies in $10.
19. There are 100 dimes in $1.
20. There are 10 dimes in $10.

Mixed Applications

21. Veronica wants to earn $100 to buy a pair of in-line skates. She is paid $10 a week to walk her neighbor's dog. How many weeks will it take her to earn $100?
22. **WRITE ABOUT IT** Tell how you would explain to a third grader how you know that 1,000 pennies equal $10.

Modeling to Compare

You will learn to model and compare numbers.

Why learn this? You can find the lowest prices when you are shopping.

Sonny and Ashley are shopping for new bicycles. Sonny found a bicycle that costs \$79. Ashley found a bicycle that costs \$89. Which bicycle costs less?

Base-ten blocks can help you model the costs.

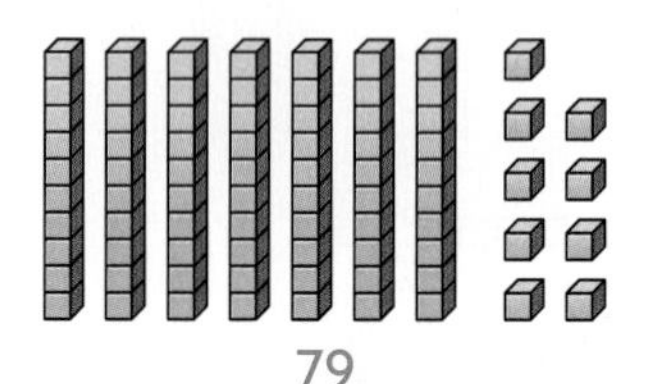

79

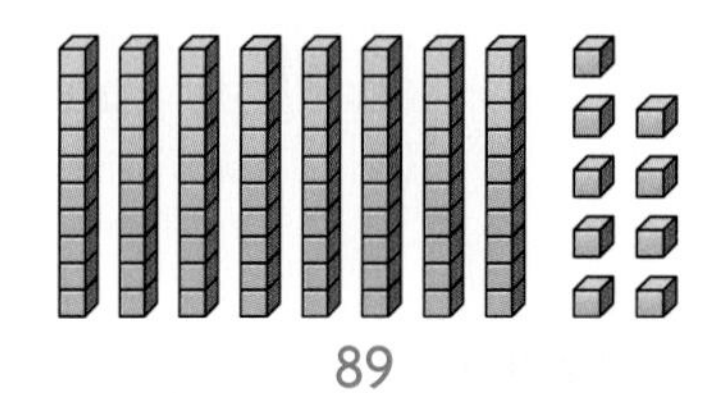

89

Notice that

- you begin comparing at the left.
- the greatest place-value position where digits are different tells you the greater number.
- the number of tens are different, and the number of ones are the same.

Compare the number of tens. Since 7 tens $<$ 8 tens, $79 < 89$.

So, the bicycle that Sonny found costs less.

REMEMBER:

$=$ means "equal to."

$>$ means "greater than."

$<$ means "less than."

The symbol points to the smaller number.

$79 < 89$

Say: seventy-nine is *less than* eighty-nine.

EXAMPLES

A.

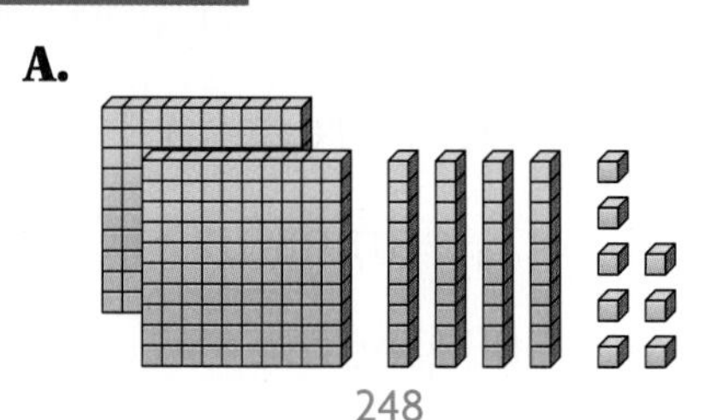

248

352

Compare the number of hundreds.
2 hundreds $<$ 3 hundreds, so $248 < 352$.

B.

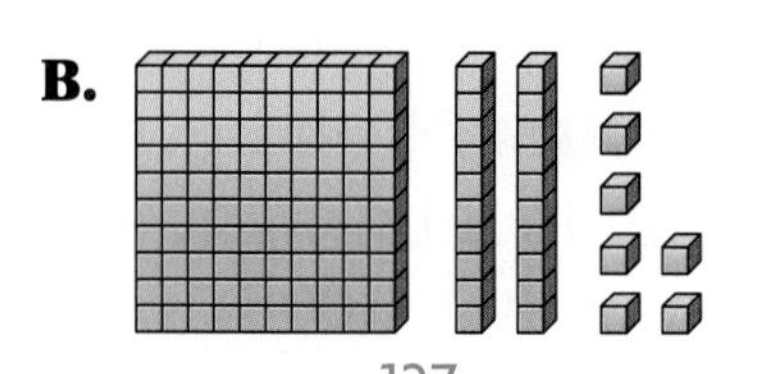

127

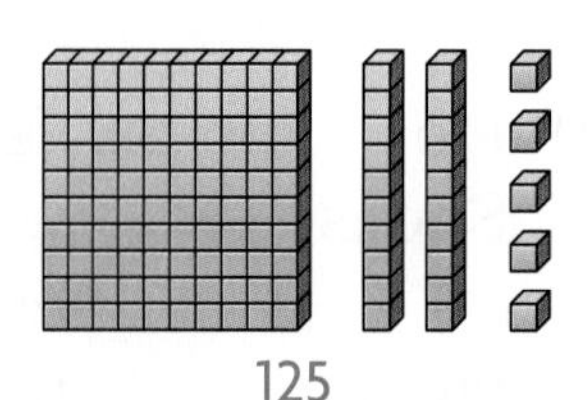

125

Compare the number of hundreds first, then the number of tens, and finally the number of ones. $7 > 5$, so $127 > 125$.

Talk About It

- For Examples A and B, in which place-value position did you find the greater number?
- How can you write the comparison in Example A using the *greater than* symbol?
- How can you write the comparison in Example B using the *less than* symbol?

PRACTICE

Write $<$ or $>$ for the ●.

1. 121 ● 111

2. 214 ● 241

Name the place-value position that tells you the greater number. Write $<$ or $>$ for the ●.

3. 23 ● 25	**4.** 52 ● 33	**5.** 16 ● 35	**6.** 68 ● 67

Compare the numbers and write $<$ or $>$ for the ●.

7. 65 ● 47	**8.** 78 ● 87	**9.** 98 ● 94	**10.** 58 ● 84
11. 284 ● 484	**12.** 215 ● 219	**13.** 131 ● 113	**14.** 651 ● 655

Mixed Applications

15. Cliff scored 371 points in the first video game he played. He scored 295 points in the second game. How many more points did he score in the first game than in the second?

16. Todd deposited $12 into his new savings account in April. He deposited $14 in May and $9 in June. His parents also deposited the same amounts into his account. How much money is in Todd's account?

17. On Friday, Amy spent 45 minutes on the telephone. On Saturday she was on the telephone for 1 hour and 10 minutes. How many more minutes was she on the telephone on Saturday?

Consumer Link

When you go shopping, you compare numbers to find the lowest prices. Which video game costs less?

Measuring Time

You will learn that the units used to measure time include minutes, hours, days, months, and years.	**Why learn this?** You can understand how the passage of time is recorded, from minutes to years.

Calendars and clocks measure time. Clocks can measure minutes and hours. Calendars can measure days, months, and years.

A. Both clocks show 23 minutes past 12 o'clock.

digital clock **analog clock**

Each day's passage of time is recorded in two 12-hour cycles on the clock.

B. These calendars show 1 month with 30 days and 1 month with 31 days.

JANUARY, FEBRUARY, MARCH, APRIL, MAY

JUNE

Sun	Mon	Tue	Wed	Thu	Fri	Sat
		1	2	3	4	5
6	7	8	9	10	11	12
13	14	15	16	17	18	19
20	21	22	23	24	25	26
27	28	29	30			

JULY, AUGUST, SEPTEMBER, OCTOBER, NOVEMBER

DECEMBER

Sun	Mon	Tue	Wed	Thu	Fri	Sat
			1	2	3	4
5	6	7	8	9	10	11
12	13	14	15	16	17	18
19	20	21	22	23	24	25
26	27	28	29	30	31	

Each year's passage of time is recorded in one 12-month cycle on the calendar.

Talk About It

- How would you show 5:05 on an analog clock?
- In Example B, on what day of the week is June 16?
- How is measuring time similar to other kinds of measuring? How is it different?

CULTURAL LINK

The Babylonians made calendars that were based on the positions of the sun, moon, and stars. The calendars were also based on the growing cycles of crops. Why was this way of measuring time important?

PRACTICE

Write *clock* or *calendar* to tell which you would use to measure each time.

1. hours spent at work in one day

2. the number of days until your birthday

3. time spent away from school in summer

4. minutes until the school bus arrives

Draw an analog clock that shows the time.

5. 3:15 **6.** 9:30 **7.** 5:45 **8.** 6:50 **9.** 1:25

10. 4:05 **11.** 11:40 **12.** 6:10 **13.** 12:35 **14.** 8:55

Write the time.

15. 

16. 

17. 

18. 

For Exercises 19–27, use the calendar.

Write the day of the week.

19. July 4 **20.** July 26 **21.** July 16

22. July 20 **23.** July 31 **24.** July 8

25. What is the date of the third Wednesday in July?

26. On what day of the week does August begin?

27. What is the date of the last Saturday in July?

JULY

Sun	Mon	Tue	Wed	Thu	Fri	Sat
1	2	3	4	5	6	7
8	9	10	11	12	13	14
15	16	17	18	19	20	21
22	23	24	25	26	27	28
29	30	31				

Mixed Applications

28. Mike's birthday is on Tuesday, July 3. Cara's birthday is July 22. On what day of the week is Cara's birthday? How many days after Mike's birthday is Cara's?

29. **Write a problem** about the calendar for July shown above.

Identifying Parts of a Graph

You will learn to name the parts of a bar graph.

Why learn this? You can read and analyze data in a bar graph to make choices.

Name the parts of the bar graph below so you can find and compare the prices of sports tickets.

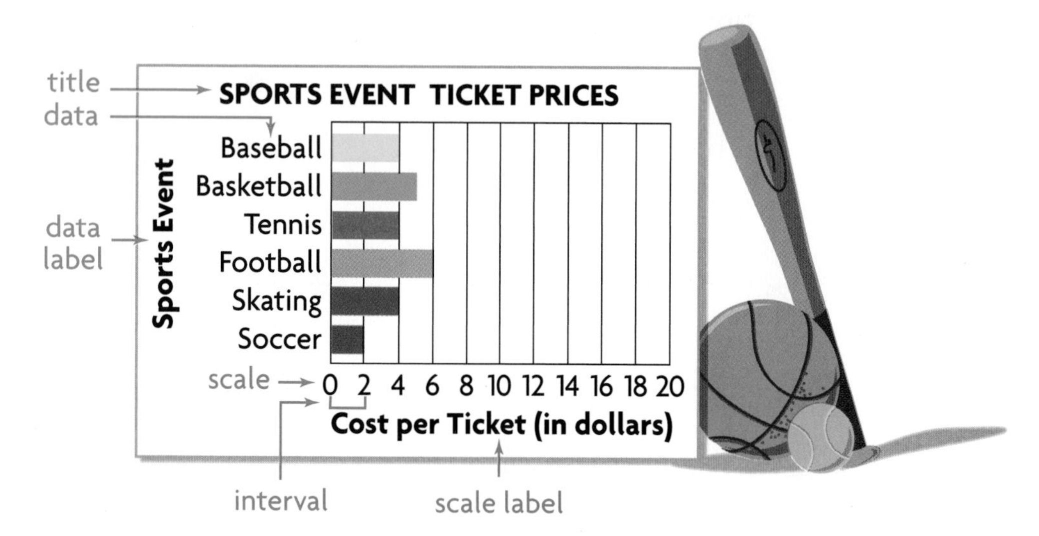

Notice that

- the *title* of the graph describes the data shown in the graph.
- the *data label* describes each item for which data are given in the graph.
- the *scale label* describes what the numbers on the scale stand for.
- each *interval* of the *scale* stands for $2.
- the bar for the basketball event ticket ends halfway between $4 and $6.

A day at the baseball game

Talk About It

- Which kind of ticket costs the least? Which costs the most?
- For which three sports events is the cost of tickets the same?
- How much more does a football ticket cost than a baseball ticket?
- How can you tell how much a basketball ticket costs?

PRACTICE

For Problems 1–7, use the bar graph about membership in school clubs.

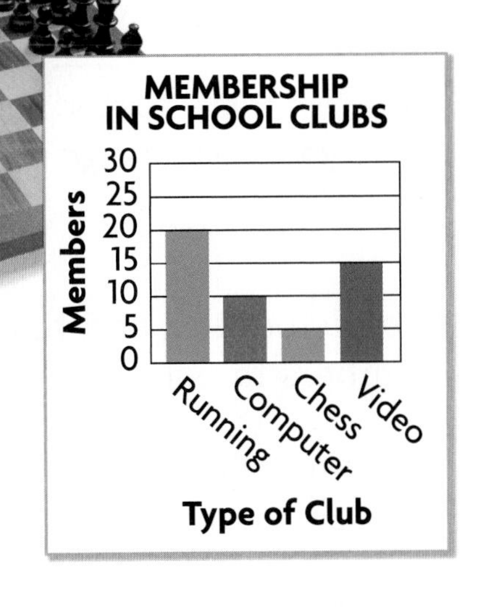

1. What is the title of the bar graph?
2. What is the data label used in the graph?
3. What do the numbers on the scale stand for?
4. What is the interval on the scale?
5. What are the kinds of clubs?
6. Which club has the most members? the fewest members?
7. What is the total number of members in all the clubs?

Mixed Applications

For Problems 8–11, use the bar graph about transportation.

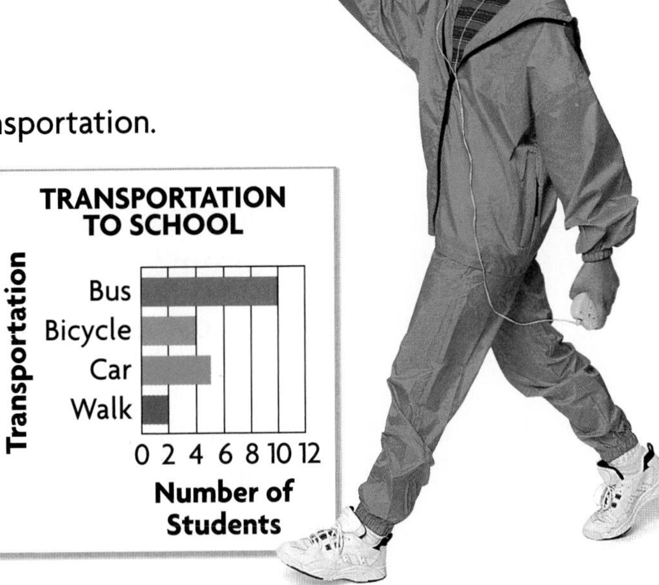

8. How many more students ride the bus than walk to school?
9. Which way of going to school is used by the most students?
10. How many students ride to school in a car?
11. How many students ride a bicycle to school?
12. The safety patrol sold 157 raffle tickets on Monday, 126 on Tuesday, and 205 on Friday. How many tickets did they sell in all?
13. There are 36 students on each of 2 school buses. There are 38 students on a third school bus. How many in all are on the 3 school buses?
14. Nick wants to buy a new bicycle that costs $119. He has saved $80. How much more money does Nick need to buy the bicycle?
15. **Write a problem** using the data from one of the bar graphs above.

Kinds of Graphs

You will learn to read and compare pictographs and bar graphs.	**Why learn this?** You can use data in graphs to find out things, such as which club has the most members.

The pictograph and bar graph show the number of members in each after-school club.

AFTER-SCHOOL CLUB MEMBERSHIP

Club	Members
Hobby Club	🧍 🧍 🧍
Writers' Club	🧍 🧍 🧍
Chess Club	🧍 🧍 🧍 ◐
Art Club	🧍 🧍 🧍 🧍
Drama Club	🧍 🧍 🧍 🧍
Science Club	🧍 🧍 🧍 🧍 🧍
Sports Club	🧍 🧍 🧍 🧍 🧍 🧍
Math Club	🧍 🧍 🧍 🧍 🧍 🧍 🧍 🧍 🧍

Key: Each 🧍 stands for 4 members.

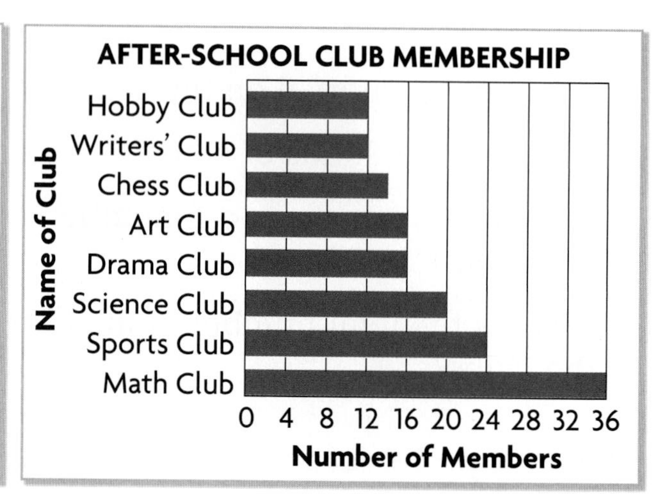

Talk About It

- How are the two kinds of graphs the same? How are they different?
- In the two graphs, how are the key and the scale related?
- How do you read the data graphed for the Chess Club in each graph?

Check Your Understanding

CRITICAL THINKING

1. Suppose each symbol in the pictograph stands for 2 members. How many symbols stand for the 36 Math Club members?
2. How would you change the scale in the bar graph to match the data in the new pictograph?
3. Would the symbols and the bars change in any way? Explain.

PRACTICE

The pictograph and bar graph below show the same data as the graphs on page H20. For Problems 4 and 5, use the graphs.

AFTER-SCHOOL CLUB MEMBERSHIP

Club	
Hobby Club	
Writers' Club	
Chess Club	
Art Club	
Drama Club	
Science Club	
Sports Club	
Math Club	

Key: Each [symbol] stands for 6 members.

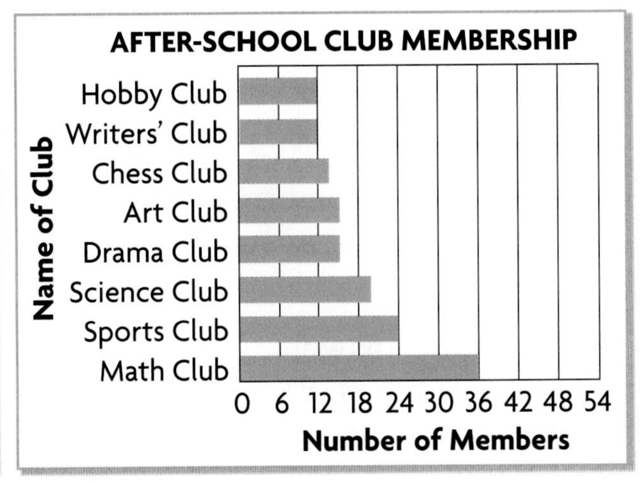

4. Describe how the graphs changed.

5. Which interval or key makes the data easier to read: 2, 4, or 6? Explain.

Mixed Applications

For Problems 6–7 and 13, use the bar graph at the right.

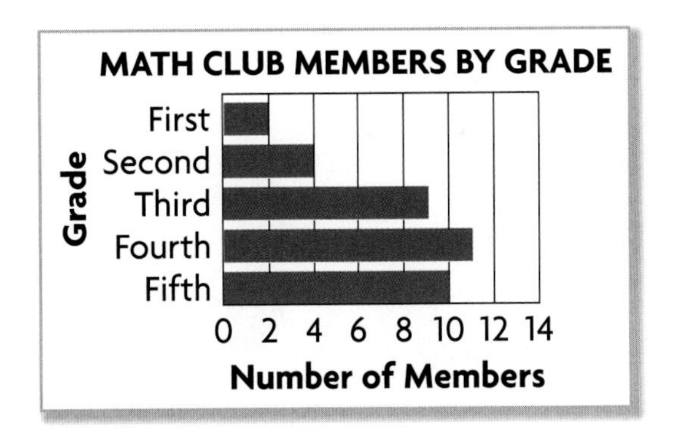

6. If you made a pictograph of these data, what key would you use?

7. How many symbols would stand for the fourth-grade members?

8. The Drama Club is putting on a play that is 1 hour and 45 minutes long. If the play begins at 7:30 P.M., at what time will it end?

9. Each of the 12 members of the Writers' Club wrote 3 short stories for a book. How many short stories did they write?

10. Sue is making a pictograph with a key in which each symbol stands for 5 students. How many symbols stand for 20 students? 25 students?

11. Beth and Ron played a number game. Beth picked a number and subtracted 5. Then, she added 8. Last, she subtracted 12. The answer was 31. What number did Beth choose?

12. Mickey bought a CD for $16.95. He gave the clerk a $20 bill. How much change did Mickey get?

13. **Write a problem** about the *Math Club Members by Grade* bar graph.

Possible Outcomes

You will learn to decide about all possible outcomes of events.

Why learn this? You can see how events, such as the weather, have certain possible outcomes.

Mrs. Foley asked her class to name all the possible kinds of weather they might have tomorrow. She listed the students' answers on the board.

The students' answers were all *possible outcomes*. Each kind of weather would be an event that could happen.

- Name a situation or an event and its possible outcomes.

Each of these events has one or more possible outcomes.

tossing a coin

rolling a number cube

spinning the pointer on a spinner

pulling a marble from a bag

Talk About It

- What are the possible outcomes of tossing a coin?
- What are the possible outcomes of rolling a number cube with numbers 1–6?
- What are the possible outcomes of spinning the pointer on the spinner above?
- What are the possible outcomes of pulling a marble from the bag above?

PRACTICE

List the possible outcomes of each event.

1. getting a grade on a math test

2. playing checkers against a computer

3. rolling a number cube with all even numbers less than 14

4. pulling a coin out of a bag of different coins

5. dropping a thumbtack and watching it land

6. tossing two coins

7.

pulling a marble from this bag

8.

tossing this two-color counter

9.

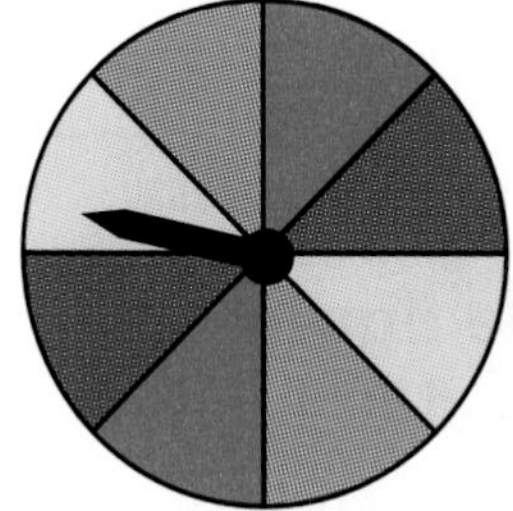

spinning the pointer on this spinner

Mixed Applications

10. Five students are waiting to use the computer. Morgan is before Kerry. Ben is between Allen and Kerry. Tim is first, and Allen is last. In what order will the students use the computer?

11. Thalia is taking a survey to find out if her classmates have pets at home. What are the possible outcomes of her survey?

12. There are 50 dimes in a roll. How many dimes does Terry have if she has 8 rolls? How much money is that?

13. Earl flips the light switch in his bedroom. What are the possible outcomes of his action?

14. Melissa started her homework at 4:30. She spent 35 minutes on it. Then she talked on the telephone for 15 minutes. After that she played a computer game for 25 minutes until she was called for dinner. At what time did Melissa have dinner?

15. **Write a problem** about possible outcomes, using this grid.

2	7	8
5	1	5
7	4	7

Characteristics of Plane Figures

You will learn the difference between open and closed figures in a plane.

Why learn this? You can read a map or draw a diagram of a fence for a pet.

WORD POWER
closed figure
open figure
plane figure

Shapes that begin and end at the same point are **closed figures**. **Open figures** do not begin and end at the same point.

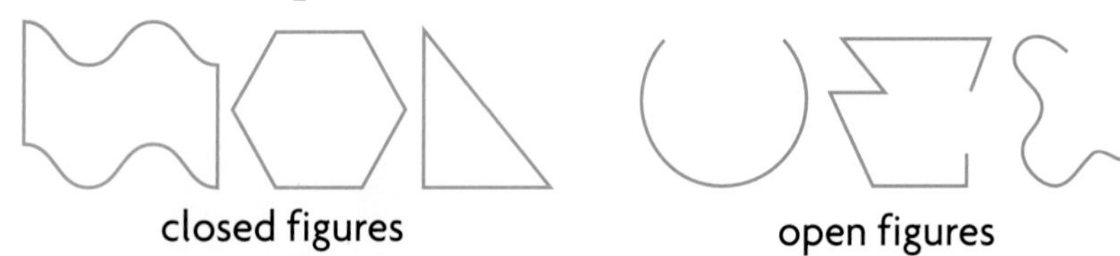

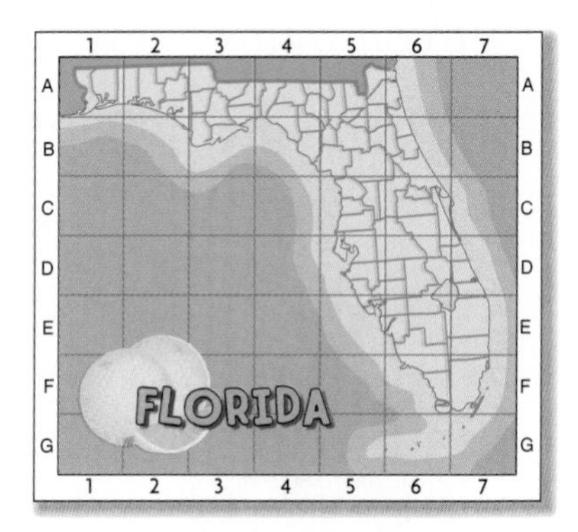

Counties on this map are closed figures.

A **plane figure** is flat and is all in one plane. It can be closed or open. Which figures below are closed? Which are open?

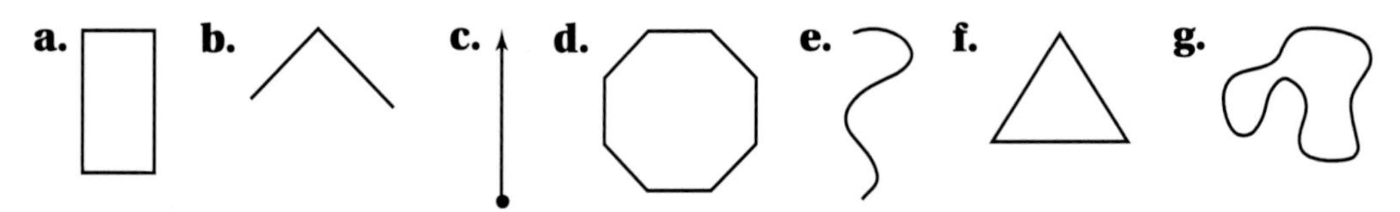

So, **a, d, f,** and **g** are closed figures; **b, c,** and **e** are open figures.

- When is a fenced yard like a closed figure? an open figure?

There are three kinds of closed plane figures.

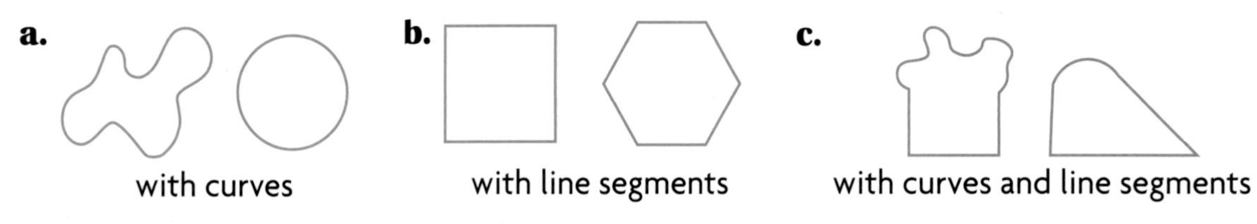

Talk About It

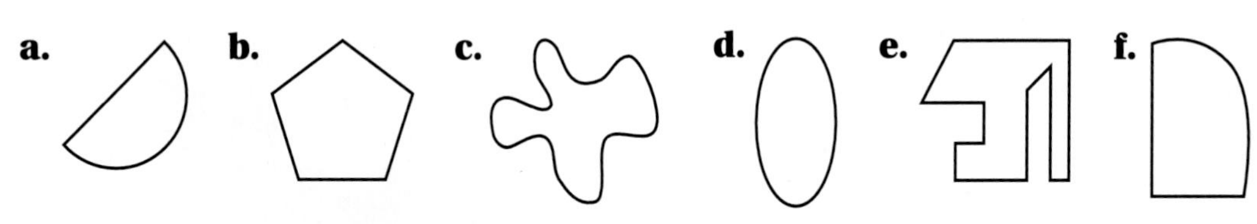

- Which kind of closed plane figure is each?
- How are figures **b** and **f** alike? How are they different?

PRACTICE

Write *open* or *closed* to describe each figure.

1. 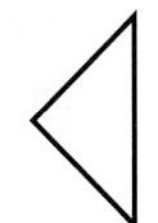

2. 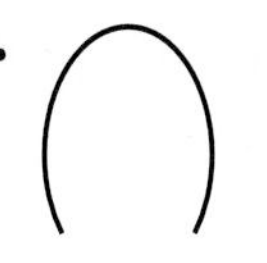

3. 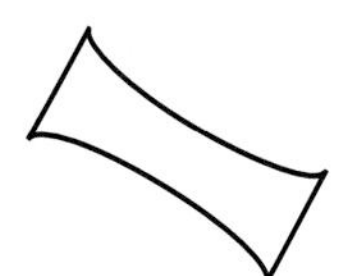

4. 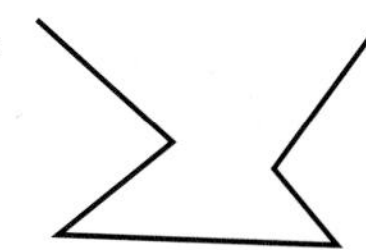

5. 

6. 

7. 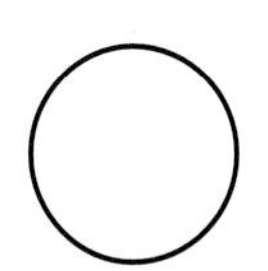

8. 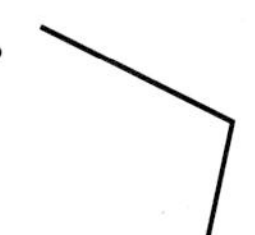

Which kind of closed plane figure is each? Write *with curves, with line segments,* or *with curves and line segments.*

9. 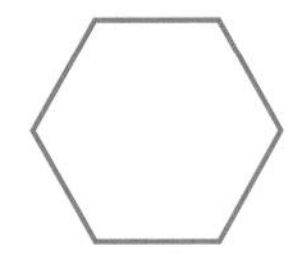

10. 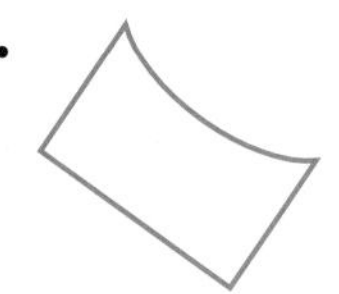

11. 

12. 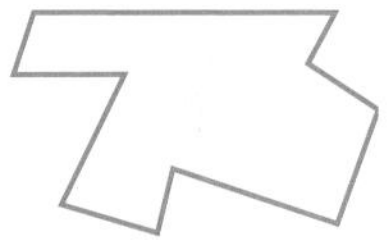

13. 

14. 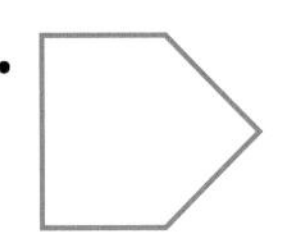

15. 

16. 

Mixed Applications

17. Belinda is drawing Lake Michigan on her map. Since it connects to Lake Huron, should she draw the lake as a closed or an open figure? Explain.

18. Imagine that you are walking around the block. How many right-hand turns do you have to make to return to where you started? Draw a picture to show your answer.

19. David collected 58 insects for a science project. He needs a total of 100 insects. How many more does he need?

20. **WRITE ABOUT IT** Francisco is looking at a map that shows the county lines of his state. Is each county shown as an open or a closed figure? Explain.

Social Studies Link

People who make maps can find distances quickly. They use tools that tell how long it takes light or radio waves to move between two points.

How can you find the distance between two points on the map?

Multiplication Facts

You will learn that there are several ways to recall the multiplication facts.

Why learn this? You can use the multiplication facts to find totals. For example, you can find how many postage stamps are in a book.

You can use different methods to help you learn multiplication facts.

Skip Counting on a Number Line

Counting by twos and fives can help you remember some facts.

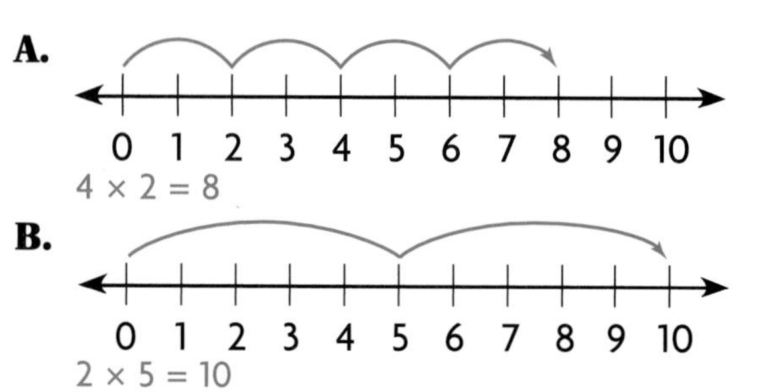

- Why is skip counting by twos and fives the same as multiplying by twos and fives?

Patterns

Discovering patterns can help you recall multiplication facts.

Facts of Nine
$9 \times 1 = 9$
$9 \times 2 = 18$
$9 \times 3 = 27$
$9 \times 4 = 36$
$9 \times 5 = 45$
$9 \times 6 = 54$
$9 \times 7 = 63$
$9 \times 8 = 72$
$9 \times 9 = 81$
$9 \times 10 = ?$

- What pattern do you see in the ones place of the products? in the tens place of the products?
- Add the digits in each product. What pattern do you see in the sums?
- How can you use patterns to find 9×10?

Order Property

Factors can be multiplied in any order. Their product will be the same.

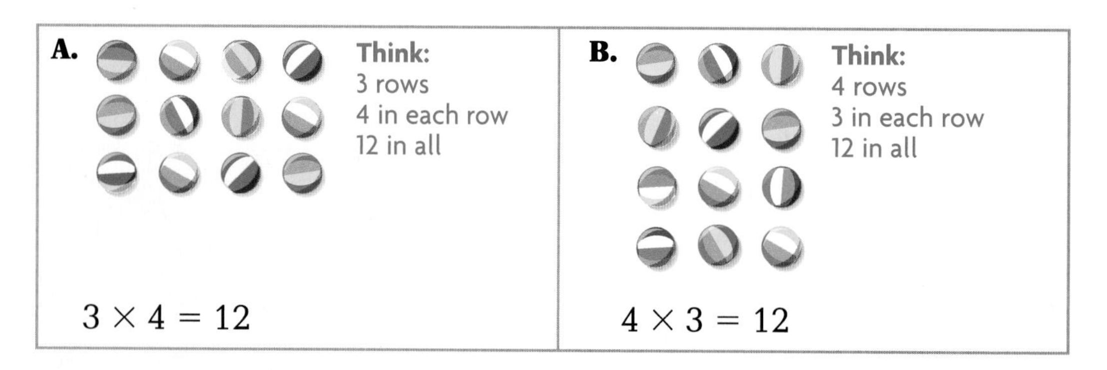

- If you know that $8 \times 3 = 24$, how does the Order Property of Multiplication help you find the product 3×8?

PRACTICE

Use the number line to find the product.

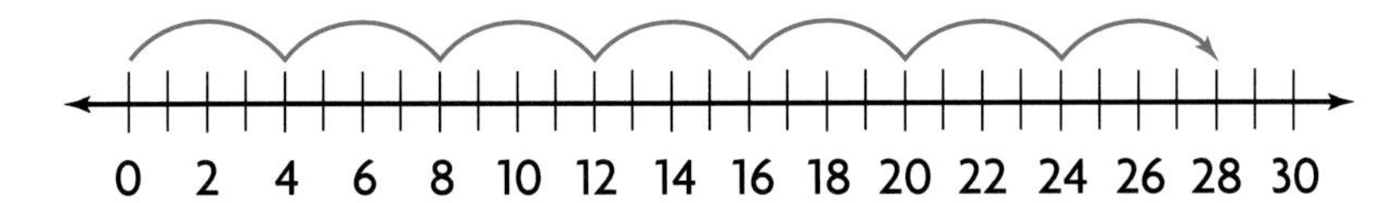

1. $7 \times 4 =$ ___?___

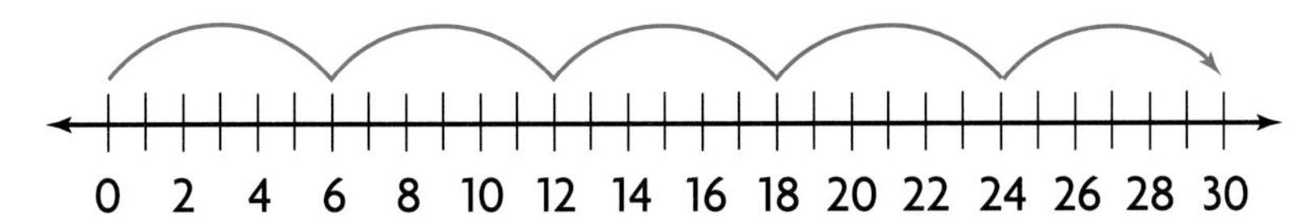

2. $5 \times 6 =$ ___?___

Use what you know about the Order Property to solve.

3. $4 \times 6 = 24$
$6 \times 4 =$ ___?___

4. $6 \times 8 =$ ___?___
$8 \times 6 = 48$

5. $8 \times 4 =$ ___?___
$4 \times 8 = 32$

6. $3 \times 5 =$ ___?___
$5 \times 3 =$ ___?___

7. $7 \times 9 =$ ___?___
$9 \times 7 =$ ___?___

Use the patterns in the facts of 9 to find the product.

8. $3 \times 9 =$ ___?___

9. $9 \times 9 =$ ___?___

10. $8 \times 9 =$ ___?___

11. $4 \times 9 =$ ___?___

12. $5 \times 9 =$ ___?___

13. $6 \times 9 =$ ___?___

Mixed Applications

14. Each of 4 students finished 2 math worksheets a day for one school week. How many did the students finish that week?

15. Alex has 3 boxes with 6 tennis balls in each. Ivan has 6 cans with 3 tennis balls in each. Who has more tennis balls? Explain.

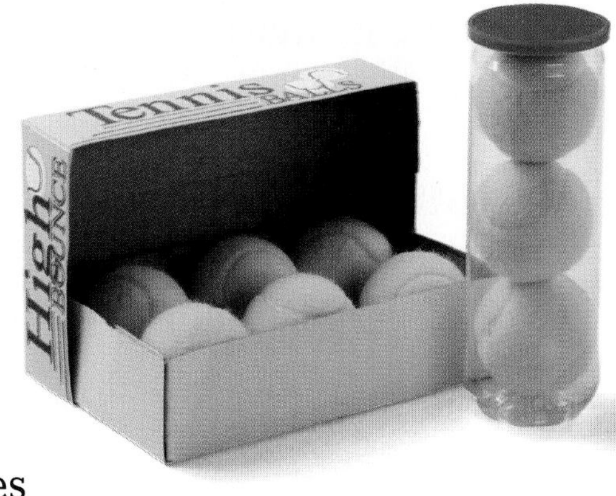

16. Lesli bought 4 packages of cups and 3 packages of plates for her class party. There were 8 cups in each package and 10 plates in each package. How many cups and plates did she buy in all?

Division Facts

You will learn that there are several ways to recall division facts.	Why learn this? You can quickly find how many in each group or how many groups.

Equal Groups

When you make equal groups, you divide. Place 1 counter in each circle. Do this until all the counters are placed equally in the 3 circles.

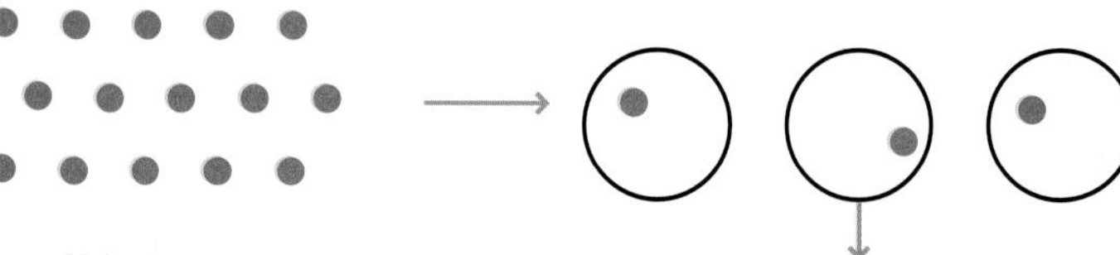

18 ÷ 3 = ?

So, 18 ÷ 3 = 6.

- How many counters are there in all? How many groups?
- How many counters are in each group?

Repeated Subtraction

Subtraction can help you understand division.

Divide. 20 ÷ 4 = ?

Start at 20 and subtract 4 until you reach 0.

$$\begin{array}{r} 20 \\ -\ 4 \\ \hline 16 \end{array} \quad \begin{array}{r} 16 \\ -\ 4 \\ \hline 12 \end{array} \quad \begin{array}{r} 12 \\ -\ 4 \\ \hline 8 \end{array} \quad \begin{array}{r} 8 \\ -4 \\ \hline 4 \end{array} \quad \begin{array}{r} 4 \\ -4 \\ \hline 0 \end{array}$$

You can subtract 4 from 20 five times.

So, 20 ÷ 4 = 5.

- Why is division called repeated subtraction?

Multiplication Facts

Since division is the inverse of multiplication, you can use multiplication facts to find quotients.

Find the missing factor.

12 ÷ 4 = ?

So, 12 ÷ 4 = 3. Think: 4 × ? = 12
4 × 3 = 12

CRITICAL THINKING How can you use multiplication facts to help you divide?

REMEMBER:

You can use the basic multiplication facts to find quotients because division is the inverse of multiplication. One operation undoes the other.

PRACTICE

Draw a model to find the number of equal groups.

1. $12 \div 3 =$? **2.** $15 \div 5 =$? **3.** $24 \div 4 =$? **4.** $18 \div 6 =$?

5. $48 \div 8 =$? **6.** $63 \div 9 =$? **7.** $16 \div 4 =$? **8.** $54 \div 6 =$?

Use repeated subtraction to divide.

9. $36 \div 4 =$? **10.** $42 \div 6 =$? **11.** $20 \div 5 =$? **12.** $27 \div 9 =$?

13. $14 \div 2 =$? **14.** $30 \div 5 =$? **15.** $40 \div 8 =$? **16.** $25 \div 5 =$?

Write the multiplication fact used to find the quotient.

17. $32 \div 8 =$? **18.** $36 \div 6 =$? **19.** $40 \div 5 =$? **20.** $28 \div 4 =$?

21. $45 \div 9 =$? **22.** $56 \div 7 =$? **23.** $49 \div 7 =$? **24.** $72 \div 8 =$?

Mixed Applications

25. Ms. James is placing her 15 students into 3 equal groups. Draw a model to show how many students will be in each group.

26. Mark is using repeated subtraction to divide the number 18. If he subtracts 6 each time, how many times does he subtract?

27. Willie is dividing 64 pencils into groups. He wants to put an equal number in each box. He has 8 boxes. How many pencils can he put in each box?

28. There are 24 students and 3 tables in the art class of Bayview School. How many students can sit at each table?

29. There are 6 students in each of the 4 relay teams in Mrs. Miller's class. How many students are in Mrs. Miller's class?

30. Mrs. Martin needs 24 paintbrushes. A package of 8 brushes costs $2.95. How much will Mrs. Martin spend on paintbrushes?

31. **WRITE ABOUT IT** Explain three ways Eric can find the quotient $30 \div 5$.

Adding and Subtracting Money

You will learn that you can add and subtract money amounts like whole numbers.	**Why learn this?** You can find out how much money you will need to purchase something, or how much change you will receive.

Anthony bought one cassette tape for $4.98, a second for $5.98, and a third for $4.69. How much did Anthony spend?

Add.

$$\begin{array}{r} {}^{2\,2}\\ \$4.98 \\ 5.98 \\ +\ 4.69 \\ \hline \$15.65 \end{array}$$

dollar sign → $15.65 ← decimal point

Add money amounts the same as whole numbers. A decimal point separates dollars and cents. Place the dollar sign and decimal point in the sum.

So, Anthony spent $15.65 for his cassettes.

Sharon bought some tennis balls on sale for $2.79. She paid $5.00. How much change will she receive?

Subtract.

$$\begin{array}{r} 4\ \ \ 9\ \ \ \\ 4\ \ 10\,10 \\ \$\not{5}\,.\,\not{0}\,\not{0} \\ -\ 2\,.\,7\,9 \\ \hline \$2\,.\,2\,1 \end{array}$$

dollar sign → $2.21 ← decimal point

Subtract money amounts as you subtract whole numbers. A decimal point separates dollars and cents. Place the dollar sign and decimal point in the difference.

So, Sharon will receive $2.21 in change.

Talk About It

- How is adding and subtracting money amounts the same as adding and subtracting whole numbers? How is it different?
- How is the placement of the dollar sign and the decimal point different?
- How would you regroup $3.00 to subtract $0.79?

Consumer Link

In 1996, the average price for a candy bar, in United States currency, was $1.06 in Japan, $0.45 in Germany, $0.35 in the United Kingdom, $0.45 in Mexico, and $0.48 in the United States. How much do 2 candy bars cost in each of these countries?

PRACTICE

Find the sum.

1. $\begin{array}{r} \$4.09 \\ 2.98 \\ +\ 3.11 \\ \hline \end{array}$

2. $\begin{array}{r} \$7.12 \\ +\ 3.22 \\ \hline \end{array}$

3. $\begin{array}{r} \$9.78 \\ 0.85 \\ +\ 6.17 \\ \hline \end{array}$

4. $\begin{array}{r} \$2.88 \\ 9.14 \\ +\ 3.74 \\ \hline \end{array}$

5. $\begin{array}{r} \$8.19 \\ 3.48 \\ +\ 7.47 \\ \hline \end{array}$

Find the difference.

6. $\begin{array}{r} \$4.76 \\ -\ 1.25 \\ \hline \end{array}$

7. $\begin{array}{r} \$7.09 \\ -\ 6.18 \\ \hline \end{array}$

8. $\begin{array}{r} \$5.26 \\ -\ 2.17 \\ \hline \end{array}$

9. $\begin{array}{r} \$6.00 \\ -\ 3.16 \\ \hline \end{array}$

10. $\begin{array}{r} \$2.45 \\ -\ 1.37 \\ \hline \end{array}$

Find the sum or difference.

11. $\begin{array}{r} \$6.78 \\ +\ 2.49 \\ \hline \end{array}$

12. $\begin{array}{r} \$5.97 \\ -\ 3.29 \\ \hline \end{array}$

13. $\begin{array}{r} \$8.21 \\ 1.81 \\ +\ 0.16 \\ \hline \end{array}$

14. $\begin{array}{r} \$1.99 \\ +\ 9.11 \\ \hline \end{array}$

15. $\begin{array}{r} \$9.00 \\ -\ 5.43 \\ \hline \end{array}$

Mixed Applications

16. Kendel and Josh went to the park at 2:15 P.M. to play basketball. They played basketball for 1 hour and 35 minutes. At what time did Kendel and Josh finish playing basketball?

17. Trisha paid $3.75 for a ticket to the movie. She bought a box of popcorn for $1.50 and pretzels for $0.89. How much change did she receive from $10.00?

18. The Brady family went to Ruby's Restaurant. John and Nancy ordered steak dinners. Lois ordered a super salad, and Frank ordered a chicken platter. How much did the Brady family spend for dinner?

19. Ms. Brown bought a dozen apples. Sam and Julie each ate two of the apples. What fraction shows how many of the apples were eaten? What fraction shows how many apples are left?

20. **Write a problem** about a time when you used decimal numbers to add or subtract.

Estimate and Measure

You will learn to estimate length and to check your estimate by measuring to the nearest inch.

Why learn this? You will be able to look at an object and estimate its length close to the exact measurement.

An estimate is an answer that is close to an exact answer. Estimate the length of each object in the picture. Make a table like the one below, and record your estimates.

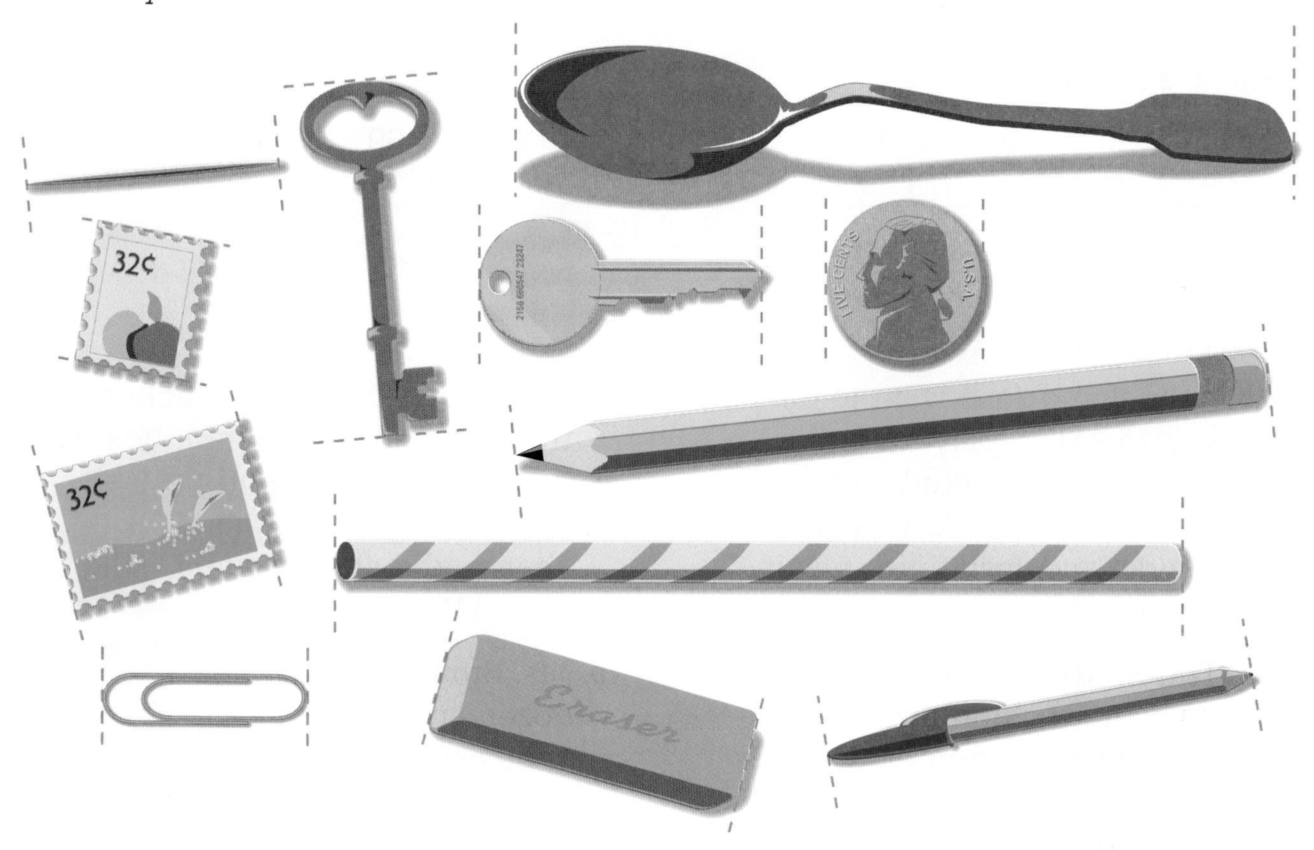

- How did you estimate the lengths of the objects?

____

Object	Estimate	Measurement
pencil		
pen		
toothpick		
paper clip		
spoon		
straw		

Now, use a ruler to measure the length of each object to the nearest inch. Record the measurements in the table.

- How do your estimates compare with your measurements? Give examples.

PRACTICE

Choose the best estimate for each object.

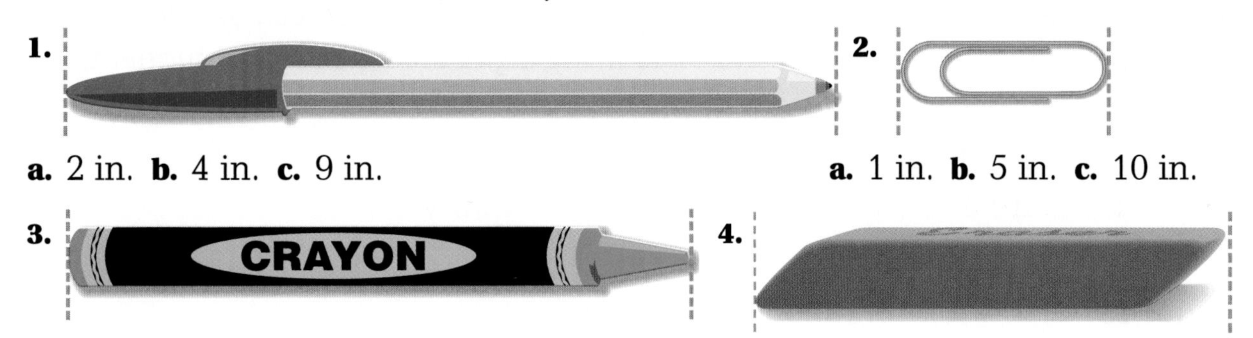

1. **a.** 2 in. **b.** 4 in. **c.** 9 in.

2. **a.** 1 in. **b.** 5 in. **c.** 10 in.

3. **a.** 2 in. **b.** 3 in. **c.** 7 in.

4. **a.** 3 in. **b.** 5 in. **c.** 1 in.

Estimate the length. Then use a ruler to measure to the nearest inch.

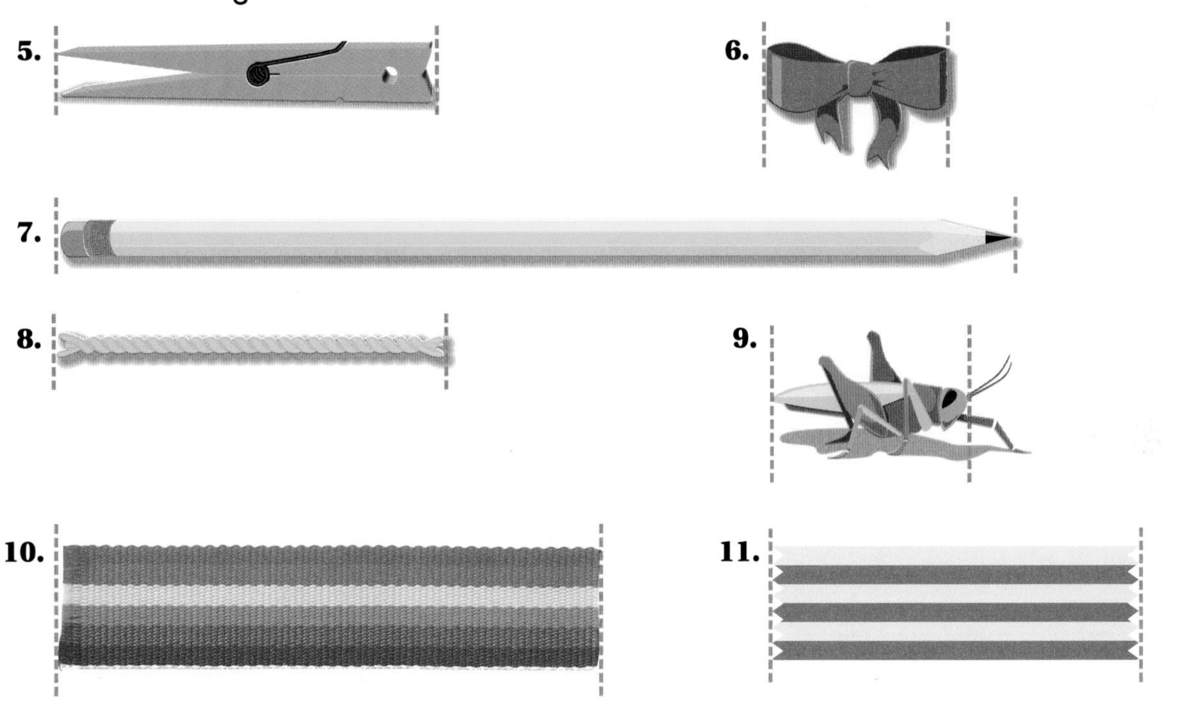

5.

6.

7.

8.

9.

10.

11.

Mixed Applications

12. Pete estimates that the perimeter of one of his school pictures is about 20 in. What could be the length and width of the picture?

13. Meg wants to cover her math book. She estimates that each side is 4 in. wide. Has Meg made a good estimate? Explain.

14. Without using a ruler, draw a line segment that you estimate to be 3 inches long. Measure your line segment. Then write the difference between your estimate and a 3-inch line segment.

15. **WRITE ABOUT IT** Why is estimation important in measurement?

Placing the First Digit

You will learn how to place the first digit in the quotient.

Why learn this? You can decide how many digits should be in the quotient.

The town library donated 157 books to the fourth grade. There are 4 fourth-grade classes. How many books did each class receive?

Divide. $157 \div 4 = n$ $\quad 4\overline{)157}$

Estimate. $160 \div 4 = 40$ **Think:** $4 \times 4 = 16$

MODEL

What is $157 \div 4$?

Step 1

Decide where to place the first digit in the quotient.

no $\quad 4\overline{)157}$ with x over the 1 — You *cannot* divide 1 by 4. There are not enough hundreds.

yes $\quad 4\overline{)157}$ with x■ over the 15 — You *can* divide 15 by 4. There are enough tens.

So, place the first digit in the tens place.

Step 2

Divide the tens. $4\overline{)15}$

Think: $4 \times n = 12$

$$\begin{array}{r} 3 \\ 4\overline{)157} \\ -12 \\ \hline 3 \end{array}$$

Multiply. 4×3
Subtract. $15 - 12$
Compare. $3 < 4$

Step 3

Bring down the ones.

Divide. $4\overline{)37}$

Think: $4 \times n = 36$

$$\begin{array}{r} 39 \text{ r1} \\ 4\overline{)157}\phantom{\text{ r1}} \\ -12\phantom{\text{ r1}} \\ \hline 37\phantom{\text{ r1}} \\ -36\phantom{\text{ r1}} \\ \hline 1\phantom{\text{ r1}} \end{array}$$

Multiply. 4×9
Subtract. $37 - 36$
Compare. $1 < 4$

Write the remainder next to the quotient.

So, each class will receive 39 books. There will be 1 book left over.

The library is a quiet place to do work.

Talk About It

- How can you decide where to place the first digit in the quotient?
- Why is it necessary to compare the remainder to the divisor?
- Where would you place the first digit in the quotient if the dividend was 857 and the divisor was 4? Explain.

PRACTICE

Copy each problem. Draw a box where the first digit in the quotient should be placed.

1. $6\overline{)195}$ **2.** $8\overline{)329}$ **3.** $2\overline{)407}$ **4.** $5\overline{)653}$ **5.** $3\overline{)287}$

6. $7\overline{)856}$ **7.** $4\overline{)932}$ **8.** $6\overline{)721}$ **9.** $5\overline{)487}$ **10.** $4\overline{)672}$

11. $9\overline{)901}$ **12.** $2\overline{)105}$ **13.** $8\overline{)982}$ **14.** $3\overline{)522}$ **15.** $7\overline{)800}$

Find the quotient.

16. $4\overline{)179}$ **17.** $7\overline{)810}$ **18.** $6\overline{)139}$ **19.** $8\overline{)658}$

20. $5\overline{)327}$ **21.** $9\overline{)222}$ **22.** $3\overline{)497}$ **23.** $6\overline{)545}$

24. $268 \div 3 = n$ **25.** $906 \div 5 = n$ **26.** $137 \div 2 = n$ **27.** $285 \div 9 = n$

28. $396 \div 5 = n$ **29.** $716 \div 7 = n$ **30.** $329 \div 6 = n$ **31.** $862 \div 9 = n$

Mixed Applications

32. There were 6 classes at the library on Monday. The 6 classes checked out 192 books in all. Each class checked out the same number of books. How many books did each class check out?

33. Elizabeth has 250 books to stack on 4 library shelves. The same number of books will fit on each shelf. How many books will be on each shelf? How many books will be left over?

34. A spinner is divided into 8 equal sections numbered 1–8. Warren gets a point if the pointer lands on an odd number. Joanne gets a point if it lands on an even number. Is this fair? Explain.

35. Dolores painted a picture on a piece of paper that was 11 inches long and 17 inches wide. What are the perimeter and area of Dolores's picture?

36. Caroline read 8 books in each month from September through December. Donald read 5 books each month during the same months. How many books did each one read? How many more books did Caroline read than Donald?

37. **Write a problem** using 186 as the dividend and 3 as the divisor.

Finding Volume

You will learn to find volume of a three-dimensional figure.

Why learn this? You can find how much a box will hold.

Volume is the measure of the space a solid figure occupies.

Find the volume of this rectangular prism in cubic units.

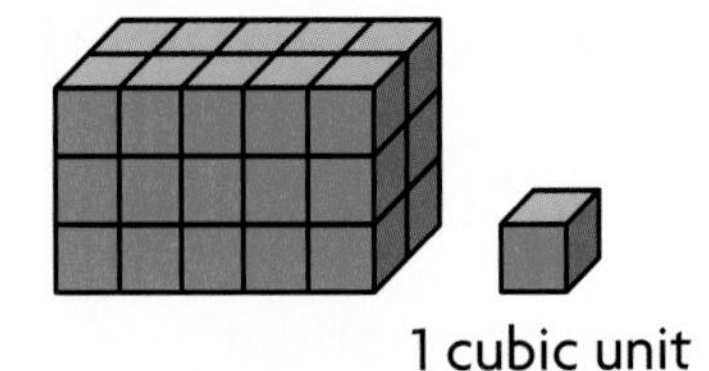

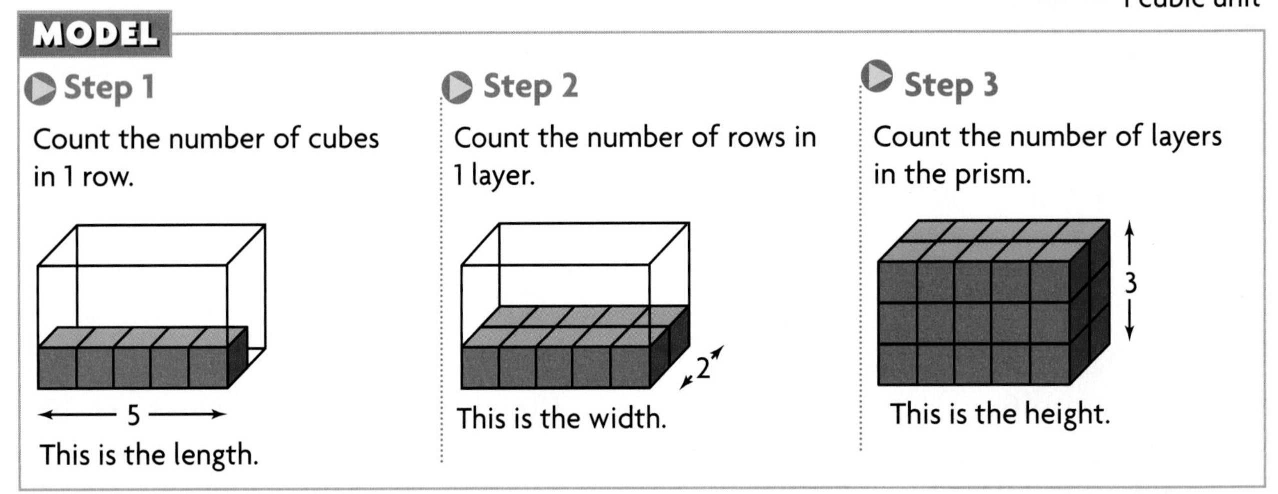

Talk About It

- How many cubes are in 1 row?
- How many rows are in 1 layer?
- How many layers of cubes are there?
- How many cubes did it take to make the prism?

FINDING VOLUME			
Length	**Width**	**Height**	**Volume**
5 cubes	2 cubes	3 cubes	? cubic units

So, the volume of the rectangular prism is 30 cubic units.

Besides counting, you can use multiplication to find the volume of a rectangular prism. Multiply length $\times$ width $\times$ height.

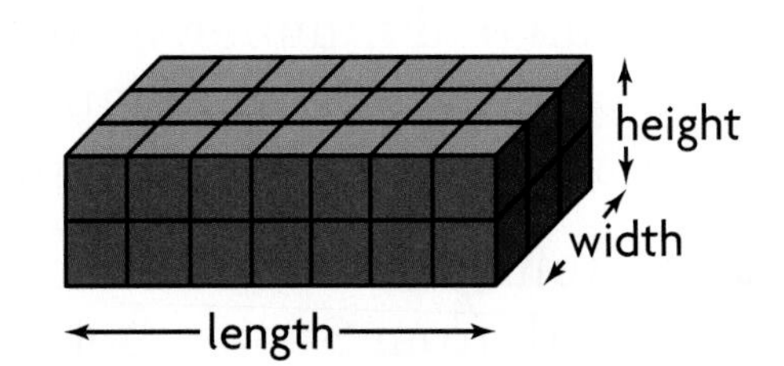

You can use a calculator.

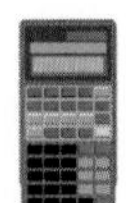

Press: 7 × 3 × 2 =   42.

So, volume = 42 cubic units.

- What are the dimensions that are multiplied to find the volume of a rectangular prism?

PRACTICE

Count or multiply to find the volume.

1. 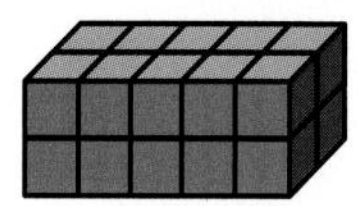

2. 

3. 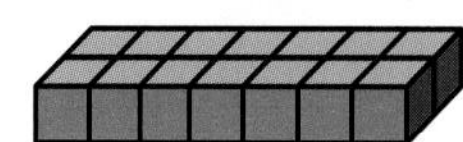

4. 

5. 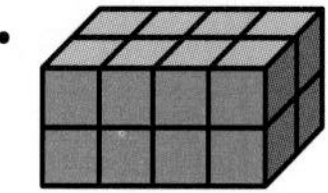

6. 

7. 

8. 

9. 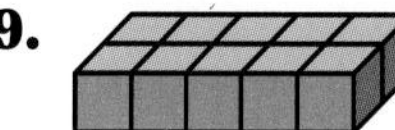

Which figure has the greatest volume?

10. **a.** 

b. 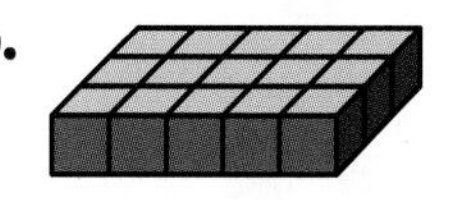

c. 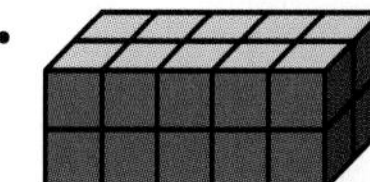

Copy and complete the table. You may use a calculator.

	MEASURING VOLUME			
	Length	**Width**	**Height**	**Volume**
11.	5 cm	3 cm	2 cm	?
12.	4 in.	6 in.	2 in.	?
13.	3 ft	3 ft	10 ft	?
14.	3 yd	7 yd	2 yd	?

Applications

You may use a calculator for Problems 15–17.

15. Julio's briefcase is 14 inches long, 10 inches wide, and 3 inches high. What is the volume of the briefcase?

16. The volume of a packing carton is 40 cubic feet. If the carton is 2 feet long and 4 feet high, how wide is it?

17. A storage room is 12 feet by 10 feet by 8 feet. What is the volume of the room?

18. **WRITE ABOUT IT** Explain to a third-grade student how to find the volume of a rectangular prism.

Making Equal Areas

You will learn that different figures can have the same areas.	**Why learn this?** You will understand that a given area can be shown in many different ways.

Use the methods you have learned to find the area of the shaded part of each figure.

a. 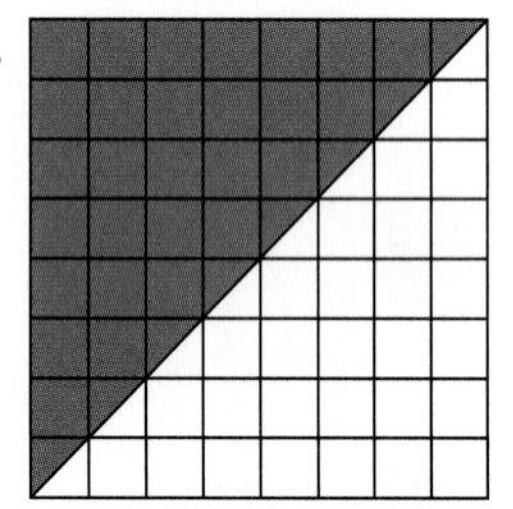

b. 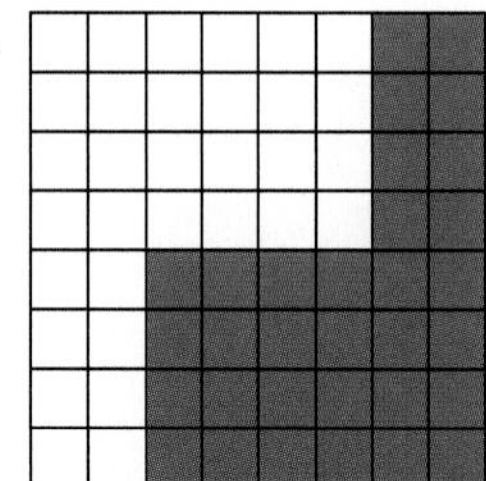

c. 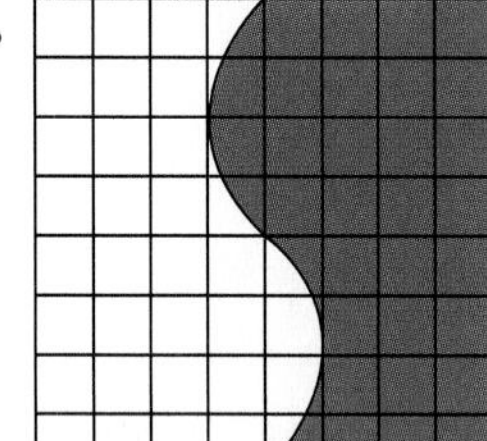

d. 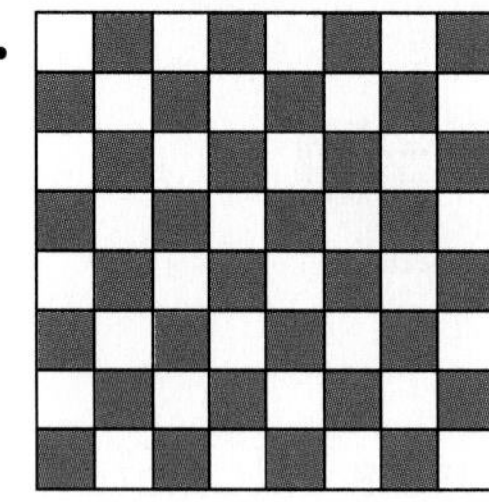

Consumer Link

Which carpet costs more? Explain.

Talk About It

- What is alike about each figure? What is different?
- How does the shaded figure compare to the unshaded figure in each square?

Check Your Understanding

MATERIALS: grid paper

Divide each grid into two figures that will cover equal areas. Shade one of the figures.

1. How many different ways can you show two equal areas on a grid?
2. How can you check each grid to see if the two figures cover equal areas?

PRACTICE

Draw each shaded area in at least four other ways. Use grid paper.

3. 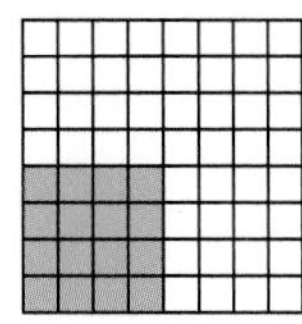

4. 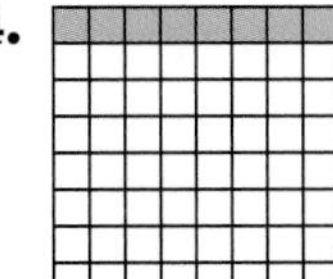

5. 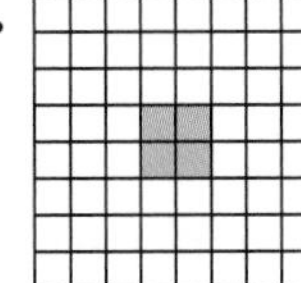

6. 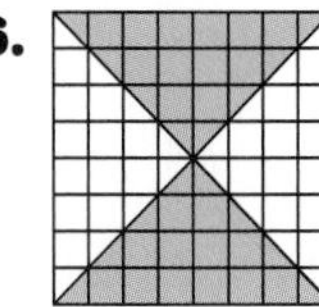

Find the area of each shaded figure. Write the letter of each shaded figure that covers the same area as the first figure.

7. 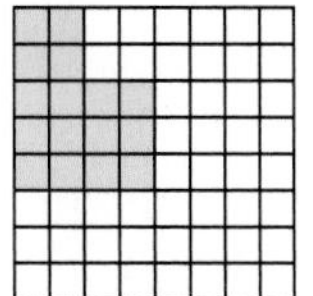
a. 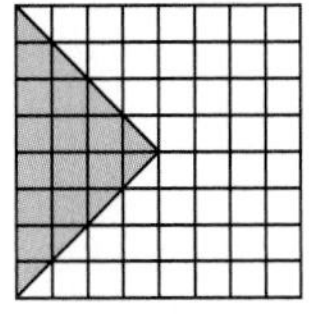
b. 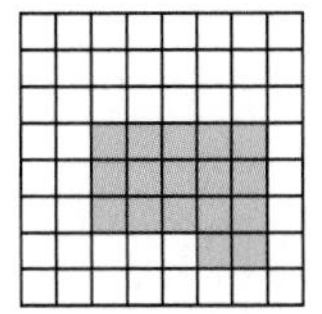
c. 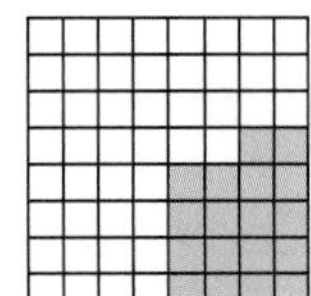
d. 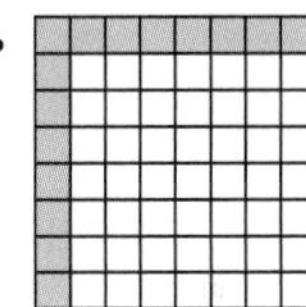

8. 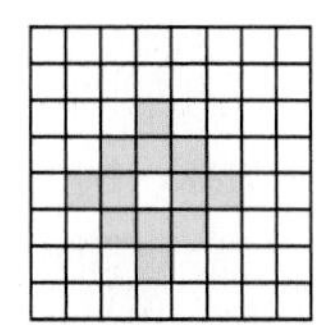
a. 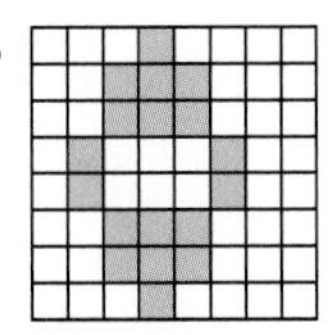
b. 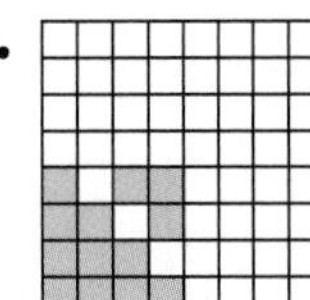
c. 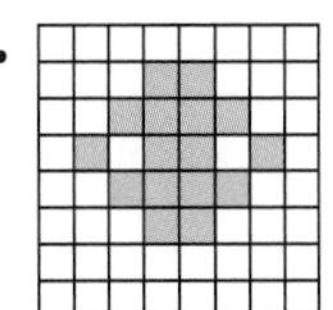
d. 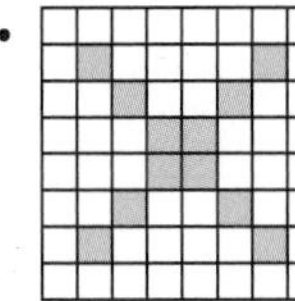

9. 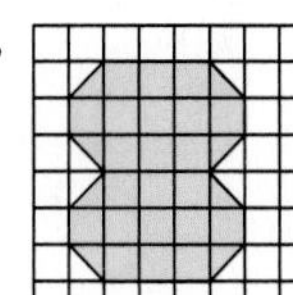
a. 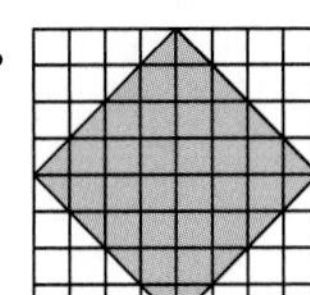
b. 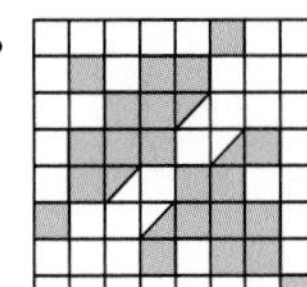
c. 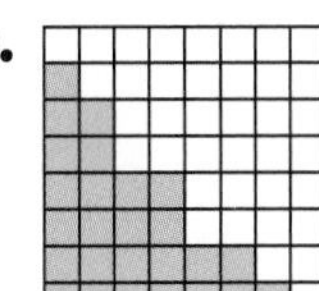
d. 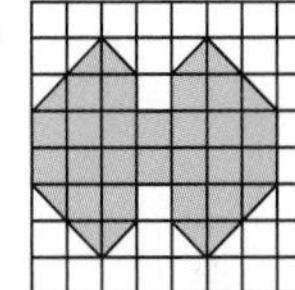

Applications

10. Three Boy Scouts want to pick up litter from their school yard. This drawing represents the school and the school yard. Copy the drawing. Then show how the school yard could be divided to give each Boy Scout an equal area to clean.

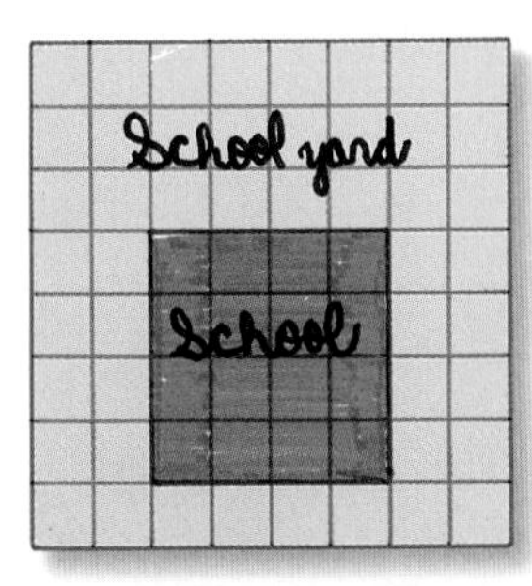

11. Rochelle stapled ten sheets of construction paper to a bulletin board. At least one side of each sheet is touching another sheet. Draw three different shapes that Rochelle might have created.

12. There are 9 desks along each of the 2 long walls in the classroom. There are 3 other rows of desks with 5 desks in each row. What is the total number of desks in the classroom?

13. José's kitchen floor is 8 feet long and 7 feet wide. The bathroom floor is 9 feet long and 6 feet wide. Which room has more area?

14. **WRITE ABOUT IT** Explain why there is more than one correct answer to Exercise 10.

Transformations in Designs

You will learn to see translations, reflections, and rotations in a design.	**Why learn this?** You can make a design by repeating a figure while making your own pattern of moves.

Many art designs are based on patterns formed by translations, reflections, and rotations.

Use 1-inch grid paper to draw a pattern.

MODEL

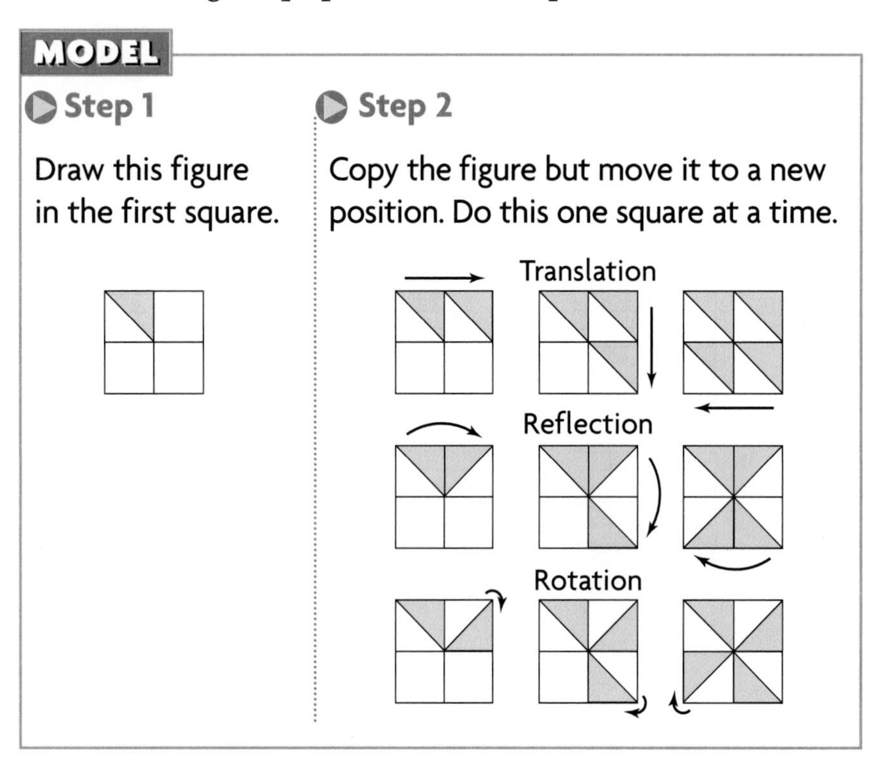

CULTURAL LINK

Native Americans use ancient designs in their baskets, beadwork, weavings, and pottery.

What shape was repeated to make the design shown here?

- How could you combine moves to make a pattern?

Check Your Understanding

Write if each pattern shows a *translation, reflection*, or *rotation*.

1.

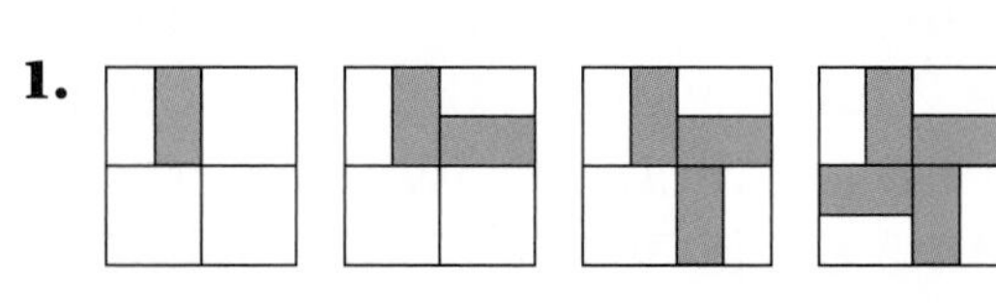

2.

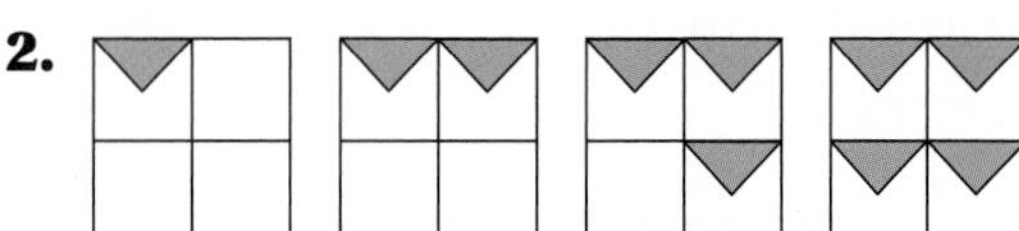

3.

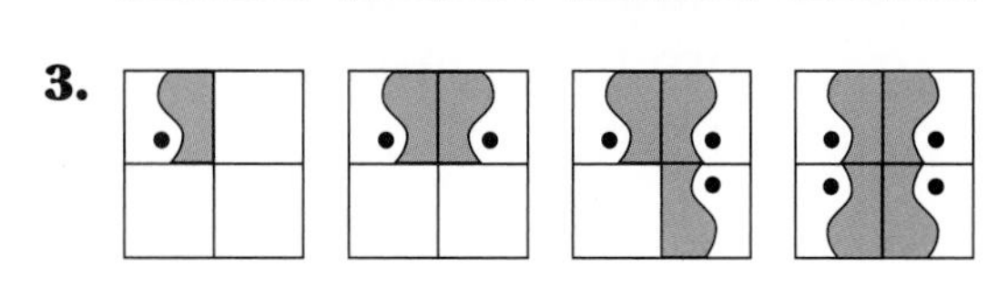

PRACTICE

Write whether each pattern shows a *translation, reflection,* or *rotation.*

4. 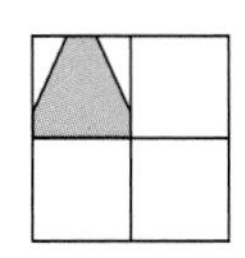 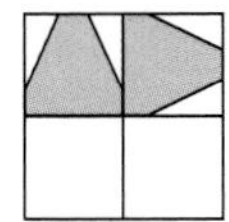 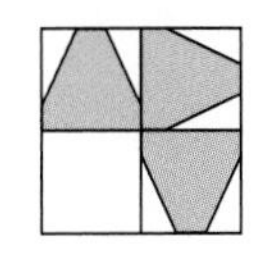 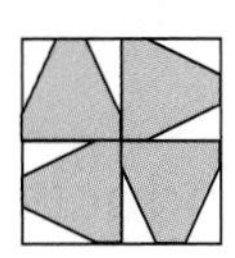

5. 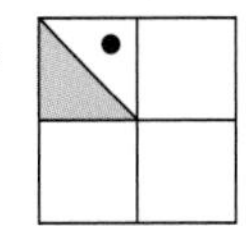 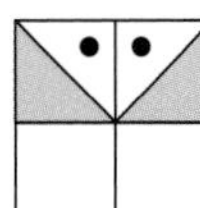 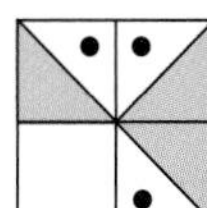 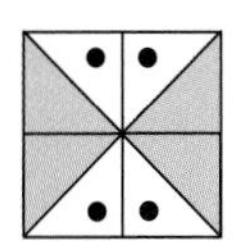

Draw the figure to complete the pattern.

6. 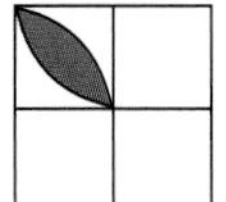 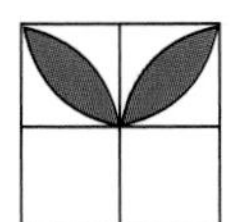 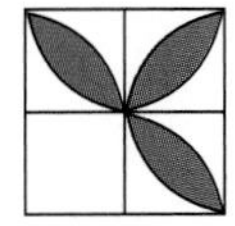 ?

7. 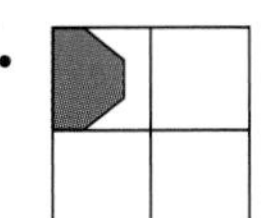 ? 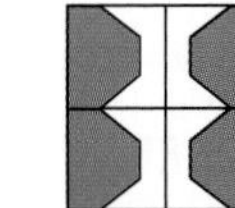

8. 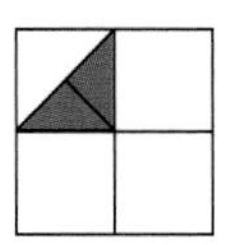 ? 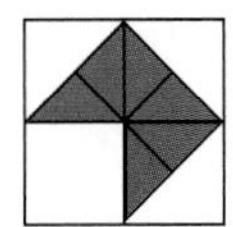 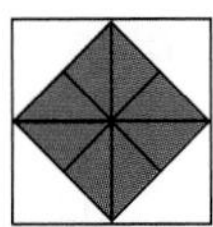

9.  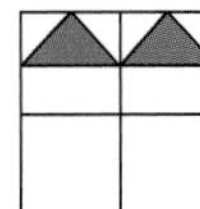 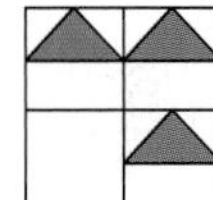 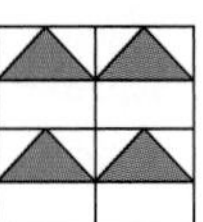

Use grid paper to make a design. Start the pattern with the first square given. Write whether your pattern shows a *translation, reflection,* or *rotation.*

10. 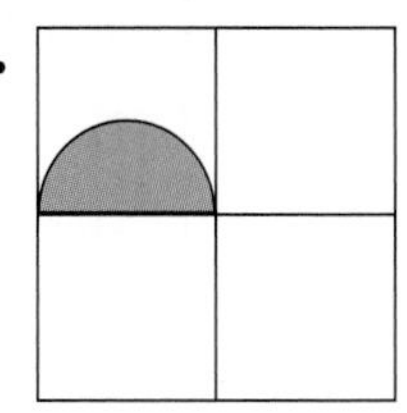

11. 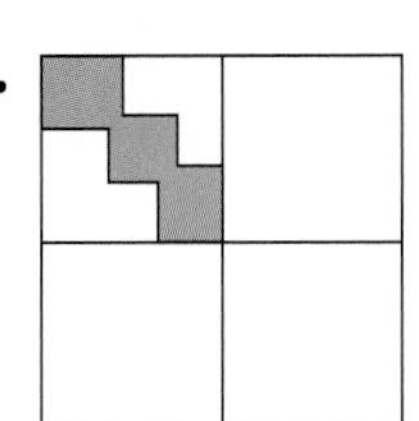

12. 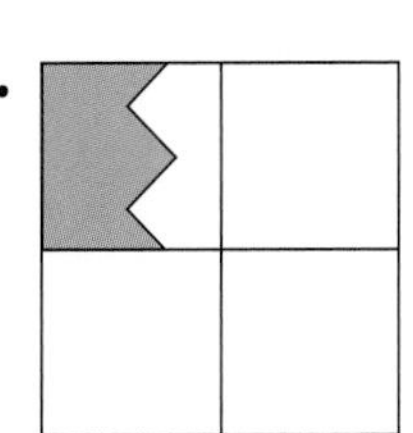

13. 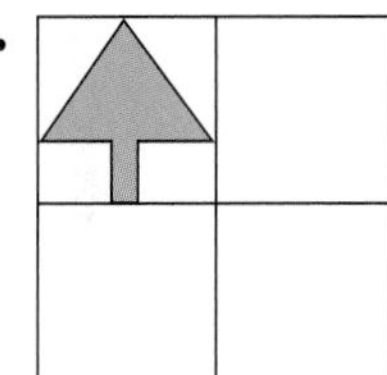

Applications

14. Michelle made a quilt design that looks like this. What figure did Michelle start with? What move did she use to finish the pattern?

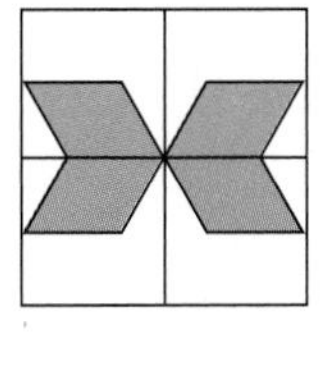

15. This design pattern is on a swimming pool. How was the design on the first tile moved to make this pattern?

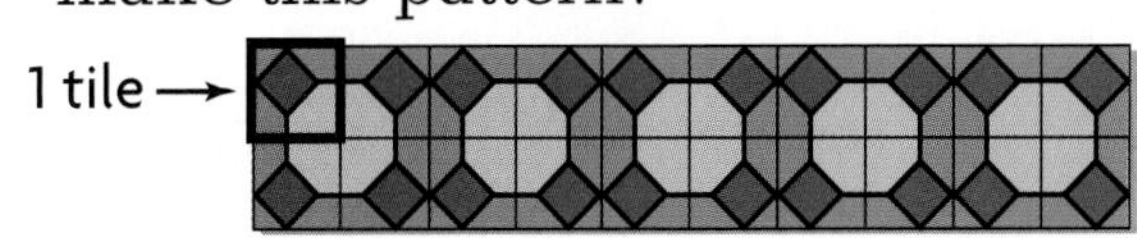

16. Jason is making a pattern for tile in his family's kitchen. It starts with the first square shown at the right. Choose a move. Use it to finish a pattern. Name the move you used.

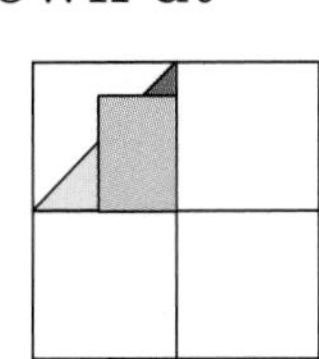

17. **WRITE ABOUT IT** Copy the figure. Finish the pattern, using only translations. Repeat, using only reflections. Are the patterns different? Explain.

Lattice Multiplication

You will learn to multiply by using a grid.	**Why learn this?** You can use the grid to find the product of two-digit numbers.

Lattice multiplication is another way to find products.

MODEL

What is 42 × 65?

Step 1

Draw a grid with 4 squares. Draw a diagonal line in each square.

One square along the top is for each digit in 65. One square along the right is for each digit in 42.

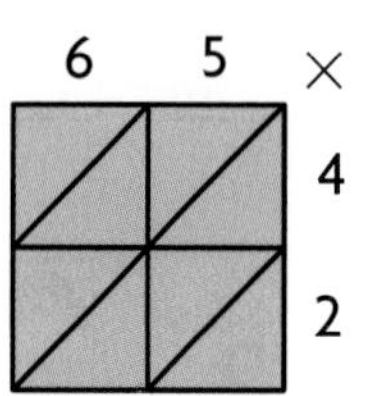

Step 2

Begin at the far right. Multiply each digit at the top of the column by the number at the right of the top row.

Record each product across the diagonal.

4 × 6 = 24 →

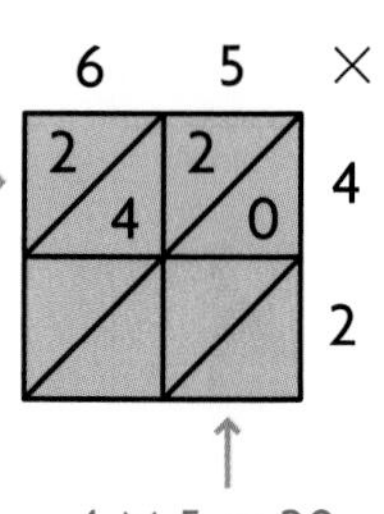

4 × 5 = 20

Step 3

Multiply each digit at the top of the column by the number at the right of the bottom row.

Record each product across the diagonal.

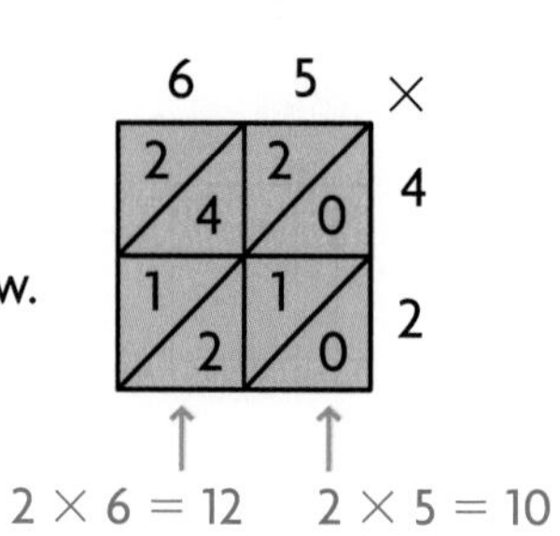

2 × 6 = 12   2 × 5 = 10

Step 4

Add along the diagonals.

Read the product down the left side and across the bottom.

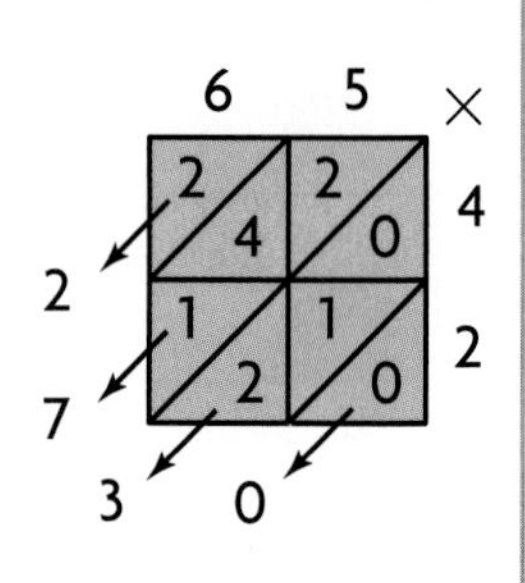

So, 42 × 65 = 2,730.

CRITICAL THINKING What is the purpose of the diagonal line in each square?

Talk About It

- What factors do you multiply to find the product?
- What place value does each diagonal row represent?
- How does using the grid help you find the product?

History Link

Early examples of lattice tables were found in a book that was printed in 1478 in Treviso, Italy. It shows four methods for multiplying 934 and 314. What method today can you use to quickly find the product of 789 and 654?

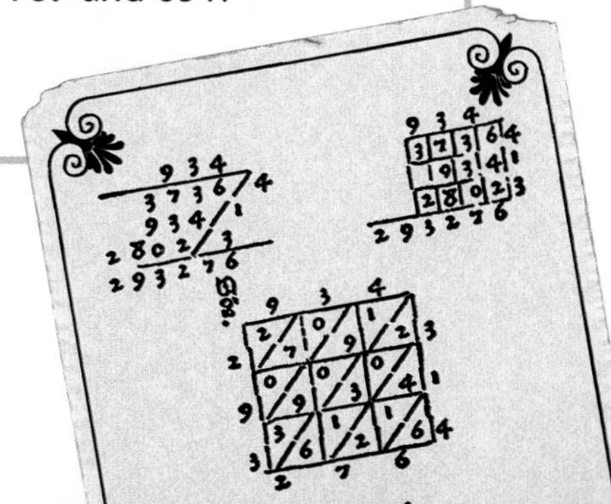

Check Your Understanding

Use a grid to find the product.

1. $23 \times 46 = n$

2. $57 \times 83 = n$

3. $39 \times 74 = n$

4. $62 \times 91 = n$

PRACTICE

Copy and complete each lattice. Find the product.

5.

5	8	
1 / 5	2 / 4	3
3 / 5	5 / ?	7

6.

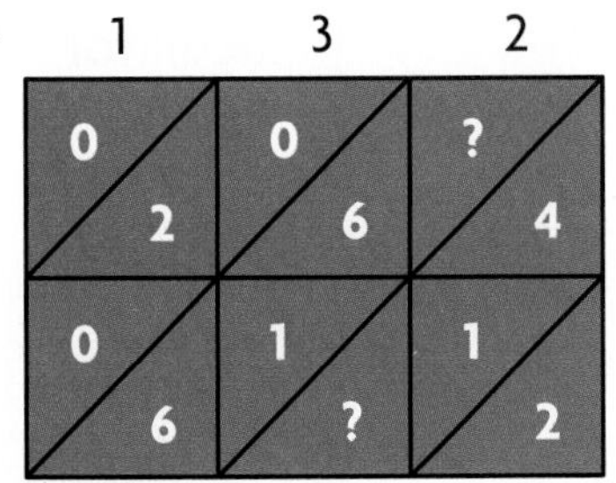

7.

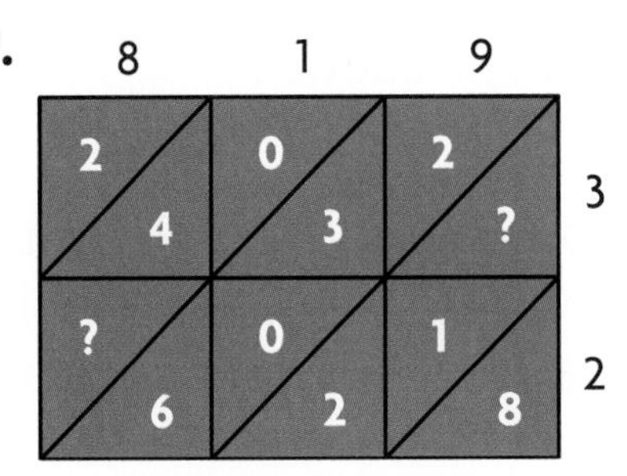

Use lattice multiplication to find the product.

8. $13 \times 75 = n$ **9.** $16 \times 37 = n$ **10.** $41 \times 56 = n$ **11.** $52 \times 85 = n$

12. $23 \times 64 = n$ **13.** $32 \times 78 = n$ **14.** $18 \times 164 = n$ **15.** $23 \times 241 = n$

16. $33 \times 605 = n$ **17.** $59 \times 423 = n$ **18.** $256 \times 118 = n$ **19.** $365 \times 489 = n$

Applications

For Problems 20–23 and 26, use the table at the right. Use lattice multiplication to find the product.

Washing Dishes	
Dishwasher (1 load—25 min cycle)	216 gal
Hand-Wash in dishpan (same number of dishes)	144 gal

20. A family washed 14 loads of dishes in the dishwasher. How much water did the family use?

21. How much water would 23 families use in one day if each washed the dishes by hand?

22. How much water would 32 families save each day if each washed the dishes by hand rather than using the dishwasher?

23. Dana uses the dishwasher 3 times a week instead of 5 times a week. How much water does she save in 4 weeks?

24. Marta cleans the kitchen after dinner. It takes her 30 minutes. She starts at 6:50 P.M. At what time does Marta finish cleaning?

25. Jamie works 4 hours a day in the Cozy Corner kitchen. She is paid $5.25 for each hour she works. How much money does Jamie earn in 5 days?

26. **Write a problem** that uses multiplication. Use the data in the table as needed.

Dividing with a Calculator

You will learn to use a calculator to find the quotient.	**Why learn this?** You can use the calculator when dividing larger numbers.

Monica and Wilhelm often travel by airplane to visit relatives. They have traveled 4,257 miles in the last 6 months. About how many miles each month have they traveled?

Estimate. $4{,}257 \div 6 = n$ **Think:** $6 \times 700 = 4{,}200$

A calculator can help you divide larger numbers.

Divide. $4{,}257 \div 6 = n$

Press: 4 2 5 7 INT÷ [I 4257]

The I in the display stands for *integer.* It means the display shows the quotient and remainder separately.

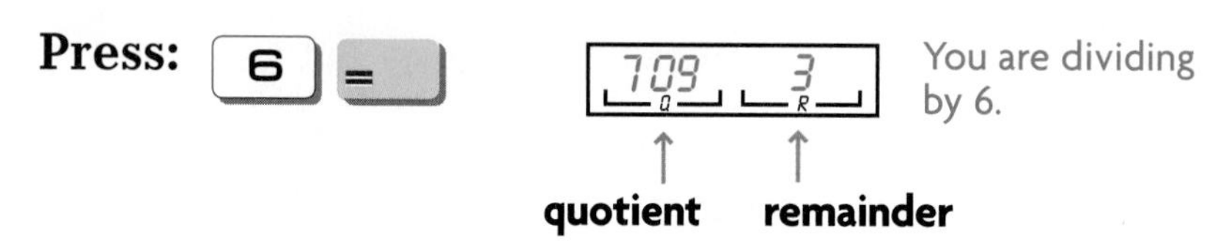

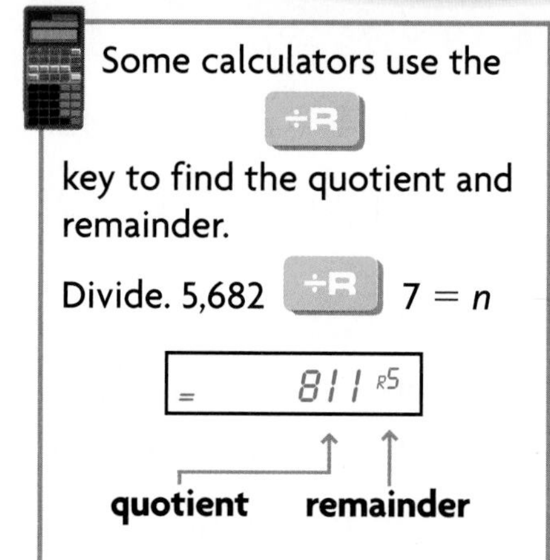

The quotient and remainder are displayed in the window.

$4{,}257 \div 6 = 709$ r3

So, Monica and Wilhelm have traveled about 709 miles each month.

Talk About It

- When you use a calculator to divide numbers, which number do you press first: the divisor or the dividend?
- Why is it important to estimate even when you are using a calculator?

You can also use a calculator to check division.

Multiply.

Press: [7] [0] [9] [×] [6] [=] → 4254

Add remainder.

Press: [+] [3] [=] → 4257

Compare your answer with the dividend. So, 709 r3 is correct.

- How can you use the calculator to check the quotient when there is no remainder?

PRACTICE

Find the quotient and remainder by using a calculator.

1. $6\overline{)1{,}421}$ **2.** $4\overline{)3{,}677}$ **3.** $3\overline{)2{,}456}$ **4.** $5\overline{)9{,}064}$

5. $9\overline{)4{,}115}$ **6.** $7\overline{)8{,}235}$ **7.** $2\overline{)5{,}607}$ **8.** $8\overline{)4{,}975}$

Divide. Check using a calculator.

9. $5\overline{)5{,}287}$ **10.** $2\overline{)9{,}263}$ **11.** $3\overline{)7{,}235}$ **12.** $6\overline{)8{,}790}$

13. $3\overline{)6{,}512}$ **14.** $7\overline{)1{,}943}$ **15.** $9\overline{)6{,}227}$ **16.** $3\overline{)5{,}891}$

Applications

For Problems 17, 18, and 20, use the menu at the right. You may use a calculator.

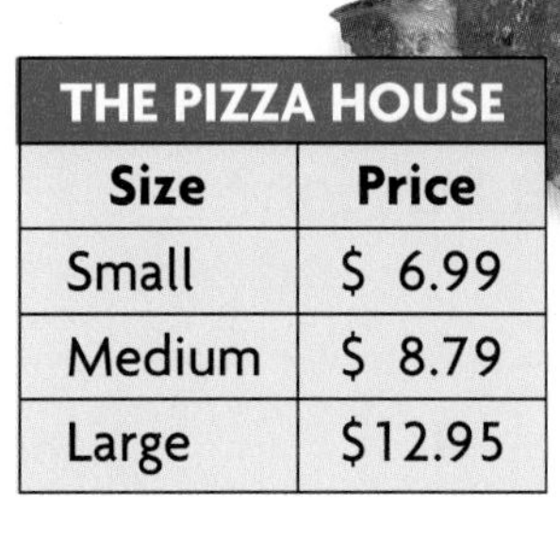

THE PIZZA HOUSE	
Size	**Price**
Small	$ 6.99
Medium	$ 8.79
Large	$12.95

17. Janine, SoHee, and Tasha shared a small pizza. They each paid the same amount. How much did each girl pay?

18. At Phil's Pizza, you can get 4 large pizzas for $50.00. How much less does 1 large pizza at Phil's cost than 1 large pizza at the Pizza House?

19. Mrs. Becker ordered 4 extra-large pizzas for a birthday party. The total cost for the pizzas was $59.80. How much did one pizza cost?

20. There are 6 friends sharing 2 medium pizzas. How much should each friend pay?

21. **WRITE ABOUT IT** Explain two ways a calculator can help you when dividing.

Fractions in Simplest Form

You will learn to find an equivalent fraction in simplest form.

Why learn this? Fractional amounts expressed in simplest form use smaller numbers and are easier to visualize.

Kevin's mom cut his birthday cake into 12 equal pieces. Kevin, Keri, and their mom and dad each ate 1 piece, or $\frac{4}{12}$ of the cake. What is $\frac{4}{12}$ in simplest form?

You can find the simplest form of a fraction by using fraction bars. A fraction is in *simplest form* when it uses the largest fraction bar possible.

Line up fraction bars to find equivalent fractions for $\frac{4}{12}$. Find the largest fraction bar possible.

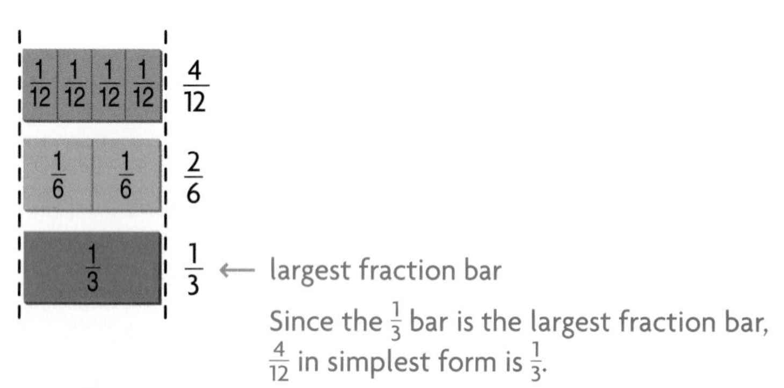

Since the $\frac{1}{3}$ bar is the largest fraction bar, $\frac{4}{12}$ in simplest form is $\frac{1}{3}$.

- How do you know when you have found the simplest form of a fraction?

EXAMPLES

A. $\frac{2}{4}$

$\frac{1}{4}$ $\frac{1}{4}$

$\frac{1}{2}$

$\frac{2}{4}$ in simplest form is $\frac{1}{2}$.

B. $\frac{3}{8}$

$\frac{1}{8}$ $\frac{1}{8}$ $\frac{1}{8}$

$\frac{1}{2}$

$\frac{1}{4}$

Since no other fraction bars line up with $\frac{3}{8}$, it is in simplest form.

C. $\frac{8}{12}$

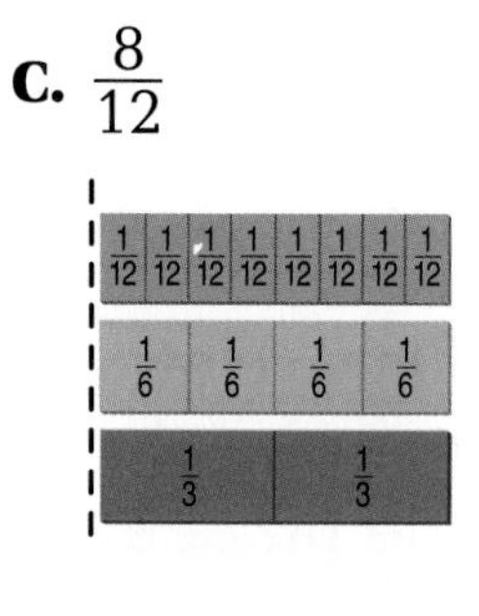

$\frac{8}{12}$ in simplest form is $\frac{2}{3}$.

D. $\frac{5}{6}$

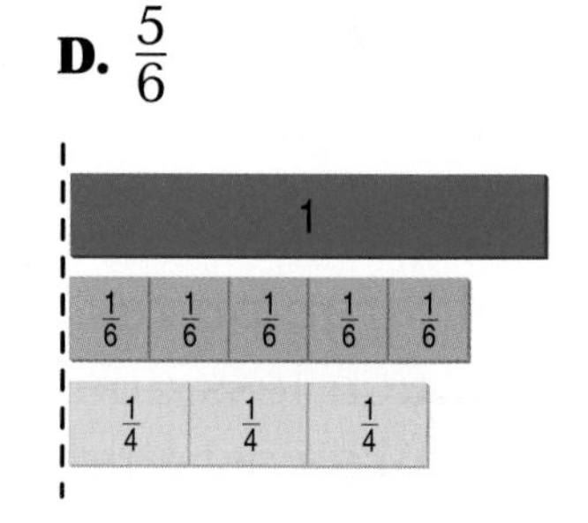

Since no other fraction bars line up with $\frac{5}{6}$, it is in simplest form.

PRACTICE

Is the fraction in simplest form? Write *yes* or *no*.

1. $\frac{2}{4}$

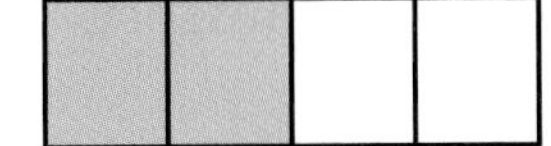

2. $\frac{1}{3}$

3. $\frac{6}{9}$

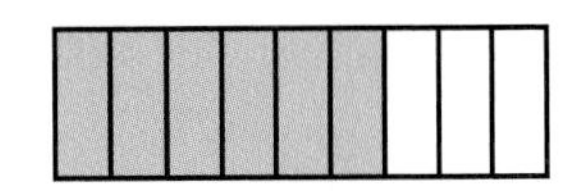

4. $\frac{3}{4}$

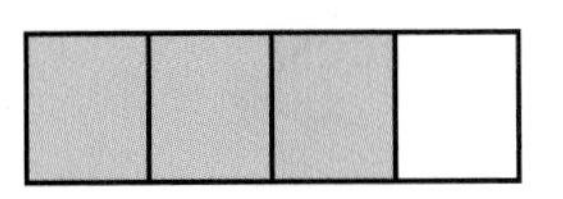

Use fraction strips to find the fraction in simplest form.
Write *a* or *b*.

5. a. $\frac{5}{10}$ **b.** $\frac{1}{2}$

6. a. $\frac{3}{5}$ **b.** $\frac{6}{10}$

7. a. $\frac{3}{4}$ **b.** $\frac{6}{8}$

8. a. $\frac{4}{6}$ **b.** $\frac{2}{3}$

9. a. $\frac{1}{4}$ **b.** $\frac{3}{12}$

10. a. $\frac{6}{9}$ **b.** $\frac{2}{3}$

Write each fraction in simplest form. Use fraction strips.

11. $\frac{2}{6}$ **12.** $\frac{4}{8}$ **13.** $\frac{1}{4}$ **14.** $\frac{3}{12}$ **15.** $\frac{8}{10}$

16. $\frac{2}{8}$ **17.** $\frac{3}{6}$ **18.** $\frac{9}{12}$ **19.** $\frac{3}{9}$ **20.** $\frac{2}{10}$

21. $\frac{6}{12}$ **22.** $\frac{6}{8}$ **23.** $\frac{1}{5}$ **24.** $\frac{3}{6}$ **25.** $\frac{6}{10}$

Applications

For Problems 26–28, use fraction strips and the cake recipe at the right.

26. Would the fraction bar used to represent the amount of sugar be longer or shorter than the fraction bar used to represent the amount of butter?

27. Write an equivalent fraction for each: the amount of butter, the amount of sugar, and the amount of salt.

28. Are the fractions used in this recipe in simplest form? How do you know?

Banana Cake Recipe

2 cups flour	$\frac{1}{2}$ cup butter
2 eggs	$\frac{3}{4}$ cup sugar
4 bananas	$\frac{3}{4}$ teaspoon vanilla
$\frac{1}{4}$ teaspoon salt	$\frac{1}{2}$ teaspoon baking soda

Mix ingredients until smooth. Bake at 350° for 1 hr.

29. **WRITE ABOUT IT** Explain why tools used to measure ingredients have measurements written in simplest form.

Estimating Sums and Differences

You will learn to round fractions and to estimate sums and differences.

Why learn this? You can estimate when an exact answer is not needed, such as checking what you need to make your favorite dessert.

Use a number line to round fractions.

Is $\frac{5}{6}$ closer to 0, $\frac{1}{2}$, or 1?

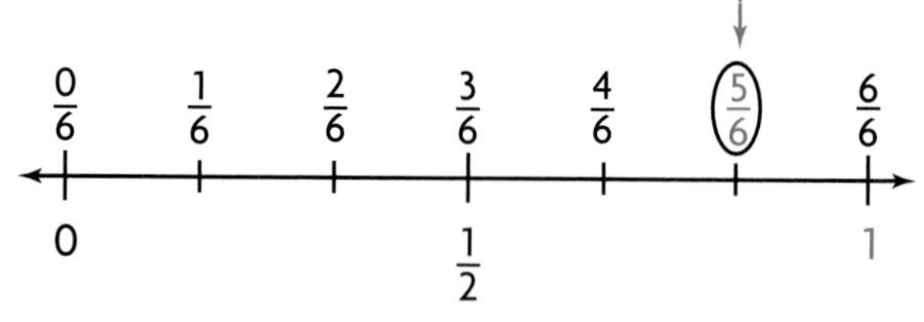

So, $\frac{5}{6}$ is closer to 1.

A.

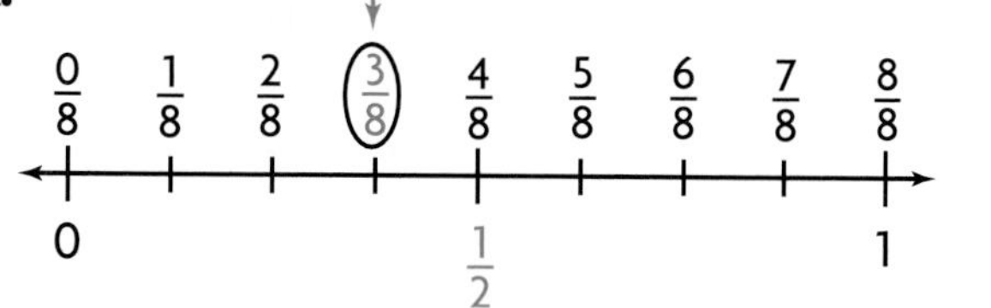

So, $\frac{3}{8}$ is closer to $\frac{1}{2}$.

B.

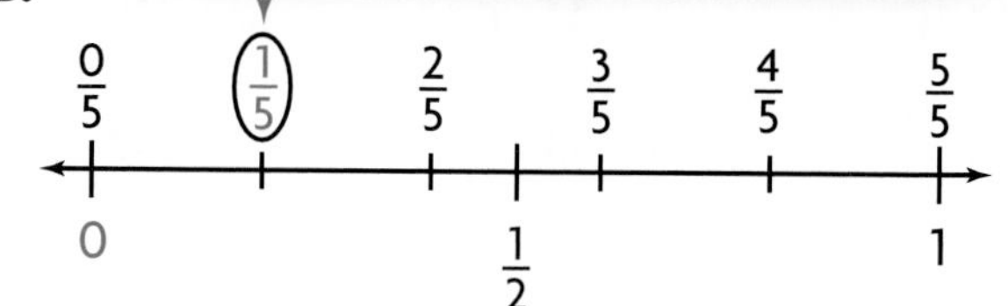

So, $\frac{1}{5}$ is closer to 0.

Rounding fractions to 0, $\frac{1}{2}$, or 1 on a number line can help you estimate sums and differences.

EXAMPLES

A. Estimate the sum $\frac{1}{3} + \frac{3}{5}$.

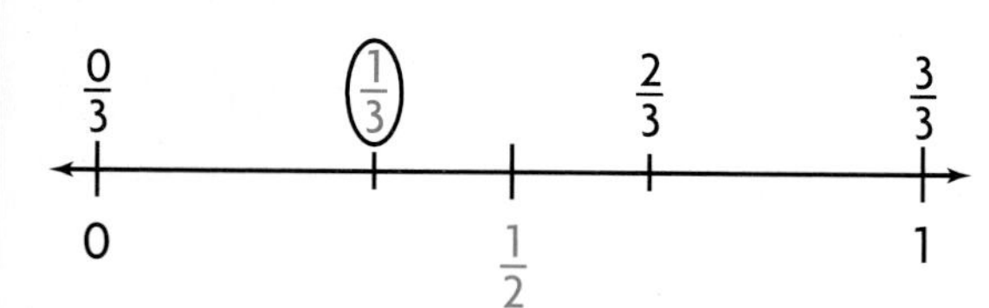

$\frac{1}{3}$ is close to $\frac{1}{2}$.

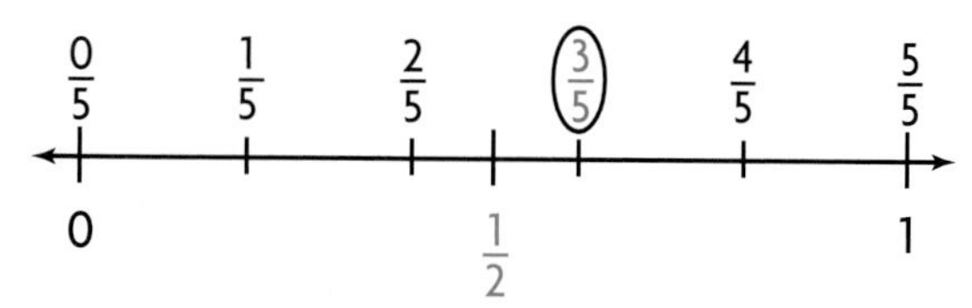

$\frac{3}{5}$ is close to $\frac{1}{2}$. $\frac{1}{2} + \frac{1}{2} = 1$

So, $\frac{1}{3} + \frac{3}{5}$ is about 1.

B. Estimate the difference $\frac{3}{5} - \frac{1}{8}$.

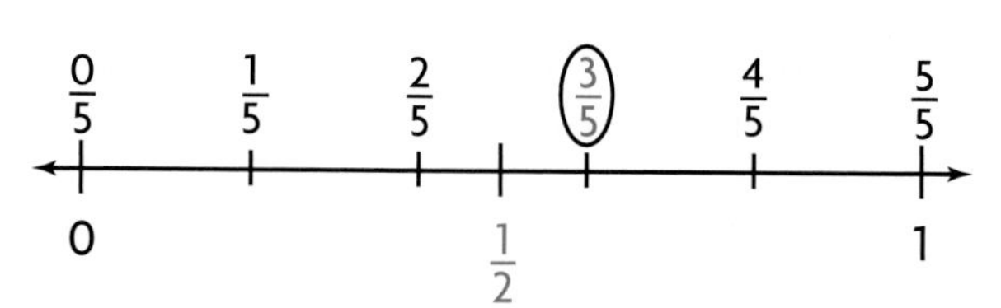

$\frac{3}{5}$ is close to $\frac{1}{2}$.

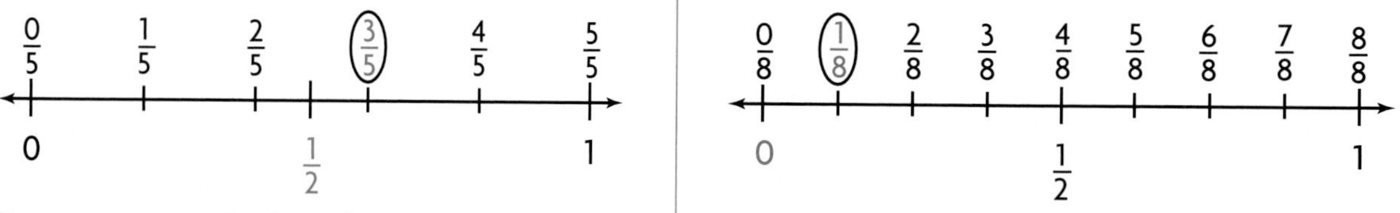

$\frac{1}{8}$ is close to 0. $\frac{1}{2} - 0 = \frac{1}{2}$

So, $\frac{3}{5} - \frac{1}{8}$ is about $\frac{1}{2}$.

PRACTICE

Use the number lines to estimate if each fraction is closer to 0, $\frac{1}{2}$, or 1.

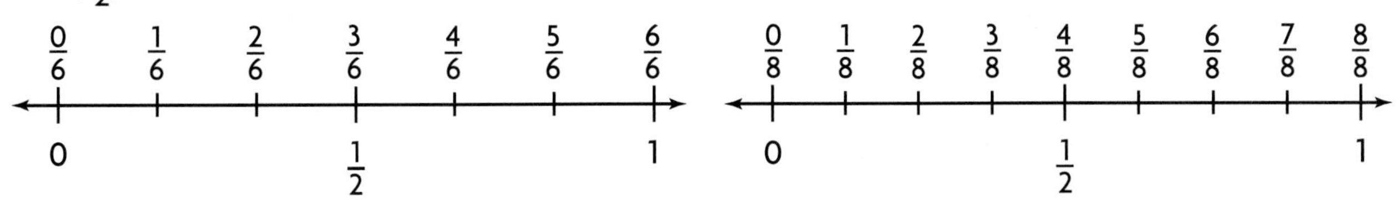

1. $\frac{5}{6}$ **2.** $\frac{3}{6}$ **3.** $\frac{2}{6}$ **4.** $\frac{1}{8}$ **5.** $\frac{5}{8}$ **6.** $\frac{7}{8}$

Write whether each fraction is closer to 0, $\frac{1}{2}$, or 1. You may use a number line.

7. $\frac{7}{8}$ **8.** $\frac{2}{3}$ **9.** $\frac{1}{6}$ **10.** $\frac{2}{10}$ **11.** $\frac{3}{4}$

12. $\frac{5}{12}$ **13.** $\frac{8}{9}$ **14.** $\frac{6}{10}$ **15.** $\frac{2}{12}$ **16.** $\frac{11}{12}$

17. $\frac{5}{6}$ **18.** $\frac{7}{12}$ **19.** $\frac{1}{8}$ **20.** $\frac{4}{9}$ **21.** $\frac{9}{10}$

Estimate the sum or difference. Write *about 0, about* $\frac{1}{2}$, or *about 1.*

22. $\frac{3}{4} + \frac{1}{9}$ **23.** $\frac{8}{9} - \frac{3}{7}$ **24.** $\frac{6}{7} - \frac{3}{4}$ **25.** $\frac{2}{5} + \frac{3}{7}$ **26.** $\frac{1}{12} + \frac{1}{8}$

27. $\frac{7}{8} + \frac{1}{10}$ **28.** $\frac{2}{5} + \frac{5}{9}$ **29.** $\frac{11}{12} - \frac{5}{8}$ **30.** $\frac{1}{10} + \frac{1}{6}$ **31.** $\frac{9}{10} - \frac{6}{7}$

Applications

32. Brad is making two kinds of dip for a party. He has 1 cup of sour cream. One kind of dip calls for $\frac{3}{8}$ cup and the other kind calls for $\frac{7}{8}$ cup. Estimate to see if Brad has enough sour cream to make both kinds of dip.

33. Amanda used $\frac{4}{8}$ cup of sugar in the cake. She used $\frac{3}{8}$ cup of sugar in the frosting. If there was 1 cup of sugar in the box to start, was the amount left closer to 0 cup, to $\frac{1}{2}$ cup, or to 1 cup?

34. If Nate gave $\frac{1}{10}$ of the cookies on a plate to Leah and $\frac{1}{10}$ to Neil, will Nate have more or less than $\frac{1}{2}$ of the cookies left?

35. **WRITE ABOUT IT** Suppose you add two fractions between $\frac{1}{2}$ and 1. Will the sum be greater than or less than 1? Explain.

Thousandths

You will learn to read and write decimal numbers to the thousandths.	**Why learn this?** You can read and understand decimal numbers, such as those used in gymnastics scores.

The United States women's gymnastics team scored 389.225 points in the 1996 Olympic team competition.

Olympic gold medalist Shannon Miller

Decimal Number: 389.225
Read: three hundred eighty-nine and two hundred twenty-five thousandths

Decimal numbers can be modeled using base-ten blocks.

If you let the cube represent 1, you can use this chart.

Ones	Tenths	Hundredths	Thousandths
one 1.0	one tenth 0.1	one hundredth 0.01	one thousandth 0.001

- Compare the base-ten blocks from right to left. How many thousandths cubes does it take to make a hundredth? a tenth? one?

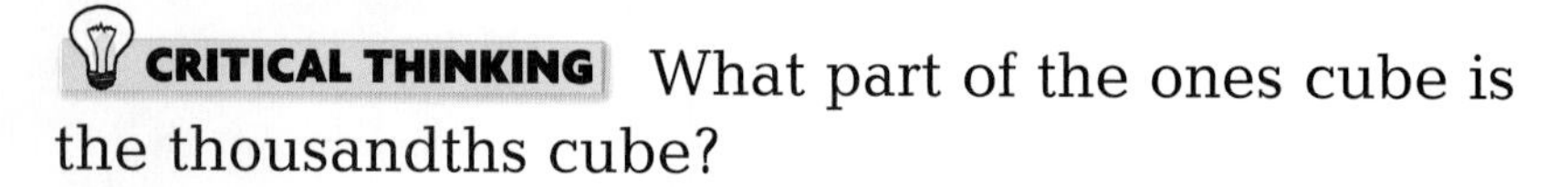

CRITICAL THINKING What part of the ones cube is the thousandths cube?

____

You can use a place-value chart to show decimal numbers.

Ones	Tenths	Hundredths	Thousandths
0 .	8	8	7
0 .	0	5	4

Read: eight hundred eighty-seven thousandths; fifty-four thousandths

When reading decimals, say the word for the place value of the digit that is farthest to the right of the decimal.

- How many places to the right of the decimal point are needed to show tenths? to show hundredths? to show thousandths?

PRACTICE

Write the decimal number.

1. eighteen hundredths
2. two hundred twenty-one thousandths
3. nine thousandths
4. one and one thousandth
5. thirty thousandths
6. eleven thousandths
7. eighty-eight thousandths
8. one hundred eleven thousandths

Write the place-value position of each underlined digit.

9. $0.\underline{6}2$
10. $2.4\underline{1}8$
11. $1.23\underline{4}$
12. $4\underline{2}.778$
13. $15.6\underline{0}9$
14. $21.63\underline{5}$
15. $849.\underline{0}07$
16. $568.29\underline{5}$
17. $101.0\underline{0}1$
18. $\underline{3}43.343$

Write each decimal number in words.

19. 0.15
20. 0.19
21. 0.441
22. 0.019
23. 0.236
24. 0.901
25. 0.001
26. 0.022
27. 0.011
28. 0.18

Applications

29. A well-known baseball player's batting average is 0.394. Write the decimal number in words.

30. A decimal number has a 6 in the tenths place and a 1 in the thousandths place. The sum of its digits is 7. Write the number.

31. I have a 9 in the thousandths place, a 7 in the hundredths place, and a 1 in the tenths place. The sum of my digits is 17. What number am I?

32. A bookstore sold 1,000 books one month. Two hundred fifty-three of those books were non-fiction. Write a decimal that shows what part of the books were non-fiction.

33. I have a 0 in the tenths place, a 5 in the hundredths place, and a 3 in the thousandths place. The sum of my digits is 8. What number am I?

34. A survey of 1,000 people found that 567 preferred the popular-music radio station to the country-music station. Write this number as a decimal.

35. There are 1,000 students at Princeton Elementary. One hundred forty-eight of those students are fourth graders. Write a decimal that shows what part of the students are fourth graders.

36. **Write a problem** about the thousandths cube and the ones cube.

Relating Metric Units

You will learn how units of metric measurement are related to place value.

Why learn this? You can understand the prefixes used to name metric measurements.

WORD POWER
milli-
centi-
deci-
kilo-

Metric units can be used to measure length, capacity, and mass.

Length		Capacity	Mass
milli *meter*	*meter*	milli *liter*	*gram*
centi *meter*	kilo *meter*	*liter*	kilo *gram*
deci *meter*			

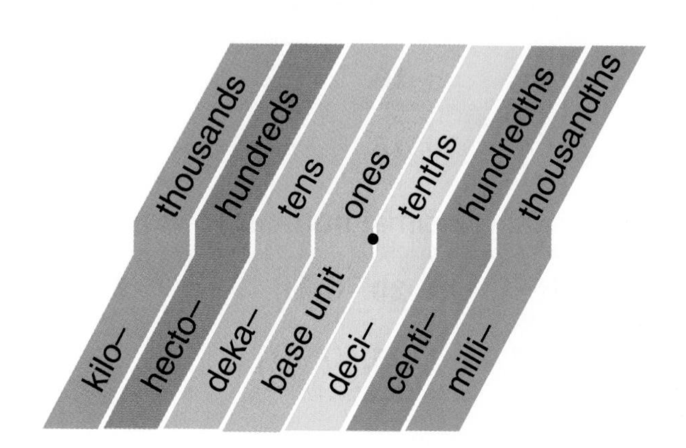

Metric units are related to place value. You can use a prefix with a base unit to change the value of the unit.

In the word *centimeter*, the prefix is *centi-* and the base unit is *meter*.

So, *centimeter* means "one-hundredth, or 0.01, meter."

Talk About It

- What does *milliliter* mean?
- What name can be used to mean the same as 1,000 meters?

____

You can change units of measure to their equivalent measures.

3 centimeters = _?_ meters	6 kilograms = _?_ grams
Think: 1 centimeter = 0.01 meter	**Think:** 1 kilogram = 1,000 grams
So, 3 centimeters = 0.03 meter.	So, 6 kilograms = 6,000 grams.

Check Your Understanding

Choose the smaller unit of measure. Write *a* or *b*. Use the prefix to help you.

1. a. liter
b. milliliter

2. a. gram
b. kilogram

3. a. decimeter
b. centimeter

PRACTICE

Choose the larger unit of measure. Write *a* or *b*. Use the prefix to help you.

4. a. meter
b. kilometer

5. a. kilogram
b. gram

6. a. milliliter
b. liter

For Exercises 7–13, fill in the missing measures.

	Meters	Decimeters	Centimeters	Millimeters
7.	6	60	?	6,000
8.	9	?	900	9,000
9.	10	100	1,000	?

	Liters	Milliliters
10.	1	?
11.	?	2,000

	Kilograms	Grams
12.	?	1,000
13.	2	?

Write the equivalent measurement.

14. 4,000 grams = _?_ kilograms

15. 40 decimeters = _?_ meters

16. 3 liters = _?_ milliliters

17. 5,000 millimeters = _?_ decimeters

18. 8 centimeters = _?_ meters

19. 4 kilograms = _?_ grams

20. 6,000 milliliters = _?_ liters

21. 7 meters = _?_ centimeters

Applications

22. Marcia paid $4 for a 2-meter fence for her flower garden. The perimeter of the garden is 20 decimeters. What did it cost Marcia to put a fence around the perimeter of her garden?

23. Crystal's gym shoes have a mass of about 2 kilograms. Heather's dance shoes have a mass of about 200 grams. Whose shoes have a greater mass?

24. Cindy drank 1 liter of orange juice after the ball game. Jean drank 1,000 milliliters of orange juice. Who drank more juice?

25. Mike's desk measures 8 decimeters long. Alan's desk measures 1 meter. Who has the longer desk?

26. Sharon needs 2 meters of ribbon. She found 2 pieces of ribbon each 75 centimeters long. Does Sharon need more ribbon? Explain.

27. **WRITE ABOUT IT** Explain how to decide if the mass of an object should be measured in grams or kilograms.

Time on a Stopwatch

You will learn to express parts of seconds shown on a stopwatch by using decimals.	**Why learn this?** You can read and understand seconds and parts of seconds on a stopwatch.

The world record for the women's 100-meter run is 10.49 seconds, or 10 seconds plus $\frac{49}{100}$ of a second. A stopwatch can be used to measure hundredths of a second.

A.

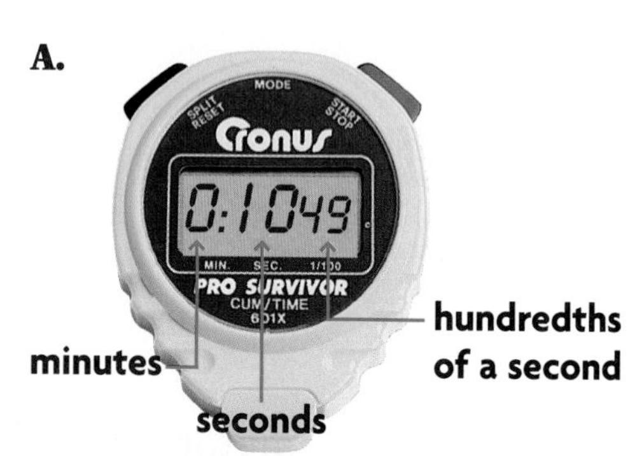

Say: 10 and 49 hundredths seconds
Write: 10.49 sec

B.

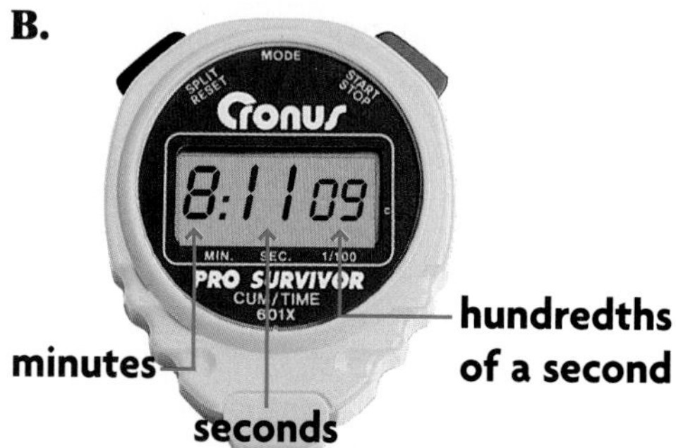

Say: 8 minutes, 11 and 9 hundredths seconds
Write: 8 min, 11.09 sec

Notice that

- the first set of numbers shows minutes, and the second set of numbers shows seconds.
- the small set of numbers shows hundredths of a second.

Talk About It

- How are the times shown on these stopwatches different from times shown on some digital clocks?
- Why is it important to be able to measure hundredths of a second, especially in races?

Check Your Understanding 

Write each time.

1. 30 and 57 hundredths seconds

2. 42 and 8 hundredths seconds

3. 2 minutes, 4 and 54 hundredths seconds

Sports Link

The closest world championship car race was in 1986. The first-place car crossed the finish line 0.014 seconds before the second-place car. Can 0.014 be shown on this stopwatch? Explain.

PRACTICE

Write each time as you would say it and write it.

4.

5.

6.

7.

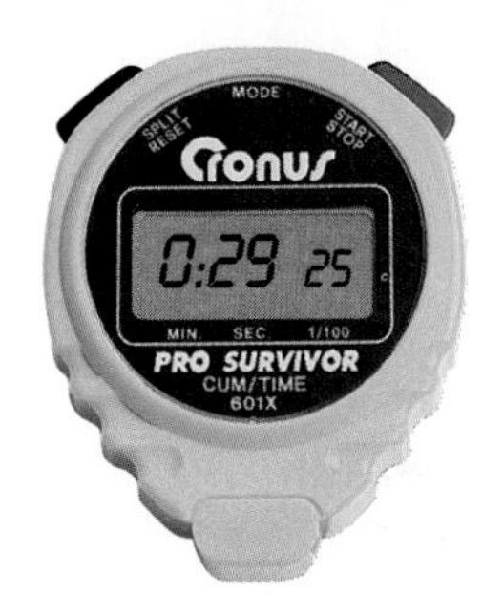

8.

9.

Write each time as you would say it.

10. 42.08 sec

11. 2 min, 23.12 sec

12. 14 min, 59.03 sec

13. 8.16 sec

14. 1 min, 50.21 sec

15. 60 min, 2.02 sec

Write each time as it would be shown on a stopwatch.

16. 52.39 sec

17. 7 min, 11.79 sec

18. 5 min, 10.15 sec

19. 4 minutes, 19 and 3 hundredths seconds

20. 8 minutes, 23 seconds

21. 34 and 17 hundredths seconds

Applications

22. Jorge ran a 10-kilometer race in 53 minutes, 24 and 59 hundredths seconds. What time was shown on Jorge's stopwatch?

23. When Ann finished 40 multiplication facts, her stopwatch showed 2:51 09. How long did it take Ann to do her work?

24. Hal ran 1 mile in 7 minutes, 45 and 3 hundredths seconds. Grace ran 1 mile in 8 minutes, 5 seconds. Who ran faster? Explain.

25. **WRITE ABOUT IT** Explain how to read a stopwatch display.

Making a Circle Graph from a Bar Graph

You will learn to make a circle graph from a bar graph.

Why learn this? You can compare the same data on different kinds of graphs.

Joanne asked 16 classmates which season was their favorite. She made a bar graph to show her data.

You can use the Favorite Seasons bar graph that Joanne made to make a circle graph.

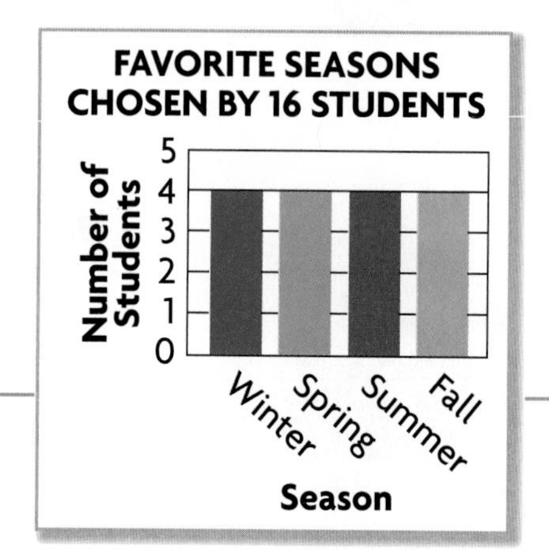

MODEL

How can you use the bar graph to make a circle graph?

Step 1

On your copy of the graph, write the name of each season inside the bar for that season. Color each bar a different color. Carefully cut out each bar.

Winter	Spring
Summer	Fall

Step 2

Tape the four bars together so that the ends do not lie over each other.

Winter	Spring	Summer	Fall

Step 3

Tape the two ends of the strip together to form a circle.

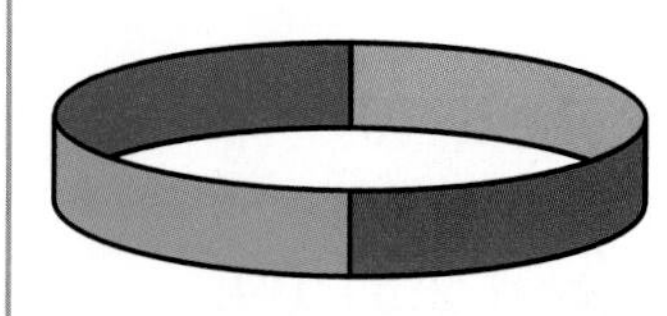

Step 4

Place your paper circle on top of the blank circle pattern. On the outside of the circle, mark the spot where each taped bar meets another taped bar.

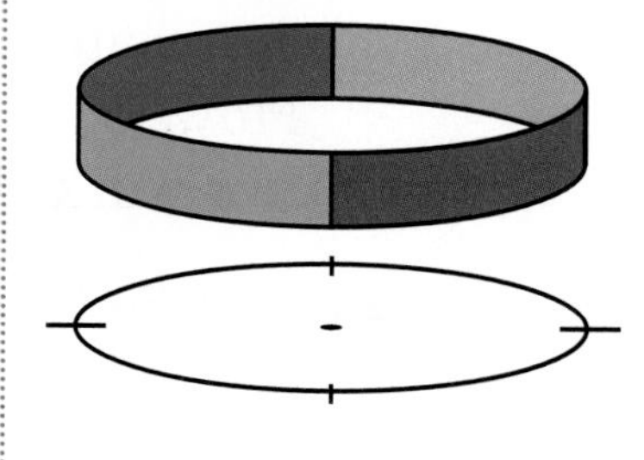

Step 5

Use a straightedge to draw a line from the center of the circle to each mark you made around the circle. Color the parts of the circle to match the colors of the strip. Label each part and title the graph.

FAVORITE SEASONS CHOSEN BY 16 STUDENTS

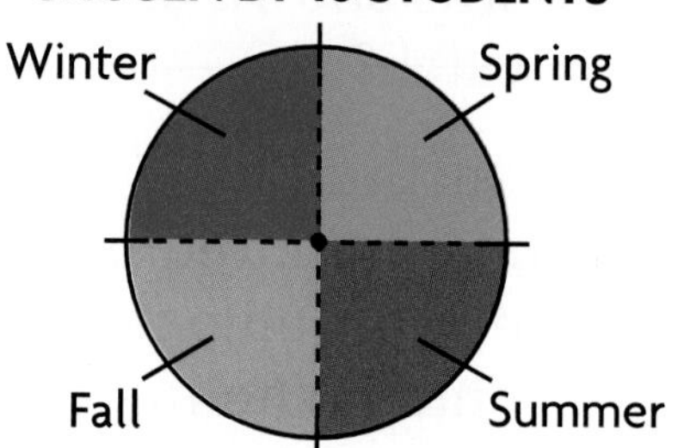

Talk About It

- What do you notice about the sizes of the parts of the circle graph? the lengths of the bars on the bar graph?
- What fraction represents the classmates who chose fall? What does the whole circle graph stand for?

CRITICAL THINKING How do you know that both the circle graph and the bar graph show the same data?

PRACTICE

Use the bar graph to make a circle graph. Write the fraction that represents each part of the circle graph.

1.

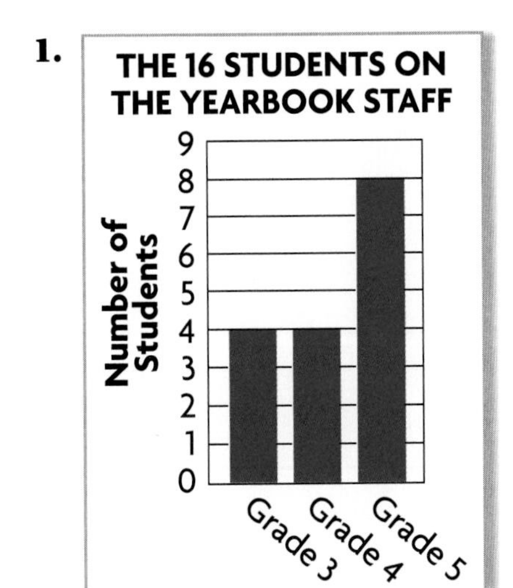

2.

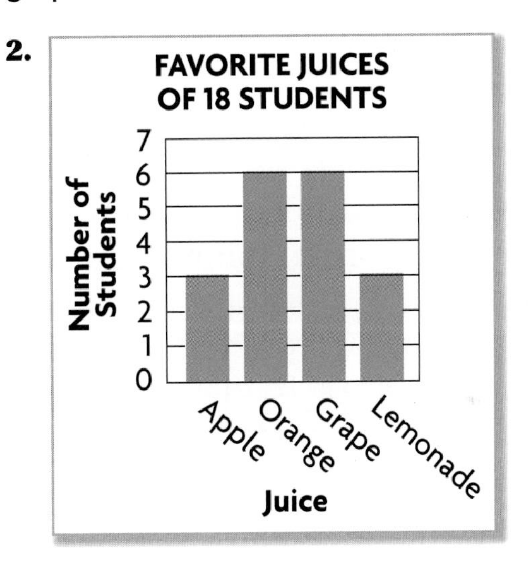

Applications

Make a bar graph. Use the bar graph to make a circle graph.

3. There were 5 girls and 5 boys at Joey's birthday party.

4. Betty has 2 dimes, 2 nickels, and 4 quarters in her pocket.

5. In Pierre's family, 3 people have brown hair, and 1 person has blond hair.

6. Jack has 4 books and 2 pencils in his school bag.

7. George has 3 fish, 2 hamsters, and 1 bird.

8. Leslie has 2 cats and 1 dog.

CALCULATOR Activities

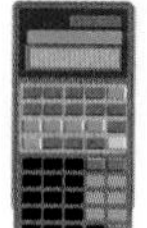

A MULTIPLE OF FUN

Number Patterns and Multiples

Look at this number pattern. It shows the first four multiples of 2.

2, 4, 6, 8

What is the seventh number in this pattern? Use your calculator to find out.

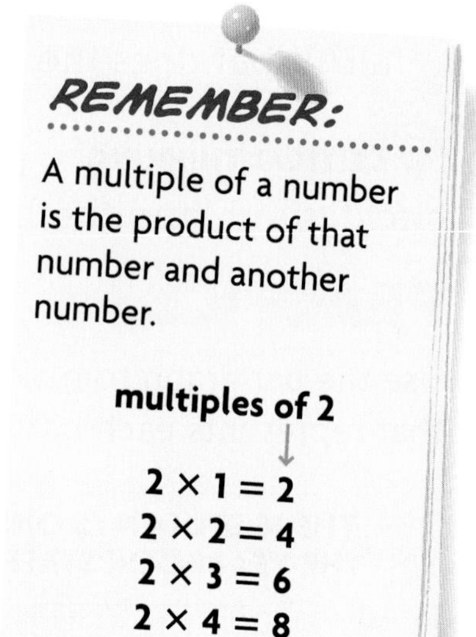

Using the Calculator

To find the seventh multiple of 2 by using the *TI Math Explorer*, enter the following:

To find the seventh multiple of 2 by using the *Casio fx-55*, enter the following:

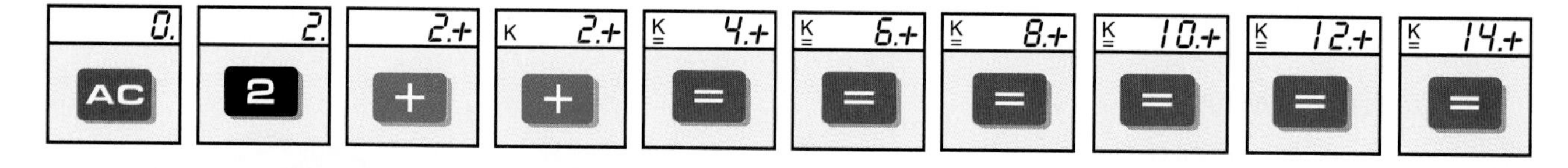

So, the seventh number in the pattern is 14.

PRACTICE

Use your calculator to solve.

1. Find the first seven multiples of 3.
2. Find the first seven multiples of 4.
3. Is 25 a multiple of 5?
4. Is 44 a multiple of 6?
5. Is 140 a multiple of 7?
6. 12 is a multiple of six numbers. Name them.
7. 28 is a multiple of six numbers. Name them.

FRUITY CALCULATIONS
Multiplication Properties

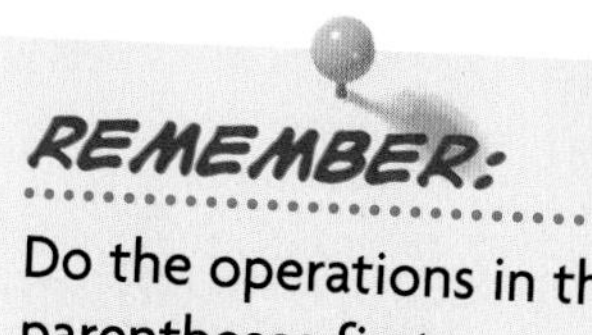

Do the operations in the parentheses first.

$(2 \times 1) + (3 \times 1) = \underline{?}$
$2 + 3 = 5$

Fred ate 3 apples and 2 bananas every week for 4 weeks. How many pieces of fruit did Fred eat in all?

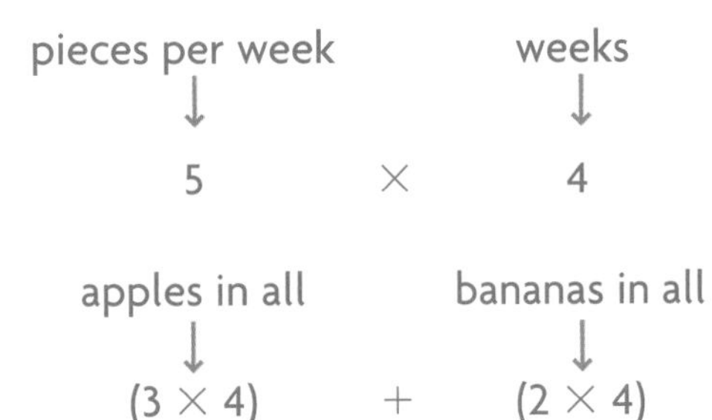

	pieces per week		weeks
You could think:	5	×	4
	apples in all		bananas in all
Or, you could spread out the multiplication:	(3 × 4)	+	(2 × 4)

Using the Calculator

Use the *TI Math Explorer* to find the value of $(3 \times 4) + (2 \times 4)$. Enter the following:

Use the *Casio fx-55* to find the value of $(3 \times 4) + (2 \times 4)$. Enter the following:

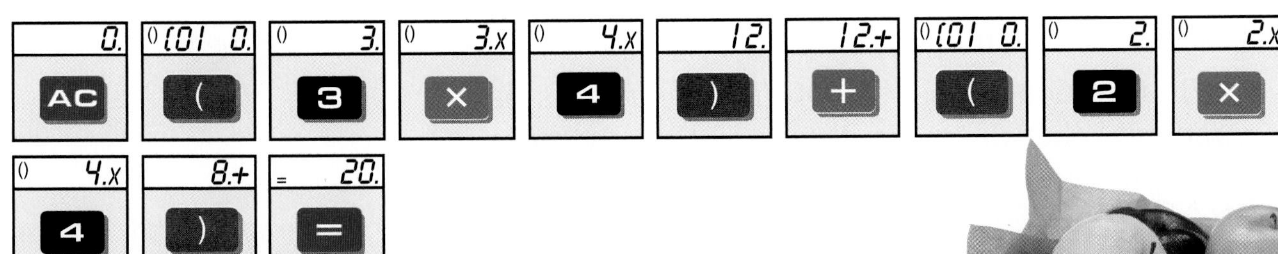

So, Fred ate 20 pieces of fruit in all.

PRACTICE

Copy and complete. Then use your calculator to solve.

1. $6 \times 3 = (4 \times 3) + (2 \times 3) = \underline{?}$
2. $8 \times 2 = (4 \times 2) + (4 \times \underline{?}) = \underline{?}$
3. $5 \times 5 = (4 \times 5) + (\underline{?} \times 5) = \underline{?}$
4. $10 \times 6 = (7 \times 6) + (\underline{?} \times \underline{?}) = \underline{?}$
5. Jack ate 3 bananas and 2 oranges every week for 6 weeks. How many pieces of fruit did Jack eat in all?

SHARE AND SHARE ALIKE

Division with Remainders

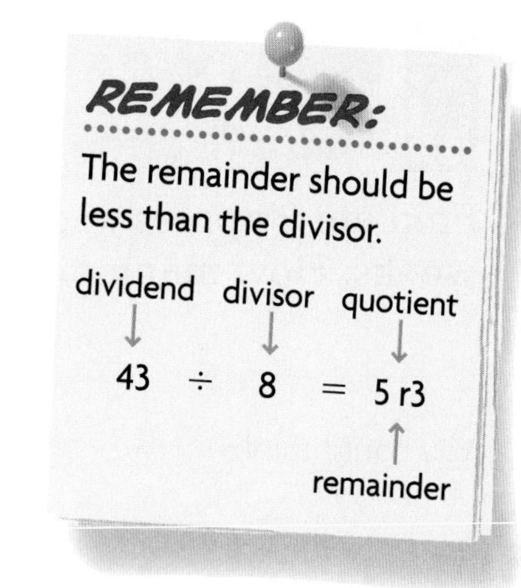

A jar contains 38 marbles. Can 5 people share the marbles equally?

- **Think:** $38 \div 5 = \underline{\ ?\ }$
- The marbles can be shared equally only if there is no remainder.
- Guess first. Then use your calculator to check.

Using the Calculator

Use the *TI Math Explorer* to find the value of $38 \div 5$. Enter the following:

Use the *Casio fx-55* to find the value of $38 \div 5$. Enter the following:

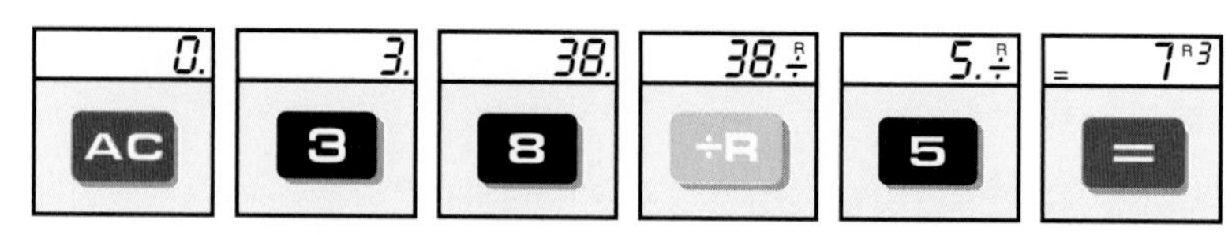

No, 5 people cannot share 38 marbles equally. Each person gets 7 marbles, but there are 3 marbles remaining.

- What do *Q* and *R* in the *Math Explorer* display mean? What does *R* in the *fx-55* display mean?

PRACTICE

Copy and complete. Use your calculator. First guess if the shares will be equal.

	Number of People	Number of Marbles	Number of Marbles Each	Number of Marbles Remaining	Equal Share?
1.	6	52	?	?	?
2.	4	63	?	?	?
3.	10	130	?	?	?
4.	20	187	?	?	?

SHOPPING SPREE

Multistep Problems

The memory keys are used to store numbers. The M+ key stores the product. The MR key recalls the product from memory.

The Minus Three Clothing Store deducts $3 from all purchase totals. Margarita bought 2 shirts and 1 belt. After the store deducted $3 from her bill, how much did Margarita pay for her purchases?

REMEMBER:

Use logical thinking to choose the correct operation.

- Choose addition or multiplication for more.
- Choose subtraction or division for less.

Minus Three Clothing Store

Item	Price
Shirts	$ 7
Jeans	$19
Sweaters	$12
Shoes	$25
Skirts	$18
Belts	$ 6

Using the Calculator

Here's how to use the memory of the *TI Math Explorer* to solve the problem.

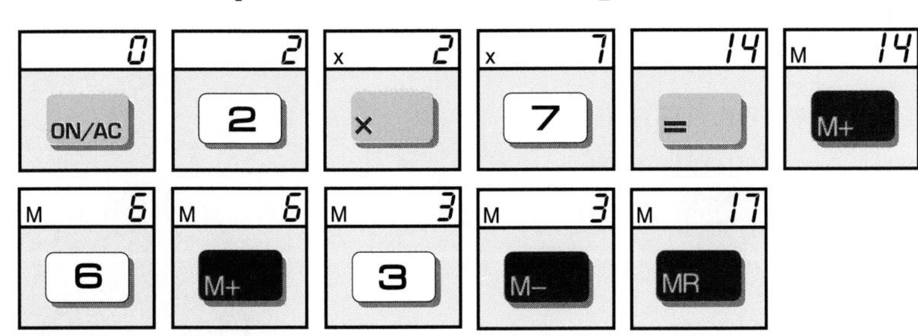

Here's how to use the memory of the *Casio fx-55* to solve the problem.

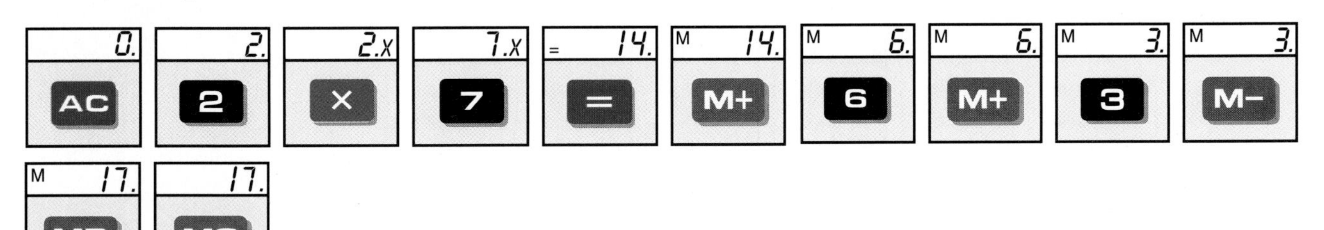

So, Margarita paid $17 for her purchases.

PRACTICE

Use the memory keys of your calculator. Figure out each total spent.

1. bought: 1 sweater
2 pairs jeans
deduction: $3
total spent: ?

2. bought: 2 pairs shoes
1 belt
deduction: $3
total spent: ?

3. bought: 3 sweaters
1 skirt
deduction: $3
total spent: ?

MAKING IT RIGHT!

Fixing Input Errors

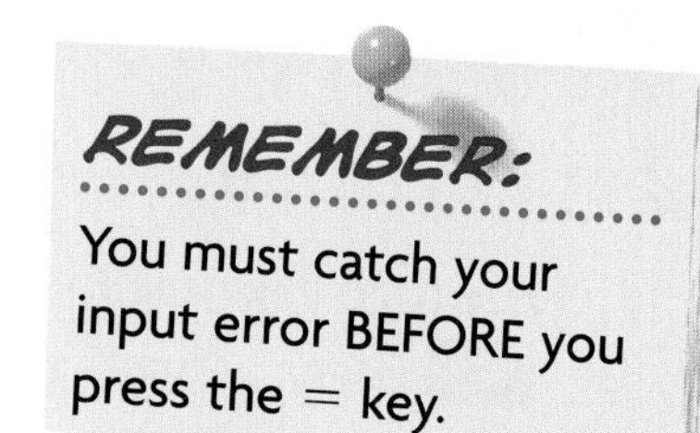

Mary doesn't have to start all over again. She can fix her input error and find the total without clearing the correct entries.

Oh, no!
I entered 688 instead of 68.
Do I have to start all over again?

Using the Calculator

Here's one way to correct an input error, using the *TI Math Explorer*.

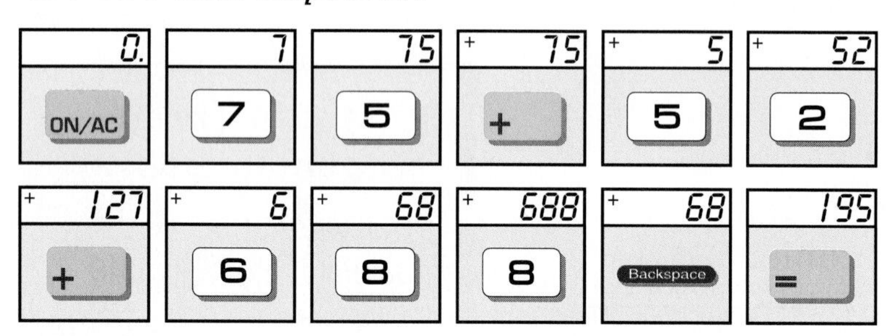

Here's one way to correct an input error, using the *Casio fx-55*. This method will also work on the *TI Math Explorer*. Use the CE/C key instead of the C key.

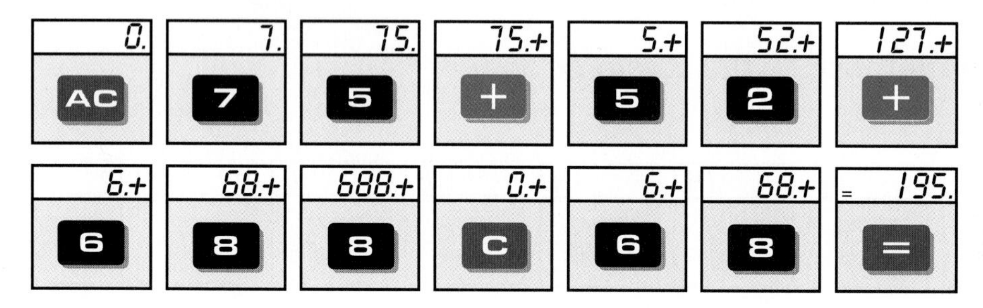

There is another way to correct an input error with the *Casio fx-55*. You can press the AC key, which will clear the entire calculation. Then you do have to start all over again!

75
52
+68

PRACTICE

Use your calculator to correct each entry. Then find each total. Try both methods.

1. Enter 35 + 12 + 419. Correct to 35 + 12 + 41.
2. Enter 201 + 125 + 367. Correct to 201 + 125 + 376.
3. Enter 3.5 + 67 + 7.2. Correct to 3.5 + 6.7 + 7.2.
4. Enter 25.1 − 13.4. Correct to 25.1 + 13.4.

BATTER'S UP!

Changing Fractions to Decimals and Decimals to Fractions

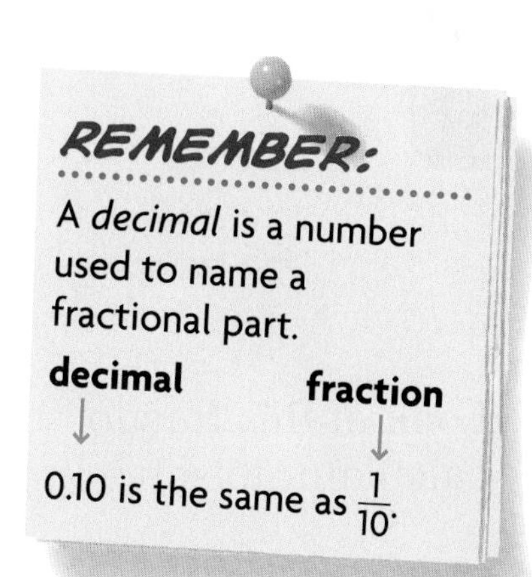

Last season Freddie the Slugger hit the ball $\frac{1}{4}$ of the times he was at bat. What decimal shows Freddie the Slugger's batting average?

Using the Calculator

Here's how to change $\frac{1}{4}$ to a decimal, using the *TI Math Explorer*.

I hit the ball $\frac{1}{4}$ of the times I was at bat.

Here's how to change $\frac{1}{4}$ to a decimal, using the *Casio fx-55*.

So, Freddie's batting average was 0.25, or 0.250. Check your answer. Use the *TI Math Explorer* to change 0.25 back to a fraction.

Here's how to change 0.25 to a fraction, using the *Casio fx-55*.

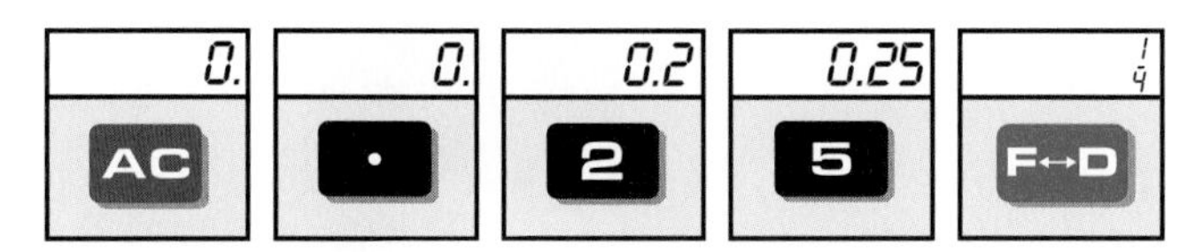

PRACTICE

Use your calculator. Change each fraction to a decimal. Check your answer by changing the decimal back to a fraction.

1. $\frac{2}{5}$ **2.** $\frac{2}{4}$ **3.** $\frac{3}{4}$ **4.** $\frac{7}{10}$ **5.** $\frac{1}{25}$ **6.** $\frac{6}{25}$

7. $\frac{9}{100}$ **8.** $\frac{11}{50}$ **9.** $\frac{13}{20}$ **10.** $\frac{4}{5}$ **11.** $\frac{11}{20}$ **12.** $\frac{11}{25}$

FRACTION FUN

Add and Subtract Fractions; Equivalent Fractions

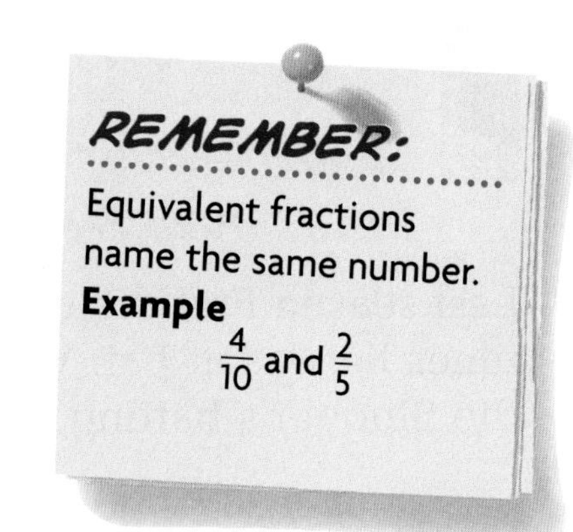

$\frac{5}{8} + \frac{2}{8} - \frac{6}{8} + \frac{3}{8} = \triangle$

Look at this fraction chain. You can use your calculator to solve it.

Using the Calculator

Here's how to add and subtract fractions with the *TI Math Explorer*.

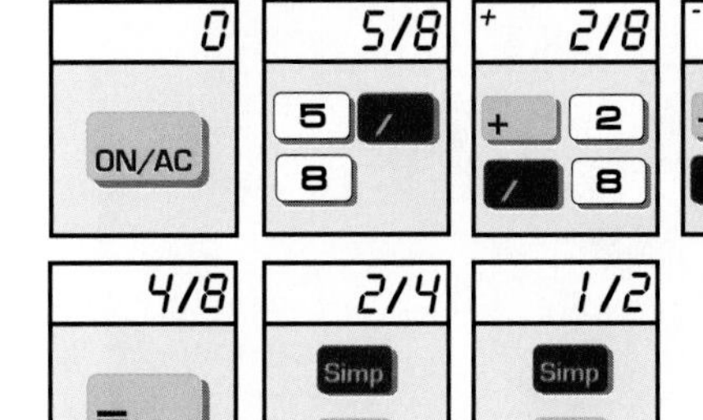

Here's how to add and subtract fractions with the *Casio fx-55*.

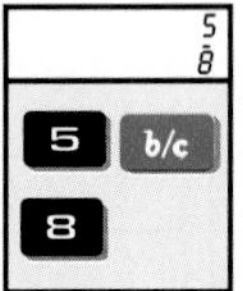

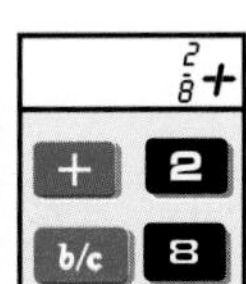

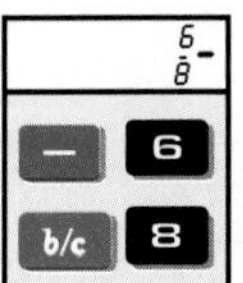

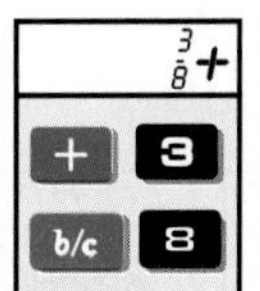

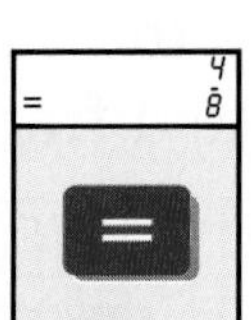

So, the answer is $\frac{1}{2}$. Did you notice that the answer $\frac{4}{8}$ was changed to simplest form? That's because $\frac{4}{8}$ and $\frac{1}{2}$ are equivalent fractions.

PRACTICE

Use your calculator to solve each fraction chain.
Use the SIMP key to find an equivalent fraction.

1. $\frac{3}{10} + \frac{5}{10} - \frac{4}{10} + \frac{1}{10} = \triangle$
2. $\frac{2}{9} - \frac{1}{9} + \frac{3}{9} - \frac{1}{9} = \triangle$
3. $\frac{7}{12} + \frac{2}{12} + \frac{2}{12} - \frac{3}{12} = \triangle$

FAST FRACTIONS

Mixed Numbers; Converting to a Mixed Number

You already know that $1\frac{2}{3}$ is a mixed number. Here's how to enter $1\frac{2}{3}$ on a calculator.

REMEMBER:

A fraction greater than 1 has a numerator that is greater than its denominator.

$\frac{5}{4}$ ← numerator / ← denominator

Using the Calculator

Using the *TI Math Explorer*

0	1	1u
ON/AC	1	Unit
1u2	1u2/	1u2/3
2	/	3

Using the *Casio fx-55*

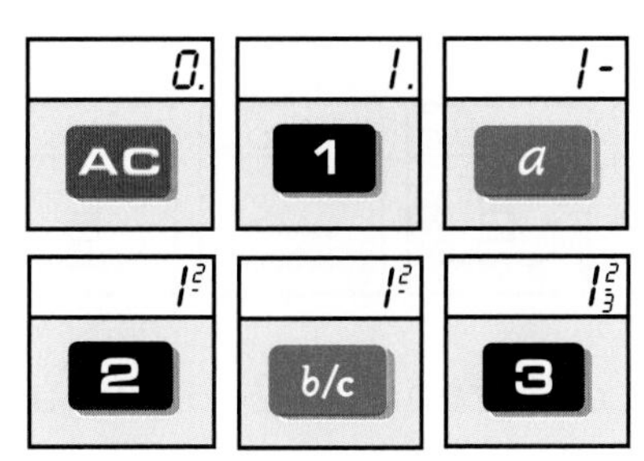

Sometimes you need to rename a fraction greater than 1 as a mixed number. Here's how to rename $\frac{8}{5}$ as a mixed number, using a calculator.

Using the *TI Math Explorer*

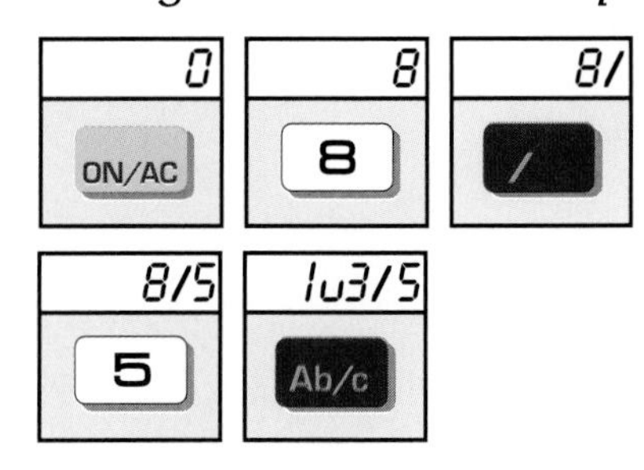

Using the *Casio fx-55*

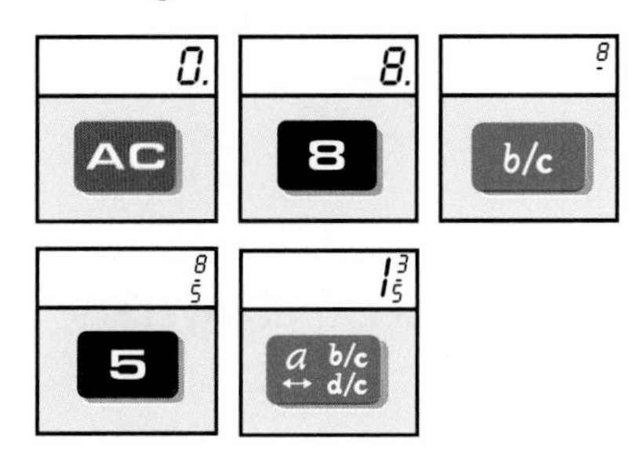

PRACTICE

You will need a watch or clock with a second hand. See how many mixed numbers you can enter in the calculator in 1 minute. Then, see how many fractions greater than 1 you can rename as mixed numbers in 1 minute. Remember to clear one entry before moving on to the next.

Mixed Numbers			Fractions		
$2\frac{1}{2}$	$4\frac{1}{3}$	$1\frac{2}{5}$	$\frac{3}{2}$	$\frac{6}{5}$	$\frac{8}{3}$
$1\frac{3}{4}$	$2\frac{6}{7}$	$3\frac{2}{3}$	$\frac{9}{4}$	$\frac{12}{11}$	$\frac{15}{5}$
$1\frac{1}{9}$	$3\frac{4}{13}$	$7\frac{2}{7}$	$\frac{17}{4}$	$\frac{11}{2}$	$\frac{16}{4}$

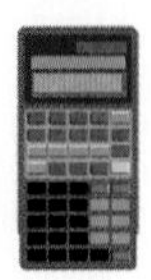

BE A DECIMAL DETECTIVE

Operate with Decimals

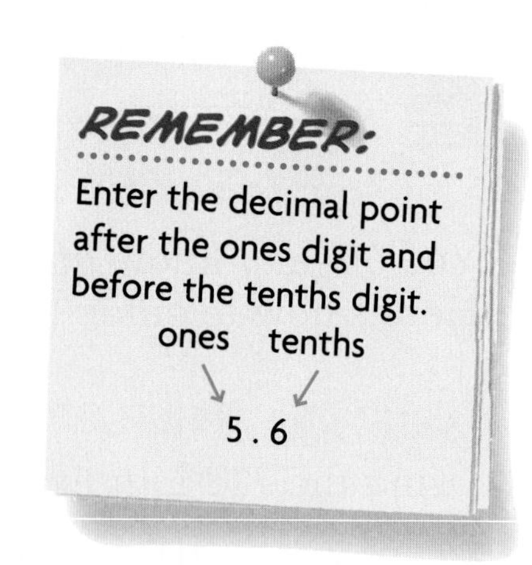

If I am added to 5.6, the sum is 8.2. Who am I?

You can solve this problem on your calculator. Start with the sum of 8.2. Then subtract 5.6.

Using the Calculator

Here's how to find the difference 8.2 − 5.6, using the *TI Math Explorer*.

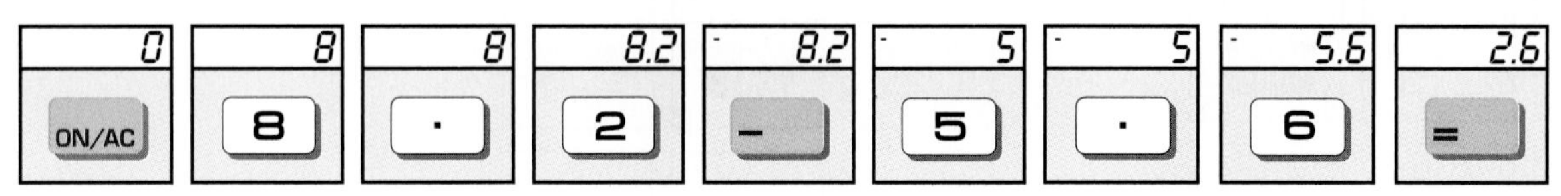

Here's how to find the difference 8.2 − 5.6, using the *Casio fx-55*.

So, I am 2.6. Use your calculator to check.
Does 5.6 + 2.6 = 8.2?

PRACTICE

Use your calculator to solve each decimal mystery.
Check your answers.

1. If I am added to 4.1, the sum is 9.7. Who am I?
2. If I am added to 12.75, the sum is 20.84. Who am I?
3. If I am subtracted from 6.2, the difference is 1.8. Who am I?
4. If I am subtracted from 23.79, the difference is 17.33. Who am I?
5. If I am added to 16.16, the sum is 20.27. Who am I?
6. If I am subtracted from 13.79, the difference is 7.58. Who am I?

ESTIMATE AND CALCULATE

Decimal Estimation; Fixing the Decimal Point

$$\begin{array}{r} 2.53 \\ +3.74 \\ \hline \end{array}$$

You can estimate sums on your calculator. By using the FIX key, you can "tell" the calculator how many decimal places you want to see in the answer. Estimate first.

REMEMBER:

Estimate the sum of decimal numbers by rounding.

1.28	rounds to 1.3
+2.41	rounds to 2.4

1.3 + 2.4 = 3.7. So, the sum is about 3.7.

Using the Calculator

Estimate the sum of 2.53 and 3.74 to one decimal place, using the *TI Math Explorer*.

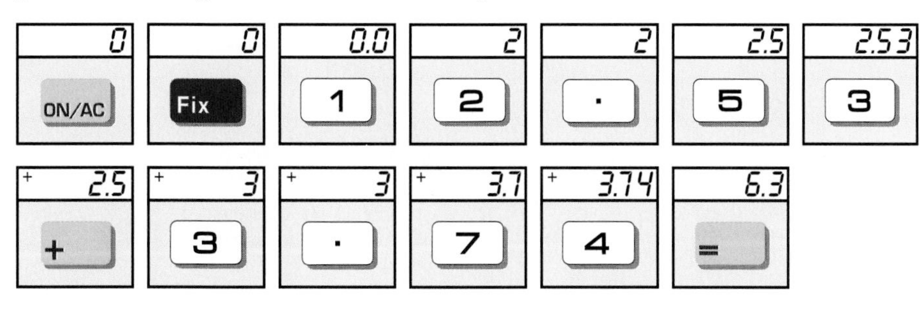

Estimate the sum of 2.53 and 3.74 to 1 decimal place, using the *Casio fx-55*.

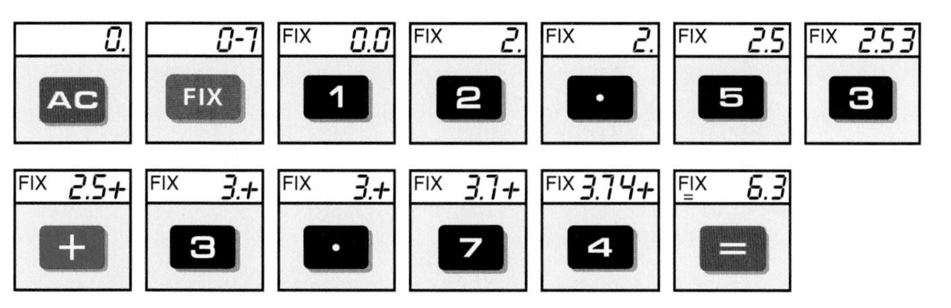

So, the sum is about 6.3.

To cancel the fix function on the *Casio fx-55*, press FIX ·.

PRACTICE

Estimate each sum to the nearest tenth. Use your calculator and the FIX key to check your answer.

1. $1.38 + 3.44 = n$

2. $5.84 + 3.57 = n$

3. $9.07 + 4.18 = n$

4. $4.11 + 6.21 = n$

5. $12.25 + 12.31 = n$

6. $6.76 + 13.19 = n$

More Practice

Chapter 1

Lesson 1.1 (pages 2–3)

Decide if you should add or subtract. Solve.

1. Juan had 9 erasers. Mary gave him some more erasers. Now he has 13 erasers. How many erasers did Mary give him?

2. Mike has 4 marbles. Shane has 8 more marbles than Mike. How many marbles does Shane have?

Lesson 1.2 (pages 4–5)

Copy and complete each equation. Show how you solved it.

1. $4 + 3 = \underline{\ ?\ } + 5$
2. $9 + 2 = \underline{\ ?\ } + 6$
3. $8 + 2 = 3 + \underline{\ ?\ }$
4. $9 + 6 = \underline{\ ?\ } + 3$
5. $8 + 4 = 5 + \underline{\ ?\ }$
6. $3 + 7 = \underline{\ ?\ } + 8$

Use mental math to complete each equation.

7. $\underline{\ ?\ } - 9 = 5 + 8$
8. $6 + \underline{\ ?\ } = 7 + 0$
9. $1 + 9 = \underline{\ ?\ } - 5$
10. $1 + 11 = \underline{\ ?\ } - 4$
11. $\underline{\ ?\ } - 2 = 8 + 8$
12. $13 + 2 = \underline{\ ?\ } + 3$

Lesson 1.3 Part 1 (pages 6–7)

Find the perimeter of each figure.

1.

7 in.

3 in. 3 in.

7 in.

2.

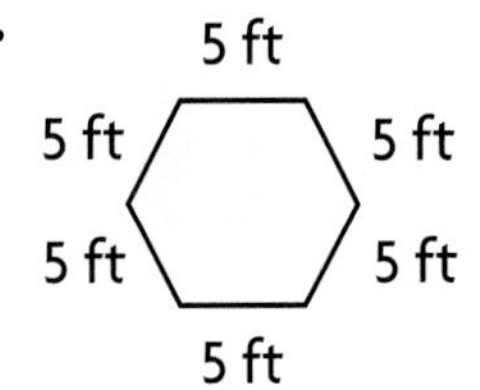

3.

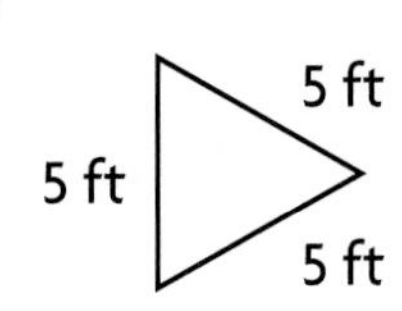

Find the sum.

4. $\begin{array}{r} 97 \\ 47 \\ +26 \\ \hline \end{array}$

5. $\begin{array}{r} 32 \\ 74 \\ +15 \\ \hline \end{array}$

6. $\begin{array}{r} 13 \\ 74 \\ +23 \\ \hline \end{array}$

7. $\begin{array}{r} 12 \\ 54 \\ +86 \\ \hline \end{array}$

8. $\begin{array}{r} 35 \\ 96 \\ +15 \\ \hline \end{array}$

Lesson 1.3 Part 2 (pages 8–9)

Make a model to solve.

1. The playground at Jonathan's school is 64 feet long and 33 feet wide. What is the perimeter of the playground?

2. The basketball court at Jamal's school is 20 feet long and 25 feet wide. What is the perimeter of the basketball court?

Lesson 1.4 (pages 10–11)

Round to the nearest *ten*.

1. 6 **2.** 18 **3.** 51 **4.** 73 **5.** 89

Round to the nearest *hundred*.

6. 67 **7.** 119 **8.** 345 **9.** 989 **10.** 450

Round $68.87 to each given amount.

11. ten cents **12.** dollar **13.** ten dollars

Estimate the sum or difference.

14. 147 + 298 + 745

15. 98 − 45

16. $1.47 + 2.98 + 7.45

17. 577 − 158

Lesson 1.5 (pages 12–13)

Find the sum or difference.

1. $3.97 + 2.95 + 1.85

2. $6.89 − 4.45

3. $7.47 + 5.67 + 9.87

4. $2.35 + 7.63

5. $3.36 − 1.99

Chapter 2

Lesson 2.1 (pages 18–19)

Use addition *and* subtraction to find the missing length.

1.

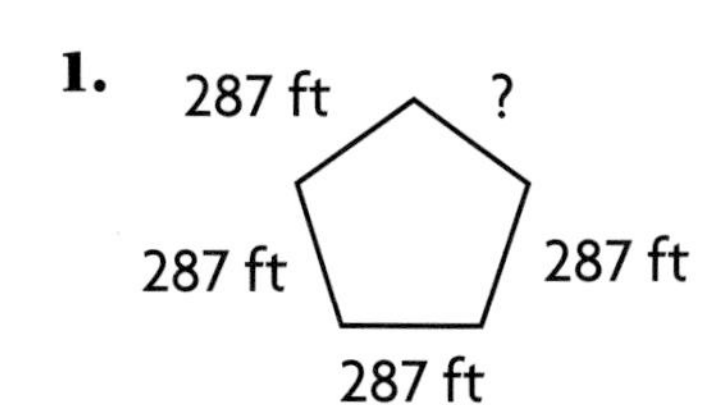

perimeter = 1,435 ft

2.

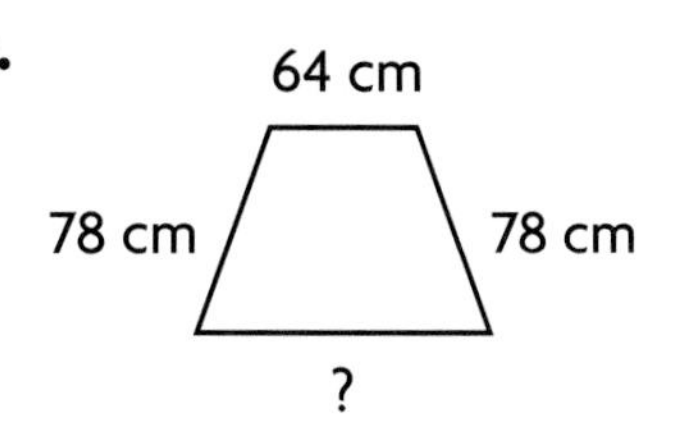

perimeter = 293 cm

3.

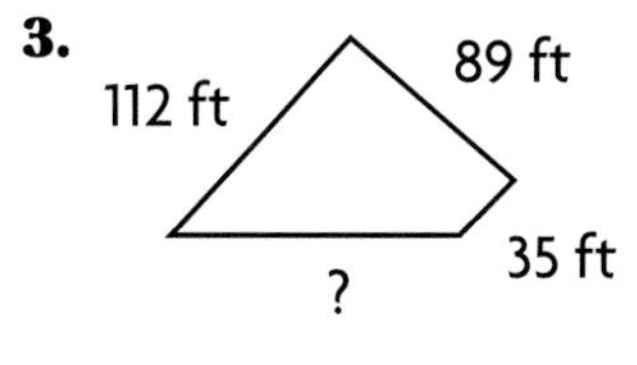

perimeter = 379 ft

Lesson 2.2 (pages 20–21)

Find the difference.

1. 200 − 119

2. 300 − 134

3. 200 − 79

4. 400 − 283

5. 300 − 275

6. 500 − 217

7. 900 − 621

8. 800 − 389

9. 600 − 411

10. 700 − 533

Lesson 2.3 Part 1 (pages 22–23)

Find the difference.

1. $\begin{array}{r} 500 \\ -164 \\ \hline \end{array}$

2. $\begin{array}{r} 700 \\ -453 \\ \hline \end{array}$

3. $\begin{array}{r} 600 \\ -332 \\ \hline \end{array}$

4. $\begin{array}{r} 900 \\ -681 \\ \hline \end{array}$

5. $\begin{array}{r} 2{,}000 \\ -1{,}190 \\ \hline \end{array}$

Lesson 2.3 Part 2 (pages 24–25)

Work backward to solve.

1. Dues of $2 each were paid by 15 new club members. They earned $45 at their bake sale. The club now has $100. How much money did the club have before the bake sale and dues?

2. Jamal and Mike played a number game. Mike chose a number and subtracted 7. Then, he added 1. Last, he subtracted 10. The result was 1. What number did Mike choose?

Lesson 2.4 (pages 26–27)

Round to the nearest *hundred.*

1. 345 2. 884 3. 523 4. 650 5. 495

Round to the nearest *thousand.*

6. 3,245 7. 9,024 8. 8,849 9. 3,500 10. 5,456

Round to the nearest *ten, hundred,* and *thousand.*

11. 2,356 12. 7,345 13. 4,677 14. 5,321 15. 9,398

Round to the nearest *ten, hundred,* or *thousand.* Estimate the sum or difference.

16. $\begin{array}{r} 360 \\ -192 \\ \hline \end{array}$

17. $\begin{array}{r} 696 \\ 405 \\ +387 \\ \hline \end{array}$

18. $\begin{array}{r} 5{,}499 \\ -3{,}132 \\ \hline \end{array}$

19. $\begin{array}{r} 545 \\ +285 \\ \hline \end{array}$

20. $\begin{array}{r} 599 \\ -109 \\ \hline \end{array}$

Lesson 2.5 (pages 28–29)

Write whether you should add or subtract to solve. Use the table to find the missing numbers and solve.

1. Juan took a vacation and went mountain climbing. He climbed _?_ feet to the top of Mt. Elbert. He then climbed _?_ feet to the top of Mt. McKinley. How many feet did Juan climb on his vacation?

TALLEST MOUNTAINS IN THE UNITED STATES	
Mt. McKinley	20,320 ft
Mt. Whitney	14,494 ft
Mt. Elbert	14,433 ft
Mt. Rainier	14,410 ft
Gannett Peak	13,804 ft
Mauna Kea	13,796 ft

2. Tonya climbed ___?___ feet to the top of Mt. Rainier. Chad climbed ___?___ feet to the top of Gannett Peak. Did Chad or Tonya climb the greater distance? How much greater?

3. Jim wanted to climb 28,000 feet in two climbs. He climbed ___?___ feet to the top of Mauna Kea and then climbed ___?___ feet to the top of Gannett Peak. Did Jim meet his goal?

Chapter 3

Lesson 3.1 (pages 34–35)

Model each problem. Solve.

1. Tim has 4 packs of baseball cards with 3 cards in each pack. How many baseball cards does Tim have?

2. Lisa has 2 bags of gum balls with 7 gum balls in each bag. How many gum balls does Lisa have?

Lesson 3.2 (pages 36–37)

Write *a, b,* or *c* to tell which property is shown.

a. Property of One   **b.** Zero Property   **c.** Order Property

1. $1 \times 35 = 35$ **2.** $8 \times 3 = 3 \times 8$ **3.** $325 \times 0 = 0$ **4.** $43 \times 1 = 43$

Use the multiplication properties to solve.

5. $\begin{array}{r} 4 \\ \times 1 \\ \hline \end{array}$ **6.** $\begin{array}{r} 9 \\ \times 0 \\ \hline \end{array}$ **7.** $\begin{array}{r} 1 \\ \times 7 \\ \hline \end{array}$ **8.** $\begin{array}{r} 8 \\ \times 0 \\ \hline \end{array}$ **9.** $\begin{array}{r} 6 \\ \times 1 \\ \hline \end{array}$ **10.** $\begin{array}{r} 0 \\ \times 1 \\ \hline \end{array}$

11. $2 \times 9 =$ ___?___
 $9 \times 2 =$ ___?___

12. $4 \times 7 =$ ___?___
 $7 \times 4 =$ ___?___

13. $8 \times 3 =$ ___?___
 $3 \times 8 =$ ___?___

14. $6 \times 5 =$ ___?___
 $5 \times 6 =$ ___?___

Lesson 3.3 (pages 38–39)

Use the array. Find the products.

1. What is 4×7?

7   4   3

4   4 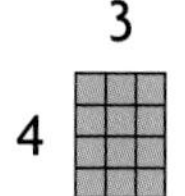   4

$4 \times 4 =$ ___?___ $4 \times 3 =$ ___?___   So, $4 \times 7 =$ ___?___.

Use grid paper. Break apart the numbers to find the product.

2. $3 \times 6 =$ ___?___   **3.** $4 \times 8 =$ ___?___   **4.** $9 \times 3 =$ ___?___   **5.** $5 \times 6 =$ ___?___

6. $5 \times 9 =$ ___?___   **7.** $8 \times 7 =$ ___?___   **8.** $6 \times 5 =$ ___?___   **9.** $9 \times 7 =$ ___?___

10. $8 \times 8 =$ ___?___   **11.** $6 \times 9 =$ ___?___   **12.** $7 \times 6 =$ ___?___   **13.** $8 \times 5 =$ ___?___

Lesson 3.4 Part 1 (pages 40–41)

Find the product.

1. $(4 \times 2) \times 3 = \underline{?}$

2. $(4 \times 4) \times 2 = \underline{?}$

3. $(1 \times 5) \times 4 = \underline{?}$

Show two ways to group Exercises 4–6 using parentheses.
Find the products.

4. $1 \times 4 \times 1 = \underline{?}$

5. $2 \times 4 \times 3 = \underline{?}$

6. $3 \times 3 \times 4 = \underline{?}$

Lesson 3.4 Part 2 (pages 42–43)

Make a model to solve.

1. At the computer store, there were 2 rows of computer disks. Each row had 3 packages of disks, and each package contained 6 disks. How many disks were there in all?

2. The store received some apples. There were 3 rows of boxes, with 3 boxes in each row. Each box contained 8 bags of apples. How many bags were there?

Lesson 3.5 (pages 44–45)

Choose the number sentences you would use to solve Problems 1–2. Then solve.

a. $7 + 2 = \underline{?}$

b. $7 \times 2 = \underline{?}$

c. $7 - 2 = \underline{?}$

d. $7 - \underline{?} = 2$

1. The boat races at the harbor had 7 events. There were 2 boats entered in each event. How many boats were entered in the races?

2. While watching the boat races, Bob was fishing from a dock. He caught 7 fish but let 2 go. How many fish did Bob keep?

Chapter 4

Lesson 4.1 (pages 50–51)

Decide whether using division will answer the question.
Write *yes* or *no*. If you write *yes*, then solve.

1. Carla has 12 folders to use for 6 subjects at school. She uses the same number of folders for each subject. How many folders does she have for each subject?

2. There are 16 people waiting to ride 4 hot-air balloons. Each balloon carries the same number of people. How many people will be in each balloon?

Lesson 4.2 (pages 52–53)

Write a related multiplication fact.

1. $9 \div 3 = 3$ **2.** $12 \div 4 = 3$ **3.** $18 \div 3 = 6$ **4.** $24 \div 8 = 3$

Complete the number sentence. Write the related multiplication fact used to find the quotient.

5. $8 \div 2 =$ _?_ **6.** $10 \div 5 =$ _?_ **7.** $14 \div 2 =$ _?_ **8.** $20 \div 5 =$ _?_

Write the fact family for each set of numbers.

9. 2, 8, 16 **10.** 3, 5, 15 **11.** 4, 7, 28

Lesson 4.3 Part 1 (pages 54–55)

Use counters to find the quotient and remainder.

1. $14 \div 3 =$ _?_ **2.** $19 \div 6 =$ _?_ **3.** $32 \div 5 =$ _?_

4. $41 \div 6 =$ _?_ **5.** $53 \div 7 =$ _?_ **6.** $61 \div 7 =$ _?_

Use the model to find the quotient.

7.

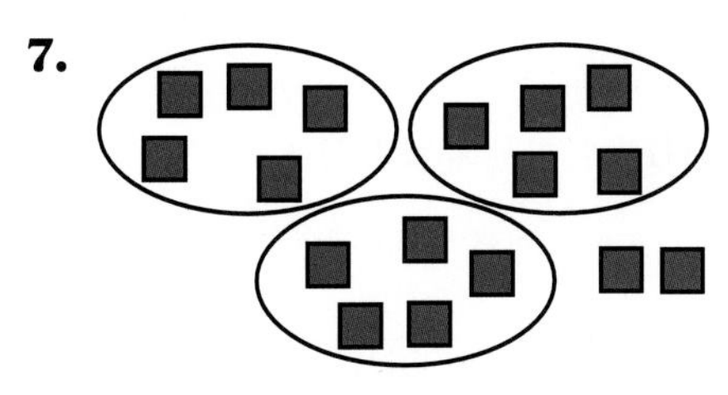

$17 \div 3 =$ _?_

8.

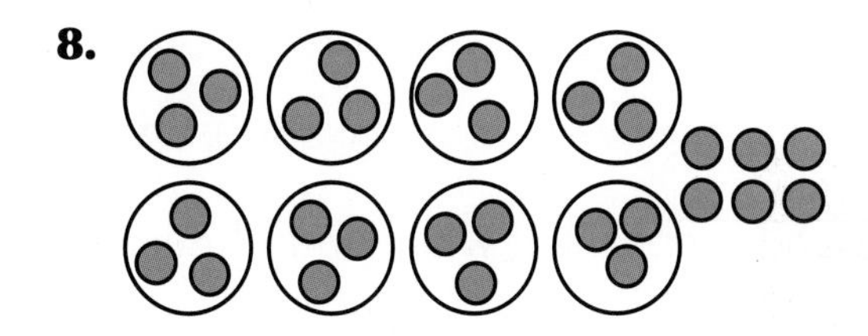

$30 \div 8 =$ _?_

Find the quotient. You may wish to use a model to help you.

9. $13 \div 5 =$ _?_ **10.** $19 \div 6 =$ _?_ **11.** $26 \div 8 =$ _?_ **12.** $45 \div 7 =$ _?_

13. $59 \div 8 =$ _?_ **14.** $67 \div 7 =$ _?_ **15.** $70 \div 8 =$ _?_ **16.** $79 \div 9 =$ _?_

Lesson 4.3 Part 2 (pages 56–57)

Make a table to solve.

1. George went to the grocery store to buy oranges. He can buy single oranges or bags of 6. In how many different ways can George buy 18 oranges?

2. Gina needs 4 tickets to ride the Ferris wheel. Tickets can be bought separately or in sets of 3. In how many different ways can Gina buy enough tickets to ride the Ferris wheel 4 times?

Lesson 4.4 (pages 58–59)

Find the quotient.

1. $8 \div 1 =$ _?_ **2.** $14 \div 2 =$ _?_ **3.** $18 \div 6 =$ _?_ **4.** $12 \div 3 =$ _?_

Lesson 4.5 (pages 60–61)

Find the quotient.

1. $12 \div 3 = \underline{?}$ **2.** $14 \div 2 = \underline{?}$ **3.** $28 \div 7 = \underline{?}$ **4.** $36 \div 6 = \underline{?}$

5. $9\overline{)36}$ **6.** $6\overline{)48}$ **7.** $7\overline{)49}$ **8.** $7\overline{)56}$

Lesson 4.6 (pages 62–63)

Choose an operation to use. Then solve.

1. The pet store sells boxes of hamster food for $1.50 each. James bought 3 boxes. What was the total amount James paid for the hamster food?

2. There are 9 cookies on the plate. If Joy and her 2 friends each eat the same number of cookies, how many cookies will each eat?

Chapter 5

Lesson 5.1 Part 1 (pages 72–73)

Tell whether each number is *cardinal, ordinal*, or *nominal*.

1. 1st **2.** 6,749 **3.** 2809 Owl Dr. **4.** 413th **5.** 11:00 A.M.

Write each number. Tell what kind of number it is.

6. your place in line with 2 people in front of you

7. the temperature outside

8. the price of a pack of gum

9. your address

Write the temperature, weight, or length shown.

10. **11.** **12.**

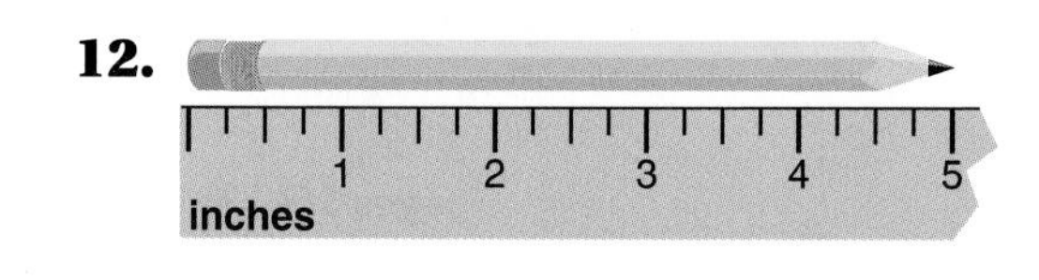

Lesson 5.1 Part 2 (pages 74–75)

Use the map to write the ordered pair for each place.

1. Police Station

2. Fire Station

3. Hospital

4. Library

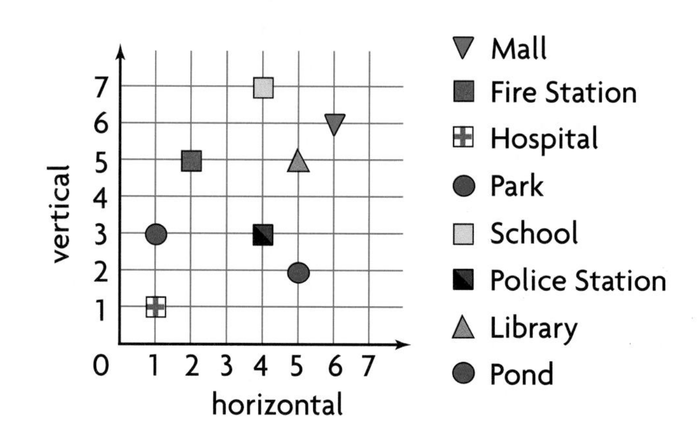

Write the name of the place for the ordered pair.

5. (6,6) **6.** (5,2) **7.** (4,7) **8.** (1,3)

Copy and complete the table. Use the ordered pair to find the landmark on the grid below.

	Ordered Pair	Landmark
9.	(6,6)	?
10.	(4,4)	?
11.	(7,2)	?
12.	(1,5)	?

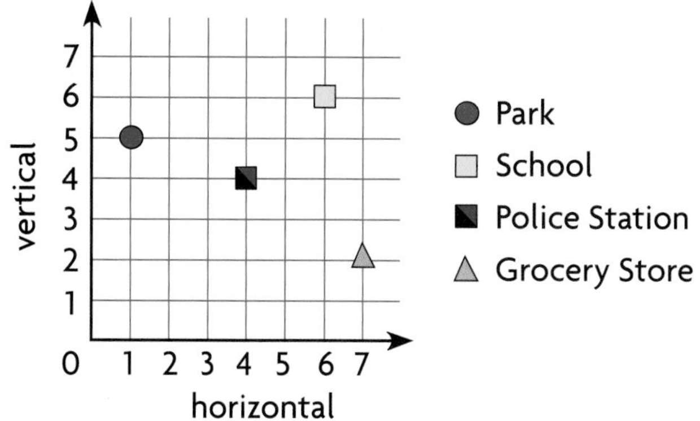

Lesson 5.2 (pages 76–77)

Look in your "1,000 Squares" book. Write the page number on which each number is found.

1. 65 **2.** 32 **3.** 198 **4.** 225

5. 399 **6.** 401 **7.** 550 **8.** 675

9. 749 **10.** 837 **11.** 943 **12.** 1,000

Lesson 5.3 Part 1 (pages 78–79)

Write the number shown by the base-ten blocks.

1. 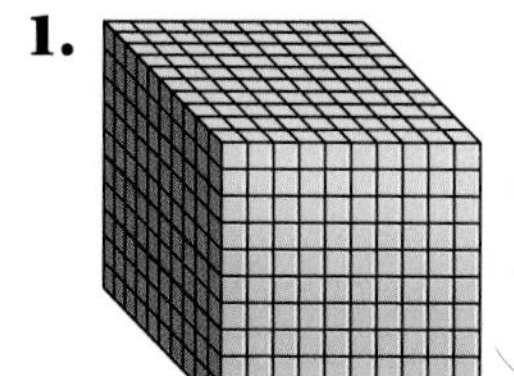 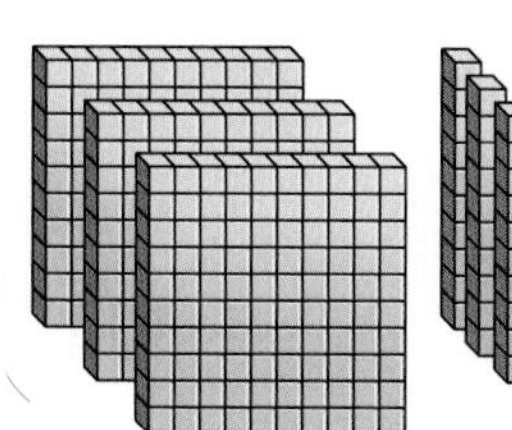 

2. 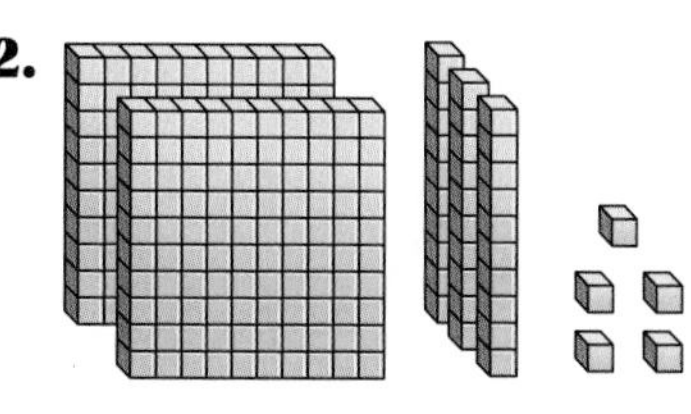

Record the number of thousands, hundreds, tens, and ones.

3. 1,909 **4.** 8,001 **5.** 3,278 **6.** 5,454 **7.** 2,187

8. 4,290 **9.** 6,005 **10.** 7,731 **11.** 9,437 **12.** 5,205

13. 8,764 **14.** 9,611 **15.** 3,856 **16.** 1,042 **17.** 7,593

Put in the comma, and write each number in words.

18. 8745 **19.** 5363 **20.** 8725 **21.** 3454 **22.** 5007

23. 3846 **24.** 4699 **25.** 2457 **26.** 1780 **27.** 4271

28. 1003 **29.** 7587 **30.** 4187 **31.** 2080 **32.** 3890

Lesson 5.3 Part 2 (pages 80–81)

Act it out to solve.

1. Lee had 12 sport cards. He gave Mike 4 of his cards. Lee now has twice as many cards as Tom. How many cards does Tom have?

2. Krista had 15 pennies. She put 3 pennies into each of several banks. In how many banks did Krista place 3 pennies?

Lesson 5.4 (pages 82–83)

Write a benchmark number for each problem. Use the benchmark to estimate.

A.

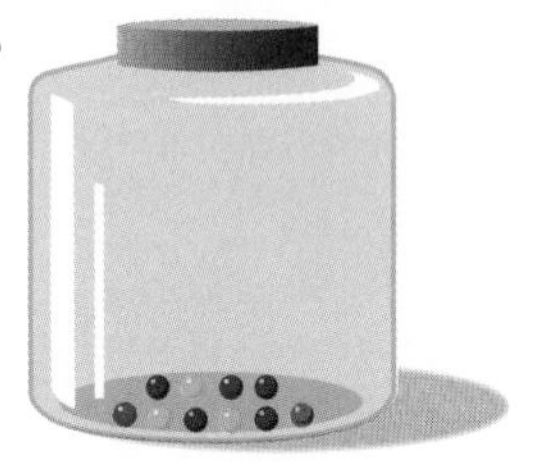

10 gum balls

B.

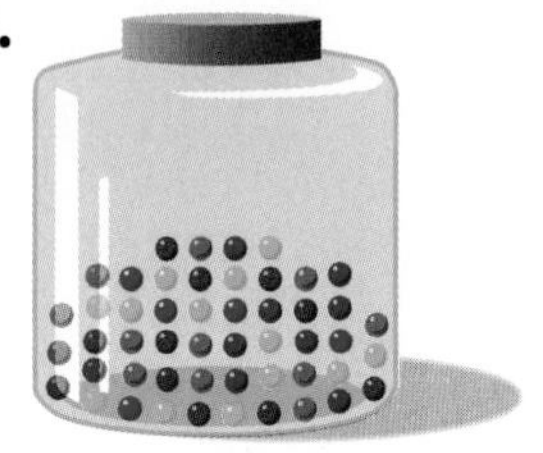

C.

1. In which jar are there about 50 gum balls?

2. In which jar are there about 100 gum balls?

3. Are there more or fewer gum balls in jar A than in jar C?

4. Are there more or fewer gum balls in jar B than in jar A?

Chapter 6

Lesson 6.1 (pages 88–89)

Write the value of each group of Egyptian symbols.

1. 𓆼𓍢∩|

2. 𓆼𓆼𓍢

3. 𓆼𓍢𓍢|||||

4. 𓆼𓆼𓍢𓍢∩||||||||

5. 𓆼𓆼𓆼𓍢𓍢𓍢𓍢∩|

6. 𓆼𓆼𓆼𓆼∩

Show the value of each digit in a place-value system.

7. 2,225 **8.** 6,798 **9.** 9,995 **10.** 999 **11.** 1,150

12. 203 **13.** 420 **14.** 7,902 **15.** 3,628 **16.** 4,051

Lesson 6.2 (pages 90–91)

Write each number in standard form.

1. forty-five

2. one thousand, one

3. four thousand, two hundred one

4. one hundred one

5. two thousand, one hundred five

6. seven thousand, fifty-six

Write each number in expanded form and written form.

7. 56 **8.** 5,084 **9.** 373 **10.** 8,835 **11.** 9,123

12. 1,723 **13.** 6,021 **14.** 4,090 **15.** 3,500 **16.** 4,006

Write each number in two other ways.

17. 499 **18.** one thousand, fifty **19.** 200 + 70 + 3

20. 6,000 + 400 + 20 + 1 **21.** 4,592 **22.** seven hundred one

Lesson 6.3 (pages 92–93)

Use place value to name each number in two different ways.

1. 50 **2.** 990 **3.** 340 **4.** 820 **5.** 8,900

Use another name for each number and solve by using mental math.

6. 100 + 300

7. 9,000 + 6,000

8. 900 + 800

9. 7,100 + 3,300

10. 8,000 + 8,000

11. 1,600 + 2,100

12. 3,200 + 6,300

13. 4,100 + 4,800

14. 5,300 + 3,900

15. 6,400 + 3,900

Lesson 6.4 (pages 94–95)

Write *true* or *false* for each statement. Rewrite false statements to make them true.

1. There are exactly 10 thousands in 1,000.

2. There are exactly 100 thousands in 10,000.

3. There are exactly 10 ten thousands in 100,000.

4. There are exactly 10 thousands in 10,000.

5. There are exactly 100 thousands in 1,000.

6. There is exactly 1 ten thousand in 100,000.

Lesson 6.5 Part 1 (pages 96–97)

Write the number as you would say it with period names.

1. 154,325 154 ___, 325

2. 3,233,104 3 ___, 233 ___, 104

3. 64,798,001 64 ___, 798 ___, 1

4. 354,340,406 354 ___, 340 ___, 406

5. 926,000,020 926 ___, 20

Write each number in standard form.

6. one hundred forty million, five hundred fifty thousand, nine hundred one

7. seventy-eight million, eight hundred twenty thousand, six hundred fifty-two

Write *yes* or *no* to tell whether each number is large enough to be counted in the hundred thousands or more.

8. the number of days in a year

9. the number of fish in the ocean

10. the number of pencils in your desk

11. the number of students in your school

12. the number of stars in the sky

13. the number of people at a football game

Lesson 6.5 Part 2 (pages 98–99)

Use the table to solve.

Population of Large U.S. Cities (people)	
New York, NY	7,322,564
Los Angeles, CA	3,485,557
Chicago, IL	2,783,726
Phoenix, AZ	983,403
Indianapolis, IN	741,952

1. Between which two cities is the greatest difference in population?

2. How many more people live in Chicago than in Indianapolis?

3. The cities with the smallest difference in population are __?__ and __?__.

4. Tim moved from New York to Phoenix. How many fewer people live in Phoenix than in New York?

5. There are a total of __?__ people living in New York and Chicago combined.

6. The city with the smallest population has __?__ fewer people than Los Angeles.

Chapter 7

Lesson 7.1 (pages 104–105)

Use the number line to compare. Use $<$ or $>$.

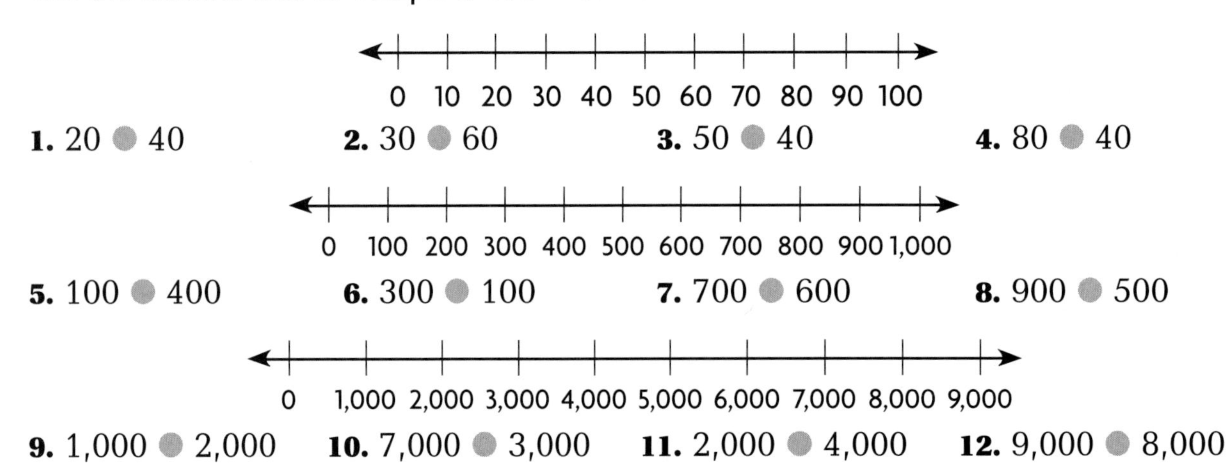

1. 20 ● 40 **2.** 30 ● 60 **3.** 50 ● 40 **4.** 80 ● 40

5. 100 ● 400 **6.** 300 ● 100 **7.** 700 ● 600 **8.** 900 ● 500

9. 1,000 ● 2,000 **10.** 7,000 ● 3,000 **11.** 2,000 ● 4,000 **12.** 9,000 ● 8,000

Compare the numbers and write < or > for the ●.

13. 5,000 ● 8,000 **14.** 3,000 ● 7,000 **15.** 9,000 ● 6,000

Lesson 7.2 Part 1 (pages 106–107)

Write the greatest place-value position in which the digits are different.
Write the greater number.

1. 25, 24 **2.** 56, 65 **3.** 125, 115 **4.** 188, 182 **5.** 456, 265

Compare the numbers. Write the comparison using <, >, or =.

6. 85
68

7. 69
96

8. 121
211

9. 388
438

10. 788
841

Lesson 7.2 Part 2 (pages 108–109)

Guess and check to solve.

1. Thomas started a club with 2 friends. In the next 3 days, his club grew to a total of 24 members. How many people joined each day for those 3 days?

2. There are 7 cows and chickens on Jenny's farm. All together, the 7 animals have 24 legs. How many cows are on Jenny's farm? How many chickens?

Lesson 7.3 (pages 110–111)

Order from the least to the greatest length.

1. a. 16 cm

b.  3 cm

c. 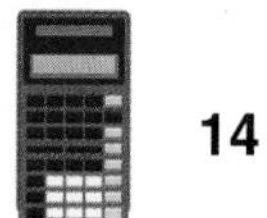 14 cm

2. a. 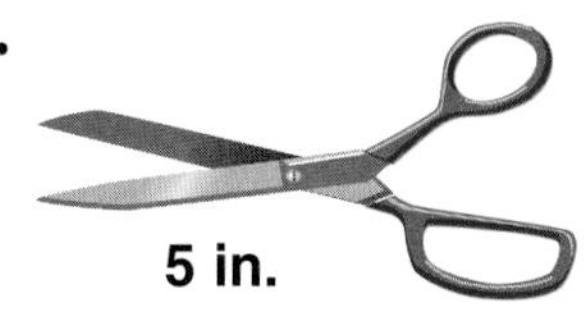 5 in.

b. 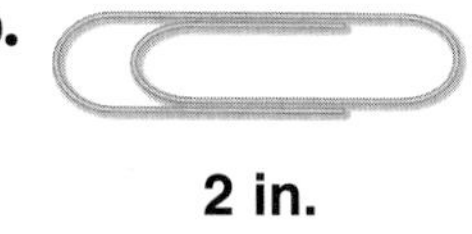 2 in.

c. 12 in.

Lesson 7.4 (pages 112–113)

Write the numbers in order from the least to the greatest.

1. 486, 152, 264 **2.** 646, 387, 984 **3.** 385, 185, 793

4. 781, 993, 312 **5.** 735, 291, 381 **6.** 981, 873, 867

Write the numbers in order from the greatest to the least.

7. 229, 250, 109 **8.** 277, 768, 312 **9.** 304, 187, 897

10. 150, 696, 646 **11.** 812, 575, 752 **12.** 899, 989, 990

Lesson 7.5 (pages 114–115)

Copy the Venn diagrams. Place the numbers where they belong.

1. 10, 34, 45, 69, 97, 101 **2.** 9, 21, 139, 99, 874, 911 **3.** 304, 441, 520, 419, 631

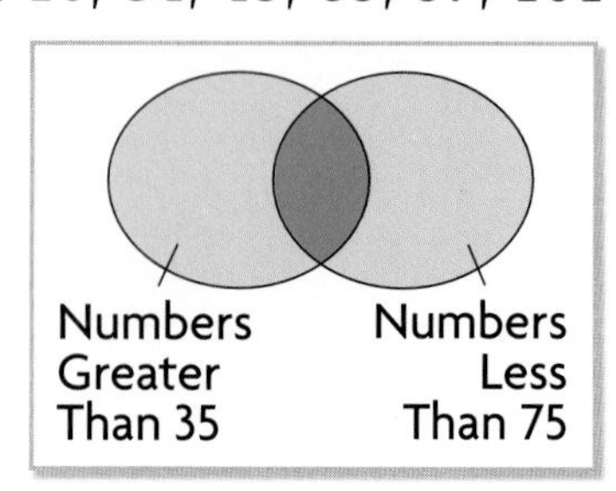

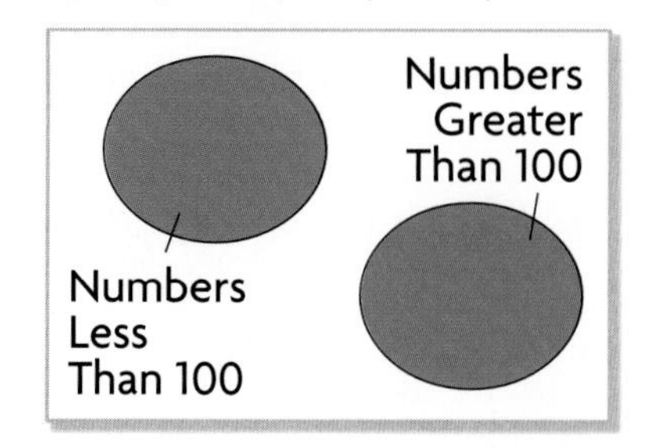

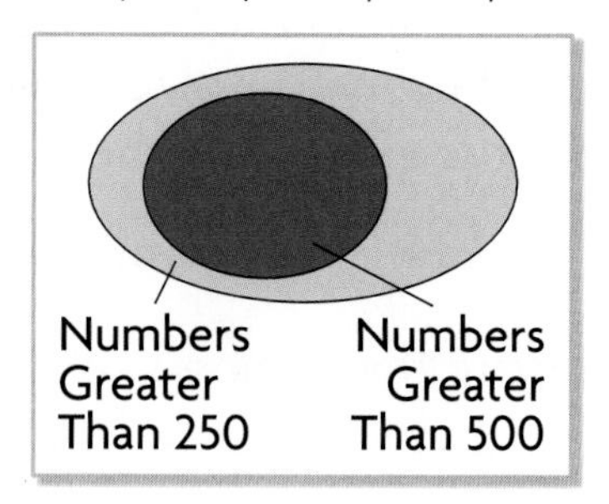

Chapter 8

Lesson 8.1 (pages 120–121)

Write the letter of the unit used to measure the time. Use each answer only once.

a. days	**c.** minutes
b. hours	**d.** seconds

1. complete your math homework

2. a dog to bark one time

3. have a good night's sleep

4. complete a book report

Write the time shown on the clock. Include seconds.

5. 

6. 

7. 

8. 

Lesson 8.2 (pages 122–123)

Write the time, using A.M. or P.M.

1. when you get out of bed

2. when you do your homework

Write the time as shown on a 24-hour clock.

3. 8:00 P.M. **4.** 5:00 A.M. **5.** 2:00 P.M. **6.** 10:00 A.M. **7.** 4:00 P.M.

Lesson 8.3 (pages 124–125)

Use an analog clock to find the elapsed time.

1. start: 4:15 P.M.
end: 7:20 P.M.

2. start: 3:00 P.M.
end: 9:25 P.M.

3. start: 5:25 P.M.
end: 1:30 A.M.

4. start: 2:15 A.M.
end: 7:45 A.M.

Write the ending time.

5. **starting time:** 10:05 P.M.
elapsed time: 2 hr 25 min

6. **starting time:** 12:15 A.M.
elapsed time: 5 hr 15 min

7. **starting time:** 5:10 P.M.
elapsed time: 3 hr 10 min

8. **starting time:** 9:55 P.M.
elapsed time: 3 hr 40 min

Lesson 8.4 Part 1 (pages 126–127)

For Problems 1–3, use the schedule.

BAYSIDE CLEANUP DAY	
Job	**Time**
Litter Cleanup	9:00 A.M.
Planting	10:30 A.M.
Weeding	11:50 A.M.
Window Washing	12:45 P.M.

1. Bayside Elementary is having a cleanup day. Each job lasts for 1 hour and 15 minutes. What time will each activity end?

2. Is it possible to be there for all four activities? Explain.

3. What is the elapsed time from the beginning of weeding to the end of window washing?

Lesson 8.4 Part 2 (pages 128–129)

Make a table to solve.

1. Cheerleading practice begins after school at 3:00. It lasts 2 hours and 30 minutes on Monday and Wednesday, and 2 hours on Friday. At what time does practice end each day?

2. Susan has swim practice on Mondays at 3:30, on Tuesdays and Thursdays at 4:15, and Wednesdays and Fridays at 4:30. Each practice lasts 1 hour 30 minutes. At what time does each session end?

Lesson 8.5 (pages 130–131)

For Problems 1–3, use the calendars.

1. Kaley's birthday is May 19. Matthew's is exactly 1 month and 3 days after Kaley's. When is Matthew's birthday?

MAY						
Sun	Mon	Tue	Wed	Thu	Fri	Sat
					1	2
3	4	5	6	7	8	9
10	11	12	13	14	15	16
17	18	19	20	21	22	23
24	25	26	27	28	29	30
31						

JUNE						
Sun	Mon	Tue	Wed	Thu	Fri	Sat
	1	2	3	4	5	6
7	8	9	10	11	12	13
14	15	16	17	18	19	20
21	22	23	24	25	26	27
28	29	30				

JULY						
Sun	Mon	Tue	Wed	Thu	Fri	Sat
			1	2	3	4
5	6	7	8	9	10	11
12	13	14	15	16	17	18
19	20	21	22	23	24	25
26	27	28	29	30	31	

2. The Tuckers are going on vacation for 2 weeks and 3 days. They will leave on June 3. When will they return?

3. How many days pass between July 6 and August 1?

Chapter 9

Lesson 9.1 (pages 140–141)

For Problems 1–7, use the frequency table.

CANNED FOODS COLLECTED		
Week	Number of Cans	Cumulative Frequency
1	27	27
2	32	59
3	21	80
4	40	120

1. How many cans of food were collected during Week 1?
2. How many cans of food were collected during Week 4?
3. By the end of Week 3, how many cans had been collected?
4. How many cans in all were collected during Weeks 2 and 3?
5. How many more cans were collected during Week 4 than during Week 1?
6. How many cans were collected in all?
7. How many more cans were collected during Weeks 3 and 4 than during Weeks 1 and 2?

Lesson 9.2 Part 1 (pages 142–143)

For Problems 1–5, use the table.

Mary and Peter made this table to organize the results of an experiment in which they tossed a two-color counter and a number cube with the numbers 1–6.

<table>
<tr><th colspan="7">EXPERIMENTAL RESULTS</th></tr>
<tr><td></td><td>1</td><td>2</td><td>3</td><td>4</td><td>5</td><td>6</td></tr>
<tr><td>Red</td><td></td><td>|</td><td>||</td><td></td><td>|</td><td>|</td></tr>
<tr><td>Yellow</td><td>|</td><td></td><td></td><td></td><td>|||</td><td></td></tr>
</table>

1. What are all the possible outcomes for this experiment?
2. How would the table change if they used a spinner with the numbers 1–4 instead of a number cube?
3. How do the parts of the table relate to all possible outcomes?
4. What are all the possible outcomes if they toss a two-color counter and spin a spinner with the numbers 1–4?
5. Which outcome happened most often?

Lesson 9.2 Part 2 (pages 144 –145)

Make an organized list to solve.

1. Ray can have one scoop of ice cream. His choices are coffee, fudge swirl, and peppermint. He may choose a waffle cone, sugar cone, or a cup. In how many possible ways can Ray have his ice cream?

2. Sierra is going to have one scoop of ice cream in a cup. She is deciding between vanilla, chocolate, and strawberry. She will have one topping. Her choices are nuts and hot fudge. In how many possible ways can she have her ice cream?

Lesson 9.3 (pages 146–147)

Tommy conducted a survey to help him decide what game to play with his friends. He asked his friends, "What is your favorite game?" The table shows the results of his survey.

FAVORITE GAME	
Game	**Votes**
Tag	|||
Hide-and-Seek	||||
Baseball	||
Basketball	卌
Soccer	|

For Problems 1–3, use the table.

1. What game is the favorite of the greatest number of Tommy's friends?

2. How do you think the survey would change if Tommy asked, "Is your favorite game baseball, basketball, or soccer?"

3. Does the survey question make it easy for Tommy to choose which game to play with his friends? Explain.

Lesson 9.4 (pages 148–149)

For Exercises 1–2, use the graphs.

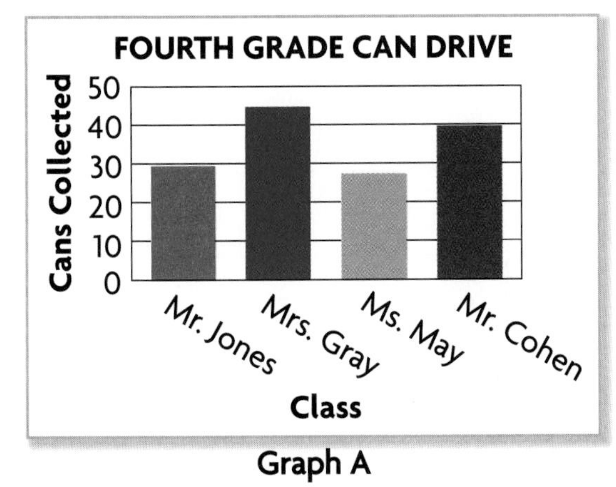

Graph A

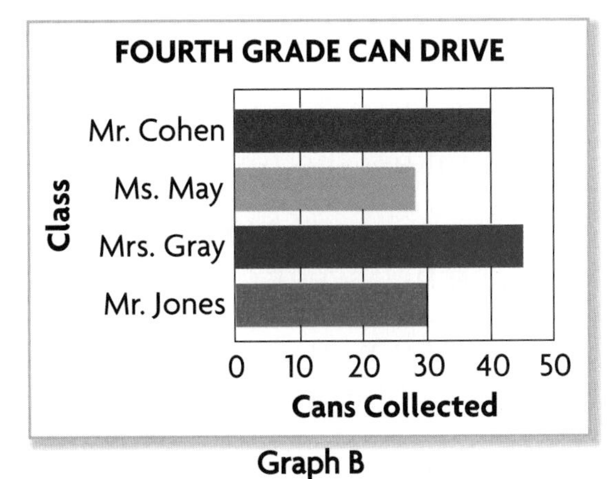

Graph B

1. How are Graphs A and B alike? How are they different?

2. How many cans did Mr. Jones's class collect?

Lesson 9.5 (pages 150–151)

Tell how the bars would change in the graph.

1. if the interval were 1
2. if the interval were 2
3. if the interval were 5
4. if the interval were 20

FOURTH GRADERS FAVORITE COOKIES

Cookies

Peanut Butter

Chocolate Chip

Sugar

Oatmeal

0 10 20 30 40

Students

Chapter 10

Lesson 10.1 (pages 156–157)

Make a double-bar graph to compare the data of Ms. Thomas's and Mr. Hoffman's classes.

1. What scale did you use? Why did you use that scale?
2. What does the key on your graph show?
3. Which sport is liked best by the same number of people in both classes?
4. Could you have made a single-bar graph to show your data? Explain why or why not.

FAVORITE SPORTS		
Sport	Ms. Thomas's Class	Mr. Hoffman's Class
Soccer	4	8
Basketball	8	7
Gymnastics	3	6
Hockey	6	2
Football	7	7

Lesson 10.2 (pages 158–159)

Mike made this line graph to show the number of mountain bikes he sold in May. Use the graph to answer Problems 1–5.

1. During which week did Mike sell the most bikes? the fewest?
2. How many bikes did he sell during the first week?
3. During which weeks did he sell more than 6 bikes?
4. Why is the point between the 10 and the 12 in Week 4?
5. Between which two weeks was there the greatest increase in the number of mountain bikes sold?

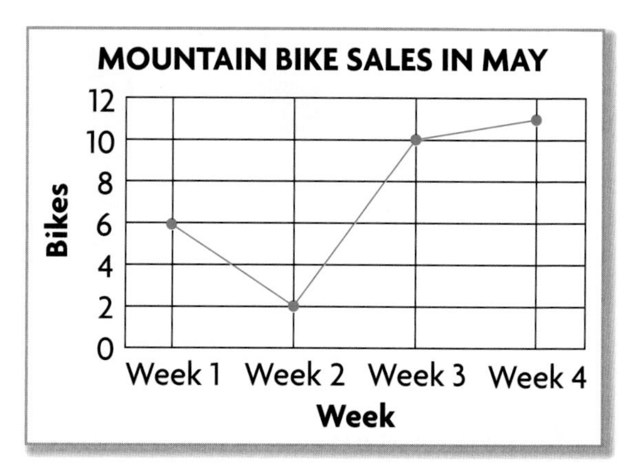

Lesson 10.3 (pages 160–161)

For Problems 1–4, use the line plot.

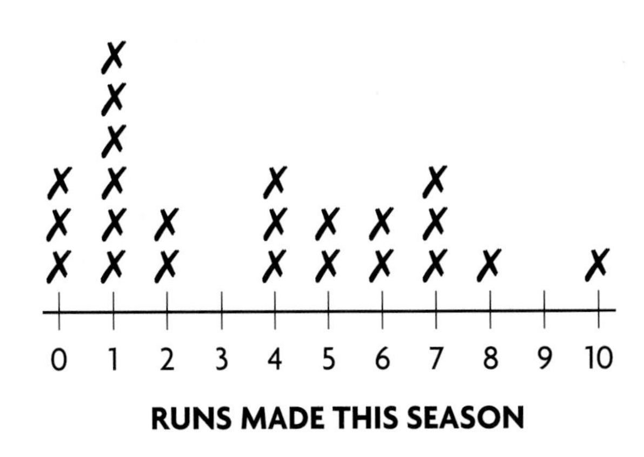

1. The X's on this line plot represent the number of players. What do the numbers on the line plot represent?

2. How many players scored 10 runs this season?

3. How many runs did the most players make?

4. What is the range used in this line plot?

Lesson 10.4 (pages 162–163)

The stem-and-leaf plot below shows spelling-test scores of Mr. Watson's class. Use it to answer Problems 1–3.

Stem	Leaves
7	8 8 9 9
8	2 5 5 5 5 6 6 7 7 9
9	0 0 1 1 2 3 3 6 8 9 9

1. What were the least and the greatest spelling-test scores?

2. What is the mode of the spelling-test scores?

3. What is the median of the spelling-test scores?

The number of students in each class at Oak Elementary is as follows: 18, 19, 22, 22, 23, 25, 25, 25, 26, 27, 27, 28, 29, 29, 29, 30, 30, 30, 30, 30, 30, 31, 31, 31, and 32.

4. Show these class sizes on a stem-and-leaf plot.

5. What is the mode of the class sizes? the median?

Lesson 10.5 Part 1 (pages 164–165)

Write the graph or plot you would choose to show data for each of the following.

1. to show favorite books of your classmates

2. to show last week's science-test scores of the students in your class

3. to compare the favorite ice-cream flavors of two classes

4. to show the scores of one football team for one season

Lesson 10.5 Part 2 (pages 166–167)

Make a graph or plot for the table or set of data.

1.

FAVORITE ICE-CREAM FLAVORS	
Ice Cream	**Students**
Chocolate	6
Cookies and Cream	4
Fudge Swirl	6
Chocolate Chip	9

2. Scores on a math test: 77, 79, 79, 81, 81, 81, 83, 84, 85, 85, 85, 86, 86, 87, 88, 88, 88, 88, 88, 89, 90, 91, 91, 91, and 92

Chapter 11

Lesson 11.1 (pages 172–173)

Tell if each event is certain or impossible. Write *certain* or *impossible*.

1. pulling a dime out of a change purse full of dimes
2. spinning a number greater than 6 on a spinner with sections numbered 1 through 5.

Lesson 11.2 (pages 174–175)

Tell whether each event is *likely* or *unlikely*.

1. pulling a green counter from a bag that has one green and six red counters
2. pulling a blue marble out of a bag that has seven blue and two yellow marbles

Lesson 11.3 (pages 176–177)

Make a six-section spinner. Color three sections red, two sections yellow, and one section green. First, predict the likely outcomes. Then, spin 20 times and record the results in a tally table. Spin 40 more times and record the results in a different tally table. Finally, answer Exercises 1–3.

1. What did you predict would be the likely outcomes in the spinner experiment? Did your results support your prediction?
2. Explain why they are likely outcomes.
3. Did the likely outcomes happen more in the 20-spin experiment or in the 40-spin experiment?

Lesson 11.4 (pages 178–179)

Look at the spinner at the right. Find the probability of spinning each.

1. the number 4

2. the number 12

3. an odd number

4. a number greater than 6

Look at the bag of marbles. Find the probability of pulling each.

5. a green marble

6. a red marble

7. a yellow marble

8. a blue marble

9. a marble that isn't blue

For Problems 10 and 11, use the spinner at the right.

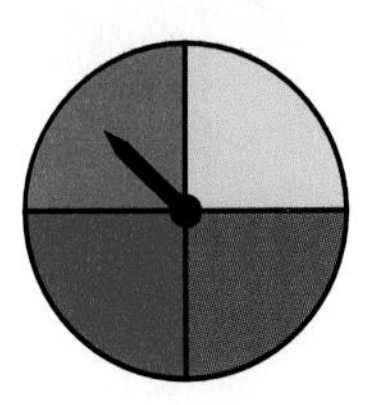

10. What is the probability of spinning red or yellow?

11. What is the probability of spinning red, yellow or green?

Lesson 11.5 Part 1 (pages 180–181)

Tell if each spinner is fair. Write *yes* or *no*. If your answer is *no*, explain why the spinner isn't fair.

1. 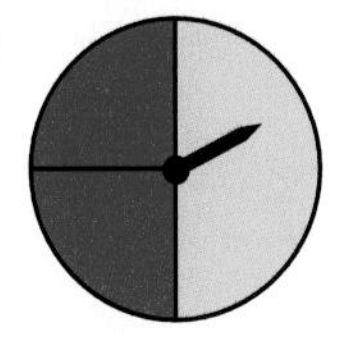

2. 

3. 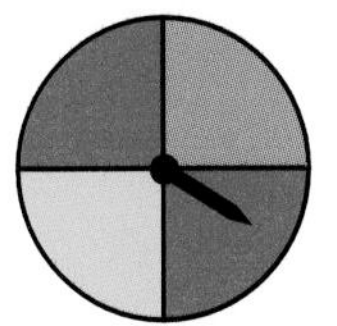

4. 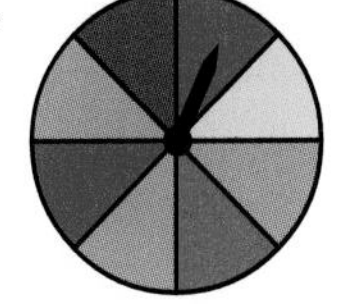

Lesson 11.5 Part 2 (pages 182–183)

Make a model to solve.

1. Julie's spinner is divided into 4 sections. The yellow section is $\frac{1}{4}$ of the spinner. The green and blue sections are the same size. The red section is the same size as the yellow section. Is Julie's spinner fair?

2. Charles made a spinner that has 4 sections. The red and blue sections are the same size. Together they are $\frac{1}{4}$ of the spinner. The orange section is the same size as the red and blue together. The rest of the spinner is yellow. Is Charles's spinner fair?

Chapter 12

Lesson 12.1 (pages 192–193)

Write *one-dimensional*, *two-dimensional*, or *three-dimensional* to describe each figure.

1. **2.** **3.** **4.**

Choose the unit that can be used to measure each. Write *feet*, *square feet*, or *cubic feet*.

5.

volume of a box

6.

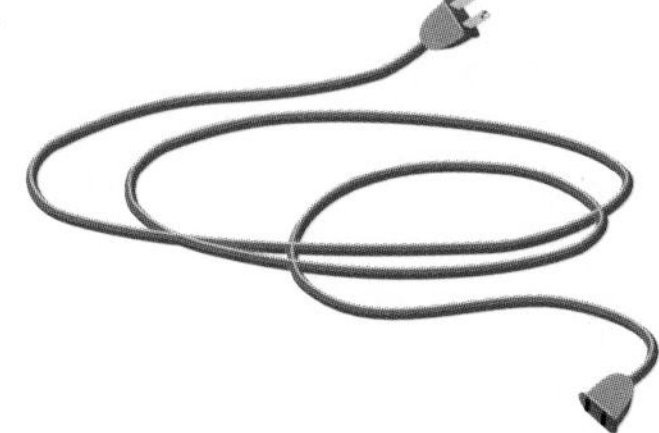

length of an extension cord

7.

area of a flag

Lesson 12.2 (pages 194–195)

Write the letter of the figure that is made with each net.

1.

2.

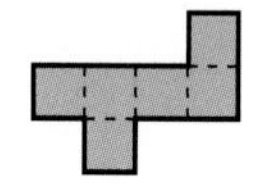

3.

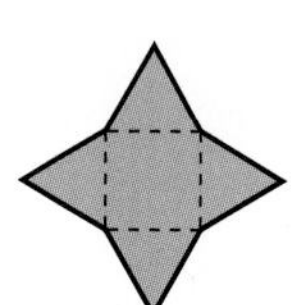

4.

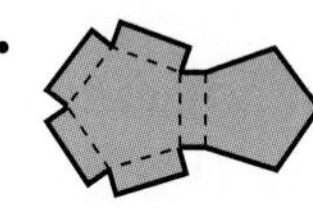

a.

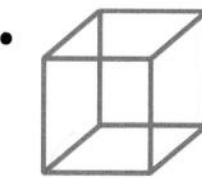

b.

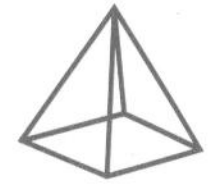

c.

d.

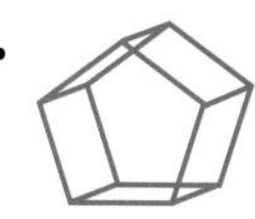

Lesson 12.3 Part 1 (pages 196–197)

Write the names of the plane figures that are the faces of each three-dimensional figure.

1.

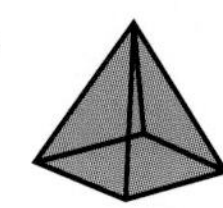

2.

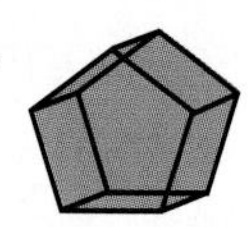

3.

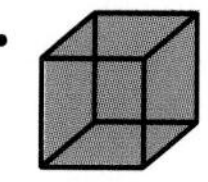

4.

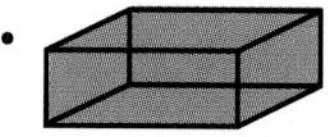

Write the names of the faces and the number of each face on the three-dimensional figure.

5. triangular pyramid **6.** cube **7.** pentagonal prism

Lesson 12.3 Part 2 (pages 198–199)

Copy the drawings. Circle each vertex, outline each edge in blue, and shade one face in yellow.

1. 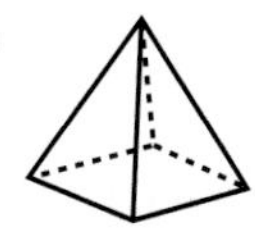

2. 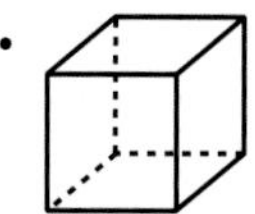

3. 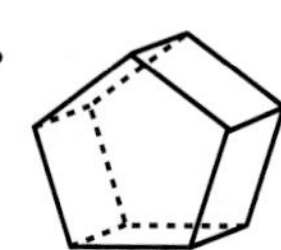

Write the letter of the figure that answers each question.

4. Which figure has more vertices?
   a. cube
   b. triangular prism

5. Which figure has all faces congruent?
   a. triangular prism
   b. cube

Lesson 12.4 (pages 200–201)

Write the ordered pairs used to draw each plane figure.

1. 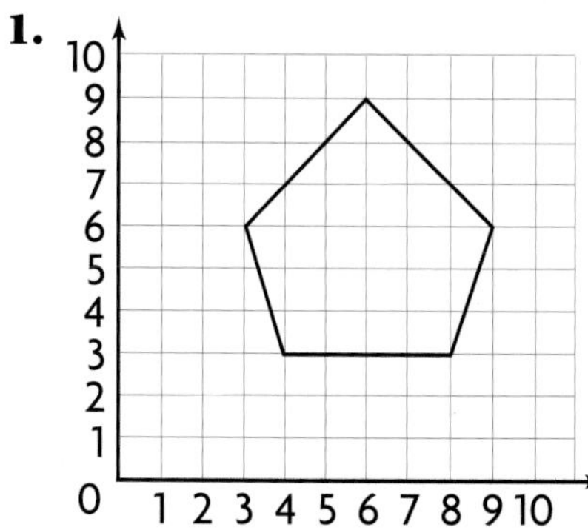

2. 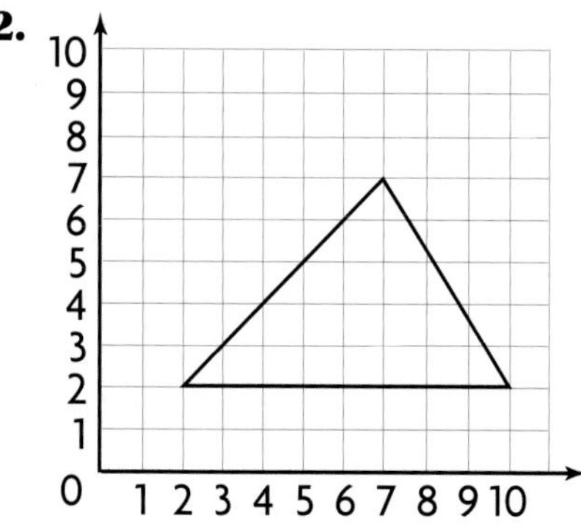

Mark the ordered pairs on grid paper. Draw a figure with vertices at the named points. Write the name of the figure.

3. (1,1), (1,4), (4,1), (4,4)

4. (6,8), (9,5), (8,2), (4,2), (3,5)

Lesson 12.5 Part 1 (pages 202–203)

Which solid figure do you see in each?

1. 

2. 

3. 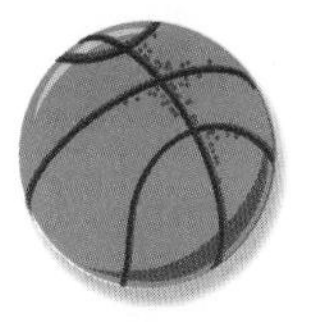

Write a label for each part of the Venn diagram.

4. 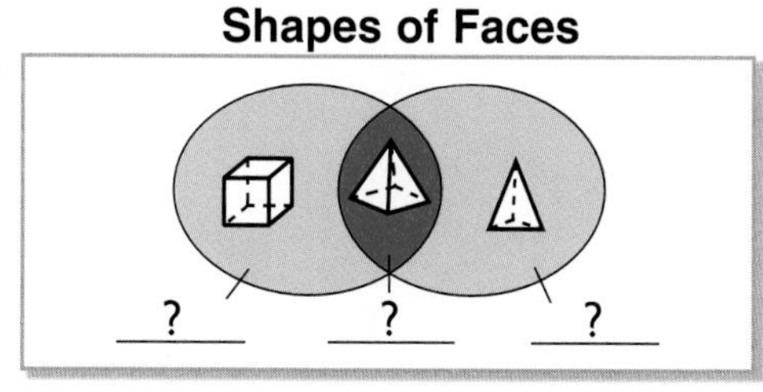

5. 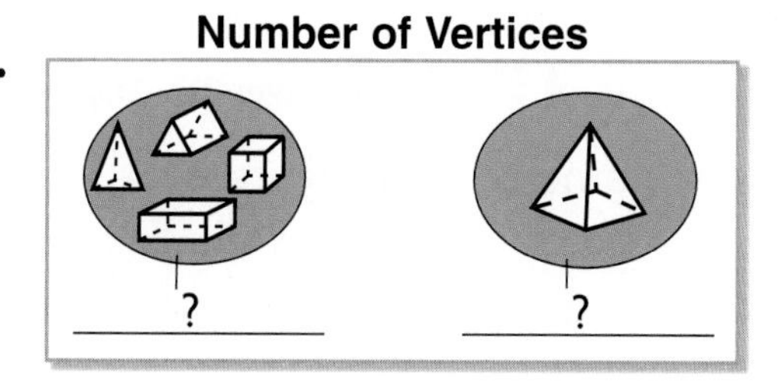

Lesson 12.5 Part 2 (pages 204–205)

Make an organized list to solve.

1. Tony went to the store to buy party supplies. He bought cans of soda, a gift box, drinking straws, party hats, and helium balloons. Sort the supplies according to the three-dimensional objects each suggests.

2. Not all three-dimensional objects have the same number of faces. List the following three-dimensional objects according to the number of faces: cube, triangular prism, square pyramid, and triangular pyramid.

Chapter 13

Lesson 13.1 (pages 210–211)

Write *points, line, line segment,* or *plane* to name each figure.

1. 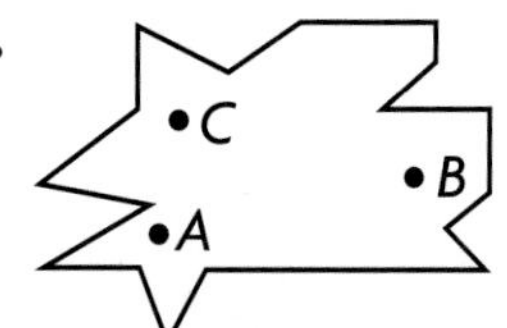

2. X Y

3. • W 

4. 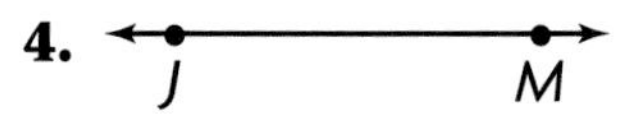

Decide if the figure is a line segment. Write *yes* or *no*.

5.

6.

7.

Write *yes* or *no* to tell if the pair of line segments is parallel.

8. 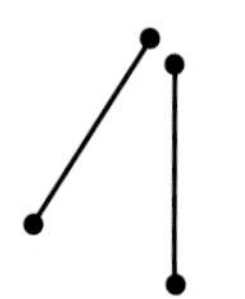

9. 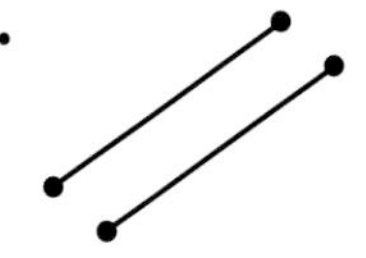

10. 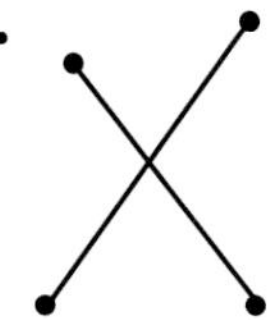

11. 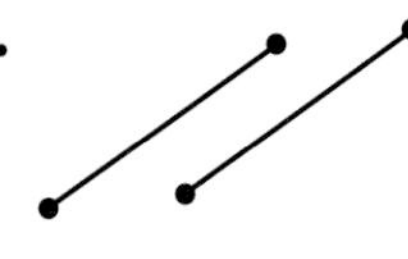

12. 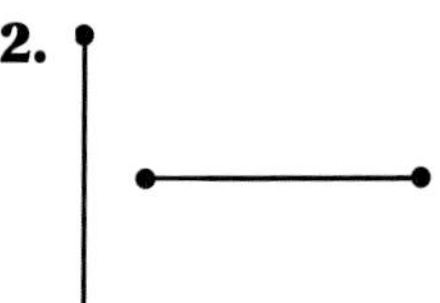

13.

Lesson 13.2 Part 1 (pages 212–213)

Write the name of each figure.

1. 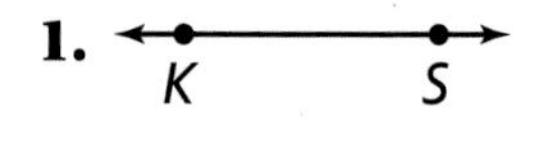

2. • J

3. 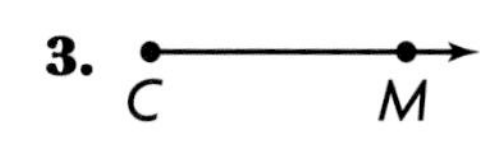

4. N M

What kind of angle is each? Write *right, acute,* or *obtuse*.

5. 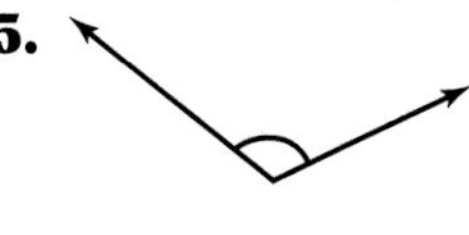
6. 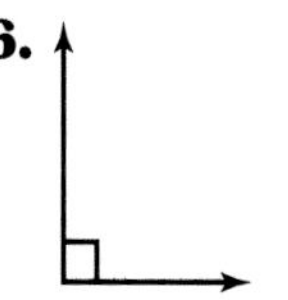
7. 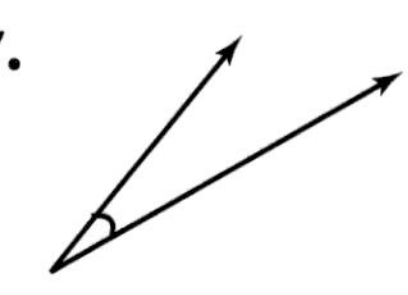
8. 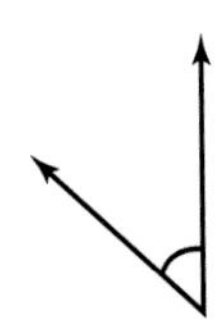

9. 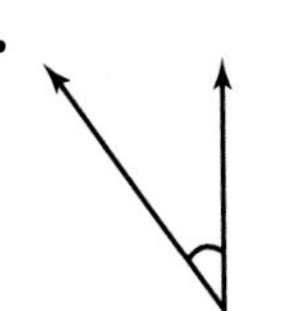
10. 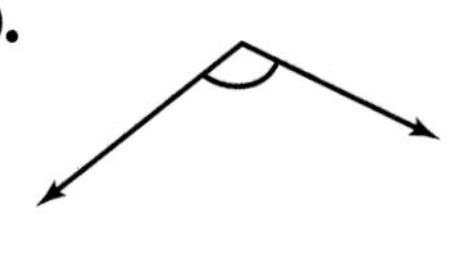
11. 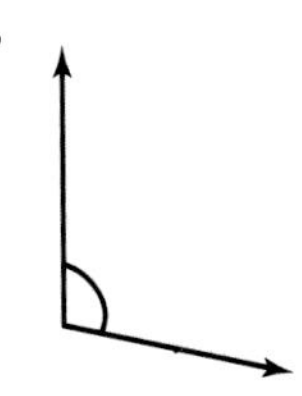
12. 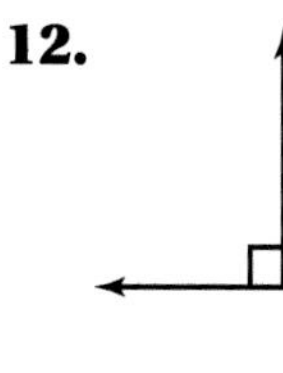

Lesson 13.2 Part 2 (pages 214–215)

What kind of line relationship is each? Write *intersecting, parallel,* or *perpendicular*.

1.
2. 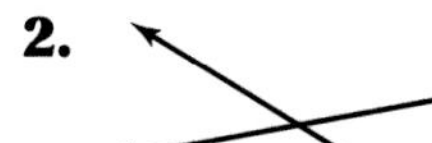
3. 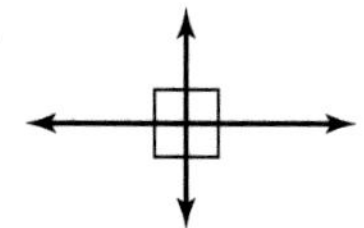

Lesson 13.3 (pages 216–217)

For Problems 1–4, use the drawing and a centimeter ruler.

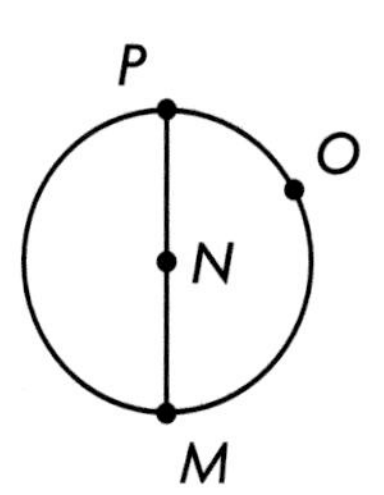

1. The center of the circle is __?__.

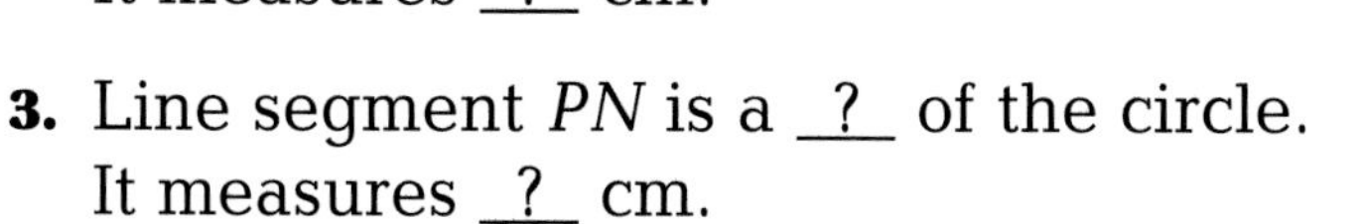

2. Line segment MP is a __?__ of the circle. It measures __?__ cm.

3. Line segment PN is a __?__ of the circle. It measures __?__ cm.

4. Three points on the circle are __?__ , __?__ , and __?__.

Lesson 13.4 (pages 218–219)

Is the figure a polygon? Write *yes* or *no*. Give a reason for your answer.

1. 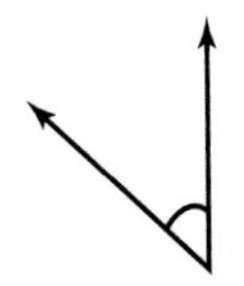
2. 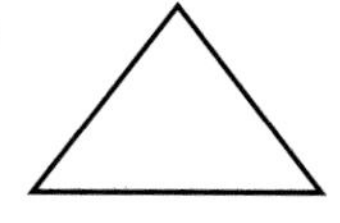
3. 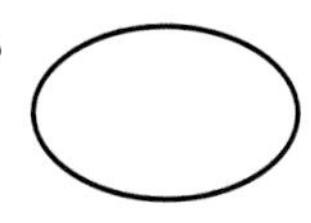

Name each polygon. Tell how many sides and angles.

4. 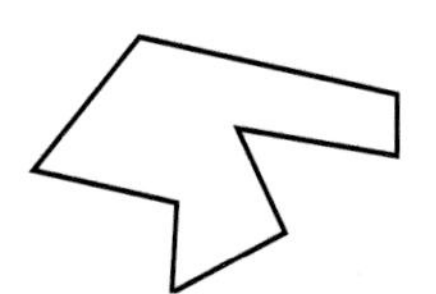
5. 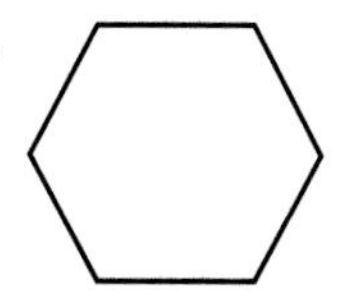
6. 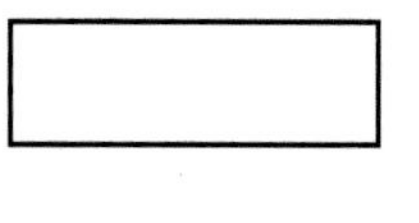
7. 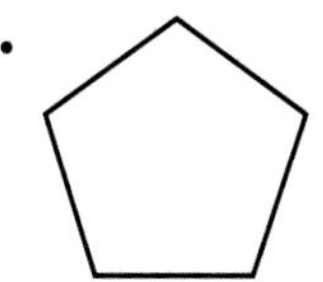

Lesson 13.5 Part 1 (pages 220–221)

Draw and name the quadrilaterals.

1. It has 4 sides of different lengths and angles, and its sides are not parallel.

2. It has 2 pairs of parallel sides, 2 obtuse angles, and 2 acute angles.

Name the kind of quadrilateral. Explain your choice.

3.  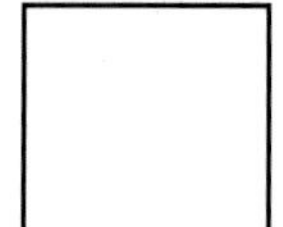

4. 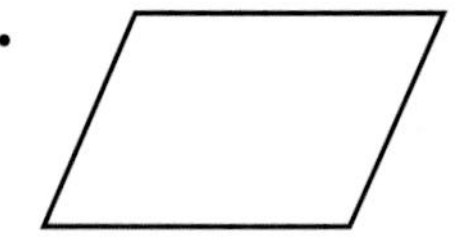

5. 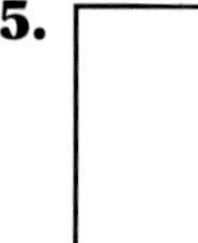

6. 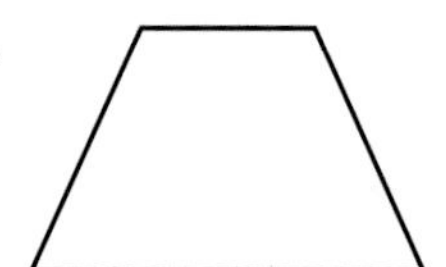

Lesson 13.5 Part 2 (pages 222–223)

Act it out to solve.

1. Five students stood in line to get their lunch. Billy was in the middle. Sydney was first in line. Veronica was last in line. Megan stood between Billy and Veronica. Where was Josh?

2. Anthony, Kristen, and Cathy walked dogs to earn money. At the end of one week they had earned 2 five-dollar bills, 6 one-dollar bills, 3 quarters, 5 dimes, 1 nickel, and 4 pennies. How much did each person earn in one week?

Chapter 14

Lesson 14.1 (pages 228–229)

Find the perimeter. Write the letter A, B, or C to show which method from page 228 you used.

1. 

2. 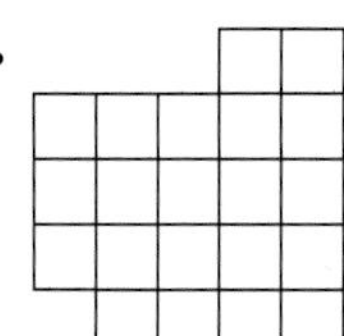

3. 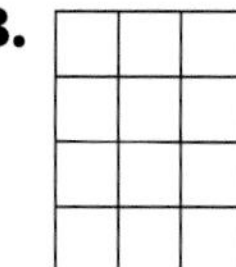

4. 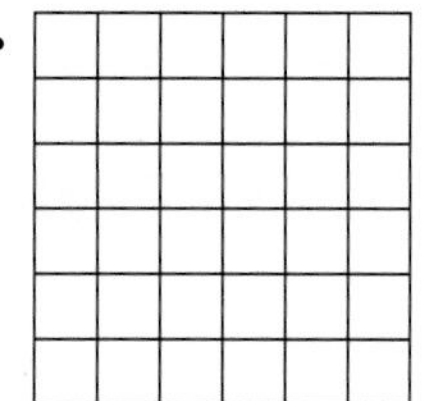

Find the perimeter.

5. 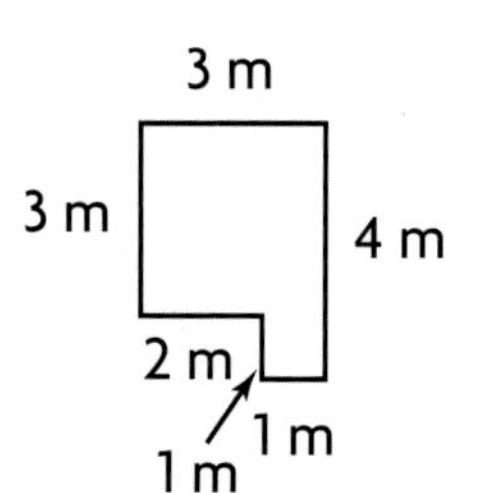

6. 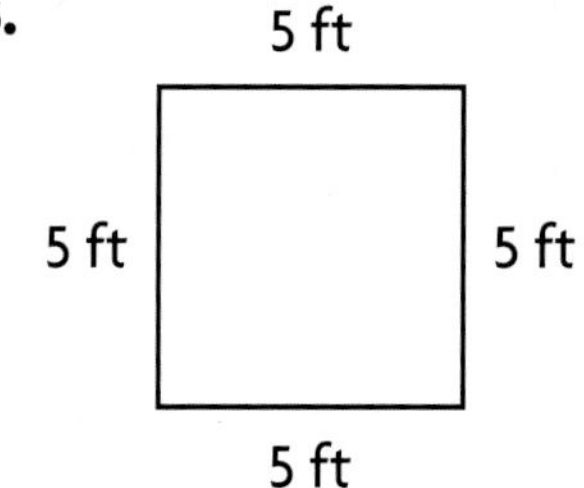

7. 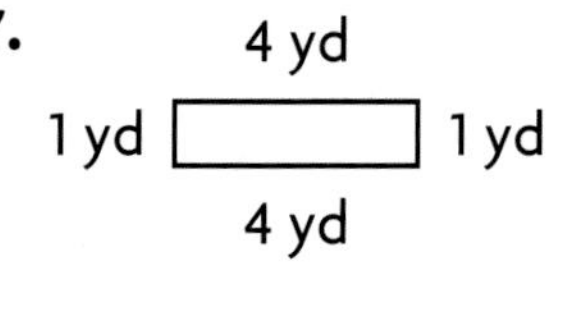

8. 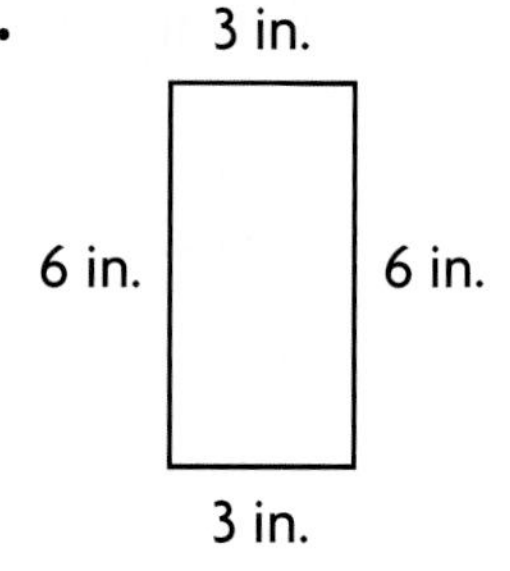

Lesson 14.2 (pages 230–231)

Find the area.

1. 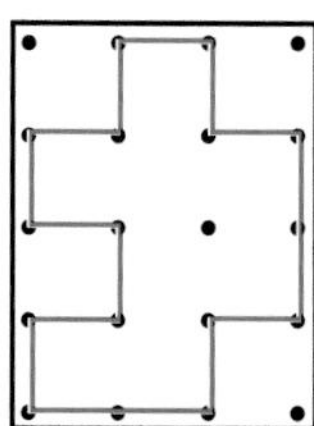

2. 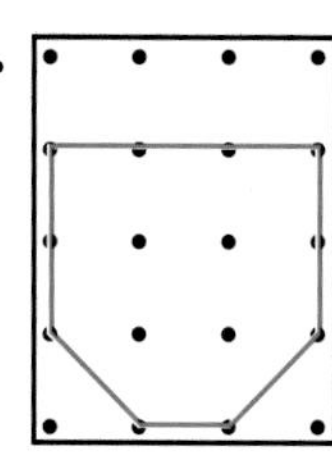

3. 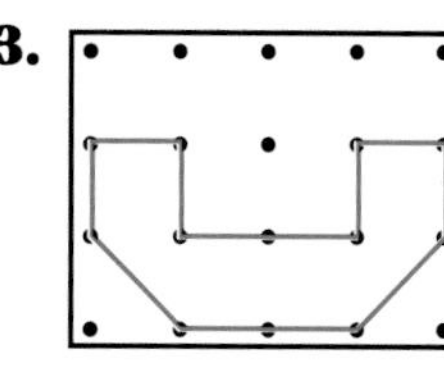

4. 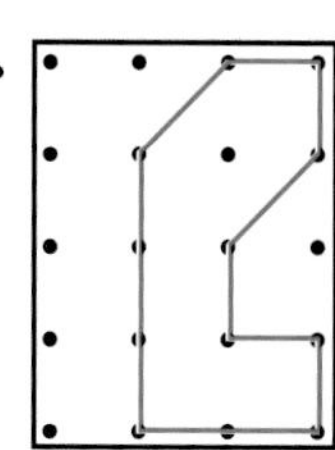

Lesson 14.3 (pages 232–233)

Copy the figure onto 1-inch grid paper. Find the area.

1. 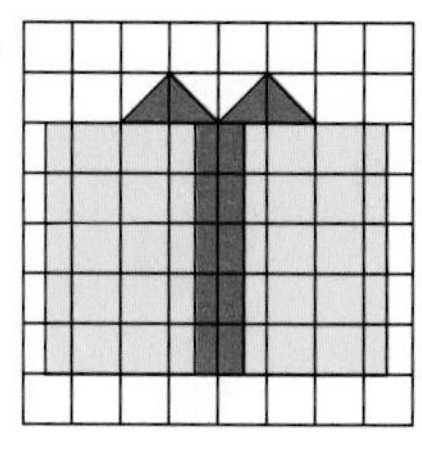

2. 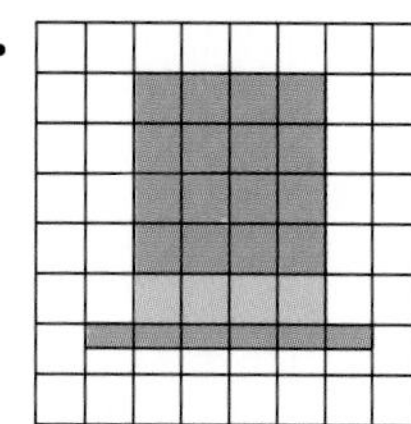

Copy the figure onto 1-inch grid paper. Estimate the area.

3. 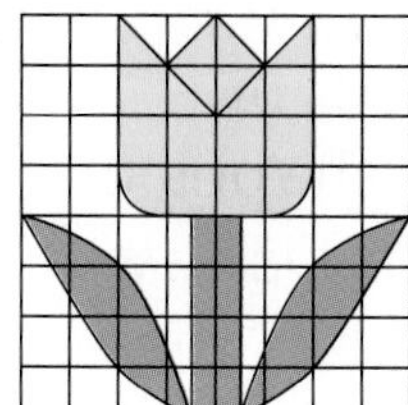

4. 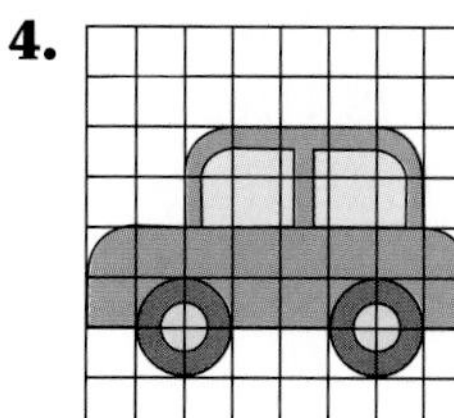

Lesson 14.4 (pages 234–235)

Find the area.

1. 16 km

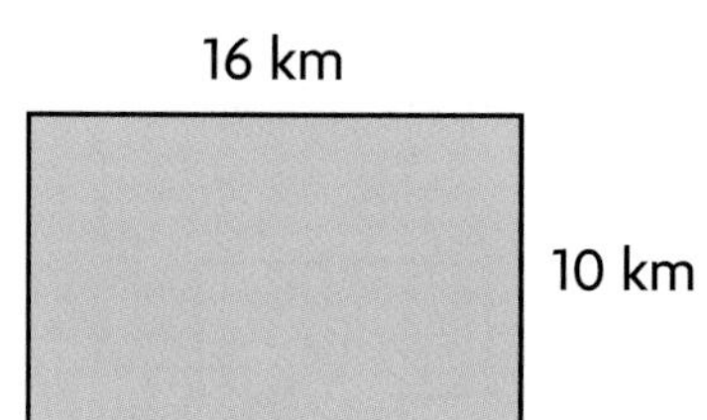

10 km

2. 3 yd

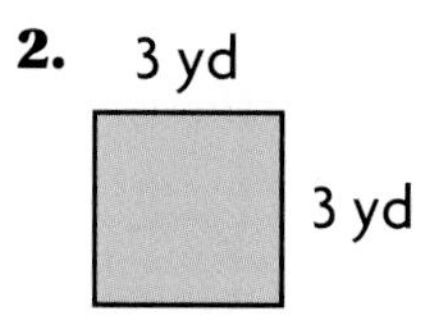

3 yd

3. 11 in.

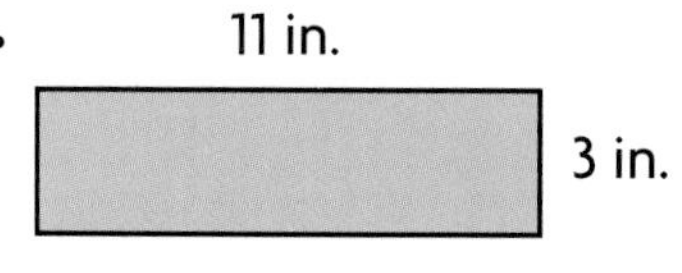

3 in.

Write the letter of the rectangle that has the greater area.

4. **a.** 6 ft

5 ft

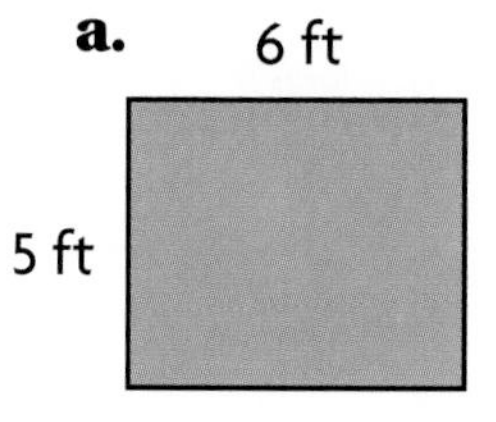

b. 7 ft

4 ft

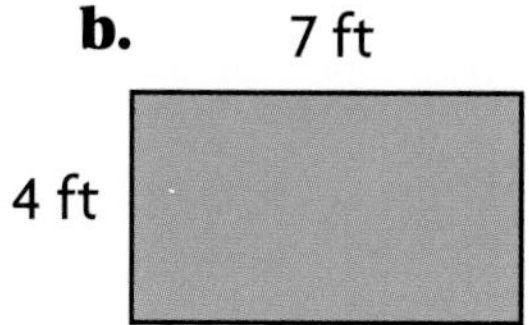

5. **a.** 11 in.

2 in.

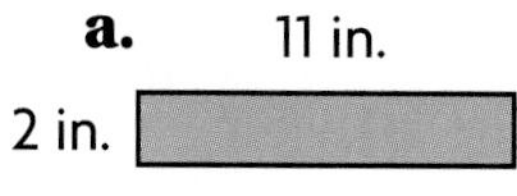

b. 5 in.

5 in.

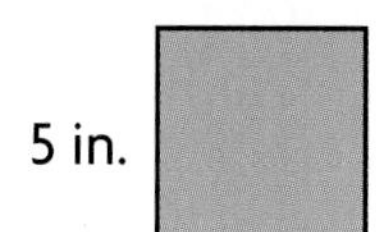

Lesson 14.5 Part 1 (pages 236–237)

Write the area and the perimeter.

1. 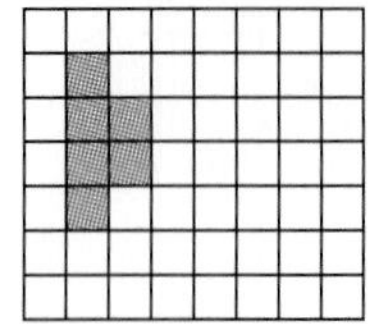

2. 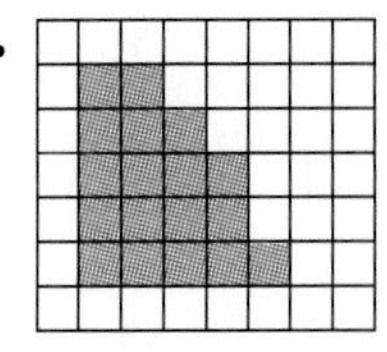

3. 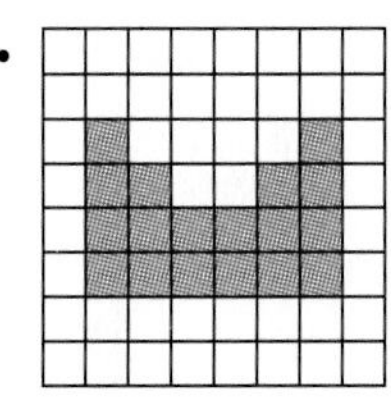

For each figure, draw another figure that has the same area but a different perimeter. You may wish to use grid paper.

4. 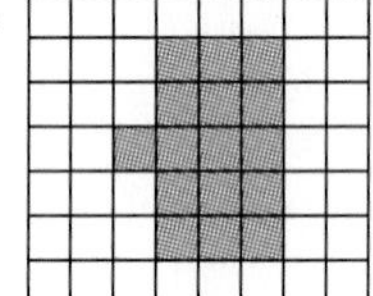

5. 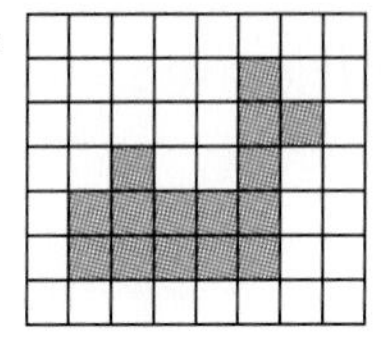

6. 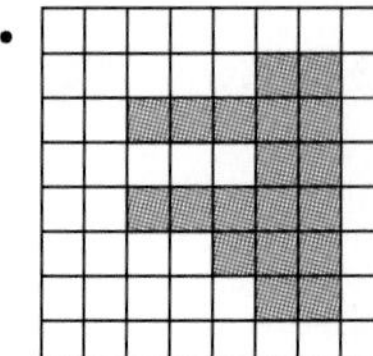

Lesson 14.5 Part 2 (pages 238–239)

Draw a diagram to solve.

1. Candace wants to put a border around a flower garden. She has 52 feet of border. What is the greatest possible area Candace can make her garden?

2. Danny wants to make the largest possible rectangular pen for his iguana. He has 28 feet of fencing. How many shapes of rectangular pens can Danny make? Which shape has the greatest possible area?

Chapter 15

Lesson 15.1 (pages 244–245)

Tell how each figure was moved. Write *translation, refection,* or *rotation.*

1. 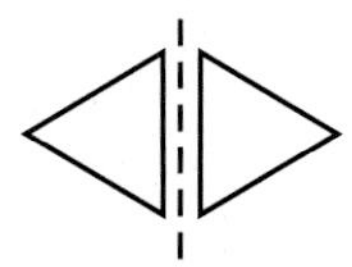

2. 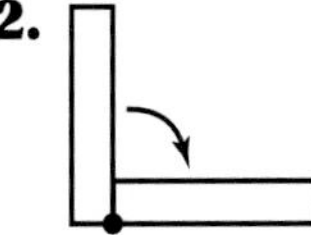

3. 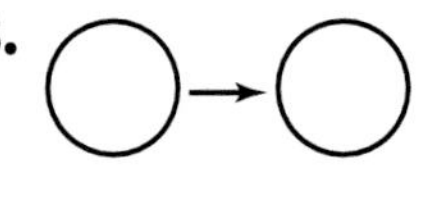

4. 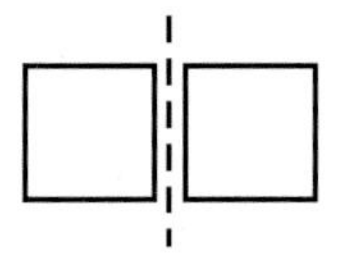

Lesson 15.2 (pages 246–247)

Is each pair of figures congruent? Write *yes* or *no.*

1. 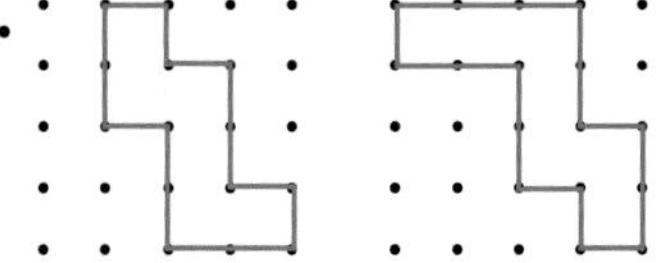

2. 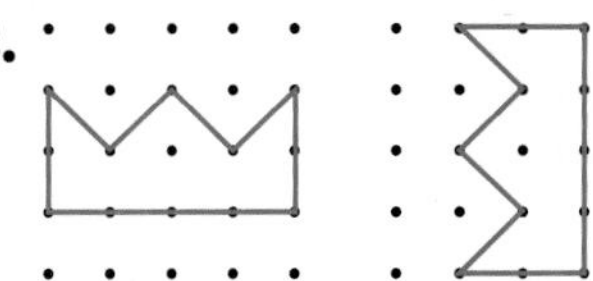

3. 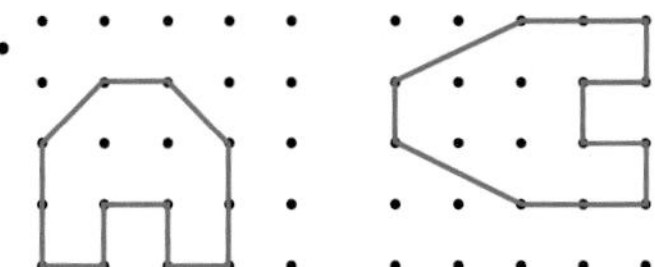

Lesson 15.3 Part 1 (pages 248–249)

Follow the steps in the model on page 248 to determine if each shape has point symmetry. Write *yes* or *no*.

1. 

2. 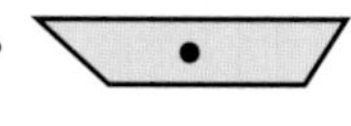

3. 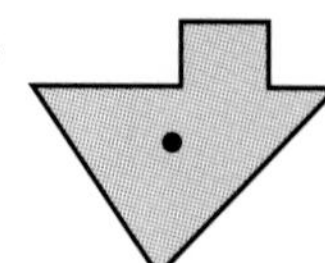

4. 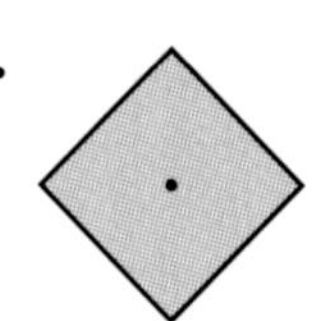

Does each figure have point symmetry? Write *yes* or *no*.

5. 

6. 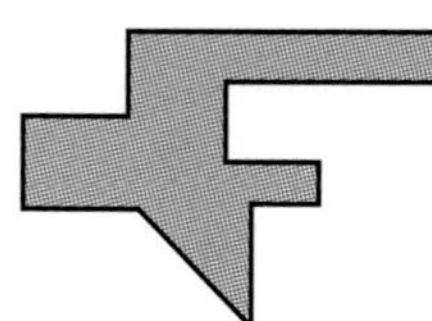

7. 

8. 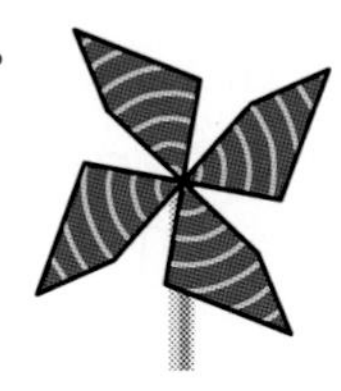

Lesson 15.3 Part 2 (pages 250–251)

Complete the design to show line symmetry.

1. 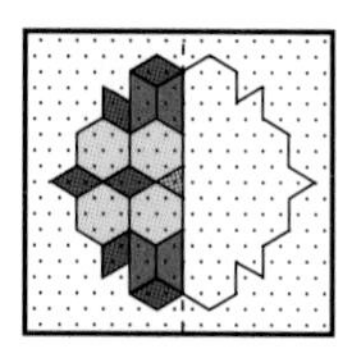

2. 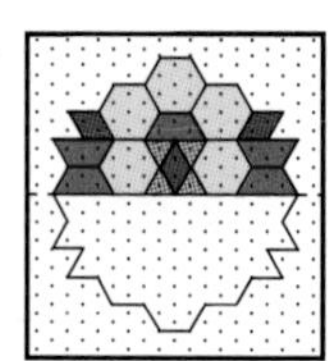

3. 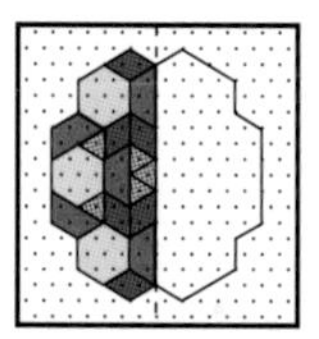

Is the blue line a line of symmetry? Write *yes* or *no*.

4. 

5. 

6. 

7. 

Lesson 15.4 (pages 252–253)

Will the figure tessellate? Write *yes* or *no*.

1. 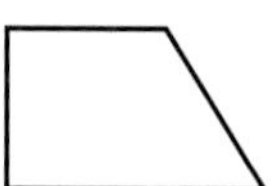

2. 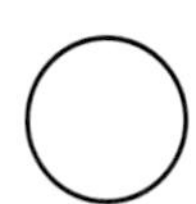

3. 

Lesson 15.5 Part 1 (pages 254–255)

Draw each figure larger on 1-inch grid paper.

1. 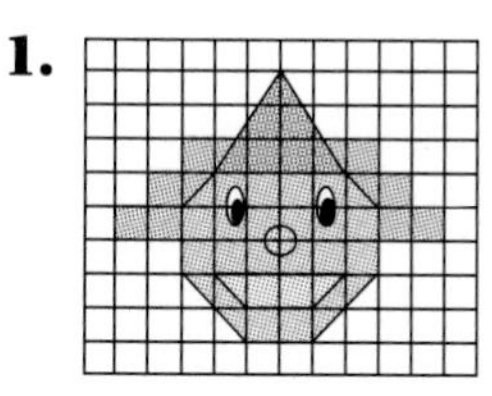

2. 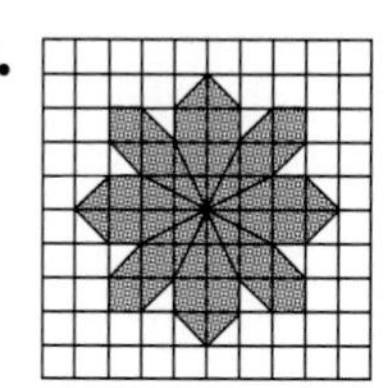

3. 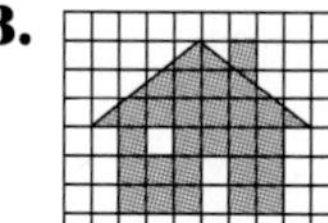

Tell whether each pair of figures is *similar*, *congruent*, or *both*.

4. 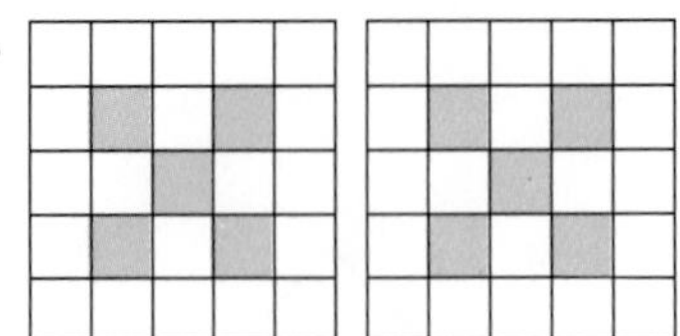

5. 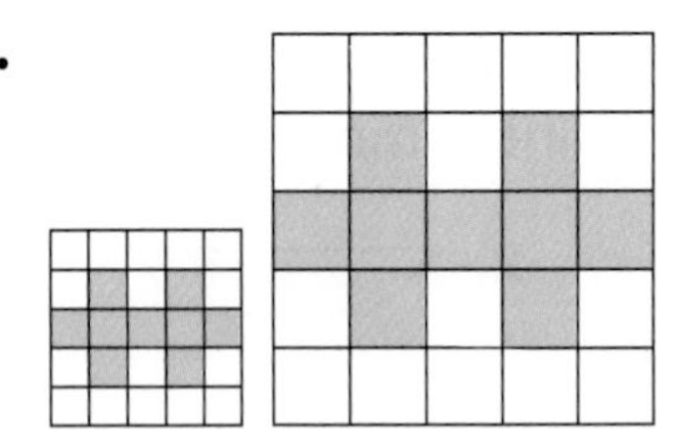

Lesson 15.5 Part 2 (pages 256–257)

Make a model to solve.

1. Holly has $2.35 in coins. She has 5 quarters and twice as many dimes as quarters. The rest of her coins are nickels. How many of each coin does Holly have?

2. Patrick wants to fence an area in his yard for a vegetable garden. He has 24 feet of fencing to use. What is the greatest possible area he can enclose with his fence?

Chapter 16

Lesson 16.1 (pages 266–267)

Finish each pattern.

1. $5 \times 30 = \underline{?}$
$\underline{?} \times 300 = 1{,}500$
$5 \times \underline{?} = 15{,}000$

2. $\underline{?} \times 20 = 120$
$6 \times 200 = \underline{?}$
$6 \times \underline{?} = 12{,}000$

3. $4 \times 40 = \underline{?}$
$\underline{?} \times 400 = 1{,}600$
$4 \times 4{,}000 = \underline{?}$

4. $7 \times \underline{?} = 140$
$7 \times 200 = \underline{?}$
$\underline{?} \times 2{,}000 = 14{,}000$

Use mental math and basic multiplication facts to find the product.

5. 700×5 **6.** $3{,}000 \times 8$ **7.** 500×9 **8.** $1{,}000 \times 3$ **9.** $4{,}000 \times 7$

10. $9 \times 1{,}000 = \underline{?}$ **11.** $6 \times 300 = \underline{?}$ **12.** $5 \times 2{,}000 = \underline{?}$

Lesson 16.2 (pages 268–269)

Find the product.

1. 25×4 **2.** 36×2 **3.** 42×5 **4.** 37×3 **5.** 71×7

6. 18×5 **7.** 46×3 **8.** 61×6 **9.** 83×2 **10.** 94×3

Lesson 16.3 (pages 270–271)

Find each product by using partial products.

1. $\begin{array}{r} 29 \\ \times\ 5 \\ \hline \end{array}$ **2.** $\begin{array}{r} 31 \\ \times\ 4 \\ \hline \end{array}$ **3.** $\begin{array}{r} 17 \\ \times\ 7 \\ \hline \end{array}$ **4.** $\begin{array}{r} 46 \\ \times\ 2 \\ \hline \end{array}$ **5.** $\begin{array}{r} 62 \\ \times\ 3 \\ \hline \end{array}$

Lesson 16.4 (pages 272–273)

Multiply. Tell in which place-value positions you need to regroup.

1. $\begin{array}{r} 125 \\ \times\ \ 4 \\ \hline \end{array}$ **2.** $\begin{array}{r} 239 \\ \times\ \ 3 \\ \hline \end{array}$ **3.** $\begin{array}{r} 163 \\ \times\ \ 3 \\ \hline \end{array}$ **4.** $\begin{array}{r} 256 \\ \times\ \ 2 \\ \hline \end{array}$ **5.** $\begin{array}{r} 325 \\ \times\ \ 3 \\ \hline \end{array}$

6. $\begin{array}{r} 339 \\ \times\ \ 4 \\ \hline \end{array}$ **7.** $\begin{array}{r} 296 \\ \times\ \ 5 \\ \hline \end{array}$ **8.** $\begin{array}{r} 359 \\ \times\ \ 7 \\ \hline \end{array}$ **9.** $\begin{array}{r} 852 \\ \times\ \ 9 \\ \hline \end{array}$ **10.** $\begin{array}{r} 976 \\ \times\ \ 6 \\ \hline \end{array}$

Lesson 16.5 Part 1 (pages 274–275)

Multiply, and record each product. Place the dollar sign and decimal point in it.

1. $\begin{array}{r} \$8.09 \\ \times\ \ \ \ 3 \\ \hline \end{array}$ **2.** $\begin{array}{r} \$6.25 \\ \times\ \ \ \ 7 \\ \hline \end{array}$ **3.** $\begin{array}{r} \$7.93 \\ \times\ \ \ \ 6 \\ \hline \end{array}$ **4.** $\begin{array}{r} \$6.77 \\ \times\ \ \ \ 2 \\ \hline \end{array}$ **5.** $\begin{array}{r} \$9.26 \\ \times\ \ \ \ 3 \\ \hline \end{array}$

6. $6 \times \$5.39 = \underline{?}$ **7.** $5 \times \$4.27 = \underline{?}$ **8.** $7 \times \$3.69 = \underline{?}$ **9.** $4 \times \$9.19 = \underline{?}$

Lesson 16.5 Part 2 (pages 276–277)

Write a number sentence to solve.

1. Peggy goes jogging for 35 minutes 4 times a week. How many minutes does Peggy jog each week?

2. Jeanne bought 6 pizzas for her party for $8.75 each. How much did Jeanne spend for the 6 pizzas?

Chapter 17

Lesson 17.1 Part 1 (pages 282–283)

Copy and complete. Use a basic fact and the pattern of zeros to help you.

1. $8 \times 40 = n$
$8 \times 400 = n$
$8 \times 4{,}000 = n$

2. $3 \times 20 = n$
$3 \times 200 = n$
$3 \times 2{,}000 = n$

3. $7 \times 80 = n$
$70 \times 80 = n$
$70 \times 800 = n$

4. $5 \times 90 = n$
$50 \times 90 = n$
$500 \times 90 = n$

Use mental math and basic facts to find the product.

5. $7 \times 90 = n$ **6.** $30 \times 400 = n$ **7.** $60 \times 800 = n$ **8.** $70 \times 500 = n$

Find the product.

9. 600×30 **10.** $7{,}000 \times 60$ **11.** $40{,}000 \times 80$ **12.** $90{,}000 \times 6$

Lesson 17.1 Part 2 (pages 284–285)

Find a pattern to solve.

1. Liz has a puzzle for her friends. When she says 6, the answer is 12. When she says 8, the answer is 16. When she says 12, the answer is 24. What is the pattern?

2. Cookies come in packages of 40 cookies. The grocery store got a shipment of 50 packages. How many cookies is that?

Lesson 17.2 (pages 286–287)

Round each factor to the nearest ten. Estimate the product.

1. 24×18 **2.** 32×25 **3.** 19×13 **4.** 56×52 **5.** 49×32 **6.** 92×24

7. 19×14 **8.** 37×24 **9.** 12×11 **10.** 19×16 **11.** 26×18 **12.** 34×12

Round each factor. Estimate the product.

13. $\$78 \times 18$ **14.** 29×22 **15.** $\$309 \times 39$ **16.** 642×43 **17.** 321×53

18. $19 \times 39 = n$ **19.** $46 \times 23 = n$ **20.** $72 \times 21 = n$ **21.** $46 \times 81 = n$

Lesson 17.3 (pages 288–289)

Make a model to find the product.

1. 17×14 **2.** 26×18 **3.** 27×11 **4.** 23×19 **5.** 13×12

6. 16×16 **7.** 21×15 **8.** 18×12 **9.** 24×11 **10.** 19×18

Lesson 17.4 (pages 290–291)

Find the product.

1. $\begin{array}{r} 42 \\ \times 37 \\ \hline \end{array}$ 2. $\begin{array}{r} 56 \\ \times 29 \\ \hline \end{array}$ 3. $\begin{array}{r} 63 \\ \times 41 \\ \hline \end{array}$ 4. $\begin{array}{r} 19 \\ \times 17 \\ \hline \end{array}$ 5. $\begin{array}{r} 92 \\ \times 73 \\ \hline \end{array}$ 6. $\begin{array}{r} 52 \\ \times 13 \\ \hline \end{array}$

7. $36 \times 27 = n$ 8. $85 \times 34 = n$ 9. $44 \times 35 = n$

Lesson 17.5 (pages 292–293)

Find the product.

1. $\begin{array}{r} 162 \\ \times\ 18 \\ \hline \end{array}$ 2. $\begin{array}{r} 293 \\ \times\ 36 \\ \hline \end{array}$ 3. $\begin{array}{r} 139 \\ \times\ 76 \\ \hline \end{array}$ 4. $\begin{array}{r} 521 \\ \times\ 43 \\ \hline \end{array}$ 5. $\begin{array}{r} 673 \\ \times\ 51 \\ \hline \end{array}$

6. $57 \times 326 = n$ 7. $39 \times 562 = n$ 8. $82 \times 3{,}468 = n$

9. $21 \times 1{,}379 = n$ 10. $46 \times 4{,}011 = n$ 11. $63 \times 6{,}021 = n$

Chapter 18

Lesson 18.1 (pages 298–299)

Make a model and solve.

1. $46 \div 2 = \underline{\ ?\ }$ 2. $90 \div 5 = \underline{\ ?\ }$ 3. $96 \div 8 = \underline{\ ?\ }$ 4. $68 \div 4 = \underline{\ ?\ }$

5. $91 \div 7 = \underline{\ ?\ }$ 6. $54 \div 2 = \underline{\ ?\ }$ 7. $72 \div 3 = \underline{\ ?\ }$ 8. $84 \div 6 = \underline{\ ?\ }$

Lesson 18.2 (pages 300–301)

Find the quotient. Check by multiplying.

1. $5\overline{)34}$ 2. $6\overline{)38}$ 3. $2\overline{)17}$ 4. $4\overline{)25}$ 5. $3\overline{)31}$

6. $8\overline{)50}$ 7. $3\overline{)26}$ 8. $9\overline{)88}$ 9. $5\overline{)82}$ 10. $7\overline{)55}$

11. $3\overline{)95}$ 12. $4\overline{)69}$ 13. $6\overline{)77}$ 14. $5\overline{)58}$ 15. $9\overline{)76}$

Lesson 18.3 (pages 302–303)

Find the quotient. Check by multiplying.

1. $4\overline{)52}$ 2. $2\overline{)47}$ 3. $3\overline{)97}$ 4. $5\overline{)75}$ 5. $9\overline{)67}$

6. $7\overline{)46}$ 7. $8\overline{)33}$ 8. $2\overline{)98}$ 9. $3\overline{)49}$ 10. $6\overline{)80}$

11. $9\overline{)59}$ 12. $6\overline{)91}$ 13. $3\overline{)51}$ 14. $7\overline{)64}$ 15. $8\overline{)75}$

Lesson 18.4 Part 1 (pages 304–305)

Copy each problem. Draw a box where the first digit in the quotient should be placed.

1. $3\overline{)42}$ **2.** $8\overline{)79}$ **3.** $2\overline{)69}$ **4.** $5\overline{)42}$ **5.** $7\overline{)88}$

6. $9\overline{)51}$ **7.** $3\overline{)29}$ **8.** $5\overline{)75}$ **9.** $7\overline{)60}$ **10.** $2\overline{)26}$

Find the quotient. Check by multiplying.

11. $4\overline{)368}$ **12.** $7\overline{)929}$ **13.** $5\overline{)365}$ **14.** $4\overline{)492}$ **15.** $3\overline{)729}$

Lesson 18.4 Part 2 (pages 306–307)

Use guess and check to solve.

1. There were 94 students at camp. After equal groups were formed, 3 campers were left over. How many groups were formed? How many campers are in each group?

2. Elizabeth bought an outfit for $34.50. The shirt cost $3.50 more than the skirt. How much was each?

Lesson 18.5 (pages 308–309)

Copy each problem. Draw a box where the first digit in the quotient should be placed.

1. $4\overline{)672}$ **2.** $9\overline{)121}$ **3.** $2\overline{)496}$ **4.** $5\overline{)453}$

5. $7\overline{)971}$ **6.** $6\overline{)508}$ **7.** $9\overline{)300}$ **8.** $5\overline{)754}$

Find the quotient. Check by multiplying.

9. $7\overline{)427}$ **10.** $5\overline{)545}$ **11.** $3\overline{)965}$ **12.** $6\overline{)126}$

13. $619 \div 2 = n$ **14.** $112 \div 8 = n$ **15.** $341 \div 4 = n$ **16.** $258 \div 9 = n$

Lesson 18.6 (pages 310–311)

Find the quotient. Check by multiplying.

1. $6\overline{)349}$ **2.** $3\overline{)852}$ **3.** $4\overline{)418}$ **4.** $5\overline{)741}$

5. $4\overline{)229}$ **6.** $3\overline{)529}$ **7.** $2\overline{)963}$ **8.** $7\overline{)632}$

9. $217 \div 8 = n$ **10.** $490 \div 5 = n$ **11.** $157 \div 9 = n$ **12.** $974 \div 4 = n$

13. $524 \div 9 = n$ **14.** $774 \div 4 = n$ **15.** $843 \div 7 = n$ **16.** $464 \div 5 = n$

Chapter 19

Lesson 19.1 (pages 316–317)

Copy and complete. Use a basic fact and a pattern of zeros to help you.

1. $480 \div n = 80$
$4{,}800 \div 6 = n$
$n \div 6 = 8{,}000$

2. $280 \div 7 = n$
$2{,}800 \div n = 400$
$n \div 7 = 4{,}000$

3. $n \div 8 = 40$
$3{,}200 \div 8 = n$
$32{,}000 \div 8 = n$

4. $360 \div n = 40$
$3{,}600 \div 9 = n$
$n \div 9 = 4{,}000$

Find the quotient.

5. $2\overline{)1{,}200}$ **6.** $4\overline{)16{,}000}$ **7.** $8\overline{)240}$ **8.** $5\overline{)3{,}500}$

9. $6\overline{)36{,}000}$ **10.** $3\overline{)270}$ **11.** $7\overline{)28{,}000}$ **12.** $9\overline{)8{,}100}$

Lesson 19.2 (pages 318–319)

Write the number of digits in each quotient.

1. $5\overline{)105}$ **2.** $4\overline{)283}$ **3.** $9\overline{)\$9.54}$ **4.** $7\overline{)890}$

Find the quotient.

5. $5\overline{)517}$ **6.** $9\overline{)907}$ **7.** $3\overline{)271}$ **8.** $4\overline{)450}$

9. $7\overline{)562}$ **10.** $2\overline{)309}$ **11.** $8\overline{)821}$ **12.** $6\overline{)360}$

Lesson 19.3 (pages 320–321)

Find the quotient. Place the dollar sign and decimal point in the quotient.

1. $4\overline{)\$4.52}$ **2.** $8\overline{)\$5.92}$ **3.** $3\overline{)\$5.01}$ **4.** $6\overline{)\$13.14}$ **5.** $7\overline{)\$10.64}$

6. $3\overline{)\$15.48}$ **7.** $4\overline{)\$28.92}$ **8.** $7\overline{)\$29.40}$ **9.** $2\overline{)\$17.84}$ **10.** $5\overline{)\$46.25}$

Lesson 19.4 Part 1 (pages 322–323)

Solve. Tell how you interpret the meaning of the remainder.

1. Cindy is putting photos in an album. She has 529 photos. She can fit 4 on a page. How many pages does she need?

2. Chris wants to make as many batches of cookies as possible with 17 cups of flour. She needs 4 cups of flour per batch. How many batches can Chris make?

Lesson 19.4 Part 2 (pages 324–325)

Solve. Account for all the possibilities.

1. Matthew mows lawns in his neighborhood to earn money. Last month he earned $77.50. He mowed 9 lawns. How much does Matthew earn for each lawn?

2. Scott has a 155-page book to read for a book report. He has 7 nights to finish the book. How many pages should he read each night? How can Scott use the time he has?

Lesson 19.5 (pages 326–327)

Find the average of each set of numbers by using unit cubes.

1. 2, 4, 6, 9, 11, 12, 12
2. 4, 7, 8, 8, 10, 12, 14
3. 12, 13, 15, 16
4. 13, 19, 21, 23
5. 8, 9, 11, 12, 13, 19
6. 21, 26, 28, 33

Lesson 19.6 (pages 328–329)

Solve. Name the operation you used.

1. Nancy and Anthony ordered 20 pictures for $2.50 each. How much did they spend on the pictures?

2. Uncle Jim drove 1,562 miles to the wedding. Cousin Katie drove 982 miles to the wedding. How many more miles did Uncle Jim drive than Cousin Katie?

Chapter 20

Lesson 20.1 (pages 338–339)

Draw a picture and shade part of it to show the fraction.

1. $\frac{2}{3}$
2. $\frac{5}{6}$
3. $\frac{1}{8}$
4. $\frac{2}{5}$
5. $\frac{1}{2}$
6. $\frac{1}{4}$

For Exercises 7–13, use the figure at the right.

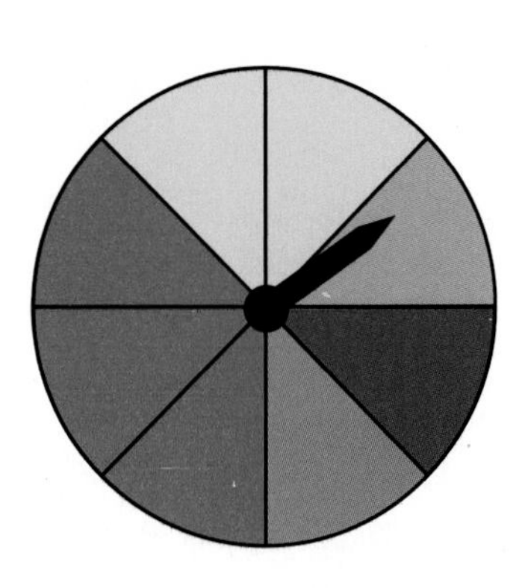

7. What fraction of the figure is red?
8. What fraction of the figure is not yellow?
9. What fraction of the figure is not yellow or green?
10. What fraction of the figure is purple?
11. What fraction of the figure is not red?
12. What color covers $\frac{2}{8}$ of the figure?
13. What two colors together cover $\frac{1}{2}$ of the figure?

Lesson 20.2 (pages 340–341)

What fraction of the parts is shaded? What fraction is not shaded?

1. 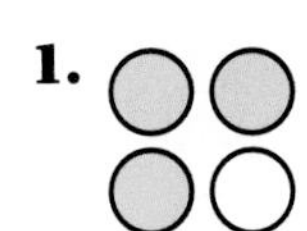

2. 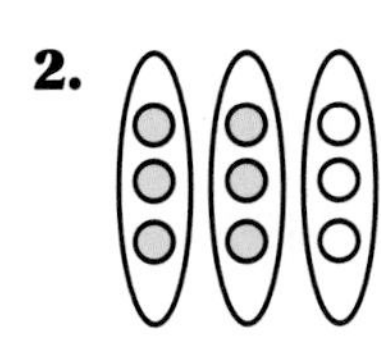

3. 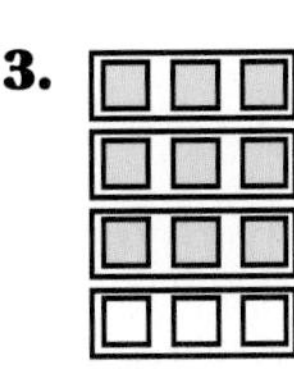

4.

Draw the picture and shade 1 part. Write the fraction for the shaded part.

5. 6 circles
   6 parts
6. 4 triangles
   2 parts
7. 6 circles
   3 parts
8. 12 squares
   4 parts

Lesson 20.3 (pages 342–343)

Find an equivalent fraction. Use fraction bars.

1. $\frac{1}{2} = \frac{?}{6}$
2. $\frac{1}{4} = \frac{?}{8}$
3. $\frac{3}{5} = \frac{?}{10}$
4. $\frac{1}{2} = \frac{?}{4}$
5. $\frac{2}{3} = \frac{?}{6}$
6. $\frac{2}{4}$
7. $\frac{2}{8}$
8. $\frac{1}{3}$
9. $\frac{3}{12}$
10. $\frac{4}{6}$

Lesson 20.4 Part 1 (pages 344–345)

Compare the fractions. Write $<$, $>$, or $=$. Use fraction bars.

1. $\frac{2}{3}$ ● $\frac{5}{6}$
2. $\frac{5}{8}$ ● $\frac{1}{2}$
3. $\frac{1}{4}$ ● $\frac{3}{12}$
4. $\frac{3}{5}$ ● $\frac{7}{10}$

Use fraction bars to order each set of fractions from greatest to least.

5. $\frac{3}{8}, \frac{7}{8}, \frac{1}{8}$
6. $\frac{3}{4}, \frac{4}{5}, \frac{2}{8}$
7. $\frac{1}{2}, \frac{1}{6}, \frac{2}{5},$
8. $\frac{5}{6}, \frac{1}{2}, \frac{3}{4}$

Use fraction bars to order each set of fractions from least to greatest.

9. $\frac{1}{4}, \frac{5}{8}, \frac{3}{5}$
10. $\frac{5}{6}, \frac{1}{6}, \frac{4}{6}$
11. $\frac{7}{10}, \frac{1}{6}, \frac{5}{6}$
12. $\frac{5}{12}, \frac{9}{10}, \frac{3}{8}$

Lesson 20.4 Part 2 (pages 346–347)

Make a model to solve.

1. A spinner has 8 equal sections. Of the sections, 3 are red, 3 are yellow, 1 is blue, and 1 is green. What two colors make up more than $\frac{1}{2}$ of the spinner?

2. David and his mom are making bread. David measures $\frac{1}{2}$ teaspoon of salt, $\frac{1}{4}$ teaspoon of pepper, and $\frac{3}{4}$ teaspoon of yeast. List the ingredients in order from least to greatest.

Lesson 20.5 (pages 348–349)

For Exercises 1–4, use the figures at the right.

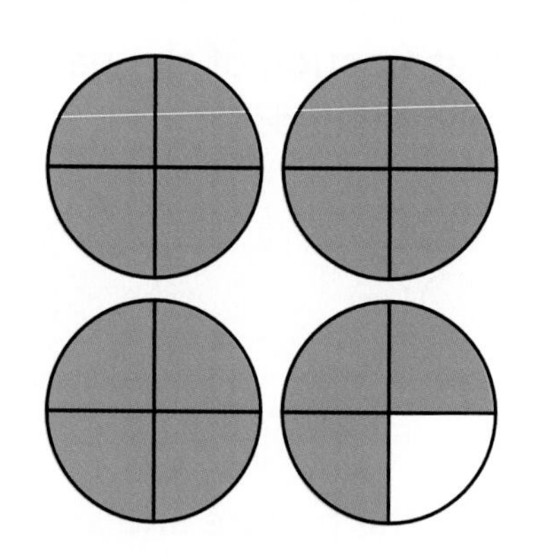

1. How many whole figures are shaded?
2. Into how many equal parts is each figure divided?
3. How many parts of the fourth figure are shaded?
4. What fraction and mixed number can you write for the picture?

Write a mixed number for each picture.

5.

6.

7.

Rename each fraction as a mixed number. You may wish to draw a picture.

8. $\frac{8}{5}$ 9. $\frac{5}{3}$ 10. $\frac{16}{5}$ 11. $\frac{7}{2}$ 12. $\frac{13}{9}$

Chapter 21

Lesson 21.1 (pages 354–355)

Use fraction bars to find the sum. Draw the bars and write the number sentence.

1. $\frac{1}{4} + \frac{2}{4} = n$
2. $\frac{3}{5} + \frac{2}{5} = n$
3. $\frac{5}{8} + \frac{4}{8} = n$
4. $\frac{2}{3} + \frac{2}{3} = n$
5. $\frac{4}{10} + \frac{3}{10} = n$
6. $\frac{2}{6} + \frac{3}{6} = n$

Write the letter of the number sentence for each model. Find the sum.

7. 1 | $\frac{1}{8}$ $\frac{1}{8}$ $\frac{1}{8}$ $\frac{1}{8}$ $\frac{1}{8}$

8. 1 | $\frac{1}{4}$ $\frac{1}{4}$ $\frac{1}{4}$

9. 1 | $\frac{1}{3}$ $\frac{1}{3}$ $\frac{1}{3}$

10. 1 | $\frac{1}{8}$ $\frac{1}{8}$ $\frac{1}{8}$ $\frac{1}{8}$ $\frac{1}{8}$ $\frac{1}{8}$ $\frac{1}{8}$

a. $\frac{1}{3} + \frac{2}{3} = n$

b. $\frac{2}{4} + \frac{1}{4} = n$

c. $\frac{5}{8} + \frac{2}{8} = n$

d. $\frac{3}{8} + \frac{2}{8} = n$

Lesson 21.2 (pages 356–357)

Write a number sentence for each problem and then find the sum.

1. five ninths plus two ninths
2. one seventh plus five sevenths
3. three sixths plus two sixths
4. four eighths plus five eighths

Find the sum.

5. $\frac{7}{10} + \frac{2}{10} = n$
6. $\frac{5}{8} + \frac{3}{8} = n$
7. $\frac{2}{5} + \frac{4}{5} = n$
8. $\frac{1}{9} + \frac{4}{9} = n$
9. $\frac{3}{6} + \frac{2}{6} = n$
10. $\frac{3}{4} + \frac{2}{4} = n$
11. $\frac{5}{12} + \frac{5}{12} = n$
12. $\frac{1}{8} + \frac{3}{8} = n$
13. $\frac{2}{9} + \frac{5}{9} = n$

Lesson 21.3 Part 1 (pages 358–359)

Use fraction bars or paper folding to find the difference. Draw a picture and write the number sentence.

1. $\frac{4}{8} - \frac{3}{8} = n$
2. $\frac{4}{6} - \frac{3}{6} = n$
3. $\frac{9}{10} - \frac{3}{10} = n$
4. $\frac{11}{12} - \frac{3}{12} = n$
5. $\frac{2}{3} - \frac{1}{3} = n$
6. $\frac{4}{5} - \frac{1}{5} = n$

Lesson 21.3 Part 2 (pages 360–361)

Make a model to solve.

1. The Martins ate $\frac{7}{12}$ of an apple pie for dessert. What fraction of the apple pie is left?
2. Laura and Wendy each ate $\frac{3}{8}$ of a pizza. What fraction of the pizza is left?

Lesson 21.4 (pages 362–363)

Find the sum. You may wish to draw a picture.

1. $5\frac{1}{5} + 3\frac{2}{5}$
2. $3\frac{4}{9} + 2\frac{1}{9}$
3. $7\frac{3}{6} + 2\frac{5}{6}$
4. $2\frac{4}{5} + 4\frac{2}{5}$
5. $9\frac{3}{8} + 2\frac{5}{8}$
6. $2\frac{1}{2} + 3\frac{1}{2}$
7. $6\frac{2}{12} + 3\frac{5}{12}$
8. $4\frac{2}{9} + 4\frac{1}{9}$
9. $5\frac{1}{6} + 6\frac{4}{6}$
10. $1\frac{3}{8} + 5\frac{1}{8}$
11. $5\frac{2}{9} + 2\frac{3}{9} = n$
12. $1\frac{3}{4} + 6\frac{1}{4} = n$
13. $8\frac{1}{3} + 3\frac{2}{3} = n$

Lesson 21.5 (pages 364–365)

Find the difference. You may wish to draw a picture.

1. $9\frac{3}{5} - 3\frac{2}{5} = n$
2. $7\frac{6}{7} - 2\frac{4}{7} = n$
3. $6\frac{9}{10} - 5\frac{7}{10} = n$
4. $8\frac{3}{4} - 4\frac{2}{4} = n$
5. $9\frac{5}{8} - 5\frac{3}{8} = n$
6. $8\frac{5}{9} - 7\frac{1}{9} = n$
7. $3\frac{5}{6} - 2\frac{1}{6} = n$
8. $8\frac{2}{3} - 1\frac{1}{3} = n$

Chapter 22

Lesson 22.1 (pages 370–371)

Write the decimal for the part that is shaded.

1. 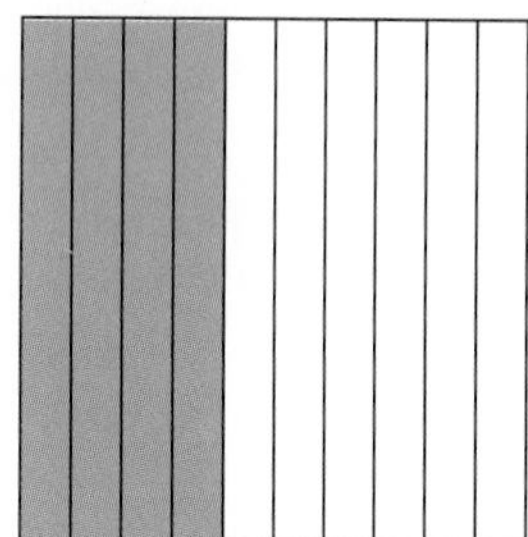
2. 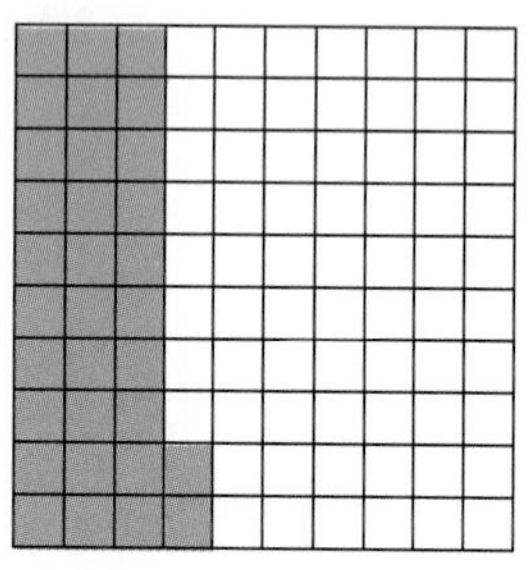
3. 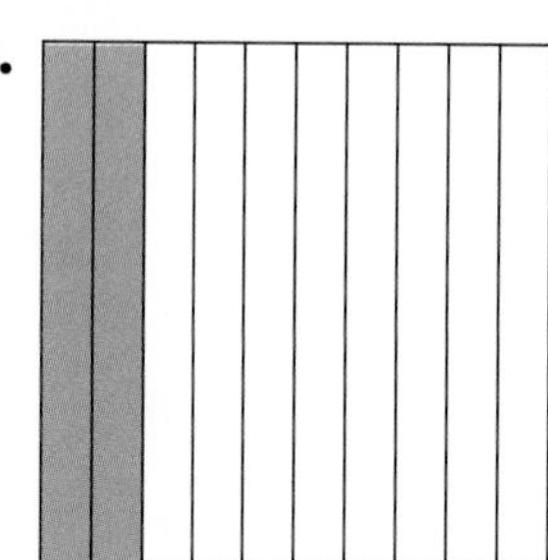
4. 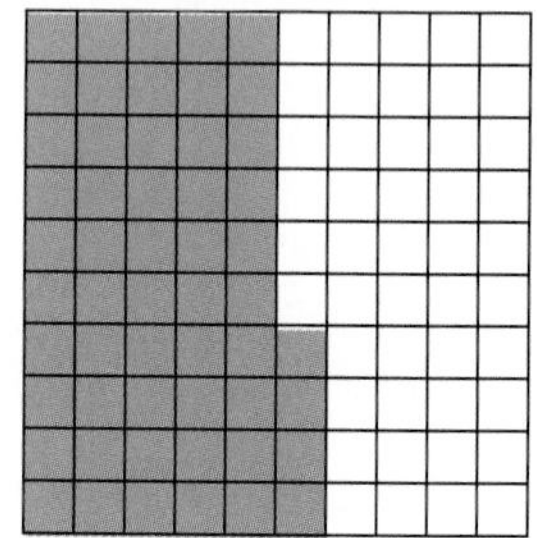

Write each fraction as a decimal.

5. $\frac{3}{10}$
6. $\frac{42}{100}$
7. $\frac{94}{100}$
8. $\frac{7}{10}$
9. $\frac{1}{10}$
10. $\frac{28}{100}$

Write each decimal as a fraction.

11. 0.6
12. 0.66
13. 0.8
14. 0.70
15. 0.3
16. 0.57
17. 0.29
18. 0.02
19. 0.11
20. 0.08
21. 0.40
22. 0.05

Lesson 22.2 (pages 372–373)

Write the amount as a fraction of a dollar, a decimal, and a money amount.

1. 36 pennies
2. 91 pennies
3. 3 dimes
4. 14 pennies

Write the decimal and the decimal name for the shaded part of each model.

5. 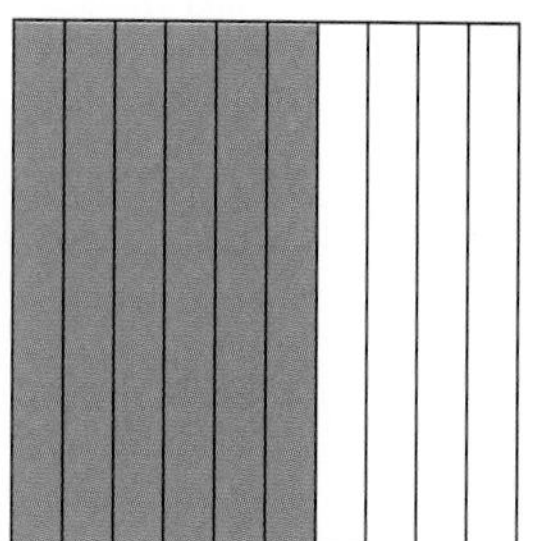
6. 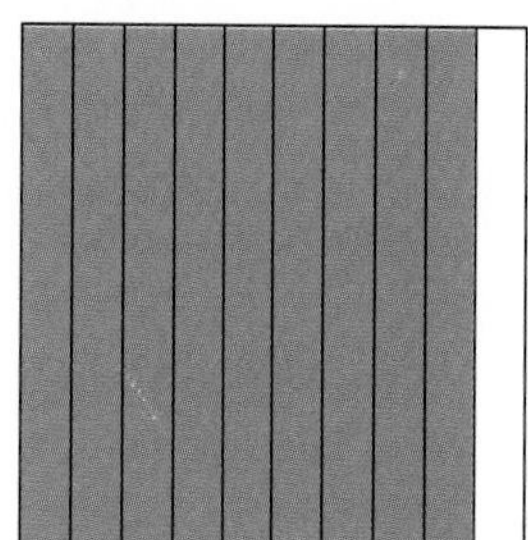
7. 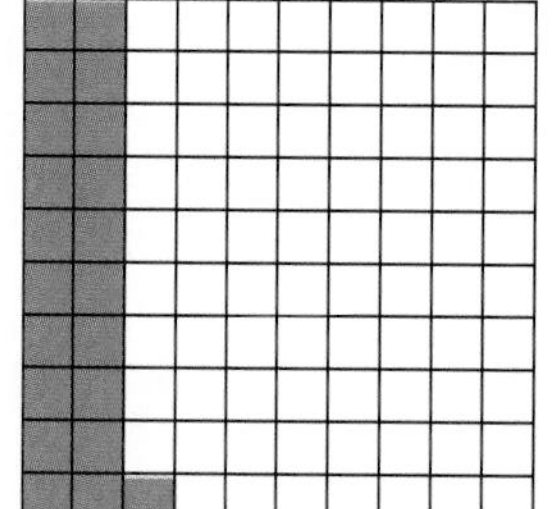
8. 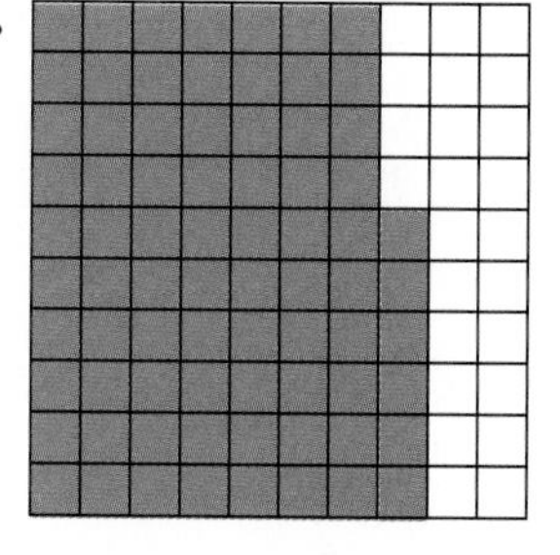

Lesson 22.3 (pages 374–375)

Write an equivalent decimal for each.
You may wish to use decimal models.

1. 0.9 **2.** 0.20 **3.** 0.6 **4.** 0.4 **5.** 0.5

Are the two decimals equivalent? Write *yes* or *no*.

6. 0.1 and 0.10 **7.** 0.6 and 0.06 **8.** 0.09 and 0.9

Lesson 22.4 (pages 376–377)

Tell which number is greater.

1. 0.72
0.91 **2.** 0.01
0.10 **3.** 0.7
0.37 **4.** 0.5
0.59 **5.** 0.92
0.29

Use the number line on page 377 to order the decimals from least to greatest.

6. 0.21, 0.12, 0.24, 0.02 **7.** 0.63, 0.06, 0.03, 0.36

Lesson 22.5 Part 1 (pages 378–379)

Write each mixed number as a mixed decimal.

1. $7\frac{3}{10}$ **2.** $9\frac{16}{100}$ **3.** $5\frac{9}{100}$ **4.** $12\frac{7}{10}$ **5.** $28\frac{8}{100}$

Write each mixed decimal as a mixed number.

6. 4.7 **7.** 3.24 **8.** 6.19 **9.** 4.9 **10.** 3.05

Write an equivalent mixed decimal for each.
You may wish to use decimal models.

11. 7.9 **12.** 21.80 **13.** 4.90 **14.** 3.1 **15.** 15.40

Lesson 22.5 Part 2 (pages 380–381)

Make a table to solve.

1. At a track meet Dante's time was 10.15 seconds, William's time was 10.42 seconds, and Andy's time was 10.35 seconds. First place goes to the runner with the least time. Who finished first? second? third?

2. In a survey of 35 fourth graders, 11 students said mysteries were their favorite books, 14 said they liked fiction best, and 10 liked humor best. According to the survey, which kind of book is the fourth graders' favorite? second favorite? third favorite?

Chapter 23

Lesson 23.1 (pages 386–387)

Use decimal squares to find the sum or difference.

1. $0.9 - 0.3 = n$ **2.** $0.7 + 0.2 = n$ **3.** $0.10 - 0.06 = n$ **4.** $0.3 + 0.3 = n$

Lesson 23.2 (pages 388–389)

Find the sum.

1. $\begin{array}{r} 0.5 \\ +0.9 \\ \hline \end{array}$ **2.** $\begin{array}{r} 0.21 \\ +0.13 \\ \hline \end{array}$ **3.** $\begin{array}{r} 0.42 \\ +0.26 \\ \hline \end{array}$ **4.** $\begin{array}{r} 0.73 \\ +0.14 \\ \hline \end{array}$ **5.** $\begin{array}{r} 0.8 \\ +0.6 \\ \hline \end{array}$

Lesson 23.3 (pages 390–391)

Find the difference.

1. $\begin{array}{r} 0.9 \\ -0.7 \\ \hline \end{array}$ **2.** $\begin{array}{r} 0.32 \\ -0.16 \\ \hline \end{array}$ **3.** $\begin{array}{r} 0.41 \\ -0.39 \\ \hline \end{array}$ **4.** $\begin{array}{r} 1.3 \\ -0.2 \\ \hline \end{array}$ **5.** $\begin{array}{r} 1.32 \\ -0.21 \\ \hline \end{array}$

Lesson 23.4 Part 1 (pages 392–393)

Find the sum.

1. $\begin{array}{r} 0.7 \\ +0.1 \\ \hline \end{array}$ **2.** $\begin{array}{r} 0.20 \\ +0.12 \\ \hline \end{array}$ **3.** $\begin{array}{r} 4.64 \\ +3.31 \\ \hline \end{array}$ **4.** $\begin{array}{r} 7.71 \\ +4.49 \\ \hline \end{array}$ **5.** $\begin{array}{r} 6.92 \\ +5.78 \\ \hline \end{array}$

Find the difference.

6. $\begin{array}{r} 0.8 \\ -0.5 \\ \hline \end{array}$ **7.** $\begin{array}{r} 0.9 \\ -0.3 \\ \hline \end{array}$ **8.** $\begin{array}{r} 4.39 \\ -3.21 \\ \hline \end{array}$ **9.** $\begin{array}{r} 7.31 \\ -5.59 \\ \hline \end{array}$ **10.** $\begin{array}{r} 9.82 \\ -6.68 \\ \hline \end{array}$

Find the sum or difference.

11. $0.93 - 0.77 = n$ **12.** $4.9 + 3.3 = n$ **13.** $6.91 - 4.69 = n$

Lesson 23.4 Part 2 (pages 394–395)

Write a number sentence to solve.

1. Noel walked 4.74 miles on Monday, 5.05 miles on Tuesday, 4.13 miles on Wednesday, and 3.94 miles on Thursday. How many miles did Noel walk in those four days?

2. In a gymnastics meet, Shannon scored 9.98 on the beam, 8.96 on the vault, 9.41 on the bars, and 9.67 on the floor. How many points did Shannon score in all?

Lesson 23.5 (pages 396–397)

Estimate the sum or difference by rounding to the nearest whole number.

1. $\begin{array}{r} 3.4 \\ -2.3 \\ \hline \end{array}$ **2.** $\begin{array}{r} 9.3 \\ -4.9 \\ \hline \end{array}$ **3.** $\begin{array}{r} 8.9 \\ +7.1 \\ \hline \end{array}$ **4.** $\begin{array}{r} 7.4 \\ +3.6 \\ \hline \end{array}$ **5.** $\begin{array}{r} 2.5 \\ -1.1 \\ \hline \end{array}$

Estimate the sum or difference by rounding to the nearest tenth.

6. $\begin{array}{r} 1.76 \\ +1.62 \\ \hline \end{array}$ **7.** $\begin{array}{r} 1.94 \\ -0.42 \\ \hline \end{array}$ **8.** $\begin{array}{r} 3.18 \\ -1.92 \\ \hline \end{array}$ **9.** $\begin{array}{r} 4.92 \\ +3.19 \\ \hline \end{array}$ **10.** $\begin{array}{r} 5.52 \\ +4.76 \\ \hline \end{array}$

11. $\begin{array}{r} 4.24 \\ +2.72 \\ \hline \end{array}$ **12.** $\begin{array}{r} 9.69 \\ -5.45 \\ \hline \end{array}$ **13.** $\begin{array}{r} 8.36 \\ +4.17 \\ \hline \end{array}$ **14.** $\begin{array}{r} 1.08 \\ -1.01 \\ \hline \end{array}$ **15.** $\begin{array}{r} 4.13 \\ -2.24 \\ \hline \end{array}$

Chapter 24

Lesson 24.1 (pages 406–407)

Choose the reasonable unit of measure. Write *in., ft, yd,* or *mi.*

1. The length of a chair leg is about 14 _?_.

2. The width of an envelope is about 13 _?_.

3. The distance from school to the grocery store is about 3 _?_.

Use a ruler to measure the length of each line to the nearest inch.

4. ______________

5. ____________________________

Name the longer measurement.

6. 22 yd or 22 in.

7. 51 in. or 51 ft

8. 3 ft or 3 mi

Lesson 24.2 Part 1 (pages 408–409)

Change the unit. You may use a calculator.

1. 3 yd = _?_ ft

2. 84 in. = _?_ ft

3. 36 ft = _?_ in.

Lesson 24.2 Part 2 (pages 410–411)

1. Maggie has a vegetable garden. She wants to plant tomato plants 6 in. apart in a 12-ft row. She will not plant on either end. How many tomato plants will she need?

2. Chris is decorating her baby's room. She wants to paint teddy bears 4 inches apart along a 10-ft wall. She will not paint either corner. How many teddy bears will she paint?

Lesson 24.3 (pages 412–413)

Measure the length of each item to the nearest $\frac{1}{4}$ in.

1.

2.

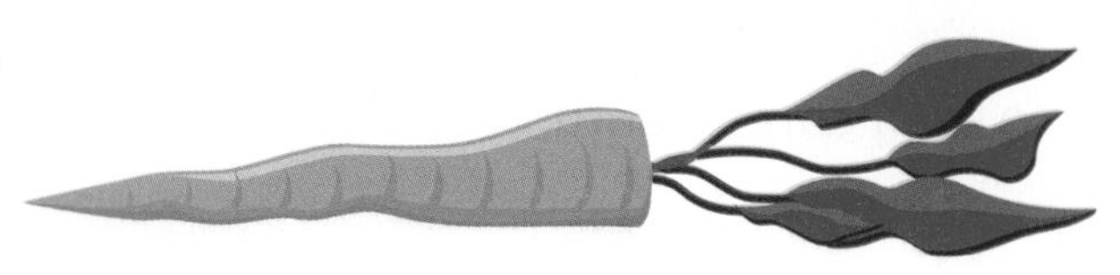

Lesson 24.4 (pages 414–415)

Write the letter of the reasonable unit.

1. 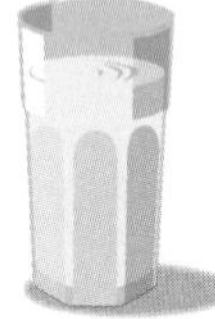

a. quart **b.** cup

2. 

a. gallon **b.** quart

3. 

a. pint **b.** gallon

Write the equivalent measurement.

4. 8 cups = _?_ quarts
5. 10 pints = _?_ quarts
6. 3 gallons = _?_ quarts

Lesson 24.5 (pages 416–417)

Choose the more reasonable measurement.

1. 

35 lb or 35 oz

2. 

1 T or 1 lb

3. 

4 T or 4 lb

Write the equivalent measurement. You may use a calculator.

4. 64 oz to _?_ lb
5. 12 lb to _?_ oz
6. 3 T to _?_ lb

Chapter 25

Lesson 25.1 (pages 422–423)

Use a centimeter ruler or a meterstick to measure each thing.
Write the measurement and unit of the measure you used.

1. length of a crayon
2. width of a magazine
3. height of a chair

Lesson 25.2 (pages 424–425)

Write the missing unit. Use a meterstick to help you.

1. 9 __?__ = 90 cm **2.** 0.02 __?__ = 2 cm **3.** 0.3 __?__ = 3 dm

Write the decimal number. Use a meterstick to help you.

4. 3 dm = __?__ m **5.** 40 cm = __?__ m **6.** 70 cm = __?__ m

Lesson 25.3 Part 1 (pages 426–427)

Would you multiply each by 10 or by 100 to change the larger units to smaller units? Write × *10* or × *100*.

1. 7 m = __?__ cm **2.** 11 m = __?__ dm **3.** 9 m = __?__ cm

4. 16 dm = __?__ cm **5.** 4 dm = __?__ cm **6.** 8 m = __?__ dm

Write the equivalent measurement. You may use a calculator.

7. 6 m = __?__ cm **8.** 3 dm = __?__ cm **9.** 14 m = __?__ cm

10. 29 m = __?__ dm **11.** 31 dm = __?__ cm **12.** 8 dm = __?__ cm

Lesson 25.3 Part 2 (pages 428–429)

Solve a simpler problem.

1. Marc caught a fish that is 1.5 meters long. How many centimeters long is Marc's fish?

2. Frank's height is 15 decimeters. Jeanne's height is 1.3 meters. Who is taller? How many decimeters taller?

Lesson 25.4 (pages 430–431)

Choose the reasonable unit of measure. Write *mL, metric cup,* or *L.*

1. a baby bottle **2.** a pond **3.** a cup of coffee **4.** a bathtub

Choose the more reasonable measurement.

5.

a. 250 L **b.** 25 L **c.** 250 mL

6.

a. 10 mL **b.** 10 L **c.** 1 L

Lesson 25.5 (pages 432–433)

Choose the reasonable unit. Write *g* or *kg*.

1. 

2. 

3. 

4. 

Choose the more reasonable measurement.

5. 

600 kg or 60 g

6. 

1 g or 1 kg

7. 

5 kg or 50 kg

8. 

2 g or 2 kg

Chapter 26

Lesson 26.1 (pages 438–439)

Write each time in a different way.

1. 2:15 **2.** 4:30 **3.** a quarter past one **4.** half past three

Use *a quarter* or *half* to express the time shown.

5. 

6. 

7. 

8. 

Lesson 26.2 Part 1 (pages 440–441)

Find the perimeter of each figure in customary and metric units.

1. 

2. 

Choose the more reasonable measure for each line segment.

3. ____________

a. 1 in. **b.** 1 cm

4. ________________

a. 4 in. **b.** 4 cm

5. ___________

a. 2.5 in. **b.** 2.5 cm

Lesson 26.2 Part 2 (pages 442–443)

Write a number sentence to solve.

1. Myrna has a square patio that measures 15 feet on each side. What is the perimeter of Myrna's patio in yards?

2. Timothy has a piece of cardboard that has 2 sides 30 centimeters long and 2 sides 40 centimeters long. What is the perimeter in meters?

Lesson 26.3 (pages 444–445)

Use the thermometers on page 444. Find the difference between the two temperatures.

1. 20°F and 35°F **2.** 10°C and 75°C **3.** 20°F and ⁻10°F

Use the thermometer to answer the question.

4. 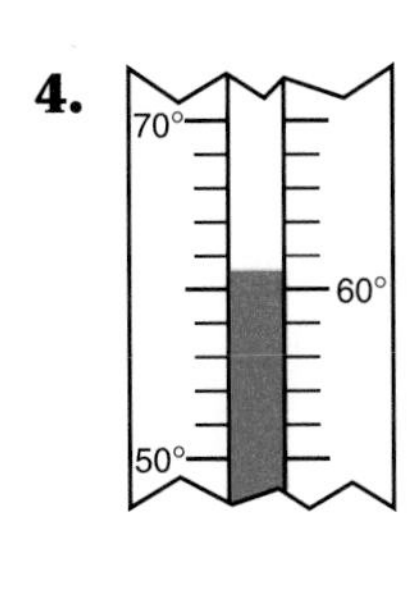

The Fahrenheit temperature at night is shown. The temperature rose 28 degrees during the day. What was the daytime high temperature?

5. 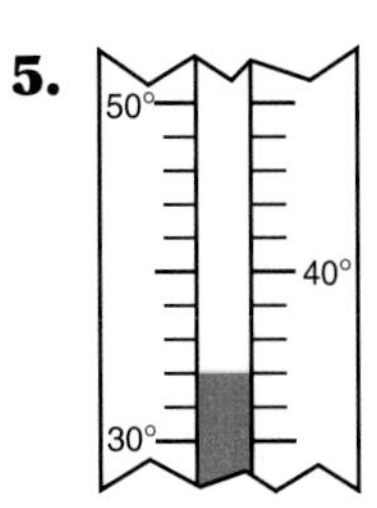

Ice begins to melt if the temperature rises above 32°F. The outside temperature is shown. Would ice begin to melt if it were placed outside?

Lesson 26.4 (pages 446–447)

Use the pattern-block shapes to model each area.

1. Use as the whole. Model $\frac{1}{6}$. **2.** Use as the whole. Model $\frac{1}{2}$. **3.** Use as the whole. Model $\frac{1}{3}$.

Chapter 27

Lesson 27.1 (pages 456–457)

Write the numbers you would use to estimate the quotients. Then write the estimate.

1. $65 \div 11 = n$ **2.** $208 \div 31 = n$ **3.** $183 \div 26 = n$ **4.** $362 \div 28 = n$

Write the basic fact that helps you find the quotient.

5. $91 \div 32 = n$ **6.** $62 \div 11 = n$ **7.** $241 \div 42 = n$ **8.** $63 \div 21 = n$

9. $345 \div 74 = n$ **10.** $322 \div 79 = n$ **11.** $177 \div 23 = n$ **12.** $201 \div 46 = n$

Lesson 27.2 (pages 458–459)

Copy each problem. Draw a box where the first digit in the quotient should be placed.

1. $20\overline{)68}$ **2.** $30\overline{)409}$ **3.** $50\overline{)369}$ **4.** $70\overline{)952}$

Find the quotient.

5. $70\overline{)862}$ **6.** $30\overline{)579}$ **7.** $40\overline{)589}$ **8.** $90\overline{)498}$

9. $50\overline{)756}$ **10.** $40\overline{)368}$ **11.** $80\overline{)263}$ **12.** $20\overline{)761}$

13. $20\overline{)999}$ **14.** $70\overline{)616}$ **15.** $60\overline{)675}$ **16.** $40\overline{)348}$

Lesson 27.3 (pages 460–461)

Make a model and find the quotient.

1. $23\overline{)72}$ **2.** $18\overline{)79}$ **3.** $14\overline{)152}$ **4.** $32\overline{)128}$

5. $29\overline{)156}$ **6.** $32\overline{)98}$ **7.** $42\overline{)183}$ **8.** $15\overline{)187}$

9. $136 \div 21 =$? **10.** $172 \div 17 =$? **11.** $149 \div 34 =$?

12. $225 \div 14 =$? **13.** $197 \div 22 =$? **14.** $616 \div 11 =$?

Lesson 27.4 Part 1 (pages 462–463)

Find the quotient. Check by multiplying.

1. $18\overline{)356}$ **2.** $41\overline{)496}$ **3.** $14\overline{)272}$ **4.** $35\overline{)536}$

5. $62\overline{)879}$ **6.** $32\overline{)426}$ **7.** $15\overline{)392}$ **8.** $22\overline{)335}$

9. $71\overline{)645}$ **10.** $26\overline{)318}$ **11.** $43\overline{)524}$ **12.** $16\overline{)419}$

13. $52\overline{)601}$ **14.** $95\overline{)722}$ **15.** $64\overline{)591}$ **16.** $76\overline{)843}$

Lesson 27.4 Part 2 (pages 464–465)

Write a number sentence to solve.

1. Roger threw a football 490 inches and Rick threw it 42 feet. What is the distance in feet that Roger threw the football? Who threw the football farther?

2. Marcus took 9 minutes to walk to Trevor's house and Steve took 560 seconds. How many minutes did it take Steve to walk to Trevor's house? Who got there faster?

Lesson 27.5 (pages 466–467)

Write *too high, too low*, or *just right* for each estimate. Find the quotient.

1. $41\overline{)393}$ estimate 8
2. $38\overline{)326}$ estimate 9
3. $18\overline{)172}$ estimate 9
4. $27\overline{)115}$ estimate 3
5. $19\overline{)168}$ estimate 7
6. $53\overline{)299}$ estimate 5
7. $45\overline{)298}$ estimate 5
8. $56\overline{)229}$ estimate 5
9. $62\overline{)341}$ estimate 6
10. $76\overline{)195}$ estimate 1
11. $58\overline{)234}$ estimate 4
12. $24\overline{)231}$ estimate 8

Chapter 28

Lesson 28.1 (pages 472–473)

Use fraction-circle pieces to make each circle graph. Draw the circle graph by tracing the pieces. Title the graph and label each part.

1. a flower bed that is $\frac{1}{3}$ roses, $\frac{1}{3}$ tulips, and $\frac{1}{3}$ daisies
2. a book collection that is $\frac{1}{2}$ fiction, $\frac{1}{3}$ mysteries, and $\frac{1}{6}$ historical
3. a spice mixture that is $\frac{1}{4}$ basil, $\frac{1}{4}$ oregano, $\frac{1}{4}$ salt, and $\frac{1}{4}$ pepper
4. a park that has $\frac{1}{2}$ jungle gyms, $\frac{1}{4}$ swings, and $\frac{1}{4}$ slides

Lesson 28.2 (pages 474–475)

For Problems 1–6, use the circle graph.

1. What fraction of the 32 students like hockey?
2. What fraction of the 32 students like swimming?
3. Which sport is most popular? least popular?
4. What fraction of the 32 students like football?
5. What fraction represents all the students in the survey?
6. What would the graph look like if the number of students who chose each sport was the same?

Lesson 28.3 Part 1 (pages 476–477)

For Problems 1–5, use the circle graph.

1. What does the whole graph show?
2. What decimal tells how many students like iced tea? lemonade? fruit punch? milk?
3. What is the most popular drink? least popular?
4. What is the sum of the four decimals?
5. What two drinks together did 0.5 of the students choose?

Lesson 28.3 Part 2 (pages 478–479)

Make a graph to solve.

1. Andrea asked 10 friends to name their favorite animal. Of her friends, 4 chose dogs, 3 chose horses, 2 chose cats, and 1 chose rabbits. What decimal tells how many friends chose dogs? horses? cats? rabbits?
2. A vote in Mrs. Thomas's class showed that 18 students live in houses, 8 in apartments, and 4 in townhouses. In Mr. Carlson's class, 15 students live in houses, 5 in apartments, and 10 in townhouses. Which class had a larger part living in houses? apartments? townhouses?

Lesson 28.4 (pages 480–481)

Match the graph with the set of data it describes.

a.

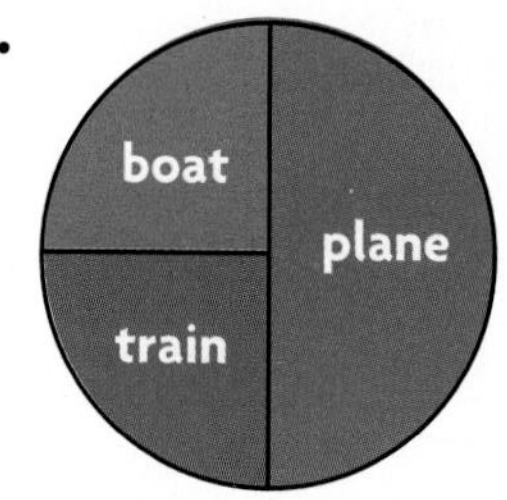

b.

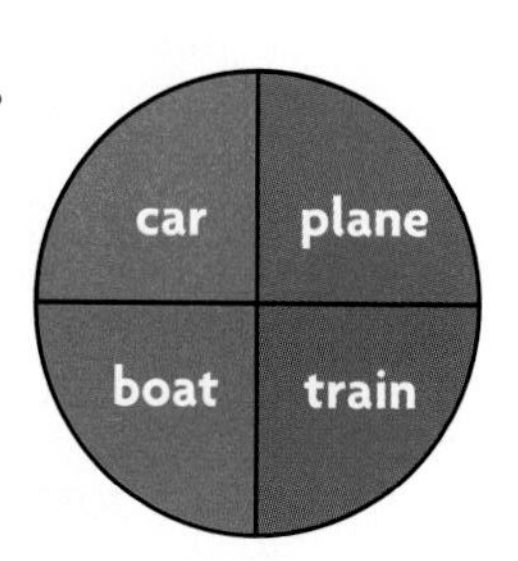

c.

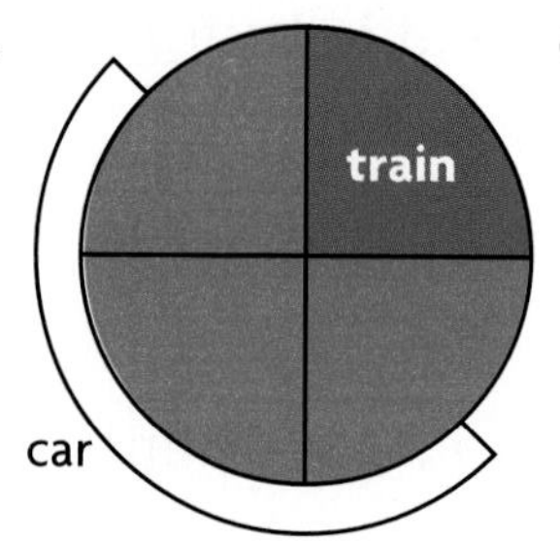

d.

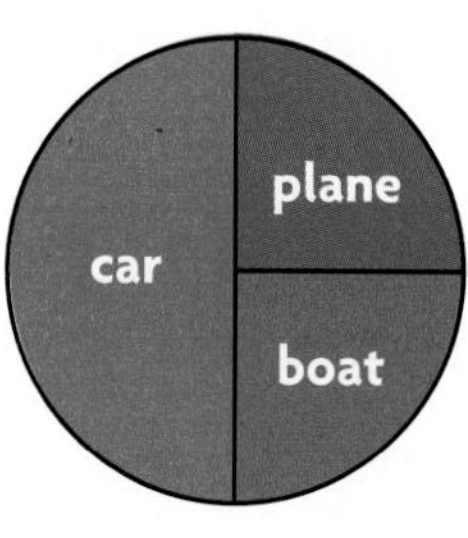
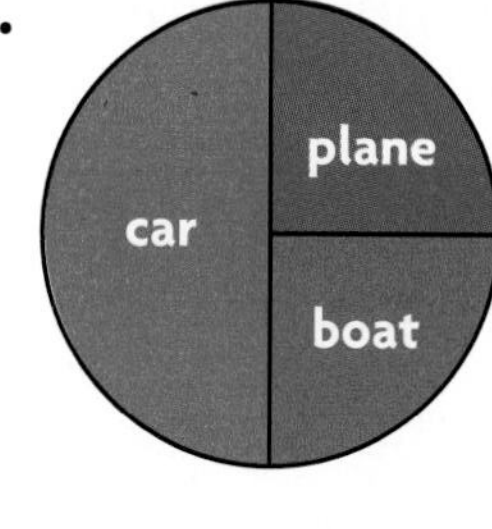

1. $\frac{3}{4}$ car

   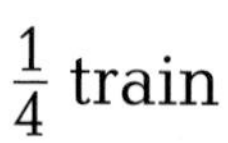
   $\frac{1}{4}$ train

2. $\frac{1}{2}$ car

   $\frac{1}{4}$ plane

   $\frac{1}{4}$ boat

3. $\frac{1}{4}$ car

   $\frac{1}{4}$ plane

   $\frac{1}{4}$ train

   $\frac{1}{4}$ boat

4. $\frac{1}{2}$ plane

   $\frac{1}{4}$ boat

   $\frac{1}{4}$ train

TABLE OF MEASURES

METRIC	CUSTOMARY
Length	
10 millimeters (mm) = 1 centimeter (cm)	1 foot (ft) = 12 inches (in.)
10 centimeters = 1 decimeter (dm)	1 yard (yd) = 3 feet, or 36 inches
10 decimeters = 1 meter (m)	1 mile (mi) = 1,760 yards, or 5,280 feet
100 centimeters = 1 meter	
1,000 meters = 1 kilometer (km)	
Weight	
1 gram (g) = 1,000 milligrams (mg)	1 pound (lb) = 16 ounces (oz)
1 kilogram (kg) = 1,000 grams	1 ton (T) = 2,000 pounds
Capacity	
1 liter (L) = 1,000 milliliters (mL)	3 teaspoons (tsp) = 1 tablespoon (tbsp)
250 milliliters = 1 metric cup	8 fluid ounces (fl oz) = 1 cup (c)
	2 cups = 1 pint (pt)
	2 pints = 1 quart (qt)
	4 quarts = 1 gallon (gal)

TIME

60 seconds (sec) = 1 minute (min)
60 minutes = 1 hour (hr)
24 hours = 1 day
7 days = 1 week (wk)

12 months (mo),
or 52 weeks,
or 365 days = 1 year (yr)
366 days = 1 leap year

MONEY

1 penny = 1 cent (¢)
1 nickel = 5 cents
1 dime = 10 cents
1 quarter = 25 cents
1 half dollar = 50 cents
1 dollar ($) = 100 cents

SYMBOLS

< is less than
> is greater than
= is equal to
°F degrees Fahrenheit
°C degrees Celsius
(2,3) ordered pair 2,3

GLOSSARY

A

acute angle An angle that has a measure less than a right angle (90°) *(page 212)*
Example:

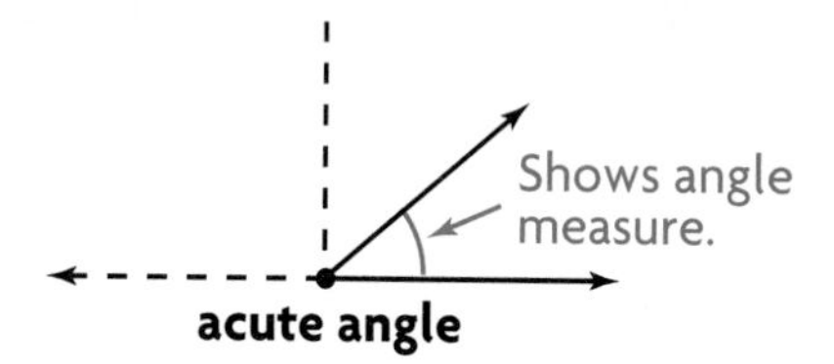

addend Any of the numbers that are added *(page 6)*

A.M. The time between midnight and noon *(page 122)*

angle A figure formed by two rays that meet at a common endpoint *(page 212)*
Example:

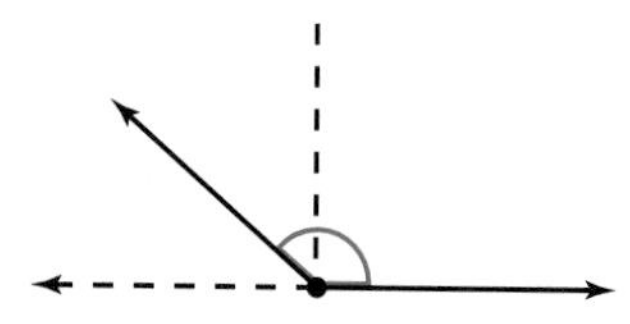

area The number of square units needed to cover a flat surface *(page 230)*

array An arrangement of objects in rows and columns *(page 34)*

average One way to find a number that best represents all the numbers in a set *(page 326)*

B

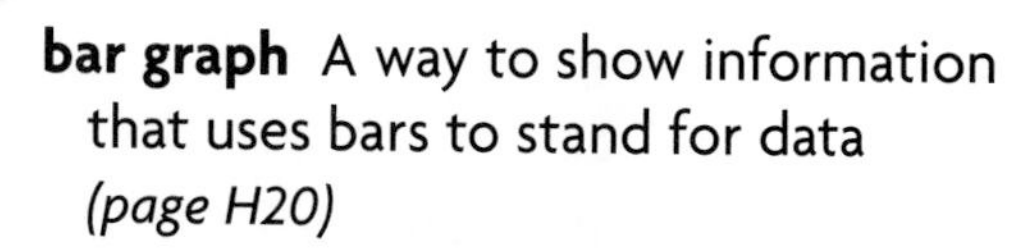

bar graph A way to show information that uses bars to stand for data *(page H20)*

benchmark A number used as a point of reference *(page 82)*

C

calendar A table that shows the days, weeks, and months of a year in order *(page 130)*

capacity The amount a container can hold when filled *(page 414)*

cardinal A number that tells how many *(page 72)*

centimeter (cm) A unit of length in the metric system *(page 422)*
100 centimeters = 1 meter

certain An event that will always happen *(page 172)*

circle graph A graph in the shape of a circle that shows data as a whole made up of different parts *(page 472)*

closed figure A shape that begins and ends at the same point *(page H24)*
Example:

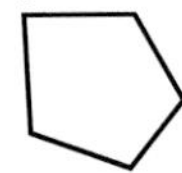

congruent figures Figures that have the same size and shape *(page 246)*
Example:

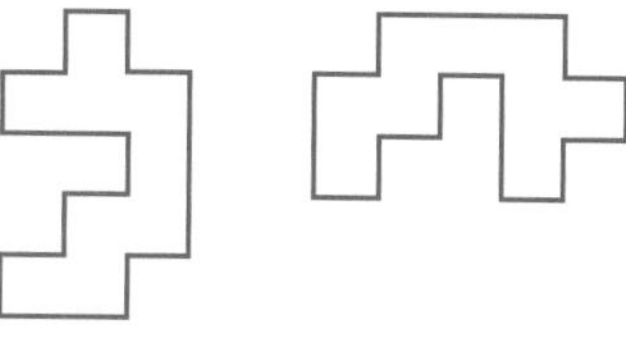

cumulative frequency The sum of the frequency of data as they are collected *(page 140)*

cup (c) A customary unit for measuring capacity *(page 414)*
8 ounces = 1 cup

decimal A number that uses place value and a decimal point to show values less than one, such as tenths and hundredths *(page 370)*

decimal point A period used in decimal numbers to separate the whole number part from the decimal part *(page 372)*

decimeter (dm) A unit of length in the metric system *(page 422)*
10 decimeters = 1 meter

degree Celsius (°C) A standard unit for measuring temperature in the metric system *(page 444)*

degree Fahrenheit (°F) A standard unit for measuring temperature in the customary system *(page 444)*

denominator The number below the bar in a fraction. It tells the total number of equal parts *(page 338)*

Example: $\frac{3}{4}$ ← denominator

diameter A line segment that passes through the center of a circle and has its endpoints on the circle *(page 217)*
Example:

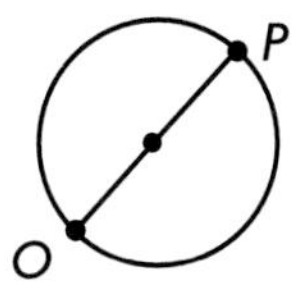

diameter *OP*

difference An answer to a subtraction problem *(page 10)*

digit Any one of the ten symbols 0, 1, 2, 3, 4, 5, 6, 7, 8, or 9 used to write numbers *(page H10)*

dimension A measure in one direction *(page 192)*

dividend The number that is being divided in a division problem *(page 60)*

divisor The number that divides the dividend *(page 60)*

double-bar graph A graph used to compare similar kinds of data *(page 156)*

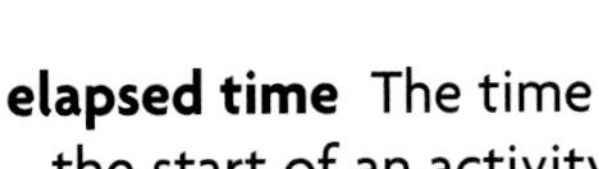

elapsed time The time that passes from the start of an activity to the end of that activity *(page 124)*

equally likely When the outcomes of an experiment have the same chance of happening *(page 176)*

equation A number sentence with an equals sign to show that two amounts are equal *(page 4)*
Examples: $3 + 7 = 10$
$4 - 1 = 3$

equivalent decimals Two or more decimals that name the same amount *(page 374)*
Example: 0.3 and 0.30

equivalent fractions Two or more fractions that name the same amount *(page 342)*
Example: $\frac{2}{4}$ and $\frac{1}{2}$ name the same amount.

estimate To find an answer that is close to the exact answer *(page 26)*

event The action that happens in an experiment that brings about an outcome *(page 174)*

expanded form A way to write numbers by showing the value of each digit *(page 90)*
Examples: $253 = 200 + 50 + 3$
$1{,}679 = 1{,}000 + 600 + 70 + 9$

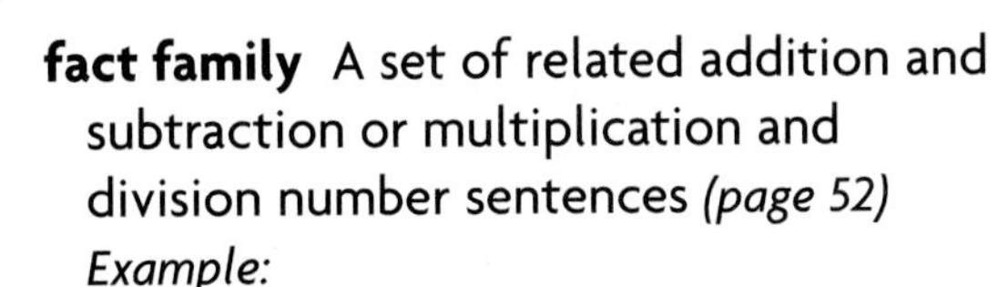

fact family A set of related addition and subtraction or multiplication and division number sentences *(page 52)*
Example:
$7 \times 8 = 56, 8 \times 7 = 56$
$56 \div 7 = 8, 56 \div 8 = 7$

factor A number that is multiplied by another number to find a product *(page H6)*
Example: $4 \times 7 = 28$
The factors are 4 and 7.

fairness When one outcome is not more likely to happen than another *(page 180)*

foot (ft) A unit of length in the customary system *(page 406)*
12 inches = 1 foot

fraction A number that names part of a whole or part of a group *(page 338)*

frequency table A table that shows the frequency of data *(page 140)*

G

gallon (gal) A customary unit for measuring capacity *(page 414)*
4 quarts = 1 gallon

gram (g) A metric unit used to measure mass *(page 432)*
1,000 grams = 1 kilogram

Grouping Property of Addition The property which states that the way addends are grouped does not change the sum *(page 6)*
Example:
$(5 + 9) + 3 = 5 + (9 + 3)$
$14 + 3 = 5 + 12$
$17 = 17$

Grouping Property of Multiplication The property which states that the way factors are grouped does not change the product *(page 40)*
Example:
$(2 \times 3) \times 4 = 2 \times (3 \times 4)$
$6 \times 4 = 2 \times 12$
$24 = 24$

H

hexagon A polygon with 6 sides and 6 angles *(page 218)*

horizontal The direction from left to right *(page 74)*

I

impossible An event that will never happen *(page 172)*

inch (in.) A unit of length in the customary system *(page 406)*

intersecting lines Two lines that cross at exactly one point *(page 214)*
Example:

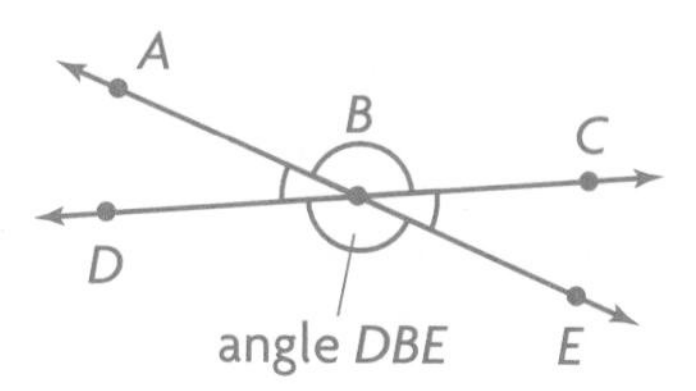

interval The distance between two numbers on the scale of a graph *(page 148)*

inverse Opposite operations, such as multiplication and division, that undo each other *(page 52)*
Example: $3 \times 4 = 12$ and $12 \div 4 = 3$

K

kilogram (kg) A metric unit used to measure mass *(page 432)*
1,000 grams = 1 kilogram

L

line A straight path in a plane, extending in both directions with no endpoints *(page 210)*

line graph A graph that uses a line to show how data change over a period of time *(page 158)*

line plot A diagram that shows the frequency of data as they are collected *(page 160)*

line segment A part of a line between two endpoints *(page 210)*
Example:

line symmetry A figure has line symmetry when it can be folded about a line so that its two parts are identical *(page 250)*
Example:

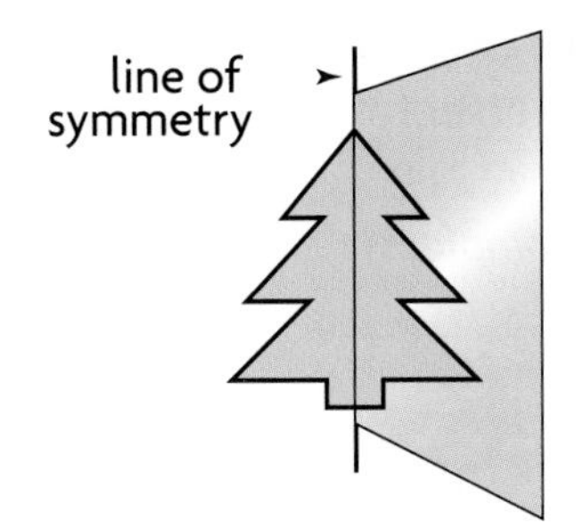

linear Units that measure in one direction, such as length, width, height, or distance *(page 406)*

liter (L) A metric unit of capacity *(page 430)*
1,000 milliliters = 1 liter

M

mass The amount of matter of an object *(page 432)*

mean One way to find a number that best represents all the numbers in a set *(page 326)*

median The middle number in an ordered series of numbers *(page 162)*

meter (m) A unit of length in the metric system *(page 422)*
100 centimeters = 1 meter

mile (mi) A unit of length in the customary system *(page 406)*
5,280 feet = 1 mile

milliliter (mL) A metric unit of capacity *(page 430)*
1,000 milliliters = 1 liter

mixed decimal A number that is made up of a whole number and a decimal *(page 378)*

mixed number A number that is made up of a whole number and a fraction *(page 348)*

mode The number that is listed the most often in a set of data *(page 162)*

multiple A number that is the product of a given number and another whole number *(page 266)*

N

net A two-dimensional pattern of a three-dimensional figure *(page 194)*
Example:

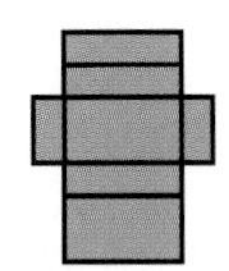

nominal A number that names something *(page 72)*

numeration system A way to count and name numbers *(page 88)*

numerator The number above the bar in a fraction. It tells how many parts are being considered. *(page 338)*
Example: $\frac{3}{4}$ ← numerator

O

obtuse angle An angle that has a measure greater than a right angle (90°) *(page 212)*
Example:

obtuse angle

octagon A polygon with 8 sides and 8 angles *(page 218)*
Example:

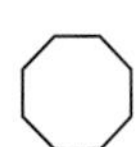

open figure A shape that does not begin and end at the same point *(page H24)*
Example:

Order Property of Multiplication The property which states that when the order of two factors is changed, the product is the same *(page 36)*
Example: $4 \times 5 = 5 \times 4$
$20 = 20$

ordered pair A pair of numbers used to locate a point on a grid. The first number tells the left-right position and the second number tells the up-down position. *(page 74)*

ordinal A number that tells position or order *(page 72)*

ounce (oz) A customary unit used to measure weight *(page 416)*
16 ounces = 1 pound

outcomes Possible results of an experiment *(page 142)*

parallel line segments Line segments that stay exactly the same distance apart *(page 210)*
Example:

parallelogram A quadrilateral with opposite sides parallel and congruent *(page 220)*
Examples:

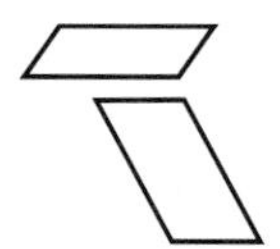

partial product A method of multiplying where the ones, tens, hundreds, and so on are multiplied separately and then the products added together *(page 270)*

pentagon A polygon with 5 sides and 5 angles *(page 218)*

perimeter The distance around a figure *(page 228)*

period Each group of three digits in a number *(page 96)*
Example:

385,643,900

perpendicular lines Two lines that intersect to form four right angles *(page 214)*
Example:

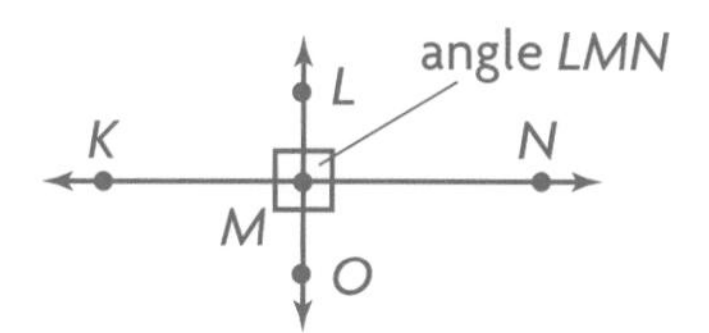

pictograph A graph that uses pictures to show and compare information *(page H20)*

pint (pt) A customary unit for measuring capacity *(page 414)*
2 cups = 1 pint

plane A flat surface that extends without end in all directions *(page 210)*

plane figure A closed figure that lies on a flat surface *(page H24)*

P.M. The time between noon and midnight *(page 122)*

point The name of a location on an object and in space *(page 210)*

point symmetry When a figure can be turned about a central point and still look the same in at least two positions *(page 248)*
Example:

polygon A closed plane figure with straight sides *(page 218)*

possible ways All the possible outcomes of an experiment *(page 176)*

pound (lb) A customary unit used to measure weight *(page 416)*
16 ounces = 1 pound

predict To tell what will happen when doing experiments *(page 172)*

probability The chance that a given event will occur *(page 178)*

product The answer to a multiplication problem *(pages 36, H6)*
Example: $6 \times 2 = 12$
The product is 12.

Property of One for Multiplication The property which states that the product of any number and 1 is that number *(page 36)*
Examples: $5 \times 1 = 5$
$12 \times 1 = 12$

quadrilateral A polygon with 4 sides and 4 angles *(page 220)*
Examples:

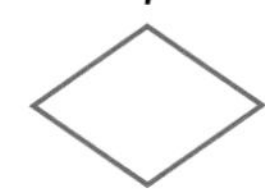
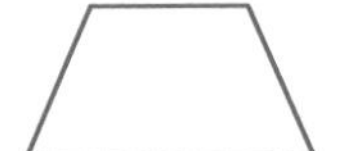

quart (qt) A customary unit for measuring capacity *(page 414)*
2 pints = 1 quart

quotient The answer in a division problem *(pages 60, H8)*

radius A line segment with one endpoint at the center of a circle and the other endpoint on the circle *(page 217)*
Example:

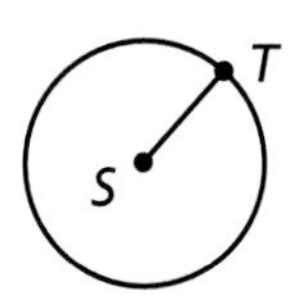

radius *ST*

range The difference between the greatest and least numbers in a set of data *(page 160)*

ray A part of a line that begins at one endpoint and extends forever in only one direction *(page 212)*
Example:

ray *FG*

rectangle A polygon with 4 sides and 4 right angles *(page 220)*

reflection The result of a figure flipped over a line *(page 244)*
Example:

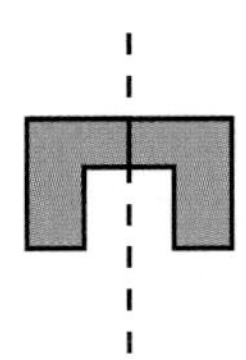

remainder The amount left over when you find a quotient *(pages 54, 300)*

rhombus A parallelogram with four congruent sides whose opposite angles are congruent *(page 220)*
Example:

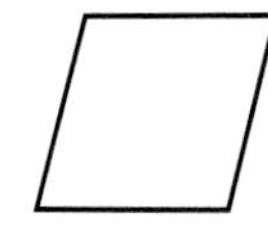

right angle An angle that forms a square corner and measures 90° *(page 212)*
Example:

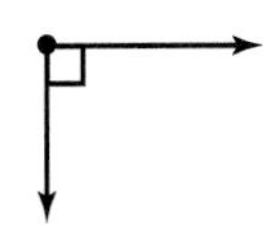

rotation The action of turning a figure around a point or a vertex *(page 244)*
Example:

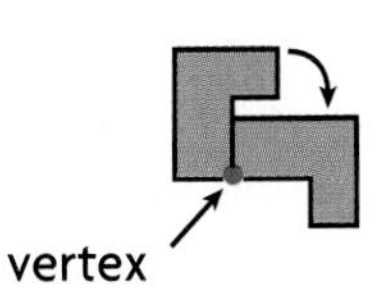

scale A series of numbers placed at fixed distances on a graph to help label the graph *(page 150)*

schedule A table that lists activities and the times they happen *(page 126)*

similar figures Figures that have the same shape but may have different sizes *(page 254)*
Example:

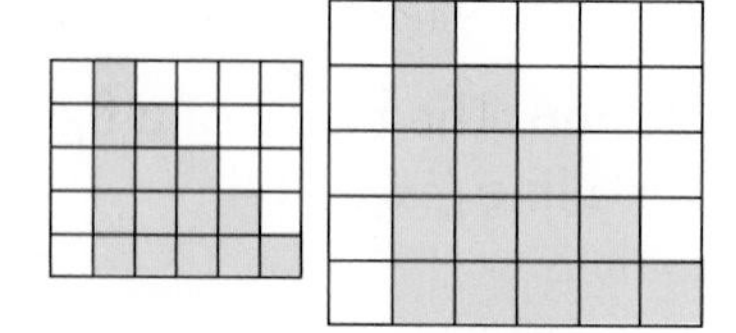

simplest form When a fraction can be modeled with the largest fraction bar possible *(page H46)*

square A polygon with 4 equal sides and 4 right angles *(page 220)*

square unit The unit used to measure area *(page 230)*
Example:
■ 1 square unit

standard form A way to write numbers by using digits *(page 90)*
Example: 3,023

stem-and-leaf plot A table that shows groups of data arranged by place value *(page 162)*

sum The answer to an addition problem *(page 6)*

survey A collection of data that lists choices *(page 146)*

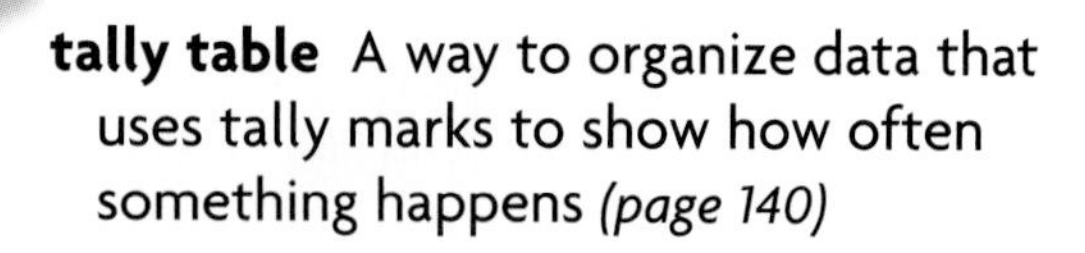

tally table A way to organize data that uses tally marks to show how often something happens *(page 140)*

tessellation An arrangement of geometric figures that covers a flat surface without leaving gaps and without overlapping *(page 252)*
Example:
These figures ▲◆ tesselate.

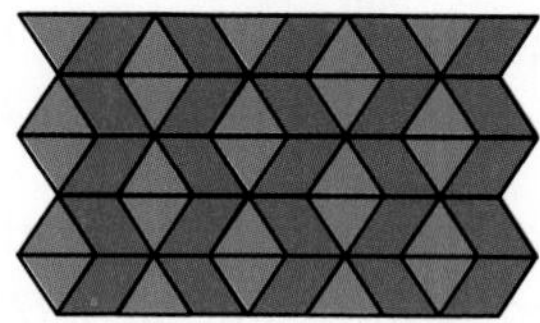

ton (T) A customary unit used to measure weight *(page 416)*
2,000 pounds = 1 ton

transformation The moving of a figure in a translation, reflection, or rotation *(page 244)*
Example:

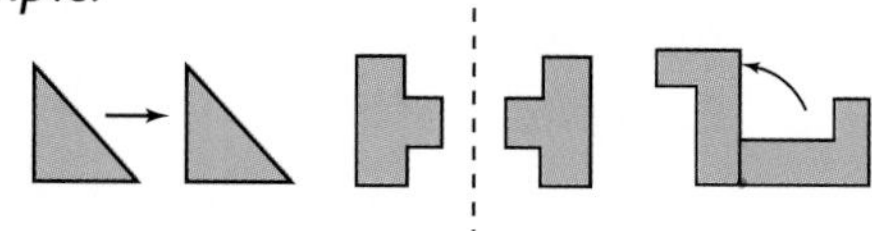

translation The action of sliding a figure in any direction *(page 244)*
Example:

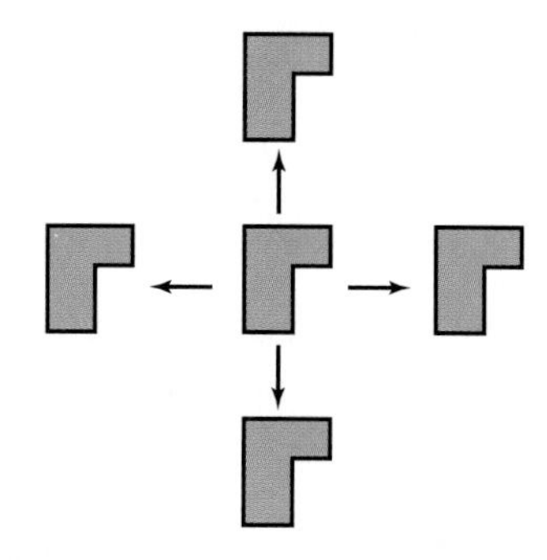

trapezoid A quadrilateral with only one pair of sides parallel *(page 220)*
Example:

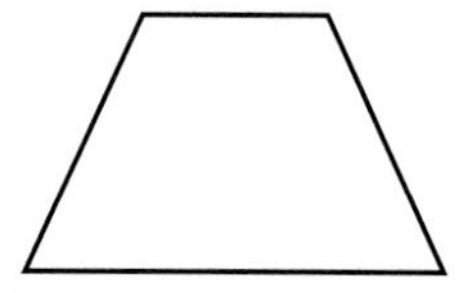

triangle A polygon with 3 sides and 3 angles *(page 218)*

24-hour clock A clock that does not use A.M. or P.M. *(page 122)*
Example:

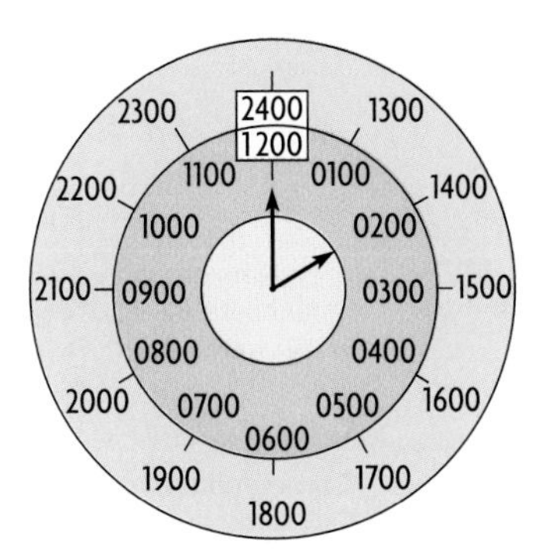

V

Venn diagram A diagram that uses circles to show relationships among sets of things *(page 114)*
Example:

vertex The point at which two rays of an angle or two or more line segments meet in a plane figure, or where three or more sides meet in a solid figure *(page 196)*
Examples:

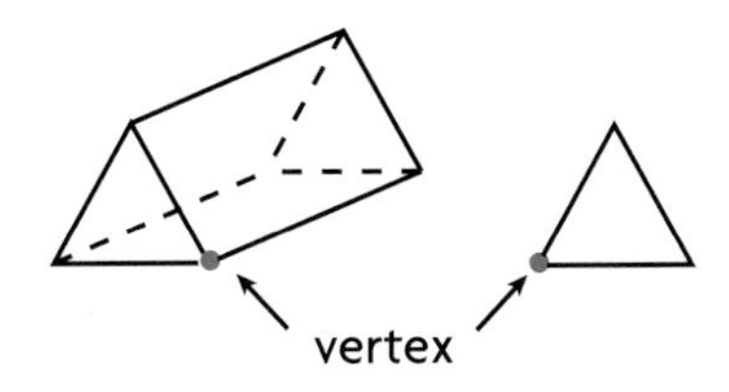

vertical The direction from top to bottom *(page 74)*

volume The measure of the space a solid figure occupies *(page H36)*
Example:

W

written form A way to write numbers by using words *(page 90)*
Example:
two hundred fifty-seven

Y

yard (yd) A unit of length in the customary system *(page 406)*
3 feet = 1 yard

Z

Zero Property for Multiplication The property which states that the product of zero and any number is zero *(page 36)*
Examples: $13 \times 0 = 0$
$0 \times 7 = 0$

INDEX

D

N

O

P

Q

R

S

T

U

V

W

Y

Z

ART CREDITS

Harcourt Brace & Company 86-87; Ortelius Design 22, 75, 100, 111, H24; Raymond Smith 89; ©Van Nostrand Reinhold Company Inc. 392; All other art not listed by The Quarasan Group, Inc.

PHOTO CREDITS

Page Placement Key: (t)-top (c)-center (b)-bottom (r)-right (l)-left

Chapter 1; Harcourt Brace & Company; 4 (cr); 5 (c); 5 (c); 5 (cr); 11 (c); 14 (br); xviii (bkg), xviii-1 (c), 2 (tr) ASG Sherman Graphics, Inc.; 2 (br) Allan Landau; 3 (tr) ASG Sherman Graphics, Inc.; 3 (cr), 8 (br) Allan Landau; 9 (br) K. & K. Ammann/Bruce Coleman, Inc.; 10 (tr) ASG Sherman Graphics, Inc.; 11 (tr), 13 (cr) Rich Franco; **Other;** 1 (cr), 5 (cr), 12 (br) PhotoDisc; **Chapter 2; Harcourt Brace & Company;** 19 (cr); 20 (tr); 27 (br); 28 (tc); 28 (tc); 28 (tr); 28 (c); 28 (cr); 17 (tr) ASG Sherman Graphics, Inc.; 17 (br), 20 (b) Allan Landau; 21 (bc) Rich Franco; 24 (r) Allan Landau; 28 (tr) Metropolitan Museum of Art, Rogers Fund, 1907; 28 (c) John F. Kennedy Library; 28 (cr) 1980 Smithsonian Institution; **Other;** 16-17 (bkg) Peter Pearson/Tony Stone Worldwide; 18 (br) Dallas & John Heaton/Stock•Boston; 21 (br) SportsChrome East/West; 22 (tr) SuperStock, Inc; 25 (tr) PhotoDisc; 26 (cr) Focus on Sports; 28 (br) SuperStock, Inc; 29 (tr) Dallas & John Heaton/Stock•Boston; 30 (c) W. Bertsch/Bruce Coleman, Inc.; 30 (cr) Bob Daemmrich/Tony Stone Worldwide; **Chapter 3; Harcourt Brace & Company;** 33 (tr); 34 (b); 43 (c); 45 (cr); 46 (t); 32 (bkg), (br), 38 (cr) ASG Sherman Graphics, Inc.; 38 (br) Allan Landau; 39 (tr) Don Mason/The Stock Market; 39 (cr) Comstock; 40 (cr) Sheri O'Neal; 43 (tr) Ed McDonald; 44 (cr) Allan Landau; 44 (br) Sheri O'Neil; **Other;** 32-33 (bkg) PhotoDisc; 35 (cr) Sue Streeter/Tony Stone Worldwide; 36 (cr) Leonard Lee Rue III/Photo Researchers, Inc.; 42 (cr) Stephen Dalton/Photo Researchers, Inc.; **Chapter 4; Harcourt Brace & Company;** 51 (tr); 52 (br); 57 (cr); 56 (br); 58 (tr); 58 (b); 49 (r) ASG Sherman Graphics, Inc.; 49 (b) Allan Landau; 53 (cr) ASG Sherman Graphics, Inc.; 54 (b) Allan Landau; 55 (tr) Rich Franco; 56 (cr) Allan Landau; 59 (cr) ASG Sherman Graphics, Inc.; 60 (cr) Rich Franco; 60 (br) ASG Sherman Graphics, Inc.; 62 (tr) Rich Franco; 63 (cr) ASG Sherman Graphics, Inc.; 68 (tr) Allan Landau; 68 (cr) Sheri O'Neal; **Other;** 48-49 (bkg) Shelley Rotner/Omni-Photo Communications; 52 (br) David Madison/Bruce Coleman, Inc.; 61 (cr) Chuck Keeler/Tony Stone Worldwide; 62 (br) Focus on Sports; 64 (tc) Benn Mitchell Image Bank; 64 (cl) Corel Co.; 64 (c), (cr) SuperStock, Inc; 64 (bc) Bill Gallery/Stock•Boston; **Chapter 5; Harcourt Brace & Company;** 81 (cr); 70 (l), (c), (bl), 71 (2) ASG Sherman Graphics, Inc.; 74 (br) SuperStock, Inc; 76 (b) Allan Landau; 78 (tr) SuperStock, Inc; 78 (cr) Rich Franco; 80 (r) Allan Landau; 82 (tr) Rich Franco; 82 (cl), (br), 83 (t), (cr) ASG Sherman Graphics, Inc.; 84 (tr) Allan Landau; **Other;** 70 (bkg) Don Smetzer/Tony Stone Worldwide; 71 (b) J.C. Carton/Bruce Coleman, Inc.; 71 (br) PhotoDisc; 72 (cr) Harry Hartman/Bruce Coleman, Inc.; 79 (br) Gerard Vandystadt/Photo Researchers, Inc.; **Chapter 6; Harcourt Brace & Company;** 99 (br); 101 (br); 87 (tr) ASG Sherman Graphics, Inc.; 87 (b) Allan Landau; 91 (c) Rich Franco; 92 (cr), (br) ASG Sherman Graphics, Inc.; 93 (cr) Rich Franco; 94 (tr), (r) Ed McDonald; 95 (t) Allan Landau; 96 (br) ASG Sherman Graphics, Inc.; 97 (cr) D. Trask/The Stock Market; 98 (br) Rodney Jones; **Other;** 86 (bkg) Lee Rentz/Bruce Coleman, Inc.; 88 (t) Bill Wassman/The Stock Market; 88 (cr) SuperStock, Inc; 95 (br) Erwin & Peggy Bauer/Bruce Coleman, Inc.; 100 (c) Guido Cozzi/Bruce Coleman, Inc.; **Chapter 7; Harcourt Brace & Company;** 107 (br); 106 (r) Allan Landau; 109 (br), 110 (t) ASG Sherman Graphics, Inc.; 110 (b) Allan Landau; 112 (b) ASG Sherman Graphics, Inc.; 113 (cl) Ed McDonald; **Other;** 102-103 (bkg) NASA; 102 (tl), (c) Bob Gathany; 105 (cr) Tony Stone Worldwide; 107 (c) Metatools; 108 (c) Young-Wolff/PhotoEdit; 111 (tr) David Madison/Bruce Coleman, Inc.; 112 (tr) Arthur Tilley/Tony Stone Worldwide; 114 (br) Bob Daemmrich/Tony Stone Worldwide; 118 (br) Ron & Valerie Taylor/Bruce Coleman, Inc.; **Chapter 8; Harcourt Brace & Company;** 124 (br); 129 (cr); 118 (c) ASG Sherman Graphics, Inc.; 121 (tr) Terry Sinclair; 122 (r) Allan Landau; 123 (cr), 124 (c), (cr) ASG Sherman Graphics, Inc.; 125 (br) Terry Sinclair; 126 (t) Allan Landau; 128 (r) Allan Landau; 129 (br) Rich Franco; **Other;** 118-119 (bkg) SuperStock, Inc; 118-119 (r) Chris A. Crumley/EarthWater Stock Photography; 119 (c), (cr) Metatools; 119 (b) Bruce Coleman, Inc.; 120 (tr) Fred McConnaughey/Photo Researchers, Inc.; 120 (br) DiMaggio/Kalish /The Stock Market; 121 (bc) Charles D. Winters/Photo Researchers, Inc.; 125 (t) Steve Weber/Tony Stone Worldwide; 126 (cr) Robert Estall/Tony Stone Worldwide; 132 (c) Bettmann Archive; 132 (cr) Granger Collection; **Chapter 9; Harcourt Brace & Company;** 147 (tc); 149 (cr); 138 (bkg), (cl), (bl), 139 (tr), (br), 140 (cr) ASG Sherman Graphics, Inc.; 141 (tr) Rich Franco; 141 (br) ASG Sherman Graphics, Inc.; 142 (b) Allan Landau; 143 (tr) ASG Sherman Graphics, Inc.; 143 (br) Rich Franco; 144 (r) Allan Landau; 145 (b), 147 (cr) ASG Sherman Graphics, Inc.; 148 (b) Allan Landau; 151 (tr) Sheri O'Neal; 152 (tr) ASG Sherman Graphics, Inc.; **Other;** 139 (bc) Scherer/StockFood America; 146 (br) Arthur Beck/The Stock Market; 147 (tr) Metatools; 147 (cr) Corel Co.; 152 (br) Michael Newman/PhotoEdit; **Chapter 10; Harcourt Brace & Company;** 157 (br); 161 (cr); 162 (b); 163 (tr); 165 (cr); 167 (tr); 154 (c), 155 (tr), (br) ASG Sherman Graphics, Inc.; 156 (b) Allan Landau; 161 (c) ASG Sherman Graphics, Inc.; 166 (bc) Allan Landau; 168 (tc) ASG Sherman Graphics, Inc.; **Other;** 154-155 (bkg) James Randkley/Tony Stone Worldwide; 158 (cr) SuperStock, Inc; 160 (br) Bob Daemmrich/Stock•Boston; 163 (cr) Metatools; 164 (cr) The Stock Market; 166 (tc) SuperStock, Inc; 168 (cr) P. Karunak/Photo Researchers, Inc.; **Chapter 11; Harcourt Brace & Company;** 170-171 (bkg); 170 (bl); 176 (br); 179 (cr); 181 (bc); 170 (c) ASG Sherman Graphics, Inc.; 170 (tr), (cl), (c), (c), (c) Allan Landau; 171 (c), 172 (br), 173 (t), 174 (c) ASG Sherman Graphics, Inc.; 176 (cr), 178 (b), 180 (cr), 182 (br) Allan Landau; **Chapter 12; Harcourt Brace & Company;** 190 (tr), (c), 191 (cr), (r), 192 (tr), 194 (tr) ASG Sherman Graphics, Inc.; 194 (b) Allan Landau; 200 (tr) ASG Sherman Graphics, Inc.; 200 (b) Allan Landau; 204 (r) Rich Franco; **Other;** 190-191 (t), 190-191 (b) NASA; 196 (br) Alex S. MacLean/Landslides; 197 (cl) Stephen Johnson/Tony Stone Worldwide; 197 (c) Michele Burgess/The Stock Market; 197 (cr) Ed Pritchard/Tony Stone Worldwide; 197 (br), 198 (br) SuperStock, Inc; 203 (cl) Robert Fried/Stock•Boston; 203 (c) John Elk III/Stock•Boston; 203 (cr) Dennis MacDonald/PhotoEdit; 206 (cl) SuperStock, Inc; 206 (c) Jeff Greenberg/PhotoEdit; **Chapter 13; Harcourt Brace & Company;** 208 (tr), (c) ASG Sherman Graphics, Inc.; 208 (r), 209 (r) Allan Landau; 211 (cr) ASG Sherman Graphics, Inc.; 212 (tr) Tony Freeman/PhotoEdit; 213 (bc) Sheri O'Neal; 216 (b) Allan Landau; 218 (br) ASG Sherman Graphics, Inc.; 219 (c) Comstock; 220 (r), 222 (tr) Allan Landau; 223 (br) Ed McDonald; **Other;** 208-209 (bkg) Jurgen Vogt/Image Bank; 210 (br) David Sailors/David Sailors Photography; 211 (cr) Bob Daemmrich/Stock•Boston; 214 (cr) Stuart L. Craig Jr./Bruce Coleman, Inc.; 215 (cr) Semitic Museum Harvard University; 221 (cr) SuperStock, Inc; 222 (br) Bettmann Archive; **Chapter 14; Harcourt Brace & Company;** 230 (tr); 226 (c) Allan Landau; 226 (br), 227 (cr), (br) ASG Sherman Graphics, Inc.; 230 (b) Allan Landau; 232 (tr) ASG Sherman Graphics, Inc.; 234 (r) Allan Landau; 235 (cr) Sheri O'Neal; 236 (br), 237 (r) ASG Sherman Graphics, Inc.; 238 (c) Allan Landau; 239 (br) Weronica Ankarorn; **Other;** 226-227 (bkg) Lawrence Migdale; 228 (tr) Paul Barton/The Stock Market; 240 (cr) John Elk III/Bruce Coleman, Inc.; **Chapter 15; Harcourt Brace & Company;** 251 (c); 242 (c), 242-243 (bkg), 244 (tr) ASG Sherman Graphics, Inc.; 244 (b), 246 (b) Allan Landau; 247 (tr) ASG Sherman Graphics, Inc.; 248 (t) Allan Landau; 252 (tr), 254 (tr) ASG Sherman Graphics, Inc.; 256 (r) Allan Landau; 257 (br) Rich Franco; 258 (cr) ASG Sherman Graphics, Inc.; **Other;** 249 (cl) Arthur Beck/Photo Researchers, Inc.; 249 (cl) Tardos Camesi/The Stock Market; 249 (c) Pete Saloutos/The Stock Market; 249 (cr) Peter Steiner/The Stock Market; 249 (cr) PhotoDisc; 250 (br) Pete Saloutos/The Stock Market; 251 (cl) SuperStock, Inc; 251 (c) Stock•Boston; 251 (cr) Pam Taylor/Bruce Coleman, Inc.; 255 (br) Jen & Des Bartlett/Bruce Coleman, Inc.; **Chapter 16; Harcourt Brace & Company;** 267 (cr); 264-265 (bkg) ASG Sherman Graphics, Inc.; 264 (l), (r) Allan Landau; 264 (br) ASG Sherman Graphics, Inc.; 265 (r) Allan Landau; 266 (t) ASG Sherman Graphics, Inc.; 268 (b) Allan Landau; 269 (r) ASG Sherman Graphics, Inc.; 270 (tr) Allan Landau; 272 (t), 273 (r), 274 (t), 275 (br) ASG Sherman Graphics, Inc.; 276 (b) Ed McDonald; **Other;** 268 (t) Rob Crandall/Stock•Boston; 272 (b) Jeff Greenberg/Stock•Boston; 278 (br) Paul Harris/Tony Stone Worldwide; **Chapter 17; Harcourt Brace & Company;** 286 (c); 291 (tr); 294 (bc); 280 (l), (c) ASG Sherman Graphics, Inc.; 281 (r), 282 (t) Allan Landau; 284 (cr) ASG Sherman Graphics, Inc.; 288 (t) Allan Landau; 290 (br), 292 (tr) Rich Franco; **Other;** 280-281 (bkg) Jean Mark Barey/Photo Researchers, Inc.; 285 (tr) PhotoDisc; 286 (tr) The Stock Market; 286 (br) SuperStock, Inc; 289 (tr) Rene Sheret/Tony Stone Worldwide; 289 (br) Metatools; 292 (br) PhotoDisc; 293 (cr) The Stock Market; **Chapter 18; Harcourt Brace & Company;** 299 (tr); 302 (tr); 309 (cr); 296-297 (bkg) ASG Sherman Graphics, Inc.; 296 (c) Allan Landau; 297 (br) ASG Sherman Graphics, Inc.; 298 (t) Allan Landau; 299 (cr) Jerry White; 300 (tr), 301 (r) Ed McDonald; 302 (b) Allan Landau; 304 (tr), 310 (tr), (b) ASG Sherman Graphics, Inc.; 311 (cr) Sheri O'Neal; **Other;** 296-297 (t) Christian Grzimek/Photo Researchers, Inc.; 298 (br) Wardene Weisser/Bruce Coleman, Inc.; 303 (tr) SuperStock, Inc; 304 (br) PhotoDisc; 307 (cr) Michal Heron/The Stock Market; 308 (tr) Bob Abraham/The Stock Market; 309 (tr) Metatools; 312 (c) Bettmann Archive; **Chapter 19; Harcourt Brace & Company;** 314-315 (bkg); 314 (c); 317 (tr); 317 (c); 325 (cr); 330 (tr); 320 (tr) Sheri O'Neal; 320 (b) Allan Landau; 321 (cr) ASG Sherman Graphics, Inc.; 322 (br), 324 (cr) Rich Franco; 327 (t) Allan Landau; 328 (b), 334 (c), 335 (br) ASG Sherman Graphics, Inc.; **Other;** 314-315 (bkg) Zao Audebert/Image Bank; 314 (cl), (cr) Tony Stone Worldwide; 316 (c) Tony Freeman/PhotoEdit; 316 (cr) Will & Demi McIntyre/Photo Researchers, Inc.; 318 (tr) PhotoDisc; 318 (br) Lawrence Midgale/Tony Stone Worldwide; 322 (tr) SuperStock, Inc; 323 (tr) Steve Bly/Tony Stone Worldwide; 334 (bkg) SuperStock, Inc; 334 (bc) Jane Burton/Bruce Coleman, Inc.; 335 (br) Hans Reinhard/Bruce Coleman, Inc.; **Chapter 20; Harcourt Brace & Company;** 339 (cr); 347 (br); 336 (c), 337 (br), 340 (t), (cl), (cr) ASG Sherman Graphics, Inc.; 342 (t), 346 (b) Allan Landau; 348 (tl) ASG Sherman Graphics, Inc.; 348 (tr) Allan Landau; 348 (cr) ASG Sherman Graphics, Inc.; 349 (cr) Rich Franco; 350 (b) Allan Landau; **Other;** 336 (bc) Jane Burton/Bruce Coleman, Inc.; 336-337 (bkg) SuperStock, Inc.; 337 (br) Hans Reinhard/Bruce Coleman, Inc.; 338 (br) Roy Morsch/The Stock Market; 341 (cr) Mark C. Burnett/Photo Researchers, Inc.; 343 (br) PhotoDisc; 345 (cr) Corel Co.; **Chapter 21; Harcourt Brace & Company;** 353 (tr); 362 (tr); 352 (cl), (cr) Allan Landau; 352 (bl), 352-353 (bkg) ASG Sherman Graphics, Inc.; 354 (b) Allan Landau; 355 (cr), 356 (t) ASG Sherman Graphics, Inc.; 356 (cr) Sheri O'Neal; 358 (b), 360 (b) Allan Landau; 365 (cr) Rich Franco; 366 (br) ASG Sherman Graphics, Inc.; 367 (bl) Rich Franco; **Other;** 352 (c) Corel Co.; 357 (cr) Jonathan Nourok/PhotoEdit; 361 (tr) The Stock Market; 363 (cr) Peter Steiner/The Stock Market; **Chapter 22; Harcourt Brace & Company;** 372 (tl); 372 (tc); 372 (tr); 372 (c); 372 (cr); 373 (cr); 378 (br); 379 (cr); 381 (cr); 368 (r) Allan Landau; 369 (r) ASG Sherman Graphics, Inc.; 374 (c), 375 (t) Allan Landau; 377 (cr) Rich Franco; 382 (br) ASG Sherman Graphics, Inc.; **Other;** 368-369 (r) Jeff Greenberg/PhotoEdit: 368-369 (bkg) Alan Thornton/Tony Stone Worldwide; 370 (t) Ed Bock/The Stock Market; 370 (br) Bettmann Archive; 371 (c) Michael Newman/PhotoEdit; 376 (tr) Focus on Sports; 380 (br) SuperStock, Inc; 382 (tr) Lawrence Migdale/Photo Researchers, Inc.; **Chapter 23; Harcourt Brace & Company;** 389 (cr); 395 (tr); 396 (b); 398 (cr); 402 (tr); 384 (cl), (cr) ASG Sherman Graphics, Inc.; 385 (b-), 386 (b) Allan Landau; 397 (cr) ASG Sherman Graphics, Inc.; **Other;** 384-385 (bkg) SuperStock, Inc; 384 (tr) Ruth Dixon/Stock•Boston; 384 (cr) Doug Peebles/Westlight; 384 (cl) Kunio Owaki/The Stock Market; 385 (tr) SuperStock, Inc; 387 (cr) Bob Daemmrich/Tony Stone Worldwide; 388 (tr) SuperStock, Inc; 390 (r) Jeff Greenberg/PhotoEdit; 391 (cr) Robin L. Sachs/PhotoEdit; 393 (r) PhotoDisc; 394 (r) Bob Daemmrich/Stock•Boston; **Chapter 24; Harcourt Brace & Company;** 407 (cr); 417 (cr); 404 (cl), (c), (cr), (r), 404-405 (b), 405 (b), 406 (cr), (b) ASG Sherman Graphics, Inc.; 407 (tr) Weronica Ankarorn; 410 (b) Allan Landau; 411 (cr), 412 (tc), (cl), (cr), (bl), (br), 413 (tl), (tr), (c) ASG Sherman Graphics, Inc.; 414 (c), (cr) Allan Landau; 414 (br) Rich Franco; 416 (r) Allan Landau; **Other;** 404-405 (bkg) SuperStock, Inc; 409 (cr) The Stock Market; 415 (tr) Felicia Martinez/PhotoEdit; 418 (tr) Don Mason/The Stock Market; 418 (br) Frankfurt Okapia/Photo Researchers, Inc.; **Chapter 25; Harcourt Brace & Company;** 425 (cr); 432 (cl); 432 (c); 432 (cr); 420 (c) ASG Sherman Graphics, Inc.; 421 (br), 423 (r) Allan Landau; 425 (c) Rich Franco; 426 (r) Allan Landau; 430 (cl), (c), (cr), (br) ASG Sherman Graphics, Inc.; 432 (tr), (b), 433 (t) Rich Franco; **Other;** 420-421 (bkg) Simon Fraser/Photo Researchers, Inc.; 423 (cl) Chris Sorensen/The Stock Market; 423 (bl) David Young-Wolff/PhotoEdit; 423 (bl) Robert P. Carr/Bruce Coleman, Inc.; 424 (c) Gerard Vandystadt/Allsport U.S.A.; 424 (cr) Gerard Vandystadt/Allsport U.S.A.; 427 (cr) Bill Gallery/Stock•Boston; 428 (cr) Charles Gupton/Stock•Boston; 428 (br) Tom Brakefield/The Stock Market; 429 (br) SuperStock, Inc; 430 (tr) David Young-Wolff/PhotoEdit; 432 (cr) Tony Freeman/PhotoEdit; 432 (br) PhotoDisc; **Chapter 26; Harcourt Brace & Company;** 441 (bl); 450 (cr); 436-437 (bkg), 436 (bkg), (tr), (c), (cr), 437 (cr), 439 (br) ASG Sherman Graphics, Inc.; 440 (cr) Allan Landau; 441 (cl), (cr) ASG Sherman Graphics, Inc.; 442 (cr), 446 (b) Allan Landau; 447 (t) Rich Franco; 449 (tl), (tr), (cl), 450 (tr), 451 (bl) ASG Sherman Graphics, Inc.; **Other;** 436-437 (bkg) Corel Co.; 438 (cr) Tony Stone Worldwide; 441 (br) James Carmichael/Bruce Coleman, Inc.; 448 (tr) Bruce Coleman, Inc.; 449 (tc) John Gerlach/Tony Stone Worldwide; 450 (c) Tony Freeman/PhotoEdit; 450 (br) Paul Conklin/PhotoEdit; 451 (bc) Mark Richards/PhotoEdit; **Chapter 27; Harcourt Brace & Company;** 460 (tr); 468 (cr); 454 (c), 455 (br) ASG Sherman Graphics, Inc.; 458 (tr) Allan Landau; 460 (b) Allan Landau; 461 (tr), 462 (tr), 463 (b) ASG Sherman Graphics, Inc.; 464 (c) Allan Landau; **Other;** 456 (tr) Metatools; 456 (cr) SuperStock, Inc; 459 (cr) Harold Hoffman/Photo Researchers, Inc.; 461 (cr) David W. Hamilton Image Bank; 466 (tr) Cathlyn Melloan/Tony Stone Worldwide; 466 (br) John Elk III/Bruce Coleman, Inc.; 467 (cr) SuperStock, Inc; **Chapter 28; Harcourt Brace & Company;** 486 (t); 470-471 (bkg), 470 (tl), (c), (cr), (br), 471 (c) ASG Sherman Graphics, Inc.; 472 (b) Allan Landau; 474 (b) Sheri O'Neal; 475 (cr) ASG Sherman Graphics, Inc.; 478 (b) Allan Landau; 482 (c) ASG Sherman Graphics, Inc.; **Other;** 470 (bc) Gilmore J. Dufresne/Uniphoto; 471 (l) StockFood America; 473 (tr) Metatools; 476 (cr) David Madison/Bruce Coleman, Inc.; 477 (cr) John Cancolor/Stock•Boston; 480 (tr), (br) SuperStock, Inc; 482 (r) Rafael Macia/Photo Researchers, Inc.; 483 (tr) PhotoDisc; **Student Handbook; Harcourt Brace & Company;** H14 (cr); H19 (r); H20 (b); H22 (t); H31 (cr); H34 (br); H49 (cr); H54 (t); H55 (t); H59 (br); H60 (cr); H60 (br); H62 (cr); H64 (r); H66 (b); H3 (br) Rich Franco; H7 (r) Ed McDonald; H9 (cr), (bl), ASG Sherman Graphics, Inc.; H10 (cr) Rich Franco; H15 (br), H17 (tr), H26 (t), H27 (b) ASG Sherman Graphics, Inc.; H28 (c) Allan Landau; H29 (b) Ed McDonald; H30 (t) ASG Sherman Graphics, Inc.; H30 (br), H35 (cr), H46 (br) Sheri O'Neal; H40 (bc), (br) San Diego Museum of Man; H45 (r) Sheri O'Neal; H46 (cr) PhotoEdit; H48 (tr) Allan Landau; H51 (br) Rich Franco; H65 (br) ASG Sherman Graphics, Inc.; **Other;** H2 (tr) SuperStock, Inc; H5 (br) Stock•Boston; H6 (br) Thomas Braise/The Stock Market; H7 (tc) Don Mason/The Stock Market; H10 (br) Bob Daemmrich/Tony Stone Worldwide; H16 (br) Erich Lessing/Art Resource, Inc.; H18 (cr) Ken Biggs/Tony Stone Worldwide; H19 (tc) PhotoDisc; H25 (br) Robert Rathe/Stock•Boston; H40 (cr) Stock•Boston; H44 (t) Jerry Wachter/Photo Researchers, Inc.; H50 (cr) Stephen Dunn/Allsport U.S.A.; H53 (tr) Stephen Frisch/Stock•Boston; H53 (cr) William Whitehurst/The Stock Market; H54 (cr) SuperStock, Inc; H54 (br) Peter Steiner/The Stock Market; H57 (br) PhotoDisc; H63 (cr) Lew Long/The Stock Market.

http://www.hbschool.com
SPLIT/RESET
SELECT
MODE
START/STOP
SET
MODEL 221
SUN MON TUE WED THU FRI SAT
MIN
SEC
1/100
SPORTLINE
WATERTIGHT